The Scarecrow Author Bibliographies

1. John Steinbeck (Tetsumaro Hayashi). 1973.
2. Joseph Conrad (Theodore G. Ehrsam). 1969.
3. Arthur Miller (Tetsumaro Hayashi). 2d ed. due 1976.
4. Katherine Anne Porter (Waldrip & Bauer). 1969.
5. Philip Freneau (Philip M. Marsh). 1970.
6. Robert Greene (Tetsumaro Hayashi). 1971.
7. Benjamin Disraeli (R. W. Stewart). 1972.
8. John Berryman (Richard W. Kelly). 1972.
9. William Dean Howells (Vito J. Brenni). 1973.
10. Jean Anouilh (Kathleen W. Kelly). 1973.
11. E. M. Forster (Alfred Borrello). 1973.
12. The Marquis de Sade (E. Pierre Chanover). 1973.
13. Alain Robbe-Grillet (Dale W. Fraizer). 1973.
14. Northrop Frye (Robert D. Denham). 1974.
15. Federico García Lorca (Laurenti & Siracusa). 1974.
16. Ben Jonson (Brock & Welsh). 1974.
17. Four French Dramatists: Eugène Brieux, François de Curel, Emile Fabre, Paul Hervieu (Edmund F. SantaVicca). 1974.
18. Ralph Waldo Ellison (Jacqueline Covo). 1974.
19. Philip Roth (Bernard F. Rodgers, Jr.). 1974.
20. Norman Mailer (Laura Adams). 1974.
21. Sir John Betjeman (Margaret Stapleton). 1974.
22. Elie Wiesel (Molly Abramowitz). 1974.
23. Paul Laurence Dunbar (Eugene W. Metcalf, Jr.). 1975.
24. Henry James (Beatrice Ricks). 1975.
25. Robert Frost (Lentricchia & Lentricchia). 1975.

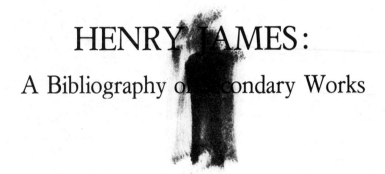

HENRY JAMES:

A Bibliography of Secondary Works

compiled by
BEATRICE RICKS

The Scarecrow Author Bibliographies, No. 24

The Scarecrow Press, Inc.
Metuchen, N.J.   1975

Library of Congress Cataloging in Publication Data

Ricks, Beatrice.
  Henry James.

    (The Scarecrow author bibliographies ; no. 24)
    Bibliography: p.
    Includes indexes.
    1. James, Henry, 1843-1916--Bibliography.
I. Title.
Z8447.R5 [PS2123]   016.813'4   75-22128
ISBN 0-8108-0853-6

Dedicated to the Staff of the
Wards Edwards Library
of
Central Missouri State University

PREFACE

This bibliography of secondary references, consisting of over 4,600 items, is comprised of the following sections: Biography; Works: critical studies of specific works arranged alphabetically according to authors under titles of novels or stories; General Criticism, alphabetically arranged by authors; Bibliography; Topical Index; and Index of Authors.

The original purpose was to compile a comprehensive bibliography of secondary works, but that endeavor has not been achieved, for even the volume of James's writing is probably exceeded by the volume of critical studies concerning his work. However, an effort has been made to gather references from the nineteenth as well as from the twentieth century, from both American and English sources, and from as many areas of study as possible.

Excellent and exhaustive bibliographies of editions have been provided by Leon Edel and Dan H. Laurence, A Bibliography of Henry James (London, 1957; 2nd edition revised, 1961); and by LeRoy Phillips, A Bibliography of the Writings of Henry James (New York, 1930; reprinted 1968). Therefore, no effort has been made to collect and list editions when such a work is preceded by a critical introduction.

Likewise, since we are indebted to Percy Lubbock for Letters of Henry James (New York, 1920; reprinted 1970), a listing of letters has been omitted. However, articles referring to specific communications of Henry James have been included, as well as commentary on James as a correspondent.

We are indebted also to Albert Mordell for Literary Reviews and Essays by Henry James on American, English, and French Literature (New York, 1957), and also to Pierre de Chaignon La Rose for an earlier work, Notes and Reviews by Henry James (Cambridge, Mass., 1921). Hence, a listing of reviews by Henry James would be repetitious although, again, a section of critical commentary on the reviews has been included under Works.

Editions of a specific critical work about James have been combined when possible. For instance, the publisher and date of the earlier work, with the publication data of a later printing, or of a revised and enlarged edition, have been combined in the same item under the same number. This method, it is hoped, will alert the student to available texts.

The Topical Index, in which cross-references are given by item numbers, has been designed to suggest facets of study, persons important in the life and work of Henry James, authors whose influence on James has been noted, or authors influenced by James, or whatever areas of interpretation or technique which critics have considered.

Although articles and books pertaining to a specific work, as stated, are listed under the novel or story, reference should be made to General Criticism, for very often many novels and stories will be examined in one study.

Acknowledgment is made of the assistance and encouragement particularly of Dr. Edward Harris, Mrs. Kathryn Erisman, Mrs. Margaret Greef, Dr. Wasyl Hucalak, Mrs. Eloise Kibbie, and Mr. William Stanton.

B. R.

TABLE OF CONTENTS

		Entry	Page
Abbreviations and Publications			
Masterlist of Bibliographic Entries			
I.	Biography	1	2
II.	Works:		
	Novels, Stories and Plays	49	8
	Drama	1586	209
	Essays and Criticism	1634	213
	The "Last Dictation"	1642	215
	Lectures	1649	215
	Letters	1653	216
	The New York Edition	1736.2	224
	Notebooks	1737.4	225
	Prefaces	1744	226
	Reviews	1755	227
	Sketches	1763	228
III.	General Criticism	1767	230
IV.	Bibliography	3731	400
Topical Index			413
Index of Critics			436

ABBREVIATIONS AND PUBLICATIONS

AB	American Bookman
Academy	London Academy
Accent	Accent
AF	Anglistische Forschungen
AH	American Heritage
AI	American Imago
AION-SG	Annali Istituto Universitario Orientale, Napoli, Sezione Germanica
AL	American Literature
Albion	New York Albion
ALR	American Literary Realism
America	America: A Journal of To-Day
AmMerc	American Mercury
AmSch	American Scholar
AN&Q	American Notes and Queries (New Haven, Conn.)
AngBbl	Anglia Beiblatt
Anglia	Anglia
AntiochR	Antioch Review
AnUBLG	Analele Universitatii Bucuresti Limbi/ germanice
AnUBLUC	Analele Universitatii Bucuresti. Literatura Universala si comparata
Apollo	Apollo
ArchF	Architecture Forum
ArchR	Architectural Review
ArlQ	Arlington Quarterly
ArQ	Arizona Quarterly
Arts	The Arts
Arts/Soc	Arts in Society (University of Wisconsin, Extension Division)
AryanP	Aryan Path
AS	American Speech
Athenaeum	Athenaeum (London)
Atl	Atlantic Monthly
ATQ	American Transcendental Quarterly
AULLA	The Australasian Universities Language and Literature Association

BAASB	British Association for American Studies Bulletin
BachA	Bachelor of Arts
Balcony	Balcony: The Sydney Review, University of Sydney
BaratR	Barat Review, Barat College, Lake Forest, Ill.
BAS	Bulletin of the Atomic Scientists
BB	Bulletin of Bibliography
BBDI	Bulletin of Bibliography and Dramatic Index
BBr	Books at Brown
BC	Book Collector
BCit	Bulletin of the Citadel
Belfagor	Belfagor (Florence)
BEM	Blackwood's Edinburgh Magazine
BJA	British Journal of Aesthetics
BLM	Bonniers Litterara Magasin (Stockholm)
BNYPL	Bulletin of the New York Public Library
BookB	Book Buyer
BookN	Book News
Books	Books
BottOS	Botteghe Oscure
BPLQ	Boston Public Library Quarterly
BRMMLA	Bulletin of the Rocky Mountain Modern Language Association
BrSE	Brno Studies in English
BSAP	(See PBSA)
BSUF	Ball State University Forum
BulCit	Bulletin of the Citadel (Charleston, South Carolina)
BungR	Bungaku Ronshu (Konan University, Japan)
BuR	Bucknell Review
BUSE	Boston University Studies in English
BYUS	Brigham Young University Studies
CAASB	Canadian Association for American Studies Bulletin
CalR	Calcutta Review
CamJ	Cambridge Journal
C&P	Character and Personality
CamR	Cambridge Review
CanL	Canadian Literature
CathW	Catholic World
CC&C	College Composition and Communication
CE	College English
CEA	CEA Critic
CEJ	California English Journal
CentR	Centennial Review (Michigan State University)

Century	Century Magazine
ChessL	Chess Life
ChiR	Chicago Review
Chm	The Churchman
CL	Comparative Literature
CLAJ	College Language Association Journal (Morgan State College, Baltimore)
CLQ	Colby Library Quarterly
CLS	Comparative Literature Studies (University of Illinois)
CM	Carleton Miscellany
Comm	Commentary
ConnR	Connecticut Review
ContR	Contemporary Review Studies
Coranto	Journal of Friends of the Libraries (U.S.C.)
Cornhill	Cornhill Magazine
CQ	Cambridge Quarterly
CR	The Critical Review (Melbourne, Sydney)
CRAS	Canadian Review of American Studies
Cresset	Cresset (Valparaiso University)
Crit	Critique: Studies in Modern Fiction
Criterion	Criterion
Critic	Critic
Critica	Critica Society
Criticism	Criticism (Wayne State University)
Critique	Critique (Paris)
CritQ	Critical Quarterly
CS	Cahiers du Sud (France)
CSE	Carnegie Series in English
CSMM	Christian Science Monitor Magazine
Cue	Cue
CurL	Current Literature
CurOp	Current Opinion
Cw	Commonweal
DA	Dissertation Abstracts
Daedalus	Daedalus
DAI	Dissertation Abstracts International
DailyN	Daily News
DailyT	Daily Telegraph
Delta	Delta (Cambridge, England)
Descant	Descant
Dial	Dial
Dickensian	Dickensian
DieuV	Dieu Vivant
Discourse	Discourse (Concordia College)
DLAJ	DeKalb Literary Arts Journal
DR	Dalhousie Review

EA	Etudes Anglaises
E&S	Essays and Studies in British and American Literature (Tokyo - Joshi Daigaku)
EBST	Edinburgh Bibliographical Society Transactions
Edda	Edda (Oslo)
EdinR	Edinburgh Review
EDK	Ehime Daigaku Kiyo
EIC	Essays in Criticism (Oxford)
EIE	English Institute Essays
EigoS	Eigo Seinen [The Rising Generation] (Tokyo)
EIHC	Essex Institute Historical Collections
EiK	Eibungakukai-Kaiho (English Literary Society of Nihon University)
EJ	English Journal
ELH	Journal of English Literary History
ELL	English Language and Literary (English Literary Society of Korea)
ELN	English Language Notes (University of Colorado)
Elsinore	Elsinore
ELT	English Literature in Transition (1880-1920)
Encounter	Encounter (London)
Eng	English, Magazine of the English Association
Eng"A"A	English "A" Analyst (Northwestern University)
English	English (London)
EngLit	English Literature (Waseda)
EngN	English Notes
EngR	English Review
EngRec	English Record (New York State English Council)
EngS	Englische Studien (Amsterdam)
ErasmusR	Erasmus Review, A Journal of the Humanities (Bayside, New York)
ES	English Studies
ESA	English Studies in Africa
ESQ	Emerson Society Quarterly
ESQ:JAR	Emerson Society Quarterly: Journal of the American Renaissance
Esquire	Esquire
Essays	Essays
EUQ	Emory University Quarterly
E-WR	East-West Review
ExEx	Exercise Exchange
Expl	Explicator
FAR	French American Review
FilmQ	Film Quarterly
FitzN	Fitzgerald Newsletter

FL	Figaro Littéraire
FLe	Le Fiera Letterària (Italy)
FMLS	Forum for Modern Language Studies (University of St. Andrews, Scotland)
FMod	Filología Moderna (Madrid)
FnR	Fortnightly Review
Forum	The Forum
ForumH	Forum (Houston)
FourQ	Four Quarters (La Salle)
FR	French Review
Freeman	Freeman
FukURLS	Fukuoka University Review of Literature and Science
Furioso	Furioso
GaR	Georgia Review
Genre	Genre
Gifthorse	Gifthorse (Ohio State University)
GreyfriarL	Greyfriar Lectures
Griffin	Griffin
G-RM	Germanisch-Romantische Monatsschrift, Neue Folge
GSE	Graduate Student of English
H&H	Hound and Horn
HarperB	Harper's Bazaar
HarperM	Harper's Magazine
HarperNMM	Harper's New Monthly Magazine
Harper's	Harper's
HarperW	Harper's Weekly
HarvardM	Harvard Monthly
HeM	Hommes et Mondes
HGM	Harvard Graduate Magazine
Hist/Today	History Today
HiyRon	Hiyoshi Ronbunshu
HLB	Harvard Library Bulletin
Horizon	Horizon
Horizontes:	Horizontes: Revista de la Universidad Católica de Puerto Rico
HSL	Hartford Studies in Literature
HudR	Hudson Review
HUL	Harvard University Library
Humanist	Humanist
Humanitas	Humanitas
HunterCS	Hunter College Studies
HUSL	Hebrew University Studies in Literature
IbadanSE	Ibadan Studies in English

IEBY	Iowa English Bulletin Yearbook
IeD	Informations et Documents
IEY	Iowa English Yearbook
IJAS	Indian Journal of American Studies
IJES	Indian Journal of English Studies
IllQ	Illinois Quarterly
ILondN	Illustrated London News
IlSim	Il Simbolismo
Independent	Independent
IntroB	Intro Bulletin
Inventario	Inventario
InvitL	Invitation to Learning
JA	Jahrbuch für Amerikastudien
JAAC	Journal of Aesthetics and Art Criticism
JAmS	Journal of American Studies
JGE	Journal of General Education
JHI	Journal of the History of Ideas
JimK	Jimbun Kenkyu (Osaka City University)
Jin-ShR	Jinbun-Shizenkagaku (Tokyo Economic College)
JKU	Journal of the Karnatak University
JML	Journal of Modern Literature (Temple University)
JNT	Journal of Narrative Technique
JO'LW	John O'London's Weekly
JourA	Journal American (New York)
JP	Journal of Philosophy
JPC	Journal of Popular Culture
JQ	Journalism Quarterly
JRUL	Journal of Rutgers University Library
JSE&AL	Journal of the Society of English and American Literature (Kwansei Gakiun University)
KAL	Kyushu American Literature (Juokuoka, Japan)
Kam	Kameron (Kameron Society)
KiplingJ	Kipling Journal
KM	Kansas Magazine
KN	Kwartalnik Neofilologiczny (Warsaw)
KR	Kenyon Review
KSMB	Keats-Shelley Memorial Bulletin (Rome)
LaHJ	Ladies Home Journal
LakeUR	Lakehead University Review (Port Arthur, Ontario)
Lamp	Lamp
LaN	La Nef (Paris)
L&L	Life and Letters Today
L&P	Literature and Psychology (University of Hartford)

Lang&L	Language and Literature
Lang&S	Language and Style
LanM	Les Langues Modernes
LaurelR	Laurel Review (West Virginia Wesleyan College)
LCrit	Literary Criterion (University of Mysore, India)
LCUT	Library Chronicle of the University of Texas
Le Monde	Le Monde
LetFran	Lettres Françaises
LetN	Lettres Nouvelles
LHR	Lock Haven Review (Lock Haven State College, Pa.)
Library	Library
Lif&L	Life and Letters Today
Life	Life
List	Listener
Lit	Literature
LitD	Literary Digest
Litera	Litera
LitR	Literature Review (Fairleigh Dickinson University, Teaneck, New Jersey)
LittleR	The Little Review
LitW	Literary World (Boston)
LivA	The Living Age
LonM	London Magazine
LonMerc	London Mercury
LonN	London News
LonQR	London Quarterly Review
LonSp	London Spectator
LSUSHS	Louisiana State University Studies, Humanities Series
LTLS	London Times Literary Supplement
LWU	Literatur in Wissenschaft und Unterricht (Kiel)
Mainstream	Mainstream
M&M	Masses and Mainstream
Mandrake	Mandrake
ManGW	Manchester Guardian Weekly
MarkR	Markham Review
MASJ	Midcontinent American Studies Journal (University of Kansas, Lawrence)
MassR	Massachusetts Review
McGUM	McGill University Magazine
MCR	Melbourne Critical Review
MD	Modern Drama
MdF	Mercure de France

Meanjin	Meanjin (University of Melbourne)
Merkur	Merkur (Deutsche Zeitschrift für europäisches Denken)
MethR	Methodist Review
MFS	Modern Fiction Studies
MHSB	Missouri Historical Society Bulletin
MichA	Michigan Academician
MichQR	Michigan Quarterly Review
MinnR	Minnesota Review
Mirror	New York Mirror
MissQ	Mississippi Quarterly
MLN	Modern Language Notes
MLQ	Modern Language Quarterly
MLR	Modern Language Review
ModA	Modern Age (Chicago)
Mon/AmLS	Monographs/American Literary Scholarship (Duke University)
Mon/Ball	Ball State Monographs (Muncie, Indiana)
Mon/BibLiège	Bibliotheque de la Faculté de Philosophie et Lettres de L'Université de Liège (Société d'Editions les Belles Lettres, Paris)
Mosaic	Mosaic: A Journal for the Comparative Study of Literature and Ideas
MSpr	Modern Sprak (Stockholm)
MTJ	Mark Twain Journal
MTQ	Mark Twain Quarterly
MunM	Munsey's Magazine
MusQ	Music Quarterly
MwQ	Midwest Quarterly (Pittsburg, Kansas)
NA	Nuova Antologia (Roma)
Names	Names
N&Q	Notes and Queries
NAR	North American Review
Nation	Nation
NatlR	National Review
NC	Nineteenth Century
NCF	Nineteenth Century Fiction
NDEJ	Notre Dame English Journal
Neophil	Neophilologus (Groningen)
NEQ	New England Quarterly
NeueR	Neue Rundschau
NewAdel	New Adelphi
NewL	New Leader
NewLR	New Left Review
New Masses	New Masses
NewRep	New Republic
Newsweek	Newsweek

NL	Nouvelles Littéraires
NLauR	New Laurel Review [Formerly, Laurel Review], The Pennington School, Pennington, New Jersey
NM	Neuphilologische Mitteilungen
NMQ	New Mexico Quarterly
NorM	Northern Miscellany
Novel	Novel: A Forum on Fiction (Brown University)
NRF	Nouvelle Revue Française
NS	Die Neueren Sprachen
NS&N	New Statesman and Nation
NSR	Newe Schweizer Rundschau
NSt	New Statesman
NVT	Nieu Vlaams Tijdschrift
NwR	Northwest Review
NY	New Yorker
NYDN	New York Daily News
NYG&BR	New York Genealogical and Biographical Record
NYHTB	New York Herald Tribune Books
NYHTBR	New York Herald Tribune Book Review
NYRB	New York Review of Books
NYT	New York Times
NYTBR	New York Times Book Review
NYTCR	New York Theatre Critics' Reviews
NYWT	New York World-Telegram
Oberon	Oberon (Tokyo)
Obs	Observer
OJES	Osmania Journal of English Studies (Osmania University, Hyderabad)
OR	The Oxford Review
Orizont	Orizont
OUR	Ohio University Review (Athens)
Outlook	Outlook
PacNQ	Pacific Northwest Quarterly
PacS	Pacific Spectator
PAH	Perspectives in American History
Paunch	Paunch (Buffalo, New York)
PBSA	Papers of the Bibliographical Society of America
PCTEB	Pennsylvania Council of Teachers of English Bulletin
Person	Personalist
Perspective	Perspective (Washington University)
PLL	Papers on Language and Literature

PMASAL	Papers of the Michigan Academy of Science, Arts, and Letters
PMHB	Pennsylvania Magazine of History and Biography
PMLA	Publications of the Modern Language Association
Poetique	Poetique
PoetLore	Poet Lore
Poetry	Poetry
PP	Philologica Pragensia
PQ	Philological Quarterly (Iowa City)
PR	Partisan Review
PrH	Przeglad Humanistyczny
Prose	Prose
PrR	Princeton Review
PrS	Prairie Schooner
PRSC	Proceedings of Royal Society of Canada
PS	Pensiero e Scuola
PSA	Papeles de Son Armadans (Mallorca) (Madrid)
PsyR	Psychoanalytic Review
PubW	Publishers Weekly
PULC	Princeton University Library Chronicle
Punch	Punch
PutM	Putnam's Monthly
QQ	Queen's Quarterly
QR	Quarterly Review
Queries	Queries (Osaka City University)
Quest	Quest (Bombay)
QuinLit	Quinzaine Littéraire
RAA	Revue Anglo-Américaine
Ramparts	Ramparts
RdF	Revue de France
RDM	Revue des deux mondes
RdP	Revue de Paris
RE: A&L	Re: Arts and Letters
Reader	Reader
REL	Review of English Literature (Leeds)
Renascence	Renascence
Reporter	Reporter
RES	Review of English Studies
RevMeta	Review of Metaphysics (New Haven)
RevR	Review of Reviews
RevUM	Revista de la Universidad de Mexico
RGB	Revue Générale Belge (Brussels)
RHM	Revista Hispánica Moderna
RikR	Rikkyo Review (Tokyo)

RITL	Revista de Istorie si Theorie Literară
RLC	Revue de Littérature Comparée
RLV	Revue des Langues Vivantes (Brussels)
RMS	Renaissance and Modern Studies (University of Nottingham)
RN	Revue Nouvelle (Brussels)
RomN	Romance Notes (University of North Carolina)
Ronko	Ronko (Kwansei Gakuin University)
RS	Research Studies (Washington State University)
RUS	Rice University Studies
RUSEng	Rajasthan University Studies in English
SA	Studi Americani (Roma)
SAB	South Atlantic Bulletin
SAQ	South Atlantic Quarterly
SatR	Saturday Review
SatRL	Saturday Review of Literature
Saturday	Saturday
SB	Studies in Bibliography: Papers of the Bibliographical Society of the University of Virginia
SCB	South-Central Bulletin: Studies
Sch&S	School and Society
Scribner's	Scribner's Magazine
Scrutiny	Scrutiny
SDD-UW	Summaries of Doctoral Dissertations (Northwestern University)
SDR	South Dakota Review
SEL	Studies in English Literature, 1500-1900
SELit	Studies in English Literature (English Literary Society of Japan, University of Tokyo)
SELL	Studies in English Literature and Language (Kyushu University, Fukuoka, Japan)
SEngL	Studies in English Literature
SFQ	Shakespeare Fellowship Quarterly
SG	Studium Generale
ShawR	Shaw Review
Shenandoah	Shenandoah: The Washington & Lee University Review
ShN	Shakespeare Newsletter
Show	Show
SHR	Southern Humanities Review
Shur	Shuryu (Doshisha University)
SIR	Studies in Romanticism
SlavR	Slavonic Review
SLN	Sinclair Lewis Newsletter
SNNTS	Studies in the Novel (North Texas State University)

SophiaT	Sophia: Studies in Western Civilization and the Cultural Interaction of East and West (Tokyo)
SoQ	Southern Quarterly (Hattiesburg, Mississippi, University of Southern Mississippi)
SoR	Southern Review (Louisiana State University)
SoRA	Southern Review: An Australian Journal of Literary Studies (University of Adelaide)
SoSpJ	Southern Speech Journal
Southerly	Southerly (Sydney)
Spectator	Spectator (London)
Spectrum	Spectrum
SR	Sewanee Review
SRAZ	Studia Romanica et Anglica Zagrabiensia
SSF	Studies in Short Fiction
SSH	Stetson Studies in the Humanities
StPR	St. Paul's Review (St. Paul's University)
Style	Style (University of Arkansas)
SUB	Stetson University Bulletin
Sun	New York Sun
Sym	Symposium
TAM	Theatre Arts Monthly
TamR	Tamarack Review
T&T	Time & Tide
T&Z	Texte und Zeichen
TCAus	Twentieth Century, An Australian Quarterly Review
TCEA&A	Travaux du Centre d'Etudes Anglaises et Américaines
TCI	Twentieth Century Interpretations
TCL	Twentieth Century Literature
ThA	Theatre Arts
Thought	Thought
TigE	The Tiger's Eye (New York)
Time	Time Magazine
TimesH	Times Herald (Dallas, Texas)
TLS	Times Literary Supplement (London)
TM	Les Temps Modernes
Tomorrow	Tomorrow
Topic	Topic: A Journal of the Liberal Arts
Torre	La Torre
TQ	Texas Quarterly (University of Texas)
TR	Table Ronde (France)
TriQ	Tri-Quarterly (Evanston, Illinois)
TSE	Tulane Studies in English
TSL	Tennessee Studies in Literature
TSLL	Texas Studies in Language and Literature

TsudaR	Tsuda Review
TuK	Text und Kritik
TVG	TV Guide
TWA	Transactions of the Wisconsin Academy of Sciences, Arts, and Letters
UCC	University of California Chronicle
UCFP	Union College Faculty Papers
UES	Unisa English Studies
UISL&L	University of Illinois Studies in Language and Literature (Urbana, Illinois)
UKCR	University of Kansas City Review
UMPAW	University of Minnesota Pamphlets on American Writers
UMSE	University of Mississippi Studies in English
UnivM	University Magazine (Montreal)
UnivR	Universal Review
UR	University Review (Kansas City, Missouri)
URev	University Review (Dublin)
URLB	University of Rochester Library Bulletin
UTQ	University of Toronto Quarterly
UTSE	University of Texas Studies in English
UWR	University of Windsor Review (Windsor, Ontario)
VAC	Vie Art Cité
Variety	Variety
Ventures	Ventures: Magazine of the Yale Graduate School
Vesy	Vesy
Vice Versa	Vice Versa (New York)
Vinduet	Vinduet (Oslo)
ViR	Viata Romaneasca (Bucharest)
VJUS	Vassar Journal of Undergraduate Studies
VL	Voprosy Literatury
VN	Victorian Newsletter
Vogue	Vogue
VQR	Virginia Quarterly Review
VS	Victorian Studies (Indiana University)
W&R	The Wind and the Rain (London)
WascanaR	Wascana Review (Regina, Sask.)
Wasp	Wasp (San Francisco)
WBEP	Wiener Beitrage zur Englischen Philologie
WeeklyR	Weekly Review
Westerly	Westerly
WestR	Western Review
WF	Western Folklore

WHR	Western Humanities Review
WR	Western Review: A Journal of the Humanities
WSLL	Wisconsin Studies in Language and Literature (University of Wisconsin)
XUS	Xavier University Studies
YB	Yellow Book
YCGL	Yearbook of Comparative and General Literature
YR	Yale Review
YSE	Yale Studies in English
YULG	Yale University Library Gazette
ZAA	Zeitschrift für Anglistik und Amerikanistik (East Berlin)

I. BIOGRAPHY

1   Aldridge, John W. "The Anatomy of Passion in the Consummate Henry James," SatR, 55 (February 12, 1972), 65-68. Essay-review of Leon Edel's <u>Henry James: The Master.</u> New York: 1972.

1.1   Allen, Gay Wilson. <u>William James: A Biography.</u> New York: Viking Press, 1967, passim.

1.2   Anderson, Quentin. <u>The American Henry James.</u> New Brunwsick, N.J.: Rutgers U. P., 1957.

1.3   _____. "Leon Edel's 'Henry James,'" VQR, 48 (Autumn, 1972), 621-630.

1.4   Anon. "The Death of Henry James," TLS (April 17, 1943), 187.

1.5   Anon. "The Matter of the Master," TLS (August 18, 1972), 957-959.

2   Barzun, Jacques. "The Jameses," TLS, 3,680 (September 15, 1972), 1060. Cf., Leon Edel. "The Jameses," TLS, 3,684 (October 13, 1972), 1226-1227.

2.1   Bewley, Marius. "Death and the James Family," <u>Masks and Mirrors.</u> New York: Atheneum Pubs., c1949, pp. 107-118.

3   Bicknell, Percy F. "Mr. James's Memories of Boyhood," Dial, 54 (May 1, 1913), 372-374.

3.1   Bliven, Naomi. "Leon Edel's Biography," NY, 48 (April 29, 1972), 137ff. Essay-review, Edel's <u>Henry James: The Master.</u>

4   Brooks, Sydney. "Henry James at Home," HarperW, 48 (October 8, 1904), 1548-1549.

5   Bruccoli, Matthew J. "Fitzgerald, Brooks, Hemingway, and James: A New Fitzgerald Letter," FitzgeraldN, 29 (Spring, 1965), 1-3. Letter about James's injury in his youth.

1

5.1   Burr, Anna Robeson. Alice James: Her Brothers, Her Jour-
       nal. New York: Dodd Mead, 1934; repr., Boston: Milford
       House, 1972.

5.2   Clemens, Katherine. "Alice James, Neglected Sister," MTQ,
       6 (Summer-Fall, 1944), 6-7.
       Relates the comments of Alice James as to Henry James
       and Mark Twain.

5.3   Clemons, Walter. Newsweek, 79 (February 14, 1972), 92.
       Essay-review, Leon Edel's Henry James: The Master.

5.4   Cowser, John. "Henry James's Ancestry," TLS (January 25,
       1957), 49; Leon Edel, ib., (March 8, 1957), 145.

6   Dunbar, Viola R. "Addenda to 'Biographical and Critical
       Studies of Henry James, 1941-1948,' AL, 20 (January, 1949),
       424-435," AL, 22 (March, 1950), 56-61.

7   Dupee, Frederick W. Henry James: His Life and Writings.
       American Men of Letters Series. William Sloane Associates,
       1951; rev., and enl., Garden City, New York: Doubleday
       Anchor, 1956; Dell, 1965.

7.1   Edel, Leon. "The Exile of Henry James," UTQ, 2 (July,
       1933), 520-532.

7.2   _____, ed. Introduction. The Diary of Alice James. New
       York: Dodd, Mead, 1964, passim.
       Cf., Anna Robeson Burr. Alice James. 1934.

7.3   _____. Henry James: Les Années Dramatiques. Paris:
       Jouve et Cie, 1931.
       Contains much biographical material.

8   _____. Henry James: The Untried Years, 1843-1870.
       New York: Philadelphia: Lippincott, 1953.
       Biographical and interpretive. Edel's five-volume set is
       here arranged in chronological order.

9   _____. Henry James: The Conquest of London, 1870-1881.
       New York: Philadelphia: Lippincott, 1962.

10   _____. Henry James: The Middle Years, 1882-1895.
       New York: Philadelphia: Lippincott, 1962.

11   _____. Henry James: The Treacherous Years: 1895-
       1901. New York: Philadelphia: Lippincott, 1969.

12   _____. Henry James: The Master, 1901-1916. New
       York: Philadelphia: Lippincott, 1972.

13   _____. "Henry James and Sir Sydney Waterlow: The Un-

published Diary of a British Diplomat, " TLS, 3, 467 (August 8, 1968), 844-845.

14   . "The Jameses, " TLS, 3, 684 (October 13, 1972), 1226-1227.
Cf. , Jacques Barzun. "The Jameses, " TLS, 3, 680 (September 15, 1972), 1060.

15   . Literary Biography: The Alexander Lectures, 1955-1956. Toronto U. P., 1957, pp. 11-12, 26-38, 99-103, passim.

15. 1   . "Time and the Biographer, " Listener, 54 (September 22, 1955), 461-462.

15. 2   . "To the Poet of Prose, " MFS, 12 (Spring, 1966), 3-6.
Commemoration of the fiftieth anniversary of James's death.

16   Edgar, Pelham. Henry James: Man and Author. Boston and New York: Houghton Mifflin, 1927. Reissued, Russell & Russell, 1964.
A critical biography of James in which his works are treated chronologically, with summaries of plot and style.

17   Ellis, Davis. "Edel's James, " Delta, 36 (Summer, 1965), 2-9.
In selection of material says that Edel shows "no sense of what might have been the important events in James's life. "

17. 1   Flower, Dean. Henry James in Northampton: Visions and Revisions. Northampton, Mass.: Friends of the Smith College Library, 1971.

17. 2   Frank, Joseph. "Henry James: The Real Thing, " SR, 63 (Winter, 1955), 168-174.
Essay-review, Edel's Henry James: The Untried Years. 1953.

18   Garis, Robert. "Anti-Literary Biography, " HudR, 23 (1970), 143-153.
An indictment of Edel's approach in Henry James: The Treacherous Years.

19   Garnett, David. The Golden Echo. New York: Harcourt, Brace & Co., 1954.
Autobiographical account of association with James.

20   Gass, William H. "A Spirit in Search of Itself, " Fiction and the Figures of Life. New York: Knopf, 1970, pp. 157-163.

21   Gosse, Edmund. "Henry James, " Aspects and Impressions.

London and New York: 1922, pp. 17-53.

22   Gould, Cecil. ["Henry James"], TLS, 3,508 (May 22, 1969),
        558.
            Cf., H. Montgomery Hyde. "Henry James," TLS, 3,507
            (May 15, 1969), 525. A defense of James's character
            which Mr. Gould says should be accepted.

23   Grattan, C. Hartley. The Three Jameses, A Family of
        Minds: Henry James, Sr., William James, Henry James.
        New York: Longmans, Green, 1932. Repr., New York Uni-
        versity Press, 1962.

24   Greene, Graham. "Henry James," NSt, 46 (July 18, 1953),
        76.
            Essay-rev., Edel's Henry James: The Untried Years.

25   Hamilton, E. C. "Biographical and Critical Studies of Henry
        James," AL, 20 (January, 1949), 424-435.

25.1   Hampshire, Stuart. "A Son and Brother," NYRB, 8 (June 29,
        1967), 3-4.

26   Hartsock, Mildred E. "Biography: The Treacherous Art,"
        JML, 1 (1970), 116-119.
            Essay-review, Leon Edel. Henry James: The Treacher-
            ous Years.

26.1   Hastings, Katherine. "William James of Albany, New York,
        and His Descendants," NYG&BR, 55 (April, July, October,
        1924).
            A full genealogy of the James family.

26.2   Hicks, Granville. "Vision Behind the Vision," SatR, 45 (No-
        vember 3, 1962), 23.
            Essay-review, Leon Edel. Henry James: Conquest of Lon-
            don, and The Middle Years.

27   Hoffman, Frederick J. "The Expense and Power of Greatness:
        An Essay on Leon Edel's Henry James," VQR, 39 (Summer,
        1963), 518-528.
            Remarks on the creative blend of biography and criticism
            in Edel's work on James.

28   Houser, Zelma Large. "Early Years of Henry James," MTQ,
        8 (Winter-Spring, 1949), 9-10.

29   Hyde, H. Montgomery. "Henry James," TLS, 3,507 (May 15,
        1969), 525.
            Cf., Cecil Gould. ["Henry James"], TLS, 3,508 (May 22,
            1969), 558.

30   _____. Henry James at Home. New York: Farrar,

Straus and Giroux, 1969.
A detailed and interesting biography, well documented.

31   _____. "The Lamb House Library of Henry James, " BC,
16 (Winter, 1967), 477-480. Repr., The Lamb House Library of Henry James. London: Collector, 1967.

32   _____. The Story of Lamb House, Rye: The Home of
Henry James. Rye, Sussex: Adams of Rye Ltd., 1966.

33   Hynes, Samuel. "A Small Literary Monument, " Cw, 77 (November 9, 1962), 172-174.
Calls Edel's definitive biography of Henry James a monument to the master.

33.1   "The Intellectual Jameses, " Newsweek, 30 (November 3, 1947),
93-94.
Essay-rev., F. O. Matthiessen's The James Family, and
Matthiessen and Murdock's The Notebooks of Henry James.

34   Jefferson, D. W. Henry James. Writers and Critics Series.
Edinburgh: Oliver and Boyd, 1960; New York: Barnes &
Noble, 1965.

34.1   Jones, Howard Mumford. "An Altar of the Living, " NewRep,
147 (November 17, 1962), 30ff.
Essay-review, Leon Edel's Conquest of London and The
Middle Years.

35   Karita, Motoshi. "Shosetsu to Denki no Shudai-sentaku to
Imi, " SophiaT, 17 (1968), 29-45.
Matter and meaning in fiction and biography in James and
Hawthorne.

35.1   Larrabee, Harold A. "The Jameses: Financier, Heretic,
Philosopher, " AmSch, 1 (October, 1932), 401-413.

36   Le Clair, Robert C. "Henry James and Minny Temple, " AL,
21 (March, 1949), 35-48.
Evidence of letters shows that James was speaking of his
cousin "Minny" Temple when he referred to "the starved
romance of my life. "

37   _____. Young Henry James, 1843-1870. New York:
Bookman Associates, 1955.

37.1   "Life of James at Rye, " CurL, 29 (August, 1900), 148.

37.2   MacCarthy, Desmond. "Money, Birth and Henry James, "
NSt, 9 (July 21, 1917), 375-376.

37.3   Maddocks, Melvin. ["Henry James"], Time, 99 (February
14, 1972), 70ff.

Essay-rev., Leon Edel's Henry James: The Master. A
laudatory review.

37.4   "The Matter of the Master," TLS, #3,677 (August 18, 1972),
       957-959.

38   Matthiessen, Francis Otto. The James Family: Including
       Selections from the Writings of Henry James, Sr., William,
       Henry, and Alice James. New York: Knopf, 1947.
       An outstanding study.

39   Moore, Rayburn S. "The Full Light of a Higher Criticism:
       Edel's Biography and Other Recent Studies of Henry James,"
       SAQ, 63 (Winter, 1964), 104-113.
       Objects to Edel's sparse documentation.

40   Mutarelli, Giorgio. "Una biografia di James," FLe, 17 (No-
       vember 25, 1962), 4.

41   Narkevich, A. Iu. "Genri Dzhems (25 let so dnia smerti).
       [Henry James (25th anniversary of his death)]. Literaturnoe
       obozrenie, 1941, no. 4, p. 79.

42   Nowell-Smith, Simon, ed. The Legend of the Master, Henry
       James. New York: Scribner's, 1948.
       Includes anecdotes about James, with a chronological table
       of his life and works.

43   Perry, Ralph Barton. The Thought and Character of William
       James. London: Oxford U. P., 1935; Boston: Little, Brown
       & Co., 1935, passim.
       Comments on the boyhood and education of Henry James.

44   Porter, Katherine Anne. "The Days Before," in The Days
       Before. New York: Harcourt, Brace & Co., 1926, 1952,
       pp. 3-22.
       An analysis of James's youth.

45   Scott, R. H. F. ["Henry James"], TLS (May 22, 1969), 558.
       Cf., Montgomery Hyde. "Henry James," TLS, 3,507 (May
       15, 1969), 525; and Cecil Gould. ["Henry James"], TLS,
       3,508 (May 22, 1969), 558.

45.1   Sharp, Robert L. "Stevenson and James's Childhood," NCF,
       8 (December, 1953), 236-237.

45.2   Stevenson, Elizabeth. "Something about Biography," EUQ, 17
       (1961), 129-132.

46   Tanner, Tony. "A Choice of Inheritance," Spectator, 7,011
       (November 9, 1962), 719-720.
            Essay-rev., Leon Edel. Henry James: The Conquest of
            London.

46.1   Trilling, Lionel. "The Jameses," TLS, 3,685 (October 20, 1972), 1257.

47   Warren, Austin. "William and Henry," The Elder Henry James. Freeport, New York: Books for Libraries Press, 1934, repr., 1970, pp. 127-161.

48   Wegelin, Christof. "Jamesian Biography," NCF, 18 (December, 1963), 283-287.
       Laudatory comment on Edel's biographical method.

48.1   Weimer, David R. ["Henry James"], Nation, 214 (April 24, 1972), 539-540.
       Essay-review, Leon Edel. Henry James: The Master.

48.2   Wiesenfarth, Joseph. ["Henry James"], Cw, 96 (March 17, 1972), 44-45.
       Essay-rev., Leon Edel. Henry James: The Master.

48.3   Wilson, Edmund. "New Documents on the Jameses," NY, 23 (December 13, 1947), 133-137.
       Essay-review, F. O. Matthiessen. The James Family.

See also AUTOBIOGRAPHY, THE MIDDLE YEARS, NOTES OF A SON AND BROTHER, and A SMALL BOY AND OTHERS

II. WORKS

NOVELS, STORIES AND PLAYS

"Abasement of the Northmores"

49   Gale, Robert L. "The Abasement of Mrs. Warren Hope,"
      PMLA, 78 (March, 1963), 98-102.
       The abasement of the Northmore family is in the mind of
       Mrs. Hope.

      See also: 270, 1740, 1794, 2198, 2229, 2352, 2637, 2637.1,
      3536, 3706

"Adina"

      See: 9, 10, 1794, 1799, 2198, 2352, 2564, 2695, 3354,
      3536, 3626, 3710, 3711

"The Altar of the Dead"

50   Monteiro, George. "Hawthorne, James, and the Destructive
      Self," TSLL, 4 (Spring, 1962), 58-71.

51   Tate, Allen. "Three Commentaries: Poe, James, Joyce,"
      SR, 58 (1950), 1-15.
       Considers this story James's greatest failure.

      See also: 8, 10, 11, 12, 38, 270, 1740, 1794, 1890, 1924,
      2006, 2028, 2062, 2198, 2205, 2208, 2229, 2258, 2352, 2380,
      2382, 2560, 2630, 2637, 2637.1, 2737, 2770, 2944, 3332,
      3417, 3521, 3536, 3702, 3702.1, 3703, 3711, 3720.1

THE AMBASSADORS

52   Alexander, Charlotte Anne. "The Emancipation of Lambert
      Strether: A Study of the Relationship Between the Ideas of
      William and Henry James," DA, 28 (Indiana: 1964), 661A-
      62A.
       Development of Strether influenced by a knowledge of Wil-
       liam's thinking.

53   Altick, Richard D. "Textual Study, " The Art of Literary Re-
        search. New York: W. W. Norton & Co., 1963, p. 49.
        Cf., Leon Edel. "The Text of The Ambassadors, " HLB,
        14 (1960), 453-460.

54   Andersen, Kenneth. "Mark Twain, W. D. Howells, and Hen-
        ry James: Three Agnostics in Search of Salvation, " MTJ, 15
        (1970), 13-16.
        The experience of Lambert Strether, and heroes of Twain
        and Howells, in the search for their destinies.

55   Aoki, Tsugio. "Strether's Imagination: On Henry James's
        The Ambassadors, " SELit, 39 (March, 1963), 33-49.

55. 1   Auchincloss, Louis. "The Ambassadors, " Horizon, 15 (Sum-
        mer, 1973), 118-119.

56   Bass, Eben. "Lemon-Colored Volumes and Henry James, "
        SSF, 1 (Winter, 1964), 113-122.
        The phrase in The Ambassadors is linked to James's con-
        tributions to The Yellow Book and to the current associa-
        tion of yellow with artistic idealism.

57   Bennett, Arnold. The Journal of Arnold Bennett, 1896-1910.
        2 vols. New York: Viking Press, 1932, I, 206.
        An uncomplimentary opinion of the novel.

58   Bennett, Joan. "The Art of Henry James: The Ambassadors, "
        ChiR, 9 (Winter, 1956), 12-26.
        The "figure in the carpet" of The Ambassadors is the con-
        flict of values.

59   Berland, Alwyn. "Americans and Ambassadors: on Henry
        James, " WascanaR, 1, ii (1966), 53-82.
        Analysis of Strether's development into the "whole man"
        provides insight into James's artistic growth.

59. 1   _____. "Henry James, " UKCR, 18 (1951), 94-108.
        A good analysis of point of view.

59. 2   Birch, Brian. "Henry James: Some Bibliographical and
        Textual Matters, " Library, 20 (1965), 108-123.
        Discussion of textual complications in The Ambassadors,
        and the deficiency of Edel and Laurence's Bibliography of
        Henry James in their not recording earlier texts.

60   _____. "Reply, " [to S. P. Rosenbaum], Library, 21
        (1966), 250-52.
        Cf., S. P. Rosenbaum. "The Editions of The Ambassa-
        dors, " Library, 21 (1966), 248-250.

61   Black, James O. "A Novel as a 'Work of Art': A Reading
        of The Ambassadors, " DA, 19 (Arkansas: 1958), 1750.

62   Blackmur, R. P. Introduction. The Ambassadors. New
        York: Dell, 1964.

62.1   _____, ed. Preface. "The Ambassadors," in The Art
        of the Novel: Critical Prefaces By Henry James. New York
        and London: Scribner's, 1934, pp. 309-310.

63   Bontly, Thomas J. "The Moral Perspective of The Ambas-
        sadors," WisSL, 6 (1969), 106-117.
        The novel demonstrates that for James there was "special
        affinity ... between the intelligence of the novelist ... and
        the intelligence of the individual as he exercises his mor-
        al prerogative.

64   Brennan, Joseph G. "Three Novels of Dépaysement," CL,
        22 (Summer, 1970), 223-236.
        Comparison of The Ambassadors and L'Immoraliste by
        André Gide and Der Zauberberg by Thomas Mann.

65   Brewster, Dorothy, and Angus Burrell. "Paris and the Puri-
        tan: The Ambassadors by Henry James," Dead Reckonings in
        Fiction.
        London: Longmans, Green, 1924, pp. 19-41.

66   Brown, Daniel Russell. "The Cosmopolitan Novel: James
        and Lewis," SLN, 1, i (Spring, 1969), 6-9.
        The ties between The Ambassadors and Dodsworth.

67   Brown, E. K. Rhythm in the Novel. Toronto: University
        of Toronto Press, 1950; repr., 1957, pp. 24-27.
        An apt discussion of characters and incidents in The Am-
        bassadors.

68   Busch, Frieder. Erzähler-, Figuren- und Leserperspektive
        in Henry James Roman "The Ambassadors." München: Max
        Hueber, 1967.
        Discussion of the techniques of The Ambassadors.

69   Cargill, Oscar. "The Ambassadors: A New View," PMLA,
        75 (September, 1960), 439-452.
        The Ambassadors owes more to James's "past accumula-
        tions" than any of his other novels.

69.1   _____. Introduction. The Ambassadors. New York:
        Washington Square Press, 1963.

70   Cecil, L. Moffitt. " 'Virtuous Attachment' in James's The
        Ambassadors," AQ, 19 (Winter, 1967), 719-724.
        James shows the difference between the moral codes of
        the New and Old Worlds, and that neither code is "moral
        enough to stand as an adequate guide for the conduct of a
        morally sensitive person. "

71   Chartier, Richard. "The River and the Whirlpool: Water
        Imagery in The Ambassadors," BSUF, 12 (Spring, 1971), 70-
        75.
            The water imagery is "the most lucid unifying element in
        the novel," operating "below the level of plot and charac-
        ter" and as "sublevel" perhaps "clearer than the surface
        level."

72   Chase, Richard. "James' Ambassadors," Twelve Original
        Essays on Great American Novels. Charles Shapiro, ed.
        Detroit: Wayne State University Press, 1958, pp. 124-127.
            "The Ambassadors is not intended to be a full-blown so-
        cial novel; it is a novel of manners...."

73   Cooper, Frederick Taber. "The Novelist's Omniscience and
        Some Recent Books," Bookman (America), 18 (January, 1904),
        530-537 [532-34].
            Defines The Ambassadors as a "study of the New England
        conscience subjected to the hot-house atmosphere of the
        Parisian Vie de Boheme."

74   Coursen, Herbert R., Jr. "The Mirror of Allusion: The
        Ambassadors," NEQ, 34, #3 (September, 1961), 382-384.
            Use of the Cleopatra allusion to characterize Madame de
        Vionnet.

74.1   Crews, Frederick C. "The Ambassadors," The Tragedy of
        Manners: Moral Drama in the Later Novels of Henry James.
        New Haven: Yale University Press, 1957, pp. 30-56.

75   Cromwell, Agnes Whitney. "Innocent Among the Lions,"
        Vogue, 15 (November, 1951), 158.
            Agnes Whitney Cromwell, in talking with James about The
        Ambassadors, was asked whether she knew what had hap-
        pened to Strether, Chad, or to Miss Gostrey after the book
        ended. When she answered in the negative, James admit-
        ted that he did not know either.

76   Davis, J. "Intention and Achievement in Narrative Tech-
        nique: Henry James's The Ambassadors," KN, 12 (3rd Qt.,
        1965), 245-254.
            Points out that James enters the story by comments on
        characters, by explaining motives, and by moderating dra-
        matic scenes.

77   Deans, Thomas R. "Henry James' The Ambassadors: The
        Primal Scene Revisited," AI, 29 (Fall, 1972), 233-256.
            An analysis of Strether's recurrent sexual fantasies, their
        course and consequence.

78   Dooley, D. J. "The Hourglass Pattern in The Ambassadors,"
        NEQ, 41 (June, 1968), 273-281.
            A good treatment of the hourglass pattern in this novel.

78.1   Dorris, George E. "Two Allusions in the Poetry of T. S.
       Eliot," ELN, 2, #1 (September, 1964), 54-57.
           The beginning of the "Fragment of an Agon" in Sweeney
       Agonistes echoes a scene in James's The Ambassadors.

79   Dort, B. "Un roman de la connaissance: 'Les Ambassa-
       deurs' d'Henry James," CS, 33 (1951), 329-333.

80   Dunn, Albert O. "Articulation of Time in The Ambassadors,"
       Criticism, 14 (Spring, 1972), 137-150.
           Time in The Ambassadors is always ultimately the pres-
       ent.

80.1   Dupee, F. W., ed. Introduction. The Ambassadors. New
       York: Rinehart, 1960.

81   Durr, Robert A. "The Night Journey in The Ambassadors,"
       PQ, 35 (October, 1956), 24-38.
           Strether's journey is comparable to the rites de passage
       and to the myths embodying the rhythm of death and re-
       birth.

82   Edel, Leon. "A Further Note on 'An Error in The Ambas-
       sadors,' " AL, 23 (March, 1951), 128-130.
           Edel notes that no reverse order of Chapters 28 and 29
       can be found in the English edition which James personally
       saw through the press.
           Cf., Robert E. Young. "An Error in The Ambassadors,"
       AL, 22 (1950-51), 246-253.

83   _____. "Henry James: The Ambassadors," Landmarks
       of American Writing. Hennig Cohen, ed. New York: Basic
       Books, 1969, pp. 182-93.

84   _____. "Henry James's Revisions for The Ambassadors,"
       N&Q, n. s., 2 (January, 1955), 37-38.
           James did not revise The Ambassadors heavily for book
       publication; he rather inserted portions left out in the seri-
       al version.

85   _____, ed. Introduction. The Ambassadors. Boston:
       Houghton Mifflin, 1960.

85.1   _____. Introduction. The Bodley Head Henry James.
       Vol. 8 The Ambassadors. (With the author's Preface.)
       London: Bodley Head, 1970.

86   _____. "A Letter to the Editors," [Rejoinder to Robert E.
       Young], AL, 24 (November, 1952), 370-372.
           The reversed chapters in The Ambassadors do not occur in
       the Methuen edition, which was the first edition. Cf., Ro-
       bert E. Young, AL, 22 (1950), 245-253.

87   _____. "The Text of The Ambassadors," HLB, 14, #3
            (Autumn, 1960), 453-460.
            On errors in current editions.

88   _____. "Time and The Ambassadors," MLN, 73 (March,
            1958), 177-179.
            Rebuttal to R. W. Stallman. "Time and the Unnamed
            Article in The Ambassadors," MLN, 72 (January, 1957),
            27-32.

88.1   Engstrom, Susanne. "Epistemological and Moral Validity in
            Henry James's The Ambassadors," Lang&L, 1, i (1971), 50-
            65.

89   Evans, Patricia. "The Meaning of the Match Image in
            James's The Ambassadors," MLN, 70 (January, 1955), 36-
            37.
            Cf., R. W. Stallman. "Time and the Unnamed Article in
            The Ambassadors," MLN, 72 (January, 1957), 27-32.

90   Fiderer, Gerald. "James's Discriminated Occasion," Crit-
            ique, 11, #2 (1969), 56-69.

90.1   Finn, C. M. "Commitment and Identity in The Ambassa-
            dors," MLR, 66, #3 (July, 1971), 522-531.
            In references in the Notebooks, Strether is more deeply
            committed to Mrs. Newsome, Woollett, and the little re-
            view than in the novel. The finished book presents an in-
            dividual who is still searching for an identity and a com-
            mitment.

91   Fisher, Neil H. Introduction. The Ambassadors. New
            York: Airmont, 1965.

92   Forster, E. M. "The Ambassadors," Aspects of the Novel.
            New York: Harcourt, 1927; renewed, 1955, pp. 218-234.

93   Fox, Hugh, Jr. "Henry James and the Antimonian James
            Household: A Study of Selfhood and Selflessness," ArQ,
            15 (Spring, 1959), 49-55.

93.1   Frederiksen, Bodil F. "Moral or Historical Validity: Henry
            James, The Ambassadors," Lang&L, 1, iii (1972), 58-66.

94   Friese, Fränze. "Auf der Suche nach dem Muster im Tep-
            pich," TuK, 15, #6 (1967), 22-43.

95   Gale, Robert L. Study Guide to Henry James' "The Ambas-
            sadors." (Pennant key-indexed). Philadelphia: Educational
            Research Associates in association with Bantam Books, New
            York: 1967.

96   Gargano, James W. "The Ambassadors and Louis Lambert,"

MLN, 75 (March 1960), 211-213.
Similarities between James's novel and Balzac's.

97   Garis, Robert E. "The Two Lambert Strethers: A New
       Reading of The Ambassadors," MFS, 7 (Winter, 1961-1962),
       305-316.
       Strether's character in the last seven chapters contrasts
       with that in the first twenty-nine chapters.

98   Geismar, Maxwell. "The Ambassadors: A New View," SA
       7 (1961), 105-132.

99   Gerber, John C., and Martin W. Sampson. Introduction.
       The Ambassadors. New York: n. d.

100   Gibson, William M. "Metaphor in the Plot of The Ambassa-
       dors," NEQ, 24 (September, 1951), 291-305.
       The "apparently disparate images and scenes" of the novel
       form an "essential element of James's meaning."

101   Goldstein, Sallie Sears. "A Critical Study of Henry James's
       The Wings of the Dove, The Ambassadors, and The Golden
       Bowl," DA, 24 (Brandeis: 1964), 5384-85.
       James's vision is negative rather than tragic.

102   Goode, John. " 'Character' and Henry James," NewLR, 40
       (November-December, 1966), 55-75.

103   Gordon, Caroline. "Some Readings and Misreadings," SR,
       61 (Summer, 1953), 387-388.

103.1 Grabo, Carl H. "Excellence of the Point of View in James's
       The Ambassadors," The Technique of the Novel. New York:
       Scribners, 1928; repr., New York: Gordian Press, 1964, pp.
       81-94.
       In The Ambassadors, more than in any other novel, the
       point of view is handled "with greater subtlety and is fur-
       ther prefaced by the author's analysis of his purpose and
       the reasons which led him to construct the novel as he
       did."

104   Hartsock, Mildred E. "The Dizzying Crest: Strether as
       Moral Man," MLQ, 26 (September, 1965), 414-425.
       The ending of the novel is a repudiation of Puritanism.
       Strether has discovered that no code will do. He antici-
       pates Camus' existentialism.

105   Hill, John S. "Henry James: Fitzgerald's Literary Ances-
       tor," FitzN, 40 (Winter, 1968), 6-10.
       Fitzgerald's debt to James's The Ambassadors has been
       overlooked.

106   Holder, Alan. "On the Structure of Henry James's Meta-

phors," ES, 41 (October, 1960), 289-297.

107 Hopkins, Viola. "Gloriani and the Tides of Taste," NCF, 18 (June, 1963), 65-71.
The author shows how James changed Gloriani, who first appeared in Hudson, when he presented the sculptor again in The Ambassadors and the Velvet Glove."

108 Horowitz, Floyd R. "The Ambassadors: A Modern Allegory," DA, 21 (Iowa: 1960), 1949.

109 Hudspeth, Robert N. "The Definition of Innocence: James's The Ambassadors," TSLL, 6 (Autumn, 1964), 354-360.
"The American innocent cannot conceive of the evil within his own culture but the American initiate can."

110 Humphreys, S. M. "Henry James's Revisions for The Ambassadors," N&Q, 1, n. s. (September, 1954), 397-399.
Comparison of the New York edition and the original version in the North American Review.

110.1 Hutton, Virgil. "James Joyce's The Dead," E-WR, 2, #2 (Winter 1965-1966), 124-139.
The essential theme is almost identical to that of James's The Ambassadors.

111 Kamerbeck, J., Jr. "Two Golden Nails: Henry James and Sainte-Beuve," RLC, 36 (July-September, 1962), 447-451.
Images in The Ambassadors and Sainte-Beuve's Le Clou d'Or.

112 Kaye, Julian B. "The Awkward Age, The Sacred Fount, and The Ambassadors: Another Figure in the Carpet," NCF 17 (March, 1963), 339-353.
Sees Strether's triumph as the resolution of conflicts dramatized earlier by Henry James.

113 Kazin, Alfred. Introduction and Commentaries. The Ambassadors. Toronto, New York: Bantam Books, 1969, pp. 541-562.

114 Kenton, Edna. "The Ambassadors--Project of a Novel," H&H, 7 (April-June, 1934), 541-562.

115 Kinoian, Vartkis. Henry James' "The Ambassadors." New York: Monarch Press, Inc., 1965.

116 Knoepflmacher, U. C. " 'O Rare for Strether!': Antony and Cleopatra and The Ambassadors," NCF, 19 (March, 1965), 333-344.
Comparison of the novel with Shakespeare's play.

117 Knox, George. "James's Rhetoric of 'Quotes,' " CE, 17

(February, 1956), 293-297.
The validity of James's use of quotation marks in The
Ambassadors.

118   Kraft, Quentin G.   "The Question of Freedom in James's
       Fiction," CE, 26 (February, 1965), 372-381.

119   Kudo, Yoshimi.   "Strether to Prufrock," EigoS, 114 (1968),
       790-791.
       James's influence on T. S. Eliot.

119.1 Lauer, Kristin, Olson.   "The Interior Monologue in The Am-
       bassadors and The Golden Bowl," DAI, 31 (Michigan State:
       1970), 6015A.

119.2 Leavis, Frank Raymond.   "The Meaning of Paris in The Am-
       bassadors: A Disagreement," The Ambassadors: An Author-
       itative Text: The Author on the Novel: Criticism. S. P.
       Rosenbaum, ed.   A Norton Critical Edition.   New York: W.
       W. Norton, 1964, pp. 438-439.

120   Lee, Brian.   "Henry James's 'Divine Consensus': The Am-
       bassadors, The Wings of the Dove, The Golden Bowl," RMS,
       6 (1962), 5-24.
       These novels show James's dependence on "the native in-
       tellectual climate" of which both father and son partook.

121   Liddell, Robert.   "A Plot Successfully Deduced from One
       Episode: The Ambassadors," A Treatise on the Novel. Lon-
       don: Jonathan Cape, 1947, repr., 1963, pp. 82-84.

122   Lodge, David.   "Strether by the River," Language of Fiction:
       Essays in Criticism and Verbal Analysis of the English Nov-
       el.   London: Routledge & Kegan Paul, 1966; New York:
       Columbia U. P., 1966, pp. 189-213.

123   Logan, Annie R. M.   "The Ambassadors," Nation, 78 (Feb-
       ruary 4, 1904), 95.
       Repr., in Twentieth Century Interpretations of "The Ambas-
       sadors." Albert E. Stone, Jr., ed.   Englewood Cliffs, New
       Jersey: Prentice-Hall, Inc., 1969, pp. 24-27.

124   Long, Robert E.   "The Ambassadors and the Genteel Tradi-
       tion: James's Correction of Hawthorne and Howells," NEQ,
       42 (March, 1969), 44-64.
       James was more expert than Hawthorne and Howells in his
       correction of the "type."

125   Lubbock, Perry.   "The Point of View: The Ambassadors,"
       The Craft of Fiction: Picture, Drama, and Point of View.
       London: Jonathan Cape, 1921, pp. 161-171, passim; New
       York: The Viking Press, 1957; reissued, 1963.

126   Mackenzie, Manfred. "Henry James: Serialist Early and
       Late," PQ, 41 (April, 1962), 492-499.

127   Maixner, Paul Roger. "Henry James and the Question of
       Formal Unity," DA, 27 (Columbia: 1966), 1828A-29A.
       The integration of moral and aesthetic values is best il-
       lustrated in The Ambassadors and "Madame de Mauves."

128   Matthiessen, F. O. "The Ambassadors," in The Question
       of Henry James. F. W. Dupee, ed. New York: Henry
       Holt, 1945, pp. 218-235.

129   Maxwell, J. C. "The Text of The Ambassadors," EIC, 11
       (January, 1961), 116.
       Reply to Ian Watt. "The First Paragraph of The Am-
       bassadors: An Explication," EIC, 10 (1960), 250-274;
       Rejoinder by Watt, EIC, 11 (1961), 116-119.

130   Maynard, Reid. "The Irony of Strether's Enlightenment,"
       LHR, 11 (1969), 33-44.
       Raises the question whether it is "not possible that James
       ... created a protagonist [Strether] who does not become
       quite so enlightened as he or Strether would like to be-
       lieve."

130.1 McCullough, Bruce. "Henry James," Representative Eng-
       lish Novelists: Defoe to Conrad. New York: Harper, 1947,
       pp. 274-302.

131   McGinty, Sister Mary Carolyn, C.S.J. "The Jamesian
       Parenthesis: Elements of Suspension in the Narrative Sen-
       tences of Henry James's Late Style," DA, 24 (Catholic Univ.:
       1964), 4193.
       Structural analysis of the "Jamesian Parenthesis" in the
       sentences of The Ambassadors.

132   McLean, Robert C. "The Completed Vision: A Study of
       'Madame de Mauves' and The Ambassadors," MLQ, 28 (De-
       cember, 1967), 446-461.
       James's early novella offered the basic material for The
       Ambassadors.

133   Michael, Mary Kyle. "Henry James's Use of the Word
       Wonderful in The Ambassadors," MLN, 75 (February, 1960),
       114-117.
       The use of the word wonderful in a "wide range of nu-
       ances, overtones, and ironies" unifies the resolution,
       Strether's "preservation of his integrity," and the art of
       the novel.

134   Mizener, Arthur. "The Ambassadors," in Twelve Great
       American Novels. New York: New American Library,
       1967, pp. 49-67.

135   Mudrick, Marvin. "Colette and Strether," HudR, 15 (Spring, 1962), 110-113.

136   Mulqueen, James E.   "Perfection of a Pattern: The Struc-
       ture of The Ambassadors, The Wings of the Dove, and The
       Golden Bowl," ArQ, 27 (Summer, 1971), 133-142.
       Similarity of pattern in all three novels.

137   Nathan, Monique. "Les 'Ambassadeurs' et les carnets de
       James," Critique, 7 (June, 1951), 492-498. [Paris]

138   Nettels, Elsa. "The Ambassadors and the Sense of the
       Past," MLQ, 31 (June, 1970), 220-235.

139   Normand, Jean. "L'Ambassadeur: Henry James, romancier
       des deux mondes," IeD, 216 (May 15, 1965), 14-19.

140   O'Grady, Walter. "On Plot in Modern Fiction: Hardy,
       James, and Conrad," MFS, 11 (Summer, 1965), 107-115.

141   Paget, Violet. [Pseud., Lee, Vernon]. "The Handling of
       Words: Meredith, Henry James," EngR, 5 (June, 1910),
       427-434.

141.1   _____. "The Handling of Words: Henry James," The
       Handling of Words and Other Studies in Literary Psychology.
       Lincoln, Nebraska: Nebraska Univ. Press, 1968, pp. 241-
       251.

142   Read, Sir Herbert Edward. "Two Notes on a Trilogy,"
       Tenth Muse: Essays in Criticism. New York: Horizon
       Press, 1957, pp. 189-197.

143   Reed, John Q. "The Ambassadors: Henry James's Method,"
       MwQ, 4 (Summer, 1962), 55-67.
       Analysis of the "four stages" in the creation of The Am-
       bassadors.

143.1   Richards, Bernard. "The Ambassadors and The Sacred
       Fount: the Artist Manqué," The Air of Reality, John Goode,
       ed. London: Methuen & Co., 1972, pp. 219-243.
       A study based on the similarities of theme and method of
       the two novels.

144   Rosenbaum, S. P., ed. The Ambassadors: An Authoritative
       Text, the Author on the Novel, Criticism. Norton Critical
       Editions. New York: W. W. Norton, 1964.

145   _____. "The Editions of The Ambassadors," Library, 21
       (1966), 248-250.
       Cf., Brian Birch, Library, 20 (1965), 108-123; and "Re-
       ply," Library, 21 (1966), 250-252.

146   Rupp, Henry R. Henry James's "The Ambassadors": Its
       Text and Evolution. Diss. NYU, n. d.

147   Ryan, Marjorie. "Forster, James, and Flaubert: A Paral-
       lel," N&Q, n. s. , 8 (March, 1961), 102-103.

147.1 Saalburg, Leslie. Illustrations and Preface. The Ambassa-
       dors. New York: Heritage Press, [1963].

148   Sampson, Martin W. Introduction. The Ambassadors. New
       York: Harper, 1930.

149   San Juan, Epifanio, Jr. "James's The Ambassadors: The
       Trajectory of the Climax," MwQ, 5 (July, 1964), 295-310.

150   Schneider, Daniel J. "The Ironic Imagery and Symbolism of
       James's The Ambassadors," Criticism, 9 (Spring, 1967), 174-
       196.
            Strether has outgrown "both the Woollett and Paris codes";
            he sees both cities as "but moulds into which 'the jelly of
            consciousness' may be poured to harden and, hardening,
            to die."

151   Schumann, Kuno. "Ethik und Ästhetik im Spätwerk von Hen-
       ry James," JA, 15 (1970), 77-87.

151.1 Sears, Sallie. "The Ambassadors," The Negative Imagina-
       tion: Form and Perspective in the Novels of Henry James.
       Ihaca, New York: Cornell Univ. Press, 1968, pp. 101-151.

152   Shriber, Michael. "Cognitive Apparatus in Daisy Miller, The
       Ambassadors, and Two Works by Howells: A Comparative
       Study of the Epistemology of Henry James," Lang&S, 2
       (1969), 207-225.
            A special study of the literary representation of "cogni-
            tion" as it reveals itself in early and later works of the
            two novelists.

152.1 Shucard, Alan R. "Diplomacy in Henry James's The Ambas-
       sadors," ArQ, 29, #2 (Summer, 1973), 123-129.
            James has woven an "intricate web of diplomacy" through
            the novel "as one of the important structural devices."

153   Sigaux, Gilbert. "Les Ambassadeurs," LaN, No. 71-2 (De-
       cember, 1950, January, 1951), 197-199.

154   Stallman, R. W. , ed. Afterword. The Ambassadors. New
       York: New American Library, 1961.

155   _____. "A Note on the Text of The Ambassadors," in
       The Houses That James Built, and Other Literary Studies.
       East Lansing, Michigan: Michigan State Univ. Press, 1961,
       pp. 51-53.

156   _____. " 'The Sacred Rage': The Time-Theme in The
           Ambassadors," MFS, 3 (Spring, 1957), 41-56.

156.1   _____. " 'The Sacred Rage': The Time-Theme in The
           Ambassadors," in The Houses That James Built. East Lan-
           sing, Michigan: Michigan State U. P., 1961, pp. 34-51.

157   _____. "Time and Mrs. Newsome's 'Blue Message': A
           Reply to Leon Edel," MLN, 76 (January, 1961), 20-23.
                Cf., Leon Edel. "Time and The Ambassadors," MLN,
                73 (1958), 177-79.

158   _____. "Time and the Unnamed Article in The Ambassa-
           dors," MLN, 72 (January, 1957), 27-32.

158.1   Stanzel, Franz K. Narrative Situations in the Novel: Tom
           Jones, Moby Dick, The Ambassadors, Ulysses. Tr., James
           P. Pusack. Bloomington, Ind.: Indiana U. P., 1971, pp.
           92-120.

159   _____. "Der personale Roman: The Ambassadors,"
           Chapter IV of Die Typischen Erzählsituationen im Roman,
           WBEP, 63. Wien: 1955, pp. 93-121.

160   Stein, William Bysshe. "The Ambassadors: The Crucifixion
           of Sensibility," CE, 17 (February, 1956), 289-292.

161   Stone, Albert E., Jr., ed. Introduction. Twentieth Century
           Interpretations of "The Ambassadors." Englewood Cliffs,
           New Jersey: Prentice-Hall, 1969.

162   Swinnerton, Frank. Introduction. The Ambassadors. Lon-
           don: Dent; New York: Dutton, 1962; Dent, 1966.

163   Tanner, Tony. "The Watcher from the Balcony: Henry
           James's The Ambassadors," CritQ, 8 (Spring, 1966), 35-52.
                Sees the balcony as an image of detached observation
                where extensions of consciousness are more important than
                mere memory.

164   Tate, Allen. "Three Commentaries," SR, 58 (Winter, 1950),
           5-10.
                Brief comparisons of "The Beast in the Jungle" and The
                Ambassadors.

165   Taylor, Gordon O. "The Friction of Existence: Henry
           James," The Passages of Thought: Psychological Represen-
           tation in the American Novel, 1870-1900. New York: Ox-
           ford U. P., 1969, pp. 42-84.

166   Terrie, Henry L. "The Image of Chester in The Ambassa-
           dors," ES, 46 (February, 1965), 46-50.
                Parallels of scene in the novel with James's essay on

Chester written for the Nation, 1872, reprinted in Trans-
atlantic Sketches, 1875.

167   Thomas, William B. "The Author's Voice in The Ambassadors," JNarT, 1, #2 (May, 1971), 108-121.
James intended to have us read the novel in its entirety
"as Strether's experience, registered by him, and relayed
by him."

168   Thurber, James; Mark Van Doren; and Lyman Bryson. "The
Ambassadors," InvitL, 1 (Winter, 1951-52), 364-371.

169   Tilford, John E., Jr. "James the Old Intruder," MFS, 4
(Summer, 1958), 157-164.
Authorial intrusions in The Ambassadors.

170   Tintner, Adeline R. "Balzac's 'Madame Firmiani,' and
James's The Ambassadors," CL, 25 (Spring, 1973), 128-135.

170.1   _____. "Balzac's Two Maries and James's The Ambassadors," ELN, 9 (1972), 284-287.

170.2   _____. "Hyacinth at the Play: The Play within the Play
as a Novelistic Device in James," JNT, 2 (1972), 171-185.
James's device in The Princess Casamassima "becomes
a technical resource of extraordinary subtlety" in The Ambassadors.

171   Veeder, William. "Strether and the Transcendence of Language," MP, 69 (November, 1971), 116-132.
Strether finally transcends language to arrive at "a truth
and a communion based upon shared receptions."

171.1   Wadden, Anthony T. "The Novel as Psychic Drama: Studies of Scott, Dickens, Eliot, and James," DAI, 31 (Iowa U.:
1970), 4737A.
"The 'anima' image of Mrs. Newsome dominates the neurosis of Strether, determining his return to America at
the end of the novel."

171.2   Wallace Ronald. "Comic Form in The Ambassadors,"
Genre, 5 (1972), 31-50.

172   Ward, J. A. "The Ambassadors as a Conversion Experi-
ence," SoR, 5, n. s. (Spring, 1969), 350-374.
Strether's transformation in Europe regarded as a typical
"Jamesian [religious] conversion."

173   _____. "The Ambassadors: Strether's Vision of Evil,"
NCF, 14 (June 1959), 45-58.
Europe provides a special "enriching [experience for
Strether] without which one is incomplete."

174   Warren, Austin. "The New England Conscience, Henry
        James and Ambassador Strether," MinnR, 2 (Winter, 1962),
        149-161.

174.1   _____. "The New England Conscience, Henry James, and
        Ambassador Strether," in Henry James's Major Novels. L.
        H. Powers, ed. Michigan State U. P., 1973, pp. 346-357.

175   Watt, Ian. "The First Paragraph of The Ambassadors: An
        Explication," EIC, 10 (July, 1960), 250-274.

176   _____. Rejoinder, EIC, 11 (1961), 116-119.
        Rejoinder to J. C. Maxwell. "The Text of The Ambassa-
        dors," EIC, 11 (1961), 116.

176.1   Wegelin, Christof. "The 'Internationalism' of The Golden
        Bowl," NCF, 11 (December, 1956), 161-181.
        The Golden Bowl is a fusion of the two points of view
        presented in The Ambassadors and The Wings of the Dove.

176.2   Weimer, David R. The City as Metaphor. New York:
        Random House, 1966, pp. 46-51.

177   Williams, Orlo. "The Ambassadors," Criterion, 8 (Septem-
        ber, 1928), 47-64.

178   Williamson, Marilyn L. " 'Almost Wholly in French': The
        Crisis in The Ambassadors," N&Q, n. s., 9 (March, 1962),
        106-107.
        Madame de Vionnet's lapse into French.

179   Wise, James N. "The Floating World of Lambert Strether,"
        ArlQ, 2 (Summer, 1969), 80-110.
        The tidal nature of Strether's journey in terms of the
        water over which it takes place.

180   Wolf, H. R. "The Psychology and Aesthetics of Abandon-
        ment in The Ambassadors," L&P, 21 #3 (1971), 133-147.
        Strether's journey is an unconscious search for identity
        and for psychic rebirth.

181   Young, Robert E. "An Error in The Ambassadors," AL, 22
        (November, 1950), 245-253.
        The reverse order of Chapters 28 and 29.

182   _____. "A Final Note on The Ambassadors," AL, 23
        (1952), 487-90.

Reviews of The Ambassadors:

        Athenaeum, 3970 (November 28, 1903), 714

Bookman (NY), 18 (January, 1904), 532-534; 20 (1905), 418-
419

Nation, 78 (February 4, 1904), 95

NoAmer, 176 (January-December, 1903), 138-60, 297-320,
459-480, 634-56, 792-816, 945-68; 177: 138-60, 297-
320, 457-80, 615-40, 779-800, 947-968

Outlook, 75 (December 19, 1903), 958; 78 (Sept. 10, 1904),
112-113

Poet-Lore, 16 (Winter, 1905), 94

Quarterly Rev, 198 (October, 1903), 358

SatR, 96, 551

TLS (October 16, 1903), 296

THE AMERICAN

183 Antush, John V. "The 'Much Finer Complexity' of History in
The American," JAmS, 6 (1972), 85-95.

183.1 Backus, Joseph M. " 'Poor Valentin' or 'Monsieur de Com-
te': Variation in Character Designation as Matter for Critical Consideration in Henry James' The American," Names,
20 (1972), 47-55.

184 Banta, Martha. "Rebirth and Revenge: The Endings of
Huckleberry Finn and The American," MFS, 15 (Summer,
1969), 191-207.
Comparison of the "social codes of revenge" in both novels.

185 Beach, Joseph Warren. Introduction. The American. New
York: Holt, Rinehart and Winston, 1949, 1964.

186 Bernard, F. V. "James's Florabella and the 'Land of the
Pink Sky,' " N&Q, 13 (1966), 70.
A passage in the Notebooks (p. 320) identifies America as
the "land of the pink sky."

186.1 Bhatnagar, O. P. "The American: A Revaluation," IJAS, 1,
iv (1971), 51-61.

187 Blackmur, R. P., ed. Introduction. The American. New
York: Dell Pub. Co., 1960.

187.1 Blasing, Mutlu. "Double Focus in The American," NCF, 28,
#1 (June, 1973), 74-84.
The double focus "reflects not only James's ambivalence toward a type like Newman but the nature of
the technical problem that confronted James in The
American."

187.2   Bosanquet, Theodora. " 'The Revised Version,' " LittleR,
        5 (August, 1918), 56-62.

188   Bosch, Louis Alan. "Henry James's The American: The
        Novel and the Play," DAI, 32 (Indiana: 1971), 5774A.
            A study of the two versions of The American, the 1877
            novel and the 1891 play, in order to determine the nature
            and causes of the failure of the play.

189   Brooks, Cleanth. "The American 'Innocence,' " Shenandoah,
        16 (Autumn, 1964), 21-37.

189.1   _____. "The American 'Innocence' in James, Fitzgerald,
        and Faulkner," in A Shaping Joy: Studies in the Writer's
        Craft. Harcourt Brace Jovanovich, Inc., 1972, pp. 181-197.

189.2   Butterfield, R. W. "The American," in The Air of Reality:
        New Essays on Henry James. John Goode, ed. London:
        Methuen & Co., 1972, pp. 5-35.
            The difference between the original edition and the revised
            New York edition.

190   Cargill, Oscar. "The First International Novel," PMLA, 73
        (September, 1958), 418-425.
            The first consciously produced international novel, The
            American, developed into a refutation of Dumas fils
            l'Etrangére, seen by James in February, 1876.

190.1   [Christopher Newman of The American], Nation, 24 (January
        11, 1877), 29.

191   Clair, John A. "The American: A Reinterpretation,"
        PMLA, 74 (December, 1959), 613-618.
            The American is not about "the innocent American lamb
            thrown to the continental wolves of Paris"; James's Pref-
            ace to the 1907 edition suggests a much deeper meaning.

192   Cook, George A. "Names in The American," CEA, 28 (Ap-
        ril, 1966), 5.
            Urbain de Bellegarde suggests "urbane," Valentin the triv-
            ial association with "valentine."

193   Creeth, Edmund. "Moonshine and Bloodshed: A Note on
        The American," N&Q, 9, n. s. (March, 1962), 105-106.
            Parallelism in appearance between Claire and Murillo's
            Madonna.

194   Duffy, John J. "Ernest Dowson and the Failure of Deca-
        dence," UR, 34 (October, 1967), 45-49.
            Dowson, perhaps the prototype of the aesthete in the 90's,
            is of interest partly for this fact but more for James's
            influence upon him.

195   Edel, Leon. Aferword. The American. New York: New
       York: New American Library, 1963.

196   Gargano, James W. "Foreshadowing in The American,"
       MLN, 74 (November, 1959), 600-601.
       The opera scene of Chapter 19 foreshadows Mme. de
       Cintré's retreat to the convent and Newman's suffering.

197   Gettmann, Royal A. "Henry James's Revision of The Amer-
       ican," AL, 16 (January, 1945), 279-295.
       The alterations in diction were toward the concrete and
       the explicit; no essential changes were made in the char-
       acters.

198   Gross, Barry. "Newman to Gatsby: This Side of Innocence,"
       PMASAL, 53 (1968), 279-289.
       The differences between these two generic characters are
       more important than the often-noted similarities.

198.1 Haas, Herta. Der Amerikaner. (Aus dem Englischen von
       Herta Haas.) Koln, Berlin: Kiepenheuer & Witsch, 1966.

199   Hoftund, Sigmund. "The Point of View in Henry James,"
       Edda, 61 (1961), 169-176.
       Negative criticism of The American.

200   Horowitz, Floyd R. "The Christian Time Sequence in Henry
       James's The American," CLAJ, 9 (1966), 234-245.
       Suggests that the use of Ash Wednesday for Newman's be-
       trothal to Claire, and the setting of the marriage for
       Palm Sunday, points to a scheme of religious symbolism.

201   Howe, Irving. "Henry James and the Millionaire," Tomor-
       row, 9 (January, 1950), 53-55.

202   James, Henry. "Preface to The American," in The Art of
       the Novel. New York: Scribner, 1934, pp. 20-39.

203   Johnson, C. "Adam and Eve and Isabel Archer," Renas-
       cence, 21 (Spring, 1969), 134-144, 167.

204   Kenney, B. G. "The Two Isabels: A Study in Distortion,"
       VN, 25 (1964), 15-17.

205   Knox, George. "Romance and Fable in James's The Ameri-
       can," Anglia, 83 (1965), 308-323.
       The American is a cultural fable of success and failure
       superimposed on fairy-tale motifs, allusions to marriage
       themes in Renaissance paintings, and the employment of
       18th century Gothic conventions.

206   Krutch, Joseph Wood. The Modern Temper: A Study and
       a Confession. New York: Harcourt, 1929, 1956, pp. 105-108.

207   Lowell, James Russell. New Letters of James Russell
        Lowell. M. A. DeWolfe Howe, ed. New York: 1932, pp.
        234-235.

208   Mackenzie, Manfred. "Henry James: Serialist Early and
        Late," PQ, 41 (April, 1962), 492-499.
            "In the case of The American the serial convention effec-
            tively helped James shape his narrative, and the result is
            a form graduated with extreme subtlety."

209   Maguire, C. E. "James and Dumas, fils," MD, 10 (1967),
        34-42.
            Influence of l'Etrangère on The American.

209.1   Millgate, Michael. American Social Fiction: James to Coz-
        zens. Edinburgh: Olive and Boyd; New York: Barnes &
        Noble, 1964.

210   Moore, John Robert. "An Imperfection in the Art of Henry
        James," NCF, 13 (March, 1959), 351-356.
            James's ignorance of the American business man vitiates
            the characterization of Christopher Newman.

211   Noda, Hisashi. "A Note on Mrs. Tristram and the Educa-
        tion of Christopher Newman," KAL, 10 (1967), 50-60.

212   Normand, Jean. "L'Ambassadeur: Henry James, romancier
        des deux mondes," IeD, 216 (May 5, 1965), 14-19.

213   Paget, Violet [Lee, Vernon] "Henry James," The Hand-
        ling of Words and Other Studies in Literary Psychology.
        Lincoln, Nebraska: Nebraska U. P., 1968 (reproduced
        from 1927 edition), pp. 241-251.

214   Parker, Hershel. "An Error in the Text of James's The
        American," AL, 37 (November, 1965), 316-318.
            Correction of error of attribution of speaker near end of
            Chapter XI in original serialization and editions derived
            from it.

215   Pearce, Roy Harvey. "Henry James and His American," in
        Historicism Once More: Problems and Occasions for the
        American Scholar. Princeton, New Jersey: Princeton U. P.,
        1969, pp. 240-260.

216   _____, and Matthew J. Bruccoli, eds. Introduction by
        Roy Harvey Pearce. A Note on the Text by Matthew J.
        Bruccoli. The American by Henry James. Boston: The
        Riverside Cambridge Press, Houghton Mifflin Co., 1962.

216.1   Poirier, Richard. "The American," The Comic Sense of
        Henry James: A Study of the Early Novels. New York:
        Oxford U. P., 1960, pp. 44-94.

"... Comedy in The American is almost entirely social
satire.... The American is concerned with the public
identity of its characters, their nationality, and their relationship to ... Parisian society...."

217   Popkin, Henry. "The Two Theatres of Henry James," NEQ,
       24 (March, 1951), 69-83.
       James's theater metaphors in The American.

218   Preston, Harriet Waters. "Mr. James's American on the
       London Stage," Atl, 68 (December, 1891), 846-848.

219   Pritchett, V. S. "Babcockism," NS&N, 59 (June 11, 1960),
       863-864.
       James's comic approach in The American and The Euro-
       peans--the free and the fixed.

220   Rosenbaum, S. P. "Two Henry James Letters on The Amer-
       ican and Watch and Ward," AL, 30 (January, 1959), 533-537.

221   Rourke, Constance. "The American," in American Humor:
       A Study of the National Character. New York: Harcourt,
       1931, pp. 235-265; repr., in Criticism. M. Schorer, and
       J. Miles, G. McKenzie, eds. New York: 1948, pp. 84-95.

222   Schneider, Sister Lucy. "Osculation and Integration: Isabel
       Archer in the One-Kiss Novel," CLAJ, 10 (December, 1966),
       149-161.

223   Schulz, Max F. "The Bellegardes' Feud with Christopher
       Newman: A Study of Henry James's Revision of The Ameri-
       can," AL, 27 (March, 1955), 42-55.
       James's revisions of The American reveal that he attempt-
       ed to deepen the feud between Newman and the Bellegardes.

224   Shumsky, Allison. "James Again: The New York Edition,"
       SR, 70 (Summer, 1962), 522-525.

225   Stafford, William T. "The Ending of James's The American:
       A Defense of the Early Version," NCF, 18 (June, 1963), 86-
       89.
       Cf., Floyd C. Watkins, "Christopher Newman's Final In-
       stinct," NCF, 12 (1957), 85-88.

225.1 _____, comp. Preface. Studies in "The American."
       Columbus, Ohio: Charles E. Merrill, 1971, pp. iii-viii.

226   Strandberg, V. H. "Isabel Archer's Identity Crisis," URev,
       34 (Summer, 1968), 283-290.

227   Swan, Michael. Introduction. The American. London:
       1949.

228   Szala, Alina. "Henry James's The American Simplified,"
        KN, 16 (1969), 61-64.
            Speculation as to liberties taken by A. Callier, trans.,
            in the Polish version, Amerykanin (1879).

228.1   Takano, Fumi, trans. The American. Tokyo: Arechi Sup-
        pansha, 1958. (In Japanese.)

228.2   Taylor, Marion A. "Henry James' American and American
        Millionaires," Litera, 9 (1968), 78-85.

229   Tick, Stanley. "Henry James's The American; Voyons,"
        SNNTS, 2 (Autumn, 1970), 276-291.
            Newman's attempt to understand the European as opposed
            to the American way of life requires a shift in vision
            rather than in moral values.

230   Traschen, Isadore. "An American in Paris," AL, 26
        (March, 1954), 67-77.
            Revisions for the New York Edition of The American.

231   _____. Henry James: The Art of Revision: A Compari-
        son of the Original and Revised Versions of "The American."
        Diss. Columbia University: 1952.

232   _____. "Henry James and the Art of Revision," PQ, 35
        (January, 1956), 39-47.

233   _____. "James's Revisions of the Love Affair in The
        American," NEQ, 29 (March, 1956), 43-62.
            Detailed examination of the revisions and their effects.

234   Van Der Beets, Richard. "A Note on Henry James's 'West-
        ern Barbarian,'" WHR, 17 (Spring, 1963), 175-178.
            Mark Twain in Innocents Abroad may have served as
            source for Newman.

235   Vanderbilt, Kermit. "James, Fitzgerald, and the American
        Self-Image," MassR, 6 (Spring, 1965), 289-304.
            A comparison of The Great Gatsby and The American.

236   Watkins, Floyd C. "Christopher Newman's Final Instinct,"
        NCF, 12 (June, 1957), 85-88.

236.1   West, Ray B., Jr. The Writer in the Room. East Lansing,
        Michigan State U. P., 1968, pp. 60-73.
            The American as an "allegory that exists on the three
            levels of social, artistic, and moral commentary."

237   Willen, Gerald, ed. Preface and Note on the Text. Henry
        James: "The American." New York: Thomas Y. Crowell, 1972.

237.1   Willett, Maurita. "Henry James's Indebtedness to Balzac,"
        RLC, 41 (April-June, 1967), 204-227.

238   Zietlow, Edward R. "A Flaw in The American," CLAJ, 9
         (1966), 246-54.
              Objection to the burning of the documents.

Reviews of The American:
         Saintsbury, George. Academy, 12 (July, 1877)
         Appleton, n. s., 3 (August, 1877), 189-90
         Athenaeum, 2593 (July 7, 1877), 14-15
         Atlantic, 39 (March 1877), (June, 1877); 40 (July, 1877),
              108-9; 68 (December 8, 1891), 846; 98 (October 3, 1891),
              461
         CatholicW, 28 (December 1878), 331-4
         Eclectic, n. s., 26 (August, 1877), 249-50
         Galaxy, 24 (July, 1877), 135-8
         Independent, 29 (May 17, 1877), 9
         Library Table, 3 (August 30, 1877), 154-5
         LiteraryW, 9 (July, 1877), 29-30
         Nation, (January 11, 1877); 24 (May 31, 1877), 325-26
         North Amr Rev, 125 (Sept., 1877), 309-15
         Picayune, (June 3, 1877), 12
         Quarterly Review, 198 (October, 1903), 358
         SatR, 44 (August 18, 1877), 214-215
         Scribner's, 14 (July, 1877), 406-7

                    THE AMERICAN SCENE

239   Auden, W. H. "Henry James's The American Scene," Hori-
         zon, 15 (February, 1947), 77-90.

240   _____. Introduction. Henry James: "The American
         Scene" Together with Three Essays from "Portraits of
         Places." New York: Scribner's, 1946.

241   Bewley, Marius. "Henry James's 'English Hours' in Masks
         and Mirrors: Essays in Criticism. New York: Atheneum
         Publishers, 1970, pp. 119-138. [The American Scene]

242   Brooks, Van Wyck. "Henry James: The American Scene,"
         Dial, 75 (July, 1923), 29-42.

243   Brown, Ashley. "Landscape into Art: Henry James and
         John Crowe Ransom," SR, 79 (Spring, 1971), 206-212.

244   Buitenhuis, Peter. "The Return of the Novelist: Henry
         James's The American Scene," CAASB, 4 (Spring-Summer,
         1969), 54-103.

244.1   Burnham, P. "View of America: The American Scene,"
         Cw, 45 (October 25, 1946), 36-40f.

245   Burtner, William Thomas, Jr. Actual and Ideal Society:

Theme and Technique in Henry James's "The American
Scene." Diss. Miami University, Oxford, Ohio: 1973.

246   Cooper, Frederick Taber. "The American Scene," NAR,
       185 (May 17, 1907), 214-218.

247   Edel, Leon. Introduction and Notes. "The American Scene"
       by Henry James. Bloomington, Indiana: Indiana U. P., 1968.

247.1 _____. "A Prophetic Vision of America: Henry James's
       The American Scene." Cincinnati: McGraw-Hill, 1969. Code
       75600. Lecture recorded at NYU for Sound Seminars. First
       appearance, "Speaking of Books: Henry James Looked Ahead,"
       NYTBR (Nov. 12, 1967), 2, 70-72.

248   Fabris, Alberta. "Note su The American Scene," SA, 6
       (1960), 255-273.

249   Hackett, Francis. "Stylist on Tour," Horizons: A Book of
       Criticism. Huebsch: 1918.

249.1 _____. "Stylist on Tour: A Re-reading of The American
       Scene," NewRep, 2 (May 1, 1915), 320-321.

250   Hall, William F. "Continuing Relevance of Henry James's
       The American Scene," Criticism, 13 (Spring, 1971), 151-165.

251   Howe, Irving. Introduction. The American Scene by Henry
       James. New York: Horizon, 1967.

252   _____. "Henry James and The American Scene," in De-
       cline of the New. New York: Harcourt, Brace & World,
       1970, pp. 112-121.

252.1 Iwase, Shitsuu. "The American Scene and James's Creative
       Method," SELit, 46 (1970), 141-152.

253   James, William. Ltr. to Henry James, May 1907 in The
       James Family by F. O. Matthiessen. New York: Knopf,
       1967, pp. 341-342.
           "... You know how opposed your whole 'third manner' of
       execution is to the literary ideals which animate my crude
       and Orsonlike breast, mine being to say a thing in one
       sentence ... and then to drop it forever; yours being to
       avoid naming it straight...."

254   Kraft, James. "On Reading The American Scene," Prose,
       6 (Spring, 1973), 115-136.

255   Morris, Wright. "Henry James's The American Scene," TQ,
       1 (Summer-Autumn, 1958), 27-42.

255.1 _____. "Use of the Past: Henry James," The Territory
       Ahead, New York: Harcourt, 1958, pp. 93-112, 187-214.

256   Pound, Ezra. The Letters of Ezra Pound, 1907-1941. D.
       D. Paige, ed. New York: Harcourt, 1950, pp. 137-138,
       passim.
            "... The American Scene is the best...."

257   Pritchett, V. S. "The Traveller Returns," NSt, 77 (Febru-
       ary 21, 1969), 259-260.

257.1 Rambeau, James M. "The American Scene and James's Late
       Fiction, (1907-1914)," DAI, 32 (Rutgers: 1971), 981A.

258   Scherman, David E., and Rosemarie Redlich. "Henry James,"
       Literary America: A Chronicle of American Writers from
       1607-1952 with 173 Photographs of the American Scene That
       Inspired Them. New York: Dodd, Mead & Co., 1952, pp.
       96-97.
            Portraits that inspired The American Scene and Washing-
       ton Square.

259   Stevens, A. Wilber. "Henry James's The American Scene:
       The Vision of Value," TCL, 1 (April, 1955), 27-33.

260   Thompson, Francis. "American Scene," in Literary Criti-
       cisms: Newly Discovered and Collected by Terence L. Con-
       nolly. New York: Dutton, 1948, pp. 301-306.

261   Trachtenberg, Allan. "The American Scene: Versions of the
       City," MassR, 8 (Spring, 1967), 281-295.

262   _____. "The Craft of Vision," Critique, 4 (Winter, 1961-
       1962), 41-55.

263   White, Sidney Howard. "Henry James's The American Scene,"
       DA, 26 (So. Calif.: 1965), 1030-31.

Reviews of The American Scene:

            Arena, 36 (July, 1906), 4-7
            Athenaeum, 41 (March 9, 1907), 282-283
            Bellman, 2 (April 20, 1907), 476
            Bookman (London), 31 (March 1907), 265-66
            Bookman (NY), 25 (April 1907), 188-190
            Churchman, 95 (March 22, 1907), 428
            CurrentLit, 39 (July, 1905), 97-9; 42 (June 1907), 634-6; 43
                (November, 1907), 526
            Critic, 48 (April 1906), 298-9
            Dial, 42 (March 16, 1907), 176-7
            Independent, 63 (July 11, 1907), 95-6
            Lit Digest, 30 (June 24, 1905), 929
            Nation, 84 (March 21, 1907), 266-7
            North Amer Rev, 185 (May 17, 1907), 214-218
            Outlook, 83 (May 5, 1906), 16-7; 85 (March 16, 1907), 622-3

Putnam's, 2 (May-July, 1907), 164-70, ˙433-42
Reader, 10 (July 1907), 215-6
SAQ, 6 (July, 1907), 313-4
Times, 12 (April 6, 1907), 221

"The Art of Fiction"

264   Ähnebrink, Lars. "Literary Credos: Henry James and 'The
        Art of Fiction,' 1884," The Beginnings of Naturalism in
        American Fiction. (Essays and Studies on American Lan-
        guage and Literature, IX). S. B. Liljegren, ed. Upsala:
        A. -B. Lundequistska Bokhandelin; Cambridge: Harvard Uni-
        versity Press, 1950, pp. 128-129.

265   Edel, Leon, ed. Introduction. The Future of the Novel:
        Essays on the Art of Fiction. New York: Vintage Books,
        1956.

265.1   _____, ed. The House of Fiction. London: Hart-Davis,
        1957.

266   Krook, Dorothea. "Critical Principles," NSt, (May 9, 1969),
        658.

267   McElderry, B. R., Jr. "Henry James's 'The Art of Fic-
        tion,'" RSSCW, 25 (March, 1957), 91-100.

268   Miller, James E., Jr., ed. Introduction. Theory of Fic-
        tion: Henry James. Lincoln, Nebraska: University of Ne-
        braska Press, 1972.

269   Roberts, Morris, ed. Henry James: The Art of Fiction
        Other Essays. New York: Oxford University Press, 1948.

"The Art of the Novel"

270   Blackmur, R. P., ed. Introduction. The Art of the Novel:
        Critical Prefaces by Henry James. New York: Scribner's,
        1934, 1962.

271   Edel, Leon, ed. Introduction. Henry James: The Future
        of the Novel: Essays on the Art of Fiction. New York:
        Vintage Books, 1956.

272   Edgar, Pelham. "The Essential Novelist? Henry James,"
        in The Art of the Novel. New York: Macmillan, 1933, pp.
        172-183; repr., in Leon Edel, ed. Henry James: A Collec-
        tion of Critical Essays. Englewood Cliffs, New Jersey:
        Prentice-Hall, 1963, pp. 92-101.

272.1   Franklin, Rosemary F. "The Art of the Novel," An Index

to Henry James's Prefaces to the New York Edition. Charlottesville, Va., 1966.

272.2 James, Henry. The Art of the Novel: Critical Prefaces.
New York: Scribner's, 1934.

"The Art of Travel"

272.3 Hicks, Granville. "Henry James as Traveler," SatR, 41
(July 19, 1958), 22f Rev.-art of The Art of Travel By Henry
James (Doubleday-Anchor, 1958).

272.4 Zabel, Morton D., ed. Introduction. The Art of Travel by
Henry James. Freeport, New York: Books for Libraries
Press, 1962, 1970.

THE ASPERN PAPERS

273   Baskett, Sam S. "The Sense of the Present in The Aspern
Papers," PMASAL, 44 (1959), 381-388.

274   Blackmur, R. P., ed. The Aspern Papers; The Spoils of
Poynton. With Introduction. New York: Dell, 1959.

275   Bottkol, Joseph M. Introduction. The Aspern Papers and
The Europeans. New York: 1950; Norfolk, Connecticut:
New Directions, 1950.

276   Brylowski, Anna S. "In Defense of the First Person Narrator in The Aspern Papers," CentR, 13 (Spring, 1969), 215-
240.

277   Edel, Leon. "The Aspern Papers: Great Aunt Wyckoff and
Juliana Bordereau," MLN, 68 (June, 1952), 392-395.
           James may have modeled Juliana on the elder sister of his
           mother's grandmother.

278   Espey, John J. "The Epigraph to T. S. Eliot's 'Burbank
with a Baedeker: Bleistein with a Cigar," AL, 29 (January,
1958), 483-84.
           Part of Eliot's epigraph to "Burbank" does not come di-
           rectly from The Aspern Papers but from a passage in
           Ford's Henry James: A Critical Study.

279   Forde, Sister Victoria. "The Aspern Papers: What Price--
Defeat," NDEJ, 6 (1970-71), 17-24.

280   Hartsock, Mildred. "Unweeded Garden: A View of The Aspern Papers," SSF, 5 (Fall, 1967), 60-68.

281   Hux, Samuel. "Irony in The Aspern Papers: The Unreliable

Symbolist," BSUF, 10 (Winter, 1969), 60-65.

281.1 James, Henry. "Preface to The Aspern Papers," in The
Art of the Novel: Critical Prefaces. New York: Scribner's,
1934, XII, x.

282   Korg, Jacob. "What Aspern Papers? A Hypothesis," CE,
23 (February, 1962), 378-381.
Cf., Robert S. Phillips. "A Note on 'What Aspern Papers? A Hypothesis,'" CE, 24 (1962), 154-155.

283   Lehmann, John. "A Question of Covering One's Tracks," in
The Open Night. London: Longmans, 1952, pp. 45-53; New
York: Harcourt, Brace, 1952, pp. 45-53.

284   McLean, Robert C. "'Poetic Justice' in James's Aspern
Papers," PLL, 3 (1967), 260-266.

285   Mellard, James M. "Modal Counterpoint in James's The
Aspern Papers," PLL, 4 (1968), 299-307.
The subject of the story is that "of one man's blindness
to the humanity he thinks he serves."

286   Murdock, Kenneth. Introduction. The Turn of the Screw
and The Aspern Papers. London: 1957.

286.1 Neider, Charles. Introduction. The Aspern Papers, in
Short Novels of the Masters. New York: Rinehart, 1948.

287   Panter-Downes, Mollie. "Letter from London," NY, 24
(September 12, 1959), 154.

288   Phillips, Robert S. "A Note on 'What Aspern Papers? A
Hypothesis,'" CE, 24 (1962), 154-155.
Cf., Jacob Korg. "What Aspern Papers? A Hypothesis,"
CE, 23 (1962), 378-381.

288.1 Redgrave, Michael. The Aspern Papers: A Comedy of Letters. London: French, 1959.

289   Reed, K. T. "Henry James, Andrew Marvell, and The Aspern Papers," NDEJ, 6 (1970-1971), 24-28.

289.1 Ross, L. Interview of Michael Redgrave. NY, 37 (October
21, 1961), 73-74.

290   Stein, William Bysshe. "The Aspern Papers: A Comedy of
Masks," NCF, 14 (September, 1959), 172-178.

291   Swan, Michael. Introduction. The Turn of the Screw, The
Aspern Papers, and Other Stories. London: New Collins
Classics, 1956.

292   Wallace, Irving. "The Real Juliana Bordereau," in The Fab-
         ulous Originals. New York: Knopf, 1956, pp. 46-80.

292.1   Wexford, Jane. Monarch Literature Notes on James's The
         Aspern Papers. Monarch, 1973.

293   Wilcox, Thomas W. "A Way into The Aspern Papers, ExEx,
         3 (December, 1955), 5-6.

Reviews of The Aspern Papers:

         Athenaeum, 3186 (November 17, 1888), 659-60
         Epoch, 4 (November 23, 1888), 290
         Nation, 48 (April 25, 1889), 353
         Quarterly Rev, 198 (October, 1903), 358
         SatR, 66 (November 3, 1888), 526-7
         TLS, January 6, 1927

Reviews: Dramatization of The Aspern Papers

         Chapman, John. "The Aspern Papers Bewitching, Tantaliz-
              ing, Beautifully Acted," NY Daily News (February 8, 1962),
              in NYTCR, 23 (1962), 357.
         Coleman, Robert. "Aspern Papers Need Editor," NY Mirror
              (February 8, 1962), in NYTCR, 23 (1962), 356.
         Kerr, Walter. "The Aspern Papers" NY Herald Tribune
              (February 8, 1962), in NYTCR, 23 (1962), 359.
         McClain, John. "Good Acting Is Wasted on Dated Vehicle,"
              NY Journal American (February 8, 1962), in NYTCR, 23
              (1962), 356.
         Nadel, Norman. "Aspern Opens at Playhouse," NY World-
              Telegram & Sun (February 8, 1962), in NYTCR, 23 (1962),
              357.
         Taubman, Howard. "Theatre: Suspense Story," NY Times
              (February 1962), 26.
         Watts, Richard. "With Fidelity to Henry James," NY Post
              (February 8, 1962), in NYTCR, 23 (1962), 358.

Other Reviews of the Dramatization:

         Cw, 75 (March 2, 1962), 597
         English, 13 (Spring, 1960), 20-21
         Illus Lond N, 235 (August 29, 1959), 150
         Nation, 194 (March 3, 1962), 200
         New Rep, 146 (February 19, 1962), 21
         NY, 35 (September 12, 1959), 153-4
         Newsweek, 59 (February 19, 1952), 88
         SatR, 45 (February 21, 1962), 36
         Spec 203 (August 21, 1959), 223-4
         Theatre Arts, 46 (April 1962), 58
         Time, 79 (February 16, 1962), 60

"At Isella"

294   Adams, John R.   " 'At Isella': Some Horrible Printing Cor-
        rected," MTQ 5 (Spring, 1943), 10, 23.
           The article lists errors and corrections.
        See also: 9, 1794, 1804, 2028, 2198, 2352, 2695, 2793,
        3354, 3711

"The Author of Beltraffio"

295   Murakami, Fujio. "The Question of the Aesthete in Henry
        James--The Case of 'The Author of Beltraffio,' " JimK, 11
        (1960), 101-114.

295.1   Pickering, Samuel F.   "The Sources of 'The Author of Bel-
        traffio,' " ArQ, 29 (Summer, 1973), 177-190.

296   Reinman, Donald H.   "The Inevitable Imitation: The Narra-
        tor in 'The Author of Beltraffio,' " TSLL, 3 (Winter, 1962),
        503-509.

297   Scoggins, James.   " 'The Author of Beltraffio': A Reappor-
        tionment of Guilt," TSLL, 5 (Summer, 1963), 265-270.

298   Winner, Viola Hopkins.   "The Artist and the Man in 'The
        Author of Beltraffio,' " PMLA, 83 (1968), 102-108.

        See also: 9, 10, 11, 270, 1740, 1794, 1804, 1862, 1924,
        1931, 1980, 2028, 2198, V; 2229, 2352, 2380, 2382, 2528,
        2581, 2637, XXI; 2637.1, 2695, 2737, 2918, 2944, 3045,
        3206, 3417, 3528, 3536, 3648, 3689, 3697, 3710, 3711

Reviews of "The Author of Beltraffio":

        Christian Union, 31 (February 26, 1885), No. 9, 21
        Critic, 6 (May 2, 1885), 206-7
        Independent, 37 (April 9, 1885), 459
        Lippincott, 35 (April, 1885), 242
        Literary W, 16 (March 21, 1885), 102
        Nation, 40 (March 12, 1885), 226

AUTOBIOGRAPHY

299   Ashton, Jean Willoughby.   "The Contact of Flint with Steel:
        A Study of History, Self, and Form in the Autobiographies of
        Howells, Adams, James, and Twain," DAI, 33 (Columbia:
        1970), 4328A.

300   Barzun, Jacques.   " 'The Blest Part of Us,' " Griffin, 5

(June, 1956), 4-13.

301   Dupee, Frederick W., ed. Introduction. Henry James:
        Autobiography. New York: Criterion Books, 1956; London:
        W. H. Allen, 1956.
           Reviews: Philip Toynbee, Obs, (December 16, 1956), 11
           David Stone, Sun. Times (December 30, 1956), 5
           DeLancy Ferguson, NYHTB (May 6, 1956), 3
           Newton Arvin, NYTB (April 29, 1956), 1
           Elizabeth Stevenson, NEQ, 29, 541-3;
           NY, (May 5, 1956), 171

302   "Extraordinary Autobiography of the Extraordinary Mr.
        James," CurOp, 56 (June, 1914), 457-458.

303   Hoffa, William. "The Final Preface: Henry James's Auto-
        biography," SR, 77 (Spring, 1969), 277-293.

304   _____. "A Study of Theme and Technique in the Autobi-
        ography of Henry James," DA, 28 (Wisconsin: 1967), 3186A.

304.1   "James the Obscure," Newsweek, 47 (May 7, 1956), 110.
           Essay-rev., F. W. Dupee's Henry James: Autobiography.
           New York: Criterion Press, 1956.

304.2   "Memories of a Mandarin," Time, 67 (May 7, 1956), 114-
        115.
           Essay-rev., F. W. Dupee, ed. Henry James: Autobiog-
           raphy.

305   Paulding, Gouverneur. "Henry James Came Home at Last,"
        Reporter, 15 (October 4, 1956), 40-42, 44.
           Essay-rev., F. W. Dupee, ed. Henry James: Autobiog-
           raphy.

305.1   Payne, James Robert. "Style and Meaning in American Auto-
        biography: William Dean Howells, Henry James, Hamlin
        Garland," DAI, 34 (Univ. of Calif., Davis: 1973), 6653A-
        54A.

305.2   Saul, Frank J. "Autobiographical Surrogates in Henry James:
        The Aesthetics of Detachment," DAI, 30 (Johns Hopkins,
        1969), 2549A-50A.

306   Sayre, Robert Freeman. The Examined Self: Henry Adams
        and Henry James and American Autobiography. Diss. Yale:
        1962.

306.1   _____. The Examined Self: Benjamin Franklin, Henry
        Adams, Henry James. Princeton: Princeton U. P., 1964.
           A study of autobiographies.

307   Schieber, Alois J. "Autobiographies of American Novelists:

Twain, Howells, James, Adams, and Garland," DA, 17 (Wisconsin: 1957), 2261.

307.1 Spiller, Robert E. "Artist of Fiction," SatR, 39 (June 9, 1956), 19-20.
Essay-rev., F. W. Dupee, ed. Henry James: Autobiography.

307.2 Walsh, William. Autobiographical Literature and Educational Thought. Leeds: University Press, 1959.
Rev., in TLS, April 10, 1959, p. 209.

307.3 Weinman, Geoffrey Stephen. "Life into Art: A Literary Analysis of Henry James's Autobiography," DA, 29 (Johns Hopkins: 1968), 1882A-83A.

THE AWKWARD AGE

308 Bass, Eben. "Dramatic Scene and The Awkward Age," PMLA, 79 (March, 1964), 148-157.
Shows that the novel has a schematic structure.

309 Colognesi, Silvana. "Apparenze e realtà in The Awkward Age," SA, 9 (1963-64), 227-248.
Study of use of implication in the novel, the development of "a mere grain of subject matter."

310 Cooney, Seamus. "Awkward Ages in The Awkward Age," MLN, 75 (March 1960), 208-211.
Inconsistencies in the ages of Vanderbank and Mr. Longdon were deliberate.

311 Donoghue, Dennis. "James's The Awkward Age and Pound's Mauberly," N&Q, 17 (February, 1970), 49-50.
Pound's indebtedness to James.

311.1 Edel, Leon, ed. Introduction. The Bodley Head Henry James. Vol. 2. The Awkward Age. London: Bodley Head, 1967.

312 Firebaugh, Joseph. "The Pragmatism of Henry James," VQR, 27 (Summer, 1951), 419-435.
The Awkward Age demonstrates not only James's craftsmanship but also his devotion to pragmatism.

313 Gargano, James W. "The Theme of 'Salvation' in The Awkward Age," TSLL, 9 (Summer, 1967), 273-287.
A good analysis of the manner in which James's "social" comedy dramatizes the struggle between two "saviors," Mrs. Brooks and Longdon.

314 Gillen, Francis. "The Dramatist in His Drama: Theory vs.

Effect in <u>The Awkward Age</u>," TSLL, 12 (Winter, 1971), 662-675.

Shows the discrepancy between James's theory and his actual practice as shown in this novel.

315   Girling, H. K.   " 'Wonder' and 'Beauty' in <u>The Awkward Age</u>," EIC, 8 (October, 1958), 370-380.

Good discussion of James's use of the words "wonderful" and "beauty" in <u>The Awkward Age</u>.

316   Gregor, Ian, and Brian Nicholas.   "The Novel of Moral Consciousness: <u>The Awkward Age</u>," in <u>Moral and the Story</u>. London: Faber and Faber, 1962, pp. 151-184.

Discussion of the theme of the innocent or guilty woman in society in certain novels, including <u>The Awkward Age</u>.

317   Hall, William F.   "James's Conception of Society in <u>The Awkward Age</u>," NCF, 23 (June, 1968), 28-48.

<u>The Awkward Age</u> is seen "as one of James's most sustained and positive statements concerning the nature of society, its ideals, its code, the relationship between it and the individual,...."

318   Hartsock, Mildred.   "The Exposed Mind: A View of <u>The Awkward Age</u>," CritQ, 9 (Spring, 1967), 49-59.

Nanda, whose developing consciousness, her concern for "knowing," is seen in this article as the center of the novel's purpose.

319   Havens, Raymond D.   "A Misprint in <u>The Awkward Age</u>," MLN, 60 (November, 1945), 497.

320   Hill, Hamlin L., Jr.   " 'The Revolt of the Daughters': A Suggested Source for <u>The Awkward Age</u>," N&Q, 8, n. s. (September, 1961), 347-349.

A series of articles by various writers appearing in British journals during the first half of the nineteenth century probably gave James details for <u>The Awkward Age</u>, and also the theme of ignorance of girls before marriage.

321   Holloway, John.   "<u>Tess of the D'Urbervilles</u> and <u>The Awkward Age</u>," in <u>The Charted Mirror: Literary and Critical Essays.</u> London: Routledge and Kegan Paul, 1960, pp. 108-117.

321.1 Isle, Walter.   "<u>The Awkward Age</u>," in <u>Experiments in Form: Henry James's Novels, 1896-1901.</u> Cambridge, Mass.: Harvard U. P., 1968, pp. 165-204.

321.2 James, Henry.   Preface.   <u>The Awkward Age.</u> Harmondsworth: Penguin Books, 1966.

322   Kaye, Julian B.   "<u>The Awkward Age, The Sacred Fount</u>, and

The Ambassadors: Another Figure in the Carpet," NCF, 17 (March, 1963), 339-351.
>   The three novels are linked by the fact that in each the central character is an unmarried man, an outsider, and that in each a woman of forty is in love with a younger man.

323   Krishna Rao, N. "The Idea of Refinement in Henry James's The Awkward Age," LCrit, 6 (1965), 56-60.
>   The pose of refinement as a cloak for corruption.

324   Levin, Gerald. "Why Does Vanderbank Not Propose?" UKCR, 27 (June, 1961), 314-318.
>   Interpretations of the final two books of The Awkward Age.

325   Lubbock, Percy. "Strategy of Point of View," in Critiques and Essays on Modern Fiction, 1920-1951. J. W. Aldridge, ed. Ronald Press, 1952, pp. 9-30.

326   Nelson, Carl. "James's Social Criticism: The Voice of the Ringmaster in The Awkward Age," ArQ, 29 (Summer, 1973), 151-168.

327   Owen, Elizabeth. "The Awkward Age and the Contemporary English Scene," VS, 11, #1 (September, 1967), 63-82.
>   Sees both the form and content of the novel "to be very much a product of its decade."

327.1 Walters, Margaret. "Keeping the Place Tidy for the Young Female Mind: The Awkward Age," in The Air of Reality. John Goode, ed. London: Methuen, 1972, pp. 190-218.
>   "It's not that Nanda is caged: she herself is the cage."

Reviews of The Awkward Age:

>   Athenaeum, 113 (May 27, 1899), 651-2
>   Bookman (London), 16 (June, 1899), 81
>   Bookman (NY), 9 (July, 1899), 472-3
>   Critic, 35 (August, 1899), 754-7
>   Dial, 27 (July 1, 1899), 21
>   HarperM, 98, Sup. 2 (April, 1899), 830
>   Independent, 51 (June 8, 1899), 1565
>   LitWorld, 30 (July 22, 1899), 227
>   Nation, 69 (August 24, 1899), 155
>   North Amer Rev, 176 (January, 1903), 125-37
>   Outlook, 62 (June 3, 1899), 314; 69 (August 24, 1899), 155
>   Quarterly Rev, 198 (October, 1903), 358
>   SatR, 87 (May 13, 1899), 598
>   Sewanee R, 8 (January 1900), 112-3
>   Spec, 82 (May 6, 1899), 647
>   Times, 4 (May 27, 1899; August 12, 19; September 2, 16, 23, 1899) 349, 540, 550, 591, 610, 622, 634

"The Beast in the Jungle"

328   Adams, Robert M. Nil: Episodes in the Literary Conquest
       of Void During the Nineteenth Century. New York: Oxford
       U. P., 1966, pp. 99-101.

329   Beardsley, Monroe, Robert Daniel and Glenn Leggett. Aids
       to Study for "Theme and Form: An Introduction to Litera-
       ture." Englewood Cliffs, New Jersey: Prentice-Hall, 1956,
       pp. 97-98.

330   Beck, Ronald. "James's 'The Beast in the Jungle': Theme
       and Metaphor," MarkR, 2, ii (February, 1970), 17-20.
       The beast metaphor organizes all thematic elements. The
       author sees the beast as paradoxically both ignorance and
       tardy awareness.

331   Cady, Edwin Harrison. "Three Sensibilities: Romancer,
       Realist, Naturalist," in The Light of Common Day: Realism
       in American Fiction. Bloomington, Indiana: Indiana U. P.,
       1971, pp. 23-52.

332   Cambon, Glauco. "The Negative Gesture in Henry James,"
       NCF, 15 (1961), 335-343.
       On renunciation by Catherine Sloper and May Bartram.

333   Conn, Peter J. "Seeing and Blindness in 'The Beast in the
       Jungle,'" SSF, 7 (Summer, 1970), 472-475.
       "Marcher and his Beast are not merely similar--they are
       one."

334   Fadiman, Clifton. Prefatory Note. The Beast in the Jungle.
       Kentfield, California: Allen Press, 1963.

335   Geismar, Maxwell. "Henry James: 'The Beast in the
       Jungle,'" NCF, 18 (June, 1963), 35-42.
       The symbolism of the beast.

336   Gottschalk, Jane. "The Continuity of American Letters in
       The Scarlet Letter and 'The Beast in the Jungle,'" WisSL,
       4 (1967), 39-45.
       Comparison of The Scarlet Letter and "The Beast in the
       Jungle" shows a "continuing tradition" in American litera-
       ture in that "both works depend on a perception of values
       that are not material."

336.1 Hansot, Elizabeth. "Imagination and Time in 'The Beast in
       the Jungle,'" in Twentieth Century Interpretations. Jane
       Tompkins, ed. Englewood Cliffs, New Jersey: Prentice-
       Hall, Inc., 1970, pp. 88-94.

336.2 Hogsett, Elizabeth A. " 'The Beast in the Jungle' and 'Old

Mr. Marblehall,' " LaurelR, 10, #2 (1970), 70-75.

337   Johnson, Courtney. "John Marcher and the Paradox of the
       'Unfortunate' Fall," SSF, 6 (1969), 121-135.
              The purpose of the article apparently is to pinpoint the na-
              ture of Marcher's limitations.

338   Jost, Edward F. "Love and Two Kinds of Existentialism,"
       EngRec, 16 (February, 1966), 14-18.
              Sees the story as an anticipation of the existentialism of
              Walter Ong or Gabriel Marcel, though James's premises
              are in contrast to those of Sartre.

339   Kerner, David. "A Note on 'The Beast in the Jungle,' "
       UKCR, 17 (Winter, 1950), 109-118.
              The law illustrated is: "It is not good for man to live
              alone."

340   Kraft, James L. "A Perspective on 'The Beast in the
       Jungle,' " LWU, 2 (1969), 20-26. Repr., in Twentieth Cen-
       tury Interpretations. Jane P. Tompkins, ed. Englewood
       Cliffs, New Jersey: Prentice-Hall, 1970, pp. 95-98.

341   Lord, James, and Marguerite Duras. "Dramatization of
       'The Beast in the Jungle,' " NY, 38 (January 12, 1963), 104.

342   Lucke, Jessie R. "The Inception of 'The Beast in the Jun-
       gle,' " NEQ, 26 (December, 1953), 529-532.
              A passage in The Blithedale Romance suggested as per-
              haps the original inspiration of James's story.

343   Miller, Betty. "Miss Savage and Miss Bartram," NC, 144
       (November, 1948), 285-292.
              Suggests analogy between Miss Bartram and John Marcher,
              and Samuel Butler and his friend, Miss Savage.

344   Monteiro, George. "Hawthorne, James, and the Destructive
       Self," TSLL, 4 (Spring, 1962), 58-71.
              Antecedents in Hawthorne of the hero of "The Beast in the
              Jungle."

345   Reid, Stephen. " 'The Beast in the Jungle' and 'A Painful
       Case,' " AI, 20 (Fall, 1963), 221-239.
              Parallels between James's story and Joyce's shorter one.

346   Rogers, Robert. "The Beast in Henry James," AI, 13
       (Winter, 1956), 427-453.
              For James the Beast was "an archetypal figure" repre-
              senting his sense of guilt.

347   Salzberg, Joel. "The Gothic Hero in Transcendental Quest:
       Poe's 'Ligeia' and James's 'The Beast in the Jungle,' " ESQ,
       18 (2nd Qt., 1972), 108-114.

348   Smith, Frances E. " 'The Beast in the Jungle': The Lim-
      its of Method," Perspective, 1 (Autumn, 1947), 33-40.

349   Stone, Edward, ed. Henry James: Seven Stories and Stud-
      ies. New York: Appleton-Century-Crofts, 1961, pp. 241-
      259.

350   _____. "James's 'Jungle': The Seasons," UKCR, 21
      (1954), 142-144.
         Imagery of the months and seasons implicit in names of
         the characters: May, Weatherend, Marcher.

351   Tate, Allen. "Three Commentaries: Poe, James, and
      Joyce, II. 'The Beast in the Jungle,' " SR, 58 (Winter, 1950),
      5-10.
      Repr. in The House of Fiction. Caroline Gordon and Allen
      Tate, eds. New York: Scribner's, 1950, pp. 228-231.

352   Tompkins, Jane P. " 'The Beast in the Jungle': An Analy-
      sis of James's Late Style," MFS, 16 (1970), 185-191.
         James's use of parenthetical statements, usually adverbial
         and often rhythmical, characteristic of his late style, are
         illustrated with evidence from "The Beast in the Jungle."

352.1 Van Kaam, Adrian, and Kathleen Healy. "Marcher in
      James's 'The Beast in the Jungle,' " in The Demon and the
      Dove: Personality Growth Through Literature. Duquesne
      U. P., 1967, pp. 197-224.
         "Marcher is fixated all his life long on existential trans-
         ference to his own ego which stunts the growth of his per-
         sonality,...."

353   Walt, James. "Stevenson's 'Will o' the Mill' and James's
      'The Beast in the Jungle,' " UES, 8 (1970), 19-25.

354   Wertham, Frederic. "Henry James' 'The Beast in the Jun-
      gle,' " in The World Within: Fiction Illuminating Neuroses
      of Our Time. Mary L. Aswell, ed. New York: McGraw-
      Hill, 1947, pp. 160-161.

354.1 Wiesenfarth, Joseph. "Illusion and Allusion: Reflections in
      'The Cracked Looking-Glass,' " FourQ, 12 (November, 1962),
      30-37.
         Comparison of Katherine Anne Porter's story with "The
         Beast in the Jungle."

      See also: 1740, 1870, 1924, 1967, 2028, 2205, 2208, 2229,
      2352, 2380, 2382, 2419.1, 2560, 2564, 2573, 2630, 2650,
      2737, 2946, 3076, 3207.1, 3297, 3332, 3346, 3417, 3423,
      3427, 3429, 3454, 3536, 3571, 3711

"The Beldonald Holbein"

355   Thorberg, Raymond.   "Henry James and the Real Thing:
       'The Beldonald Holbein,' " SHR, 3 (Winter, 1968), 78-85.
           Apparent contradictions of James's aesthetic theories ap-
           pear in this story, which is based more fully on actual
           incidents and which reflects James's "increasing emphasis
           in his later career upon the value of life."

       See also: 11, 1740, 1794, 1804, 1980; 2198, XI; 2229, 2352,
       2380, 2382; 2637, XXIII; 2637.1, XVIII; 2737, 3626, 3689,
       3706, 3711

"The Bench of Desolation"

356   Lynskey, Winifred, ed.   Reading Modern Fiction.   3rd ed.
       New York: Scribner's, 1962, pp. 306-307.

357   Segal, Ora.   "The Weak Wings of Pride: An Interpretation
       of James's 'The Bench of Desolation,' " NCF, 20 (Summer,
       1965), 145-154.
           Conclusion is that though Herbert Dodd's acceptance of
           Kate Cookham at the end seems to be a renunciation of
           his past, the reconciliation strikes a sad rather than a
           bitter note.

       See also: 12, 1740, 1840; 2198, XII; 2229, 2352, 2380,
       2382, 2558, 2560, 2603; 2637, XVIII; 2737, 2944, 3536,
       3582, 3711

"Benvolio"

       See: 9, 10, 639, 1794, 1804, 1883, 2028; 2198, III; 2352,
       2637, XXIV; 2695, 3198, 3536, 3710

"The Better Sort"

       See: 38, 1740, 2320, 2321, 2380, 2737, 3010, 3542

Reviews of "The Better Sort":

       Athenaeum, 3941 (May 9, 1903), 591
       Boynton, H. W. Atl, 92 (August, 1903), 278
       Bookman (London), 24 (April, 1903), 30
       Current Lit. 34 (May, 1903), 625
       Dial, 34 (June 1, 1903), 374
       Nation, 76 (June 4, 1903), 460
       Outlook, 74 (May 16, 1903), 184
       Public Op, 34 (March 26, 1903), 410

Schuyler, M. Lamp, 26 (April, 1903), 231-235
Times, 8 (March 21, 1903), 184

"The Birthplace"

358   Arms, George. "James's 'The Birthplace': Over a Pulpit-
        Edge," TSL, 8 (1963), 61-69.
            Religious imagery suggests that James may have intended
            his story as an allegory, which also shows his concern
            with the general problem of religious belief.

359   Hartsock, Mildred E. "The Conceivable Child: James and
        the Poet," SSF, 8 (Fall, 1971), 569-574.
            A good study which surveys other interpretations and con-
            cludes that the story is "about a fully realized human be-
            ing whose imagination enables him honestly to transcend
            a moral problem."

360   Holleran, James V. "An Analysis of 'The Birthplace,'"
        PLL, 2 (Winter, 1966), 76-80.
            Sees the real theme of the story as a serious condemna-
            tion of public taste and moral standards.

361   Ross, Morton L. "James's 'The Birthplace': A Double
        Turn of the Narrative Screw," SSF, 3 (1966), 321-328.
            In this story there are actually two turns of the Jamesian
            narrative screw: "a process whereby the apparently ob-
            vious point is qualified or even reversed by a turn in the
            narrative until the casual reader's initial response is no
            longer adequate."

362   Stafford, William T. "James Examines Shakespeare: Notes
        on the Nature of Genius," PMLA, 73 (March, 1958), 123-
        128.
            A little-known introduction which James wrote to The
            Tempest helps explain "The Birthplace."

        See also: 12, 270, 1740, 1794, 1799, 1804, 2198, XI; 2229,
        2258, 2352, 2380, 2382, 2581; 2637, XXII; 2637.1, XVII;
        3403, 3417, 3427, 3536, 3711

Reviews of "The Birthplace":

Book News, 21 (April, 1903), 557
Independent, 55 (March 26, 1903), 741
LitW, 34 (April, 1903), 73
Tribune, 2 (March 14, 1903), 12

THE BOSTONIANS

363   Anderson, Charles R. "James's Portrait of the Southerner,"

AL, 27 (November, 1955), 309-331.
Shows the limitations of James' knowledge of the Southerner and his acceptance of myth about the South.

364   Arvin, Newton. Herman Melville. New York: Sloane, 1950;
        Toronto: Macmillan, 1957; New York: Viking Compass
        Books, 1957, passim.

365   Bewley, Marius. "James's Debt to Hawthorne (I): The
        Blithedale Romance and The Bostonians," Scrutiny, 16 (Sept.,
        1949), 178-195.

366   Bland, D. S. "The Bostonians," TLS, 18 (April, 1952), 265.
        An argument for the value of James's notebooks in the un-
        derstanding of his aims and methods.

367   Bogan, Louise. "James on a Revolutionary Theme," Nation,
        146 (April 23, 1938), 471-474.

368   _____. "The Portrait of New England," Nation, 161 (De-
        cember 1, 1945), 582-583.

368.1   _____. "The Portrait of New England," Selected Criti-
        cism. New York: The Noonday Press, 1955, p. 297.

369   Burns, Graham. "The Bostonians," CR, 12 (1969), 45-60.
        An excellent interpretive view.

369.1   [Clemens, Samuel Langhorne] Mark Twain-Howells Letters.
        Henry Nash Smith and William M. Gibson, eds. Cambridge,
        Mass.: The Belknap Press of Harvard University Press,
        1960, II, 533-34.
        Clemens' dislike of The Bostonians.

370   Cox, James M. "Henry James: The Politics of Internation-
        alism," SoR, 8 (July, 1972), 493-506.
        The Bostonians and The Princess Casamassima are overt-
        ly political.

371   Dunlap, George A. The City in the American Novel, 1789-
        1900. Philadelphia: University of Pennsylvania Press, 1934,
        pp. 160-162.

371.1   Edel, Leon, ed. Introduction. The Bodley Head Henry
        James. Vol. 3. The Bostonians. London: Bodley Head,
        1967.

372   Goldfarb, Clare R. "Names in The Bostonians," IEY, 13
        (1968), 18-23.
        Believes that the names reveal character and prefigure
        plot.

373   Green, David B. "Witch and Bewitchment in The Bostonians,"

PLL, 3 (1967), 267-269.
Analysis of witchcraft images in The Bostonians.

374   Grewall, Om Prakash.   "Henry James and the Ideology of
      Cultures: A Critical Study of The Bostonians, The Princess
      Casamassima and The Tragic Muse," DAI, 30 (Rochester:
      1970), 5444A-45A.

375   Grossman, Edward.   "Henry James and the Sexual-Military
      Complex," Commentary, 53 (April, 1972), 37-50.   Also:
      Discussion, 53 (April, 1972), 7-9; 54 (August, 1972), 12.

376   Habegger, Alfred.   "The Disunity of The Bostonians," NCF,
      24 (September, 1969), 193-209.
           The narrative techniques of Book First (Chapters I-XX)
      compared with Books Second and Third.

377   Hamblen, Abigail Ann.   "Henry James and the Freedom
      Fighters of the Seventies," GaR, 20 (Spring, 1966), 35-44.
           The central interest in The Bostonians is James's recogni-
      tion that seekers for equality really want vengeance.

378   _____.   "Henry James and the Transcendentalists," Cres-
      set, 26 (December, 1962), 16-17.
           The Bostonians depicts a society which clings to a devital-
      ized transcendentalism, "seized upon by all sorts of vulgar
      influences."

379   Harris, Joel Chandler.   "Provinciality in Literature: A De-
      fense of Boston," in Joel Chandler Harris, Editor and Essay-
      ist: Miscellaneous Literary, Political and Social Writings.
      Julia C. Harris, ed.   Chapel Hill: University of North Caro-
      lina Press, 1931, pp. 186-191.

380   Hartsock, Mildred E.   "Henry James and the Cities of the
      Plain," MLQ, 29 (September, 1968), 297-311.

381   Haslam, Gerald.   "Olive Chancellor's Painful Victory in The
      Bostonians," RS, 36 (September, 1968), 232-237.
           The "victory" at the end of the novel is in Olive's willing-
      ness to face a crowd that may well hiss her.

381.1 Howard, David.   "The Bostonians," in The Air of Reality.
      John Goode, ed.   London: Methuen, 1972, pp. 60-80.

382   Howe, Irving.   Introduction.   The Bostonians.   New York:
      Modern Library, 1956, pp. xxviii.

383   Kimmey, John L.   "The Bostonians and The Princess Casa-
      massima," TSLL, 9 (1968), 537-546.
           A study of the parallels and contrasts in the two novels to
      support the thesis that the major influence on The Princess
      was James's conviction of his failures with The Bostonians.

384   Long, Robert E. "The Society and the Masks: The Blithe-
        dale Romance and The Bostonians," NCF, 19 (September,
        1964), 105-122.
             James saw in Hawthorne's novel "an unconscious allegory
             of democracy."

385   _____. "A Source for Dr. Mary Prance in The Boston-
        ians," NCF, 19 (June 1964), 87-88.
             The author suggests that the name for James's character
             is a play on the name of Dr. Mary Walker, a well-known
             supporter of women's rights in James's day.

385.1   Maglin, Nan B. "Fictional Feminists in The Bostonians and
        The Odd Women," in Images of Women in Fiction: Feminist
        Perspectives. Susan K. Cornillon, ed. Bowling Green,
        Ohio: Bowling Green University, Popular Press, 1972, pp.
        216-236.

386   Martin, W. R. "The Use of the Fairy-Tale: A Note on the
        Structure of The Bostonians," ESA, 2 (March, 1959), 98-109.

387   Mauriac, Francois. "En marge des Bostoniennes," FL, 10
        (August 6, 1955), 1, 9.

388   _____. Memoires Interieurs. Gerard Hopkins, trans.
        New York: Farrar, Straus and Cudahy, 1961, pp. 227-230.

389   McLean, Robert C. "The Bostonians: New England Pastor-
        al," PLL, 7 (Fall, 1971), 374-381.
             James's controlling motif is derived from pastoral litera-
             ture.

390   McMurray, William. "Pragmatic Realism in The Bostonians,"
        NCF, 16 (March, 1962), 339-344.
             James's realism in The Bostonians is a "dramatic illustra-
             tion of pragmatism. Reality in the novel is such that all
             absolutisms, when tested by experience, either must yield
             their claims to sanctity or fall in disaster."

390.1   _____. "Pragmatic Realism in The Bostonians," in Henry
        James: Modern Judgments. Tony Tanner, ed. London:
        Macmillan, 1968, pp. 160-183.

391   Meldrum, Ronald M. "Three of Henry James's Dark Ladies,"
        RS, 37 (1969), 54-60.
             Olive is the "dark lady" in The Bostonians.

392   Miller, Theodore C. "The Muddled Politics of Henry James's
        The Bostonians," GaR, 26 (Fall, 1972), 336-346.
             James's shift of political allegiance in the 1880's from
             liberal to conservative is demonstrated in The Bostonians
             in which liberal ideas are treated with scorn.

392.1   Netherby, Wallace. "Tragedy of Errors: A Note on The
        Bostonians," Coranto, 8, ii (1972), 34-41.

393   Oliver, Clinton. "Henry James as a Social Critic," AR, 7
        (June, 1947), 243-258.

394   Powers, Lyall H. "James's Debt to Alphonse Daudet," CL,
        24 (Spring, 1972), 150-162.
            "Similarities in theme and structure" suggest The Boston-
        ians is James's attempt to rewrite l'Evangeliste.

395   Putt, S. Gorley. "A Henry James Jubilee, II," Cornhill,
        160 (Spring, 1947), 284-297.
            Critical notes on The Bostonians and The Princess Casa-
        massima.

395.1   _____. "The Private Life and the Public Life: The
        Princess Casamassima and The Bostonians," in Scholars of
        the Heart: Essays in Criticism. London: Faber and Faber,
        1962, pp. 174-203.

396   Rahv, Philip. Introduction. The Bostonians. New York:
        Dial Press, 1945.

397   Schultz, Elizabeth. "The Bostonians: The Contagion of Ro-
        mantic Illusion," Genre, 4 (March, 1971), 45-59.
            The author sees this novel as a "proving ground not only
        for the value of the romantic vision but also for the truth
        of romantic conventions."

397.1   Scudder, H. E. "James, Crawford, and Howells," Atl, 57
        (1886), 850-857.

398   Selig, Robert L. "The Red Haired Lady Orator: Parallel
        Passages in The Bostonians and Adam Bede," NCF, 16
        (September, 1961), 164-169.
            Similarities and differences between James's Verena Tar-
        rant and Eliot's Dinah Morris.

399   Smith, Herbert F., and Michael Petnovich. "The Boston-
        ians: Creation and Revision," BNYPL, 73 (May, 1969), 298-
        308.
            An informative history of the serial publication of The
        Bostonians, and the nature of James's revisions for the
        first book version.

400   Solotaroff, Theodore. The Bostonians: A Social and Liter-
        ary Study. Diss. Chicago. n. d.

401   Stone, Geoffrey. Melville. New York: Sheed & Ward,
        1949, p. 290.
            Ungar, a character in Melville's Clarel, has some intel-
        lectual "affinities" with the Southern hero of James's The
        Bostonians.

402   Ticknor, Caroline. "Henry James's 'Bostonians,'" in
        Glimpses of Authors. Boston: Houghton Mifflin, 1922, pp.
        243-256.

403   Trilling, Lionel. "The Bostonians," in The Opposing Self:
        Nine Essays in Criticism. New York: Viking, 1955, pp.
        104-117.

404   _____. Introduction. The Bostonians. London: J. Leh-
        mann, 1952.

404.1   Walcutt, Charles Child. "Discourse on Feminism: The Bos-
        tonians," Man's Changing Mask: Modes and Methods of Char-
        acterization in Fiction. Minneapolis: Minnesota U. P., 1966,
        pp. 182-193.

405   Woodward, Comer, Vann. "A Southern Critique for the
        Gilded Age," The Burden of Southern History. Baton Rouge,
        Louisiana State University Press, 1960, 1968, pp. 109-140.

Reviews of The Bostonians:

        Athenaeum, 30 (March 6, 1886), 323
        CathW, 43 (April, 1886), 130
        Critic, 8 (April 17, 1886), 191-2
        Dial, 7 (May 1886), 14-15
        Independent, 38 (April 22, 1886), 495
        LitW, 17 (April 17, 1886), 137
        Nation, 42 (May 13, 1886), 407-8
        Picayune, 11 (Apr, 1886), p. 14
        SatR, 61 (June 5, 1886), 791-2
        SR, 11 (July, 1903), 360

                        "Broken Wings"

        See: 11, 270, 1794, 1804; 2198, XI; 2352, 2380, 2564, 2581;
        2637, XXI; 2637.1, XVI; 2737, 2918, 3582, 3706, 3711

                        "Brooksmith"

406   Dow, Eddy. "James' 'Brooksmith' [Paragraphs 4 and 5],"
        Expl, 27 (January, 1969), Item 35.
            The butler is cogently named as one who is able "to direct
            through a smiling land, between suggestive shores, a sinu-
            ous stream of talk."

406.1   Frantz, Jean H. "A Probable Source for a James 'Nouvelle,'"
        MLN, 74 (March, 1959), 225-226.
            A comparison of the situation and main character in
            "Brooksmith" and "In the Cage."

See also: 11, 270, 272.2, 1740, 1794, 1804; 2198, VIII;
2229, 2258, 2352, 2380, 2382, 2581; 2637, XXIII; 2637.1,
XVIII; 2737, 2944, 3536, 3706, 3711

"A Bundle of Letters"

407 Onishi, Akio. "An Approach to Henry James--Through an
'International' Trilogy," BungR, 12 (January, 1963), 1-45.
On "A Bundle of Letters," "The Point of View" and "The
Pension of Beaurepas."

See also: 8, 9, 10, 270, 272.2, 1740, 1794, 1804, 2028;
2198, IV; 2229, 2258, 2352, 2380, 2382, 2564; 2637, XIX;
2637.1, XIV; 2695, 2737, 3536, 3626, 3711

Review of "A Bundle of Letters": SatR, 51 (March 19, 1881), 372-
373.

"The Chaperon"

See: 10, 12, 270, 272.2, 1740, 1794, 1804, 2096; 2198,
VIII; 2229, 2352, 2630; 2637, XV; 2637.1, X; 2944

"Collaboration"

See: 8, 9, 10, 1740, 1794, 1804; 2198, VIII; 2229, 2352;
2637, XXVII; 3417, 3689, 3711

Reviews of "Collaboration":

Atl, 73 (April, 1894), 568
Nation, 57 (November 30, 1893), 417

CONFIDENCE

408 Hamblen, Abigail A. "Confidence: The Surprising Shadow of
Genius," UR, 36 (Winter, 1969), 151-154.
An effort to find modern "situation ethics" in this early
novel.

409 Levy, Leo B. "Henry James's Confidence and the Development of the Idea of the Unconscious," AL, 28 (November,
1956), 347-358.
Contains a good survey of James's use of the "unconscious."

409.1 Poirier, Richard. "Confidence and Washington Square," The
Comic Sense of Henry James. New York: Oxford U. P.,
1960, pp. 145-182.

410   Pritchett, V. S. "Birth of a Hermaphrodite," NSt (Novem-
        ber 30, 1962), 779-780.
            The early Henry James and William James--"Confidence."

411   Ruhm, Herbert, ed. Introduction, Notes, and Bibliography.
        Confidence. New York: Grosset and Dunlap, 1962.
            Textual variants from the manuscript and first serial pub-
            lication.

412   Thorberg, Raymond. "Henry James and the 'New England
        Conscience,' " N&Q, 16 (June, 1969), 222-223.
            The phrase "New England Conscience," which Austin War-
            ren could not find before 1895, when James used it in his
            Notebooks, actually occurs in James's Confidence, pub-
            lished serially in Scribner's 1879-1880.

413   Wilson, Edmund. "The Ambiguity of Henry James," in The
        Triple Thinkers. New York: Harcourt, Brace, 1938; rev.
        ed. , New York: Oxford U. P. , 1948, p. 134.
            "Is the fishy Bernard Longueville ... really intended for
            a sensitive and interesting young man or is he a prig in
            the manner of Jane Austen?"

414   Woolf, Virginia. Roger Fry: A Biography. New York:
        Harcourt, Brace & Co. , 1940, pp. 273-274.
            The influence of Confidence on Roger Fry.

        See also: 9, 10, 11, 12, 38, 639, 1740, 1794, 1804, 1871,
        1980, 2028, 2070, 2352, 2380, 2382, 2560, 2695, 2793,
        2944, 3010, 3147, 3672.1, 3711

Reviews of Confidence:

        Athenaeum, 2723 (January, 1880), 16
        Atl, 46 (July, 1880), 125-6; 46 (July, 1880), 140-1
        Californian, 1 (July, 1880), 92
        Christian Union, 21 (April 28, 1880), 398
        Churchman, 41 (May 1, 1880), 490-1
        Eclectic, 31, n. s. (May, 1880), 634-5
        Harper's, 60 (May, 1880), 945-6
        Independent, 32 (March 18, 1880), 11
        Lit World, 11 (April 10, 1880), 119-20
        Nation, 30 (March 25, 1880), 289-90
        PubOp, 10 (February 21, 1891), 482
        SatR, 49 (January 3, 1880), 25-6
        Scribner's, 20 (June, 1880), 311

        "Cousin Maria"--See "Mrs. Temperly"

"Covering End"

Reviews of "Covering End":

Athenaeum, 3704 (October 22, 1898), 564-5
Bookman (London), 25 (November, 1898), 54
Dixie, I (January, 1899)
Nation, 67 (December 8, 1898), 432
Outlook, 60 (October 29, 1898), 537
Picayune, 27 (November 1898), 10
QtRev, 198 (October, 1903), 358
SR, 7 (January, 1899), 124

See also: 10, 11, 12, 1740, 1794, 1804, 2229, 2352, 2380,
2382, 2630, 2788, 2793, 2944, 3711

"The Coxon Fund"

See: 10, 12, 38, 270, 1740, 1794, 1804, 1862; 2198, IX;
2229, 2352, 2380, 2382, 2630; 2637, XX; 2637.1, XV; 2651,
3417, 3427, 3536, 3689

"Crapy Cornelia"

415   Purdy, Strother B. "Language as Art: The Ways of Know-
       ing in Henry James's 'Crapy Cornelia,' " Style, 1 (Spring,
       1967), 139-149.
           "Crapy Cornelia" hinges upon the uses of a small number
       of words: "Tone" on the thematic level, and "know" in
       the dialogue in which two characters carry on what
       amounts to courting in word-play.

See also: 12, 1740, 1804, 1930, 1931, 2028; 2198, XII;
2229, 2352, 2380, 2382, 2564; 2637, XXVIII; 2695, 2917,
3332, 3346, 3536, 3711

"Crawford's Consistency"

See: 8, 9, 2028, 2352, 2695, 2948, 2701, 3711

DAISY MILLER

415.1   Alexandrescu, Sorin. Introduction. "Henry James sau
        Poezia Enigmei." (Henry James, or the Poetry of the Puz-
        zle). In Henry James's Daisy Miller. The Great Short Nov-
        els. Bucuresti: Editura pentru literatură, 1968, pp. x-
        xxxiii.

416   Anzilotti, Rolando. "Un racconto italiano di Henry James:
        Daisy Miller," in Study e Ricerche di Letteratura Ameri-
        cana. Florence: La Nuova Italia, 1968, pp. 173-181.
            The author regards Winterbourne as less a character than
            a "punto di vista." Also discusses "ambiguità" in the
            story.

417   Arms, George, and William M. Gibson. "Silas Lapham,
        Daisy Miller, and the Jews," NEQ, 16 (March, 1953), 118-
        122.
            In Howells' novel, Hartley Hubbard had used the phrase
            "Daisy Millerism" in writing up his interview with Lap-
            ham. ["The Rise of Silas Lapham," Century, 29 (Nov.,
            1884), 20.] Howells had replied in Century, January,
            1885.

418   Baxter, Annette K. "Archetypes of American Innocence:
        Lydia Blood and Daisy Miller," in The American Experience:
        Approaches to the Study of the United States. Hennig Cohen,
        ed. New York: Houghton, 1968, pp. 148-156.

419   Bewley, Marius. "Maisie, Miles and Flora, the Jamesian
        Innocents," Scrutiny, 17 (Autumn, 1950), 258.

420   Bicanic, Sonia. "Writing for the Magazines," SR&A, 13-14
        (July-December, 1962), 13-30.
            Those who published serially in Cornhill between 1860 and
            1880 often used the installments like acts in a drama to
            reinforce the desired effect, e.g., James in Daisy Miller.

421   Buitenhuis, Peter. "From Daisy Miller to Julia Bride,"
        AQ, 11 (Summer, 1959), 136-146.
            Relation between the sexes James had treated uncritically
            in Daisy Miller and critically appraised in Julia Bride.

422   Burrell, John A. "Henry James: A Rhapsody of Youth,"
        Dial, 63 (September 27, 1917), 260-262.

423   Canady, Nicholas, Jr. "Portrait of Daisy: Studies of James
        and Fitzgerald," Forum (Texas), 4 (Summer, 1966), 17-20.
            A comparison of Daisy Miller and Daisy Buchanan (The
            Great Gatsby).

424   Cargill, Oscar. Introduction. Washington Square and Daisy
        Miller. New York: 1956.

425   Coffin, Tristram P. "Daisy Miller, Western Hero," WF,
        17 (October, 1958), 273-275. Repr., in James's Daisy Mil-
        ler. William T. Stafford, ed. New York: Scribner's,
        1963, pp. 136-137.

425.1   Davis, O., comp. "Daisy Miller," in Introduction to the
        Novel. New York: Hayden Book Co., 1969.

426   Deakin, Motley F. "Daisy Miller, Tradition, and the Euro-
        pean Heroine," CLS, 6 (March, 1969), 45-59.
            The author shows that the literary heroines of Turgenev,
        Cherbuliez, George Sand, and Mme. de Staël are as much
        the source of James's character as real American girls
        he may have observed.

427   Draper, R. P. "Death of a Hero? Winterbourne and Daisy
        Miller," SSF, 6 (Fall, 1969), 601-608.
            "It is the hero's slow, lingering, and almost comically un-
        dramatic death that is the main theme...."

428   Dunbar, Viola. "A Note on the Genesis of Daisy Miller,"
        PQ, 27 (April, 1948), 184-186.
            Shows a parallel with Cherbuliez's Paule Méré.

429   _____. "The Revision of Daisy Miller," MLN, 65 (May,
        1950), 311-317.
            The author finds the revision more poetic than the origi-
        nal.

429.1   Dupee, F. W. Henry James. New York: William Sloane,
        1951, pp. 107-113. Rev. ed., New York: Doubleday, 1956,
        pp. 91-97. Repr., in James's Daisy Miller. William T.
        Stafford, ed. New York: Scribner's, 1963, pp. 147-149.

430   Durham, Frank M. "Henry James' Dramatization of His
        Novels," BCit, 6 (November, 1942), 50-64.
            Dramatization of Daisy Miller.

431   Edel, Leon, ed. Henry James: Selected Fiction. New York:
        Dutton, 1953, x-xi. Repr., in James's Daisy Miller. Willi-
        am T. Stafford, ed. New York: Scribner's, 1963, p. 154.

432   Fiedler, Leslie A. ["Daisy: The Good Bad Girl"] in Love
        and Death in the American Novel. Rev. ed., New York:
        Stein and Day, Publishers, 1966, pp. 310-312; repr., in
        James's Daisy Miller. William T. Stafford, ed. New York:
        Scribner, 1963, pp. 140-141.

433   Gargano, James W. "Daisy Miller: An Abortive Quest for
        Innocence," SAQ, 59 (Winter, 1960), 114-120.
            A study of Winterbourne.

434   Geist, Stanley. "Fictitious Americans--Portraits from a
        Family Album: Daisy Miller," HudR, 5 (1952), 203-206. Repr.,
        James's Daisy Miller. William T. Stafford, ed. New York:
        Scribner, 1963, 131-133.

435   Gibson, W. M., and G. R. Petty. "Project Occult: The Or-
        dered Computer Collation of Unprepared Literary Text," in
        Art and Error: Modern Textual Editing. Ronald Gottesman,
        and Scott Boyce Bennett, eds. Bloomington, Indiana:

Indiana U. P., 1970, pp. 279-300.
In Appendix C, the authors present variant readings found
in a collation of the first London edition and the revised
New York edition texts of Daisy Miller.

435.1   Gioli, Giovanna M.   "Racconto psicologico e Romance in
        Daisy Miller," SA, 16 (1970), 231-254.

436   Goodspeed, Edgar J.   "Footnote to Daisy Miller," Atl, 153
        (February, 1934), 252-253.
        "... a very recent tragedy in the American colony at
        Rome was the germ of Daisy Miller."

437   Greene, Bertram.   "Summer of Daisy Miller," NY, 39 (June
        8, 1963), 126ff; ThA, 47 (August, 1963), 11ff.
        Dramatization of Daisy Miller.

438   Hagopian, John V., and Martin Dolch, eds.   Insight I: An-
        alyses of American Literature.   Frankfurt am Main: Hirsch-
        graben Verlag, 1962, 134-139.

439   Hamblen, Abigail Ann.   "Two Almost-Forgotten Innocents,"
        Cresset, 30 (October, 1967), 16-17.
        Tarkington's Claire Ambler (1928) duplicates James's
        Daisy Miller.

440   Hassan, Ihab.   Radical Innocence: Studies in the Contempo-
        rary American Novel.   Princeton, New Jersey: Princeton
        U. P., 1961, p. 41.

441   Hirsch, David H.   "William Dean Howells and Daisy Miller,"
        ELN, 1 (December, 1963), 123-128.

441.1   Hoffman, Michael J.   "Realism as Vision and Style: Daisy
        Miller and the Social Octopus," in Michael J. Hoffman's The
        Subversive Vision: American Romanticism in Literature.
        Port Washington, New York: Kennikat Press, 1973, pp. 117-
        128.

442   Holloway, John.   Introduction.   Daisy Miller, A Study.   Cam-
        bridge, England.   Printed for the members of the Limited
        Editions Club at the University Printing House, 1969.

443   Houghton, Donald E.   "Attitude and Illness in James' Daisy
        Miller," L&P, 19 (1969), 51-59.
        Interpretation of American illness as a psychosomatic mani-
        festation of American negative attitudes toward the European
        environment.

444   Howells, Mildred, ed.   Life in Letters of William Dean
        Howells.   New York: Doubleday, Doran & Co., 1928, I, 271.
        William Dean Howells to James Russell Lowell apropos
        Daisy Miller.

445   [Howells, William Dean] "The Contributor's Club," [Daisy
        Miller], Atl, 43 (February, 1879), 252-262.

445.1   _____. "The Contributor's Club," [Daisy Miller], Atl,
        43 (March, 1879), 392-404.

446   _____. "Mr. James's Daisy Miller," in Heroines of Fic-
        tion. 2 vols. London and New York: Harper & Bros.,
        1901, pp. 164-176.

447   _____. Introduction. Daisy Miller. New York: Modern
        Library, 1918.

448   _____. "Henry James, Jr.," Century, 25 (November,
        1882) 25-29. [Daisy Miller]

449   _____. "Mr. James's Masterpiece," HarpersB, 36 (Jan-
        uary, 1902), 9-14.
        Daisy Miller.

449.1   _____. "The Latest Avatar of American Girlhood," Lit,
        n. s., 2 (July 28, 1899), 57-58.

450   Hoxie, Elizabeth F. "Mrs. Grundy Adopts Daisy Miller,"
        NEQ, 19 (December, 1946), 474-484.
        Authorities on etiquette appropriated James's heroine and
        displayed her as an example of what American girls should
        not be and do.

450.1   Humma, John B. "The 'Engagement' of Daisy Miller," RS,
        39 (1971), 154-155.

451   James, E. Anthony. "Henry James's Mrs. Walker: Proper
        Matron or Possessive Mistress," PCTEB, 13 (May, 1966),
        15-22.
        A possible and ingenious interpretation of Mrs. Walker as
        Winterbourne's "possessive mistress."

452   James, Henry. "Daisy Miller: A Study," Cornhill, 37 (June,
        1878), 678-698, and 38 (July, 1878), 44-67.
        Said to be the original version.

452.1   _____. "Letter to Mrs. Lynn Linton," in Mrs. Lynn Lin-
        ton. George S. Layard, ed. London: Methuen, 1901, pp.
        233-234. Repr., in James's Daisy Miller. William T. Staf-
        ford, ed. New York: Scribner, 1963, pp. 115-116.

453   _____. Preface to Daisy Miller. The Novels and
        Tales of Henry James. New York: Scribner's, 1909, XVIII,
        v-viii.

454   Kar, Annette. "Archetypes of American Innocence: Lydia
        Blood and Daisy Miller," AQ, 5 (Spring, 1953), 31-38.

A comparative study of innocence as representative of extreme provincialism and Americanism in Howells' The Lady of the Aroostook and James's Daisy Miller.

455   Kennedy, Ian. "Frederick Winterbourne: The Good Bad Boy in Daisy Miller," ArQ, 29 (Summer, 1973), 139-150.
       Winterbourne, in contrast to Daisy, "the Bad Good Girl," is the "archetypal, dangerous Good Bad Boy."

456   Lanier, Sidney. The English Novel and Essays on English Literature. Clarence Gohdes, ed. Baltimore: Johns Hopkins Press, 1945, pp. 198-200.

457   Mann, Jona J. "Is There an Angel in the House?" IEBY, 21 (Fall, 1971), 39-50.
       Daisy as an example of the "Good Bad Girl," the "transitional anti-virgin figure" of the early part of this century.

458   McElderry B. R., Jr. "The 'Shy Incongruous Charm' of Daisy Miller," NCF, 10 (September, 1955), 162-165.
       Reprint of letter from James to Mrs. Lynn Linton reaffirming Daisy's innocence.

459   Mendelsohn, Michael J. " 'Drop a tear': Henry James Dramatizes Daisy Miller," MD, 7 (May, 1964), 60-64.
       Restates the unfavorable judgment of the play reached by previous commentators.

460   Monteiro, George. " 'Girlhood on the American Plan'--A Contemporary Defense of Daisy Miller," BBr, 19 (May, 1963), 89-93.
       Shows that a review (Atl, March, 1879), previously assigned to Howells, was written by John Hay.

461   _____. "William Dean Howells: Two Mistaken Attributions," PBSA, 56 (2nd Qt., 1962), 254-257.
       Two notes on Daisy Miller attributed to Howells identified as by Constance F. Woolson and John Hay.

461.1 Murray, D. M. "Candy Christian as a Pop-Art Daisy Miller," JPC, 5 (1971), 340-348.
       Comparison of Terry Southern's Candy and Daisy Miller. "Daisy Miller," the author concludes, "you've come a long way...."

462   "New Books," [Daisy Miller], BEM, 126 (July, 1879), 88-107.

462.1 "Novels of the Week," Athenaeum (March 1, 1879), 275-277.

463   Ohmann, Carol. "Daisy Miller: A Study of Changing Intentions," AL, 36 (March, 1964), 1-11.
       Use of James's preface and various revisions to show that

James "began by criticising Daisy in certain ways and ended simply by praising her."

464   Phelps, William Lyon. "James," in Howells, James, Bryant, and Other Essays. New York: 1924, pp. 123-155.

465   Randall, John H. "The Genteel Reader and Daisy Miller," AQ, 17 (Fall, 1965), 568-581.
       James may have intended Daisy Miller as an attack upon stereotyped American gentility.

466   Rollins, A. W. "Ad Absurdum," Critic, 27, n. s., 24 (September 28, 1895), 193.

467   Sampson, Martin W. Introduction. Daisy Miller and an International Episode. New York: Macmillan Co., 1927.

468   Shriber, Michael. "Cognitive Appartus in Daisy Miller, The Ambassadors, and Two Works by Howells: A Comparative Study of the Epistemology of Henry James," Lang&S, 2 (1969), 207-225.

469   Stafford, William T., ed. James's Daisy Miller: The Story, The Play, The Critics. Scribner Research Anthologies. New York: Scribner's, 1963.
       A very useful work.

470   Stone, Edward. "A Further Note on Daisy Miller and Cherbuliez," PQ, 29 (April, 1950), 213-216.
       Similarities of characterization and plot between Daisy Miller and Victor Cherbuliez's Paule Méré.

471   Tadokoro, Nobushige. "The Castle of Chillon and the Colosseum," FukURLS, 7 (March, 1963), 273-292.
       A consideration of the structure of James's Daisy Miller.

471.1 Vedder, Henry Clay. "Henry James," American Writers of Today. New York and Boston: Silver & Burdett, 1894, 1910, pp. 73-74.
       Discussion of the angry criticism roused by Daisy Miller.

472   Volpe, Edmond L. "The Reception of Daisy Miller," BPLQ, 10 (January, 1958), 55-59.
       The author questions the tradition that Daisy Miller was not well received by the American critics, and asserts that a search of periodicals reveals that the story was well received.

473   Wasserstrom, William. Heiress of All the Ages: Sex and Sentiment in the Genteel Tradition. Minneapolis: Minnesota U. P., 1959, pp. 61-64; repr., in James's Daisy Miller. William T. Stafford, ed. New York: Scribner's, 1963, pp. 138-139.

474   White, Richard Grant. "Recent Fiction," NAR, 128 (Janu-
       ary, 1879), 96-110.

475   Wood, Ann. "Reconsideration--Daisy Miller," NewRep, 167
       (December, 1972), 31-33.
            "... She is so vulnerable, this Daisy Miller, an Ameri-
       can girl whose superficiality is her complexity...."

475.1 Woolson, Constance Fenimore. "Contributor's Club," Atl,
       43 (February, 1879), 258-259.
            The author saw Daisy Miller "an an exquisitely loyal serv-
       vice to American girlhood."

Reviews of Daisy Miller:

            Atlantic, 71 (January, 1893), 124
            Continent, 3 (April 18, 1883), 508
            Harper's, 58 (January, 1879), 310
            NAR, 150 (June, 1890), 687
            Nation, 27 (December 19, 1878), 386-389
            Overland, 2d S2 (November, 1883), 554-6
            Picayune, 24 (November, 1878), 5; (October 7, 1883), 7
            Quarterly Rev, 198 (October, 1903), 358
            SatR, 47 (May 3, 1879), 561-562
            Times (November 10, 1878), 10
            Times (New York) (June 4, 1879), 4; (September 9, 1883),
               10

                        "A Day of Days"

       See: 1794, 1804, 2028; 2198, I; 2352; 2637, XXV; 2695,
       2793, 2773, 3417, 3536

                      "The Death of the Lion"

475.2 Hetherington, Hugh W.   Melville's Reviewers, British and
       American, 1846-1891.   Chapel Hill, North Carolina: North
       Carolina U. P., 1961, p. 267.
            Pierre, in Melville's novel, is compared to Neil Paraday
       in James's "The Death of the Lion."

475.3 Nicholas, Charles A. "A Second Glance at Henry James's
       'The Death of the Lion,'" SSF, 9 (1972), 143-146.

475.4 Smith, William Francis, Jr. "Sentence Structure in Three
       Representative Tales of Henry James," DA, 31 (Michigan
       State Univ.: 1970), 3520A.

       See also: 10, 12, 38, 272.2, 1740, 1804, 1862, 1924,
       1943, 2062; 2198, IX; 2229, 2352, 2380, 2382, 2448, 2560,

2564, 2581, 2630, 2637, 2637.1, 2650, 2916, 3332, 3417, 3427, 3536, 3711

"De Grey"

476   Tytell, John. "Henry James and the Romance," MarkR, 5 (May, 1969), 1-2.
The story represents an "important example of a young writer assimilating the lessons of two earlier masters, Hawthorne and Poe, and then veering off in his own direction."

See also: 8, 1794, 1804, 1871, 2028, 2198, I; 2205, 2208, 2229, 2352, 2695, 2701, 2773, 2793, 3711

"The Diary of a Man of Fifty"

477   Garnett, David. <u>Fourteen Stories by Henry James.</u> London: Rupert Hart-Davis, 1946.

478   Leavis, Q. D. "Henry James: The Stories," Scrutiny, 14 (Spring, 1947), 226.

See also: 9, 10, 1740, 1794, 1804, 2028; 2198, IV; 2352; 2637, XXV; 2695, 2793, 3536, 3689, 3710, 3711

EMBARRASSMENTS

Reviews:

Athenaeum, 108 (August 1, 1896), 158
Atlantic, 79 (January, 1897), 137
Chatauqua, 23 (September, 1896), 783
Critic, 29 (ns 26) (July 25, 1896), 52
Independent, 48 (July 30, 1896), 1037
Nation, 63 (July 30, 1896), 91
Public Opinion, 21 (July 30, 1896), 152
Spec, 77 (August 29, 1896), 273

"English Hours"

479   Lowe, Alma Louise. Introduction. <u>English Hours.</u> Illustrations by Anthony Gross. London: Readers Union, Heinemann, 1962.

479.1   Pennell, Joseph, illustrator. <u>English Hours.</u> New York: Horizon Press, 1969.

Reviews of "English Hours":

> Bookman (London), 29 (December, 1905), 140
> Book News, 24 (December, 1905), 324
> Churchman, 92 (December 9, 1905), 962
> Critic, 48 (May, 1906), 470
> Dial, 39 (December 1, 1905), 381
> Nation, 81 (December 28, 1905), 528
> Reader, 7 (February, 1906), 336-337
> Review of Revs, 33 (January, 1906), 121
> Times, 10 (December 2, 1905), 826
> Tribune, 6 (November 25, 1905), 11

"Eugene Pickering"

See: 8, 9, 10, 1774, 1804, 2028; 2198, III; 2352; 2637,
XXIV; 2695, 3015, 3711

"Europe"

480   Gettmann, Royal A., and Bruce Harkness, eds. Teacher's
       Manual for a Book of Stories. New York: Rinehart, 1955,
       pp. 36-39.

480.1 Hall, James B. Teacher's Manual for "The Realm of Fic-
       tion: 61 Short Stories." New York: McGraw-Hill, 1965,
       pp. 36-37.

481   Han, Pierre. "Organic Unity in 'Europe,' " SAB, 35, iii
       (1970), 40-41.
          Shows that the first sentence of "Europe" starts a unify-
       ing rhetorical pattern which is elaborated later.

481.1 Knoll, Robert E. Instructor's Manual for "Contrasts," 2nd
       ed. New York: Harcourt, Brace, 1959, p. 68.

481.2 Magalaner, Marvin, and Edmond L. Volpe, eds. Twelve
       Short Stories. New York: Macmillan, 1961, pp. 205-209.

482   Stone, Edward, ed. Henry James: Seven Stories and Stud-
       ies. New York: Appleton, Century, Crofts, 1961.

       See also: 272.2, 1740, 1804, 2028, 2198, 2229, 2258, 2380,
       2382; 2637, XXI; 2637.1, XVI; 2651, 2917, 3417, 3427,
       3429, 3536, 3626, 3711

THE EUROPEANS

483   Austin, Deborah. "Innocents at Home: A Study of The
       Europeans of Henry James," JGE, 14 (July, 1962), 103-129.

484   Bass, Eben. "James's The Europeans," Expl, 23 (Sept.,
        1964), Item 9.
            Notes a comic mythological reference to Diana when the
            Baroness is described as "prudent archer."

485   Bewley, Marius. "Henry James and 'Life,' " HudR, 11 (Sum-
        mer, 1958), 167-185.
            This work shows that Europe was a testing ground for
            American character.

486   Bottkol, Joseph M. Introduction. The Aspern Papers and
        The Europeans. New York: 1950.

487   Buitenhuis, Peter. "Comic Pastoral: Henry James's The
        Europeans," UTQ, 31 (January, 1962), 152-163.
            James favors the Europeans in the battle between sophisti-
            cation and Puritanism in The Europeans.

487.1   Edel, Leon, ed. Introduction. The Bodley Head Henry James.
        Vol. 1. The Europeans and Washington Square. London:
        Bodley Head, 1967.

487.2   Kossick, Shirley. "Henry James: The Europeans," Unisa
        EngS (May, 1969), 29-38.

488   Leavis, F. R. "The Novel as Dramatic Poem (III): The
        Europeans," Scrutiny, 15 (Summer, 1948), 209-221.

489   Macauley, Robie. " 'Let Me Tell You About the Rich...,' "
        KR, 27 (Autumn, 1965), 648-649.

490   Poirier, Richard. Afterword. The Europeans. New York:
        New Amer Lib., 1964.

490.1   _____. "The Europeans," in The Comic Sense of Henry
        James. New York: Oxford U. P., 1960, pp. 95-144.

491   Preston, Harriet Waters. "The Europeans," Atl, 43 (January,
        1879), 106-108.

492   Pritchett, V. S. "Babcockism," NS&N, 59 (June 11, 1960),
        863-864.

493   Sackville-West, Edward. Introduction. The Europeans.
        London: J. Lehmann, 1952.

494   Tanner, Tony. Introduction. Three Novels: The Europeans,
        The Spoils of Poynton, The Sacred Fount. New York: Harp-
        er & Row, 1968.

495   Vandermoer, H. "Baroness Munster's Failure," ES, 50
        (1969), 47-57.
            Eugenia and Robert Acton together represent a Europe and

an America that can never meet.

496   Ward, J. A.   "James's The Europeans and the Structure of
        Comedy," NCF, 19 (June, 1964), 1-16.
             Considers this novel "a nearly perfect comic perform-
             ance."

496.1   _____.   "The Europeans and the Structure of Comedy," in
        Henry James: Modern Judgments.   Tony Tanner, ed.   Lon-
        don: Macmillan, 1968, pp. 128-142.

Reviews of Eugenia (1957) by Randolph Carter, based on The Euro-
        peans:

        Atkinson, Brooks.   "Theatre: Henry James Dramatized," NY
             Times (January 31, 1957), 20
        Coleman, Robert.   "Tallu Makes Much Ado About Nothing,"
             NY Daily Mirror, (February 2, 1957) in NYTCR, 18
             (1957), 367
        Donnelly, Tom.   "A Tedious Time with Tallulah," NYWT&
             Sun (January 31, 1957), in NYTCR, 18 (1957), 367
        Kerr, Walter.   "Eugenia," NYHT (January 31, 1957), in
             NYTCR, 18 (1957), 368
        McClain, John.   "Bankhead Still Tallu--but Play's a Snafu,"
             NY Journal American (January 31, 1957) in NYTCR, 18
             (1957), 366
        McHarry, Charles.   "Tallulah Shines in a Weak Play," NYDN
             (January 31, 1957) in NYTCR, 18 (1957), 369
        Watts, Richard.   "Tallulah Bankhead and Something,"
             NYPost (January 31, 1957) in NYTCR, 18 (1957), 366.

Other Reviews of the Dramatization:

        Cw, 65 (March 22, 1957), 638
        Newsweek, 49 (February 11, 1957), 67
        New Yorker, 32 (February 5, 1957), 74-75
        Theatre Arts, 41 (April, 1957), 16
        Time, 69 (February 11, 1957), 70

Reviews of the novel, The Europeans:

        Appleton's, n. s., 6 (January, 1879), 94-95
        Athenaeum, 2658 (October 5, 1878), 431
        Atl, 43 (February, 1879), 167-173
        Christian Union, 18 (October 30, 1878), 361
        Eclectic, n. s., 29 (January, 1879), 123
        Harper's, 58 (January, 1879), 309
        Independent, 30 (November 21, 1878), 9
        International Rev, 6 (January 1879), 95-96
        Library Table, 4 (Aug. 31, Dec. 7, 1878), 383, 511-512
        Literary World, 10 (January, 1879), 28
        North Amer, 128 (January, 1879), 101-106

Quarterly Rev, 198 (October, 1903), 358
Scribner's, 17 (January, 1879), 447
Sunday Afternoon, 2 (December, 1878), 574

"The Figure in the Carpet"

497   Baumgaertel, Gerhard. "The Concept of the Pattern in the
        Carpet: Conclusions from T. S. Eliot," RLV, 25 (1959),
        300-306.
        On Eliot's interpretation of the story.

497.1   Beach, Joseph Warren. "The Figure in the Carpet," in The
        Question of Henry James. F. W. Dupee, ed. New York:
        Henry Holt, 1945, pp. 92-104.

498   Bragdon, Claude. "The Figure in Mr. James's Carpet,"
        Critic, 44 (February, 1904), 146-150.

499   Canavaggia, Marie. "Traduction et Presentation de "L'image
        dans le tapis." Paris: Editions Pierre Horay, 1957.

500   Feidelson, Charles, Jr. "Art as Problem in 'The Figure in
        the Carpet' and 'The Madonna of the Future,'" in Twentieth
        Century Interpretations. Jane P. Tompkins, ed. Englewood
        Cliffs, New Jersey: Prentice-Hall, 1970, pp. 47-55.

501   Finch, G. A. "A Retreading of James' Carpet," TCL, 14
        (July, 1968), 98-101.
        Finds the interest of the story more in the narrator-critic
        than in the artist Vereker.

502   Gide, André. Journal, 1889-1939. Paris: 1948, p. 847.
        "The Figure in the Carpet" is "one of the great parables
        of literature for our times."

503   Gossman, Ann. "Operative Irony in 'The Figure in the Car-
        pet,'" Descant, 6 (Spring, 1962), 20-25.
        The author sees the reader of the story as the victim of
        James's irony in that, like the narrator, he never pene-
        trates the secret of the figure.

504   Hofmann, Gert. Interpretationsprobleme Bei Henry James.
        ["The Turn of the Screw," "The Sacred Fount," "The Fig-
        ure in the Carpet"]. Diss. Freiburg: 1957.

505   Kanzer, Mark. "The Figure in the Carpet," AI, 17 (Winter,
        1960), 339-348.
        A psychological study of the story.

506   Kaye, Julian B. "The Awkward Age, The Sacred Fount, and
        The Ambassadors: Another Figure in the Carpet," NCF, 17
        (March, 1963), 339-353.

507   Lainoff, Seymour. "Henry James's 'The Figure in the Car-
        pet,'" BUSE, 5 (Summer, 1961), 122-128.
            Discusses Quentin Anderson's view of the story in The
            American Henry James.

508   _____. "James and Eliot: The Two Gwendolens," VN,
        21 (Spring, 1962), 23-24.

509   Levy, Leo B. "A Reading of 'The Figure in the Carpet,'"
        AL, 33 (January, 1962), 457-465.
            Finds that the meaning of the story is that the novelist
            works with ideas, feelings, attitudes, symbols, that to be
            meaningful must be shared and understood.

510   Powers, Lyall H. "A Reperusal of James's 'The Figure in
        the Carpet,'" AL, 33 (May, 1961), 224-228.
            The story is "concerned with the importance of attending
            to the work of the artist, or practising the 'exercise of
            penetration.'"

511   Roditi, Edouard. Oscar Wilde. New York: 1947, p. 111.
            "The Figure in the Carpet."

512   Scholes, Robert. The Fabulators. New York: Oxford U. P.,
        1967, p. 162.
            In the story, "The Figure in the Carpet," James "sees
            the literary artist and the critic as totally separate in
            their functions...."

513   Tyler, Parker. "The Child as 'The Figure in the Carpet,'"
        ChiR, 11 (Winter, 1958), 31-42.
            In "The Figure in the Carpet" James insists indirectly on
            the sexual passion as a ritual mystery, which is Vere-
            ker's "figure" as well as James's.

513.1   _____. "The Figure in the Carpet," in Every Artist His
        Own Scandal: A Study of Real and Fictive Heroes. New
        York: Horizon Press, 1964, pp. 225-237.

514   Westbrook, Perry D. "The Supersubtle Fry," NCF, 8 (Sep-
        tember, 1953), 134-140.
            Suggests that James had a "satirical intention" in "The
            Figure in the Carpet" and "The Middle Years."

        See also: 9, 10, 1740, 1794, 1804, 1924, 1943, 2006, 2198,
        IX; 2229, 2352, 2380, 2382, 2448, 2560, 2581, 2630; 2637,
        XX; 2637.1, XV; 2857, 3536, 3711, 3720.1

THE FINER GRAIN

515   Bennett, Arnold. "Henry James," Books and Persons, Being
        Comments on a Past Epoch, 1908-1911. New York: Chatto,
        1917, pp. 263-266.

516   _____. "The Finer Grain," New Age, n. s., 7 (October,
         1910), 614-15.

517   Hackett, Francis. "Finer Grain, Henry James," Horizons:
         A Book of Criticism. Huebsch, 1918, pp. 74-82.

         See also: 1740, 1794, 2028, 2229, 2380, 2382, 2560, 2737

Reviews of The Finer Grain:

         Athenaeum, 4332 (November 5, 1910), 552
         Book Buyer, 35 (January, 1911), 231
         Bookman (London), 39 (November 1910), 95-96
         Book News, 29 (January, 1911), 333-334
         Chicago Even Post, 2 (December 2, 1910), 1
         Harper's Wky, 54 (December 10, 1910), 35
         Nation, 91 (December 1, 1910), 522-523
         North Amer, 193 (February, 1911), 302
         Review of Revs, 43 (January, 1911), 120
         SatR, 110 (October 29, 1910), 553-54
         Spec, 105 (November 19, 1910), 864-5
         Times, 2 (November 5, 1910), 614
         TLS, (October 13, 1910), 377

                         "Flickerbridge"

518   Bement, Douglas, and Ross M. Taylor. "Henry James:
         Miss Wenham," The Fabric of Fiction. New York: Har-
         court, Brace & World, 1943, p. 264.

519   Shulman, Robert. "Henry James and the Modern Comedy of
         Knowledge," Criticism, 10 (Winter, 1968), 41-53.
             "Flickerbridge" as example of a "form" which James de-
         veloped most fully in other works.

         See also: 11, 270, 272.2, 692, 712, 1740, 1804; 2198, XI;
         2229, 2352, 2380, 2382; 2637, XXIII; 2637.1, XVIII; 3332,
         3711, 3536, 3706

                         "Fordham Castle"

         See: 270, 272.2, 1740, 1794, 1804; 2198, XII; 2229, 2352;
         2367, XXI; 2637.1, XVIII; 2651, 3010, 3536, 3711

                       "The Four Meetings"

520   Aziz, Maqbool. " 'Four Meetings': A Caveat for James
         Critics," EIC, 18 (1968), 258-274.
             The story is used as a plea for more "intelligent atten-
         tion" to James's revisions.

520.1 Bosanquet, Theodore. "The Revised Version," LittleR, 5
       (August, 1918), 56-62.

521   Felheim, Martin, Franklin Newman, and William Steinhoff.
       Study Aids for Teachers for "Modern Short Stories." New
       York: Oxford U. P., 1951, pp. 39-42.

522   Griffin, Robert J. "Notes toward an Exegesis: 'Four Meet-
       ings,'" UKCR, 29 (October, 1962), 45-49.
            Negative moral judgment of the narrator on Caroline Spen-
       cer.

523   Gurko, Leo. "The Missing Word in Henry James's 'Four
       Meetings,'" SSF, 7 (Spring, 1970), 298-307.
            Happy, uncompleted, and alive are the words suggested.

524   Iwase, Shitsuyu. "Henry James: 'Four Meetings' Revised,"
       Queries, 3 (June, 1962), 9-22.
            Importance of the narrator in the revised edition.

525   Jones, Leonidas M. "James's 'Four Meetings,'" Expl, 20
       (1962), Item 55.
            Caroline Spencer compared to a "medieval saint."

525.1 Loomis, Roger S., and Donald L. Clark, eds. Modern Eng-
       lish Readings. 6th ed. New York: Rinehart, 1950, pp.
       1029; 7th ed., 1965, pp. 1047-1048.

525.2 Sale, William, James Hall, and Martin Steinmann, Critical
       Discussions for Teachers Using "Short Stories": Tradition
       and Direction. Norfolk, Conn.: New Directions, 1945, pp.
       11-14.

526   Tartella, Vincent. "James's 'Four Meetings': Two Texts
       Compared," NCF, 15 (June, 1960), 17-28.
            A comparison of the original, published in 1877, and the
       1907-09 revision.

526.1 Thorp, Willard. The Madonna of the Future: and Other
       Early Stories. New York: New American Library, 1962.

       See also: 8, 9, 10, 1740, 1804, 1973, 2028, 2096, 2149;
       2198, IV; 2229, 2258, 2352, 2380, 2382, 2603; 2637, XXI;
       2637.1, XVI; 2695, 2773, 2944, 3422, 3536, 3648, 3689,
       3710, 3711

FRENCH POETS AND NOVELISTS

527   Edel Leon. Introduction. Henry James, French Poets and
       Novelists. New York: Grosset and Dunlap, 1964.

527.1 Patrick, Michael D. "Henry James's Literary Criticism,"

IllQ, (December, 1972), 20-33.

527.2   Stafford, William T.   "Lowell 'Edits' James: Some Revi-
        sions in 'French Poets and Novelists,' " NEQ, 32 (March,
        1959), 92-98.

527.3   Starkie, Enid.   <u>Flaubert: The Master--A Critical and Bio-
        graphical Study</u> (1856-1880).   New York: Atheneum, 1971,
        passim.

        See also: 9, 10, 12, 38, 1740, 2380, 2382, 2564, 2695,
        2793, 3015, 3724, 3725

Reviews:

        Atl, 42 (July, 1878), 118-9; (October, 1878), 508-510
        Christian Union, 29 (March 27, 1884), 305
        Churchman, 38 (July 6, 1878), 14; 51 (January 3, 1885), 15
        Dial, 5 (May 1884), 16-17
        Harper's, 56 (May, 1878), 939-940
        Independent, 30 (July 25, 1878), 13
        Library Table, 4 (March 30, 1878), 197
        Literary World, 15 (April 19, 1884), 129
        Penn Mo, 9 (May, 1878), 402-403

                    "The Friends of the Friends"

        See: 11, 12, 1035, 1740, 1804; 2198, IX; 2205, 2208, 2229,
        2352, 2380, 2382; 2637, XXII; 2637.1, XVII; 2737, 3536,
        3703, 3711

                    "The Future of the Novel"

528   Edel, Leon, ed.   <u>The Future of the Novel: Essays on the
        Art of Fiction.</u>   New York: 1956.

529   Hoskins, K.   "Henry James and the Future of the Novel,"
        SR, 54 (January, 1946), 87-101.

530   Monteiro, George.   "Addendum to Edel and Laurence: Henry
        James's 'Future of the Novel,' " PBSA, 63 (1969), 130.

                    "Gabrielle de Bergerac"

        See: 8, 1774, 1794, 1804; 2198, II; 2352, 2695, 2701, 2773,
        2793, 3045, 3123, 3536, 3711

"George Sand"

Reviews:

Liv Age, 281 (June, 13, 1914), 643-657
Quart. 220 (April, 1914), 315-338

"Georgina's Reasons"

See: 8, 10, 12, 1740, 1794, 1804; 2198, VI; 2229, 2352,
2380, 2382; 2637, XXV; 3010, 3711

"The Ghostly Rental"

531   Andreach, Robert J. "Literary Allusion as a Clue to Mean-
ing: James's 'The Ghostly Rental' and Pascal's Pensées,"
CLS, 4 (1967), 299-306.
James's story has two explicit references to Pascal's
Pensées.

See also: 8, 9, 1794, 2028; 2198, IV; 2205, 2208, 2352,
2695, 2701, 2948, 3711

"The Given Case"

See: 1740; 2198, X; 2637, XXVII

"Glasses"

See: 639, 1740; 2198, IX; 2637, XXVII

THE GOLDEN BOWL

532   Allott, Miriam. "Romola and The Golden Bowl," N&Q, 198
(March, 1953), 124.
Resemblances suggest James's indebtedness.

532.1 Anderson, Quentin. "The Golden Bowl as a Cultural Artifact,"
in The Imperial Self: An Essay in American Literary and
Cultural History. New York: Knopf, 1971, pp. 201-244.

533   _____. "Henry James and the New Jerusalem," KR, 8
(1946), 515-566.
Suggests that Adam is "divine wisdom," Maggie, "divine
love."

534   Bareiss, Dieter. "Henry James' The Golden Bowl und D. H.

Lawrence's Women in Love," Die Vierpersonenkonstellation
im Roman: Strukturuntersuchungen Zur Personenfuhrung.
Bern: Herbert Lang, 1969. (Europaische Hochschulschriften,
Reihe (14:I).

535   Bayley, John. "Love and Knowledge: The Golden Bowl," in
The Characters of Love: A Study in the Literature of Personality. New York: Basic Books, 1961, pp. 203-262.

536   Bebeau, Donald. "A Search for Voice: A Sense of Place in
The Golden Bowl," SDR, 7 (Winter, 1969-1970), 79-86.

537   Bewley, Marius. "Appearance and Reality in Henry James,"
Scrutiny, 17 (Summer, 1950), 96-102.

537.1   Birch, Brian. "Henry James: Some Bibliographical and
Textual Matters," Library, 20 (1965), 108-123.
James's revisions of The Golden Bowl in the New York
Edition.

538   Blackmur, R. P. Introduction. The Golden Bowl. New
York: Dell Publishing Co., 1963.

539   Bleich, David. "Artistic Form as Defensive Adaptation:
Henry James and The Golden Bowl," PsyR, 58 (Summer-Fall,
1971), 223-244.
A careful analysis of James's life at the time he was writing The Golden Bowl to show his relationship to the novel.

540   Bompard, Paola. "Una Nota Su The Golden Bowl," SA, 2
(1956), 143-162.

541   Bragdon, Claude. "The Golden Bowl," Critic, 46 (January,
1905), 20-22.

542   Brown, E. K. "James and Conrad," YR, 35 (December,
1945), 265-285.
Comparison of the two writers in regard to The Golden
Bowl.

543   Brumm, Ursula. "Symbolism and the Novel," PR, 25 (1958),
327-342. Repr., in The Theory of the Novel. Philip Stevick, ed. New York: Free Press; London: Macmillan,
1967, pp. 354-368.
"... Only in The Golden Bowl do we have symbolism in
the full sense of the term...."

543.1   Byrd, Scott. "Fractured Crystal in Middlemarch and The
Golden Bowl," MFS, 18 (Winter, 1972-73), 551-554.
A comparison of the two novels.

544   _____. "The Spoils of Venice: Henry James's 'Two Old
Houses and Three Young Women' and The Golden Bowl," AL

43 (November, 1971), 371-384.
James's sketch (1909), written in 1899, provides clues as to James's characterization of Prince Amerigo in The Golden Bowl.

545   Coles, Merivan Robinson. "Form and Meaning in The Golden Bowl," DA, 21 (Bryn Mawr: 1960), 2712.

545.1   La Coupe d'Or. Paris: R. Laffont, 1955.

546   Cox, C. B. "The Golden Bowl," EIC, 5 (April, 1955), 190-193.
Sees Maggie as battling for her rights as an individual.

547   Crawford, William, artist. "Crack in the Golden Bowl," Newspaper Enterprise Association, May, 1973.
Cartoon of the "cracked" golden bowl as a symbol of the scandals in American democracy.

547.1   Crowl, Susan R. "The Beholder's Eye: Romantic and Critical Perspective Through Style in James's 'Turn of the Screw,' The Wings of the Dove, and The Golden Bowl," DAI, 31 (Indiana: 1970), 5357A.
"The Turn of the Screw" in this study is seen as almost a parody of themes and means instrumental to the reading of The Golden Bowl and The Wings of the Dove.

547.2   Edel, Leon, ed. Introduction. The Bodley Head Henry James. Vol. 9. The Golden Bowl. London: Bodley Head, 1971.

548   Enck, John J. "Wholeness of Effect in The Golden Bowl," TWASAL, 47 (1958), 227-240.
The literary and figurative language in The Golden Bowl "provides one way of apprehending the wholeness of the novel."

549   Fergusson, Francis. "The Drama in The Golden Bowl," H&H, 7 (April-June, 1934), 407-413.
An interpretation.

550   _____. "The Golden Bowl Revisited," SR, 63 (January-March, 1955), 13-28.
A discussion of Quentin Anderson's thesis that The Golden Bowl is part of "an elaborate allegory" based upon the Swedenborgianism of James's father.

551   Firebaugh, Joseph J. "The Ververs," EIC, 4 (October, 1954), 400-410.
Sees the novel as more than social criticism: it is criticism of the very basis on which the notion of the absolute stands.

552   Gale, Robert L.   "James' The Golden Bowl, II, 307," Expl,
       19 (October, 1960), Item 5.
          The Minos, Ariadne, Theseus legend alluded to in the gar-
          den scene parallels the relationships between Maggie,
          Adam, and the Prince.

553   Gard, A. R.   "Critics of The Golden Bowl," MCR, 6 (1963),
       102-109.
          A good survey of pertinent interpretations.

554   Girling, H. K.   "The Function of Slang in the Dramatic Po-
       etry of The Golden Bowl," NCF, 11 (September, 1956), 130-
       147.
          In critical moments James "feels the need for a simplicity
          comparable to Shakespeare" and he employs slang phrases
          which often "crystalize" the complex situations.

555   Goldstein, Sallie Sears.   "A Critical Study of Henry James's
       The Wings of the Dove, The Ambassadors, and The Golden
       Bowl," DA, 24 (Brandeis: 1964), 5384-85.

556   Gordon, Caroline.   "Mr. Verver, Our National Hero," SR,
       63 (Winter, 1955), 29-47.
          The author is sympathetic to Adam but calls Charlotte a
          "monster."

557   Halperin, John W.   "The Language of Meditation: Four Stud-
       ies in Nineteenth-Century Fiction," DAI, 32 (Johns Hopkins:
       1972), 6976A-77A.
          The Golden Bowl is studied.

558   Hamblin, Abigail Ann.   "Literary Ramble: Architectural
       Imagery in The Golden Bowl," ArchitF, 139 (July, 1973), 98f.

558. 1 Heston, Lilla A.   "A Study of the Point of View in Three
       Novels by Henry James: The Spoils of Poynton, The Wings
       of the Dove, and The Golden Bowl," DA, 26 (Northwestern:
       1965), 3533.

559   Holder, Alex.   "On the Structure of Henry James's Meta-
       phors," ES, 41 (October, 1960), 289-297.
          On The Golden Bowl and The Ambassadors.

560   James, Henry.   "Preface to The Golden Bowl," The Art of
       the Novel.   New York: Scribner, 1934, 1946, pp. 327-348.

560. 1 James, William.   Letter to Henry James, October, 1905, in
       The James Family by F. O. Matthiessen.   New York: 1947,
       p. 339.
          ". . . why won't you, just to please Brother, sit down and
          write a new book . . . with great vigor and decisiveness in
          the action, no fencing in the dialogue, no psychological
          commentaries, and absolutely straightness in the style?

... I should think it would tempt you, to embark on a
'fourth manner'...."

Cf., Henry James.   Letter, November 1905, in reply to
William James. The Letters of Henry James. Percy
Lubbock, ed. New York: 1920, 1970, II, 44-55.
"... let me say, dear William, that I shall greatly be hu-
miliated if you do like it [The Golden Bowl], and thereby
lump it, in your affection with things of the current age,
that I have heard you express admiration for and that I
would sooner descent to a dishonoured grave than have
written...."

561   Kimball, Jean. "Henry James's Last Portrait of a Lady:
         Charlotte Stant in The Golden Bowl," AL, 28 (January, 1957),
         449-468.
         "... the evidence in the novel and in the author's preface
         [is] that James intended that Charlotte's predicament, the
         drama of her struggle, be the focus of interest in The
         Golden Bowl."

562   Krook, Dorothea. "The Golden Bowl," CamJ, 7 (1954), 716-
         737.
         Considers Maggie the "scapegoat and redeemer."

562.1   _____. "The Golden Bowl," (I), (II), in The Ordeal of
         Consciousness in Henry James. Cambridge: University
         Press, 1962, pp. 232-279, 280-324.

562.2   Lauer, Kristin Olson. "The Interior Monologue in The Am-
         bassadors and The Golden Bowl," DAI, 31 (Michigan State,
         1970), 6015A.

563   Lebowitz, Naomi. "Magic and Metamorphosis in The Golden
         Bowl," SR, 73 (January-March, 1965), 58-73.
         The author supports Dorothea Krook in ranking this novel
         as James's greatest achievement.

564   Lee, Brian. "Henry James's 'Divine Consensus': The Am-
         bassadors, The Wings of the Dove, The Golden Bowl," RMS
         6 (1962), 5-24.

564.1   Marks, Sita P. S. "Character Patterns in Henry James's
         The Wings of the Dove and The Golden Bowl," DAI, 31 (Mich-
         igan: 1970), 6063A.

565   Mercer, Caroline G. "Adam Verver, Yankee Businessman,"
         NCF, 22 (December, 1967), 251-269.
         A "crucial study" of The Golden Bowl. "... in his por-
         trait of Verver as an American in action, James is show-
         ing a businessman and maneuverer who belongs in many
         ways to the old American, and especially Yankee, tradi-
         tion...."

566   Mooney, Stephen L. "James, Keats, and the Religion of Consciousness," MLQ, 22 (December, 1961), 399-401.
The author believes that Keats's sonnet on Chapman's Homer is central, thematically, to The Golden Bowl.

567   Mulqueen, James L. "Perfection of a Pattern: The Structure of The Ambassadors, The Wings of the Dove, and The Golden Bowl," ArQ, 27 (Summer, 1971), 133-142.

568   Murakami, Fujio. "The Creation of The Golden Bowl," JimK, 10 (July, 1959), 117-131.
The process by which James created The Golden Bowl.

568.1 Naik, M. K. "The Draught from the 'Golden Bowl,'" JKU, 7 (1963), 199-217.

568.2 Nash, Deanna C. "The Web as an Organic Metaphor in The Marble Faun, Middlemarch: A Study of Provincial Life, and The Golden Bowl: The Growth of Contextualism as an Aesthetic Theory in the Nineteenth Century," DAI, 31 (North Carolina, Chapel Hill: 1971), 4131A.

569   Nuhn, Ferner. "The Enchanted Kingdom of Henry James-- The Golden Bowl," in The Wind Blew from the East: A Study in the Orientation of American Culture. New York and London: Harper & Row, 1940, 1942, pp. 116-158.

570   Ochshorn, M. G. "Henry James: The Golden Bowl," NMQ, 22 (Autumn, 1952), 340-349.

571   Owen, Elizabeth. "The 'Given Appearance' of Charlotte Verver," EIC, 13 (October, 1963), 364-374.
A study of the "scheming duplicity of Charlotte" which requires the aggressive actions of Maggie.

571.1 Pearson, Gabriel. "The Novel to End All Novels: The Golden Bowl," in The Air of Reality. John Goode, ed. London: Methuen, 1972, pp. 301-362.
"... imaginatively it [The Golden Bowl] figures, in its imagery, the whole past and future of the novel form."

571.2 Perrin, Edwin N., and C. B. Cox. ["The Ververs"] EIC, 5 (April, 1955), 189-191.
Cf., J. J. Firebaugh. "The Ververs," EIC, 4 (1954), 400-410.

572   Rahv, Philip. "The Heiress of All the Ages," PR, 10 (May-June, 1943), 232.
Calls the marriage in The Golden Bowl "symbolic of the reconciliation of their competing cultures."

572.1 Reddick, Bryan D. "Tone in Dramatic Narrative," DAI, 31 (Calif., Davis: 1970), 2397A.

"In James's The Golden Bowl, the reader is 'distanced' from any single character by changes in narrative focus, idiosyncratic style, elaborate images, summaries, and 'overlapping' time segments...."

572.2   Richmond, Lee J.   "Henry James and the Comedy of Love: The Golden Bowl," ErasmusR, 1, i (1971), 47-62.
Provides a helpful list of parallels between the Commedia dell-arte tradition and the characterization, tone, and structure of The Golden Bowl.

573   Roberts, Morris.   "Henry James and the Art of Foreshorten- ing," RES, 22 (July, 1946), 207-214.
An analysis of James's technique of foreshortening princi- pally in The Golden Bowl.

574   Rose, Alan.   "The Spatial Form of The Golden Bowl," MFS, 12 (1966), 103-116.
The author shows that "by relating scenes, symbols and images in space, and by employing a prose style that abounds in grammatical focuses, James has succeeded in concreting the narrative flow. He thereby effects his theme, which deals essentially with a spatial complex of relationships among characters, moralities, backgrounds, environments and attitudes."

574.1   Sears, Sallie.   "The Golden Bowl" in The Negative Imagina- tion: Form and Perspective in the Novels of Henry James. Ithaca, New York: Cornell U. P., 1968, pp. 155-222.

574.2   Sharp, Sister M. Corona.   "Fatherhood in Henry James," UTQ, 35 (1966), 279-292.

575   Snow, Lotus.   " 'A Story of Cabinets and Chairs and Tables': Images of Morality in The Spoils of Poynton and The Golden Bowl," ELH, 30 (December, 1963), 413-435.
A study of the furniture imagery in The Golden Bowl.

576   Spencer, James L.   "Symbolism in James's The Golden Bowl," MFS, 3 (Winter, 1957-1958), 333-344.
A careful study of the symbolism.

577   Spender, Stephen.   "The Golden Bowl," in The Question of Henry James. F. W. Dupee, ed. New York: Henry Holt, 1945, pp. 236-245.

578   Tanner, Tony.   "The Golden Bowl and the Reassessment of Innocence," LonM, 1 (November, 1961), 39-49.

579   Theobald, John R.   "New Reflections on The Golden Bowl," TCL, 3 (April, 1957), 20-26.
According to the author, the motivation of the novel is in- adequate.

580   Thompson, Francis. "The Golden Bowl," in Literary Criti-
        cisms: Newly Discovered and Collected. New York: Dut-
        ton, 1948, pp. 298-301.

581   Todasco, Ruth T. "Theme and Imagery in The Golden
        Bowl," TSLL, 4 (Summer, 1962), 228-240.
            The bowl is a grail-like symbol marking Maggie's sacri-
        fice.

582   Trieschmann, Margaret. "The Golden Bowl: An Analysis
        of the Sources of Evil in Human Relationships," IEY, 12
        (1967), 61-67.
            The author sees the Prince's "Roman venality" and Mag-
        gie's "Wilful ignorance of human suffering" as sources of
        evil.

583   Ward, Joseph A. "Evil in The Golden Bowl," WHR, 14
        (1960), 47-59.
            James develops the point, according to the author, that
        evil may stem from differences in personal as well as
        from national traits.

584   Watanabe, Hisayoshi. "Past Perfect Retrospection in the
        Style of Henry James," AL, 34 (May, 1962), 165-181.

585   Wegelin, Christof. "The 'Internationalism' of The Golden
        Bowl," NCF, 11 (December, 1956), 161-181.
            This novel, a "prophetic fable," represents a fusion of
        the two points of view shown in The Wings of the Dove
        and The Ambassadors. James synthesized values in The
        Golden Bowl with a succesful international marriage.

585.1   Weinstein, Philip M. "Fusion and Confusion: The Golden
        Bowl," in Henry James and the Requirements of the Imagina-
        tion. Cambridge, Mass.: Harvard U. P., 1971, pp. 165-
        194.

586   Welsh, A. "The Allegory of Truth in English Fiction," VS,
        9 (September, 1965), 7-28.

587   Wilson, James Southall. "Henry James and Herman Mel-
        ville," VQR, 21 (Spring, 1945), 281-286.

588   Wright, Walter. "Maggie Verver: Neither Saint Nor Witch,"
        NCF, 12 (June, 1957), 59-71.
            Wright defends Maggie against critics who hold her to be
        a malicious antagonist of Charlotte Stant. The article al-
        so provides a summary of criticism.

Reviews of The Golden Bowl:

        Academy, 68 (February, 1905), 128-129

Athenaeum, 4038 (March 18, 1905), 332
Atl, 95 (May, 1905), 696
Bookman (NY), 20 (January, 1905), 418-9
Book News, 23 (December, 1904), 275-6
Churchman, 91 (March 4, 1905), 334
Critic, 46 (January, 1905), 20-2
Current Lit, 37 (December, 1904), xvii
Independent, 57 (November 17, 1904), 1137
Lamp, 29, (1905), 583
Nation, 80 (January 26, 1905), 74
Outlook, 78 (December 3, 1904), 865
Reader, 5 (February, 1905), 380-2
Rev. of Revs, 31 (January, 1905), 116
Times (November 26, 1904)
TLS (February 10, 1905), 47
Tribune, 4 (December 10, 1904), 11
Vesy, 6 (1905), 63-64

"The Great Condition"

See: 11, 1740, 1794, 1804; 2198, X; 2229, 2352, 2637,
XXVII; 3728

"The Great Good Place"

589   DeFalco, Joseph M.   " 'The Great Good Place': A Journey
        into the Psyche," L&P, 8 (Spring, 1958), 18-20.

590   Herx, Mary Ellen.   "The Monomyth in 'The Great Good
        Place,' " CE, 24 (March, 1963), 439-443.
              Finds that James in this story follows patterns of myth
              and dream, "symbolic of the primordial experience of a
              hero's departure from the physical world, his discovery
              of and initiation into his spiritual realm, and his return,
              ... to his natural existence."

591   Silverstein, Henry.   "The Utopia of Henry James," NEQ,
        35 (December, 1962), 458-468.
              Shows that James in "The Great Good Place" withdraws
              George Dane from a busy life and creates for him a se-
              rene dreamworld, the keynote of which is simplicity.

591.1   Tintner, Adeline R.   "The Influence of Balzac's L'Envers
        de l'Histoire Contemporaine on James's 'The Great Good
        Place,' " SSF, 9 (1972), 343-51.

        See also: 11, 38, 240, 1794, 1804, 1883, 1924; 2198, XI;
        2205, 2208, 2229, 2258, 2352, 2380, 2382, 2581; 2637; XXI;
        2637.1, XVI; 2737, 2915.1, 2944, 3198, 3346, 3417, 3536,
        3702, 3702.1, 3703, 3710, 3711, 3720.1

"Greville Fane"

592   Hall, James B., and Joseph Langland. <u>The Short Story.</u>
New York: Macmillan, 1956, pp. 346-347.

See also: 270, 1740, 1804; 2198, VIII; 2229, 2352, 2380,
2382, 2448, 2581; 2637, XXI; 2637.1, XVI; 3417, 3536, 3706

"The Guest's Confession"

See: 9, 12, 38, 1794, 1804, 2028; 2198, II; 2352, 2695,
2793, 3536

GUY DOMVILLE

593   Edel, Leon. Introduction and Biographical Chapters: "Henry James: The Dramatic Years." <u>Guy Domville: A Play
in Three Acts.</u> With Comments by Bernard Shaw, H. G.
Wells and Arnold Bennett. London: Rupert Hart-Davis,
1961; Philadelphia: Lippincott, 1960.

594   Hatcher, Joe B. "Shaw the Reviewer and James's <u>Guy Domville,</u>" MD, 14 (December, 1971), 331-334.
Although Shaw thought the play lacked color and force, he
defended it because it did not follow the usual codes of
sentimentality.

594.1 Michaels, H. S. "An Unpublished Letter of Henry James,"
CLQ, Ser. 3 (May, 1951), 23-26.
In a letter written during a rehearsal of <u>Guy Domville,</u>
James commended Miss Marion Terry for her acting.

594.2 Putt, S. Gorley. "Henry James Haggles over Terms for
<u>Guy Domville,</u>" TLS, 3,749 (January 11, 1974), 35-36.

594.3 [Scott, Clement] "<u>Guy Domville</u> at the St. James's Theatre,"
The Daily Telegraph (January 7, 1895).

595   Shou [Shaw], B. "Dve novye p'esy ("Gai Domvill")" [Two new
plays ("Guy Domville")]. In: Shaw, B. <u>O drame i teatre</u>
[On drama and the theater]. Moscow, 1963, pp. 126-130.

596   Shaw, George Bernard. "Two New Plays: Guy Domville,"
<u>Dramatic Opinions and Essays with an Apology by Bernard
Shaw.</u> 2 vols. London: Constable & Co., Ltd., 1910, I,
7-11.

597   _____. "Two New Plays," in <u>Plays and Players: Essays
on the Theatre.</u> Oxford: 1952, pp. 1-9.

598   Walkley, A. B.   "Mr. Henry James's Guy Domville,"
        HarperW, 39 (March 2, 1895), 199.

598.1   Ward, A. C.   Introduction.   Plays and Players: Essays on
        the Theatre.   Oxford, 1952, pp. 1-9.

        See also: 10, 11, 38, 1740, 1794, 1924, 2062, 2229, 2352,
        2380, 2382, 2560, 2630, 2793, 3010, 3417, 3536

Reviews:
        Athenaeum, 105 (January 12, 1895), 57
        Critic, 26 (January 12, 19, 26, 1895), 38, 40, 53, 70-1; 29
            (November 28, 1896), 340-1
        Dial, 17 (September 1, 1894), 125; 18 (March 1, 1895), 156
        Lit World, 25 (June 30, 1894), 202
        Nation, 58 (June 28, 1894), 491; 60 (January 31, 1895), 18
        SatR, 79: 43

                              HAWTHORNE

599   Anderson, Quentin.   Introduction.   Hawthorne.   New York:
        Collier Books, 1966; London: Collier-Macmillan, 1966.

599.1   Bewley, Marius.   "Hawthorne and Henry James," in The
        Complex Fate: Hawthorne, Henry James, and Some Other
        American Writers.   New York: Gordian Press, Inc., 1967.

600   Buitenhuis, Peter.   "Henry James on Hawthorne," NEQ, 32
        (June, 1959), 207-225.
            James's appraisals of Hawthorne.

600.1   Cameron, Kenneth Walter.   Hawthorne Among His Contempo-
        raries.   Hartford: Transcendental Books, 1968, passim.

601   Chislett, William.   "A Henry James Paragraph on Hawthorne,"
        Moderns and Near-Moderns: Essays on Henry James, Stock-
        ton, Shaw, and Others.   Grafton Press, 1928, pp. 107-108.

602   Eliot, T. S.   "The Hawthorne Aspect," LittleR, 5 (August,
        1918), 44-53.   Repr., in The Question of Henry James.   F.
        W. Dupee, ed.   New York: 1945, pp. 112-119.

603   Grover, P. R.   "A Tanner in the Works," CamR, 89A (May
        3, 1968), 430-431.

603.1   Howells, William Dean.   "Henry James's Hawthorne," Atl
        45 (February, 1880), 280f.   Repr., in Naomi Lebowitz.
        Discussions of Henry James.   Boston: D. C. Heath, 1962,
        pp. 1-3.

603.2   Patrick, Michael D.   "Henry James's Literary Criticism,"
        IllQ, 35 (December, 1972), 20-33.

James saw Hawthorne as the "last pure American who learned of European traditions too late to be influenced by them to any great extent."

604   Tanner, Tony, ed.   Introduction and Notes. "<u>Hawthorne</u>"
<u>By Henry James.</u> London: Macmillan, 1967; New York: St. Martin's Press, 1967.

604.1 Trilling, Lionel. "Afterword," <u>Hawthorne Centenary Essays.</u>
Roy Harvey Pearce, ed. Ohio State U. P., 1964.

604.2 _____. "Our Hawthorne," PR, 31 (Summer, 1964), 329-
351.

Reviews:

Atl, 45 (Feb., 1880), 282-5
Appleton's, n. s., 8 (March, 1880), 282-4
Christian Union, 21 (February 11, 1880), 133-4
Eclectic, n. s., 31 (March 1880), 378-9
Harper's 60 (March 1880), 633
Independent, 32 (February 26, 1880), 12
International Rev, 8 (April, 1880), 447-50
Lippincott's 25 (March, 1880), 388-9
Lit. World, 11 (February 14, 1880), 51-3
Nation 30 (January 29, 1880), 80-1
Scribner's 19 (April, 1880), 943-4

"The High Bid"

604.2 Beerbohm, Max. "The High Bid," SatR (February 27, 1909); repr., in <u>Around Theatres.</u> New York: Alfred A. Knopf, 1930, II, 667.

604.3 Levy Babette May. " 'The High Bid' and the Forbes-Robertsons," CE, 8 (March, 1947), 284-292.
Forbes-Robertson told James that "The High Bid" had "the best audience of any of the set of plays" presented in the series. The article also contains a good survey of reviews of the play.

"The Impression of a Cousin"

605   Havens, Raymond D. "Henry James's 'The Impressions of a Cousin,'" MLN, 65 (May, 1950), 317-319.
The author feels there is danger in reading the final versions of the story in terms of the Notebooks.

See also: 10, 1740, 1804, 2028; 2198, V; 2352; 2637, XXIV; 3626, 3689

"In the Cage"

606   Aswell, E. Duncan. "James's 'In the Cage': The Telegraph-
       ist as Artist," TSLL, 8 (Fall, 1966), 375-384.
           According to Aswell, it is James's intention to use the
       voice of the young girl "to comment ironically on high and
       low society, but the last laugh is always at the expense of
       the girl herself as she unwittingly reveals traits and feel-
       ings identical with those she most condemns in others."

607   Blackall, Jean Frantz. "James's 'In the Cage': An Approach
       through the Figurative Language," UTQ, 31 (January, 1962),
       164-179.

608   Frantz, Jean H. "Henry James and Saintine," N&Q, 7 (July,
       1960), 266-268.
           Suggests that Joseph Xavier Boniface, a 19th-century
       French dramatist, is a possible influence on the story.

609   _____. "A Probable Source for a James Nouvelle,"
       MLN, 74 (March, 1959), 225-226.

610   Friend, Albert C. "A Forgotten Story by Henry James,"
       SAQ, 53 (January, 1954), 100-108.
           "In the Cage" is an "attempt to render a modern story in
       terms of a classical myth, Everard being Jove.

611   Füger, Wilhelm. " 'In the Cage'--Versuche zur Deutung
       einer umstrittenen Henry James Novelle," NS, 15 (1966), 506-
       513.
           An attempt to dramatize the problems of knowing.

612   Gass, William H. "In the Cage," Fiction and the Figures of
       Life. New York: Alfred A. Knopf, 1971, pp. 164-176.

613   Knights, L. C. "Henry James and the Trapped Spectator,"
       SoR, 4 (January, 1939), 600-615.
           According to Knights, the girl is typical of James's trapped
       spectators.

614   McFarlane, I. D. "A Literary Friendship--Henry James and
       Paul Bourget," CamJ, 4 (December, 1950), 144-161.
           James and Bourget both wrote on the subject of James's
       story.

614.1 Stone, William B. "On the Background of James's 'In the
       Cage,' " ALR, 6 (Summer, 1973), 242-248.

615   Wiesenfarth, Brother Joseph. "Illusion and Allusion: Reflec-
       tions in 'The Cracked Looking-Glass,' " FourQ, 12 (Novem-
       ber, 1962), 30-37.
           A comparison of Katherine Anne Porter's story with "In
       the Cage."

616   Zabel, Morton D.   Introduction.   Henry James's "In the
        Cage" and Other Tales.   London: Hart-Davis;   New York:
        Doubleday, 1958, pp. 21-22.

        See also: 11, 12, 270, 272.2, 1804;   2198, X;   2229, 2352,
        2380, 2382, 2630;   2637, XVI;   2637.1, XI;   2711, 2737, 2944,
        2948.1, 3417, 3474, 3582, 3664, 3711

Reviews of "In the Cage":

        Athenaeum, 3704 (October 22, 1898), 564-5
        Bookman (London), 14 (September, 1898), 165-6
        Critic, 33 (December, 1898), 523
        Nation, 67 (December, 1898), 432
        SatR, 86 (September 3, 1898), 319-20
        Spec, 81 (August 20, 1898), 249

                    AN INTERNATIONAL EPISODE

617   Brooks, Van Wyck.   "Henry James: An International Epi-
        sode," Dial, 75 (September, 1923), 225-238.

618   Daniels, Howell.   "Henry James and An International Episode,"
        BAASB, n. s., 1 (1960), 3-35.

618.1   Preston, Harriet Waters.   Atl, 43 (June, 1879), 758-759.
        Essay-rev., of An International Episode.

619   Sampson, Martin W.   Introduction.   Daisy Miller and an In-
        ternational Episode.   New York: Macmillan Co., 1927.

        See also: 38, 1676;   2198, IV;   2560;   2637, XIX;   2637.1, XIV;
        2651, 2695, 2737, 2773, 2793, 2944, 3205.1, 3206, 3326,
        3416, 3422, 3582, 3626, 3711

                        ITALIAN HOURS

619.1   Byrd, Scott.   "Two Old Houses and Three Young Women,"
        PBSA, 65 (4th Qt., 1971), 383-389.
        The sketch first appeared in "Italian Hours" in 1909.

620   Mitgang, Herbert.   Introduction.   Italian Hours.   With Illus-
        trations by Joseph Pennell.   New York: Horizon Press,
        1968.

620.1   _____.   "Springtime for Henry," SatR, 51 (April 6, 1968),
        46-47.
            "The splendor of Italian Hours is that it enables the read-
            er to walk the crooked streets with James himself as a
            young American in Italy."

See also: 11, 12, 1980, 2380, 2382, 2654, 3710

Reviews of Italian Hours:

> Churchman, 100 (December 4, 1909), 843
> Dial, 47 (December 1, 1909), 450-1
> Lit Digest, 39 (December 11, 1909), 1073
> Nation, 89 (December 9, 1909), 569
> North American, 191 (May 1910), 698-9
> Outlook, 94 (January 1, 1910), 41-2
> Rev of Reviews, 41 (February, 1910), 250

THE IVORY TOWER

621   Beebe, Maurice. "Henry James: The Ideal of Detachment,"
       in Ivory Towers and Sacred Founts: The Artist as Hero in
       Fiction from Goethe to Joyce. New York: New York Univer-
       sity Press, 1964, pp. 197-231, passim.

622   Buitenhuis, Peter. " 'The Fresh Start and the Broken Link':
       Henry James's The Ivory Tower," UTQ, 33 (July, 1964),
       355-368.
           The author suggests that this novel might have been the
           "artistic correlative" of Veblen's Theory of the Leisure
           Class, and, if completed, would have been James's best
           novel on American life.

623   Pound, Ezra. "Henry James," Instigations. New York:
       1920, pp. 106-107. Also in Make It New: Essays by Ezra
       Pound. New Haven: Yale U. P., 1935, pp. 251-307.
           Outline of ideas and technique used by James in develop-
           ing The Ivory Tower.

623.1 _____. "The Notes to The Ivory Tower," LittleR, 5
       (August, 1918), 62f.

624   Putt, S. Gorley. "Henry James: An Unfinished Master-
       piece," Eng, 16 (Summer, 1966), 44-48.
           The Ivory Tower is a "teasingly truncated masterpiece."
           Believes that had James lived to finish the work, his so-
           cial ideas might have appeared more fully and forced a
           revaluation of his work as a whole.

624.1 _____. "Unfinished Novels: The Sense of the Past and
       The Ivory Tower," in Henry James: A Reader's Guide.
       Ithaca, New York: Cornell U. P., 1966, pp. 401-413.
           Agrees with Professor Cargill that "no partially finished
           work by a great artist is capable of inspiring more re-
           grets for its incompleteness than The Ivory Tower."

625   Schneider, Marcel. "Henry James et Benjamin Britten,"
       NRF, 25 (April, 1965), 713-716.

Benjamin Britten imitates James in The Ivory Tower.

See also: 12, 38, 1931, 2070, 2229, 2380, 2351, 2352, 2561, 2946, 2898, 2915.1, 3161, 3386, 3417, 3603

Review of The Ivory Tower:

Bookman (London), 53 (December, 1917), 107-8

"John Delavoy"

See: 11, 12, 1740, 1794, 1804; 2198, IX; 2229, 2352, 2637, XXVII; 2737, 3417

"The Jolly Corner"

626   Blackmur, R. P. "The Sacred Fount," KR, 4 (1942), 328-352.
       Sees Brydon "as exorcising a partly living self."

627   Delbaere-Garant, J. "The Redeeming Form: Henry James's 'The Jolly Corner,' " RLV, 33 (1967), 588-596.

628   Freedman, William A. "Universality in 'The Jolly Corner,' " TSLL, 4 (Spring, 1962), 12-15.
       A comparison of "The Jolly Corner" with "The Beast in the Jungle."

629   Geismar, Maxwell. "The Ghost in the Jolly Corner," Henry James and the Jacobites. Boston: Houghton Mifflin Co., 1963, pp. 355-364.

630   Johnson, Courtney. "Henry James' 'The Jolly Corner': A Study of Integration," AI, 24 (Winter, 1967), 344-359.
       According to Professor Johnson, the imagery in the story suggests duality which "corresponds to Spencer Brydon's own psychological ambivalence, leading to a final symbol of ambivalence, the two finger stumps on the apparition at the end, and a uniting of ambivalence in the final scene with Alice."

630.1 MacKenzie, Manfred. "Theory of Henry James's Psychology," YR, 63 (Spring, 1974), 347-371.
       "The Jolly Corner" is given as an illustration of the author's theory of James's psychology because "it reads so much like a concentrated abstract" of James's work.

631   Mays, Milton A. "Henry James, or, The Beast in the Palace of Art," AL, 39 (January, 1968), 467-487.
       If "The Jolly Corner" is read metaphorically as the story of James himself, Brydon may not have been defeated.

632   Rogers, Robert. "The Beast in Henry James," AI, 13
        (Winter, 1956), 427-453.

633   Rosenfield, Claire. "The Shadow Within: The Conscious
        and Unconscious Use of the Double," Daedalus, 92 (Spring,
        1963), 326-344.
        Comment on "The Jolly Corner."

634   Rovit, Earl. "The Ghosts in James's 'The Jolly Corner,' "
        TSL, 10 (1965), 65-72.
        Sees allegorical emphasis in the dreams of Alice Staver-
        ton.

634.1   Smith, William Francis, Jr. "Sentence Structure in Three
        Representative Tales of Henry James," DA, 31 (Michigan
        State: 1970), 3520A.
        "The Jolly Corner" is one of the tales studied.

635   Stone, Edward, ed. Henry James: Seven Stories and Stud-
        ies. New York: Appleton-Century-Crofts, 1961.

636   Stovall, Floyd. "Henry James's 'The Jolly Corner,' " NCF,
        12 (June, 1957), 72-84.
        Sees Brydon and his ghost as a "double consciousness."

636.1   _____. "Henry James's 'The Jolly Corner,' " Henry
        James: Seven Stories and Studies. Edward Stone, ed.
        New York: Appleton-Century-Crofts, 1961, p. 304.

637   Thomson, Fred C. "James's 'The Jolly Corner,' " Expl,
        22 (December, 1963), Item 28.
        A study of the sea-world imagery.

637.1   Travis, Mildred K. "Hawthorne's 'Egotism' and 'The Jolly
        Corner," ESQ, 63 (1971), 13-18.

        See also: 8, 11, 12, 38, 270, 1740, 1786, 1794, 1804,
        1883, 1924, 1931, 2006, 2028, 2096; 2198, XII; 2205, 2208,
        2229, 2258, 2352, 2380, 2382, 2564, 2575; 2637, XXII;
        2637.1, XVII; 2737, 2793, 2915.1, 2990, 3197, 3265, 3297,
        3326, 3332, 3346, 3417, 3429, 3536, 3689, 3711, 3720.1

                            "Julia Bride"

638   Bruitenhuis, Peter. "From Daisy Miller to Julia Bride:
        'A Whole Passage of Literary History,' " AQ, 11 (Summer,
        1959), 136-146.

        See also: 12, 272.2, 1740, 1794, 1804, 1924, 2028; 2198,
        XII; 2229, 2352, 2380, 2382, 2560; 2637, XXII; 2637.1,
        XVII; 2917, 3073, 3326, 3536, 3626, 3711

Reviews of "Julie Bride":

       Churchman, 100 (October 30, 1909), 628
       Chicago Even Post, Friday Lit Rev, 1 (November 26, 1909),
          1
       Harper's, 116 (March, April, 1908), 489-502; 705-13; 119
          (Oct., 1909), xi
       Independent, 68 (January 1910), 51
       Lit Digest, 39 (November 27, 1909), 92
       North Amer, 190 (December 1909), 836
       Outlook, 93 (October 30, 1909), 515
       Rev. of Reviews, 41 (January, 1910), 124

"Lady Barberina"

638.1 M. L. H. "Tales of Three Cities," LitW, 15 (September,
      1884), 308-309.
      A disparaging critique of "Lady Barberina."

639   Ruhm, Herbert. Introduction, Notes, and Bibliography.
      Lady Barberina, and Other Tales. New York: Grosset and
      Dunlap, 1961.

639.1 Ticknor, Caroline. Glimpses of Authors. Boston: Hough-
      ton Mifflin, 1922, pp. 248, 249.

      See also: 9, 10, 270, 272.2, 1701, 1740, 1794, 1804, 1924;
      2198, V; 2229, 2352, 2380, 2382, 2564; 2637, XIX; 2637.1,
      XIV; 2650, 2737, 2944, 3206, 3326, 3417, 3536, 3626

"A Landscape Painter"

640   Allott, Miriam. " 'The Lord of Burleigh' and Henry James's
      'A Landscape Painter,' " N&Q, n. s., 2 (May, 1955), 220-
      221.
      James's story is a reply to a narrative poem by Tenny-
      son in the 1830's.

640.1 Melchiori, Giorgio. "Il dejeuner sur l'herbe de Henry
      James," SA, 10 (1964), 201-228.

      See also: 8, 1794, 1804, 2028; 2198, I; 2229, 2352; 2637,
      XXV; 2695, 2773, 3326, 3417, 3536, 3689

"The Last of the Valerii"

      See: 9, 10, 11, 679, 1794, 1804, 1871; 2198, III; 2205,
      2208, 2229, 2352, 2564; 2637, XXVI; 2695, 3326, 3354,
      3626, 3711

"The Lesson of Balzac"

640. 2 Cary, Elizabeth. "Balzac and James: An Impression of the
        Art of the Author of The Golden Bowl, Suggested by His Lec-
        ture on the Author of the Comedie Humaine," Times, 10 (May
        27, 1905), 337-338.

640. 3 Dunbar, Olivia H. "Henry James as a Lecturer," Critic,
        47 (July, 1905), 24-25.

Reviews of "The Lesson of Balzac":

        Bookman, 21 (March, 1905), 71-2
        Book News, 23 (February, 1905), 485-7
        Critic, 48 (January, 1906), 90; 46 (April, 1905), 307
        Dial, 39 (November 16, 1905), 311
        Nation, 80 (January 19, 1905), 53
        Reader, 6 (August, 1905), 336
        Rev. of Reviews, 33 (January, 1906), 121
        Tribune, 4 (July 29, 1905), 12

"The Lesson of the Master"

641   Broun, Heywood. Introduction. The Turn of the Screw, The
        Lesson of the Master By Henry James. New York: The
        Modern Library, 1930.

642   Huneker, J. G. "The Lesson of the Master," Bookman (New
        York) 51 (May, 1920), 364-368.

643   Lynd, Robert. "Literary Life," Books and Writers. Fore-
        word by Richard Church. New York: Macmillan, 1952, pp.
        113-117.

644   Nowell-Smith, Simon. "Legend of the Master," NS&N, 35
        (February, 28, 1948), 177.

645   Robinson, Edwin Arlington. Untriangulated Stars. Letters
        of E. A. Robinson to Harry de Forest Smith, 1890-1905.
        Denham Sutcliffe, ed. Cambridge: Harvard U. P. ; London:
        Oxford U. P. , 1947, p. 239.
        "... Three or four days ago, I took the liberty to borrow
        Henry James's 'The Lesson of the Master' and have read
        it to find that Henry James is a genius. No smaller word
        will do it for the man who produced such work as this...."

646   Rovit, Earl. "James and Emerson: The Lesson of the Mas-
        ter," AmSch, 33 (Summer, 1964), 434-440.

647   Smith, Charles R.   " 'The Lesson of the Master': An Inter-
        pretive Note," SSF, 6 (1969), 654-658.
            Sees the story as a reflection of James's attitudes toward
            art, artists, and critics.

647. 1 Swan, Michael, ed. Introduction. Lesson of the Master and
        Other Stories. London: Lehmann, 1948.

648   Wade, David.   "Shadows of Henry James," List (March 10,
        1966), 365.

        See also: 9, 10, 38, 272.2, 1740, 1804, 1943; 2198, VII;
        2352, 2380, 2382, 2448, 2560, 2581, 2630; 2637, XX; 2637.1,
        XV; 2737, 2765, 2918, 3244, 3326, 3417, 3422, 3528, 3536,
        3626, 3706, 3711

Reviews of "The Lesson of the Master":

        Athenaeum, 3360 (March 19, 1892), 369-70
        Atl, 69 (May, 1892), 711
        Bookman (London), 2 (April, 1892), 27
        Book Buyer, 9 (April, 1892), 115-6
        Christian Union, 47 (May 20, 1892), 981
        Churchman, 65 (April 9, 1892), 460
        Cosmopolitan, 13 (September, 1892), 630
        Nation, 54 (April 28, 1892), 326
        Picayune (April 1892), 12
        SatR, 73 (May 14, 1892), 575

                        "The Liar"

649   Kane, Robert J.   "Hawthorne's 'The Prophetic Pictures' and
        James's 'The Liar,' " MLN, 65 (April, 1950), 257-258.
            Suggests a possible source for "The Liar" in Hawthorne's
            story.

650   Powers, Lyall H.   "Henry James and the Ethics of the Art-
        ist: 'The Real Thing' and 'The Liar,' " TSLL, 3 (Autumn,
        1961), 360-368.
            James's two short stories indicate the artist's privilege to
            make use of people.

651   Rosenberry, Edward H.   "James's Use of Hawthorne in 'The
        Liar,' " MLN, 76 (March, 1961), 234-238.
            Similarities of ideas and images in the two stories.

652   Segal, Ora.   " 'The Liar': A Lesson in Devotion," RES, 16
        (August, 1965), 272-281.

653   Stone, Edward, ed. <u>Henry James: Seven Stories and Stud-
        ies.</u> New York: Appleton-Century-Crofts, 1961, pp. 102-
        106.

        See also: 10, 12, 272.2, 1740, 1794, 1804, 1929, 1930,
        1967, 1980; 2198, VI; 2229, 2258, 2352, 2380, 2382; 2637,
        XVII; 2637.1, XII; 2944, 3326, 3417, 3427, 3536, 3645,
        3689, 3711

Review:

        Critic, 15 (July 6, 1889), 3

                        "A Light Man"

654   Cantwell, Robert. "A Little Reality," H&H, 6 (1934), 503.

655   Fish, Charles K. "Description in Henry James's 'A Light
        Man,' " ELN, 2 (March, 1965), 211-215.
                Professor Fish sees "A Light Man" as a good example of
        James's skill in developing themes and characters through
        description of setting.

        See also: 8, 12, 1794, 1804; 2198, II; 2352; 2637, XXV;
        2695, 2773, 3417, 3536

                  "A Little Tour in France"

Review:

        Bookman (London) 63 (October, 1922), 70

                        "A London Life"

655.1   Howells, William Dean. "The Editor's Study," Harper's, 79
        (August, 1889), 447.
                Howells objected to the charge that James had caricatured
        Americans abroad.

        See also: 9, 10, 270, 1740, 1794, 1804, 1924, 1930; 2198,
        VII; 2096, 2229, 2352, 2380, 2382, 2564, 2630; 2637, XV;
        2637.1, X; 2737, 2793, 2944, 3010, 3015, 3332, 3417, 3536,
        3582, 3626, 3711

Reviews of "A London Life":

        Athenaeum, 3211 (May 11, 1889), 597-8
        Catholic World, 49 (August, 1889), 688-92
        Christian Union, 39 (May 16, 1889), 638
        Epoch, 5 (July 19, 1889), 389

Harper's, 79 (August, 1889), 477
LitW, 20 (May 25, 1889), 178
Nation, 49 (July 25, 1889), 77
SatR, 68 (July 13, 1889), 47-8

"Longstaff's Marriage"

See: 8, 9, 10, 12, 1804; 2198, IV; 2352; 2637, XXIV; 2695,
2793, 3326

"Lord Beaupre"

See: 1740, 1794, 1804; 2198, VIII; 2229, 2352, 2637, XVII;
3689

Reviews of "Lord Beaupre":

Athenaeum, 3428 (July 8, 1893), 60-1
Atlantic, 72 (November, 1893), 695-6
Godey's, 127 (November, 1893), 620
Nation, 57 (November 30, 1893), 416-7
Quarterly Rev, 198 (October, 1903), 358
SatR, 76 (July 8, 1893), 46-7

"Louisa Pallant"

656   Fadiman, Clifton, ed. The Short Stories of Henry James.
       New York: Random House, 1945, pp. 123-125.

657   Nicoloff, Philip L. "At the Bottom of All Things in Henry
       James's 'Louisa Pallant,' " SSF, 7 (Summer, 1970), 407-420.
       A very perceptive explication of the story.

658   Wright, Walter F. The Madness of Art: A Study of Henry
       James. Lincoln: Nebraska U. P., 1962, pp. 158-160.

       See also: 10, 270, 1676, 1740, 1794, 1804, 2062; 2198, VI;
       2229, 2352, 2380, 2382; 2637, XVIII; 2637.1, XIII; 3326,
       3626

"Madame de Mauves"

659   Bewley, Marius. "Henry James and 'Life,' " HudR, 11
       (Summer, 1958), 167-185.
       Notes the resemblances to Hawthorne.

660   Bouraoui, H. A. "Henry James and the French Mind: The
       International Theme in 'Madame de Mauves,' " Novel, 4
       (Fall, 1970), 69-76.

660.1 Cervo, Nathan A. " 'Our Lady of the Gulls': A Case of
        Polite Revenge," BaratR, 6 (Fall-Winter, 1971), 22-32.
              Sees Euphemia as the "lady of the Gulls", i.e., fools, in
              "Madame de Mauves."

661   Gleckner, Robert F. "James's 'Madame de Mauves' and
        Hawthorne's The Scarlet Letter," MLN, 73 (December, 1958),
        580-586.
              There are similarities between the two novels, the author
              says, as to characters, themes, and structure.

662   Kaplan, Charles. "James's 'Madame de Mauves,' " Expl,
        19 (February, 1961), Item 32.
              Sees the observer in the story as confused and disappoint-
              ed.

663   Kirkham, E. Bruce. "A Study of Henry James' 'Madame de
        Mauves,' " BSUF, 12 (Spring, 1971), 63-69.
              An exhaustive study of the story which examines the sym-
              bolic names, settings, the two cultures represented, the
              generations, and, as well, the characterization of Long-
              more.

664   Kraft, James. " 'Madame de Mauves' and Roderick Hudson:
        The Development of James's International Style," TQ, 11, iii
        (Autumn, 1968), 143-160.
              A study of James's treatment of the international theme.

665   Ludwig, Richard, and Marvin B. Perry, Jr. Nine Short
        Novels. Boston: Heath, 1952, pp. xxiii-xxix.

666   Maixner, Paul R. "Henry James and the Question of For-
        mal Unity," DA, 27 (Columbia: 1966), 1828A-29A.

667   McCormick, John O. "The Rough and Lurid Vision: Henry
        James, Graham Greene, and the International Theme," JA,
        2 (1957), 158-167.

668   McLean, Robert C. "The Completed Vision: A Study of
        'Madame de Mauves' and The Ambassadors," MLQ, 28 (De-
        cember, 1967), 446-461.
              A study of the parallels between the story and the novel
              in characterization, scenic structure, and theme.

669   _____. "The 'Disappointed Observer' of 'Madame de
        Mauves,' " RSW, 33 (1965), 181-196.
              Professor McLean sees the theme of the story as the con-
              sciousness of Longmore as he is attracted to the title
              character.

670   Patterson, Rebecca. "Two Portraits of a Lady," MQ, 1
        (Summer, 1960), 343-361.
              Believes that James treats the protagonist's inability to

love satirically in "Madame de Mauves" and tragically in Portrait of a Lady.

671   Rountree, Benjamin C. "James's 'Madame de Mauves' and Madame de La Fayette's Princess De Clèves," SSF, 1 (Summer, 1964), 264-271.
      A study of the parallels between James's story and the seventeenth century romance.

672   Simon, John K. "A Study of Classical Gesture: Henry James and Madame de Lafayette," CLS, 3 (December, 1966), 273-284.
      Reviews the likelihood that "Madame de Mauves" owes something to Madame de Lafayette's La Princesse De Clèves.

673   Ward, J. A. "Structural Irony in 'Madame de Mauves,' " SSF, 2 (Winter, 1965), 170-182.
      A study of the complex technique of the story.

      See also: 9, 10, 127, 132, 272.2, 712, 1804, 1854, 1932, 2062, 2148, 2229, 2352, 2380, 2382, 2560, 2564, 2650, 2651, 2695, 3015, 3206, 3244, 3326, 3386, 3388, 3416, 3417, 3536, 3582, 3626, 3648, 3711

                    "The Madonna of the Future"

674   Bellman, S. I. "Henry James's 'The Madonna of the Future' and Two Modern Parallels," CEJ, 1 (1965), 47-53.
      Finds parallels between James's story and works by Bernard Malamud and Robert Towers.

675   Buckler, William, and Arnold B. Sklare. Stories from Six Authors. New York: McGraw-Hill, 1960, pp. 416-418.

676   Feidelson, Charles, Jr. "Art as Problem in 'The Figure in the Carpet' and 'The Madonna of the Future,' " in Twentieth Century Interpretations of "The Turn of the Screw" and Other Tales: A Collection of Critical Essays. Jane P. Tompkins, ed. Englewood Cliffs, New Jersey: Prentice-Hall, Inc., 1970, pp. 47-55.

677   Havighurst, Walter. Instructor's Manual: Masters of the Modern Short Story. New York: Harcourt, 1955, pp. 15-16.

678   Niess, Robert J. "Henry James and Emile Zola: A Parallel," RLC, 30 (January-March, 1956), 4-6.
      James's story as possible source of Zola's L'Oeuvre.

678.1 Smith, William Francis, Jr. "Sentence Structure in Three Representative Tales of Henry James," DA, 31 (Michigan

State University: 1970), 3520A.
"The Madonna of the Future" is one of the stories studied.

679   Thorp, Willard. "Foreword." Henry James: The Madonna
      of the Future and Other Early Stories. New York: New
      American Library, 1962.

      See also: 9, 10, 12, 38, 1804, 2028; 2198, III; 2229, 2352,
      2380, 2382, 2560, 2564, 2581; 2637, XVIII; 2637.1, XIII;
      2650, 2695, 2770, 2916, 2918, 3175, 3417, 3493, 3536, 3626,
      3689

Review of "The Madonna of the Future":

Athenaeum, 2715 (November 8, 1879), 593-4

                        "The Marriages"

680   Kramer, Dale and Cheris. "James's 'The Marriages': De-
      signs of Structure," UR, 33 (October, 1966), 75-80.

680.1 Stone, Edward, ed. Henry James: Seven Stories and Stud-
      ies. New York: Appleton-Century-Crofts, 1961.

681   Tilton, Eleanor. Foreword. Henry James: The Marriages
      and Other Stories. New York: New American Library, 1961.

      See also: 12, 270, 272.2, 1740, 1794, 1804; 2198, VIII;
      2229, 2352; 2637, XXIII; 2637.1, XVIII; 2944, 3474, 3605,
      3706

                       "Master Eustace"

See: 9, 1794, 1804, 2028; 2198, II; 2352; 2637, XXVI; 2695,
3417

                       "Maud-Evelyn"

682   D'Avanzo, Mario L. "James's 'Maud-Evelyn': Source, Allu-
      sion, and Meaning," IEY, 13 (1968), 24-33.
      A study of Browning's "Evelyn Hope" as a major source
      of James's story.

      See also: 8, 11, 12, 1035, 1740, 1804, 1871, 1945; 2198,
      XI; 2205, 2208, 2229, 2352; 2637, XXVIII; 3244, 3326, 3417,
      3536, 3711

Review of "Maud-Evelyn":

Atlantic, 85 (April, 1900), 439-55

THE MIDDLE YEARS (Autobiographical)

683   Gilman, Lawrence. "Henry James in Reverie," NAR, 207
       (January, 1918), 130-135.
       Essay-rev., of The Middle Years.

684   Littell, Philip. "Henry James's Quality," NewRep, 6 (March
       11, 1916), 152-154.

684.1 _____. " 'Middle Years,' " in Books and Things. New
       York: Harcourt, Brace, 1919, pp. 215-223, 224-229.

685   Woolf, Virginia S. "Henry James: The Old Order," Col-
       lected Essays. New York: Harcourt, Brace & World, 1966,
       pp. 270-276.

       See also: 8, 9, 10, 11, 12, 38, 1740; 2198, IX; 2229,
       2352, 2382, 2695, 3427, 3714

Reviews:

       Bookman (London) 53 (February, 1918), 162-3
       Scribner's, 62 (1917), 465-76, 608-15

"The Middle Years" (Story)

686   Gale, Robert L. "James's 'The Middle Years,' " Expl, 22
       (November, 1963), Item 22.
       Considers that the printing of the Roman numeral "I" af-
       ter the title of the story in the revised edition is intended
       as a joke on the reader; the discovery that there is no
       second part emphasizes that a belief in a second chance
       is indeed an illusion.

686.1 Robinson, J. J. "Henry James and Schulberg's 'The Disen-
       chanted,' " MLN, 67 (November, 1952), 472-473.
       Schulberg's indebtedness to James's "The Middle Years."

687   Westbrook, Perry D. "The Supersubtle Fry," NCF, 8 (Sep-
       tember, 1953), 134-140.
       "The Middle Years" and "The Figure in the Carpet" both
       have satirical intention.

687.1 Wright, Austin McGiffert. "Appendix E: Narrative and
       Scenes in 'The Middle Years' ..." in The American Short
       Story in the Twenties. Chicago: Chicago U. P., 1961, p.
       291.
       Division into dramatic scenes and narrative sections.

       See also: 272.2, 1794, 1804, 1924, 1980, 2149, 2258, 2560,
       2564, 2581, 2630, 2637.1, XVI; 2737, 2916, 2918, 3244,

3326, 3417, 3536, 3626, 3710

Review of "The Middle Years," (Story):

Scribner's 13 (May, 1893), 609-20

"Miss Gunton of Poughkeepsie"

See: 11, 1740, 1804; 2198, XI; 2229, 2352, 2637, XXI; 2637.1, XVI; 3536, 3626, 3706, 3710

"The Modern Warning"

See: 10, 1740, 1794, 1804, 2028; 2198, VII; 2229, 2352, 2637, XXVI; 3417, 3536, 3626

"Mora Montravers"

See: 1740, 1804; 2198, XII; 2229, 2352; 2637, XXVIII; 2737, 3689, 3711

"A Most Extraordinary Case"

See: 8, 38, 1794, 1804; 2198, I; 2028, 2352; 2637, XXVI; 2695, 2773, 2915.1, 3326, 3711

"Mrs. Medwin"

688   Bernard, Kenneth. "Henry James's Unspoken Discourse in 'Mrs. Medwin,'" Disc, 6 (Autumn, 1963), 310-314.
       The story is given as an example of the manner in which James employs unspoken communication.

689   Fadiman, Clifton, ed. The Short Stories of Henry James. New York: Random House, 1945, pp. 484-485.

See also: 1740, 1794, 1804; 2198, XI; 2229, 2352, 2380, 2382; 2637, XXIII; 2637.1, XVIII; 3417, 3706

"Mrs. Temperly"

See: 1740, 1794, 1804; 2198, VI; 2229, 2352; 2637, XXVI; 3326, 3689

"My Friend Bingham"

See: 679, 1871, 2198, I; 2695, 2701, 2773, 2944, 3536

"A New England Winter"

See: 10, 1740, 1804, 2028; 2198, VI; 2229, 2352, 2637,
XXV; 3689

"The Next Time"

690 Gale, Robert L. "James's 'The Next Time,' " Expl, 21 (December, 1962), Item 35.
Suggests that the two writers whose work Lambert's wife
so much prefers are probably Thomas Anstey Guthrie
(1856-1934) and Francis Marion Crawford (1854-1909).

691 Lind, Ilse Dusoir. "The Inadequate Vulgarity of Henry
James," PMLA, 66 (December, 1951), 886-910.
A thorough account is given of the New York Tribune affair. The author adds that the "first episode of the story,
["The Next Time"] is narrated with almost no fictional in-
ventiveness.... So strong is the fidelity of fiction to fact
that one can guess only that James's need to disburden
himself of an oppressive memory was compelling."

692 Shulman, Robert. "Henry James and the Modern Comedy of
Knowledge," Criticism, 10 (Winter, 1968), 41-53.
An examination of "The Next Time" and "Flickerbridge"
as examples of form.

See also: 9, 10, 11, 38, 270, 272.2, 1673, 1740, 1794,
1804, 1862, 1943, 1967; 2198, IX; 2229, 2352, 2380, 2564,
2581, 2630; 2637, XX; 2637.1, XV; 2651, 2811, 2918, 3244,
3326, 3417, 3536

"Notes on Novelists"

692.1 Bredvold, Louis I. "Essays on the Novel," Dial, 57 (November 1, 1914), 332-333.
A favorable critique.

692.2 Harrison, Henry Sydnor. " 'Notes on Novelists,' with Some
Other Notes," YR, n. s., 4 (April, 1915), 608-611.

692.3 Littell, Philip. "Henry James as Critic," NewRep, 1 (No-
vember 21, 1914), 26-8.
Urges that every young novelist consider this body of
James's "aesthetic doctrine."

692.4   Matthews, Brander. "Notes on Novelists," Bookman, 40
        (December, 1914), 460-462.
            Described the book as a "rich feast of criticism."

Reviews of "Notes on Novelists":

        Catholic World, 100 (February, 1915), 695
        Current Lit, 58 (February, 1915), 115-116
        Independent, 80 (November 16, 1914), 243
        Rev. of Reviews, 50 (December, 1914), 763

                    NOTES OF A SON AND BROTHER

693   Tompkins, Jane P. "The Redemption of Time in Notes of a
        Son and Brother," TSLL, 14 (Winter, 1973), 681-690.

        See also: 10, 12, 38, 1794, 1924, 1980, 2229, 2352, 2382,
        2695, 2737, 3326, 3417, 3626, 3700

Reviews of Notes of a Son and Brother:

        America, 11 (June 20, 1914), 235
        Bookman, 39 (April, 1914), 117-120
        Book News, 22 (May, 1914), 451
        Churchman, 109 (June 27, 1914), 842
        Dial, 56 (April 1, 1914), 289-91
        DublinR, 155 (July, 1914), 197-8
        EngR, 17 (April, 1914), 139-41
        Independent, 78 (June 1, 1914), 366-8
        Nation, 99 (July 2, 1914), 16-7
        NoAmer, 200 (October, 1914), 632-5
        Spec, 113 (October 3, 1914), 446-7
        Times, 19 (March 15, 1914), 117-8
        Tribune, 74 (May 2, 1914), 10
        YaleR, n. s. 4 (January, 1915), 414-5

                        "Nona Vincent"

        See: 11, 1740, 1804; 2198, VIII; 2205, 2208, 2352; 2637,
        XXVI; 3332

                       "Osborne's Revenge"

        See: 8, 2028; 2198, II; 2352, 2695, 2701, 2773, 2948, 3326

                        "The Other House"

694   Bowden, Edwin T. ["The Other House"], The Themes of
        Henry James. New Haven: Yale U. P., 1956, pp. 79ff.

695   Edel, Leon, ed. Introduction. <u>The Other House.</u> London:
        Rupert Hart-Davis, 1948; New York: 1948; Norfolk, Conn.:
        New Directions, 1948.

695.1   Isle, Walter. "The Other House," <u>Experiments in Form:</u>
        <u>Henry James's Novels, 1896-1901.</u> Cambridge, Mass.:
        Harvard U. P., 1968, pp. 39-76.

695.2   K., Q.   "The Other House," NewRep, 16 (September 7,
        1918), 172.
            "The Other House," one of three stories which James
            wrote with the theatre in mind, was not successful as a
            play.

696   Kirby, David K.   "Henry James's "The Other House: From
        Novel to Play," MarkR, 3 (1972), 49-53.

696.1   McElderry, B. R., Jr.   "Henry James's Neglected Thriller:
        'The Other House,' " ArQ, 8 (Winter, 1952), 328-332.

        See also: 9, 10, 11, 12, 1740, 1794, 1804, 1980, 2070,
        2229, 2352, 2382, 2630, 2781, 2793, 2944, 3198, 3521, 3711

Reviews of "The Other House":

        Athenaeum, 3601 (October 31, 1896), 597
        Atlantic, 79 (January, 1897), 137
        Bookman (London), 11 (November, 1896), 49
        Bookman (NY), 4 (December, 1896), 359-60
        Chautauquan, 24 (February, 1897), 630-1
        Critic, 29 (n. s., 26) (November 28, 1896), 335
        Current Lit, 20 (December, 1896), 486-7; 21 (May, 1897),
            388-9
        Dial, 22 (January 1, 1897), 22
        Independent, 48 (December 10, 1896), 1693
        LitWorld, 27 (December 26, 1896), 476
        Nation, 64 (January 28, 1897), 71
        NYTSRB&A, 1 (October 31, 1896), 4
        Overland, 2d S, 29 (January, 1897), 106
        QuarterlyRev, 198 (October, 1903), 358
        SatR, 82 (October 31, 1896), 474-75

                        "The Others"

697   Banta, Martha.   "Henry James and 'The Others,' " NEQ, 37
        (June, 1964), 171-184.
            Considers that James's "The Others" is related to the
            great interest in spiritualism in the later nineteenth cen-
            tury.

698   _____.   "The Two Worlds of Henry James: A Study in
        the Fiction of the Supernatural," DA, 26 (Indiana: 1965),
        1035-1036.

"The Outcry"

699   Edel, Leon.   "Henry James and 'The Outcry,' " UTQ, 18
        (July, 1949), 340-346.
              The death of Edward VII is said to have caused the col-
              lapse of production plans for this play.   The next year
              James converted the play into a novel, but the play was
              privately produced in 1917.

700   Havens, Raymond D.   "Henry James on 'The Outcry,' " MLN,
        70 (February, 1955), 105-106.

701   MacCarthy, Desmond.   " 'The Outcry,' " NSt, 9 (July 21,
        1917), 375-376.

701.1 Putt, S. Gorley.   "The Outcry"--"Marriage and Society" in
        Henry James: A Reader's Guide.   Ithaca, New York: Cor-
        nell U. P., 1966, pp. 262-263.
              " 'The Outcry' (1911), the last novel published in James's
              lifetime,... reverts somewhat wearily to the form of an-
              other melodrama of money.... "

        See also: 1701, II; 1740, 1804, 1871, 1980, 2070, 2229,
        2321, 2352, 2380, 2382, 2560, 2630, 2944, 3332, 3626

Reviews of "The Outcry":

        Bellman, 11 (December 2, 1911), 722
        Bookman, 34 (December, 1911), 434-5
        Bookman (London), 41 (November, 1911), 94-5
        Book News, 30 (December, 1911), 278
        CurLit, 52 (February, 1912), 235-6
        Independent, 71 (November 2, 1911), 982
        Lit Digest, 43 (November 18, 1911), 924
        Nation, 93 (November 9, 1911), 444-5
        NoAmer, 195 (January, 1912), 141-3
        Outlook, 99 (October 21, 1911), 405-6
        Rev of Revs, 45 (January, 1912), 122
        Spec, 107 (October 21, 1911), 648
        Times, 17 (October 29, 1911), 687

"Owen Wingrave"

        See: 8, 11, 270, 272.2, 1740, 1804; 2198, IX; 2204, 2205,
        2208, 2229, 2352, 2380, 2382, 2560; 2637, XXII; 2637.1,
        XVII; 2651, 3265, 3417, 3703

Reviews of "Owen Wingrave":

        Atlantic, 73 (April, 1894), 568
        Nation, 57 (November 30, 1893), 416-7

"Pandora"

702   Gale, Robert L. " 'Pandora' and Her President," SSF, 1
       (Spring, 1964), 222-224.
            The "funny" president in James's story is Hayes; his suc-
            cessor is Garfield.

703   Vandersee, Charles. "James's 'Pandora': The Mixed Conse-
       quences of Revision," SB, 21 (1968), 93-108.
            A study of the revisions made in the story in all the print-
            ings, but attention is also given to the biographical con-
            cerns of the author between versions.

       See also: 8, 10, 11, 270, 272.2, 1740, 1790, 1804, 2027,
       2028; 2198, V; 2229, 2352, 2380, 2382; 2637, XXIII; 2637.1,
       XVIII; 2898, 2917, 3536, 3626

"The Papers"

       See: 12, 1740, 1804; 2198, XII; 2229, 2352; 2637, XXVIII;
       2737, 3417

PARTIAL PORTRAITS

704   Edel, Leon. New Introduction. Partial Portraits. Ann
       Arbor: Michigan U. P., 1970.

705   Noble, James Ashcroft. "Partial Portraits," Academy, 33
       (June 16, 1888), 406-407.

706   Patrick, Michael D. "Henry James's Literary Criticism,"
       IllQ, 35 (December, 1972), 20-33.
            Because of James's interest in character and conscience,
            his first mature criticism took the form of literary por-
            traits. The articles in Partial Portraits represent "in
            certain ways the pinnacle of his [James's] critical achieve-
            ment."

       See also: 10, 12, 38, 2028, 2695, 3326, 3417

Reviews:

            Atlantic, 62 (October, 1888), 564-8
            Book Buyer, n. s., 5 (September, 1888), 313
            Churchman, 58 (October 13, 1888), 458
            Critic, 12 (June 9, 1888), 278-9
            Epoch, 3 (July 13, 1888), 456-7
            Independent, 40 (June 21, 1888), 786
            Lit World, 19 (June 23, July 7, 1888), 203, 212
            Nation, 47 (July 26, 1888), 75-6
            Public Opinion, 5 (September 8, 1888), 483

A PASSIONATE PILGRIM

707   Gegenheimer, Albert Frank. "Early and Late Revisions in
       Henry James's A Passionate Pilgrim," AL, 23 (May, 1951),
       233-242.

708   Howells, William Dean. "James's Passionate Pilgrim and
       Other Tales," Atl, 35 (April, 1875), 490-495. Repr., in
       Discovery of a Genius: William Dean Howells and Henry
       James. Albert Mordell, ed. New York: 1961, pp. 63-74.

709   Josephson, Matthew. "A Passionate Pilgrim," in Portrait of
       the Artist as American. New York: Octagon Books, Inc.,
       1964, pp. 98-138.

710   Melchiori, Giorgio. "Locksley Hall Revisited: Tennyson and
       Henry James," REL, 6 (October, 1965), 9-25.

711   Nakazato, Haruhiko. "Henry James's 'A Passionate Pil-
       grim,' " StPR, 12 (August, 1962), 1-21.

712   Putt, S. Gorley. " 'The Passionate Pilgrim': An Aspect of
       Henry James," W&R, 4 (1948), 230-232.

712.1 _____. "The Passionate Pilgrim: The Sense of the Past,"
       Henry James: A Reader's Guide. Ithace, New York: Cor-
       nell U. P., 1966, pp. 55-84.

713   Wright, Walter F. ["A Passionate Pilgrim"] The Madness
       of Art: A Study of Henry James. Lincoln: Nebraska U. P.,
       1962, pp. 115-118.

       See also: 8, 9, 11, 12, 34, 38, 270, 272.2, 1740, 1794,
       1804, 2028, 2062; 2198, II; 2229, 2268, 2352, 2380, 2382,
       2564; 2637, XVIII; 2637.1, XIII; 2650, 2695, 3015, 3326,
       3417, 3536, 3626, 3689

Reviews:

       Appleton's, 14 (February 13, 1875), 214-5
       Independent, 27 (March 25, 1875), 10
       LitWorld, 5 (March 1, 1875), 157
       Nation, 20 (June 24, 1875), 425-7
       SatR, 39 (April 24, 1875), 550
       Scribner's, 9 (April, 1875), 766-7
       Unitarian Rev, 4 (July, 1875), 108-9

                              "Paste"

714   Davis, Robert G. Instructor's Manual for Ten Modern Mas-
       ters: An Anthology of the Short Story. New York:

Harcourt, Brace, 1953, pp. 38-40.

715 Highet, Gilbert. "Paste," People, Places, and Books. New York: Oxford U. P., 1953, pp. 189-190.

715.1 James, Henry. The Art of the Novel: Critical Prefaces. New York: Scribner, 1934, pp. 237-238.

716 Knieger, Bernard. "James's 'Paste,' " SSF, 8 (Summer, 1971), 468-469.
Insists that the story "centrally dramatizes Arthur's hypocrisy rather than Charlotte's 'scrupulousness.' "

717 Kuhn, Bertha M. "Study Questions and Theme Assignments on Henry James's 'Paste,' " ExEx, 4 (April, 1957), 4-5.

717.1 Lief, Leonard, ed. Story and Critic. New York: Harper & Row, 1963, pp. 330-331.

718 Segnitz, T. M. "The Actual Genesis of Henry James's 'Paste,' " AL, 36 (May, 1964), 216-219.
Suggests that James's story may have a closer parallel with Maupassant's "Les Bijoux" rather than with "La Parure," which James may have confused with "Les Bijoux."

See also: 11, 270, 272.2, 1740, 1794, 1804; 2198, X; 2229, 2352, 2544.2; 2637, XXI; 2637.1, XVI; 3706

"The Patagonia"

See: 10, 1740, 1804; 2198, VII; 2229; 2637, XXIII; 2637, XVIII; 3417, 3473, 3711

"The Path of Duty"

See: 1740, 1804, 1929, 1930; 2198, VI; 2352; 2637, XXV, 2793, 3326, 3536, 3678, 3711

"The Pension Beaurepas"

718.1 Aziz, Maqbool. "Revisiting 'The Pension Beaurepas: The Tale and Its Texts," EIC, 23 (July, 1973), 268-282.
"What the revision finally achieves is that, by using a variety of the right 'brush-strokes,' it brings the final version closer to the archetype of the intention in the author's mind...."

719 Onishi, Akio. "An Approach to Henry James--Through an 'International' Trilogy," BungR, 12 (January, 1963), 1-45.

One of the stories studied is "The Pension Beaurepas."

See also: 9, 10, 270, 272.2, 1794, 1804, 2028; 2198, IV;
2229, 2352, 2380, 2382, 2637, XIX; 2637.1, XIV; 2651,
2695, 2990, 3582, 3626, 3711

Reviews of "The Pension Beaurepas":

Atlantic, 51 (May, 1883), 706-7
Nation, 36 (April 5, 1883), 301
SatR, 51 (March 19, 1883), 372-3

"The Point of View"

720   Onishi, Akio. "An Approach to Henry James--Through an
       'International' Trilogy," BungR, 12 (January, 1963), 1-45.
       "The Point of View" is one of the stories studied.

       See also: 9, 10, 270, 272.2, 1740, 1794, 1804, 2028; 2198,
       IV; 2229, 2352, 2380, 2382; 2637, XIX; 2637.1, XIV; 2651,
       2859.1, 2917, 2944, 3010.1, 3326, 3417, 3536, 3626

Reviews of "The Point of View":

Atlantic, 51 (May, 1883), 706-7
Nation, 36 (April 5, 1883), 301
SatR, 51 (March 19, 1883), 372-3

"Poor Richard"

See: 8, 38, 1774, 1804, 1871, 2028; 2198, I; 2352; 2637,
XXV; 2695, 2773, 3417, 3711

THE PORTRAIT OF A LADY

721   Abel, Darrel. American Literature. New York: Barron's
       Educational Series, 1963, III, 256-269.

722   Allen, Walter. The English Novel: A Short Critical History.
       London: Phoenix House, 1956, pp. 253-256; New York:
       Dutton, 1957, pp. 314-318.

723   _____. The Urgent West: The American Dream and Mod-
       ern Man. New York: E. P. Dutton & Co., Inc., 1969,
       passim.

724   Anderson, Charles R. Introduction. The Portrait of a Lady.
       New York: Collier Books, 1962.

725   _____. "Person, Place, and Thing in James's The Por-

trait of a Lady," Essays on American Literature in Honor of
Jay B. Hubbell. Clarence Gohdes, ed. Durham, North Carolina: Duke University Press, 1967, pp. 164-182.

726   Anderson, Quentin. Introduction. The Portrait of a Lady.
       New York: Washington Square Press, 1963.

727   _____. "News of Life," The American Henry James.
       New Brunswick, New Jersey: Rutgers U. P., 1957, pp. 187-
       192.

728   Anon. "Novels of the Week," [The Portrait of a Lady],
       Athenaeum (November 26, 1881), 699.

729   Aplash, Madhu. "Methods of Characterization in The Por-
       trait of a Lady," in Variations on American Literature.
       Darshan Singh Maini, ed. New Delhi: U.S. Educ. Founda-
       tion in India, 1968, pp. 58-63.

730   Bazzanella, Dominic J. "The Conclusion to The Portrait of
       a Lady Re-examined," AL, 41 (March, 1969), 53-63.
            Suggests that the revision of the ending represents " 'the
            later James'--the more mature craftsman consciously at-
            tempting to move towards the stance of a 'disinterested'
            narrator.... It seems reasonable to conclude ... that
            ... the mature development of James's style also prompted
            his 1908 revisions of the conclusion to The Portrait of a
            Lady."

731   Beer, Thomas. "Henry James and Stephen Crane," in The
       Question of Henry James. F. W. Dupee, ed. New York:
       Henry Holt and Company, 1945, pp. 105-107.

732   Bielenstein, Gabrielle Maupin. "Affinities for Henry James,"
       Meanjin, 16 (Winter, 1957), 196-199.
            Contrasts the treatment of "the shared plot" in The Por-
            trait of a Lady (1881) and in Rosa Praed's Affinities
            (1886).

733   Blackmur, R. P. Introduction. The Portrait of a Lady.
       New York: Dell Publishing Co., 1961.

734   Blehl, Vincent F. "Freedom and Commitment in James's
       Portrait of a Lady," Person, 42 (July, 1961), 368-381.
            Discussion of the paradoxical ending.

735   Bochner, Jay. "Life in a Picture Gallery: Things in The
       Portrait of a Lady and The Marbel Faun," TSLL, 11 (Spring,
       1969), 761-777.
            Compares James and Hawthorne in their treatment of old
            houses and pictures, and concludes that for James "sym-
            bolic meaning ... is particular and human, a matter of
            personal, not of social or religious, morality."

736   Bonincontro, Marilia. "Le ascendenze austeniane del Por-
       trait of a Lady di Henry James," PS, 4, ii (1968), 31-39.

737   Bowden, Edwin T. "The Mighty Individual," The Dungeon
       of the Heart. New York: Macmillan, 1961, pp. 89-102.

738   _____. "The Theme of Moral Decision" [The Portrait of
       a Lady], The Themes of Henry James. New Haven: Yale
       U. P., 1956, pp. 54-60.

739   Bowman, Sylvia E. "Les Heroines d'Henry James dans The
       Portrait of a Lady et d'Ivan Tourguéniev dans A. La Veillé,
       EA, 11, #2 (Avril-Juin, 1958), 136-149.
       A comparison of the methods of the two writers.

740   Broderick, John C. " 'Henry James and Gestation': A Re-
       ply," CE, 21 (May, 1960), 497-499.
          Cf., H. G. Flinn and Howard C. Key. "Henry James and
          Gestation," CE, 21 (December, 1959), 173-175; Howard C.
          Key. "Author's Comment," CE, 21 (May, 1960), 499-500;
          Jack E. Wallace. "Isabel and the Ironies," CE, 21 (May,
          1960), 497. John Broderick says Flinn and Key are con-
          fused, and their inferences are offensive.

741   Brown, E. K. "Two Formulas for Fiction: Henry James
       and H. G. Wells," CE, 8 (October, 1946), 7-17.

742   Brownell, William C. "James's Portrait of a Lady," Nation,
       34 (February 2, 1882), 102-103.

743   Buitenhuis, Peter, ed. Introduction. Twentieth Century In-
       terpretations of "The Portrait of a Lady": A Collection of
       Critical Essays. Englewood Cliffs, New Jersey: Prentice-
       Hall, 1968.

744   Burrell, John A. "Henry James: A Rhapsody of Youth,"
       Dial, 63 (September 27, 1917), 260-262.

745   Cargill, Oscar. Afterword. The Portrait of a Lady. New
       York: Signet, 1964, pp. 547-556.

746   _____. "The Portrait of a Lady: A Critical Reappraisal."
       MFS, 3 (Spring, 1957), 11-32.

747   _____. "The Portrait of a Lady," in The Novels of Henry
       James. New York: Macmillan, 1961, pp. 78-119. Repr.,
       in Perspectives on "The Portrait of a Lady": A Collection
       of Critical Essays. William T. Stafford, ed. New York:
       1966, pp. 256-296.

748   Cazan, Ileana. Henry James. In Portretul unei doamne.
       (The Portrait of a Lady.) Bucuresti: Editura pentru litera-
       tură universală. 1969, pp. 563-576.

749   Chan, Lois M. "Figures in the Carpet: A Study of Leading
        Metaphors in Six Realistic Novels," DAI, 31 (Kentucky:
        1971), 5354A.
        "In James's Portrait of a Lady, the imagery of the house
        and garden, ... represents the confrontation of freedom
        and the conventional, i.e., James's international theme.
        Isabel Archer's story unfolds in terms of her relationship
        and psychological reactions to various houses in the novel. "

750   Chanda, A. K. "Art and Artists in the Portrait of a Lady,"
        IJES, 10 (1969), 109-121.
        James shows through Madame Merle and Gilbert Osmond
        that it is impossible to make life a work of art and to
        seek perfection in that attempt.

751   Chase, Richard. "The Portrait of a Lady," in The Ameri-
        can Novel and Its Tradition. New York: Doubleday & Co.,
        1957, pp. 117-135.

751.1   Chauhan, P. S. "The Portrait of a Lady: Its Moral De-
        sign," LitC, 6 (Summer, 1964), 56-70.

752   Clark, A. F. Bruce. "Henry James," McGUM, 18 (Febru-
        ary 19, 1919), 45-68.

753   Cox, C. B. "Henry James and the Art of Personal Relation-
        ships," The Free Spirit. New York: Oxford U. P., 1963,
        pp. 42-46.

754   Craig, G. Armour. "A Series of Exercises on The Educa-
        tion of Henry Adams and The Portrait of a Lady," ExEx,
        1 (1954(?), 1-6.

755   Daiches, David. "Sensibility and Technique: Preface to a
        Critique," KR, 5 (Autumn, 1943), 569-579.

756   Dixson, Robert J. The Portrait of a Lady. Simplified and
        Adapted with Exercises for Study and Vocabulary Drill. New
        York: Regents Publishing Co., 1954.

757   Donoghue, Denis. "Plot, Fact, and Value," The Ordinary
        Universe: Soundings in Modern Literature. New York:
        Macmillan, 1968, pp. 51-77.

758   Dove, John R. "Tragic Consciousness in Isabel Archer,"
        Studies in American Literature. Waldo McNeir and Leo B.
        Levy, eds. (LSUSHS, #8), Baton Rouge: Louisiana State
        U. P., 1960, pp. 78-94.

759   Drew, Elizabeth. "The Game of Art: Henry James, The
        Portrait of a Lady," in The Novel: A Modern Guide to Fif-
        teen English Masterpieces. New York: W. W. Norton,
        1963, pp. 224-244.

759.1 Dumitriu, Gheorghita. "Middlemarch si geneza Isabelei
       Archer." (Middlemarch and the genesis of Isabel Archer.)
       AnUBLUC, 18 #2 (1969), 77-84.

760   Dupee, F. W. "Escape from Innocence," Henry James.
       New York: William Sloane Associates, Inc., 1951, 1956, p.
       105.

761   Edel, Leon. "The Choice So Freely Made," NewRep, 133
       (September 26, 1955), 26-28.
       Reassessment of The Portrait of a Lady.

762   _____. Henry James: The Conquest of London: 1870-
       1881. New York: Lippincott, 1962, pp. 417-436.

763   _____, ed. Introduction. The Portrait of a Lady. Bos-
       ton: Houghton Mifflin, 1963, pp. v-xx.

764   _____, ed. Introduction and Preface. The Bodley Head
       Henry James. Vol. 5: The Portrait of a Lady. London:
       Bodley Head, 1968.

765   _____. "Who Was Gilbert Osmond?" MFS, 6 (Summer,
       1960), 164.
       Cf., Martin Halpern. "Henry B. Brewster," AQ, 14
       (1962), 464-482; R. W. Stallman. "Who Was Gilbert Os-
       mond?" MFS, 4 (1958), 127-135

766   Edgar, Pelham. "Isabel's Pride," Henry James: Man and
       Author. Boston: Houghton Mifflin Company, 1956, pp. 245-
       255. Repr., in Twentieth Century Interpretations of "The
       Portrait of a Lady." Peter Buitenhuis, ed. Englewood
       Cliffs, New Jersey: 1968, pp. 112-113.

767   Falk, Robert P. "The Eighties: James, The Middle Years,"
       The Victorian Mode in American Fiction, 1865-1885. East
       Lansing: Michigan State U. P., 1965, pp. 138-156.

768   Feidelson, Charles. "The Moment of The Portrait of a
       Lady," Ventures, 8, #2 (1968), 47-55.
       According to Charles Feidelson, the novel demonstrates
       James's discovery of the dramatic uses of consciousness.

769   Fisher, Neil H. Introduction. The Portrait of a Lady.
       New York: Airmont Publishing Co., 1966.

770   Flinn, H. G., and Howard C. Key. "Henry James and Ges-
       tation," CE, 21 (December, 1959), pp. 173-175.
       Cf., John C. Broderick. " 'Henry James and Gestation':
       A Reply," CE, 21 (May, 1960), 497-499; Howard C. Key.
       "Author's Comment," CE, 21 (May, 1960), 499-500; Jack
       E. Wallace. "Isabel and the Ironies," CE 21 (May, 1960),
       497.

770.1 Foley, Richard N. "The Portrait of a Lady," in Criticism
       in American Periodicals of the Works of Henry James from
       1866 to 1916. Washington: Catholic University of America
       Press, 1944, pp. 26-30.

771   Frederick, John T. "Patterns of Imagery in Chapter 42 of
       Henry James's The Portrait of a Lady," ArQ, 25 (Summer,
       1969), 150-156.
          Shows the use of imagery in patterns of opposition: im-
          prisonment to freedom, dark to light, cold to heat.

772   Friend, Joseph H. "The Structure of The Portrait of a
       Lady," NCF, 20 (June, 1965), 85-95.
          James's frequent use of irony shown as one means of
          avoiding the sentimental cliches associated with the pat-
          tern of a "quest novel."

773   Gale, Robert L. "A Possible Source for Elements in The
       Portrait of a Lady," SA, 11 (1965), 137-162.

774   Galloway, David. Henry James: The Portrait of a Lady.
       London: Edward Arnold, 1967.

775   Garg, Neera. "The Return of Isabel Archer," Variations
       on American Literature. Darshan Singh Maini, ed. New
       Delhi: U.S. Educational Foundation in India, 1968, pp. 64-
       69.

776   Gass, William H. "The High Brutality of Good Intentions,"
       Accent, 18 (Winter, 1958), 65-70.
          In The Portrait of a Lady James first uses the theme of
          the evil of human manipulation.

777   Geismar, Maxwell. "Nostalgic Poison," Henry James and
       the Jacobites. Boston: Houghton Mifflin Company, 1962,
       pp. 40-47.

778   Greene, Graham. Introduction. The Portrait of a Lady.
       New York: Oxford University Press, 1956; London: Oxford
       University Press, 1962.

779   _____. "The Portrait of a Lady," in Collected Essays.
       New York: Viking Press, 1969, pp. 54-61.

780   _____. "The Portrait of a Lady," The Lost Childhood
       and Other Essays. New York: Viking Press, 1952, pp. 40-
       44.

781   Greene, Mildred S. E. "Love and Duty: The character of
       the Princesse de Clèves as Reflected in Certain Later Eng-
       lish and American Novels," DA, 28 (New Mexico: 1967),
       230A-31A.

782   Grenander, M. E., Beverly J. Rahn, and Francine Valvo.
        "The Time-Scheme in The Portrait of a Lady," AL, 32 (May,
        1960), 127-135.
                Everything before and after adjusted to the date of No-
                vember 1, 1876, Ned Rosier's arrival in Rome.

783   Hafley, James. "Malice in Wonderland," ArQ, 15 (1959),
        5-12.
                In Poe's "The Oval Portrait," the woman dies as her por-
                trait is completed. In The Portrait of a Lady Isabel
                Archer loses "her life to become one of Gilbert Osmond's
                collector's items."

784   Haggard, H. Rider. "About Fiction," ContR (February,
        1887), 172.
                An attack on James's heroines, especially Isabel Archer.

784.1   Halperin, John W. "The Language of Meditation: Four
        Studies in Nineteenth-Century Fiction," DAI, 32 (Johns Hop-
        kins: 1972), 6976A-77A.

785   Halpern, Martin. "Henry B. Brewster (1850-1908): An In-
        troduction," AQ, 14 (Fall, 1962), 464-482.
                The subject of controversy is whether Gilbert Osmond is
                Henry B. Brewster, an American writer-philosopher, and
                friend of Henry James.
                Cf., Leon Edel. "Who Was Gilbert Osmond?" MFS, 6
                (1960), 164; R. W. Stallman. "Who Was Gilbert Osmond?"
                MFS, 4 (1958), 127-135; Leon Edel. Reply to Stallman,
                MFS, 4 (1958), 135.

786   Harvey, W. J. "Work in Progress I: Character and the Con-
        tent of Things," EIC, 13 (January, 1963), 50-66.
                The Portrait of a Lady is an interplay of aesthetics and
                ethics.

787   _____. Character and the Novel. Ithaca, New York:
        Cornell University Press, 1965, pp. 46-50, passim.

787.1   Hawthorne, Julian. "Agnosticism in American Fiction," PrR,
        13 (January, 1884), 1-15.

788   Heilbrun, Carolyn. "The Woman as Hero," TQ, 8 (Winter,
        1965), 132-141.
                James's Isabel Archer is given as an example of the wom-
                an hero (not heroine) who flourished between 1880 and
                1930 and who needed "to love" and to be herself "freely
                and strongly."

789   James, Henry. "Preface to The Portrait of a Lady," The
        Art of the Novel: Critical Prefaces. New York: Scribner,
        1934, pp. 40-58.

790   Johnson, Courtney. "Adam and Eve and Isabel Archer,"
        Renascence, 21 (1969), 134-144, 167.

791   Kenney, Blair Gates. "The Two Isabels: A Study in Distor-
        tion," VN, 25 (Spring, 1964), 15-17.
            A comparison of Isabel Archer with Isabel Boncassen, cen-
            tral character in Trollope's The Duke's Children, published
            in All the Year Round just before The Portrait of a Lady
            appeared serially in Macmillan's.

792   Kettle, Arnold. "Henry James: The Portrait of a Lady," in
        An Introduction to the English Novel. London: Hutchinson &
        Co., Ltd., 1953, pp. 13-34; New York: Harper & Row, pp.
        196-214.

793   Key, Howard C. "Author's Comment," CE, 21 (May, 1960),
        499-500.
            James's dating of Isabel's marriage in June was over-
            looked. Cf., John C. Broderick. " 'Henry James and
            Gestation,' A Reply," CE, 21 (May, 1960), 497-499; Jack
            E. Wallace, "Isabel and the Ironies," CE, 21 (1960), 497.

794   Kinoian, Vartkis. Henry James: The Portrait of a Lady.
        New York: Monarch Press, Inc., 1965.

795   Kleinberg, Seymour. "Ambiguity and Ambivalence: The Psy-
        chology of Sexuality in Henry James's The Portrait of a Lady,"
        MarkR, 5 (May, 1969), 2-7.
            James's most intricate treatment of the theme of sexual
            ambivalence may be found in the character of Isabel Arch-
            er.

796   Kohli, Raj K. "Huck Finn and Isabel Archer: Two Re-
        sponses to the Fruit of Knowledge," Banasthali Patrika, 11
        (July, 1968). Special Number on American Literature. Gup-
        ta Rameshwar, ed. (Proceedings of the Seminar on Ameri-
        can Literature, 2-3, March, 1968, at Banasthali Vidyapath.),
        pp. 73-82.

797   _____. "Isabel Archer and Huck Finn: Two Responses to
        the Fruit of Knowledge," Indian Essays in American Litera-
        ture: Papers in Honour of Robert Spiller. Sujit Mukherjee,
        and D. V. K. Raghavacharyulu, eds. Bombay: Popular Pra-
        kashan, 1969, pp. 167-178.

798   Krause, Sydney J. "Henry James's Revisions of The Por-
        trait of a Lady: A Study in Literature Portraiture and Per-
        fectionism," DA, 16 (Columbia: 1956), 1256-57.

799   _____. Henry James's Revisions of "The Portrait of a
        Lady": A Study of Literary Portraiture and Perfectionism.
        Ann Arbor: University Microfilms, 1956.

800   _____. "James's Revisions of the Style of The Portrait
of a Lady," AL, 30 (March, 1958), 67-88.
Maintains that James's purpose in the revisions was to
gain clarity, economy, concreteness, as well as infor-
mality.

801   Krook, Dorothea. "Two Problems in The Portrait of a Lady,"
Appendix A, The Ordeal of Consciousness in Henry James.
Cambridge: At the University Press, 1962, pp. 357-369.

802   Leavis, F. R. "George Eliot (IV): Daniel Deronda and The
Portrait of a Lady," Scrutiny, 14 (December, 1946), 102-
131.

803   _____. "Henry James: (I) To The Portrait of a Lady,"
in The Great Tradition: George Eliot, Henry James, Joseph
Conrad. New York: New York University Press, 1963, pp.
126-153.

804   _____. "The Portrait of a Lady Reprinted," Scrutiny, 15
(Summer, 1948), 235-241.
Comparison of James's novel with Meredith's The Egoist.

805   Leavis, Q. D. "A Note on Literary Indebtedness: Dickens,
George Eliot, Henry James," HudR, 8 (August, 1955), 423-
428.
Parallel passages in Little Dorritt, Middlemarch, and The
Portrait of a Lady.

806   Levine, George. "Isabel, Gwendolen, and Dorothea," ELH,
30 (September, 1963), 244-257.
Finds a closer parallel between James's Isabel and Dorothea Casaubon in Eliot's Middlemarch than with Gwendolen
Harleth in Eliot's Daniel Deronda.

807   Liebman, Sheldon W. "The Light and the Dark: Character
Design in The Portrait of a Lady," PLL, 6 (Spring, 1970),
163-179.
James's character design and light and dark imagery in
this novel show that he is primarily concerned with Isabel
Archer's moral and psychological development.

808   _____. "Point of View in The Portrait of a Lady," ES,
52 (April, 1971), 136-147.
Isabel discovers "that points of view are as numerous as
people who have them.... that [they] ... are not one but
multi-dimensional, and that any position has its advantages
and disadvantages."

809   Lydenberg, John. "Romanciers Américains ... A la Recher-
che d'un Monde Perdu," TCEA&A, 1 (1962), 29-46.
Isabel Archer turns not to the west but to the decadent Old
World, and is betrayed there by her compatriots, not by
Europeans.

810   Mackenzie, Manfred. "Ironic Melodrama in The Portrait of
        a Lady," MFS, 12 (Spring, 1966), 7-23.
            "The Portrait is constructed from the materials of melo-
        drama, and its intensities arise from the action of James's
        irony upon these materials; it might best be described as
        an ironic melodrama."

811   Marcell, David W. "High Ideals and Catchpenny Realities in
        James's The Portrait of a Lady," SSH, 1 (1963), 23-34.
        Repr., in Essays in Modern American Literature. Richard
        E. Langford, ed. Deland, Florida: Stetson U. P., 1963,
        pp. 26-34.
            James's novel may be analyzed as "a study of an unfold-
        ing ideal and a growing consciousness."

812   Matthiessen, F. O. "Free Will and Determinism," in Henry
        James: The Major Phase. New York: Oxford University
        Press, 1946, pp. 185-186.

813   _____. From the Heart of Europe. New York: Oxford
        University Press, 1948, pp. 44-46.
            "... through Isabel Archer, James made one of his fresh-
        est studies of the American's discovery of Europe...."

814   _____. "The Painter's Sponge and Varnish Bottle: Henry
        James's Revision of The Portrait of a Lady," AmB, 1 (Win-
        ter, 1944), 49-68. Repr., as Appendix to Henry James:
        The Major Phase. New York: 1944, pp. 152-186.
            The two most extensive revisions reveal James's concep-
        tion of dramatic structure, and his desire to strengthen
        the climax.

814.1   Mazzella, Anthony J. "James' The Portrait of a Lady,"
        Expl, 30 (January, 1972), Item 37.
            The endings to both volumes of the novel in the New York
        Edition are significantly revised, and in parallel fashion.
        In revising the single-volume 1881 American Edition with
        fifty-five consecutive chapters, James seems to have capi-
        talized on the novel's being cut nearly in half in the New
        York Edition.

815   McMaster, Juliet. "The Portrait of Isabel Archer," AL, 45
        (March, 1973), 50-66.

816   Millett, Fred B. Introduction. The Portrait of a Lady.
        New York: Modern Library, 1951, 1966.

817   Mills, A. R. "The Portrait of a Lady and Dr. Leavis,"
        EIC, 14 (October, 1964), 380-387.
            Rejection of Leavis' opinion that The Portrait is "one of
        the two most brilliant novels in the language," and calls
        it "blatantly moralistic."

818   Monteiro, George. "John Hay's Review of The Portrait of
         a Lady," BBr, 19 (1963), 95-104. Repr., in Henry James
         and John Hay: The Record of a Friendship. Providence:
         Brown U. P., 1965, pp. 65-76.
             Notes Hay's favorable review in the New York Daily Trib-
         une.

819   _____. "The New York Tribune on Henry James, 1881-
         1882," BNYPL, 67 (February, 1963), 71-81.
             A detailed study of Hay's review, Howell's article in the
         Century, as well as attacks on James as a leader of the
         "new school."

819.1   Montgomery, Judith H. "The American Galatea," CE, 32
         (1971), 890-899.
             An interpretation of The Portrait of a Lady, The Blithe-
         dale Romance, and The House of Mirth.

820   Montgomery, Marion. "The Flaw in the Portrait: Henry
         James vs. Isabel Archer," UKCR, 26 (March, 1960), 215-
         220.
             The "flaw" is that the events of the early years of Isa-
         bel's marriage are not dramatized.

821   Moody, A. D. "James's Portrait of an Ideal," MCR, 4
         (1961), 77-92.
             The ambiguous conclusion in Portrait of a Lady is due to
         James's confusion about Isabel.

822   Moss, Leonard Jerome. "Transitional Devices in Henry
         James," CEA, 22 (February, 1960), 1, 6, 12.
             Asserts that James's novel illustrates that "the key to
         sophisticated exposition lies in the proper handling of
         transitional devices."

822.1   Moynahan, Julian. "Pastoralism as Culture and Counter-
         Culture in English Fiction, 1800-1928," Novel, 6 (Fall,
         1972), 20-35.
             James's Isabel Archer seen as one of the examples of the
         "death of pastoralism" which "can be seen in the declin-
         ing fate of fictional heroines...."

823   Mukherji, N. "The Role of Pansy in The Portrait of a
         Lady," CalR, n. s., 1 (1969), 585-594.
             Pansy provides a contrast with Isabel Archer and Henri-
         etta Stackpole, helps unify the novel, and helps motivate
         Isabel at the conclusion.

823.1   _____. "Sense of Place in The Portrait of a Lady,"
         LCM (Winter, 1968), 12-25.

824   Mull, Donald L. "Freedom and Judgment: The Antimony
         of Action in The Portrait of a Lady," ArQ, 27 (Summer,

1971), 124-142.
> Focus is on Isabel's decision to marry Osmond, which he describes as made "against choice ... [in order] to make over to--or against--the man with the best taste in the world, the material agency of choice."

825   Murray, Donald M. The Critical Reception of Henry James in English Periodicals, 1875-1916. Diss. New York University, 1951.

826   Namekata, Akio. "The Ordeal of Isabel in James's The Portrait of a Lady," Essays, 15 (December, 1962), 44-59.

827   Newton, J. M. "Isabel Archer's Disease and Henry James," CQ, 2 (1967), 3-22.
> An explanation of Isabel's marriage to Osmond in terms of James's own attraction to the "ideal" represented by Osmond.

828   Nowell-Smith, Simon. "Texts of The Portrait of a Lady, 1881-1882: The Bibliographical Evidence," PBSA, 63 (4th Qt., 1969), 304-310.
> A very careful and thorough study of the various texts of The Portrait of a Lady.

829   Offen, Susan. "Isabel Archer: An Analysis of Her Fate," HunterCS, 2 (1964), 41-50.

830   Patterson, Rebecca. "Two Portraits of a Lady," MWQ, 1 (Summer, 1960), 343-361.
> The two portraits are in The Portrait of a Lady and "Madame de Mauves."

831   Perloff, Marjorie. "Cinderella Becomes the Wicked Stepmother: The Portrait of a Lady as Ironic Fairy Tale," NCF, 23 (March, 1969), 413-433.
> Isabel as a stepmother makes the same mistakes in her relations with Pansy as in her choice of Osmond as her husband.

832   Poirier, Richard. "The Portrait of a Lady," in The Comic Sense of Henry James. London: Chatto & Windus, Ltd., 1960, pp. 237-246; New York: Oxford U. P., 1960, pp. 183-246.

833   _____ . "Henry James: The Portrait of a Lady," in The American Novel from James Fenimore Cooper to William Faulkner. Wallace Stegner, ed. New York: Basic Books, 1965, pp. 47-60.

834   Powers, Lyall H. "The Portrait of a Lady: 'The Eternal Mystery of Things,' " NCF, 14 (September, 1959), 143-155.
> This novel "has indeed the unity which James claimed for

it. The career of Isabel Archer has the completeness of
form of the familiar pattern of redemption, of the fortun-
ate fall...."

835   _____, ed. Studies in "The Portrait of a Lady." Merrill Studies. Columbus, Ohio: Charles E. Merrill, 1970.

836   Randall, D. A. "The Portrait of a Lady," Collations by D.
A. Randall. Notes by J. T. Winterich. PubW, 140 (June
19, 1941), 186-187.

837   Reid, Stephen. "Moral Passion in The Portrait of a Lady
and The Spoils of Poynton," MFS, 12 (Spring, 1966), 24-43.
A study of James's moral ideas as revealed in these novels.

837.1   Roberts, James L. The Portrait of a Lady: A Critical
Study. Lincoln: Nebraska University Press, 1965.

838   Rochner, J. "Life in a Picture Gallery: Things in The Portrait of a Lady and The Marble Faun," TSLL, 11 (Spring,
1969), 761-777.

839   Rodenbeck, John. "The Bolted Door in James's Portrait of
a Lady," MFS, 10 (Winter, 1964-1965), 330-340.
The recurrent image of the bolted door serves to explain
Isabel's character and development.

839.1   Sabiston, Elizabeth J. "The Prison of Womanhood," CL, 25
(Fall, 1973), 336-351.
James's treatment of Isabel Archer.

840   _____. "The Provincial Heroine in Prose Fiction: A
Study in Isolation and Creativity," DAI, 30 (Cornell: 1969),
1150A.

841   Sackville-West, Edward. "The Code of Ladyhood: Henry
James's Portrait of a Lady," NS&N, 25 (April 17, 1943),
259.

842   _____. "The Personality of Henry James," in Inclinations.
Port Washington, New York: Kennikat Press, 1949, 1967,
pp. 42-71.

842.1   Salisbury, Howard E. "Wish-Fulfillment as Moral Crisis in
the Fiction of Henry James," DA, 24 (Univ. of Washington:
1962), 304.

843   Sandeen, Ernest. "The Wings of the Dove and The Portrait
of a Lady: A Study of James's Later Phase," PMLA, 69 (December, 1954), 1060-1075.

844   Schneider, Sister Lucy, C.S.J. "Osculation and Integration:

Isabel Archer in the One-Kiss Novel," CLAJ, 10 (December, 1966), 149-161.
> The conclusion is that Isabel's "return to Rome is to her previous experiences in her European adventures what Caspar's kiss is to the kisses that have preceded it."

845   Scudder, Horace E. "The Portrait of a Lady and Dr. Breen's Practice," Atl, 49 (January, 1882), 126-130.
> In his comparison of two novels, one of James and one of Howells, Scudder noted their similarities in that both Isabel Archer and Grace Breen were reflections of "modern womanly life."

846   Sharp, Sister Corona. Confidantes in The Portrait of a Lady," in The Confidante in Henry James: Evolution and Moral Value of a Fictive Character. South Bend: Notre Dame U. P., 1963, pp. 67-96.

847   Smith, Thomas F. "Balance in Henry James's The Portrait of a Lady," FourQ, 13 (May, 1964), 11-16.
> A defense of the novel's ending on the basis of repeated examples of balance in the general structure.

848   Snow, Lotus. "The Disconcerting Poetry of Mary Temple: A Comparison of the Imagery of The Portrait of a Lady and The Wings of the Dove," NEQ, 31 (September, 1958), 312-339.
> The Portrait and The Wings ("a grimmer and a richer book"), have the same "germ": Mary Temple's tragedy. To compare the imagery of the two novels is to compare "James's youthful and his mature vision of the qualities of life."

849   Sparshott, F. E. "An Aspect of Literary Portraiture," EIC, 15 (July, 1965), 359-360.

850   Stafford, William T., ed. Introduction. Perspectives on "The Portrait of a Lady": A Collection of Critical Essays. London: University of London Press; New York: New York University Press, 1967.

851   Stallman, R. W. "The Houses that James Built--The Portrait of a Lady," TQ, 1 (Winter, 1958), 176-196.
> The cathedral and opera house scenes are pivotal in the novel's structure, the cathedral emblematic of the spiritual, the opera house emblematic of the mundane.

852   _____. "The Houses that James Built--The Portrait of a Lady," in The Houses that James Built. East Lansing: Michigan University Press, 1961, pp. 1-33. Revised and expanded version of essay, "The Houses that James Built," TQ, 1 (Winter, 1958), 176-196.

853   _____. Introduction. The Portrait of a Lady. Illustrations by Colleen Browning. Baltimore: Printed for the Limited Editions Club by the Garamond Press, 1967.

854   _____. "Who Was Gilbert Osmond?" MFS, 4 (Summer,
1958), 127-135.
    Henry B. Brewster as the model for Osmond. Cf., Leon
Edel. "Who Was Gilbert Osmond!" MFS, 6 (1960), 164;
Martin Halpern. "Henry B. Brewster," AQ, 14 (1962),
464-482.

855 Stein, William Bysshe. "The Portrait of a Lady: Vis In-
ertiae," WHR, 13 (Spring, 1959), 177-190.
    Henry Adams' disparagement of Henry James's knowledge
of female character results from Adams' misunderstanding
of the author's intent in The Portrait of a Lady.

856 Stewart, J. I. M. Eight Modern Writers. New York: Oxford University Press, 1963, pp. 87-92.

857 Stewart, Randall. American Literature and Christian Doctrine. Baton Rouge, La.: Louisiana State U. P., 1958, p.
104.
    The Portrait of a Lady compared with Hawthorne's story,
"Egotism, or the Bosom Serpent." "The insidiousness of
egotism was James's great concern...." Osmond is also
compared with Aylmer in "The Birthmark."

858 Strandberg, Victor H. Isabel Archer's Identity Crisis: The
Two Portraits of a Lady," UR, 34 (June, 1968), 283-290.
    The structure of the novel is studied through Isabel's "cre-
ation of an identity, and ... her discovery of what her
true identity has been all along, underneath the glamorous
surface she has so assiduously been cultivating."

859 Tanner, Tony. "The Fearful Self," CritQ, 7 (Autumn, 1965),
205-219.
    The conclusion is that Isabel is defined by her fears.

860 Taylor, Gordon O. "The Friction of Existence: Henry
James," The Passages of Thought: Psychological Representa-
tion in the American Novel, 1870-1900. New York: Oxford
University Press, 1969, pp. 42-84.

861 Thorberg, Raymond. " 'Flavien,' 'Tenants,' and The Portrait of a Lady," SAB, 34 (May, 1969), 10-13.
    James probably drew hints from Riviere's "Flavien."

862 Tribble, Joseph L. "Cherbuliez's Le Roman D'Une Honnête
Femme: Another Source of James's The Portrait of a Lady,"
AL, 40 (November, 1968), 279-293.
    Similarities of the two works suggest a possible source.

863 Van Ghent, Dorothy. "On The Portrait of a Lady," The

English Novel: Form and Function. New York: Rinehart, 1953; repr., in Interpretations of American Literature. Charles Feidelson, Jr., and Paul Brodtkorb, Jr., eds. New York: Oxford U. P., 1959, pp. 244-261.

863.1 _____. "On The Portrait of a Lady," The Proper Study: Essays on Western Classics. Quentin Anderson and Joseph A. Mazzeo, eds. New York: St. Martin's Press, 1962, pp. 564-580.

864   Verney, Lady F. P. "The Americans as Painted by Them-selves," ContR, 46 (October, 1884), 549.
      An attack on James's heroines, especially Isabel Archer.

865   Volpe, Edmond Loris. "Henry James and the Conduct of Life: A Study of the Novelist's Moral Values," DA, 14 (Columbia University: 1954), 1735.

866   _____. "James's Theory of Sex," NCF, 13 (Spring, 1958), 36-[46]-47.
      "... As the historian of man's inner life, James was not interested in depicting overt actions, unless they revealed the drama of the inner world...."

867   Wagner, Linda Welshimer. "The Dominance of Heredity in the Characterizations of Henry James," SDR, 2 (Spring, 1965), 69-77.
      Analysis of characters in The Portrait of a Lady and Roderick Hudson shows that for James heredity and not environment is influential in making a man what he is.

868   Wallace, Jack E. "Isabel and the Ironies," CE, 21 (May, 1960), 497.
      Cf., H. G. Flinn and Howard C. Key. "Henry James and Gestation," CE, 21 (1959), 173-174; John C. Broderick, "'Henry James and Gestation': A Reply," CE, 21 (1960), 497-499; Howard C. Key, "Author's Comment," CE, 21 (1960), 499-500.

869   Wasiolek, Edward. "Tolstoy's The Death of Ivan Ilyich and Jamesian Fictional Imperatives," MFS, 6 (Winter, 1960-1961), 314-324.

870   Watanabe, Toshiro. "Henry James: A Study of the Heroine of The Portrait of a Lady," EiK, 13 (1963), 34-62.

871   Wegelin, Christof. "The American as a Young Lady," in The Image of Europe in Henry James. Dallas: Southern Methodist University Press, 1958, pp. 72-78.

871.1 Weinstein, Philip M. "The Drama of 'Motionless Seeing': The Portrait of a Lady," in Henry James and the Requirements of the Imagination. Cambridge, Mass: Harvard U. P., 1971, pp. 31-71.

872   Wiesenfarth, Brother Joseph. "Henry James: Action and
       the Art of Life," FourQ, 15 (January, 1966), 18-26.
          A comparison of James's novel with Austen's Pride and
          Prejudice.

873   Wilding, Michael. "James Joyce's 'Eveline' and The Por-
       trait of a Lady," ES, 49 (December, 1968), 552-556.

874   _____. "Portrait of a Lady and the World and Choice,"
       Balcony, 1 (1965), 28-35.

875   Willey, Frederick. "The Free Spirit and the Clever Agent
       in Henry James," SoR, 2 (Spring, 1966), 315-328.
          "... the relationship between seeing and feeling in the
          Jamesian pursuit of moral justice and of the harmonious
          personality...."

876   Williams, Paul O. "James's The Portrait of a Lady," Expl,
       22 (March, 1964), Item 50.
          An interpretation of the subtle self-revelation in Osmond's
          candlestick image (New York Ed., II, 309).

877   Wright, Nathalia. "Henry James and the Greenough Data,"
       AQ, 10 (Fall, 1958), 338-343.
          Acquaintance with the Greenoughs probably influenced The
          Portrait of a Lady.

878   Wright, Walter F. ["Puritanism and Isabel"] The Madness
       of Art: A Study of Henry James. Lincoln, Nebraska: Ne-
       braska U. P., 1962, pp. 146-148.
          "James remarks that she [Isabel] is 'not a daughter of the
          Puritans.' But in describing her independence in adversity,
          he writes, 'The old Protestant tradition had never faded
          from Isabel's imagination....' "

Reviews of The Portrait of a Lady:

          Athenaeum, 2822 (November 26, 1881), 699
          Atlantic, 49 (January, 1882), 126-30
          Blackwood's, 131 (January, 1882), 136-61; (March, 1882),
             374-82
          Californian, 5 (January, 1882), 86-7
          Catholic World, 34 (February, 1882), 716-7
          Century, 3 (November, 1882), 25-9
          Churchman, 45 (January 28, 1882), 97-8
          Critic, 1 (December 3, 1881), 333-4; 2 (January 14, 1882), 1
          Dial, 2 (January, 1882), 214-5
          Harper's 64 (February, 1882), 474
          Independent, 34 (January 19, 1882), 11
          Lippincott, 29 (February, 1882), 213-5
          Lit World, 12 (December 17, 1881), 473-4; 13 (January 14,
             1882), 10-1

Nation, 34 (February, 1882), 102-103
Natl. Rev. 1 (April, 1883), 257-68
Penn Mo, 13 (March, 1882), 233-4
Quarterly Rev, 155 (January, 1883), 201-29; 198 (October,
    1903), 358
SatR, 52 (December 3, 1881), 703-4
Zagranichnyi vestnik, October-December, 1881, t, 1, otd.
    II, p. 244

Reviews: The Portrait of a Lady (1954), a dramatization by William
Archibald:

Atkinson, Brooks. "Theatre: of Henry James," NYTIMES,
    (December 22, 1954), 27
Chapman, John. "New ANTA Playhouse Is a Beauty, but
    "Portrait of a Lady Is a Bore," NY Daily News (Decem-
    ber 22, 1954) in NYTCR, 15 (1954), 213.
Coleman, Robert. "Portrait of a Lady Well Framed in
    ANTA," NY Daily Mirror (December 22, 1954) in NYTCR,
    15 (1954), 212.
Hawkins, William. "Costumes Sparkle in Portrait of a Lady,"
    NY World-Telegram & Sun (December 22, 1954) in NY-
    TCR, 15 (1954), 214.
Kerr, Walter F. "Portrait of a Lady," NY Herald Tribune
    (December 22, 1954) in NYTCR, 15 (1954), 211.
McClain, John. "Effort at a Mood Lacks Excitement," NY
    Journal American (December 22, 1954), in NYTCR, 15
    (1954), 212.
Watts, Richard. "Attempt to Dramatize Henry James," NY
    Post (December 22, 1954) in NYTCR, 15 (1954), 213.

Dramatization: Other Reviews:

America, 92 (January 15, 1955), 407
Commonweal, 61 (January 21, 1955), 429
Nation, 180 (January 8, 1955), 36
New Yorker, 30 (January 1, 1955), 42ff
SatR, 38 (January 8, 1955), 25
Theatre Arts, 39 (March 1955), 91-92
Time, 65 (January 3, 1955), 35

PORTRAITS OF PLACES

878.1 Finch, George Alvin, ed. Portraits of Places. With an Es-
       say on James as a Traveller by George Alvin Finch. New
       York: Lear Publishers, 1948.
           Rev. by Henry James Forman in NYTB, July 25, 1948,
           by Henry Seidel Canby in SRL, May 29, 1948, XXXI, 15-
           16; by John Farrelly in NR, July 5, CXVIII, 24-5.

See also: 38, 1794, 1980, 2320, 2321, 2382, 2695

Reviews of Portraits of Places:

> Atlantic, 53 (April, 1884), 569-70
> Dial, 4 (March, 1884), 286-7
> Independent, 36 (February 14, 1884), 204
> Lit World (Boston), 15 (March 8, 1884), 305

THE PRINCESS CASAMASSIMA

879   Berland, Alwyn. "James and Forster: The Morality of
       Class," CamJ, 6 (February, 1953), 259-280.
              Considers the aesthetic experience to be moral for James.

879. 1 Blotner, Joseph L. "Henry James: The Breakup of Victor-
       ian Tranquillity," The Political Novel. Garden City, New
       York: Doubleday & Co. , 1955, pp. 20-21.
              "The Princess Casamassima ... is one of the novels
              which focused upon the revolutionary currents beginning to
              stir beneath the surface of English political life...."

879. 2 Bluefarb, Sam. "The 'Radicalism' of the Princess Casamas-
       sima," BaratR, 6 (Spring-Summer, 1971), 68-73.
              An attempt to see in the "type" represented by the princ-
              ess the modern radical, one who craves "bizarre adven-
              ture and a dash of sentimental philanthropy...."

879. 3 Bogan, Louise. "James on a Revolutionary Theme," Nation,
       146 (April 23, 1938), 471-474.

880   Cargill, Oscar. "The Princess Casamassima: A Critical
       Reappraisal," PMLA, 71 (March, 1956), 97-117.
              A review of criticism and an interpretation.

880. 1 Cox, James M. "Henry James: The Politics of Internation-
       alism," SoR, 8 (July, 1972), 493-506.

881   Delbaere-Garant, Jeanne. "Henry James's Divergences from
       His Russian Model in The Princess Casamassima," RLV, 37
       #5 (1971), 535-544.
              A study of the similarities between James's novel and
              Turgenev's Terre Vierges.

882   Dove, John Roland. "The Alienated Hero in Le Rouge et le
       Noir and The Princess Casamassima," LSUS, 11 (1962), 130-
       154.

883   Dubler, Walter. "The Princess Casamassima: Its Place in
       the James Canon," MFS, 12 (Spring, 1966), 44-60.
              Concludes that this novel marks the turning point between
              the early and the "major" James.

883. 1 Edel, Leon, ed. Introduction. The Bodley Head Henry

James. Vol. 10. The Princess Casamassima. London:
Bodley Head, 1972.

883.2   Edwards, Oliver. "Christina Light." Times (March 1,
        1956), 11.

884   Elliott, G. P. "Getting Away from the Chickens," HudR, 12
        (Autumn, 1959), 386-396.
        A personal account of a summer in the author's youth
        when he read James's The Princess of Casamassima.

885   Firebaugh, Joseph J. "A Schopenhauerian Novel: James's
        The Princess Casamassima," NCF, 13 (December, 1958),
        177-197.
        The significant Schopenhauerian qualities which the author
        sees in The Princess Casamassima are misogyny, oscil-
        lation of the characters between satiety and ennui, and
        traits of the main character, Hyacinth Robinson.

885.1   Freeman, Arthur. "To the Editor," TLS, 3602 (March 12,
        1971), 296.
        Another model for The Princess Casamassima is Turgen-
        ev's The Background.

886   Fukuma, Kin-ichi. "The Ambiguity of The Princess Casa-
        massima," KAL, 2 (May, 1959), 6-11.

887   Grenander, M. E. "Henry James's Capricciosa: Christina
        Light in Roderick Hudson and The Princess Casamassima,"
        PMLA, 75 (June, 1960), 309-319.

888   Grewal, Om Prakash. "Henry James and the Ideology of
        Culture: A Critical Study of The Bostonians, The Princess
        Casamassima and The Tragic Muse," DAI, 30 (Rochester:
        1970), 5444A-45A.

889   Grover, P. R. "Two Modes of Possessing--Conquest and
        Appreciation: The Princess Casamassima and L'Education
        Sentimentale," MLR, 66 (October, 1971), 760-771.
        A contrastive study of James and the French realistic tra-
        dition, especially as it is represented by Flaubert.

890   H., J. "Henry James and Dumas, fils," N&Q, 185 (August
        28, 1943), 132-133.
        The relevance of James's review of L'Affaire Clemenceau
        and its possible influence on The Princess Casamassima
        and Roderick Hudson.

891   Halliburton, D. G. "Self and Secularization in The Princess
        Casamassima," MFS, 11 (Summer, 1965), 116-128.
        An exploration of the problem of society and self in Hya-
        cinth who has a positive commitment to revolution.

892   Hamilton, Eunice C. "Henry James's The Princes Casamas-
       sima and Ivan Turgenev's Virgin Soil," SAQ, 61 (Summer,
       1962), 354-364.
       Says Turgenev's novel is one of the sources used.

893   Hartsock, Mildred E. "The Princess Casamassima: The
       Politics of Power," SNNTS, 1 (Fall, 1969), 297-309.

894   Harvey, William J. Character and the Novel. Ithaca, New
       York: Cornell University Press, 1965, pp. 81-89.
       Finds a failure of "inner coherence in the characteriza-
       tions" of The Princess Casamassima probably because
       James "did not know enough."

895   Hoffman, Frederick J. "The Princess Casamassima: Vio-
       lence and Decorum," in his The Mortal No: Death and the
       Modern Imagination. Princeton: Princeton University Press,
       1964, pp. 41-49.
       Sees the suicide of Hyacinth Robinson as ambiguous.

896   Howe, Irving. "The Future of the Novel: The Political Nov-
       el," Tomorrow, 10 (May, 1951), 51-58.

897   _____. "Henry James and the Political Vocation," WestR,
       18 (Spring, 1954), 199-208.
       A study of The Princess Casamassima.

898   _____. "Henry James: The Political Vocation," Politics
       and the Novel. New York: Horizon Press, 1957, pp. 139-156.
       "The Princess Casamassima fascinated him [Henry James]
       as a virtuoso flight--or descent--to the world of anarch-
       ist London in the 1880's, a world that had recently been
       brought to anxious public attention by the Trafalgar Square
       riots...."

899   James, Henry. "Preface to The Princess Casamassima,"
       The Art of the Novel: Critical Prefaces. New York: Scrib-
       ner, 1936, pp. 59-78.

900   Kane, Robert J. "Virgin Soil and The Princess Casamas-
       sima," Gifthorse (1949), 25-29.

900.1 Keating, P. J. The Working Classes in Victorian Fiction.
       London: Routledge and Kegan Paul; New York: Barnes and
       Noble, 1971. pp. 46-52.
       A brief account of The Princess Casamassima is given to
       illustrate that even when a good novelist attempts to de-
       pict the British working classes in fiction in this period
       he uses the usual conventions to avoid depicting them di-
       rectly.

901   Kimmey, John L. "The Bostonians and The Princess Casa-
       massima," TSLL, 9 (Winter, 1968), 537-546.

902   _____. "The Princess Casamassima and the Quality of
           Bewilderment," NCF, 22 (June, 1967), 47-62
                Hyacinth, "the plot that enmeshes him, the world he in-
                habits, his friends, and the very diction and imagery that
                reveal him," are seen as a manifestation of the guiding
                principle of contradictory opposites.

903   Kocmanova, Jessie. "The Revolt of the Workers in the Nov-
           els of Gissing, James, and Conrad," BrSE, 1 (1959), 119-
           139.

904   Kretsch, Robert W. "Political Passion in Balzac and Henry
           James," NCF, 14 (December, 1959), 265-270.
                A comparison of Balzac's Histoire des Treize and James's
                The Princess Casamassima illustrates for the author the
                "extremes between which 19th century novelists waver."
                Balzac's novel is dominated by the "passion-principle,"
                but James portrays the individual who submerges himself
                in "a group that stands or falls in the inspiration of its
                founder."

904.1   Langbaum, Robert. "Thoughts for Our Time: Three Novels
           on Anarchism," ASch, 42 (Spring, 1973), 227-250.
                The Princess Casamassima is one of the novels studied.
                Personal values supersede political ones in James's novel
                as Hyacinth refuses to carry out the promised assassina-
                tion.

904.2   Leavis, F. R. "Henry James and Dickens," TLS, 3,601
           (March 5, 1971), 271; 3,603 (March 19, 1971), 324.

905   Lucas, E. V. The Colvins and Their Friends. New York:
           Scribner, 1928, p. 161.
                Letter from Mrs. Robert Louis Stevenson to Sidney Colvin
                giving her opinion of The Princess Casamassima.

906   Lucas, William John. "Conservatism and Revolution in the
           1880's," Literature and Politics in the Nineteenth Century.
           Methuen (Distributed by Barnes & Noble), 1971, pp. 173-219.

907   Luecke, Sister Jane Marie. "The Princess Casamassima:
           Hyacinth's Fallible Consciousness," MP, 60 (May, 1963),
           274-280.
                Hyacinth's "ideals" were more "real" than reality, for,
                overvaluing Paul Muniment, he commits suicide under false
                assumptions.

908   Monteiro, George. "Another Princess," PQ, 41 (April,
           1962), 517-518.
                Princess Maria Belgiojoso, as well as her mother, the
                Princess Christiana Belgiojoso, suggested as sources for
                James's Princess. Cf., Bebe Spanos. "The Real Princ-
                ess Christina," PQ, 38 (October, 1959), 488-496.

909   _____. "The Campaign of Henry James's Disinherited
             Princess," ES, 45 (December, 1964), 442-454.
                  Sess Christina Light as not "a bad heroine." She be-
                  comes, ironically, the heiress, "the genuine keeper of hu-
                  man wisdom," in defeat.

910   Nies, Frederick J. Henry James's The Princess Casamas-
             sima: Its Revisions, Background, and Reception. Diss.
             South Carolina: n. d.

911   O'Leary, Sister Jeanine, R.S.H.M. "The Function of City
             as Setting in Dickens' Our Mutual Friend, Trollope's The
             Way We Live Now, James's The Princess Casamassima, and
             Conrad's The Secret Agent," DA, 26 (Notre Dame: 1966),
             6048-49.
                  Traces the use of the city as a means of representing
                  character development.

912   Oliver, Clinton F. "Henry James as a Social Critic,"
             AntiochR, 7 (June, 1947), 243-258.

913   _____, ed. Introduction. The Princess Casamassima.
             New York: Harper, 1959.

913.1   Putt, S. Gorley. "Henry James and Dickens," TLS, 3,599
             (February 19, 1971), 213.
                  Refutes the claim of F. R. Leavis in his Dickens, the
                  Novelist. London: 1970, p. 247, n.1, that Henry James
                  was "dependent upon memories of Dickens for his pictures
                  of London Life...."

913.2   _____. "Henry James and Dickens," TLS, 3,602 (March
             12, 1971), 296.
                  A rejoinder to F. R. Leavis, TLS, 3,601 (March 5, 1971),
                  271.

913.3   _____. "Henry James and Dickens," TLS, 3,604 (March
             26, 1971, 353.

914   _____. "A Henry James Jubilee, II," Cornhill, 160
             (Spring, 1947), 284-297.
                  Critical notes on The Princess Casamassima and The Bos-
                  tonians.

914.1   _____. "The Private Life and the Public Life:
             The Princess Casamassima...." in Scholars of the Heart:
             Essays in Criticism. London: Faber & Faber, 1962, pp.
             174-203.

914.2   _____. " 'Slashing Out in Bewilderment,'--The Public and
             the Private Life:.... The Princess Casamassima...," Henry
             James: A Reader's Guide. Ithaca, New York: Cornell Uni-
             versity Press, 1966, pp. 161-199.

915   Raleigh, John H. "The Novel and the City: England and
        America in the Nineteenth Century," VS, 11 (1968), 291-328.
        A comprehending study of "city" novels containing a sec-
        tion on The Princess Casamassima as "one of the most
        ambitious, fullest, most sensitive, and most convincing
        pictures of a large city in English or American fiction."

916   Salzberg, Joel. "Love, Identity, and Death: James' The
        Princess Casamassima Reconsidered," BRMMLA, 26 (1972),
        127-135.

917   Spanos, Bebe. "The Real Princess Christina," PQ, 38 (Oc-
        tober, 1959), 488-496.
        Cf., George Monteiro. "Another Princess," PQ, 41
        (1962), 517-518.

918   Stoehr, Taylor. "Alexander Herzen's My Past and Thoughts,"
        SoR, 3, ii (1968), 168-179.
        Comparison with James's The Princess Casamassima.

919   _____. "Words and Deeds in The Princess Casamassima,"
        ELH, 37 (March, 1970), 95-135.
        A significant study of The Princess Casamassima, relat-
        ing the novel to the linguistic theory and practice of an-
        archists.

920   Tilley, Wesley H. The Background, the Writing and the Re-
        ception of "The Princess Casamassima." Diss. Chicago:
        1964.

920.1   _____. The Backgrounds of "The Princess Casamassima."
        (University of Florida Monographs, Humanities, No. 5.)
        Gainesville: University of Florida Press, 1961.

921   Tillyard, E. M. W. The Epic Strain in the English Novel.
        Fair Lawn, New Jersey: Essential Books, 1958, pp. 121-
        125.

921.1   Tintner, Adeline R. "The Elgin Marbles and Titian's 'Bac-
        chus and Ariadne': A Cluster of Keatsian Associations in
        Henry James," N&Q, 20 (July, 1973), 250-252.
        Believes the Elgin Marbles and the "Bacchus and Ariadne"
        of Titian are joined in James's The Princess Casamas-
        sima.

922   _____. "Hyacinth at the Play: The Play Within the Play
        as a Novelistic Device in James," JNT, 2 (1972), 171-185.
        A discussion of possible borrowings from Hamlet and Balz-
        ac in The Princess Casamassima.

923   _____. "Keats and James and The Princess Casamassima,"
        NCF, 28 (September, 1973), 179-193.

924   Trilling, Lionel. Introduction. <u>The Princess Casamassima.</u>
       New York: The Macmillan Co. , 1948.

925   _____. "<u>The Princess Casamassima</u>," in <u>The Liberal</u>
       <u>Imagination.</u> New York: The Viking Press, 1950, pp. 58-
       92.

926   _____. "<u>The Princess Casamassima</u>" in <u>The Modern Crit-</u>
       <u>ical Spectrum.</u> Gerald Jay Goldberg and Nancy Marmer
       Goldberg, eds. New York: Prentice-Hall, 1962, pp. 134-
       155.

927   _____. "<u>The Princess Casamassima</u>," Horizon, 17 (April,
       1948), 267-295.

928   Vidan, Ivo. "James's Novel of 'Looming Possibilities,' "
       <u>Renaissance and Modern Essays Presented to Vivian de Sola</u>
       <u>Pinto.</u> G. R. Hibbard, ed. London: Routledge and Kegan
       Paul, 1966, pp. 137-145.
             Parallels of Turgenev's <u>On the Eve</u> and Dostoievsky's <u>The</u>
             <u>Possessed</u> in <u>The Princess Casamassima.</u>

929   _____. "<u>The Princess Casamassima</u> Between Balzac and
       Conrad," SRAZ, Nos. 21-22 (1966), 259-276.

930   Wilkins, M. S. "A Note on <u>The Princess Casamassima</u>,"
       NCF, 12 (June, 1957), 88.
             Suggests the Princess Obolensky as the prototype of
             James's Princess.

931   Woodcock, George. "Henry James and the Conspirators,"
       SR, 60 (April-June, 1952), 219-229.
             Believes that James depended on journalistic views of
             anarchists.

Review of <u>The Princess Casamassima:</u>

       Athenaeum, 3080 (November 6, 1886), 596-7
       Catholic World, 44 (January, 1887), 559
       Critic, 7 (December, 1886), 189
       Epoch, 1 (February 11, 1887), 19
       Harper's, 74 (April, 1887), 829
       Independent, 38 (December 23, 1886), 1665
       Lippincott, 39 (March, 1887), 359
       Lit World, 18 (January 8, 1887), 5
       Nation, 44 (February 10, 1887), 123-4
       Picayune, November 28, 1886, p. 7
       SatR, 62 (November 27, 1886), 728-9

"The Private Life"

932   Blackmur, R. P.   "In the Country of the Blue," The Ques-
        tion of Henry James.   F. W. Dupee, ed.   New York: 1945,
        p. 205.
            "Of this little piece ["The Private Life"] what does one
            say but that the ghost story is the most plausible form of
            the fairy tale; it makes psychological penetration ominous
            because not verifiable...."

933   Lind, Sidney E.   "James's 'The Private Life' and Browning,"
        AL, 23 (November, 1951), 315-322.

933.1   Putt, S. Gorley.   "Tales of the Uncanny--'The Private Life,'"
        Henry James: A Reader's Guide.   Ithaca, New York: 1966,
        pp. 390-392.

        See also: 10, 11, 12, 270, 272.2, 1740, 1804, 2062; 2198,
        VIII; 2205, 2208, 2229, 2352, 2380, 2630; 2637, XXII;
        2637.1, XVII; 2650, 3326, 3417, 3536, 3711

Reviews of "The Private Life":

        Athenaeum, 102 (July 8, 1893), 60-1
        Atlantic, 72 (November, 1893), 606
        Book Buyer, 10 (October, 1893), 364-5
        Christian Union [Outlook], 48 (November 18, 1893), 906
        Critic, 23 (ns 20) (October 14, 1893), 236
        Dial, 15 (October 16, 1893), 228
        HarperM, 87, Sup. 4 (September, 1893), 648
        Independent, 45 (October 26, 1893), 1453
        Lit World, 24 (September 9, 1893), 291
        Nation, 57 (November 30, 1893), 417
        Spec, 71 (July 22, 1893), 117.

"A Problem"

See: 1794, 2198, I; 2695, 2701, 2773, 2948, 3536, 3711

"Professor Fargo"

See: 1804, 2028; 2198, III; 2352, 2695, 3326, 3541, 3711

"The Pupil"

933.2   Canavan, Thomas L.   "The Economics of Disease in James's
        "The Pupil,'"   Criticism, 15 (Summer, 1973), 253-264.

934   Cummins, Elizabeth.   "The Playroom of Superstition: An

Analysis of Henry James's 'The Pupil,' " MarkR, 2 (May, 1970), 13-16.
> Either Morgan Moreen, or Pemberton, his tutor, could be the "pupil" of the title because each tries to instruct the other in values and attitudes.

934.1 Fadiman, Clifton. "A Note on 'The Pupil,' " The Short Stories of Henry James. New York: Modern Library, 1945, pp. 268-277.

934.2 Griffith, John. "James's 'The Pupil' as Whodunit: The Question of Moral Responsibility," SSF, 9 (1972), 257-268.

934.3 Hagopian, John V. "In Defense of the Affective Fallacy," SoR, 1, iii (1965), 72-77.
> Cf., Mark Spilka. "The Affective Fallacy Revisited," SoR, 1 (1965), 57-70.

935 _____. "Seing Through 'The Pupil' Again," MFS, 5 (Summer, 1959), 169-171.
> Says that, like Captain Vere in Billy Budd, Pemberton made a tragic decision out of "stern necessity." Cf., Terence Martin. "James's 'The Pupil': The Art of Seeing Through," MFS, 4 (1958-1959), 335-345.

935.1 James, Henry. Preface. The Novels of Henry James...." "The Pupil," Vol. XI. New York: Scribner's, 1908, p. xv.

936 Kenney, William. "The Death of Morgan in James's 'The Pupil,' " SSF, 8 (Spring, 1971), 317-322.
> "In many ways Morgan is the 'heart' of the family, and his own diseased organ analogously gives out as the Moreens fall apart...."

937 Lainoff, Seymour. "A Note on Henry James's 'The Pupil,' " NCF, 14 (June, 1959), 75-77.
> Sees Pemberton as "at least accessory to the crime." The failure of his friendship underscores the basic theme of the story--"the isolation, the eternal loneliness, of the human spirit."

937.1 Leyris, Pierre. Glossateur de James. L'Elève et Autres Nouvelles. Paris: Union Générale d'Editions, 1963.

938 Martin, Terence. "James's 'The Pupil': The Art of Seeing Through," MFS, 4 (Winter, 1958-1959), 335-345. Repr., in Twentieth Century Interpretations, Jane Tompkins, ed., pp. 11-21.
> Cf., John V. Hagopian, MFS, 5 (1959), 169-171.

939 McElderry, Bruce R. Henry James. New York: Twayne, 1965, pp. 111-112.

939.1 Putt, S. Gorley. "Tales of the Uncanny--'The Pupil,' "
       Henry James: A Reader's Guide. Ithaca, New York: 1966,
       pp. 390-391.

940   Short, Raymond W., and Richard B. Sewall. A Manual of
       Suggestions for Teachers Using Short Stories for Study. 3rd
       ed. New York: Henry Holt, 1956, pp. 39-42.

941   Spilka, Mark. "The Affective Fallacy Revisited," SoR, 1,
       #3 (1965), 57-70.
           Cf., John V. Hagopian. "In Defense of the Affective Fal-
           lacy," SoR, 1, #3 (1965), 72-77.

942   _____. "Hagopian Revisited," SoR, 1, #3 (1965), 77-79.

943   Stein, William B. " 'The Pupil': The Education of a Prude,"
       ArQ, 15 (Spring, 1959), 13-22.

943.1 Stone, Edward, ed. Henry James: Seven Stories and Stud-
       ies. New York: Appleton-Century-Crofts, 1961.

943.2 Trilling, Lionel. The Experience of Literature. New York:
       1967; Holt, Rinehart & Winston, 1969. (The 1969 version
       does not contain commentary.)
           Calls Pemberton a "moral agent."

       See also: 8, 10, 11, 12, 1740, 1745, 1794, 1804, 1924,
       1967; 2198, VII; 2206, 2229, 2258, 2352, 2380, 2382, 2560,
       2630, 2637, XVI; 2637.1, XI; 2651, 3069, 3206, 3326, 3374,
       3417, 3427, 3429, 3536, 3565, 3697, 3710, 3711

Reviews of "The Pupil":

       Book Buyer, 9 (April, 1892), 115-6
       Christian Union, 47 (May 20, 1892), 981
       Churchman, 65 (April 9, 1892), 460
       Cosmopolitan, 13 (September, 1892), 630
       Lit World, 23 (March 26, 1892), 110
       Nation, 54 (April 28, 1892), 326

                    "Pyramus and Thisbe"

943.3 McElderry, B. R. "The Uncollected Stories of Henry James,"
       AL, 21 (1949), 286.
           "... The three remaining uncollected pieces are technical-
           ly not stories, but 'farces' or conversation pieces....
           The first ["Pyramus and Thisbe"] is, surprisingly, the
           best...."

"The Question of Our Speech"

943.4 "Henry James on 'Newspaper English,' " CurL, 39 (August,
       1905), 155-156.

943.5 Mays, Milton A. "Down-Town with Henry James," TSLL,
       14 (1972), 107-122.

See also the Section entitled "Lectures"

Reviews of "The Question of Our Speech":

    Book News, 23 (July, 1905), 856-7
    Critic, 48 (January, 1906), 90; 46 (April, 1905), 307
    Dial, 39 (November 16, 1905), 311
    Nation, 58 (January 19, 1905), 53
    Rev of Revs, 33 (January, 1906), 121
    Tribune, 4 (August 5, 1905), 12.

"The Real Right Thing"

See: 12, 15, 1740, 1794, 1804; 2198, X; 2205, 2208, 2229;
2637, XXII; 2637.1, XVII; 3536, 3711

"The Real Thing"

944   Anderson, Quentin. "The Two Henry Jameses," Scrutiny,
       14 (September, 1947), 242-251.
            Sees the narrator as sinning against art as well as against
            himself in collecting fixed aesthetic values of the Monarchs.

945   Berkelman, Robert. "Henry James and 'The Real Thing,' "
       UKCR, 26 (Winter, 1959), 93-95.
            The "quiet heroism of the Monarchs" reveals that there is
            a "real thing in life as well as in art and the narrator
            learns a valuable lesson from them."

946   Bernard, Kenneth. "The Real Thing in James's 'The Real
       Thing,' " BYUS, 5 (1962), 31-32.
            The realization of the artist-narrator that he can trans-
            form only unreality into art is the "permanent harm"
            which he suffers.

947   Fadiman, Clifton. "On James' 'The Real Thing,' " Reading
       for a Liberal Education. Louis Glenn Locke, et al, eds.
       New York: Rinehart, 1948, II, 333-334; 1952, II, 330-331.

948   Foff, Arthur, and Daniel Knapp, eds. Story: An Introduc-
       tion to Prose Fiction. Belmont, California: Wadsworth,
       1964, pp. 366-368.

949   Gale, Robert L.   "A Note on Henry James's 'The Real
        Thing,'" SSF, 1 (Fall, 1963), 65-66.
                Gale sees the artist's reference to "black and white" il-
                lustrations as satirical allusion to the Black and White
                periodical in which the story first appeared.

950   Horne, Helen.   "Henry James: 'The Real Thing' (1890):
        An Attempt at Interpretation," NS, 5 (May, 1959), 214-219.
                The story examines the nature of art and reality, reveal-
                ing different views of the two.

951   Kehler, Harold.   "James's 'The Real Thing,'" Expl, 25
        (1967), Item 79.
                Kehler reads "Churm" as East End London patois for
                "charm."

952   Labor, Earle.   "James's 'The Real Thing': Three Levels of
        Meaning," CE, 23 (February, 1962), 376-378.
                The three levels of meaning are the social, aesthetic, and
                the moral, the last of which makes the story more mean-
                ingful.

953   Lainoff, Seymour.   "A Note on Henry James's 'The Real
        Thing,'" MLN, 71 (March, 1956), 192-193.
                The story illustrates James's theory of "nominal real-
                ism." The artist must give an "air of reality to that
                which may not be real."

954   Marquardt, William F.   "A Practical Approach to 'The Real
        Thing,'" Eng"A"A, No. 14 (1949)

955   Matsuhara, Iwao.   Introduction and Notes.   The Real Thing.
        Tokyo: Yamaguchi Shoten, 1958.

955.1   McMahon, Helen.   "Patterns of Realism in the Atlantic"--
        "The Real Thing," Criticism of Fiction: A Study of Trends
        in "The Atlantic Monthly," 1857-1898.   New York: Bookman
        Associates, 1952, pp. 34-35.

956   Mueller, Lavonne.   "Henry James: The Phenomenal Self as
        the 'Real Thing,'" ForumH, 6 (Spring, 1968), 46-50.
                Interprets the story as "an analysis of a unit, the Mon-
                archs against the artist--an endless struggle for the phe-
                nomenal self to escape its own destruction by destroying
                the 'alien' self."

957   Munson, Gorham.   "'The Real Thing': A Parable for
        Writers of Fiction," UKCR, 16 (Summer, 1950), 261-264.
                Suggests that the fiction writer's problems are in James's
                mind in "The Real Thing" for it shows that the "copying
                of life-models for fiction is bad business."

958   O'Faolain, Sean.   "'The Real Thing' by Henry James,"

<u>The Short Story</u>. New York: Devin-Adair Co., 1964, pp. 301-332.

959   Powers, Lyall H. "Henry James and the Ethics of the Art-
       ist: 'The Real Thing' and 'The Liar,' " TSLL, 3 (Autumn,
       1961), 360-368.
           The two stories complement each other. In "The Liar"
           Oliver Lyon sacrifices the artist by using himself to "sat-
           isfy the mean desires" of himself as man; in "The Real
           Thing," the artist improves and humanizes the Monarchs
           by sacrificing them to the ends of art.

960   Raeth, Claire. "The Real Approach to 'The Real Thing,' "
       Eng"A"A, No. 15 (1949).

960.1 Scudder, Horace E. Review of <u>Owen Wister: Red Man and</u>
       <u>White,</u>" Atl, 77 (February, 1896), 265.
           Comments on "The Real Thing": "Mr. James, in one of
           the subtlest of his stories, 'The Real Thing,' has touched
           most firmly this interesting truth in art, that the actual
           is not by any means the real." Cf., Horace E. Scudder's
           review of Mrs. Humphry Ward's <u>Sir George Tressady</u>,
           Atl, 78 (December, 1896), 841.

960.2 Stone, Edward, ed. <u>Henry James: Seven Stories and Stud-</u>
       <u>ies</u>. New York: Appleton-Century-Crofts, 1961.

961   Toor, David. "Narrative Irony in Henry James' 'The Real
       Thing,' " UR, 34 (December, 1967), 95-99.
           The author believes the irony in James's story is turned
           toward the narrator, not the Monarchs, thus showing that
           the narrator's theory of art is faulty.

962   Uroff, M. D. "Perception in James's 'The Real Thing,' "
       SSF, 9 (Winter, 1972), 41-46.
           "The story is certainly about the real thing of perception;
           but its point seems to be that the real thing is everywhere
           elusive."

963   Wright, Walter F. "The Real Thing," RSSCW, 25 (March,
       1957), 85-90.
           Believes the story is not an illustration of the antithesis
           between art and life but an admiring portrait of good
           breeding (the Monarchs) in adversity.

       See also: 11, 12, 272.2, 1740, 1794, 1799, 1804, 1980;
       2198, VIII; 2205, 2229, 2258, 2382, 2560, 2564, 2581, 2630,
       2637, XXIII; 2637.1, XVIII; 2650, 2737, 2918, 3244, 3255,
       3429, 3536, 3689, 3711

Reviews of "The Real Thing":

       Athenaeum, 3420 (May 13, 1893), 601-2

Atl, 72 (November, 1893), 695-6
Book Buyer, 10 (May, 1893), 153-4
Chautauquan, 17 (May, 1893), 485-6
Cottage Hearth, 19 (May, 1893), 245
Critic, 22 (ns 19) (April 15, 1893), 230
Dial, 14 (June 1, 1893), 341
Godey's, 126 (June, 1893), 771
Independent, 45 (August 24, 1893), 1154
Lit World, 24 (April 8, 1893), 113
Overland, 2d S, 21 (June, 1893), 660
SatR, 75 (June 3, 1893), 602

"The Reprobate" See: THEATRICALS

THE REVERBERATOR

964   Anderson, Charles R. "Henry James's Fable of Carolina,"
        SAQ, 54 (April, 1954), 249-257.
            Discussion of James's limited background of knowledge for
        his Carolina characters.

965   Durkin, Sister Mary Brian. "Henry James's Revisions of the
        Style of The Reverberator," AL, 33 (November, 1961), 330-
        349.
            A comparison of the serialized version of 1888 and the
        revised edition of 1908.

965.1   Howells, William Dean. "The Editor's Study," Harper's, 77
        (October, 1888), 802.
            "Francie Dosson, with her beauty, her fineness, her good-
        ness, and her helpless truth, is a marvelous expression
        of the best in American girlhood."

965.2   James, Henry. "Preface to The Reverberator," The Art of
        the Novel: Critical Prefaces. New York: Scribner, 1934.

966   Knox, George. "Reverberations and The Reverberator,"
        EIHC, 95 (October, 1959), 348-354.

967   Nowell-Smith, Simon. Introductory Note. The Reverbera-
        tor. New York: Grove Press, 1957.

968   Weber, Carl J. "Henry James and Thomas Hardy," MTQ,
        5 (Spring, 1942), 3-4.
            Quotes Hardy as saying in regard to The Reverberator:
        "After this kind of work one feels inclined to be purpose-
        ly careless in detail.... James's subjects are those one
        could be interested in at moments when there is nothing
        larger to think of."

See also: 10, 270, 1740, 1790, 1980, 2062, 2070; 2198,

XVIII; 2382, 2560; 2637.1, XIII; 2646.1, 2651, 2944, 3326,
3536, 3626, 3711

Reviews of The Reverberator:

Athenaeum, 3164 (June 16, 1888), 759
Catholic World, 48 (December, 1888), 402-5
Christian Union, 38 (August 2, 1888), 130
Churchman, 58 (August 11, 1888), 173
Critic, 13 (September 15, 1888), 123
Epoch, 4 (August 24, 1888), 55
Harper's, 77 (October, 1888), 802
Independent, 40 (December 13, 1888), 1609
Lit World, 19 (September 29, 1888), 313
Nation, 47 (October 2, 1888), 273
NoAmer Rev, 147 (November, 1888), 599

RODERICK HUDSON

969   Altick, Richard D.   "The Spirit of Scholarship," in The Art
        of Literary Research.   New York: W. W. Norton & Co.,
        1963, p. 15.
                F. R. Leavis in The Great Tradition quoted from the New
                York Edition of Roderick Hudson to show James's capabil-
                ity early in his career.

970   Bercovitch, Sacvan.   "The Revision of Rowland Mallet,"
        NCF, 24 (September, 1969), 210-221.
                The New York Edition indicates that Mallet is not a hero,
                nor an innocent observer, but a "complex and intricately
                conceived Center of Consciousness."

971   Bewley, Marius.   "Henry James and 'Life,' " HudR, 11 (Sum-
        mer, 1958), 167-185.
                Considers Europe a "testing ground" for American char-
                acter.

972   Conn, Peter J.   "Roderick Hudson: The Role of the Ob-
        server," NCF, 26, #1 (1971-72), 65-82.
                Rejects the claim that Rowland Mallet is a "personified
                surrogate for James's moral imagination."   He is instead,
                the "Observer," who assumes "control on all levels."

973   Cooney, Séamus.   "Grammar vs. Style in a Sentence from
        Roderick Hudson.   N&Q, n. s. 6, #1 (January, 1959), 32-
        33.
                The penultimate sentence of Roderick Hudson went through
                three revisions, but the third, appearing in the New York
                Edition, Cooney finds grammatically incorrect.   The sent-
                ence can be made satisfactory by dropping the word "who."

974   Daiches, David.   "Sensibility and Technique (Preface to a

Critique)," KR, 5 (Autumn, 1943), 569-579.
Roderick Hudson contains "specific" and "overt" morality.

975   Dunbar, Viola R.   "The Problem of Roderick Hudson," MLN,
        67 (February, 1952), 109-113.
        The problem is "that of the freedom of the individual will
        and man's share in determining his own destiny." In no
        other of James's novels "is expressed such unqualified
        faith in the freedom of the will."

976   _____. "A Source for Roderick Hudson," MLN, 63 (May,
        1948), 303-310.
        Striking similarities in plot, characters, and ideas between
        James's novel and L'Affaire Clémenceau: Mémoire de
        L'Accusé, of Dumas, fils, reviewed by James in Nation,
        October 11, 1866.

977   Earnest, Ernest.   "The American Ariel," SAQ, 65 (Spring,
        1966), 192-200.
        James's Roderick Hudson is given as an "unattractive"
        predecessor of the "Ariel" character, the artist figure
        "with a longing to be free and a lack of lasting human af-
        fections."

978   Edel, Leon.   "Henry James and Vernon Lee," PMLA, 69
        (June, 1954), 677-678.
        Refutes the idea that James had put Miss Lee into his nov-
        el, Roderick Hudson, in the personality of Christina Light,
        late Princess Casamassima.   James would have had to
        meet her before 1874, since Roderick Hudson was written
        during that year and published in 1875. Cf., Carl J.
        Weber. "Henry James and His Tigercat," PMLA, 68
        (1953), 672-695.

979   _____.   Introduction. Roderick Hudson. New York:
        Harper, 1961; London: Rupert Hart-Davis, 1961.

980   Engelberg, Edward.   "James and Arnold: Conscience and
        Consciousness in a Victorian 'Kunstlerroman,' " Criticism,
        10 (Spring, 1968), 93-114.
        Claims that, from a modern perspective. Roderick Hudson
        is the first in English fiction to take the artist's dilemma
        seriously, and that in so doing, James prepared the way
        for a significant progeny.

980.1   _____.   "The Tyranny of Conscience:... James's Renuncia-
        tion of Fables: Roderick Hudson," The Unknown Distance:
        From Consciousness to Conscience. Goethe to Camus.   Cam-
        bridge, Mass.: Harvard University Press, 1972, pp. 154-
        172.

981   Gale, Robert L.   "Roderick Hudson and Thomas Crawford,"
        AQ, 13 (Winter, 1961), 495-504.

James's central character owes much to Thomas Crawford, American sculptor, whose wife James knew in Rome
after Crawford's death.

982   Gardner, Burdett. "An Apology for Henry James's 'Tiger-
        Cat,' " PMLA, 68 (September, 1953), 688-695.
        Violet Paget as model for Christina Light. Cf., Carl
        Weber. "Henry James and His Tiger-Cat," PMLA, 68
        (1953), 672-687.

983   Goodman, Charlotte. "Henry James's Roderick Hudson and
        Nathaniel Parker Willis's Paul Fane," AL, 43 (January,
        1972), 642-644.
        Similarities between the two novels suggest a possible in-
        fluence.

984   Grenander, M. E. "Henry James's Capricciosa: Christina
        Light in Roderick Hudson and The Princess Casamassima,"
        PMLA, 75 (June, 1960), 309-319.
        The development of Christina Light through the two novels.

984.1   H., J. "Henry James and Dumas, fils," N&Q, 185 (August
        28, 1943), 132-133.
        The influence of L'Affaire Clémenceau on James's Rod-
        erick Hudson.

985   Harvitt, Hélène. "How Henry James Revised Roderick Hud-
        son," PMLA, 39 (March 1924), 203-227.

986   Havens, Raymond D. "The Revision of Roderick Hudson,"
        PMLA, 40 (1925), 433-434.

987   Hoff, Lloyd M. The Revision of "Roderick Hudson: Its
        Extent, Nature and Result. Diss. Ohio State: 1930.

988   Hoffman, Frederick J. The Mortal No: Death and the Mod-
        ern Imagination. Princeton, New Jersey: Princeton Univer-
        sity Press, 1964, pp. 41-50.

989   Hopkins, Viola. "Gloriani and the Tides of Taste," NCF,
        18 (June, 1963), 65-71.
        The characterization of the sculptor Gloriani in Roderick
        Hudson.

990   James, Henry. "Preface to Roderick Hudson," The Art of
        the Novel: Critical Prefaces. New York: Scribner, 1934.

991   Kinnaird, John. "The Paradox of an American 'Identity,' "
        PR, 25 (Summer, 1958), 380-381.

992   Kraft, James L. " 'Madame de Mauves' and Roderick Hud-
        son: The Development of James's International Style," TQ,
        11, iii (Autumn, 1968), 143-160.

"... both [works] show James beginning to handle with as-
surance his important international theme and its contrasting faces."

993   Kraft, Quentin G. "The Central Problem of James's Fictional Thought: From The Scarlet Letter to Roderick Hudson," ELH, 36 (June, 1969), 416-439.
Life versus form the central problem of both novels.

993.1 Leavis, F. R. "Henry James's First Novel," Scrutiny, 14
(September, 1947), 235-301.

994   Marovitz, Sanford E. "Roderick Hudson: James's Marble
Faun," TSLL, 11 (Winter, 1970), 1427-1443.
"... the themes, the settings, several of the primary
characters, and, to a large extent, the methods of construction are very similar" in Hawthorne's late romance
and James's early novel.

995   Maxwell, J. C. "The Revision of Roderick Hudson," ES, 45
(June, 1964), 239.
Repeats Gordon N. Ray's remark about F. R. Leavis's
confusion of late James revisions with early James. The
confusion has been proved as immaterial.

996   Monteiro, George. "Another Princess," PQ 41 (April, 1962),
517-518.
Suggests the possibility that James "was also touched by
the immediate gestures of irreverence--close to his Christina's characteristic élan--of the living example." Cf.,
Bebe Spanos. "The Real Princess Christina," PQ, 38
(1959), 488-496.

997   _____. "The Campaign of Henry James's Disinherited
Princess," ES, 45 (December, 1964), 442-454.
In Roderick Hudson and The Princess Casamassima, there
is "a strong internal consistency and resilient bravery" in
the central figure. However, Monteiro rejects Edel's
characterization of her as a "good-bad heroine."

998   Morooka, Hirashi. "On Henry James's Roderick Hudson,"
RikR, 14 (1952), 95-113.

999   Nettels, Elsa. "Action and Point of View in Roderick Hudson," ES, 53 (June, 1972), 238-247.

1000   Newlin, Paul A. "The Development of Roderick Hudson:
An Evaluation," ArQ, 27 (Summer, 1971), 101-123.
Hawthorne's The Marble Faun and its ties to the Rome of
the American sculptor William Wetmore Story is the major
"indirect link between these two novels of Italian settings."

1000.1 Poirier, Richard. "Roderick Hudson," in The Comic

<u>Sense of Henry James.</u>   New York: Oxford University Press, 1960, pp. 11-43.

1001   Putt, S. Gorley. Editorial Note. <u>Roderick Hudson.</u> Baltimore: Penguin Books, 1969.

1001.1   _____. " 'Everyone Was a Little Someone Else': <u>Roderick Hudson</u>,...: Tales of Split Personality," <u>Henry James: A Reader's Guide.</u> Ithaca, New York: 1966, pp. 85-106.

1002   Rao, N. Krishna. "The Idea of Refinement in James' <u>Roderick Hudson</u>," <u>Indian Essays in American Literature: Papers in Honour of Robert E. Spiller.</u> Sujit Mukherjee, and D. V. K. Raghavacharyulu, eds. Bombay: Popular Prakashan, 1969, pp. 139-147.

1003   Ray, Gordon. "The Importance of Original Editions," in <u>Nineteenth Century English Books.</u> Urbana, Illinois, 1952, p. 22.

1004   "Rossetti, and Henry James," N&Q, 184 (June 5, 1943), 327-328.

1005   Scherting, John. "<u>Roderick Hudson:</u> A Re-evaluation," ArQ, 25 (Summer, 1969), 101-119.
        "... the central meaning of the novel is intimately bound up with Roland's character, motives, and deeds. If these are examined closely, the work emerges with a different meaning...."

1006   Shumsky, Allison. "James Again: The New York Edition," SR, 70 (Summer, 1962), 522-525.

1007   Snow, Lotus. " 'The Prose and the Modesty of the Matter': James's Imagery for the Artist in <u>Roderick Hudson</u> and <u>The Tragic Muse</u>," MFS, 12, i (Spring, 1966), 61-82.
        Illustrates the development of imagery from conventional figures in the early story to more original and revealing ones in the latter.

1008   Spanos, Bebe. "The Real Princess Christina," PQ, 38 (October, 1959), 448-496.

1009   Speck, Paul. "A Structural Analysis of James's <u>Roderick Hudson</u>," SNNTS, 2 (Autumn, 1970), 292-305.
        Rowland Mallet, not Roderick Hudson, provides the basic theme in the novel, and also its pivotal structure.

1010   Takahashi, Michi. "The Design and 'Point of View' of Henry James's <u>Roderick Hudson</u>," E&S(T), 11 (Summer, 1963), 1-29.

1011   Taylor, Gordon O. <u>The Passages of Thought: Psychological</u>

Representation in the American Novel, 1870-1900. New
York: Oxford University Press, 1969, pp. 42-84.

1011.1 Wagner, Linda Welshimer. "The Dominance of Heredity in
the Characterizations of Henry James," SDR, 2 (Spring,
1965), 69-77.
Analysis of main characters in Roderick Hudson indicates
that for James, heredity and not environment is influential
in making a man what he is.

1012   Watanabe, Hisayoshi. "Past Perfect Retrospection in the
Style of Henry James," AL, 34 (May, 1962), 165-181.

1013   Weinstein, Philip M. "The Romantic and the Real: Beliefs
and Roles in Roderick Hudson," in Henry James and the Requirements of the Imagination. Cambridge, Mass.: Harvard
U. P., 1971, pp. 8-30.

Reviews of Roderick Hudson:

Appleton, 14 (December 18, 1875), 793
Athenaeum, 2697 (July 5, 1879), 12-3
Atl, 37 (February, 1876), 237-8
Independent, 27 (December 23, 1875), 8
Library Table, 1 (January, 1876), 16-7
NoAmer Rev, 122 (April, 1876), 420-5
Poet-Lore, 16 (Winter, 1905), 95-6
Quarterly Rev, 198 (October, 1903), 358
Scribner's, 11 (February, 1876), 588-9

"The Romance of Certain Old Clothes"

1014   Allot, Miriam. "James Russell Lowell: A Link between
Tennyson and Henry James," RES, 6 (October, 1955), 397-
99.
Lowell supplied James with the plot for his "The Romance
of Certain Old Clothes," and Tennyson for his poem "The
Ring."

1015   Havens, Raymond D. "Henry James on One of His Early
Stories," AL, 23 (March, 1951), 131-133.

See also: 8, 38, 1740, 1794, 1804, 2028; 2198, I; 2205,
2208; 2229; 2637, XXVI; 2695, 2773, 3536, 3711

"Rose-Agathe"

See: 1794, 2352, 2363

"A Round of Visits"

1015.1 Chapman, Sara S. "The 'Obsession of Egotism' in Henry
James's 'A Round of Visits,' " ArQ, 29 (Summer, 1973),
130-138.

1016 Purdy, Strother B. Conversation and Awareness in Henry
James's 'A Round of Visits,' " SSF, 6 (1969), 421-432.

See also: 10, 12, 1740, 1804, 1924, 1931, 2028; 2198, XII;
2229, 2352, 2380, 2382; 2637, XXVIII; 2737, 2915.1, 2917,
2990, 3326, 3417, 3536, 3582, 3626, 3711

THE SACRED FOUNT

1017 Allott, Miriam. "Henry James and the Fantasticated Conceit," NorM, 1 (Autumn, 1953), 76-86.

1018 Anderson, Quentin. "The Sacred Fount" in The American
Henry James. New Brunswick, New Jersey: Rutgers U. P.,
1957, passim.

1019 Andreach, Robert J. "Henry James's The Sacred Fount:
The Existential Predicament," NCF, 17 (December, 1962),
197-216.
A definition of the existential predicament as the "dichot-
omy that occurs between the real experiencing of the
world and the logical apprehension of the world."

1020 Andreas, Osborn. "The Sacred Fount" in Henry James and
the Expanding Horizon. Seattle: Washington U. P., 1948,
passim.
"... Intellectual adventure versus romantic adventure is
the theme of The Sacred Fount."

1021 Beach, Joseph Warren. "Henry James--The Sacred Fount"
in The Cambridge History of American Literature. Wm. P.
Trent, et al, eds. New York: Macmillan, 1936, pp. 98,
106.

1022 _____. "Technial Exercises:... The Sacred Fount," in
The Method of Henry James. New Haven: Yale U. P.,
1918, Philadelphia: Saifer, 1954, pp. 250-251.

1023 Beebe, Maurice. "Henry James: The Ideal of Detachment,"
Ivory Towers and Sacred Founts: The Artist as Hero in
Fiction from Goethe to Joyce. New York: New York U. P.,
1964, pp. 197-231.

1024 Bellringer, Alan W. "The Sacred Fount: The Scientific
Method," EIC, 22 (July, 1972), 244-264.

The novel's narrator shows a "scientific" curiosity about
human relationships as well as signs of remorse for the
consequences of his meddling in the affairs of others.

1025   Berthoff, Warner. "The Sacred Found" in The Ferment of
Realism: American Literature, 1884-1919. New York:
The Free Press, 1965, pp. 118-119.
"... The title of this work and much of its language sug-
gest an allegory of the expense and renewal of life it-
self. ..."

1026   Blackall, Jean Frantz. Jamesian Ambiguity and "The Sacred
Fount." Ithaca, New York: Cornell University Press, 1965.
A very significant study of this novel.

1027   _____. "The Sacred Fount as a Comedy of the Limited
Observer," PMLA, 78 (September, 1963), 384-393.
Finds the novel "high comedy wonderfully well sustained."

1028   Blackmur, R. P. "The Sacred Fount" KR, 4 (Autumn, 1942),
328-352.
The Sacred Fount should be approached in the light of
James's earlier ghost stories; it may be called "the last
lucid nightmare of James's hallucinated struggle with his
conscience as a novelist."

1029   _____. "In the Country of the Blue," KR, 5 (Autumn,
1943), 595-617, specifically, p. 597.

1030   Brooks, Van Wyck. "The Sacred Fount," in The Pilgrimage
of Henry James. New York: Octagon Books, 1972, pp. 88-
105.

1031   Burlingame, Roger. Of Making Many Books: A Hundred
Years of Reading, Writing and Publishing. New York:
Scribner's, 1946.

1032   Burns, Landon C., Jr. "Henry James's Mysterious Fount,"
TSLL, 2 (Winter, 1961), 520-528.
The artist in his detachment can see things more clearly
than those involved. Because of his art he is withdrawn
from life but therefore lacks the "tone" of one who experiences the things the artist depicts.

1033   Cargill, Oscar. "The Sacred Fount," in The Novels of Henry James. New York: Macmillan Co., 1961, pp. 280-299.

1034   Edel, Leon. Henry James: The Treacherous Years. Philadelphia, New York: J. B. Lippincott, 1969, pp. 338-347;
349-350.

1035   _____. Introduction. The Sacred Fount. New York:
Grove Press, 1953; London: Hart-Davis, 1959.

1036   Finkelstein, Sidney. "The 'Mystery' of Henry James's The
        Sacred Fount," MassR, 3 (Summer, 1962), 753-776.

1037   Foley, Richard N. "The Sacred Fount," Criticism in Amer-
        ican Periodicals of the Works of Henry James From 1866 to
        1916. Washington, D.C.: Catholic University of America
        Press, 1944, pp. 80-82.

1038   Follett, Wilson. "Henry James's Portrait of Henry James,"
        NYTBR (August 23, 1936), 2, 16.
            Suggests that The Sacred Fount reveals James's philosophy
        of fiction in a farcical setting.

1039   _____. "The Simplicity of Henry James," AmR, 1 (May-
        June, 1923), 315-325.

1040   Folsom, James K. "Archimago's Well: An Interpretation of
        The Sacred Fount," MFS, 7 (Summer, 1961), 136-145.

1041   Gale, Robert L. "The Marble Faun and The Sacred Fount:
        A Resemblance," SA, 8 (1962), 151-199.

1042   Gard, Roger, ed. "The Sacred Fount," in Henry James:
        The Critical Heritage. London: Routledge and Kegan Paul;
        New York: Barnes & Noble, 1968, pp. 306-316.

1043   Geismar, Maxwell. "Henry James: The Psychology of the
        Key Hole," Ramparts, 1 (March, 1963), 57-64.

1044   _____. "The Literary Orphan," Nation, 176 (May 2,
        1953), 374.

1045   Hinchliffe, Arnold P. "Henry James's The Sacred Fount,"
        TSLL, 2 (Spring, 1960), 88-94.

1046   Hoffmann, Charles G. "The Art of Reflection in James's
        The Sacred Fount," MLN, 69 (November, 1954), 507-508.

1047   _____. "The Sacred Fount," in The Short Novels of Hen-
        ry James. New York: Bookman Associates, 1957, pp. 104-
        107, 125-126, passim.
            The essay in MLN is incorporated in The Short Novels.

1048   Hofmann, Gert. Interpretationsprobleme Bei Henry James.
        ("The Turn of the Screw," The Sacred Fount, "The Figure
        in the Carpet"). Diss. Freiburg, 1957.

1048.1 Isle, Walter. "The Sacred Fount," in Experiments in Form:
        Henry James's Novels, 1896-1901. Cambridge, Mass.:
        Harvard U. P., 1968, pp. 205-233.

1049   _____. "The Romantic and the Real: Henry James's
        The Sacred Fount," RUS, 51 (Winter, 1965), 29-47.

Sees the narrator as "a romantic confronting the materials of reality."

1050   Kaye, Julian B. "The Awkward Age, The Sacred Fount and The Ambassadors: Another Figure in the Carpet," NCF, 17 (March, 1963), 339-351.

1050.1 Krook, Dorothea. "The Sacred Fount," in The Ordeal of Consciousness in Henry James. New York: Cambridge University Press, 1962, pp. 191-194.

1951   L. R. F. O. "The Sacred Fount," Speaker, N. S., 3 (February 23, 1901), 580-581.

1052   Lebowitz, Naomi. "The Sacred Fount: An Author in Search of His Characters," Criticism, 4 (Spring, 1962), 148-159.
         "No novelist ever trusted his characters to share the developing burdens and blessings of full consciousness so much as James."

1053   Levy, Leo B. "What Does The Sacred Fount Mean?" CE, 23 (February, 1962), 381-384.
         "James's novel describes the extravagant case of the artist attempting to find in the world precise models of the works of art that it is his mission to invent."

1054   Littell, Philip. "James's Sacred Fount," NewRep, 3 (July 3, 1915), 234. Repr., under title "The Middle Years" in Books and Things. New York: 1919, p. 224.

1055   Marshall, James Morse. "Patterns of Freedom in Henry James's Later Novels," DA, 23 (Syracuse: 1962), 634.
         "The Sacred Fount stands as a germinal work in the context of James's later novels."

1056   Melchiori, Giorgio. "Cups of Gold for the Sacred Fount: Aspects of James's Symbolism," CritQ, 7 (Winter, 1965), 301-316.
         A survey of possible influences on the increasing symbolism of James's later stories.

1057   Mortimer, Raymond. "Henry James: 15 April 1843--28 February 1916," Horizon, 7 (May, 1943), 318.

1058   Ozick, Cynthia. "The Jamesian Parable: The Sacred Fount," BuR, 11 (May, 1963), 55-70.
         Insists that the novel is a parable, "not universally applicable, but inevitable in its own case." The meaning of the parable is that the person who attempts "to become what he is not ... negates the integrity ... of his personality."

1059   Paik, Nak-chung. "Henry James' The Sacred Fount as a

Work of Art and as the Portrait of a Consciousness," ELL,
16 (June, 1964-1965), 105-136.

1060   Perlongo, Robert A.   "The Sacred Fount: Labyrinth or Par-
        able," KR, 22, #4 (1960), 635-647.
            The Sacred Fount is a parable of artistic morality; "its
            final message seems to be a preaffirmation of life as a
            quantity to be valued for itself, and not merely for what
            the artist may make of it."

1061   Perry, Bliss. Quoted in Of Making Many Books by Roger
        Burlingame. New York: Scribner's, 1946, pp. 134-135.

1062   Phillips, Norma.   "The Sacred Fount: The Narrator and the
        Vampires," PMLA, 76 (September, 1961), 407-412.
            The key to interpretation is the narrator's dynamic role
            in the vampire theme through his relationship with other
            characters, especially with Mrs. Brissenden.

1063   Putt, S. Gorley.   "Marriage and Society ... The Sacred
        Fount...." Henry James: A Reader's Guide. Ithaca, New
        York: 1966, pp. 239-263.

1064   Raeth, Claire J.   "Henry James's Rejection of The Sacred
        Fount," ELH, 16 (December, 1949), 308-324.
            Believes The Sacred Fount was omitted from the New
            York Edition because James noted its failure of form aris-
            ing from his use of a narrator instead of the more objec-
            tive "center of consciousness."

1065   Ranald, Ralph A.   "The Sacred Fount: James's Portrait of
        the Artist Manqué," NCF, 15 (December, 1960), 239-248.
            "The Sacred Fount ... is about life and the relationship
            of art to life...."

1066   Reaney, James.   "The Condition of Light: Henry James's
        The Sacred Fount," UTQ, 31 (January, 1962), 136-151.
            The Sacred Fount presents images of man's fight against
            darkness and ignorance. The theme is "the condition of
            light," or man's observation as regards his progress in
            knowing and controlling the hostile world around him.

1066.1 Richards, Bernard.   "The Ambassadors and The Sacred
        Fount; The Artist Manqué," in The Air of Reality. John
        Goode, ed. London: Methuen & Co., 1972, 219-243.

1066.2 Roberts, Morris.   "Henry James's Final Period," YR, n. s.,
        37 (Autumn, 1947), 60-67, specifically 60, 64-65.
            The suspense and excitement of the novel are stressed.

1067   Sackville-West, Edward.   "The Sacred Fount," NS&N, 34
        (October 4, 1947), 273. Repr., in Inclinations. London:
        1949, pp. 63-71.

1067.1 _____. "The Personality of Henry James," Inclinations.
London: Secker and Warburg, 1949, pp. 42-71.

1068   Samuels, Charles Thomas. "At the Bottom of the Fount,"
Novel, 2 (Fall, 1968), 46-54.
The narrator was confused at the outset in his theory of
the Fount.

1068.1 _____. "At the Bottom of the Fount," The Ambiguity of
Henry James. Urbana: Illinois U. P., 1971, pp. 25-39.

1069   Schrero, Elliot M. "The Narrator's Palace of Thought in
The Sacred Fount," MP, 68 (February, 1971), 269-288.

1070   Seaman, Owen. Borrowed Plumes: Parodies. New York:
Holt, 1902, pp. 133-149.
Contains a parody of The Sacred Fount.

1071   Sherman, Stuart P. "The Aesthetic Idealism of Henry
James," On Contemporary Literature. New York: 1917,
pp. 245-246. Repr., in The Question of Henry James. F.
W. Dupee, ed. New York: Henry Holt, 1945, pp. 70-91.

1072   Stein, William Bysshe. "The Sacred Fount and British Aestheticism: The Artist as Clown and Pornographer," ArQ, 27
(Summer, 1971), 161-173.
"Like too many of the British aesthetes and decadents,
James's protagonist perverts the function of the imagination, channeling its energies into the fruitless creation of
pornographic fancies of illicit wish-fulfillment."

1073   _____. "The Sacred Fount: The Poetics of Nothing,"
Criticism, 14 (Fall, 1972), 373-389.
"... life in the closed society degenerates into a charade
... The purpose of James's parody is to strip away these
disguises and to expose the silly vanities that they conceal
...." The novel is a serious work of art "whose meaning has to be derived from its method."

1074   Tanner, Tony. "Henry James's Subjective Adventurer: The
Sacred Fount," E&S, 16 (London: John Murray, 1963), 37-
55.
Suggests that the narrator stands for the artist type,
Shaftesbury's "second maker" whose lies may be better
than truth.

1075   Tyler, Parker. "The Sacred Fount: 'The Actuality Preten-
tious and Vain' vs. 'The Case Rich and Edifying,' " MFS, 9
(Summer, 1963), 127-138.
The narrator is interpreted as James, and Mrs. Brissen-
den as a typical woman reader, fascinated but skeptical.

1076   _____. "The Sacred Fount," in Every Artist His Own

<u>Scandal.</u> New York: Horizon Press, 1964, pp. 209-224.

1076.1 Weinstein, Philip M. "The Exploitative and Protective Imag-
ination: Aspects of the Artist in <u>The Sacred Fount</u>," <u>Henry
James and the Requirements of the Imagination.</u> Cambridge,
Mass.: Harvard U. P., 1971, pp. 97-120.

1077   _____. "The Exploitative and Protective Imagination: Unreliable Narration in <u>The Sacred Fount</u>," <u>The Interpretation
of Narrative: Theory and Practice.</u> Morton W. Bloomfield,
ed. Harvard English Studies 1. Cambridge, Mass.: Harvard University Press, 1970, pp. 189-209.

1077.1 Wiesenfarth, Joseph. "<u>The Sacred Fount</u> and the Perspective
Achievement," <u>Henry James and the Dramatic Analogy: A
Study of the Major Novels of the Major Period.</u> New York:
Fordham U. P., 1963.

Reviews of <u>The Sacred Fount</u>:

    Academy, 60 (February 23, 1901), 165-166.
    Athenaeum, 3827 (March 2, 1901), 272
    Atlantic, 91 (January, 1903), 77-82
    Book Buyer, 22 (March, 1901), 148
    Bookman, 13 (July, 1901), 442; 16 (November, 1902), 259-60
    Churchman, 83 (May 4, 1901), 552
    Critic, 38 (April, 1901), 368-70
    Current Lit, 30 (April, 1901), 493
    Harper's, 102 (May, 1902), 974
    Independent, 53 (March 14, 1901), 619-20
    Literature, 8 (February 23, 1901), 144
    Lit Rev, 5 (April, 1901), 32
    NoAmer Rev, 176 (January, 1903), 125-37
    NYTBR (February 16, 1901), 112
    Outlook, 67 (March 2, 1901), 554
    Quarterly Rev, 198 (October, 1903), 358
    SatR, (London), 91 (May 4, 1901), 574
    Spectator, 86 (March 2, 1901), 318-19
    Times (London) (May 4, 1901), 5
    Times, 6 (February, 1901), 112; 7 (October 4, 1903), 658

THE SENSE OF THE PAST

1078   Beams, David W. "Consciousness in James's 'The Sense of
the Past,'" Criticism, 5 (Spring, 1963), 148-172.
    Sees this incomplete novel as an illustration of "the artist
who makes life by making awareness of it."

1078.1 Edel, Leon. "The Visitable Past," <u>Henry James: The
Treacherous Years, 1895-1901.</u> Philadelphia, New York:
J. B. Lippincott, 1969, pp. 328-336.

1079 Perosa, Sergio. "Teme e tecnica in The Sense of the Past," SA, 12 (1966), 169-199.

1079.1 Putt, S. Gorley. "The Passionate Pilgrim: The Sense of the Past," Henry James: The Reader's Guide. Ithaca, New York: Cornell U. P., 1966, pp. 55-84.

1079.2 _____. "Unfinished Novels: The Sense of the Past, The Ivory Tower," Henry James: A Reader's Guide. Ithaca: New York: 1966, pp. 415-424.

1080 Stone, Edward. "From Henry James to John Balderston: Relativity and the '20's," MFS, 1 (May, 1955), 2-11.
Balderston's dramatic adaptation of The Sense of the Past, retitled Berkeley Square, reflects the then current thinking on relativity and the popularity of new concepts of time.

1081 _____. "Henry James's Last Novel," BPLQ, 2 (October, 1950), 348-353.

See also: 1701, 1740, 1786, 1924, 2070, 2382, 2630; 2637.1, XXVI; 2651, 2915.1, 2944, 3326, 3386, 3427, 3536, 3582, 3603, 3711

Review of The Sense of the Past:

Bookman (London) 53 (December 8, 1917), 107-8

"The Siege of London"

1082 Brooks, Van Wyck. "The Siege of London" in The Pilgrimage of Henry James. New York: Octagon Books, 1972, pp. 69-87.

1082.1 Habegger, Alfred. " 'The Siege of London': Henry James and the Pièce Bien Faite," MFS, 15 (Summer, 1969), 219-230.
The influence of Alexandre Dumas fils on James.

1082.2 Samuels, Charles Thomas. "Comic Criticism" ["The Siege of London"] The Ambiguity of Henry James. Urbana: Illinois U. P., 1971, pp. 141-144.

See also: 9, 10, 11, 12, 270, 272.2, 1740, 1804; 2198, V; 2229, 2352, 2380, 2564; 2637, XIX; 2637.1, XIV; 3010, 3206, 3626, 3417, 3689, 3711

Reviews of "The Siege of London":

Atl, 51 (May, 1883), 706-7
Churchman, 47 (April 14, 1883), 405

Dial, 3 (April, 1883), 280
Lit World, 14 (March 24, 1883), 90
Nation, 36 (April 5, 1883), 301
SatR, 51 (March 19, 1883), 372-3

"Sir Dominick Ferrand"

See: 10, 12, 1477.1, 1522, 1740, 1804; 2198, VIII; 2205,
2208, 2229,. 2352, 2637, XXIV; 3711

"Sir Edmund Orme"

See: 270, 272.2, 1740, 1804; 2198, VIII; 2205, 2208, 2229,
2352; 2637, XXII; 2637.1, XVII; 3265, 3326, 3711

A SMALL BOY AND OTHERS

1082.1 Brooks, Van Wyck. "A Small Boy and Others," in A Pilgrimage of Henry James. New York: 1972, pp. 1-26.

1083   Colby, F. M. "Henry James's A Small Boy and Others,"
HarperW, 57 (May 3, 1913), 18.

1083.1 Edel, Leon. "The Early Governesses" [A Small Boy and
Others], Henry James: The Treacherous Years, 1895-1901.
Philadelphia, New York: pp. 262-263.

See also: 8, 11, 12, 38, 1924, 2028, 2229, 2352, 2695,
2737, 3010, 3326, 3417, 3536, 3711

Reviews of A Small Boy and Others:

Bookman, 37 (August, 1913), 595-8
Churchman, 107 (May 10, 1913), 610
Dial, 54 (May 1, 1913), 372-4
Independent, 75 (July 3, 1913), 43
Nation, 97 (July 24, 1913), 79-80
NYHTB (July 28, 1962), 10
Sewanee R, 22 (January, 1914), 111-14
Spectator, 110 (May 3, 1913), 757-8
Times, 18 (April 13, 1913), 217
Yale R, n. s., 3 (October, 1913), 186-9

THE SOFT SIDE

Reviews of The Soft Side:

Athenaeum, 3805 (September 29, 1900), 410
Book Buyer, 21 (November, 1900), 299-300

Bookman (London), 19 (October, 1900), 28
Catholic World, 73 (May, 1901), 249
Churchman, 82 (October, 1900), 450
Current Lit, 29 (November, 1900), 626-7
Harper's, 102 (January, 1901), 318-9
Independent, 52 (November 1, 1900), 2638
Lit World, 32 (June 1, 1901), 92-3
Nation, 71 (November 29, 1900), 430
Outlook, 66 (October 13, 1900), 423
Picayune, (October 21, 1900), II, 9
Rev of Revs, 22 (December, 1900), 767
SatR, 90 (October 13, 1900), 464
Times, 5 (October 20, 1900), 717

"The Solution"

See: 9, 10, 1740, 1794, 1804; 2198, VII. 2352; 2637, XXVI;
3536, 3711

"The Special Type"

See: 11, 1740, 1804; 2198, XI; 2637, XXVIII; 2737, 3536,
3689, 3711

THE SPOILS OF POYNTON

1084   Ashmore, Basil. "Henry James on Stage," TLS, 3528 (Oc-
        tober 9, 1969), 1158.
            Reference to September 11 review of James's play Spoils,
        at Mayfair Theatre. Cf., "Commentary," TLS, 3524
        (September 11, 1969), 1,000.

1085   Aubry, G. Jean. Joseph Conrad, Life and Letters. Garden
        City, New York: Doubleday, 1927, I, 201-202.
            Joseph Conrad's appreciative criticism of The Spoils of
        Poynton.

1086   Auchincloss, Louis. Introduction. The Spoils of Poynton,
        and Other Stories. New York: Doubleday, 1971.

1087   Baym, Nina. "Fleda Vetch and the Plot of The Spoils of
        Poynton," PMLA, 84 (January, 1969), 102-111.
            An excellent study. James's Notebook entries, compared
        to the novel, show that James began the story as Mrs.
        Gereth's and that he created Fleda as a minor plotting de-
        vice. She became more important and James made the
        hero fall in love with her.

1088   Bellringer, Alan W. "The Spoils of Poynton: The 'Facts,' "
        EIC, 18 (July, 1968), 357-359.

Cf., John Lucas. "James Intentions: The Spoils of Poynton," EIC, 18 (1968), 107-111.

1089   _____. "The Spoils of Poynton: James's Intentions," EIC, 17 (April, 1967), 238-243.

1090   _____. "The Spoils of Poynton: James's Unintended Involvement," EIC, 16 (April, 1966), 185-200.
Rejoinder by John Lucas, EIC, 16 (1966), 482-489.

1091   Blackmur, R. P., ed. Introduction. The Spoils of Poynton. New York: Dell Publishing Company, 1959.

1092   Broderick, John C. "Nature, Art, and Imagination in The Spoils of Poynton," NCF, 13 (March, 1959), 295-312.
The Spoils is an "esthetic parable."

1093   Butler, John F. Exercises in Literary Understanding. Chicago: Scott-Foresman, 1956, pp. 34-38.

1094   Cary, Joyce. "Experience and Word," in Art and Reality: Ways of the Creative Process. New York: Harper, 1958, pp. 94-98.

1095   "Commentary," TLS, 3524 (September 11, 1969), 1,000.
Cf., Basil Ashmore, TLS, 3528 (October 9, 1969), 1158; Leon Drucker, TLS, 3525 (September 18, 1969), 1027; Robert Manson Myers, TLS, 3529 (October 16, 1969), 1211.

1096   Connolly, Francis X. "Literary Consciousness and Literary Conscience," Thought, 25 (December, 1950), 663-680.

1097   Dankleff, Richard. The Composition, Revisions, Reception, and Reputation of Henry James's "The Spoils of Poynton." Diss. Chicago, 1959.

1098   Drucker, Leon. "Henry James on Stage," TLS, 3525 (September 18, 1969), 1027.
Comment on the dramatization of The Spoils.

1099   Edel, Leon, ed. Introduction. The Bodley Head Henry James. Vol. 4. The Spoils of Poynton. London: Bodley Head, 1967.

1099.1   _____. "The Spoils of Poynton: Houses and Old Things," Henry James: The Treacherous Years, 1895-1901. Philadelphia, New York: 1969, pp.[145-146], 161-164.

1100   Edelstein, Arnold. " 'The Tangle of Life': Levels of Meaning in The Spoils of Poynton," HSL, 2 (1970), 133-150.
A very significant study of the novel.

1101   Fiderer, Gerald. "Henry James's 'Discriminated Occasion,'"
       Crit, 11, ii (1969), 56-69.
           A defense of Fleda Vetch by associating her with Strether
           (The Ambassadors) and with Densher (The Wings of the
           Dove).

1102   Gargano, James W. "The Spoils of Poynton: Action and Re-
       sponsibility," SR, 69 (October-December, 1961), 650-660.
           James intended to show "the complex considerations that
           mass behind a single brave act."

1103   Ghiselin, Brewster, ed. Introduction. The Creative Proc-
       ess: A Symposium. 2nd pr., Berkeley and Los Angeles:
       California U. P., 1954.

1104   Goldsmith, Arnold. "The Maltese Cross as Sign in The
       Spoils of Poynton," Renascence, 16 (Winter, 1964), 73-77.
           The cross is destroyed in the fire, Goldsmith thinks, be-
           cause Fleda was intended "not to have got anything" by
           her sacrifice.

1105   _____. "The Poetry of Names in The Spoils of Poynton,"
       Names, 24 (September, 1966), 134-142.
           Suggests that "Mona" is intended to recall Mona Lisa,
           "Brigstock" prison, and "Vetch" a climbing, twisting plant.

1106   Greene, Philip L. "Point of View in The Spoils of Poynton,"
       NCF, 21 (March, 1967), 359-368.
           A defense of Fleda Vetch as "a reliable reflector" of the
           novel's values. "She is the renouncing sensibility who is
           capable of love."

1107   Hartsock, Mildred E. "A Light Lamp: The Spoils of Poyn-
       ton as Comedy," ES (Anglo-Amer. Supp): (1969), xxix-
       xxxvii.

1108   Heston, Lilla A. "A Study of Point of View in Three Novels
       by Henry James: The Spoils of Poynton, The Wings of the
       Dove, and The Golden Bowl," DA, 26 (Northwestern: 1965),
       3533.

1109   Hunt, Thomas G. "Moral Awareness in The Spoils of Poyn-
       ton," Discourse, 9 (Spring, 1966), 255-262.
           Finds the moral conflict real; Fleda does renounce Owen
           on high moral ground.

1110   Isle, Walter. "The Spoils of Poynton," Experiments in Form:
       Henry James's Novels, 1896-1901. Cambridge: Harvard U.
       P., 1968, pp. 77-119.

1111   Izak, Emily K. "The Composition of The Spoils of Poynton,"
       TSLL, 6 (Winter, 1965), 460-471.
           Inconsistencies result from James's change of plan after

he published the opening chapters.

1112   James, Henry. Preface. "The Spoils of Poynton": The Art
       of the Novel. Richard P. Blackmur, ed. New York: Scrib-
       ner's, 1934.

1113   Lucas, John. "The Spoils of Poynton: James's Intended Un-
       involvement," EIC, 16 (October, 1966), 482-489.

1114   _____. "James's Intentions: The Spoils of Poynton," EIC,
       18 (January, 1968), 107-111.
               Cf., A. W. Bellringer, EIC, 18 (1968), 357-359.

1115   McLean, Robert C. "The Subjective Adventure of Fleda
       Vetch," AL, 36 (March, 1964), 12-30.
               Owen, "who appears to be ineffective and morally weak,
       proves to be the strongest as well as the most humane fig-
       ure in the book."

1116   Myers, Robert Manson. "Henry James on Stage," TLS,
       3529 (October 16, 1969), 1211.
               Has reference to Basil Ashmore's dramatization of The
       Spoils.

1117   Namekata, Akio. "Some Notes on The Spoils of Poynton,"
       SELit [Eng. No.] (1970), 19-35.

1118   Okoshi, Tishiko. "The Spoils of Poynton: Between Reality
       and Art," EngLit (Waseda Univ.), 21 (March, 1962), 34-41.

1118.1 Putt, S. Gorley. "Marriage and Society: The Spoils of
       Poynton,...." Henry James: A Reader's Guide. Ithaca,
       New York, 1966, pp. 239-263.

1119   Quinn, Patrick F. "Morals and Motives in The Spoils of
       Poynton," SR, 62 (Autumn, 1954), 563-577.

1120   Reid, Stephen. "The Source of Moral Passion in The Por-
       trait of a Lady and The Spoils of Poynton," MFS, 12 (Spring,
       1966), 24-43.

1121   Roper, Alan H. "The Moral and Metaphorical Meaning of
       The Spoils of Poynton," AL, 32 (May, 1960), 182-196.

1122   Rosenbaum, Stanford Patrick. "Henry James and Creativity:
       'The Logic of the Particular Case,' " Criticism, 8 (Winter,
       1966), 44-52.
               Notes the discrepancies between James's notebook entries
       about The Spoils of Poynton and the Preface written ten
       years after the first publication of the story.

1123   _____. "The Spoils of Poynton," TLS, (June 26, 1959),
       385.

On the text of the early editions.

1124 _____. "The Spoils of Poynton: Revisions and Editions,"
SB, 19 (1966), 161-174.
Collation of the four texts from 1896 to 1908 and comment
on the revisions.

1125 _____. "Studies for Definitive Edition of Henry James's
The Spoils of Poynton," DA, 21 (Cornell: 1961), 3792.

1126 Salisbury, Howard E. "Wish-Fulfillment as Moral Crisis in
the Fiction of Henry James," DA, 24 (Wash. Univ.: 1963),
304.
Fleda in The Spoils.

1126.1 Samuels, Charles Thomas. "The Joys of Renunciation"
[The Spoils of Poynton], The Ambiguity of Henry James.
Urbana: Illinois U. P., 1971, pp. 61-88.

1127 Schneider, Daniel J. "The 'Full Ironic Truth' in The Spoils
of Poynton," ConnR, 2, ii (April, 1969), 50-66.
"The whole ironic truth about Fleda is that she is the
slave of her insatiable contradictory desires: she wants,
finally, everything, and everything on her own terms...."

1128 Smith, Logan Pearsall. "Saved from the Salvage," Horizon,
7 (March, 1943), 154-155.

1129 Snow, Lotus. " 'A Story of Cabinets and Chairs and Tables':
Images of Morality in The Spoils of Poynton and The Golden
Bowl," ELH, 30 (December, 1963), 413-435.
A comparison of the two novels, showing how James's im-
agery demonstrates "the absolute union of art and moral-
ity."

1130 Spender, Stephen. "A World Where the Victor Belonged to
the Spoils," NYTBR (March 12, 1944), 3.
Critical opinion is divided as to whether Fleda's action in
sending Owen back to Mona is an affirmation or a denial.

1131 Stein, William Bysshe. "The Method at the Heart of Madness: The Spoils of Poynton," MFS, 14 (Summer, 1968),
187-202.
Fleda is one whose "reforms, protests, and rebellions
... devolve into pitiably comic grimaces, perversions of
the heroic ideal...." "Yet ... she brings a temporary,
limited perfection" to her life.

1132 Tilley, Winthrop. "Fleda Vetch and Ellen Brown, or, Henry
James and the Soap Opera," WHR, 10 (Spring, 1956), 175-
180.

1133 Tintner, Adeline R. " 'The Old Things': Balzac's Le Curé

de Tours and James's The Spoils of Poynton," NCF, 26
(1971-72), 436-455.
　　　Compares the two works.

1134 　　　　　　. "The Spoils of Henry James," PMLA, 61 (March,
1946), 239-251.
　　　James's use of symbols and metaphors principally in The
　　　Spoils of Poynton.

1135 Volpe, Edmond L. "The Spoils of Art," MLN, 74 (November, 1959), 601-608.
　　　Characterization of Fleda Vetch is a failure of art.

1136 Wiesenfarth, Joseph. Henry James and the Dramatic Analogy. New York: Fordham University Press, 1963.

1137 Willey, Frederick. "The Free Spirit and the Clever Agent
in Henry James," SoR, 2 (Spring, 1966), 315-328.
　　　Fleda is one who has "acuteness and intensity, reflexion
　　　and passion." Owen is "not his own man and therefore
　　　cannot become hers."

Reviews of The Spoils of Poynton [Published originally as Old
Things]:

　　　Athenaeum, 3619 (March 6, 1897), 308-9
　　　Book Buyer, 14 (April, 1897), 303-5
　　　Bookman (NY), 5 (May, 1897), 258-9; (London) 12 (May,
　　　　　1897), 42-3
　　　Book News, 15 (April, 1897), 389
　　　Critic, 30 (May 1, 1897), 301
　　　Dial, 22 (May 16, 1897), 311
　　　Independent, 49 (July 29, 1897), 980
　　　Lit Rev, 1 (March 15, 1897), 41
　　　Lit World, 28 (April 17, 1897), 126-7
　　　Nation, 65 (July 1, 1897), 18
　　　Outlook, 55 (February 27, 1897), 610
　　　Public Opinion, 22 (March 11, 1897), 312
　　　Quarterly Rev, 198 (October, 1903, 358
　　　Spec, 78 (February 27, 1897), 309
　　　Times, 2 (February 20, 1897), 1

"Still Waters"

1138 McElderry, B. R. "The Uncollected Stories of Henry
James," AL, 21 (1949), 279-291, especially 286-287.

See also: 2695

"The Story in It"

See: 11, 38, 270, 272.2, 1740, 1794; 2198, XI; 2229,
2352, 2363, 2380, 2581; 2637, XXIII; 2637.1, XVIII; 2737,
2916, 2918, 3080.1, 3536, 3706, 3711

"The Story of a Masterpiece"

1139   Fish, Charles K. "Indirection, Irony, and the Two Endings
of James's 'The Story of a Masterpiece,' " MP, 62 (February, 1965), 241-243.

1139.1 Martineau, Barbara. "Portraits Are Murdered in the Short
Fiction of Henry James," JNT, 2 (1972), 16-25.
"The Story of a Masterpiece" is one of the stories stud-
ied.

1139.2 McElderry, B. R. "The Uncollected Stories of Henry
James," AL, 21 (1949), 279-291, especially 283-284.

See also: 8, 38, 1980, 2028; 2198, I; 2352, 2363, 2695,
2701, 2773, 2948, 3323, 3326, 3536, 3689, 3710, 3711

Reviews of "The Story of a Masterpiece":

Nation, 6 (January 30, 1868), 94; 6 (May 28, 1868), 434

"The Story of a Year"

1139.3 Samuels, Charles Thomas. "The Joys of Renunciation"--
"The Story of a Year," The Ambiguity of Henry James. Urbana: Illinois U. P., 1971, pp. 61-88.

See: 8, 38, 1794, 1885, 2028; 2198, I; 2352, 2380, 2382,
2560, 2695, 2701, 2773, 2917, 2948, 3265, 3417, 3536

"The Sweetheart of M. Briseux"

See: 1794, 1804, 2198, III; 2352, 2695, 3326, 3536, 3689,
3711

TALES OF THREE CITIES

Reviews:

Athenaeum, 2981 (December 13, 1884), 767
Critic, n. s., 5 (December 27, 1884), 304
Dial (December, 1884), 206-7

Harper's, 70 (February, 1885), 492-3
Independent, 36 (November 27, 1884), 154
Lippincott's, 35 (February, 1885), 215-6
Lit World, 15 (September 20, 1884), 308-9
Nation, 39 (November 20, 1884), 442
Overland Mo, 2d. S, 5 (January, 1885), 108-9

TENANTS - See THEATRICALS

TERMINATIONS

1139.4 Roselli, Daniel N.   "Max Beerbohm's Unpublished Parody of
       Henry James," RES, 22 (1971), 61-63.
          Discussion of a "pencilled in" parody of James at an un-
          known date in Beerbohm's copy of James's Terminations.

Reviews of Terminations:

Athenaeum, 3529 (June 15, 1895), 769-70
Atlantic, 76 (October, 1895), 565
Critic, 27 (August 3, 1895), 67-8
HarperW, 39 (July 27, 1895), 701
HarperM, 91, Sup 3 (1895), 648
LitRev, 26 (July 13, 1895), 218
Nation, 41 (July 25, 1895), 63
Spec, 75 (September 28, 1895), 405

THEATRICALS

Theatricals: First Series: Two Comedies - "Disengaged" and
"Tenants":

Review of "Disengaged":
Forum, 41 (April, 1909), 342-3
Putnam's, 6 (May, 1909), 254

"Tenants"

1139.5 Thorberg, Raymond.   " 'Flavien,' 'Tenants' and The Portrait
       of a Lady," SAB, 34 (1969), 10-13.

Review of "Tenants":
Critic, 26 (ns 23) (January 12, 1895), 38

"Disengaged" and "Tenants" -

Reviews:
Athenaeum, 104 (November 17, 1894), 685
HarperM, 90, Sup 1 (March, 1895), 654
Nation, 58 (June 28, 1894), 491

Theatricals, 2nd Series:

"Album" and "Reprobate"

Reviews:
Athenaeum, 105 (January 19, 1895), 93
Bookman (London), 7 (January 1895), 120-1
Critic, 29 (ns 26) (November 28, 1896), 340-1
HarperM, 90, Sup, 1 (March, 1895), 654
Nation, 60 (January 3, 1895), 18

"Theodolinde" - See "Rose-Agathe"

"The Third Person"

See: 11, 1740, 1794, 1804; 2198, XI; 2205, 2208, 2229,
2363, 2637, XXVII; 3326, 3427, 3689, 3711

"The Tone of Time"

1139.6 Millett, Fred B. Reading Fiction: A Method of Analysis
with Selections for Study. New York: Harpers, 1950, pp.
199-200.

See also: 11, 1740, 1804, 1980; 2198, XI; 2229, 2258, 2352,
2363, 2380, 2382, 2581; 2637, XXVII; 2737, 3689, 3711

"A Tragedy of Error"

1140   Edel, Leon. "Prefatory Note" [to] 'A Tragedy of Error':
James's First Story," NEQ, 29 (September, 1956), 291-317.
This story is authenticated as James's earliest-known
work of fiction.

1141   _____. Prefatory Note. "A Tragedy of Error": James's
First Story. Brunswick, Me., 1956.

1142   Gale, Robert L. "A Note on Henry James's First Story,"
MLN, 72 (February, 1957), 103-107.
Added proof of authenticity may be found by comparison of
"figurative and near-figurative language in the story" with
that of James's later fiction.

See also: 8; 2198, I; 2352, 2363, 2380, 2382, 3536, 3711

THE TRAGIC MUSE

1142.1 Baker, Robert S. "Gabriel Nash's 'House of Strange Idols':
Aestheticism in The Tragic Muse," TSLL, 15 (Spring, 1973),
149-166.

1143   Bellringer, Alan W. "The Tragic Muse: The Objective Center," JAmS, 4 (July, 1970), 73-89.

1144   Blackmur, R. P. Introduction. The Tragic Muse. New
York: Dell Publishing Co., 1961.

1145   Bogan, Louise. "James on a Revolutionary Theme," Nation,
146 (April 23, 1938), 471-474.

1146   Brown, Ivor. "The Tragic Muse--Adapted for dramatization
by Hubert Griffith from the Novel of Henry James," SatR,
146 (July 7, 1928), 14.

1147   Cargill, Oscar. "Gabriel Nash--Somewhat Less than Angel?"
NCF, 14 (December, 1959), 231-239.
Cf., Rebuttal by Lyall Powers. "Mr. James's Aesthetic
Mr. Nash--Again," NCF, 13 (1959), 341-349.

1148   _____. "Mr. James's Aesthetic Mr. Nash," NCF, 12
(December, 1957), 171-187.
Gabriel Nash "equals" Oscar Wilde.

1149   Edel, Leon. Introduction. The Tragic Muse. New York:
Harper, 1960.

1150   Falk, Robert. "The Tragic Muse: Henry James's Loosest,
Baggiest Monster?" in Themes and Directions in American
Literature, Essays in Honor of Leon Howard. Ray B.
Browne and Donald Pizer, eds. Lafayette, Ind.: Purdue
University Studies, 1969, pp. 148-162.

1151   Frank, Joseph. The Widening Gyre. New Brunswick, New
Jersey: Rutgers U. P., 1963, p. 157.

1151.1 Gordon, D. J., and John Stokes. "The Reference of The
Tragic Muse," in The Air of Reality. John Goode, ed. London: Methuen, 1972, pp. 81-167.

1152   Grewal, Om P. "Henry James and the Ideology of Culture:
A Critical Study of The Bostonians, The Princess Casamassima and The Tragic Muse. DAI, 30 (Rochester: 1970),
5444A-45A.

1153   Hall, William F. "Gabriel Nash: 'Famous Centre' of The
Tragic Muse," NCF, 21 (September, 1966), 167-184.
Sees Nash as the prime mover and the representative of

James's ideal artistic consciousness.

1154   James, Henry.   Preface to The Tragic Muse, in The Art of
        the Novel: Critical Prefaces.   New York: Scribner, 1934,
        pp. 79-97.

1155   Kimmey, John L.   "The Tragic Muse and Its Forerunners,"
        AL, 41 (January, 1970), 518-531.
        The structure of The Tragic Muse gives it a "bright ad-
        vantage" over The Bostonians and The Princess Casamas-
        sima.

1156   Lockridge, Ernest H.   "A Vision of Art: Henry James's
        The Tragic Muse," MFS, 12 (Spring, 1966), 83-92.
        Asserts that in this novel art is represented as an ideal
        pursuit, greater than politics or love, comparable to
        Yeats's "Byzantium."

1157   Monteiro, George.   "The Manuscript of The Tragic Muse,"
        AN&Q, 1 (January, 1963), 68-69.
        An exchange of letters between Hay and James in 1890 in-
        dicates that at Hay's request the manuscript of The Tragic
        Muse was sent to him.   However, the manuscript was not
        among Hay's papers.

1158   Murakami, Fujio.   "The Aesthete in The Tragic Muse,"
        JimK, 12 (June, 1961), 96-108.

1159   Powers, Lyall.   "Mr. James's Aesthetic Mr. Nash--Again,"
        NCF, 13 (March, 1959), 341-349.
        Cf., Oscar Cargill.   "Gabriel Nash--Somewhat Less than
        Angel," NCF, 14 (1959), 231-239.

1160   _____.   "James's The Tragic Muse: Ave atque Vale,"
        PMLA, 73 (June, 1958), 270-274.
        The Tragic Muse is the metaphorical expression of
        "James's attitude on bidding farewell to the novel and hail
        to the theater."

1160.1 Putt, S. Gorley.   " 'Something about Art,' The Tragic Muse,
        Tales of the Artistic Life," in Henry James: A Reader's
        Guide.   Ithaca, New York: 1966, pp. 201-238.

1161   Robson, W. W.   "Henry James's The Tragic Muse," Man-
        drake, 2 (Autumn-Winter, 1954-1955), 281-295.
        Sees the weakness in The Tragic Muse as the lack of any
        deep psychological interest.

1161.1 Schneider, Daniel J.   "Theme of Freedom in James's The
        Tragic Muse," ConnR, 7 (April 1974), 5-15.

1162   Snow, Lotus.   " 'The Prose and the Modesty of the Matter':
        James's Imagery for the Artist in Roderick Hudson and The

Tragic Muse," MFS, 12 (Spring, 1966), 61-82.

1163   Wallace, Ronald. "Gabriel Nash: Henry James's Comic
        Spirit," NCF, 28 (September, 1973), 220-224.

Reviews of The Tragic Muse:

        Athenaeum, 3274 (July 26, 1890), 124
        Atlantic, 66 (September, 1890), 419-22
        Book Buyer, 7 (August, 1890), 289-9
        Chautauquan, 11 (August, 1890), 649
        Christian Union, 41 (June 26, 1890), 913
        Churchman, 62 (July 26, 1890), 109
        Cosmopolitan, 11 (July, 1891), 381
        Cottage Hearth, 16 (September, 1890), 294
        Critic, 16 (ns 13) (May 17, 1890), 250; 17 (ns 14) (Aug 2,
            1890), 55
        Dial, 11 (August, 1890), 92-3
        Epoch, 8 (September 5, 1890), 77
        Godey's 121 (August, 1890), 172
        Harper's, 81 (September, 1890), 639-41
        Lippincott's, 46 (September, 1890), 423
        Lit World, 21 (July, 1890), 231-2
        Nation, 51 (December 25, 1890), 505-5
        Overland, 2d S, 16 (October, 1890), 437
        Public Opinion, 9 (September, 1890), 539
        SatR, 70 (August 2, 1890), 141
        Spec, 65 (September 27, 1890), 409-10

                    TRANSATLANTIC SKETCHES

Reviews:

        Atlantic, 36 (July, 1875), 113-5
        Christian Union, 12 (October 27, 1875), 344
        Harper's, 51 (August, 1875), 452
        Independent, 27 (May 6, 1875), 9
        Nation, 20 (June 24, 1875), 425-7
        Scribner's, 10 (July, 1875), 389-90
        Unitarian Rev, 4 (July, 1875), 109

                    "Travelling Companions"

See: 1794, 1798, 1871; 2198, II; 2695, 2773, 2793, 3354

Review: NewRep, 19 (July 30, 1919), 422

                    "The Tree of Knowledge"

1164   Bellman, Samuel Irving. "Henry James's 'The Tree of

Knowledge': A Biblical Parallel," SSF, 1 (Spring, 1964), 226-228.
Suggests the story may be a parody of Christ's relation to Peter. The story may also be linked to James's frequent emphasis on artistic failure.

1165   Truss, Tom J., Jr. "Anti-Christian Myth in James's 'The Tree of Knowledge,' " UMSE, 6 (1965), 1-4.

See also, 270, 652, 1740, 2149; 2198, XI; 2258, 2363, 2581, 2637, XXI; 2637.1, XVI

THE TURN OF THE SCREW

1166   Aldrich, C. Knight. "Another Twist to The Turn of the Screw," MFS, 13 (Summer, 1967), 167-178.
Concludes that the story "is a tragedy about an evil older woman who drove an unstable younger woman completely out of her mind, and whose jealousy was the indirect cause of a little boy's death."

1167   Allott, Miriam. "Mrs. Gaskell's 'The Old Nurse's Story': A Link Between Wuthering Heights and The Turn of the Screw," N&Q, n. s., 8 (March, 1961), 101-102.

1168   Anderson, Quentin. "The American Henry James," DA, 14 (Columbia: 1954), 115-116.
Suggests various approaches to a study of The Turn of the Screw.

1169   Andreas, Osborn. Henry James and the Expanding Horizon. Seattle: University of Washington Press, 1948, pp. 46-47.

1170   Archibald, William. The Innocents: A New Play ... Based on "The Turn of the Screw." New York: Coward-McCann, Inc., 1950, pp. x, 78.

1171   _____. "The Quick and the Dead," ThA, 34 (June, 1950), 22-23, 92-93.
The author explains some of the changes he made in the play.

1172   Arnavon, Cyrille. Les Lettres Américaines Devant La Critique Française. Paris: Societe d'edition des belles lettres, 1951, p. 92.

1173   Arvin, Newton. "Henry James and the Almighty Dollar," H&H, 7 (April-May, 1934), 434-443.

1174   Aswell, E. Duncan. "Reflections of a Governess-Image and Distortion in The Turn of the Screw," NCF, 23 (June, 1968), 49-63.

Declares that the "inability" of the governess "to distin-
guish growth from corruption makes her the agent of the
very evil she dedicates herself to combating."

1175   Atkinson, Brooks. "First Night at the Theatre," NYT, 99
(February 2, 1950), 30.

1176   Baker, Ernest A. The History of the English Novel: The
Day Before Yesterday. London: H. F. & G. Witherby,
Ltd., 1938, IX, 254-255.

1177   Ballorain, Rolande. " 'The Turn of the Screw'--L'adulte et
l'enfant, ou les deux regards," EA, 22 (July-September,
1969), 250-258.
Shows how central the story is to an understanding of
James's other work.

1178   Bangs, John Kendrick. "The Involvular Club, or, The Return of the Screw," in The Antic Muse: American Writers
in Parody. R. P. Falk, ed. New York: Grove Press,
1955, pp. 136-141.

1179   Barnes, Howard. NYTCR (1950), 11 (February 6, 1950),
360.

1180   Barzun, Jacques. "Henry James, Melodramatist," KR, 5
(Autumn, 1943), 508-521. Repr., in The Question of Henry
James. F. W. Dupee, ed. New York: 1945, p. 261.

1181   Beach, Joseph Warren. The Twentieth Century Novel. New
York: The Century Company, 1932, pp. 208-209, passim.

1182   Beckley, Paul V. "The New Movie: 'The Innocents,' "
NYHT (December 26, 1961), 9.

1183   Bedford, Sybille. "Fantasy without Whimsy," SatR, 43 (November, 1960), 29.

1184   Beer, Thomas. "Henry James and Stephen Crane," in The
Question of Henry James. F. W. Dupee, ed. New York:
Henry Holt, 1945, p. 107.

1185   Beerbohm, Max. "The Mote in the Middle Distance," in A
Christmas Garland. New York: Oxford University Press,
1936, pp. 3-10. Repr., in The Question of Henry James,
Dupee, ed., pp. 40-43.
A parody.

1186   Beers, Henry A. "Fifty Years of Hawthorne," YR, 4 #2
(January, 1915), 307.

1187   Behrman, S. N. "Conversation with Max," NY, 36 (February 27, 1960), 88-89.

1188   Benson, E. F. As We Were: A Victorian Peep Show.
        London: Longmans, Green and Co., 1930, pp. 278-279.
        Benson was present during James's visit to Addington in
        January 1895, the occasion on which the Archbishop was
        supposed to have related the anecdote related to the sub-
        sequent story.

1189   Berland, Alwyn. "The Complex Fate," SR, 61 (Spring,
        1953), 326.

1190   Berner, Robert L. "Douglas in The Turn of the Screw,"
        EN, 3 (Winter, 1968-1969), 3-7.
        A defense of the "non-apparitionist" reading emphasizing
        the importance of the introductory comments by Douglas.

1191   Bewley, Marius. "Appearance and Reality in Henry James,"
        Scrutiny, 17 (Summer, 1950), 104, 106-107, 109-111.

1192   _____. "Correspondence: The Relation between William
        and Henry James," Scrutiny, 17 (March, 1951), 331-334.

1193   _____. "Maisie, Miles and Flora, the Jamesian Inno-
        cents: A Rejoinder," Scrutiny, 17 (Autumn, 1950), 255-263.
        A study of "the dissolution of the ties between appearance
        and reality which seems to threaten in many of James's
        stories."

1194   _____. The Complex Fate. New York: Grove Press,
        1954, pp. 132-143.

1195   Birkhead, Edith. The Tale of Terror. New York: E. P.
        Dutton & Co., 1921, p. 196.

1196   Blackmur, Richard P. "The Critical Prefaces," H&H, 7
        (April-May, 1934), 459.

1197   _____. "The Sphinx and the Housecat," Accent, 6 (Aut-
        umn, 1945), 60-63.
        On ambiguity in The Turn of the Screw.

1198   Bontly, Thomas J. "Henry James's 'General Vision of
        Evil' in The Turn of the Screw," SEL, 9 (1969), 721-735.
        The Story can be examined "as a parable in which the
        fantasy of one level of meaning ironically reveals the mor-
        al and psychological reality of another level of meaning."

1199   "Books and Authors," Outlook, 60 (October 29, 1898), 536-
        544.

1200   Booth, Wayne. "The Turn of the Screw as Puzzle," The
        Rhetoric of Fiction. Chicago: University of Chicago Press,
        1961, pp. 311-323, passim.

1201   Bosanquet, Theodora. "Henry James," FnR, 107 (June,
        1917), 996.

1202   Bowen, Elizabeth. English Novelists. London: William
        Collins, 1946, p. 42.

1203   Brewster, Dorothy. Modern Fiction. New York: Columbia
        University Press, 1935, p. 403.

1204   Britten, Benjamin. The Turn of the Screw, Opera in Two
        Acts. Libretto by Myfanwy Piper, adapted from the story by
        Henry James. London; New York: Boosey and Hawkes,
        1955.

1205   Bronson, Walter C. A History of American Literature.
        New York: D. C. Heath & Co., 1919, pp. 303-304.

1206   Broun, Heywood. Introduction. The Turn of the Screw
        [and] The Lesson of the Master. New York: Modern Library,
        1930, 1957.

1207   Brown, John Mason. "Seeing Things," SatR, (February 25,
        1950), 32-36.

1207.1 Byers, John R., Jr. " 'The Turn of the Screw': A Hellish
        Point of View," MarkR, 3 (1971), 101-104.
            Views the governess as herself an evil spirit and able to
            do with humans whatever she liked.

1208   Cameron, Kate. "Criterion Presents Classic Ghost Story,"
        DailyN (New York), (December 26, 1961), 48.

1209   Cargill, Oscar. "Henry James as Freudian Pioneer," ChiR,
        10 (Summer, 1956), 13-29.

1210   _____. "The Turn of the Screw and Alice James," PMLA,
        78 (June, 1963), 238-249. Repr., as Afterword in Toward
        a Pluralistic Criticism. Carbondale: Southern Illinois U. P.,
        1965, pp. 95-117.
            A revised version of "Henry James as Freudian Pioneer."

1210.1 Carnell, Corbin S. Notes and Exercises. Two Short Nov-
        els. Englewood Cliffs, New Jersey: Prentice-Hall, 1963.

1211   Cary, Elisabeth Luther. "Henry James," Scribner's, 36
        (October, 1904), 394-400.

1212   Castellanos, Rosario. "El fin de la inocencia," RevUM, 7
        (July, 1963), 4-7.

1213   Chapman, John. NYTCR, 11, #4 (February 6, 1950), 359.

1214   Chase, Richard. The American Novel and Its Tradition.

Garden City, New York: Doubleday, 1957, pp. 237-241.

1215   Chesterton, G. K. The Victorian Age in Literature. Lon-
        don: Oxford University Press, 1955, p. 141.

1216   Chislett, William, Jr. Moderns and Near-Moderns. New
        York: The Grafton Press, 1928, pp. 40, 61.

1216.1 "Clayton's 'The Innocents,' " NYT (December 24, 1961), 9.

1217   Clurman, Harold. "Theatre: Change of Mood," NewRep,
        122 (February 27, 1950), 20-21.

1217.1 Cole, Robert C. "These Strange Relations: Henry James'
        The Turn of the Screw," DAI, 32 (Lehigh: 1971), 382A.

1218   Coleman, J. "The Innocents," NSt, 62 (December, 1961),
        854.

1219   Coleman, Robert. NYTCR, 11, iv (February 6, 1950), 360.

1220   Collins, Carvel. "James' The Turn of the Screw," Expl,
        13 (June, 1955), Item 49.
        An additional ambiguity: the possibility that Douglas, who
        owns the governess's manuscript, is little Miles grown
        up.

1221   Cook, Alton. "Oldtime Ghost Tale, NYWT (December 26,
        1961), 15.

1222   Costello, Donald P. "The Structure of The Turn of the
        Screw," MLN, 75 (April, 1960), 312-321.
        James built the story around thirteen sequences in which
        the governess is the central figure. She becomes the
        "magnetic focus" of the novel.

1223   Cowley, Malcolm. "The Return of Henry James," NewRep,
        112 (January 22, 1945), 121-122.

1224   Cranfill, Thomas, and Robert Clark, Jr. An Anatomy of
        "The Turn of the Screw." Austin: University of Texas
        Press, 1965.
        A significant survey of criticism. Concludes that the
        children are victims of the governess' harassment, stim-
        ulated by her hallucinations.

1225   _____. "Caste in James's The Turn of the Screw,"
        TSLL, 5 (Summer, 1963), 189-198.
        The authors show that ideas of caste, considered by
        James for a story (Notebooks, Oct. 18, 1895), have a
        bearing on the interpretation of statements by the govern-
        ess and by Mrs. Grose.

1226   _____. "James's Revisions of The Turn of the Screw,"
NCF, 19 (March, 1965), 394-398.
      James's revisions improve the story's clarity, concise-
      ness, and strength, and also increase the sense of horror
      in the governess's reactions.

1227   _____. "The Provocativeness of The Turn of the Screw,"
TSLL, 12 (Spring, 1970), 93-100.
      A description of the popularity of the story.

1228   Critic, 33 (December, 1898), 523-524.

1229   Crowl, Susan. "Aesthetic Allegory in The Turn of the
Screw," Novel, 4 (Winter, 1971), 107-122.
      An analysis of the ties between the story and James's lit-
      erary career at the time of its composition so that "per-
      haps fartherest in of the nest of forms and coiled ironies
      of ... [the story] is James's own confessed creed of the
      symbolic reach of style beyond the grip of passion or of
      doubt, and his pity of the cost of that conversion."

1229.1   _____. "The Beholder's Eye: Romantic and Critical Per-
spective Through Style in James's The Turn of the Screw,
The Wings of the Dove, and The Golden Bowl." DAI, 31
(Indiana: 1970), 5357A.

1230   Crowther, Bosley. "Screen: 'The Innocents,' " NYT (December 26, 1961), 15.

1230.1 Daiches, David. "Sensibility and Technique (Preface to a
Critique)," KR, 5 (Autumn, 1943), 569-579.
      Rejects Wilson's interpretation.

1231   Davis, Douglas M. "The Turn of the Screw Controversey:
Its Implications for the Modern Critic and Teacher," GSE, 2
(Winter, 1959), 7-11.
      An analysis of criticism and James's comments to illus-
      trate the dangers of the "inexorable demand for cleverness
      in explication."

1232   De Bellis, Jack. "Andrew Lytle's A Name for Evil: A
Transformation of The Turn of the Screw," Crit, 8 (Spring-
Summer, 1966), 26-40.

1233   De Blois, Frank. "A Part for Miss Bergman," TVG, 7,
#42 (October 17, 1959), 17-19.

1234   Demuth, Charles. Charles Demuth. A. E. Gallatin, ed.
New York: Rudge, 1927.
      Contains Demuth's sketches which illustrate Edna Kenton's
      article, "Henry James to the Ruminant Reader: The Turn
      of the Screw," Arts, 6 (1924), 245-255.

1235   Dent, A. "The Innocents," LondN, 239 (December 9, 1961),
       1030.

1236   Derleth, August. Writing Fiction. Boston: The Writer,
       Inc., 1946, pp. 101, 114.

1237   De Voto, Bernard. The World of Fiction. Boston: Hough-
       ton Mifflin Co., 1950, pp. 213-214.

1238   Dickinson, Thomas H. The Making of American Literature.
       New York: The Century Co., 1932, p. 585.

1239   Dolmatch, Theodore B. "Edmund Wilson as Literary Critic,"
       UKCR, 17 (Spring, 1951), 213-219.

1240   Domaniecki, Hildegard. "Complementary Terms in The Turn
       of the Screw: The Straight Turning," JA, 10 (1965), 206-
       214.
          Regards the terms "straight" and "turn" as consistently
          symbolic in the story.

1241   _____. "Die Daumenschrauben der Erziehung: Eine Inter-
       pretation der short story 'The Turn of the Screw,' " TuK, 15/
       16 (1967), 44-61.

1242   Dove, George N. "The 'Haunted Personality' in Henry
       James," TSL, 3 (1958), 99-106.
          A study of "haunted personalities" in six other short sto-
          ries of James may be an aid to analysis of the governess.

1243   Duncan-Jones, E. E. "Some Sources of Chance," RES, 20
       (November, 1969), 468-471.
          Suggests that the story of Flora de Barral and her govern-
          ess is reminiscent of The Turn of the Screw.

1244   Dyne, Michael. The Others. National Broadcasting Company
       Matinee Theatre. (February 15, 1957).
          A dramatization of The Turn of the Screw.

1245   Edel, Leon. "Letters to the Editors," TLS, 2458 (March 12,
       1949), 169.

1246   _____. Prefatory Note to "A Pre-Freudian Reading of
       The Turn of the Screw," by Harold C. Goddards, NCF, 12
       (1957), 2.

1247   Efron, Arthur. "Spilka on The Turn of the Screw," Paunch,
       17 (January 10, 1964), 13-15.
          Cf., Mark Spilka. "Turning the Freudian Screw: How Not
          to Do It," L&P, 13 (1963), 105-111.

1248   Egan, Maurice Francis. "The Revelation of an Artist in Lit-
       erature," CathW, 111 (June, 1920), 293.

1249   Elton, Oliver. Modern Studies. London: Edward Arnold,
        1907, pp. 255-256.

1250   Evans, Oliver. "James's Air of Evil: The Turn of the
        Screw," PR, 16 (February, 1949), 175-187. Repr., in A
        Casebook on Henry James's "The Turn of the Screw." Ger-
        ald Willen, ed. New York: 1960, pp. 201-211.
            The ghosts are real ghosts, and the fundamental theme is
            that of appearance versus reality.

1250.1 "Evil Emanations," Time, 79 (January 5, 1962), 59.

1251   Fadiman, Clifton, ed. Introduction. The Short Stories of
        Henry James. New York: Random House, 1945.

1252   _____. "The Revival of Interest in Henry James,"
        NYHTBR, 21 (January 14, 1945), 1-2.

1253   Fagin, Nathan B. "Another Reading of The Turn of the
        Screw," MLN, 56 (March, 1941), 196-202. Repr., in A
        Casebook on "The Turn of the Screw." Gerald Willen, ed.
        New York: 1960, pp. 154-159.

1254   Falk, Robert P., ed. "A Few New Turns of the Screw,"
        in American Literature in Parody: A Collection of Parody,
        Satire, and Literary Burlesque of American Writers, Past
        and Present. New York: Twayne Publishers, 1955, pp.
        127-145.

1255   _____. "Henry James and the 'Age of Innocence,'"
        NCF, 7 (December, 1952), 171-188.

1256   Fay, Gerard. "The Innocents," Spec, 6472 (July 11, 1952),
        65.

1257   Feinstein, Herbert. "Two Pairs of Gloves: Mark Twain
        and Henry James," AI, 17 (Winter, 1960), 349-387.
            The glove symbol in Innocents Abroad and The Turn of
            the Screw.

1258   Feuerlicht, Ignace. "'Erlkönig' and The Turn of the Screw,"
        JEGP, 58 (January, 1959), 68-74.
            Parallels between Goethe's ballad and James's story.

1259   Fiedler, Leslie A. No! In Thunder. Boston: Beacon
        Press, 1960, p. 286.

1260   _____. "The Profanation of the Child," NewL, 41 (June
        23, 1958), 26-29.
            Provides a list of fictional children, some of which are
            "objects of ambiguous adult desire.... Other children,
            descending from The Turn of the Screw, are frankly 'in-
            struments of the diabolic'...."

1261   Firebaugh, Joseph J.   "Inadequacy in Eden: Knowledge and
        The Turn of the Screw," MFS, 3 (Spring, 1957), 57-63.
        Repr. , in A Casebook on "The Turn of the Screw." Gerald
        Willen, ed.   New York: 1969, pp. 291-297.
        Denial of knowledge is a major theme.

1261. 1 Fitzpatrick, Kathleen Elizabeth.   "Notes on Henry James and
        'The Turn of the Screw,' " Meanjin, 9 (Summer, 1950), 275-
        278.

1262   Follett, Wilson.   "Henry James and the Untold Story," Dial,
        63 (December 6, 1917), 579-581.

1263   _____. The Modern Novel. New York: Alfred A. Knopf,
        1923, pp. 306, 315.

1264   Ford, Ford Madox.   "The Master," LonMerc, 33 (November,
        1935), 46-52.

1265   _____. "Techniques," SoR, 1 (July, 1935), 22, 31.

1266   Fraser, John.   "The Turn of the Screw Again," MwQ, 7
        (July, 1966), 327-336.
        Points out the "peculiarly American nature" of the govern-
        ess.

1267   Freeman, John.   The Moderns. London: Robert Scott, 1916,
        p. 228.

1268   Gabriel, Gilbert W.   "New Plays on Broadway," Cue, (Feb-
        ruary, 1950), 18.

1269   Gale, Robert L.   "Art Imagery in Henry James's Fiction,"
        AL, 29 (March, 1957), 47-63.

1270   _____. The Caught Image: Figurative Language in the
        Fiction of Henry James. Chapel Hill: University of North
        Carolina Press, 1954, pp. 221-222, passim.

1271   _____. Plots and Characters in the Fiction of
        Henry James. Hamden, Conn. : Archon Books, 1965, pp.
        83-84, passim.

1272   Gargano, James W.   "The Turn of the Screw," WHR, 15
        (Spring, 1961), 173-179.
        James's construction of the story demonstrates the "author-
        ity" of the governess and the accuracy of her account.

1273   Garland, Robert.   NYTCR, 11 #4 (February 6, 1950), 361.

1274   Geismar, Maxwell.   Writers in Crisis. Boston: Houghton
        Mifflin Co. , 1942, p. 172.

1274.1 Genda, Shuighi, ed. <u>Neji no Kaiten eno Apurochi</u> (Studies of
'The Turn of the Screw'). Tokyo Bunri-Shoin, 1970, p. 88.

1275   Gerould, Gordon Hall. <u>The Patterns of English and American Fiction</u>. Boston: Little, Brown & Co., 1942, p. 444.

1276   Gibbs, Wolcott. NY, 25 #51 (February 11, 1950), 44.

1277   Gilbert, Justin. " 'The Innocents' Lacks Impact," Mirror
(December 26, 1961), 21.

1278   Girling, H. K. "The Strange Case of Dr. James and Mr.
Stevenson," WascanaR, 3, #1 (1968), 65-76.
       Jekyll's fate "prophesies" that the "brute force of a pas-
       sionate story" is fiction's glory. James's answer may
       well be <u>The Turn of the Screw</u>.

1279   Goddard, Harold C. "A Pre-Freudian Reading of <u>The Turn
of the Screw</u>," NCF, 12 (June, 1957), 1-36. Repr., in <u>A
Casebook on Henry James's "The Turn of the Screw."</u> Gerald Willen, ed., 1969, pp. 244-272; <u>Twentieth-Century Inter-
pretations</u>. Jane Tompkins, ed. Englewood Cliffs, N. J.,
Prentice-Hall, 1970, pp. 60-87.
       Goddard argues that the governess reveals her insanity,
       forces the housekeeper to believe her hallucinations, and
       causes the suffering of the children.

1280   Gosse, Edmund. <u>Aspects and Impressions</u>. London: Cassell and Company, Ltd., 1922, p. 38.

1281   Grabo, Carl H. "The Technique of James's <u>The Turn of the
Screw</u>," <u>The Technique of the Novel</u>. New York: Scribner's
1928, pp. 204-214.

1282   Greene, Graham. "Books in General," NS&N, 39 (January
28, 1950), 101-102.

1283   Griffiths, T. "The Haunted House," a painting by T. Griffiths. Christmas Number, <u>Black and White</u> (1891).
       Griffiths' picture which appeared in the <u>Black and White</u>
       magazine, for a weekly illustrated London review, sug-
       gested as a possible source for <u>The Turn of the Screw</u>.
       Cf., R. L. Wolff. "The Genesis of 'The Turn of the
       Screw,' " AL, 13 (March, 1941), 1-8.

1284   Haggin, B. H. "<u>The Turn of the Screw</u>: Operatic Version
by B. Britten," HudR, 15 (Summer, 1962), 260-261.

1285   Hamilton, Clayton. <u>Materials and Methods of Fiction</u>. New
York: Baker and Taylor Co., 1908, pp. 147, 177-178.
       Defines <u>Turn of the Screw</u> as a short story "in the techni-
       cal sense of the term."

1286   Haney, Charles William. "The Garden and the Child: A
        Study of Pastoral Transformation," DA, 26 (Yale: 1965),
        2212.
            Suggests in the fifth chapter that in The Turn of the Screw
            the children may be the victimizers.

1286.1 Hart, James D. The Oxford Companion to American Litera-
        ture. London: Oxford University Press, 1941, p. 365.

1287   Hartman, Geoffrey. "The Heroics of Realism," YR, 53 (Oc-
        tober, 1963), 26-35.
            "... Where does the truth lie in The Turn of the Screw,
            with the governess or the children?"

1288   Hawkins, William. NYTCR, 11, #4 (February 6, 1950), 361.

1289   Haycraft, Howard, ed. American Authors. Stanley J. Kun-
        itz, ed. New York: H. W. Wilson Co., 1938, p. 412.

1290   Heilman, Robert B. "Foreword," SoR, 7 (January, 1971),
        6-8. Heilman's Foreword explains his relationship to Eric
        Voegelin. Cf., Eric Voegelin. "Postscript: On Paradise
        and Revolution," SoR, 7 (January, 1971), 25-48.

1291   _____. "The Freudian Reading of The Turn of the Screw,"
        MLN, 62 (November, 1947), 433-445.
            A review of the Freudian interpretations of the story.
            Finds no valid evidence for such reading.

1292   _____. "The Lure of the Demonic: James and Dürren-
        matt," CL, 13 (Fall, 1961), 346-357.
            Compares The Turn of the Screw with Dürrenmatt's The
            Pledge.

1293   _____. "The Turn of the Screw as Poem," UKCR, 14
        (Summer, 1948), 277-289.
            In this story may be found "the Christian dualism of good
            and evil: this substance James has projected by poetic
            method into numerous details of symbolic language and
            action of which the implications may ... almost be missed.
            For ... James's [poetic statement] is not direct." The
            above article is repr., in Five Approaches to Literary
            Criticism. Wilbur Stewart Scott, ed. New York: 1962,
            pp. 283-301; A Casebook on "The Turn of the Screw."
            Gerald Willen, ed. 1969, pp. 174-188; Forms of Modern
            Fiction. William Van O'Connor, ed. Minnesota U. P.,
            1948, pp. 211-228.

1294   Hoffman, Charles G. "Innocence and Evil in James' The
        Turn of the Screw," UKCR, 20 (Winter, 1953), 97-105.
            Since James presents innocence as a lack of knowledge of
            evil, it is the governess, not the children, who is inno-
            cent. Repr., "A Casebook on the Turn of the Screw."

Gerald Willen, ed. 1969, pp. 212-222.

1295   _____. The Short Novels of Henry James. New York:
Bookman Associates, 1957, pp. 70-96, 108-109, passim.

1296   Hofmann, Gert. Interpretationsprobleme Bei Henry James
(The Turn of the Screw, The Sacred Fount, and The Figure
in the Carpet). Diss. Freiburg, 1957.

1297   Hogarth, Basil. The Technique of Novel Writing. London:
John Lane, 1934, p. 164.

1298   Hoshioka, Motoko. "On The Turn of the Screw," JSE&AL
7 (March, 1963), 87-96.
         An essay on the effect of ambiguity in James's story.
         (In Japanese.)

1299   Hughes, Helen A. The History of the Novel in England.
Boston: Houghton Mifflin Co., 1932, p. 340.

1299.1   "Ingrid Bergman on TV," The Times (New York) (October
4, 1958), 76, 77.

1299.2   " 'The Innocents,' " ThA, 34 (April, 1950), 16.

1300   Irle, Gerhard. "Auswirkung des Wahns auf eine Geimein-
schaft: Eine Untersuchung anhand von Henry James The
Turn of the Screw," SG, 20 (1967), 700-708.

1301   Ives, C. B. "James's Ghosts in The Turn of the Screw,"
NCF, 18 (September, 1963), 183-189.
         "In summary, the ghosts of Quint and Miss Jessel fol-
         lowed the patterns of inactivity in the 'psychical' ghosts
         described by James in the Preface, although the Preface
         pretended that they were active and therefore supernatur-
         al...."

1302   Jennings, Richard. "Fair Comment," NC, 133 (May, 1943),
230.

1303   Jones, Alexander E. "Point of View in The Turn of the
Screw," PMLA, 74 (March, 1959), 112-122.
         The "conventional interpretation" is probably correct. The
         governess cannot be a "pathological liar," and James has
         gone to great pains "to give her authority."

1304   Jones, Howard Mumford. Major American Writers. New
York: Harcourt, Brace & Co., 1952, p. 1443.

1305   Josephson, Matthew. Portrait of the Artist as American.
New York: Harcourt, Brace and Co., 1930, p. 254.

1306   Kael, Pauline. "The Innocents and What Passes for Experience," FilmQ, 15, iv (1962), 21-36.

1307   Katan, M. "A Causerie on Henry James's <u>The Turn of the</u>
        <u>Screw</u>," <u>The Psychoanalytic Study of the Child.</u> New York:
        International Universities Press, 1962, pp. 473-493. Repr.,
        in <u>A Casebook on The Turn of the Screw.</u> Gerald Willen,
        ed. New York: Thomas Y. Crowell, 1969, pp. 319-
        337.

1308   Kenton, Edna. "Henry James to the Ruminant Reader: <u>The</u>
        <u>Turn of the Screw</u>," Arts, 6 (November, 1924), 245-255.
              Cf., R. B. Heilman. "The Freudian Reading of <u>The Turn</u>
              <u>of the Screw</u>," MLN, 62 (November, 1947), 433-445.

1309   Keown, Eric. "At the Play," Punch, 211, #5524 (Novem-
        ber 6, 1946), 408.

1310   _____. "At the Play," Punch, 223, #5831 (July 16,
        1952), 127.

1311   Kimbrough, Robert, ed. <u>Henry James: "The Turn of the</u>
        <u>Screw": An Authoritative Text and Background and Sources</u>:
        <u>Essays in Criticism.</u> New York: W. W. Norton & Co.,
        1966.
              A most helpful study.

1312   Kirby, David K. "Two Modern Versions of the Quest,"
        SHR, 5 (Fall, 1971), 387-395.
              James's story and Thomas Pynchon's <u>The Crying of Lot</u>
              <u>49</u> exemplify the Quest motif.

1313   Knight, Arthur. "Innocents Abroad," SatR, 44 (December
        23, 1961), 38-39.

1314   Knight, Grant C. <u>American Literature and Culture.</u> New
        York: Ray Long and Richard R. Smith, Inc., 1932, p. 384.

1315   _____. <u>The Novel in English.</u> New York: Richard R.
        Smith, Inc., 1931, pp. 278, 286.

1316   _____. <u>Superlatives.</u> New York: Alfred A. Knopf, 1925,
        pp. 143, passim.

1317   Knox, George. "Incubi and Succubi in <u>The Turn of the</u>
        <u>Screw,</u>" WF, 22 (April, 1963), 122-123.
              Reminds us of the terms for male and female demons and
              suggests a rivalry for possession in the ghosts of Peter
              Quint and Miss Jessel.

1318   Krook, Dorothea. "Edmund Wilson and Others on <u>The Turn</u>
        <u>of the Screw</u>," Appendix B, <u>The Ordeal of Consciousness in</u>
        <u>Henry James</u>. London, New York: Cambridge University
        Press, 1962, pp. 370-389.

1319   Lane, Margaret. "The Disappearing Ghost-Story: Some Re-

flections on Ghost-Stories, in Particular on Henry James's
The Turn of the Screw," Cornhill, 1052 (Summer, 1967),
136-146.

1320   Lang, Hans-Joachim. "The Turns in The Turn of the Screw,"
        JA, 9 (1964), 110-128.
            Associates the story with the Gothic tradition of Poe and
            Hawthorne.

1321   Lanier, Henry Wysham. "Fiction, Poetry, and the Lighter
        Note in the Season's Books," RevR, 18 (December, 1898),
        732-733.

1322   Leach, Anna. "Henry James: An Appreciation," Forum, 55
        (May, 1916), 551-564.

1322.1 Leavis, Q. D. "Henry James: The Stories," Scrutiny, 14
        (Spring, 1947), 223-229.

1323   Levin, Harry. The Power of Blackness. New York: Vintage
        Books, 1960, p. 64.

1324   Levy, Leo B. "The Turn of the Screw as Retaliation," CE,
        17 (February, 1956), 286-288.
            The story might be interpreted as "retaliation" by James
            upon the spectators who had decried his play, Guy Dom-
            ville.

1325   _____. Versions of Melodrama: A Study of the Fiction
        of Henry James, 1865-1897. Berkeley: University of Cali-
        fornia Press, 1957, p. 31.

1326   Lewis, Eugene. "Turning 'The Screw' into Opera," TimesH,
        (February 21, 1963), 12.

1327   Lewisohn, Ludwig. The Story of American Literature. New
        York: Modern Library, 1939, pp. 264, 269.

1328   Liddell, Robert. "The 'Hallucination' Theory of The Turn of
        the Screw," in A Treatise on the Novel. London: Jonathan
        Cape, 1947, pp. 128-145; repr. University of Chicago Press,
        1969.
            James's "conscious intelligence" was "triumphantly at work
            ... making a great work of art out of a diabolically dirty
            story, treating the theme both with candour and with crys-
            talline purity...."

1329   _____. Some Principles of Fiction. London: Jonathan
        Cape, 1953, p. 66.

1330   Liljegren, S. B. American and European in the Works of
        Henry James. Lund: Lunds Universitets Arsskrift, 1920,
        pp. 45, 50-51.

1331   Lind, Sidney E. "The Turn of the Screw: The Torment of
        Critics," CentR, 14 (Spring, 1970), 225-240.
            Provides a survey of important previous scholarship and
            offers significant comment on James's relationship to psy-
            chological studies in his own time.

1332   Linn, James W., with H. W. Taylor. A Foreword to Fic-
        tion. New York: Appleton-Century Co., 1935, pp. 66, 192.

1332.1 "Literary Chat," MunM, 20 (February, 1899), 820-823.

1332.2 LitW (Boston), 29, #23 (November 12, 1898), 367.

1332.3 LitW (London), 58 #1519 (December 9, 1898), 456.

1333   Lydenberg, John. "Comment on Mr. Spilka's Paper," L&P,
        14 (1964), 6-8, 34.
            Cf., Mark Spilka. L&P, 13 (1963), 105-111.

1334   _____. "The Governess Turns the Screws," NCF, 12
        (June, 1957), 37-58. Repr., A Casebook on The Turn of
        the Screw," Gerald Willen, ed. 2nd ed., 1969, pp. 278-290.
            "The story [is] a covert, if unconscious attack" upon New
            England Puritanism.

1335   Macdonald, Dwight. "The Innocents," Esquire, 57 #341
        (April, 1962), 24.

1336   Machen, Arthur. "Arthur Machen Pays Tribute," MTQ, 5
        #4 (1943), 8.

1337   Mackenzie, Manfred. "The Turn of the Screw; Jamesian
        Gothic," EIC, 12 (January, 1962), 34-38.

1338   Male, Roy R., Jr. "The Dual Aspects of Evil in 'Rappac-
        cini's Daughter,'" PMLA, 69 (March, 1954), 101.
            A comparison of Beatrice and the governess.

1339   Marshall, Margaret. "Drama," Nation (February 11, 1950),
        140-141.

1340   McCarthy, Harold T. Henry James: The Creative Process.
        New York: Thomas Yoseloff, 1958, pp. 107, 110.

1341   McMaster, Juliet. "'The Full Image of a Repetition' in The
        Turn of the Screw," SSF, 6 (Summer, 1969), 377-382.
            An analysis based on the times the governess replaces the
            ghosts to "recreate the 'full image' of her own perception."

1342   Mégroz, R. L. Walter de la Mare. London: Hodder and
        Stroughton, 1924, pp. 179-181.

1343   Meldrum, Ronald M. "Three of Henry James' Dark Ladies,"

RS, 37 (March, 1969), 54-60.
One lady is in The Turn of the Screw.

1344   Milano, Paolo. Henry James o il Proscritto Volontario.
        Arnoldo Mondadori Editore, 1948, pp. 111-114.

1344.1 Motoda, Yuichi. Henry James, Neji No Kaiten E No Ap-
        proach. Tokyo: Bunri Shoin, 1970.
        An approach to James's The Turn of the Screw.

1344.2 "Mr. James's New Stories," Athenaeum, 3704 (October 22,
        1898), 564-565.

1345   Mukherji, Nirmal. "The Problem of Evil in The Turn of the
        Screw--A Study in Ambiguity," CalR, 168 (July, 1963), 63-
        70.

1346   Murdock, Kenneth. Introduction. The Turn of the Screw and
        The Aspern Papers. London: J. M. Dent, 1957, pp. v-xi.

1347   Nation, 67, #1745 (December 8, 1898), 432.

1348   "New Plays: 'The Innocents,'" Newsweek, 35 (February 13,
        1950), 80-81.

1349   NYT (December 3, 1961), 86.

1350   Northrup, Clark Sutherland. "The Novelists," A Manual of
        American Literature. Theodore Stanton, ed. New York and
        London: G. P. Putnam's Sons, 1909, p. 194.

1350.1 Norton, Rictor Carl. "Studies of the Union of Love and
        Death:...IV. The Turn of the Screw: Coincidentia Oppositor-
        um," DAI, 33 (Florida State University: 1972), 5190-A.

1350.2 _____. "The Turn of the Screw: Coincidentia Oppositor-
        um," AI, 28 (Winter, 1971), 373-390.

1351   "The Novels of Henry James," LivA, 310 (July 30, 1921),
        270.

1352   Nuhn, Ferner. The Wind Blew from the East. New York:
        Harper & Bros., 1940, pp. 140-141, passim.

1353   Orage, A. R. "Henry James and the Ghostly," The Little
        Review Anthology. New York: Hermitage House, Inc., 1953,
        pp. 230-232.

1354   Pelswick, Rose. "The Innocents," JourA (December 26,
        1961), 16.

1355   Penzoldt, Peter. The Supernatural in Fiction. London:
        Peter Nevill, Ltd., 1952, pp. 218-223.

1356   Phelan, Kappo. "The Innocents," Cw, 51, #19 (February 17,
       1950), 509-510.

1357   Phelps, William Lyon. Howells, James, Bryant and Other
       Essays. New York: Macmillan Co., 1924, pp. 141-145.

1357.1 Porat, Tsfira. "Ha'aman Ve-ha-omenet." Mo'oznayim, 33
       (1971), 240-246.

1358   Powys, John Cowper. "John Cowper Powys on Henry James,"
       The Little Review Anthology. New York: Hermitage House,
       Inc., 1953, pp. 28-30.

1359   Pritchard, John Paul. Criticism in America. Norman:
       University of Oklahoma Press, 1956, p. 275.

1360   Putt, S. Gorley. Introduction. The Turn of the Screw, and
       Other Stories. Harmondsworth: Penguin, 1969.

1361   Quinn, Arthur Hobson. "Some Phases of the Supernatural in
       American Literature," PMLA, 25, #1 (1910), 132-133.

1361.1 Rao, Adapa R. "Gleams and Glooms: A Reading of The
       Turn of the Screw," OJES, 8, i (1971), 1-9.

1362   Reed, Glenn. "Another Turn on James's The Turn of the
       Screw," AL, 20 (January, 1949), 413-423.
            Internal evidence and James's own critical comments on
       the story, show there is little basis for the current psy-
       chological interpretation.

1363   Rees, Richard. "Miss Jessel and Lady Chatterley," in For
       Love or Money. Carbondale: Southern Ill. University Press,
       1961, pp. 115-124.

1364   Reid, Charles. "At the Opera," Punch, 227, #5952 (Oc-
       tober 13, 1954), 487.

1365   Reid, Forrest. Walter de la Mare. London: Faber and
       Faber, Ltd., 1929, pp. 221-223.

1366   Roberts, Morris. "Henry James," SR, 57 (Summer, 1949),
       521-525.

1367   Roellinger, Francis X., Jr. "Psychical Research and The
       Turn of the Screw," AL, 20 (January, 1949), 401-412.
            Striking parallels in the Proceedings of the Society for
       Psychical Research show that James's apparitions were
       constructed much more in terms of the "mere modern
       'psychical' case" than he cared to admit.

1368   Rubin, Louis D., Jr. "One More Turn of the Screw,"
       MFS, 9 (Winter, 1963-1964), 314-328.

Argues that Douglas, the character in the prologue who pro-
duces the governess' story, is in fact Miles.

1368.1 _____. "One More Turn of the Screw," The Curious
Death of the Novel. Baton Rouge: Louisiana State University Press, 1967, pp. 67-87.

1369 Samuels, Charles Thomas. "Giovanni and the Governess,"
AmSch, 37 (Autumn, 1968), 655-678.
A comparison of James's story with "Rappaccini's Daugh-
ter" reveals that "James is a poorer [writer] than we
have been told...." James's "house of fiction ... isn't
a house at all" and "the rest of its author's world ...
can be strewn with the house's rubble."

1369.1 _____. "The Governess," in The Ambiguity of Henry
James. Urbana: Illinois University Press, 1971, pp. 11-22.

1370 Sanna, Vittoria. "Considerazioni intorno a The Turn of the
Screw," AION-SG, 6 (1963), 101-137.

1371 Schneider, Marcel. "Henry James et Benjamin Britten,"
NRF, 13 (April, 1965), 713-716.
Praises the opera based on James's story.

1372 Schonberg, Harold C. "Opera: Turn of the Screw Presented," NYT, (March 27, 1962), 15.

1373 Schorer, Mark, ed. "The Turn of the Screw," The Story:
A Critical Anthology. New York: Prentice-Hall, Inc.,
1950.

1374 "The Season's Books," Outlook, 60, #14 (December 3, 1898),
875-884.

1374.1 Seiffert, Alice. Schraubendrehungen, Aus Dem Amerikanis-
schen Ubertragen von Alice Seiffert. Mit einem Nachwort von
Rudolf Suhnel. Stuttgart, Reclam, 1970.

1375 Siegel, Eli. James and the Children: A Consideration of
Henry James's "The Turn of the Screw." Martha Baird, ed.
New York: Definition Press, 1968.
Says that the story ends "with the awareness of evil but
not the full conquering of it, and not the full love of what
is different."

1376 Siegel, Paul N. " 'Miss Jessel': Mirror Image of the Governess," L&P, 18, #1 (1968), 30-38.
Interprets Miss Jessel as a projection of the governess, a
shadowy portion of her personality which she does not wish
to recognize.

1377 Silver, John. "A Note on the Freudian Reading of The Turn

of the Screw," AL, 29 (May, 1957), 207-211. Repr., A
Casebook on "Turn of the Screw." Gerald Willen, ed., 2nd
ed., 1969, pp. 239-243.
> Supports the Freudian reading of the story by textual evi-
> dence that the governess "knew a good deal about Quint
> and Jessel and that James has her skillfully cloak her
> knowledge.

1378   Slabey, Robert M. " 'The Holy Innocents' and The Turn of
        the Screw," NS, 12 (April, 1963), 170-173. (In German)
> Douglas reads the manuscript containing the story of the
> Governess during the Christmas season, possibly on the
> Feast of the Holy Innocents (December 28), "called Chil-
> dermas in England." The significance does "add some-
> thing to the reader's appreciation of James's craft."

1379   _____. "The Turn of the Screw: Grammar and Optics,"
        CLAJ, 9 (September, 1965), 68-72.
> Cites three ambiguities in the use of pronouns, and notes
> the unusually acute vision attributed to the governess.
> These notations are part of a pattern as to the nature of
> imaginative truth as fiction.

1380   Slaughter, Martina. "Edmund Wilson and The Turn of the
        Screw," Henry James: "The Turn of the Screw." Norton
        Critical Edition. Robert Kimbrough, ed. W. W. Norton,
        1966, pp. 211-214. Repr., Twentieth-Century Interpretations.
        Jane Tompkins, ed. New York: 1970, pp. 56-59.

1381   Smith, Roland M. "Anglo-Saxon Spinsters and Anglo-Saxon
        Archers," MLN, 64 (May, 1949), 312-315.

1382   Snell, George. The Shapers of American Fiction, 1798-1947.
        New York: E. P. Dutton and Company, Inc., 1947, p. 120.

1383   Solomon, Eric. "The Return of the Screw," UKCR, 30
        (March, 1964), 205-211.
> On the villainy of Mrs. Grose.

1384   Spilka, Mark. "Turning the Freudian Screw: How Not To
        Do It," L&P, 13 (Fall, 1963), 105-111.
> On the governess as a prurient example of "Victorian hot-
> house purity and domesticity." Cf., Arthur Efron. Paunch,
> 17 (1964), 13-15; John Lydenburg. L&P, 14 (1964), 6-8,
> 34.

1385   Squires, Radcliffe. "Allen Tate's The Fathers," VQR, 46
        (Autumn, 1970), 629-649.
> An incidental but noteworthy comparison with James's
> story.

1386   Stanford, Donald E. "A Prefatory Note," SoR, 7 (January,
        1971), 3-5.

Cf., Eric Voegelin. SoR, 7 (1971), 9-24; SoR, 7 (1971), 25-48.

1387   "A Star at Work," Times (New York), 10 (October 18, 1959), 19, Sec. 2.

1388   Stoll, Elmer Edgar. "Symbolism in Coleridge," PMLA, 63 (March, 1948), 229-233.
        Refutes psychological interpretation of The Turn of the Screw.

1389   Stone, Albert E., Jr. "Henry James and Childhood: The Turn of the Screw," SUB, 61 (April, 1961), [18-p. pamphlet.]
        On "original sin in the minds of the very young."

1390   "The Story ... Is Distinctly Repulsive," Outlook, 60 (October 29, 1898), 537.

1390.1 _____. "Henry James and Childhood: The Turn of the Screw," in American Character and Culture: Some Twentieth Century Perspectives. John Allen Hague, ed. DeLand, Florida: Everett Edwards Press, 1964, pp. 85-100.
        Emphasizes the importance of class stratification as a factor in the story.

1391   Swan, Michael. Introduction. Henry James: The Turn of the Screw, The Aspern Papers, and Seven Other Stories. London: New Collins Classics, 1956; New York: Dell, 1956.

1392   Tadokoro, Nobushige. "The Problem of Hallucination in The Turn of the Screw," KAL, 8 (1965), 25-35.

1393   "The Theatre," ["The Innocents"], Time, 55 (February 13, 1950, 52-53.

1394   Thomas, Glen R. "The Freudian Approach to James's The Turn of the Screw: Psychoanalysis and Literary Criticism," DAI, 31 (Emory: 1970), 770A.

1395   Thomson, A. W. "The Turn of the Screw: Some Points on the Hallucination Theory," REL, 6 (October, 1965), 26-35.
        Some of the ambiguities in the story, Thomson thinks, may result from a change of intention as James wrote the story.

1396   Thorp, Willard. Foreword. The Turn of the Screw, and Other Short Novels. New York: New American Library, 1962.

1397   Thurber, James. "The Wings of Henry James," NY, 35, #38 (November 7, 1959), 188-201.

1398   Tindall, William York. Forces in Modern British Literature.

New York: Vintage Books, 1956, p. 191.

1399   Tompkins, Jane P. , ed. Introduction. Twentieth-Century
        Interpretations of "The Turn of the Screw" and Other Tales.
        Englewood Cliffs, New Jersey: Prentice-Hall, Inc. , 1970.

1400   Tournadre, C. "Propositions pour une psychologie sociale
        de The Turn of the Screw," EA, 22 (July-September, 1969),
        259-269.
            Develops the theory that "La situation [sociale] de la
            gouvernante comme celle de Miss Jessel est ... ambigué
            et va se trouver à l'origine de frustrations constantes."

1401   Trachtenberg, Stanley. "The Return of the Screw," MFS,
        11 (Summer, 1965), 180-182.
            Argues that Miles was corrupt, and that as Douglas he has
            hidden the truth for many years. Cf. , Louis D. Rubin.
            MFS, 9 (1963-64), 314-328.

1402   Trewin, J. C. "The World of the Theatre," ILonN, 221,
        #5905 (July 19, 1952), 108.

1403   Troy, William. "The Altar of Henry James," in The Ques-
        tion of Henry James. F. W. Dupee, ed. New York: Hen-
        ry Holt & Co. , 1945, pp. 267-272.

1403.1 Tuveson, Ernest. "The Turn of the Screw: A Palimpsest,"
        SEL, 12 (1972), 783-800.
            Believes The Turn of the Screw belongs to the genre of
            märchen, in the Romantic tradition.

1404   "TV: Powerful Portrayal," Times (October 21, 1959), 87.

1405   "The Two Magics," Independent, 51, #2614 (January 5,
        1899), 73.

1406   Updike, John. "Beerbohm and Others," NY, 37 (September
        16, 1961), 173.

1407   Uzzell, Thomas H. The Technique of the Novel. New York:
        J. B. Lippincott, 1947, p. 285.

1408   Van Aken, Paul. "Crisis en Eenzamheid in de Jeugd (II),"
        NVT, 23 (May-June, 1970), 504-520. [In Flemish]
            Comparison of the story with Ina Seidel's Unser Freund
            Peregrin.

1409   Van Doren, Carl. Introduction. The Turn of the Screw.
        New York: Heritage Press, 1949.

1410   Van Doren, Mark, ed. Preface. "Henry James: The Turn
        of the Screw," in The New Invitation to Learning. New
        York: Random House, 1942, pp. 221-235. Repr. , A

Casebook on Henry James's "The Turn of the Screw." Gerald Willen, ed. 2nd ed., 1969, pp. 160-170.
    Symposium: Katherine Anne Porter, Allen Tate, Mark
    Van Doren, on The Turn of the Screw.

1411   Voegelin, Eric. "A Letter to Robert Heilman," SoR, 7 #1
(January, 1971), 9-24.
    Cf., Robert B. Heilman. SoR, 7 (1971), 6-8; MLN, 62
    (1947), 433-445.

1412   _____. "Postscript: On Paradise and Revolution," SoR,
7 (January, 1971), 25-48.
    A significant study.

1413   _____. "The Turn of the Screw," SoR, 7 (January,
1971), 3-48.
    Cf., Donald E. Stanford. "A Prefatory Note," SoR, 7
    (1971), 3-5.

1414   Waldock, Arthur John Alfred. "Mr. Edmund Wilson and The
Turn of the Screw," MLN, 62 (May, 1947), 331-334. Repr.,
A Casebook on "The Turn of the Screw." Gerald Willen, ed.
2nd ed. 1969, pp. 171-173.
    A refutation of the psychological. Cf., Edmund Wilson.
    "The Ambiguity of Henry James," H&H, 7 (1934), 385-
    406.

1415   Walpole, Hugh. "England," Tendencies of the Modern Novel.
London: George Allen and Unwin, Ltd., 1934, p. 17.

1416   Ward, Alfred C. Aspects of the Modern Short Story. London: University of London Press, 1924, pp. 90-101.

1417   Watts, Richard, Jr. "The Case of the Haunted Children,"
NYTCR, 11 (February 6, 1950), 359.

1418   Weales, Gerald. American Drama Since World War II. New
York: Harcourt, Brace & World, Inc., 1962, pp. 166-168.
    The dramatization of the story.

1419   Wescott, Glenway. "A Sentimental Contribution," H&H, 7,
#3 (April-May, 1934), 523-534.

1420   West, Katharine. Chapter of Governesses: A Study of the
Governess in English Fiction, 1800-1949. London: Cohen
and West, 1949, pp. 179-182.

1421   West, Muriel. "The Death of Miles in The Turn of the
Screw," PMLA, 79 (June, 1964), 283-288. Repr., A Casebook on "The Turn of the Screw." Gerald Willen, ed. 2nd
ed. 1969, pp. 338-349.
    Reads the story with more attention to "the physical vio-
    lence of the governess ... [who] may much more

reasonably be said to cause his [Miles'] death."

1422 _____. A Stormy Night with The Turn of the Screw."
Phoenix, Arizona: Frye and Smith, 1964.

1423 Wilde, Oscar. The Letters of Oscar Wilde. Rupert Hart-
Davis, ed. New York: Harcourt, Brace & World, Inc.,
1962, p. 776.
"I think it [The Turn of the Screw] is a most wonderful,
lurid, poisonous little tale, like an Elizabethan tragedy."

1424 Willen, Gerald, ed. Preface. A Casebook on Henry James's
"The Turn of the Screw." New York: Thomas Y. Crowell
Co., 1960, 2nd ed., 1969.
Contains many of James's own comments on the story, to-
gether with articles treating many facets of The Turn of
the Screw. A very helpful volume.

1425 Wilson, Edmund. "The Ambiguity of Henry James," H&H, 7
(April-June, 1934), 385-406. Revised version in The Question of Henry James. F. W. Dupee, ed. New York: Henry
Holt, 1954, pp. 160-190.
Develops the thesis that The Turn of the Screw is a fig-
ment of the narrator's imagination by reason of sex repression.

1426 _____. "The Ambiguity of Henry James," Criticism.
Schorer, Miles, McKenzie, eds. New York: 1948, pp. 147-
162. Repr., from The Triple Thinkers: Ten Essays in Literature. New York: 1938, pp. 122-164.

1427 _____. "A Treatise on Tales of Horror," NY, 20, #15
(May 27, 1944), 72.

1428 Winsten, Archer. "The Innocents," Post (New York) (December 26, 1961), 24.

1429 Wolff, Robert Lee. "The Genesis of The Turn of the Screw,"
AL, 13 (March, 1941), 1-8.
On the possible influence of a picture, "The Haunted
House," in the Christmas number of the Black and White
Magazine, and also a fragmentary story of E. W. Benson.

1430 Woolf, Virginia. "Henry James's Ghost Stories," TLS (December 22, 1921); repr., in Granite and Rainbow. London:
Hogarth Press; New York: Harcourt, 1958, pp. 65-72.

1431 Worsley, T. C. "The Massacre of the Innocents," NS&N,
44 (July 12, 1952), 39-40.

1432 Wright, Walter F. ["The Turn of the Screw"] in "The Quest
for Reality," The Madness of Art: A Study of Henry James.

Lincoln: University of Nebraska Press, 1962, pp. 176-185.

1432.1 Yu, Frederick Y.   "Andrew Lytle's A Name for Evil as a
Redaction of The Turn of the Screw," MQR, 11 (1972), 186-
190.

1433   Zimmerman, Everett.   "Literary Tradition and The Turn of
the Screw," SSF, 7 (Fall, 1970), 634-637.
Shows that literary references in the story "create a sense
of horror by providing a viewpoint too limited for succeed-
ing events...."

Reviews: Dramatization of "The Innocents":

Atkinson, Brooks.   "At the Theatre," NY Times (February
2, 1950), 30.
Barnes, Howard.   "Has a Ghost of a Chance," NYHT (Febru-
ary 2, 1950) in NYTCR, 11 (1950), 360.
Chapman, John.   " 'The Innocents' a Weird Thriller, Admir-
ably Set, Staged and Acted," NY Daily News (February 2,
1950), in NYTCR, 11 (1950), 359.
Coleman, Robert.   " 'The Innocents' Nebulous but Beautifully
Staged," NY Daily Mirror (February 2, 1950), in NYTCR,
11 (1950), 360.
Garland, Robert.   "Eerie and Arresting--Truly Spellbinding,"
NY Jour. Amer. (February 2, 1950), in NYTCR, 11 (1950),
361.
Hawkins, William.   " 'The Innocents,' Is Splendidly Cast,"
NY World-Telegram & Sun (February 2, 1950), in NYTCR,
11 (1950), 361.
Watts, Richard.   "The Case of the Haunted Children," NY
Post (February 2, 1950), in NYTCR, 11 (1950), 359.

Other reviews of the dramatization:

CathW, 170 (March, 1950), 469; 189 (July 1959), 321
Cw, 51 (February 17, 1950), 509
Life, 28 (April, 1950), 91-92f
Nation, 170 (February 11, 1950), 141
NewRep, 122 (February 27, 1950), 20
NSt, 44 (July 12, 1952), 39-40
Newsweek, 35 (February 13, 1950), 80
NY, 25 (February 11, 1950), 44; 35 (Oct. 17, 1959), 141-142
SatR, 33 (February 25, 1950, 32f
Sch&Soc, 17 (April 8, 1950), 214-15
ThA, 34 (April 1950), 16; (June, 1950), 22-23f; 35 (January,
1951), 58-88
Time, 55 (February 13, 1950), 52-53

Early Reviews of The Turn of the Screw:

Ainslee's, 2 (December, 1898), 518

Athenaeum, 3704 (October 22, 1898), 564-5
Book Buyer, 17 (December, 1898), 437
Bookman (London), 15 (November, 1898), 54
Chautauquan, 28 (March, 1899), 630
Critic, 33 (December, 1898), 524
Dixie, 1 (January, 1899), 59-60
Independent, 51 (January 5, 1899), 73
Nation, 67 (December 8, 1898), 432
Outlook, 60 (October 29, 1898), 537
Overland Mo., 32 (November, 1898), 493
Picayune (November 27, 1898), 10
Qt. Rev, 198 (October, 1903), 358
Rev of Revs, 18 (December, 1898), 732-3
SewaneeR, 7 (January, 1899), 124

"Two Countries"--See "The Modern Warning"

"The Two Faces"

1434   Amacher, Richard E. "Henry James's 'The Two Faces,' "
        Expl, 12 (December, 1953), Item 20.
            The relationship of Sutton ("the true and sentient hero of
        this story"), and Mrs. Grantham. Cf., Henry R. Rupp.
        "James's 'The Two Faces,' " Expl, 14 (1956), Item 30.

1435   Bement, Douglas, and Ross M. Taylor. "Henry James:
        Miss Banker," The Fabric of Fiction. New York: Harcourt,
        Brace & World, 1943, p. 271.
            An analysis.

1436   Rupp, Henry R. "Henry James's 'The Two Faces,' " Expl,
        14 (1956), Item 30.
            "... What has ultimately repelled Sutton is not that Mrs.
        Grantham has refused to suffer but rather ... that she is
        incapable of suffering, while Lady Gwyther's face ... is
        made for 'unimaginable pathos,' a factor of immeasurable
        importance to Shirley Sutton, who is, as Mr. Amachar
        says, 'the true and sentient hero of this story.' " Cf.,
        Richard E. Amacher. Expl, 12 (1953), Item 20.

See also: 270, 1740; 2198, XI; 2637, XVII; 2637.1, XII;
2948.1, 3326, 3711

THE TWO MAGICS

(The Two Magics contained "The Turn of the Screw" and
"Covering End," originally written as a play.)

Reviews of The Two Magics:

Athenaeum, 3704 (October 22, 1898), 564-5
Bookman (London), 25 (November, 1898), 54
Dixie, 1 (January, 1899), 59-60
LitW, 29 (November 12, 1898), 367-8
Nation, 67 (December 8, 1898), 432
Outlook, 60 (October 29, 1898), 537
Picayune, (November 27, 1898), 10
Quarterly Rev, 198 (October, 1903), 358
Rev of Revs, 18 (December, 1898), 732
SewaneeR, 7 (January, 1899), 124
The Times, 3 (October 15, 1898), 681

"Two Old Houses and Three Young Women"

1437   Byrd, Scott. "Henry James's 'Two Old Houses and Three
        Young Women': A Problem in Dating and Assemblage,"
        PBSA, 65, #4 (4th Qt., 1971), 383-389.
            Speculates as to this travel sketch which first appeared in
            Italian Hours in 1909, bearing the date of 1899.

1438   _____. "The Spoils of Venice: Henry James's 'Two Old
        Houses and Three Young Women' and The Golden Bowl," AL,
        43 (November, 1971), 371-384.

"The Velvet Glove"

1439   Hönnighausen, Lothar. " 'The Velvet Glove'--Zur Erzähltech-
        nik in Henry James' Spätwerk," G-RM, n. s., 17, #3 (July,
        1967), 307-322. (In German.)
            In "The Velvet Glove" may be found the motif of the early
            story, "Four Meetings." Such thematic affinity allows the
            different art of representation in James's late work to
            show more clearly.

1440   Hopkins, Viola. "Gloriani and the Tides of Taste," NCF, 18
        June, 1963), 65-71.

1441   Tintner, Adeline R. "James's Mock Epic: 'The Velvet
        Glove,' " Edith Wharton, and Other Late Tales," MFS, 17
        (Winter, 1971-1972), 483-499.
            Says that this story is a mock-epic in which James used
            imagery from mythology to launch a literary joke, of
            which Edith Wharton is both heroine and butt. It also

relates to the other six stories of 1909.

See also: 1740, 1889; 2198, XII; 2352, 2363; 2637, XXVIII; 2737, 3417, 3711

"The Visits"

See: 1740; 2198, VIII; 2352, 2363; 2637, XXVII; 3711, 3714

WASHINGTON SQUARE

1442   Auchincloss, Louis S. Introduction. Washington Square. Illustrated by Lawrence Beall Smith. Mount Vernon, New York: Printed for Members of the Limited Editions Club at the Thistle Press, 1971.

1443   Berkley, James, ed. [Washington Square] Romance and Realism: An Introduction to the Study of the Novel. New York: Odyssey Press, 1961.

1444   Bicanic, Sonia. "Writing for the Magazines," SR&A, 13-14 (July-December, 1962), 13-30. Cites Washington Square as one of the examples of serial installments used "constructionally."

1445   Blackmur, R. P. Introduction. Washington Square. New York: Dell Publishing Co., 1959.

1446   Cambon, Glauco. "The Negative Gesture in Henry James," NCF, 15 (March, 1961), 335-343. Catherine Sloper in Washington Square is a typical Jamesian heroine. Says her withdrawal was influenced by Hawthorne style.

1447   Cargill, Oscar. Introduction. Washington Square and Daisy Miller. New York: Harper, 1956.

1448   Coy Ferrer, Juan J. "Washington Square o el folletín bien hecho," PSA, 55 (1969), 26-47.

1449   Dickins, Bruce. "The Story of Washington Square," TLS (October, 1961), 690. Suggests that the unhappy affair between Henry Kemble and Mary Ann Thackeray was used by Henry James as a basis for his novel.

1450   Dobree, Valentine. Introduction. Washington Square. London: 1949.

1451   Edel, Leon, ed. Introduction. The Bodley Head Henry James: Vol. 1. The Europeans and Washington Square.

London: Bodley Head, 1967.

1452   Fadiman, Clifton. Introduction. Washington Square. New
         York: Modern Library, 1950.

1453   Gordon, David J. "Washington Square: A Psychological
         Perspective," in Washington Square by Henry James. Ger-
         ald Willen, ed. New York: Thomas Y. Crowell & Co.,
         1970, pp. 263-271.

1454   Gurko, Leo. "The Dehumanizing Mind in Washington Square,"
         Washington Square By Henry James. Gerald Willen, ed.
         New York: Thomas Y. Crowell Co., 1970, pp. 230-243.

1455   Hopkins, Viola. "Gloriani and the Tides of Taste," NCF, 18
         (June, 1963), 65-71.

1456   Kenney, William. "Doctor Sloper's Double in Washington
         Square," UR, 36 (June, 1970), 301-306.
             Points out similarities between Sloper and Townsend.

1457   Kronenberger, Louis, ed. The Pleasure of Their Company:
         An Anthology of Civilized Writing. New York: Knopf, 1946.

1457.1   _____. "Washington Square," in The Polished Surface: Es-
         says in The Literature of Worldliness. New York: Knopf,
         1969, pp. 233-245.
             "... Though Henry James excluded Washington Square from
         his great New York edition, it may conceivably be his best
         novel--which is not for a moment to say his greatest."

1458   Lamb, Lynton. Lithographs, Washington Square. London:
         Folio Society, 1963.

1459   Las Vergnas, Raymond. "Lettres anglo-americaines: Henry
         James," HeM, 9 (February, 1954), 445-447.
             On Washington Square and Wings of the Dove.

1459.1   Long, Robert Emmet. "James's Washington Square: The
         Hawthorne Relation," NEQ, 46 (December, 1973), 573-590.

1459.2   Lucas, John. "Washington Square," in The Air of Reality:
         New Essays on Henry James. John Goode, ed. London:
         Methuen & Co., 1972, pp. 36-59.
             "... the brilliance of James's novel depends on the way in
         which its comic surface is played off against the tragic
         events.... It is the ordinariness which is so extraordinary
         about Washington Square."

1460   Macauley, Robie. " 'Let Me Tell You About the Rich....' "
         KR, 27 (Autumn, 1965), 649-650.

1461   Nakazato, Haruhiko. "Henry James: Washington Square,"

Kam, 4 (Spring, 1962), 60-74.
On the novel as a "tale purely American."

1462   Pearce, Brian. "Perpetuated Misprints," TLS (June 4, 1970), 613.
Textual errors in Washington Square.

1463   Pendo, Mina. "Reason under the Ailanthus," in Washington Square By Henry James. Gerald Willen, ed. New York: Thomas Y. Crowell & Co., 1970, pp. 243-252.

1464   Poirier, Richard. " 'Confidence' and Washington Square," in The Comic Sense of Henry James. New York: Oxford University Press, 1960, pp. 145-182.

1465   Rahv, Philip. La Heredera de Todos Los Tiempos [The Heiress of All Ages], Sur, 1943, p. 108.

1466   Raymond, John. "Beyond the Usual," NSt, (May 30, 1969), 778-779.
A comparison of Trollope's Can You Forgive Her? with James's Washington Square.

1467   Roddman, Philip. "The Critical Sublime: A View of Washington Square," Washington Square By Henry James. Gerald Willen, ed. New York: Crowell, 1970, pp. 253-263.

1468   Salisbury, Howard E. "Wish-Fulfillment as Moral Crisis in the Fiction of Henry James," DA, 24 (University of Washington: 1963), 304.
Catherine Sloper in Washington Square.

1468.1 Samuels, Charles Thomas. "Comic Criticism," in Washington Square. The Ambiguity of Henry James. Urbana: Illinois University Press, 1971, pp. 144-149.

1469   Scherman, David E. and Rosemarie Redlich. "Henry James," Literary America: A Chronicle of American Writers from 1607 to 1952. New York: Dodd, Mead, 1952, pp. 96-97.
Portraits that inspired The American Scene and Washington Square.

1470   Van Doren, Mark. Introduction. Washington Square. New York: Bantam Books, 1963.

1471   Weales, Gerald. American Drama Since World War II. New York: Harcourt, Brace & World, 1962, pp. 166-168.

1472   Willen, Gerald, ed. Washington Square: A Critical Edition. New York: Thomas Crowell Co., 1970.

1473   Woelfel, Karl. Dramaturgische Wandlungen Eines Epischen Themas Bei Dramatisierung und Verfilmung, Dargestellt An

Henry James "Washington Square." Diss. Erlangen, 1955.

Reviews: The Heiress (1947), a dramatization by Ruth and Augustus Goetz, based on Washington Square

Atkinson, Brooks. "The Play," NY Times, (September 30, 1947), 22

Barnes, Howard. "Old Lace, but Tattered," NYHT (September 30, 1947), in NYTCR, Rachel W. Coffin, ed., 8 (1947), 336

Chapman, John. " 'The Heiress' A Carefully Staged Costume Drama for Wendy Hiller," NY Daily News (September 30, 1947), in NYTCR, 8 (1947), 335.

Coleman, Robert. "B'way Has New Hit in 'Heiress,' " NY Daily Mirror, (September 30, 1947), in NYTCR, 8 (1947), 337.

Garland, Robert. "Flawless Cast Offers Superb Period Play," NY Jour Amer (September 30, 1947), in NYTCR, 8 (1947), 338.

Hawkins, William. " 'The Heiress' a Bitter Play of Frustrated Love," NY World-Telegram, (September 30, 1947), in NYTCR, 8 (1947), 337.

Kronenberger, Louis. "No Longer a Work of Art, but an Interesting Drama," PM (October 1, 1947), in NYTCR, 8 (1947), 338.

Morehouse, Ward. " 'The Heiress' a Taut, Bitter Play, Expertly Staged and Played at Biltmore," NY Sun (September 30, 1947), in NYTCR, 8 (1947), 336.

Watts, Richard. "The Season's First Hil Finally Arrives," NY Post (September 30, 1947), in NYTCR, 8 (1947), 336.

Other Reviews of The Heiress:

CathW, 166 (November, 1947), 168
Cw, 47 (October 17, 1947), 16
Forum, 108 (December, 1947), 370-1
Life, 23 (November 3, 1947), 149-50, 153
Nation, 165 (October 18, 1947), 425-6
New Rep, 117 (October 13, 1947), 36
NY, 23 (October 11, 1947), 50
Newsweek, 30 (October 13, 1947), 80
PubW, 153 (February 28, 1948), 1130
Sch&Soc, 67 (February 28, 1948), 167
ThA, 31 (December, 1947), 12-13; 32 (April, 1948), 32; (October, 1948, 21; 34 (April, 1950), 18; 47 (January, 1963), 17
Time, 50 (October 13, 1947), 70

Reviews of Washington Square:

Appleton's, n. s., 10 (March, 1881), 274-5
Athenaeum, 2781 (February 12, 1881), 228

Atl, 47 (May, 1881), 709-10
Californian, 3 (April, 1881), 376-7
Dial, 1 (January, 1881), 195-6
HarperM, 90, Sup, 2-3 (April, 1895), 816
Independent, 47 (May 30, 1895), 737
Lippincotts, 27 (February, 1881), 214-5
LitWorld, 12 (January 1, 1881), 10
Nation, 30 (June 24, 1880), 474
Scribner's, 21 (March, 1881), 795-6
SatR, 51 (March 19, 1881), 372-3

WATCH AND WARD

1474   Edel, Leon. "An Inalienable Mistrust--Watch and Ward," in
       Henry James: The Treacherous Years, 1895-1901. Phila-
       delphia, New York: J. B. Lippincott, 1969, pp. 258-259;
       260-261.

1474.1 _____, ed. Introduction. Watch and Ward. London:
       Rupert Hart-Davis, 1960; New York: Grove Press, 1960.

1475   Farrer, Alison. "Watch, Ward, the Jamesian Themes,"
       Balcony, 1 (1965), 23-27.

1476   Fish, Charles. "Form and Revision: The Example of
       Watch and Ward," NCF, 22 (September, 1967), 173-190.
           Sees James's revision in 1878 as achieving several im-
       provements.

1476.1 Goldfarb, Russell M. Sexual Repression and Victorian Lit-
       erature. Lewisburg: Bucknell University Press, 1970, pp.
       59-61, 63.
           Believes James was probably unaware of the sexual impli-
       cations of certain passages in Watch and Ward.

1477   Gow, Ronald. "A Boston Story": A Comedy [in three acts]
       Based on a Novel, "Watch and Ward," By Henry James.
       London: English Theatre Guild, 1969.

1478   Grosso, Luigi. "Attualità di Henry James," Fle, 15 (March
       13, 1960), 5.
           Occasioned by a reprint of Watch and Ward.

1478.1 Johnson, Lee Ann. " 'A Dog in the Manger': James's De-
       piction of Roger Lawrence in Watch and Ward," ArQ, 29
       (Summer, 1973), 169-176.
           "... James's hero is seen to emerge as an ambiguous fig-
       ure, neither wolf nor lamb but a curious mixture of the
       two...."

1478.2 Leavis, F. R. "Henry James's First Novel," Scrutiny, 14
       (September, 1947), 295-301.

1479   Levy, Leo B. "The Comedy of Watch and Ward," ArlQ, 1
        (Summer, 1968), 86-98.

1480   McElderry, B. R., Jr. "Henry James's Revision of Watch
        and Ward," MLN, 67 (November, 1952), 457-460.
                An analysis of the stylistic changes James made in his
                early novelette Watch and Ward.

1481   Rosenbaum, S. P. "Two Henry James Letters on The Amer-
        ican and Watch and Ward," AL, 30 (January, 1959), 533-537.
                Letters to Osgood, 1877, about revisions.

1482   Stone, Edward. "Henry James's First Novel," BPLQ, 2
        (April, 1950), 167-171.
                James's first novel, although excluded from his collected
                works, foreshadows the author's later greatness in its
                irony, pathos, and characterization. It also contains a
                sense of "the air of the past."

1482.1 Taylor, Gordon O. "The Hinging-Point of Great Emotions,"
        The Passages of Thought: Psychological Representation in
        the American Novel, 1870-1900. New York: Oxford Univer-
        sity Press, 1969, pp. 17-41.

1483   Veeder, William R. "Watch and Ward: The Mixed Beginning,"
        DAI, 31 (Berkeley, California: 1970), 772A.

1484   Ward, Joseph A. "The Double Structure of Watch and Ward,"
        TSLL, 4 (Spring, 1963), 613-624.
                Roger "wants not to master life, but to combine adult ex-
                perience ... with the security and ease he had known in
                childhood."

Reviews of Watch and Ward:

                Appleton, n. s., 5 (August, 1878), 189
                Athenaeum, 2650 (August 10, 1878), 177
                Christian Union, 18 (October 16, 1878), 313
                Cottage Hearth, 5 (August, 1878), 286
                Independent, 29 (May 17, 1878), 9
                Library Table, 4 (June 22, 1878), 301-2
                Lit World, 9 (August, 1878), 47
                Nation, 13 (August 3, 31, Sept. 28, Nov. 2, 30, 1871), 78,
                    148, 212, 295, 358; 27 (August 22, 1878), 117-8
                Round Table, 7 (June 27, 1869), 411
                Sunday Afternoon, 2 (October, 1878), 384

WHAT MAISIE KNEW

1485   Banta, Martha. "The Quality of Experience in What Maisie
        Knew," NEQ, 42 (December, 1969), 483-510.
                Provides a good survey of critical views.

1486   Bewley, Marius. "Appearance and Reality in Henry James,"
        Scrutiny, 17 (Summer, 1950), 102-114.

1487   _____. "Maisie, Miles and Flora, the Jamesian Inno-
        cents," Scrutiny, 17 (Autumn, 1950), 255-263.
            "... dissolution of the ties between appearance and real-
            ity...."

1488   _____. "Maisie, Miles and Flora, the Jamesian Inno-
        cents: A Rejoinder," in The Complex Fate. New York:
        Gordian Press, Inc., 1967, pp. 132-143.
            Cf., F. R. Leavis. "What Maisie Knew: A Disagree-
            ment," in The Complex Fate, pp. 114-131.

1489   Brebner, Adele. "How to Know Maisie," CE, 17 (February,
        1956), 283-285.

1490   Cambon, Glauco. "What Maisie and Huck Knew," SA, 6
        (1960), 203-220.

1490.1 Dyson, A. E. "On Knowing What Maisie Knew Perhaps," in
        On the Novel: A Present for Walter Allen on His 60th Birth-
        day from His Friends and Colleagues. B. S. Benedikz, ed.
        London: Dent, 1971, pp. 128-139.
            Maisie's "last choice" is "between two evils, with adult
            demands having so effectively outpaced her 'knowledge'
            that she must renounce the one in life she really loves."

1490.2 Edel, Leon, ed. Introduction. The Bodley Head Henry
        James. Vol. 6. What Maisie Knew. London: Bodley Head,
        1969.

1491   Fahey, Paul. "What Maisie Knew: Learning Not to Mind,"
        CritQ, 14 (1971), 96-108.
            "... the pressure of the book is towards acceptance of
            the view that, ... human relationships are inadequate to
            the essential needs of the developing individual, even
            though such relationships are necessarily the means of dis-
            covering what those needs are."

1492   Fiedler, Leslie A. "From Redemption to Initiation," NewL,
        41 (May 26, 1958), 20-23.
            Notes that many novelists follow James in What Maisie
            Knew in their treatment of the initiation theme.

1493   Gargano, James W. "Age and Innocence in What Maisie
        Knew," RSWSU, 37 (September, 1969), 218-226.
            Says that by establishing Maisie's age from the time of
            her parents' divorce to her departure for France, we can
            see her innocence and maturity at the end of the novel.

1494   _____. "What Maisie Knew: The Evolution of a 'Moral
        Sense,' " NCF, 16 (June, 1961), 33-46.

The structure of the novel, as well as James's Preface,
show that James intended Maisie's development to be a
progressive expansion of vision and moral awareness.

1494.1 Girgus, Sam B. "The Other Maisie: Inner Death and Fatalism in What Maisie Knew," ArQ, 29 (Summer, 1973), 115-
122.
"It is only natural that Maisie should think in terms of
death, for the world into which Maisie is born is incapable
of adequately providing for her...."

1495   Greet, Thomas Y. The Child's Eye: A Study of American
Fiction Written from the Child's Point of View, Leading from
"Huckleberry Finn" and "What Maisie Knew." Diss. Wis-
consin: n. d.

1496   Habegger, Alfred. "Reciprocity and the Market Place in The
Wings of the Dove and What Maisie Knew," NCF, 25 (March,
1971), 455-473.
Concludes that the focus in both novels is on reciprocity,
of "freely giving in return," an appealing ethic for James
because it was "closely affiliated with James's feeling for
symmetrical form."

1497   Hamblen, Abigail A. "Henry James and the Power of Eros:
What Maisie Knew," MQ, 9 (Summer, 1968), 391-399.
Places emphasis on the sexual implication of the story.

1498   Hynes, Joseph A. "The Middle Way of Miss Farange: A
Study of James's Maisie," ELH, 32 (December, 1965), 528-
553.
Examines the story as the process, shape, and value of
renunciation.

1498.1 Isle, Walter. "What Maisie Knew," in Experiments in Form:
Henry James's Novels, 1896-1911. Cambridge, Mass.: Harvard U. P., 1968, pp. 120-164.

1499   James, Henry. Preface to What Maisie Knew, in The Art of
the Novel: Critical Prefaces. New York: Scribner, 1934,
pp. 140-158.

1500   Jefferson, Douglas. Introduction. What Maisie Knew. London: Oxford University Press, 1966.

1501   Leavis, F. R. "James's What Maisie Knew: A Disagreement," Scrutiny, 17 (Summer, 1950), 115-127.

1501.1 _____. "What Maisie Knew: A Disagreement," in The
Complex Fate by Marius Bewley. New York: Gordian
Press, Inc., 1967, pp. 114-131.

1501.2 _____. "What Maisie Knew," in Anna Karenina and Other

Essays. New York: Pantheon Books, A Division of Random House, [1933], 1967, pp. 75-91.

1502 McCloskey, John C. "What Maisie Knows: A Study of Childhood and Adolescence," AL, 36 (January, 1965), 485-513.
Reviews criticism of the novel and concludes that Maisie has grown hard and selfish, with "an ego that will satisfy itself at the cost of what it regards as everything."

1502.1 Mitchell, Juliet. "What Maisie Knew: Portrait of the Artist as a Young Girl," in The Air of Reality. John Goode, ed. London: Methuen, 1972, pp. 168-189.

1502.2 Porcher, Frances. "What Maisie Knew: Henry James's Story of Divorce," Mirror, 7 (December 23, 1897), 7-8.

1502.3 Putt, S. Gorley. "Marriage and Society ... "What Maisie Knew," in A Reader's Guide to Henry James. Ithaca, New York: 1966, pp. 239-263.

1502.4 Samuels, Charles Thomas. "The Pupils" [What Maisie Knew], The Ambiguity of Henry James. Urbana: Illinois U. P., 1971, pp. 178-209.

1503 Stevens, Harriet S. "Lo que James Sabía," Torre, 13 (1965), 171-193.
Finds the novel a blend of form and theme which leaves Maisie and Sir Claude memorable and distinct.

1504 Swan, Michael. Introductory Note. What Maisie Knew. London: John Lehmann, Ltd., 1947.

1505 Tytell, John. "The Jamesian Legacy in The Good Soldier," SNNTS, 3 (Winter, 1971), 365-373.
The influence of James's What Maisie Knew.

1506 Walsh, William. "Maisie in What Maisie Knew," in The Use of the Imagination. London: Chatto & Windus, 1959, pp. 148ff.

1507 Wasiolek, Edward. "Maisie: Pure or Corrupt?" CE, 22, #3 (December, 1960), 167-172.
One can only speculate about Maisie's later development.

1507.1 Weinstein, Philip M. "Resisting the Assault of Experience: What Maisie Knew," Henry James and the Requirements of the Imagination. Cambridge, Mass.: Harvard U. P., 1971, pp. 72-96.

1508 Wilson, Harris W. "What Did Maisie Know?" CE, 17 (February, 1956), 279-282.
Treats the novel as Maisie's initiation into evil. The basic theme is "the violation of innocence," the "corruption of

a sensitive child" by her parents and step-parents. Cf.,
Edward Wasiolek, CE, 22 (1960), 167-172.

1509   Wolf, H. R. "What Maisie Knew: The Rankian Hero," AI,
23 (Fall, 1966), 227-234.
Uses Otto Rank's The Myth of the Birth of the Hero (1957),
as basis for interpretation of James's novel.

1510   Worden, Ward S. "A Cut Version of What Maisie Knew,"
AL, 24 (January, 1953), 493-504.
A study of the effect of excisions made in the serialized
version in the British New Review, February-September,
1897.

1511   _____. "Henry James's What Maisie Knew: A Comparison with the Plans in the Notebooks," PMLA, 68 (June,
1953), 371-383.
Regards Maisie as possessing "innate, absolute morality."

Reviews of What Maisie Knew:

        Athenaeum, 3654 (November 6, 1897), 629
        Book Buyer, 16 (February, 1898), 66-8
        Bookman (London), 13 (October, 1897), 22
        Bookman (NY), 6 (February, 1898), 562
        Book News, 16 (December, 1897), 289
        Critic, 32 (January 8, 1898), 21
        Independent, 49 (December 16, 1897), 1660
        Lit World, 28 (December 11, 1897), 454-5
        Nation, 66 (February 17, 1898), 135
        Outlook, 57 (November 13, 1897), 670
        Picayune, (November 17, 1897), 6
        Public Opinion, 23 (December 30, 1897), 855
        Quarterly Rev, 198 (October, 1903), 358
        Rev of Revs, 16 (December, 1897), 727
        SatR, 84 (November 20, 1897), 537-38
        Spec, 79 (October 30, 1897), 603
        Times, 2 (November 27, 1897), 9

                    "The Wheel of Time"

1511.1 Brooks, Van Wyck. "The Wheel of Time," The Pilgrimage
of Henry James. New York: Octagon Books, 1972, pp.
106-123.

See also: 10, 1740, 1794, 1804, 2006, 2198, VIII; 2229,
2352, 2363; 2382, 2637, XXVII; 3326, 3711

Reviews of "The Wheel of Time":

        Atlantic, 73 (April, 1894), 568

Critic, n. s., 23 (October 21, 1893), 253
Dial, 15 (December 1, 1893), 344
HarperM, 87, Sup. 2-3 (October, 1893), 810
Lit World, 24 (November 4, 1893), 367
Nation, 57 (November 30, 1893), 417

"The Whole Family"

1512   Jordan, Elizabeth. Three Rousing Cheers. New York: Appleton-Century, 1938, pp. 208-212, 216-220, 269-273.

1513   McElderry, B. R., Jr. "Henry James and 'The Whole Family,'" PacS, 4 (Summer, 1950), 352-360.
        The story shows James at work.

1514   Walbridge, Earle F. "'The Whole Family' and Henry James," PBSA, 52 (2nd Qt., 1958), 144-145.

        See: 12, 1674, 2070, 2352

WILLIAM WETMORE STORY AND HIS FRIENDS

1515   Hudson, Gertrude Reese, ed. Introduction and Notes. Browning to His American Friends: Letters Between the Brownings, The Storys and James Russell Lowell, 1841-1890. New York: Barnes & Noble, 1965.
        Henry James had access to and used some of the correspondence in his William Wetmore Story and His Friends.

1515.1 Hynes, Joseph Anthony, Jr. "Henry James's 'William Wetmore Story and His Friends': A Critical Commentary," DA, 21 (Michigan: 1961), 3458.

        See also: 1000, 1740, 1980, 3711

Reviews:

        Athenaeum, 2 (1903), 605-6
        Atlantic, 93 (January, 1904), 80-1
        Blackw, 174 (November, 1903), 659-68
        Churchman, 88 (November 14, 1903), 599
        Critic, 44 (February, 1904), 175-7
        Dial, 35 (November 16, 1903), 348-51
        Lamp, 27 (November, 1903), 333-7
        Living Age, 239 (December 5, 1903), 595-603
        Nation, 77 (November 5, 1903), 365-6
        Times, 8 (December 5, 1903), 886
        Tribune, 3 (December 5, 1903), 15

THE WINGS OF THE DOVE

1516   Allott, Miriam. "The Bronzino Portrait in Henry James's
        The Wings of the Dove," MLN, 68 (January, 1953), 23-25.
              The portrait is that of Lucrezia Panciatichi in the Uffizi
              Gallery in Florence.

1517   _____. "Form versus Substance in Henry James," REL,
        3 (January, 1962), 53-66.

1518   _____. "James Russell Lowell: A Link between Tenny-
        son and Henry James," RES, 6 (October, 1955), 397-399.

1519   _____. "A Ruskin Echo in The Wings of the Dove," N&Q,
        201 (n. s., 3) (February, 1956), 87.
              To characterize Mrs. Lowder in The Wings of the Dove,
              James borrowed an image from Ruskin's The Crown of
              Wild Olive.

1519.1 Aoki, Tsugio. "Language of Love and Language of Things:
        Henry James's The Wings of the Dove," SELit (Eng. No.) 48
        (1971), 55-71.
              A reading of the novel as to symbolic equations between
              Milly and an idea of America, indicative as she is of a
              dying civilization and a "nevertheless resurrected 'language
              of love.'"

1520   Atherton, Gertrude. Adventures of a Novelist. New York:
        Liveright, Inc., 1932, passim.
              The Wings of the Dove "still seems to me one of the great-
              est novels in the history of fiction."

1521   Bell, Millicent. "The Dream of Being Possessed and Pos-
        sessing: Henry James's The Wings of the Dove," MassR, 10
        (Winter, 1969), 97-114.
              A review of the plot with possessiveness and money in
              mind.

1522   Bersani, Leo. "The Narrator as Center in The Wings of the
        Dove," MFS, 6 (Summer, 1960), 131-144.
              Suggests that James saw human relations as "chaos" and
              found a solution only in renouncing "life in society for soli-
              tary integrity."

1523   Bewley, Marius. "James's Debt to Hawthorne (II): The Mar-
        ble Faun and The Wings of the Dove," Scrutiny, 16 (Winter,
        1949), 301-317. Also in The Complex Fate. New York:
        1967, pp. 31-54.

1523.1 Birch, Brian. "Henry James: Some Bibliographical and Tex-
        tual Matters," Library, 20 (1965), 108-123.
              Revisions of The Wings of the Dove made by James in the

New York Edition.

1524   Blackmur, R. P.   Introduction.   The Wings of the Dove.
       New York: Dell Publishing Co., 1958.

1525   Brown, E. K.   "James and Conrad," YR, 35 (December,
       1945), 265-285.

1526   Brown, R. Christiani.   "The Role of Densher in The Wings
       of the Dove," MSpr, 65 (1971), 5-11.

1527   Chen, Lucy M.   The Ancestry of "The Wings of the Dove."
       Diss.   Chicago: 1949.

1528   Clark, Harry Hayden.   "Henry James and Science: The
       Wings of the Dove," TWA, 52 (1963), 1-15.
       A discussion of the social Darwinism in the imagery of the
       novel.

1529   Colby, Frank M.   "In Darkest James," Bookman (America),
       16 (November 1902), 259-260.
       In The Wings of the Dove there is "the same absorption
       in the machinery of motive" and "mental processes."

1530   Conger, Sydney M.   "The Admirable Villains in Henry
       James's The Wings of the Dove," ArQ, 27 (Summer, 1971),
       151-160.
       James gives his reader "a refined notion of what is ethi-
       cal," showing that the "distance between seeming and actu-
       al virtue is often barely perceptible."

1531   Crow, Charles R.   "The Style of Henry James: The Wings
       of the Dove," EIE, 4 (1958), 172-189.   Also in Style in
       Prose Fiction.   Harold Clark Martin, ed.   Columbia U. P.,
       1959, pp. 172-189.
       The later James style is not a "monotone."   Examination
       of passages in The Wings of the Dove "reveals a style full
       of modulations."

1532   Crowl, Susan R.   "The Beholder's Eye: Romantic and Criti-
       cal Perspective Through Style in James's The Turn of the
       Screw, The Wings of the Dove and The Golden Bowl," DAI,
       31 (Indiana: 1971), 5357A.

1533   Dupee, F. W.   Afterword.   The Wings of the Dove.   New
       York: New American Library, 1964.

1533.1 Edel, Leon, ed.   Introduction.   The Bodley Head Henry
       James.   Vol. 7.   The Wings of the Dove.   London: Bodley
       Head, 1969.

1534   Elton, Oliver.   "The Novels of Mr. Henry James," QR, 198
       (October, 1903), 358-379; LivA, 240 (January 2, 1904), 1-

14; also in <u>Modern Studies</u>. London, 1907, pp. 245-284; New
York: 1907.
>Despite the title, <u>The Wings of the Dove</u> constitutes the
>"major part" of the discussion, and is described as "the
>most remarkable book that Mr. James has written."

1535   Firebaugh, Joseph J. "The Idealism of Merton Densher,"
UTSE, 37 (1958), 141-154.

1536   Geismar, Maxwell. "<u>The Wings of the Dove</u>: or, False
Gold," Atl, 212 (August, 1963), 93-98.
>In the novel's "multicircle or con-circular narrative," the
>attraction for the reader is James's manipulation of char-
>acters through their complex conflicts among illusions.

1537   Goldstein, Sallie Sears. <u>A Critical Study of Henry James's</u>
<u>The Wings of the Dove, The Ambassadors, and The Golden</u>
<u>Bowl.</u> DA, 24 (Brandeis: 1964), 5384-85.

1538   Goode, John. "The Pervasive Mystery of Style: <u>The Wings</u>
<u>of the Dove</u>," in <u>The Air of Reality</u>. London: Methuen,
1972, pp. 244-300.
>"... James finds something so different from <u>merde</u> in
>the coffers of the millionaire that it becomes, in effect,
>the root of innocence and the flower of imagination...."

1538.1 Grabo, Carl H. "Fusion of Exposition in Narrative" [<u>The</u>
<u>Wings of the Dove</u>], <u>The Technique of the Novel</u>. New York:
Scribner's, 1928; Gordian Press, 1964, pp. 106-108; 238ff.

1539   Greene, Mildred S. E. <u>Love and Duty: The Character of the</u>
<u>Princess de Clèves as Reflected in Certain Later English and</u>
<u>American Novels,</u> DA, 28 (New Mexico: 1967), 230A-31A.
>The novels examined are <u>The Wings of the Dove</u> and <u>The</u>
><u>Portrait of a Lady.</u>

1540   Habegger, Alfred. "Reciprocity and the Market Place in <u>The</u>
<u>Wings of the Dove</u> and <u>What Maisie Knew</u>," NCF, 25 (March,
1971), 455-473.

1541   Hagan, John. "A Note on a Symbolic Pattern in <u>The Wings</u>
<u>of the Dove</u>," CLAJ, 10 (March, 1967), 256-262.
>The symbolic imagery in the early cliff scene prefigures
>a larger pattern which recapitulates Milly Theale's three-
>part development from "initial acceptance of London soci-
>ety, through disillusionment, to the renunciation she first
>disdains."

1542   Hamblen, Abigail Ann. "Henry James and Disease," DR, 44
(Spring, 1964), 57-63.
>Notes that although James is not usually specific about ill-
>ness, in <u>The Wings of the Dove</u> he makes good use of ill-
>ness and death to purify and clarify character.

1543 _____. "The Inheritance of the Meek: Two Novels by
Agatha Christie and Henry James," Discourse, 12 (Summer,
1969), 409-413.
   A comparison of Endless Night with The Wings of the Dove.

1544 Heston, Lilla A. "A Study of the Point of View in Three
Novels by Henry James: The Spoils of Poynton, The Wings
of the Dove, and The Golden Bowl. DA, 26 (Northwestern:
1965), 3533.

1545 Holland, Laurence B. "The Wings of the Dove," ELH, 26
(December, 1959), 549-574.

1545.1 _____. ["The Wings of the Dove"]. The Expense of Vision: Essays on the Craft of Henry James. Princeton, New
Jersey: 1964, pp. 287-288.

1546 Itagaki, Konomu. " 'Merciful Indirection' in The Wings of
the Dove," SELit, 41 (March, 1965), 165-181.

1547 James, Henry. Preface. The Wings of the Dove: The Art
of the Novel: Critical Prefaces. New York: Scribner,
1934, pp. 288-306.

1548 Kimball, Jean. "The Abyss and The Wings of the Dove:
The Image as a Revelation," NCF, 10 (March, 1956), 281-
300.
   An attempt to restore Milly Theale to the center of the
   novel and "to look at the whole of the action from her
   point of view."

1549 Koch, Stephen. "Transcendence in The Wings of the Dove,"
MFS, 12 (Spring, 1966), 93-102.
   Thinks the design of the novel forced James to give a
   transcendent rather than a realistic quality to Milly.

1549.1 Kornfeld, Milton. "Villainy and Responsibility in The Wings
of the Dove," TSLL, 14 (Summer, 1972), 337-346.

1550 Kraft, Quentin G. "Life Against Death in Venice," Criti-
cism, 7 (Summer, 1965), 217-223.
   In omitting a narrative account of the actual death of Milly,
   James practiced the "art of selective omission." Milton
   Densher now sees Milly as the "princess of life" in the
   face of death.

1551 Krook, Dorothea. "The Wings of the Dove," CamJ, 7 (Aug-
gust, 1954), 671-689.
   Says that James's purpose in this novel was "to exhibit the
   world ... in the fullness of its glory and horror; and to
   exhibit it, ... as a world prepared for the descent of the
   Dove."

1551.1 _____. "The Wings of the Dove," The Ordeal of Consciousness in Henry James. New York: 1962; rev. ed.,
1967, pp. 195-231.

1552   Lang, P. H. "The Wings of the Dove" [The Operatic Version by D. Moore], MusQ, 48 (January, 1962), 101-102.

1553   Las Vergnas, Raymond. "Lettres anglo-américaines: Henry
James," HeM, 9 (1954), 445-447.
       Has reference to The Wings of the Dove and Washington
       Square.

1554   Lebowitz, Naomi. ["The Wings of the Dove"], The Imagination of Loving: Henry James's Legacy to the Novel. Detroit: Wayne State U. P., 1965, pp. 73-78, 84-85, 99-107,
passim.

1555   Lee, Brian. "Henry James's 'Divine Consensus': The Ambassadors, The Wings of the Dove, The Golden Bowl," RMS,
6 (1962), 5-24.

1556   Lewis, R. W. B. "The Histrionic Vision of Henry James,"
JA, 4 (1959), 39-51.

1557   _____. "The Vision of Grace: James's The Wings of the
Dove," MFS, 3 (Spring, 1957), 33-40.
       Merton's experience leads him to a fragmentary vision of
       grace.

1557.1 Marks, Sita Patricia. "Character Patterns in Henry James's
The Wings of the Dove and The Golden Bowl," DAI, 31 (Michigan State: 1970), 6063A.
       "Once the patterns are defined in each novel, one can
       trace the development of James's conception of good and
       evil from the modes of innocence and experience to pat-
       terns of moral perception and moral blindness."

1558   _____. "The Sound and the Silence: Nonverbal Patterns
in The Wings of the Dove," ArQ, 27 (Summer, 1971), 143-
150.
       "Each division of The Wings of the Dove has as its sub-
       ject the concealment of feeling or fact...."

1559   McDowell, B. D. "The Use of 'Everything' in The Wings of
the Dove," XUS, 2 (Spring, 1972), 13-20.

1559.1 McLean, Robert C. " 'Love by the Doctor's Direction': Disease and Death in The Wings of the Dove," PLL, 8, Supp.
(1972), 128-148.
       Says that the nature of Milly Theale's illness is crucial to
       understanding the novel.

1560   Meldrum, Ronald M. "Three of Henry James' Dark Ladies,"

RS, 37 (March, 1969), 54-60.

1561   Moore, D. "Wings of the Dove" [Operatic Version], HudR,
        14 (Winter, 1961-1962), 595-596.

1562   Muecke, D. C. "The Dove's Flight," NCF, 9 (June, 1954),
        76-78.

1563   Mulqueen, James E. "Perfection of a Pattern: The Struc-
        ture of The Ambassadors, The Wings of the Dove, and The
        Golden Bowl," ArQ, 27 (Summer, 1971), 133-142.

1564   Piccinato, Stefania. "The Wings of the Dove: Dal progetto
        alla forma," SA, 15 (1969), 131-168.

1565   Price, Reynolds. Introduction. The Wings of the Dove.
        Columbus, Ohio: Charles E. Merrill: 1970.

1566   Putt, S. Gorley. "The Wings of the Dove: A Study in Con-
        struction," Scholars of the Heart: Essays in Criticism.
        London: Faber & Faber, 1962, pp. 204-235.

1567   _____. "The Wings of the Dove (A Note on Henry James),"
        Orion: A Miscellany. C. Day Lewis, et al, eds. London:
        Nicholson & Watson, 1946, III, 120-143.

1567.1 _____. "The Wings of the Dove," A Reader's Guide to
        Henry James. Ithaca, New York: 1966, pp. 307-339.

1568   Read, Herbert. Introduction. The Wings of the Dove. Lon-
        don: Eyre and Spottiswood, 1948.

1569   Rowe, John Carlos. "The Symbolization of Milly Theale:
        Henry James's The Wings of the Dove," ELH, 40 (Spring,
        1973), 131-164.
            "... Milly's symbolic 'absence' places her in the stream
            of life and consciousness itself. Milly becomes the sym-
            bol of the mystery at the heart of our language and our
            art...."

1570   Rypins, Harold L. "Henry James in Harley Street," AL, 24
        (January, 1953), 481-492.

1570.1 Samuels, Charles Thomas. "The Joys of Renunciation"
        [The Wings of the Dove], The Ambiguity of Henry James.
        Urbana: Illinois U. P., 1971, pp. 61-88.

1571   Sandeen, Ernest. "The Wings of the Dove and The Portrait
        of a Lady: A Study of Henry James's Later Phase," PMLA,
        69 (December, 1954), 1060-1075.
            Reads each phase in reference to Minny Temple.

1572   Snow, Lotus. "The Disconcerting Poetry of Mary Temple:

A Comparison of Imagery of The Portrait of a Lady and The Wings of the Dove," NEQ, 31 (September, 1958), 312-339.

1573   Taylor, C. "The Wings of the Dove" [Dramatization], reviews: ILondN, 243 (December 21, 1963), 1044; NSt, 66 (December 13, 1963), 889.
        The reviewer of this 1963 dramatization remarked on the interest of "the unique Jamesian idiom--with its slangy primness." [NSt.]

1574   Thorberg, Raymond. 'Germaine, James's Notebooks, and The Wings of the Dove," CL, 22 (1970), 254-264.
        An analytic source study which indicates that James probably wove elements from Edmond About's Germaine into The Wings of the Dove.

1575   Thurber, James. "Onward and Upward with the Arts, the Wings of Henry James," NY, 35 (November 7, 1959), 184-197.
        On dramatic adaptations of The Wings of the Dove.

1576   Tyler, Parker. "Milly and Billy as Proto-Finnegans," in Every Artist His Own Scandal: A Study of Real and Fictive Heroes. New York: Horizon Press, 1964, pp. 239-255.
        On James's Milly Theale and Billy Budd.

1577   Van Cromphout, Gustaaf. "The Wings of the Dove: Intention and Achievement," MinnR, 6 (1966), 149-154.
        Insists that James did not intend to evoke a fairy-tale motif to raise the theme to the level of a more universal truth. The theme becomes highly universal owing to James's transcending the usually international traits of his action and characters.

1578   Vincec, Sister Stephanie. "A Significant Revision in The Wings of the Dove," RES, 23 (February, 1972), 58-61.
        Suggests that James's revision in this novel, in which he gives proper place in the Piazza of St. Marks to a statue of St. Theodore rather than St. Mark, probably derives from his reading of Ruskin.

1579   Ward, J. A. "Social Disintegration in The Wings of the Dove," Criticism, 2 (Spring, 1960), 190-203.
        In this novel, James "dramatizes both the cause--the disassociation of appearance and meaning in western culture --and the effect--the need for the individual to acquire identity as an isolated person--of the collapse of civilization."

1580   Wegelin, Christof. "Henry James's The Wings of the Dove as an International Novel," JA, 3 (1958), 151-161.

1581   _____. "The 'Internationalism' of The Golden Bowl,"

NCF, 11 (December, 1956), 161-181.
James's novel is a "prophetic fable" representing a fusion
of two points of view presented in The Wings of the Dove
and The Ambassadors.

1581.1 _____. "The Lesson of Spiritual Beauty: The Wings of
the Dove," in The Image of Europe in Henry James. Dallas:
Southern Methodist U. P., 1958. Repr., in Discussions of
Henry James. Naomi Lebowitz, ed. Boston: 1962, pp. 71-
79.

1582 Westbrook, James Seymour, Jr. "Sensibility and Society: A
Study in Themes," DA, 35 (Columbia: 1964), 3560.
Includes a chapter on The Wings of the Dove. The study
analyzes how five novelists, including James, treated sensibility within a social framework.

1583 Wharton, Edith. A Backward Glance. New York: Appleton-
Century, 1934, pp. 189-192.

1584 Wilson, R. B. J. "An Attempt to Define the Meaning of
Henry James's The Wings of the Dove," AULLA, 2 (1964),
76-78.
Discusses the changing relationship between Kate Croy and
Densher, and the skill with which James executes the cli-
max of the novel.

Reviews: "Child of Fortune" (1956), dramatization by Guy Reginald
Bolton, based on The Wings of the Dove:

Atkinson, Brooks. "Theatre: An Old-Fashioned Tale," NY
Times, (November 14, 1956), 41
Chapman, John. "Child of Fortune Is Not Long for World,"
NY Daily News (November 14, 1956), in NYTCR, 17 (1956),
210
Coleman, Robert. "Child of Fortune Misses the Mark," NY
Daily Mirror, (November 14, 1956), in NYTCR, 17 (1956),
209
Donnelly, Tom. "It's Mighty Weak Medicine," NY World-
Telegram & Sun (November 14, 1956), in NYTCR, 17
(1946), 211
Kerr, Walter. "Child of Fortune," NY Herald Tribune, (No-
vember 14, 1956), in NYTCR, 17 (1956), 212
McClain, John. "James Novel Adaptation Is Ungratifying,"
NY Journal American (November 14, 1956), in NYTCR, 17
(1956), 210
Watts, Richard. "Effort to Dramatize Henry James," NY
Post (November 14, 1956), in NYTCR, 17 (1956), 211.

Other reviews of the dramatization:

Cw, 65 (January 11, 1957), 383

NY, 32 (November 24, 1956), 124-125
SatR, 39 (December 1, 1956), 50
ThA, 41 (January, 1957), 27
Time, 68 (November 26, 1956), 58

Reviews of the novel, The Wings of the Dove:

Athenaeum, 3907 (September 13, 1902), 346
Atl, 91 (January, 1903), 77-82
Bookman (London), 23 (October, 1902), 24-25
Bookman (NY), 16 (November, 1902), 259-60
Book News, 21 (October, 1902), 68-9
Churchman, 86 (September 27, 1902), 364
Critic, 41 (November, 1902), 409-14
HarperW, 47 (February 14, 1903), 273; 47 (April 4, 1903),
    552
Independent, 54 (November 13, 1902), 2711-2
Lit Digest, 26 (February 28, 1903), 300-1
Nation, 75 (October 23, 1902), 330-1
North Amer Rev, 176 (January, 1903), 125-37
Outlook, 72 (December 6, 1902), 789
Quarterly Rev, 198 (October, 1903), 358
Reader, 1 (November, 1902), 88-90
Rev of Revs, 26 (October, 1902), 446
SatR, 95 (January 17, 1903), 79-80
Times, 7 (October 4, 1902), 658
TLS, (September, 1902), 263
Tribune Wk Rev, 1 (September 20, 1902), 13

"Within the Rim"

1585   Woolf, Virginia. "Henry James: 'Within the Rim,' " Col-
        lected Essays. London: Hogarth Press, 1966; New York:
        Harcourt, Brace & World, 1967, pp. 267-269.

1585.1 _____. "Henry James: 'Within the Rim,' " The Death of
        the Moth and Other Essays. London: The Hogarth Press,
        1942, pp. 83-86.

Reviews of "Within the Rim":

Fortn, 108 (August, 1917), 161-71
Harper, 136 (December, 1917), 55-61
LivAge, 294 (September 8, 1917), 579-86

DRAMA

(See also Theatricals, as well as references under individual plays)

1586   Alexander, Elizabeth. "Henry James as a Playwright," DA,
        29 (Wisconsin: 1969), 3123A.
           Believes that James's most successful pieces were writ-
           ten under the influence of Ibsen.

1587   Anon. "Henry James' Failure as a Dramatist Exposed by a
        London Critic," CurOp, 63 (October, 1917), 247.

1588   Anon. "James the Dramatist," TLS, #2501 (January 6,
        1950), 8.
           Says James is a better critic than a dramatist, but his
           dramas (and his interest in the drama) occupied a greater
           part of his writing time than is generally realized.

1589   Barnes, Howard. New York Theatre Critics' Reviews, 1950,
        11, #4 (February 6, 1950), 360f.
           Contains general critical comments.

1590   Barzun, Jacques. "James the Melodramatist," KR, 5 (Au-
        tumn, 1943), 508-521. Also in his The Energies of Art.
        New York: 1956, pp. 227-244; The Question of Henry James.
        F. W. Dupee, ed. New York: 1945, pp. 261-266.

1591   Beerbohm, Max. "Jacobean and Shavian," Around Theatres.
        New York: Knopf, 1930, pp. 260-265, 323-326. Repr., in
        Henry James: A Collection of Critical Essays. Leon Edel,
        ed. Englewood Cliffs, New Jersey: 1963, 22-26.

1592   Beyer, William. "The State of the Theatre," Sch&S, 71
        (April 8, 1950), 213-217.

1593   Clark, E. "Idiosyncrasy of the Master," SatRL, 32 (No-
        vember 12, 1949), 16.
           Essay-rev., The Complete Plays of Henry James. Leon
           Edel, ed. New York: Lippincott, 1949.

1594   D'Agostino, Nemi. "Sul Teatro di Henry James," SA, 2
        (1956), 163-177.

1595   Daly, Joseph Francis. The Life of Augustin Daly. New
        York: Macmillan Co., 1917, pp. 551-554, 566.
           Correspondence about a play James was to write for the
           Daly Company.

1596   Dupee, Frederick W. "Henry James and the Play," Nation,

171 (July 8, 1950), 40-42.
James's playwriting represents a transitional phase between his early and late fiction.

1597   Durham, F. H. "Henry James's Dramatizations of His Novels," BulCit, 6 (November, 1942), 51-64.

1598   Edel, Leon. Henry James: Les Années Dramatiques. Paris: Jouve, 1931.
Discusses relationship between the late novels and the
plays.

1599   _____, ed. Foreword and Introduction. The Complete
Plays of Henry James. New York: J. B. Lippincott, 1949.

1600   _____. "Henry James Flopped as a Playwright, but His
Novels Succeed as Dramas," TVG, 21, #12 (March 24, 1973),
35, 37-38.

1601   _____. "The Text of Henry James's Unpublished Plays,"
HLB, 3 (August, 1949), 395-406.
A description, listing and evaluation of typescripts and
prompt-books of the unpublished plays collated for The
Complete Plays of Henry James.

1602   Fenton, Edna. "The Plays of Henry James," ThA, 12 (May,
1928), 347-352.

1603   Fergusson, Francis. "James's Idea of Dramatic Form,"
KR, 5 (Autumn, 1943), 495-507.
James ideas of form and techniques of presentation in his
critical prefaces and his last group of novels throw as
much light on drama as on fiction.

1604   _____. "James's Idea of Dramatic Form," American Drama and Its Critics: A Collection of Critical Essays. Alan
S. Downer, ed. Chicago: Chicago U. P., 1965, pp. 177-
187.

1605   Forbes, Elizabeth L. "Dramatic Lustrum: A Study of the
Effect of Henry James's Theatrical Experience on His Later
Novels," NEQ, 11 (March, 1938), 108-120.

1606   Furbank, P. N. "Henry James: The Novelist as Actor,"
EIC, 1 #4 (1951), 404-420.

1607   Gifford, Henry. "Henry James: The Drama of Discrimina-
tion," in The Modern Age. Boris Ford, ed. Pelican Guide
to English Literature, Volume 7. Baltimore: Penguin Books,
1961, pp. 103-118.

1608   Grattan, Clinton Hartley. "Theatre and Friendship: Letter
from James to Elizabeth Robbins," Nation, 135 (October 12,

1932), 335.

1609   Greene, Graham. "Books in General," [Appeal of the The-
        atre to Henry James], NS&N, 39 (January 28, 1950), 101-
        102.
           On James as a playwright: "Unwillingly we have to con-
           demn the Master for a fault we had previously never sus-
           pected the possibility of his possessing--incompetence."

1610   _____. "The Plays of Henry James," Collected Essays.
        New York: Viking Press, 1969, pp. 62-68. Also in Lost
        Childhood and Other Essays. London: Heinemann, 1951,
        pp. 45-48.

1610.1 "Henry James's Failure as a Dramatist Exposed by a Lon-
        don Critic," CurOp, 63 (October, 1917), 247.

1610.2 "Henry James's Failure as a Dramatist," LitD, 65 (May 8,
        1920), 48.

1611   Isle, Walter. "The Early Nineties and the Drama," Experi-
        ments in Form: Henry James's Novels, 1896-1901. Cam-
        bridge, Mass.: Harvard U. P., 1968, pp. 18-38.

1611.1 James, Henry. "A Most Unholy Trade," Letters on the Dra-
        ma by Henry James. Cambridge, Mass.: The Scarab Press,
        priv. printed, 1923.
           "The four letters here printed for the first time are part
           of Henry James's informal correspondence with William
           Heinemann. ... They concern themselves with James's im-
           pressions of Ibsen's 'Little Eyolf' and contain some gener-
           al remarks on the drama."

1612   _____. Note. Two Comedies: Tenants, Disengaged By
        Henry James. London: Osgood, McIlvaine & Co., 1894;
        repr., St. Clair Shores, Michigan: Scholarly Press, 1971.

1613   K., Q. "Before the Play," NewRep, 16 (September 7, 1918),
        172.

1614   Kenton, Edna. "The Plays of Henry James," ThA, 12 (May,
        1928), 347-352.

1615   King, Kimball. "Theory and Practice in the Plays of Henry
        James," MD, 10 (May, 1967), 24-33.
           Explains why James's early plays were failures and the
           last ones improved.

1616   Kossman, Rudolph R. Henry James: Dramatist. Groningen,
        Netherlands: Wolters-Noordhoff, 1969.

1617   Levy, Leo B. Versions of Melodrama: A Study of the Fic-
        tion and Drama of Henry James, 1865-1897. Berkeley:

University of California Press, 1957.

1618   Long, Robert Emmet. "Adaptations of Henry James's Fic-
        tion for Drama, Opera, and Films: With a Checklist of New
        York Theatre Critics' Reviews," ALR, 4 (Summer, 1971),
        268-278.

1619   Matthews, Brander. "Henry James and the Theatre," Book-
        man, 51 (June, 1920), 389-395. Also in Playwrights on
        Playmaking, and Other Studies of the Stage. New York and
        London: 1923, pp. 187-204.
            Discusses eight plays by James.

1620   McDougal, Edward D. "Henry James," TLS (November 13,
        1969), 1313.

1621   Peacock, Ronald. "Henry James and the Drama," The Poet
        in the Theatre. New York: 1946, pp. 26-46; London: Rout-
        ledge, 1945.

1622   Popkin, Henry. "Pretender to the Drama," ThA, 33 (De-
        cember, 1949), 32-35, 91.
            A study of James's failures in drama and their effect on
        his fiction.

1623   _____. "The Two Theatres of Henry James," NEQ, 24
        (March, 1951), 69-83.
            The only way for drama to be "theoretically or hypotheti-
        cally acted," James found, was for it to leave the stage
        entirely and to appear in a novel rather than in a play.

1624   Robins, Elizabeth. Commentary. Theatre and Friendship:
        Some Henry James Letters. Freeport, New York: Books
        for Libraries Press, 1969.

1625   Steer, Helen Vane. "Henry James on Stage: A Study of
        Henry James's Plays, and of Dramatization by Other Writers
        Based on Works by James," (2 vols.), DA, 28 (Louisiana
        State University: 1967), 826A.

1626   Tomlinson, M. The Drama's Laws," TCAus, 16 (1962),
        293-300.

1627   Wade, Allen. "Henry James as Dramatic Critic," ThA, 27
        (December, 1943), 735-740.
            Preface to a collection of James's notes on the drama, to
        be published after the war.

1628   _____, ed. Introduction and Notes. The Scenic Art:
        Notes on Acting and the Drama, 1872-1901. New York:
        Hill and Wang, 1957. Also New Brunswick: Rutgers Uni-
        versity Press, 1948.

1629   Walbrook, H. M. "Henry James and the English Theater,"
        NC, 80 (July, 1916), 141-145; LivA, 290 (August 19, 1916)
        505-509.

1630   _____. "Henry James and the Theater," LonM, 20 (Oc-
        tober, 1929), 612-616.
            Asks why "such a master of the long and short story and
            [one] so perceptive [as] a critic of the plays of other
            writers" should have had so little success as a dramatist.

1631   _____. Nights at the Play. Ham-Smith, 1911.
            Reprint of reviews from The Pall Mall Gazette, including
            James.

1632   Walkley, Arthur Bingham. "Henry James and the Theater,"
        and "Talks at the Martello Tower," in Pastiche and Preju-
        dice, London: 1921, pp. 155-159, 206-210; New York:
        Knopf, 1921.

1633   Wyld, Lionel D. "Drama vs. the Theatre in Henry James,"
        FourQ, 7 (May, 1958), 17-23.
            "That James could have been a better dramatist had he
            followed other idols and been more du theatre, in his atti-
            tude as well as in his art, seems valid.

Reviews:

        Athenaeum, 104 (November 17, 1894), 685; 105 (January 19,
            1895), 93
        Bookman (London), 7 (January, 1895), 120-1
        Critic, 29 (ns 26) (November 28, 1896), 340-1
        HarperW, 40 (November 21, 1896), 1150; 41 (January 23,
            February 6, 20, March 27, April 24, June 5, 26, July
            31, August 21, 1897), 78, 134-5, 183, 315, 411, 562-3,
            639-40, 754, 834
        HarperM, 90 (Sup 1) (March, 1895), 654
        Nation, 58 (June 28, 1894), 491; 60 (January 3, 1895), 18

ESSAYS AND CRITICISM

1634   Bewley, Marius. "The Verb to Contribute," Spectator, 6839
        (July 24, 1959), 114-115.
            Essay-review of Literary Reviews and Essays By Henry
            James.

1635   Buitenhuis, Peter, ed. Introduction. French Writers and
        American Women: Essays. Bradford, Conn.: Compass
        Pub. Co., 1960.

1635.1 Cook, David A. "James and Flaubert: The Evolution of
       Perception," CL, 25 (Fall, 1973), 289-307.
       James's development as a critic.

1636   Edel, Leon, ed. Introduction. The American Essays of
       Henry James. New York: Vintage Books, 1956.

1637   _____, ed. Introduction. The House of Fiction: Essays
       on the Novel By Henry James. London: R. Hart-Davis,
       1957.

1638   Harrier, R. C. " 'Very Modern Rome'--An Unpublished Es-
       say of Henry James," HLB, 8 (Spring, 1964), 125-140.

1638.1 Leavis, F. R. "James as Critic," in Henry James: Se-
       lected Literary Criticism. Morris Shapira, ed. New York:
       Horizon Press, 1964.

1639   Mordell, Albert, ed. Introduction. Literary Reviews and
       Essays: on American, English and French Literature By
       Henry James. New York: Grove Press, 1957.

1639.1 Patrick, Michael D. "Henry James's Literary Criticism,"
       IllQ, 35 (December, 1972), 20-33.
       Says that James raised criticism to an art by the use of
       "central consciousness."

1640   Roberts, Morris. Henry James's Criticism. Cambridge,
       Mass. : Harvard U. P. , 1929; New York: Haskell House,
       1965.

1640.1 _____. Introduction. The Art of Fiction and Other Es-
       says By Henry James. Oxford U. P. , 1948.

1640.2 Stafford, William. An Index to Henry James' Criticism and
       Essays. NCR Microcard Editions, Washington, D.C. , 1973.

1640.3 Stewart, J. I. M. "House of Fiction: Essays on the Novel,"
       NSt, 54 (October 26, 1957), 535.
       Essay-review: Leon Edel. House of Fiction. London:
       1957.

1641   Sweeney, John L. , ed. Introduction. Henry James: The
       Painter's Eye. Cambridge, Mass. : Harvard U. P. , 1956.

Reviews:

       Atl, 73 (February, 1894), 267-8
       Critic, 23 (ns 20) (November 18, 1893), 315
       Dial, 16 (January 1, 1894), 25
       HarperM, 88 (sup. 2-3) (December, 1893), 164
       Nation, 57 (November 30, 1893), 416

The "Last Dictation"

1642 Edel, Leon. "The Deathbed Notes of Henry James," Atl, 221, #6 (June, 1968), 103-105.

1643 _____. "Henry James's 'Last Dictation,' " TLS, 3453 (May 2, 1968), 459-460.

1644 _____. "Henry James's 'Last Dictation,' " TLS, 3456 (May 23, 1968), 529.

1645 _____. "James's 'Last Dictation,' " TLS, 3458 (June 6, 1968), 597.

1646 Hyde, H. Montgomery. "Henry James's 'Last Dictation,' " TLS, 3454 (May 9, 1968), 481.

1647 _____. "Henry James's 'Last Dictation,' " TLS, 3457 (May 30, 1968), 553.

1648 _____. "Henry James's 'Last Dictation,' " TLS, 3459 (June 13, 1968), 621.

LECTURES

1649 Dunbar, Olivia Howard. "Henry James as a Lecturer," Critic, 47 (July, 1905), 24-25.

1649.1 France, Wilmer Cave. "Henry James as a Lecturer," Bookman (New York), 21 (March, 1905), 71-72.

1650 Garland, Hamlin. Companions on the Trail. New York: Macmillan, 1931, pp. 259-260.
     James's appearance as a lecturer.

1651 Harris, Marie P. "Henry James, Lecturer," AL, 23 (November, 1951), 302-314.
     James lectures during the latter part of his 1904-1905 stay in America were "successful," but, ironically, "he was not only misunderstood but also abused for what he had not said and disliked for what he had not been."

1652 Picon, Gaëtan. "Lecture d'Henry James," NRF, 2 (June, 1954), 1080-1086.

     See also references under specific titles of lectures.

Reviews:

      Bookman, 21 (March, 1905), 71-2
      Book News, 23 (February, 1905), 485-7
      Reader, 6 (August, 1905), 336

LETTERS

1653   Adams, Henry. Letters of Henry Adams (1892-1918).
        Worthington Chauncy Ford, ed. Boston: 1938, II, 33nl.
          Correspondence with Henry James.

1654   Anon. "A Henry James Centenary Exhibition," CLQ, 1 (June,
        1943), 33-44.
          Henry James's letters reproduced from autograph.

1655   Anon. "Letters and Comment," YR, 13 (October, 1923),
        206-8.

1656   Bailey, John. "Henry James's Letters," LivAge, 306 (July
        3, 1920), 55-59.
          Essay-review, The Letters of Henry James. Percy Lub-
          bock, ed. 1920. 2 vols.

1657   Benson, E. F., ed. Introduction. Henry James: Letters
        to A. C. Benson and Auguste Monod. London: 1930; Fol-
        croft, Pa.: Folcroft Press, 1969.
          A collection of theretofore unpublished letters.

1658   Bishop, Ferman. "Henry James Criticizes The Tory Lover,"
        AL, 27 (May, 1955), 262-264.
          Letter to Sarah Orne Jewett, October 5, 1901.

1659   Bixler, J. Seelye. "Letters from Henry James to Theodule
        A. Ribot," CLQ, 1 (1945), 153-161.

1660   _____. "James Family Letters in Colby College Li-
        brary," CLQ, 9 (1970), 35-47.

1661   Bode, Carl. "Henry James and Owen Wister," AL, 26 (May,
        1954), 250-252.
          Letter from James, August 7, 1902, praising The Virgin-
          ian.

1662   Bragdon, Claude. "The Letters of Henry James," Freeman,
        1 (September 8, 1920), 619.

1663   Brewster, Henry. "Henry James and the Gallo-American,"
        BottOs, 19 (Spring, 1957), 170-181.
          Discovery of James's letters among family papers.

1664 _____. "Henry James: Fourteen Letters," BottOs, 19 (Spring, 1957), 182-194.
Letters to Henry B. Brewster.

1665 Brome, Vincent. "James and Andersen," TLS (June 13, 1968), 621.
Letter relative to correspondence between James and Hendrik Christian Andersen.

1666 Bruneau, Jean. "Une Lettre Inédite de Henry James à Gustave Flaubert: Autour de Monckton Milnes, Lord Houghton," RLC, 42 (October-December, 1968), 520-533.

1667 Cary, Richard. "Henry James Juvenilia: A Poem and a Letter," CLQ, 9 (1970), 58-62.
Discusses the meager extant hints that James wrote a little poetry.

1667.1 [Conrad, Joseph. James's Letters to] Twenty Letters to Joseph Conrad. G. Jean Aubry, ed. London: The First Editions Club, 1926.
Contains three letters of James to Conrad, one of which is reprinted in Selected Letters of Henry James. Leon Edel, ed.

1668 Coward, T. R. "The Letters of Henry James," Freeman, 1 (September 8, 1920), 618-619.

1669 Dahlberg, Edward, and Herbert Read. "A Literary Correspondence," SR, 67 (Spring, 1959), 177-203; (Summer, 1959), 442-445.
Includes remarks on Henry James.

1670 Davray, Henry D. "Un déraciné Anglo-Américain: Henry James, d'après sa correspondance," MercF, 146 (February 15, 1921), 68-84.

1671 Donovan, Alan B. "My Dear Pinker: The Correspondence of Henry James with His Literary Agent," YULG, 36 (October, 1961), 78-88.
James's letters to his agent reveal James's concern with details, both financial and artistic, and provide insight into his methods and opinions.

1671.1 Edel, Leon. "Henry James Discoveries," TLS (London) (July 29, 1939), 460.
A letter, reprinted from the New York Tribune, August 4, 1889.

1672 _____. "Henry James Letters," TLS (June 17, 1965), 523.
Gives the correct text of a letter to Edmund Gosse, miscopied in Mrs. Phyllis Grosskurth's recent book; in August

19 issue of TLS, correction was accepted.

1673 _____, and Ilse Dusoir Lind, eds. Henry James:
Parisian Sketches, Letters to the New York Tribune, 1875-
1876. New York: 1961.

1674 _____, and Lyall H. Powers. "Henry James and the
Bazar Letters," BNYPL, 62 (February, 1958), 75-103.
Publication of James's correspondence with Harper's
Bazar. Cf., Earle F. Walbridge. " 'The Whole Fam-
ily' and Henry James," PBSA, 52 (1958), 144-145.

1675 _____. "A Letter to the Editors," AL, 24 (1952), 370-
372.
On the order of chapters in The Ambassadors.

1676 _____, ed. Introduction. The Selected Letters of Henry
James. Garden City, New York: Doubleday, 1960; London:
Hart-Davis, 1956.

1677 Edgar, Pelham. "The Letters of Henry James," QQ, 28
(January, 1921), 283-287.

1678 Gale, Robert L., ed. "Four Letters to Francis Marion
Crawford: From Theodore Roosevelt, Clyde Fitch, Julia
Ward Howe, Henry James," LitR, 3 (Spring, 1960), 438-443.

1679 _____. "A Letter from Henry James to Francis Marion
Crawford," SA, 4 (1958), 415-420.

1680 Gardner, Burdett. "An Apology for Henry James's 'Tiger-
Cat,' " PMLA, 68 (1953), 688-695.
Excerpts of James's correspondence with Violet Paget
[pseud., Vernon Lee].

1681 Gilman, Lawrence. "The Letters of Henry James," NAR,
211 (May, 1920), 682-690.
Essay-Review, Letters of Henry James. Percy Lubbock,
ed.

1682 Harrier, Richard C. "Letters of Henry James, Transcribed
from the Original Manuscripts in the Colby College Library,"
CLQ, 3 (May, 1953), 153-164.
Nine letters to Edmund Gosse and one to James R. Osgood.

1683 Hasler, Jörg. Switzerland in the Life and Work of Henry
James: The Clare Benedict Collection of Letters from Henry
James. Diss. Basel: 1966.

1684 _____. Switzerland in the Life and Work of Henry James:
The Clare Benedict Collection of Letters from Henry James.
Berne: Francke, 1966.

1685   Howe, M. DeWolfe. "The Letters of Henry James to Mr.
        Justice Holmes," YR, 38 (Spring, 1949), 410-433.
            Twenty-one letters by James and one by Holmes.

1686   Howells, Mildred, ed. Life in Letters of William Dean
        Howells. Garden City, New York: Doubleday, 1928, passim.
            Letters of James to Howells.

1687   Hudson, Gertrude Reese, ed. Introduction and Notes.
        Browning to His American Friends: Letters Between the
        Brownings, the Storys and James Russell Lowell, 1841-1890.
        New York: Barnes & Noble, 1965.
            Cf., Joseph Anthony Hynes, Jr. "Henry James's 'William
            Wetmore Story and His Friends': A Critical Commentary,"
            DA, 21 (Michigan: 1961), 3458.

1688   "The Illuminating Letters of Henry James," CurOp, 68 (May,
        1920), 676-678.
            Essay-review, The Letters of Henry James. Percy Lub-
            bock, ed.

1689   James, Henry. "A Letter to Mr. Howells," NAR, 195 (Ap-
        ril, 1912), 558-562.

1690   _____. Letters of Henry James to Walter Berry. Paris:
        Black Sun Press, 1928.

1691   _____. "Three Unpublished Letters and a Monologue by
        Henry James," LonMerc, 6 (September, 1922), 492-501.

1692   _____. "Two Unpublished Letters," H&H, 7 (April-June,
        1934), 414-416.
            Letters to William Heinemann and Richard Watson Gilder.

1693   James, William. The Letters of William James. Henry
        James, II, ed., [son of William James]. Boston: Atlantic
        Monthly Press, 1920. New York: Kraus Reprint, 1969.

1694   Karl, Frederick R. "Three Conrad Letters in the Edith
        Wharton Papers," YULG, 44 (January, 1970), 148-151.
            One letter is to Henry James, July 24, 1916.

1695   Keynes, Geoffrey. "Henry James in Cambridge," LonM, 6
        (March, 1959), 50-61.

1696   Kirk, Rudolf. "Five Letters of Henry James," JRUL, 12
        (June, 1949), 54-58.
            The letters are to Sir J. E. Boehme, William B. Squire,
            Sir Edmund Gosse, and Mathilda B. Bentham-Edwards.

1697   _____. "Henry James: Correction," JRUL, 16 (1953),
        63.
            A letter attributed to James in JRUL, 12 (1949), 54-58,

is by Sir Henry James, Victorian barrister.

1697.1 Kozol, Clara Barbara. "Creator and Collector: The Unpublished Letters of Henry James to Isabella Stewart Gardner,"
DAI, 34 (Columbia U.: 1973), 3407A.

1698 LaFarge, John. "Henry James's Letters to the LaFarges,"
NEQ, 22 (June, 1949), 173-192.
Twelve hitherto unpublished letters of James ranging in
dates from 1869 to 1914.

1699 Lawrence, D. H. "Henry James and Stevenson Discuss 'Vile'
Tess," CLQ, 3, #10 (1953), 164-168.
The text of disapproving remarks in letters of 1892-1893.

1699.1 Leary, Lewis. "Over Henry's Shoulder," SatR, 39 (April 7,
1956), 19.
Essay-review, The Selected Letters of Henry James.
Leon Edel, ed.

1700 Littell, Philip. "Books and Things," NewRep, 23 (June 9,
1920), 63-64.
Essay-review, The Henry James Letters. Percy Lubbock,
ed.

1701 Lubbock, Percy, ed. Introduction. The Letters of Henry
James. New York: Scribner's, 1920; Octagon Books, 1970.

1702 _____. "The Mind of an Artist," in The Question of Henry James, F. W. Dupee, ed. New York: Holt, 1945, pp.
54-69.
[The Introduction to The Letters of Henry James. Percy
Lubbock, ed. New York: 1920.]

1703 Major, John C. "Henry James, Daudet, and Oxford," N&Q,
13 (February, 1966), 69-70.
In regard to the Daudet family's visit.

1704 McClary, Ben Harris. "In Abject Terror of Rising': An Unpublished Henry James Letter," ELN, 3 (March, 1966), 208-
211.
James's letter to Clement Shorter, August 18, 1909, refusing to speak at a meeting of the Whitefriars Club.

1705 McElderry, B. R., Jr. "Published Letters of Henry James:
A Survey," BB, 20 (January-April, 1952), 165-171; 20 (May-
August, 1952), 187.

1706 McLane, James. "A Henry James Letter," YR, n. s., 14
(October, 1924), 205-208.
A letter to Lilla Cabot Perry (Mrs. Thomas Sergeant
Perry), not included in the Lubbock collection.

1707   Michaels, Herbert S. "An Unpublished Letter of Henry
        James," CLQ, 3 (May, 1951), 23-26.
            A letter written in December, 1894, to commend actress
            Marion Terry for her "perfectly beautiful" performance
            in Guy Domville.

1708   Michaud, Régis. "William et Henry James d'après leur
        correspondance," RdF (September, 1922), 141-159.

1708.1 Monteiro, George. "Henry James [letters of] and John Hay,"
        BB, 19 (May, 1963), 69-88.

1709   _____. ["Henry James and John Hay,"] Henry James and
        John Hay: The Record of a Friendship. Providence, Rhode
        Island: Brown U. P., 1965.
            Includes letters.

1710   _____. "Letters to a 'Countryman': John Hay to Henry
        James," BBr, 19 (1963), 105-112.

1711   _____, ed. "Letters of Henry James to John Hay,"
        TSLL, 4 (Supp., 1963), 641-695.
            Thirty-six letters from James to Hay and two to Mrs.
            Hay.

1712   _____. "An Unpublished Henry James Letter," N&Q, 10
        (April, 1963), 143-144.
            James's reply to Mrs. Hay for any letters of Hay's which
            he might have.

1713   Moses, Montrose, Jr. "Henry James as a Letter Writer,"
        Outlook, 125 (May 26, 1920), 167-168.

1714   Nowell-Smith, Simon. "First Editions, English and Ameri-
        can," [Letter], Library, 20 (March, 1966). 68.

1715   Perrin, Noel. "The Henry James Papers," NY, 36 (Novem-
        ber 12, 1960), 191-198.
            The discovery of some James letters in England.

1716   Phillips, John N. "A Twaddle of Graciousness," BottOs, 19
        (Spring, 1957), 195-202.
            Descendant of recipient of James's letters refuses to pub-
            lish them.

1717   Robins, Elizabeth. Theatre and Friendship: Some Henry
        James Letters: with a Commentary. London: Jonathan
        Cape, 1932.
            Letters dealing with Ibsen plays and with the theatre in
            general.

1718   Rosenbaum, S. P. "Letters to the Pell-Clarkes from Their
        'Old Cousin and Friend' Henry James," AL, 31 (March,

1959), 46-58.

1719 _____. "Two Henry James Letters on The American and
Watch and Ward," AL, 30 (January, 1959), 533-537.
Two letters by James (1877) to his publisher.

1720 Russell, John. "Henry James and the Leaning Tower,"
NS&N, 25 (April 17, 1943), 254-255.
Unpublished letters from James to Edward Warren indicate his attitude toward the war, toward France, and toward his naturalization.

1721 Seznac, Jean. "Lettres de Tourguéneff à Henry James,"
CL, 1 (Summer, 1949), 193-209.
Fifteen letters from Tourgueneff to James written between
1874 and 1882, showing that James got from Tourgueneff
"des préceptes de métier" and found in him "un idéal
d'homme et artiste qui réspondait à ses exigences, et qui
l'a aidé a definir le sien."

1722 Sherman, Stuart Pratt. "Special Case of Henry James," in
Emotional Discovery of America, and Other Essays. New
York: Farrar, 1932, pp. 35-47.
Letters.

1723 Shuman, R. B. "A New Edmund Gosse Letter," N&Q, 6
(January, 1959), 33.

1724 Smith, Janet Adam, ed. Introduction. Henry James and Ro-
bert Louis Stevenson: A Record of Friendship and Criticism.
London: Rupert Hart-Davis, 1948.
Letters.

1725 Spiller, Robert E., ed. The Van Wyck Brooks-Lewis Mumford Letters: The Record of a Literary Friendship, 1921-
1963. New York: E. P. Dutton, 1970.
The letters reveal that Brooks was uneasy while he wrote
the biography, The Pilgrimage of Henry James, and called
one draft of it a "tract."

1726 Squire, J. C. "Three Unpublished Letters and a Monologue
by Henry James," LonM, 6 (1922), 492-501.

1727 Standley, Fred L. "Henry James to Stopford Brooke: An
Unpublished Letter," VN, 27 (Spring, 1965), 29.
In a short, undated letter James recommends Vallombrosa,
Italy, to Stopford Brooke as a place to stay.

1728 Swan, Michael. "Henry James and the Heroic Young Master,"
LonM, 2 (May, 1955), 78-86.
James's relationship with Hendrik Christian Andersen,
sculptor, based on seventy-seven letters written by James
to Andersen, 1800-1915; published also in Harper's

Bazaar, September 1955, pp. 226-227, 270, 272.

1729 _____. "Henry James and H. G. Wells: A Study of Their Friendship Based on Their Unpublished Correspondence," Cornhill, 165 (Autumn, 1953), 43-65.

1730 Tharp, Louise Hall. Mrs. Jack. Boston: Little, Brown, 1965.
Includes a few letters from James.

1730.1 " 'Very Modern Rome'--An Unpublished Letter of Henry James," HLB, 8 (Spring, 1954), 125-140.

1731 Walbridge, Earle F. " 'The Whole Family' and Henry James," PBSA, 52 (2nd Qt., 1958), 144-145.
Bibliographical corrections to "Henry James and the Bazar Letters," BNYPL, 62 (1958), 75-103, by Edel and Powers.

1732 Walkley, Arthur Bingham. "Henry James and His Letters," FnR, n. s., 107 (June, 1920), 864-873.

1733 Weber, Carl J. "Henry James and His 'Tiger-Cat,' " PMLA, 68 (1953), 672-687.
The James-Paget Letters. Cf., Burdett Gardner. "An Apology for Henry James's 'Tiger-Cat,' " PMLA, 68 (1953), 688-695.

1734 Wharton, Edith. "Henry James in His Letters: The Friend," QR (London), 234 (July, 1920), 188-202.
A vivid and delightful description of James as a friend and letter writer. Second half of article repr., in Henry James: A Collection of Critical Essays. Leon Edel, ed. pp. 31-36.

1735 _____. "The Man of Letters," Henry James in His Letters. Percy Lubbock, ed. New York: Macmillan, 1920.

1736 Whitford, Robert Calvin. "The Letters of Henry James," SAQ, 19 (October, 1920), 371-372.

1736.1 Woolf, Virginia. "The Letters of Henry James," The Death of the Moth and Other Essays. London: The Hogarth Press, 1942, pp. 92-100. Also in Collected Essays. New York: Harcourt, Brace & World, 1966, I, 277-285.

Reviews:

Bookman (London), 58 (May, 1920), 76-77
CurOp, 68 (May, 1920), 676-8
LivAge, 306 (July 3, 1920), 55-9
New Rep, 23 (June 9, 1920), 63-4
NoAmer, 211 (May, 1920), 682-90

THE NEW YORK EDITION

1736.2 Bertolotti, David Santo. "A Concordance of Foreign Words and Phrases for the New York Edition of Henry James," DAI, 33 (Michigan State: 1972), 2361A.

1736.3 Edel, Leon. "The Architecture of James's 'New York Edition,' " NEQ, 24 (June, 1951), 169-178.

1736.4 _____. "The Enduring Fame of Henry James," NYTBR (September 3, 1961), 1, 16-17.
Essay-review of the reprinting of the first two volumes of the New York Edition.

1736.5 Herrick, Robert. "A Visit to Henry James," YR, n. s., 12 (July, 1923), 724-741; n. s., 13 (October, 1923), 206-208.
James's revision of the New York Edition.

1737   Hicks, Priscilla Gibson. " 'The Story in It': The Design of Henry James's 'New York Edition,' " DA, 21 (Boston: 1960), 895-896.

1737.1 Leonard, Vivien Rose. "An Introductory Study of Imagery in the Prefaces of the New York Edition of the Novels and Tales of Henry James," DA, 27 (Columbia: 1966), 1826A-1827A.

1737.2 Raunheim, John P. "A Study of the Revisions of the Tales Included in the New York Edition," DAI, 33 (NYU: 1972), 733A.

1737.3 Shumsky, Allison. "James Again: The New York Edition," SR, 70 (Summer, 1962), 522-525.

Reviews of The New York Edition:

       Atl, 95 (April, 1905), 103-113
       Bookman, 28 (September, 1908), 12-3
       CurLit, 44 (February, 1908)
       LitDig, 36 (March 21, 1908), 418; 39 (August 21, 1909), 275-6
       Nation, 86 (January 2, 1908), 11; (March 5, 1908), 215; (April 23, June 4, 1908), 376, 511; 87 (August 6, December 17, 1908), 115-6, 601; 88 (April 8, 22, 29, 1909), 359, 410, 439; 89 (July 1, August 19, 1909), 11-2, 159
       Times, 12 (December 7, 1907), 776; 13 (January 11, 1908), 13-5; January 18, 1908), 30; 13 (February 29, 1908), 3; (March 7, 1908), 128; (April 11, 1908), 199; (May 30, 1908), 306
       Tribune (April 5, 1908), 6-7

NOTEBOOKS

1737.4 Beach, Joseph Warren. "The Sacred and Solitary Refuge,"
Furioso, 3 (Winter, 1947), 23-37.
Essay-review, The Notebooks of Henry James. Matthies-
sen and Murdock, eds. 1947.

1738   . "The Witness of the Notebooks," in Forms of
Modern Fiction. Minneapolis: Minnesota U. P., 1948, pp.
46-60.

1738.1 Breit, Harvey. "Repeat Performances," NYTB (May 8,
1955).
"Mr. James, ... unsurprisingly, is a fantastic keeper of
the Notebooks, the editors have done them justice,...."

1739   Highet, Gilbert. People, Places, and Books. New York:
Oxford University Press, 1953, 187-190.

1739.1 "The Intellectual Jameses," Newsweek, 30 (November 3,
1947), 93-94.
Essay-review, The Notebooks of Henry James. Matthiessen and Murdock, eds.

1740   Matthiessen, Francis Otto, and Kenneth B. Murdock, eds.
Introduction. The Notebooks of Henry James. New York:
Oxford University Press, 1947. Reissued, George Brazil-
ler, 1955. New ed., New York, London: Oxford U. P.,
1961.
An excellent and useful work.

Reviews of Matthiessen and Murdock edition

Anderson, Q. MLN, 64 (1949), 116-19
Angel, Richard C. NMQ, 31 (1962), 77-82
Arvin, Newton. NEQ, 21 (1948), 110-111
Blackmur, R. P. KR, 10 (1948), 313-17
Brown, E. K. YR, 37 (1948), 530-3
Dupee, F. W. Nation, 165 (1947), 685-6
Gohdes, Clarence. AL, 20 (1948), 64-5; SAQ, 47 (1948),
416-18
Gordon, D. J. RES, 1 (1947), 179-83
Hoskins, Katherine, HR, 1 (1948), 120-6
M. R. More Books, 23 (1948), 32
Roberts, M. SR, 56 (1948), 510-14
Russell, John. Sun Times (August 29, 1948), 3
Schorer, Mark. NYTB (December 7, 1947), 5
Thorp, W. VQR, 24 (1948), 117-22
TLS (September 25, 1948), 540
Troy, William. PR, 15 (1948), 377-9

1741   Pritchett, V. S. "The Notebooks of Henry James," <u>Books in</u>
        <u>General</u>. New York: Harcourt, 1952, pp. 43-49.

1742   Thorberg, Raymond. "<u>Germaine</u>, James's <u>Notebooks</u>, and
        <u>The Wings of the Dove</u>," CL, 22 (Summer, 1970), 254-264.
              Despite his disclaimer in the <u>Notebook</u> entries, Thorberg
              believes James borrowed considerably from About's <u>Ger-
              maine</u>.

1742.1 Wilson, Edmund. "New Documents on the Jameses," NY,
        23 (December 13, 1947), 133-137.
              Essay-review, <u>Notebooks of Henry James</u>. Matthiessen
              and Murdock, eds.

1743   Worden, Ward S. "Henry James's <u>What Maisie Knew</u>: A
        Comparison with the <u>Notebooks</u>," PMLA, 68 (June, 1953),
        371-383.

PREFACES

1744   Blackmur, Richard P. "The Critical Prefaces," H&H, 7
        (April-June, 1934), 444-477.
              Discussion of James's Prefaces for the New York Edition.

1745   _____, ed. Introduction. <u>The Art of the Novel: Critical</u>
        <u>Prefaces By Henry James</u>. New York: Scribner's, 1934;
        1962.

1746   _____. "Critical Prefaces of Henry James," <u>Double</u>
        <u>Agent: Essays in Craft and Elucidation</u>. Arrow Editions,
        1935, pp. 234-268. Repr., Gloucester, Mass.: Peter
        Smith, 1962, pp. 234-268.

1747   _____. "Critical Prefaces of Henry James," <u>The Lion and</u>
        <u>the Honeycomb: Essays in Solicitude and Critique</u>. New
        York: Harcourt, 1955, pp. 240-267.

1748   Edel, Leon. <u>The Prefaces of Henry James</u>. Diss. Paris:
        1932.

1748.1 _____. <u>The Prefaces of Henry James</u>. Paris: Jouve,
        1931.
              Revs., Cantwell, R. Nation, (August 17, 1932), 149-50;
              H. R., Crit, 11 (July, 1932), 753-4; Kelley, C. P., JEGP,
              31 (July, 1932), 452-4.

1749   Gale, Robert L. "Imagery in James's Prefaces," RLV, 30,
        #5 (1964), 431-445.
              James's imagery in both his prefaces and fiction represent
              the same major categories: "water, flowers, and animal,
              war, art, and religion."

1750   Ghiselin, Brewster, ed. Introduction. The Creative Proc-
       ess: A Symposium. 2nd pr., Berkeley and Los Angeles:
       California University Press, 1954, p. 1.
           "Perhaps the greatest body of ... writing is the monu-
           mental work of Henry James, the prefaces to the New
           York edition of his work."

1751   Gretton, M. Sturge. "Mr. Henry James and His Prefaces,"
       ContR, 101 (January, 1912), 69-78; LivA, 272 (February 3,
       1912), 287-295.

1751.1 James, Henry. The Art of the Novel: Critical Prefaces By
       Henry James. Richard P. Blackmur, ed. New York: Scrib-
       ner's, 1934.

1752   Leonard, Vivien Rose. "An Introductory Study of Imagery in
       the Prefaces to the New York Edition of the Novels and Tales
       of Henry James," DA, 27 (Columbia: 1966), 1826A-1827A.

1753   Stafford, William T. "Literary Allusions in James's Pref-
       aces," AL, 35 (March, 1963), 60-70.
           Finds references which indicate James's wide reading.

1754   Volpe, Edmond L. "The Prefaces of George Sand and Henry
       James," MLN, 70 (February, 1955), 107-108.

REVIEWS BY HENRY JAMES (Criticism of)

1755   Brooks, Van Wyck. "Henry James as a Reviewer," Sketches
       in Criticism. New York: E. P. Dutton, 1932, pp. 190-196.

1756   Chaignon la Rose, Pierre de, ed. Preface. Notes and Re-
       views By Henry James. Cambridge, Mass.: Dunster House,
       1921; repr., Freeport, New York: Books for Libraries
       Press, Inc., 1968.
           A collection of twenty-five early reviews during the years
           1864-1866.

1757   Edel, Leon. "Autobiography in Fiction: An Unpublished Re-
       view by Henry James," HLB, 11 (Spring, 1957), 245-257.

1757.1 Houghton, Walter E., ed. "Henry James," The Wellesley
       Index to Victorian Periodicals, 1824-1900. London: Rout-
       ledge & Kegan Paul; Toronto: University of Toronto Press,
       1966.

1758   Kraft, James. "An Unpublished Review by Henry James,"
       SB, 20 (1967), 267-273.

1758.1 Maguire, Charles E. "James and Dumas, fils," MD, 10

(May, 1967), 34-42.
James's review of L'Etrangère in his March 25, 1876, letter to the Tribune.

1758.2 McMahon, Helen. Criticism of Fiction: A Study of Trends in the Atlantic Monthly, 1857-1898. New York: Bookman Associates, 1952.

1759   Monteiro, George. "Henry James and His Reviewers: Some Identifications," PBSA, 63 (4th Qt., 1969), 300-304.
A very helpful study.

1760   Mordell, Albert, ed. Introduction. Literary Reviews and Essays on American, English and French Literature By Henry James. New York: Twayne Publishers, 1957; Grove Press, 1958.
An indispensable work.

1761   Phelps, William Lyon. "Henry James, Reviewer," LitR, 1 (June 4, 1921), 4.

1762   Phillips, LeRoy, ed. Introduction. Views and Reviews by Henry James. Boston: The Ball Pub. Co., 1908; Freeport, New York: Books for Libraries Press, 1968.

1762.1 Prausnitz, Walther G. The Craftsmanship of Henry James: A Study of the Critical Reviews, 1864-1884. Diss. Chicago: 1956.

1762.2 _____. The Craftsmanship of Henry James: A Study of the Critical Reviews, 1864-1884. Chicago: Library Department of Photographic Reproductions. University of Chicago, 1956.

SKETCHES

1763   Bewley, Marius. "Henry James's English Hours," in Masks and Mirrors: Essays in Criticism. New York: Atheneum Pubs., 1970, pp. 119-138.

1764   Edel, Leon, and Ilse Dusoir Lind, eds. Introduction. Henry James: Parisian Sketches. New York: New York University Press, 1957.

1764.1 Emerson, Donald. "Henry James: A Sentimental Tourist and Restless Analyst," TWA, 52 (1963), 17-25.

1765   Greenwood, di Clarissa. Introduction. Città e Paesaggi di Toscana Visti da Henry James. Firenze: G. Barbera, 1961.

1765.1 Lowe, Alma. The Travel Writing of Henry James. Diss.
        Rice Institute: 1955.

1766   Zabel, Morton Dauwen. Introduction. The Art of Travel:
       Scenes and Journeys in America, England, France, and Italy,
       from the Travel Writings of Henry James. New York:
       Doubleday, 1958.

III.   GENERAL CRITICISM

1767   Aagemann, E. R.   " 'Unexpected Light in Shady Places':
Henry James and 'Life,' 1883-1916," WHR, 24 (1970), 241-
50.

1767.1 Abel, Darrel.   American Literature.   Great Neck, New
York: Barron's Educational Series, 1963, III, 215-363.

1768   _____, ed.   " 'Howells or James?'--An Essay by Henry
Blake Fuller," MFS, 3 (Summer, 1957), 159-164.
The first publication of a paper written in 1885 contending
that Howells, more American than James, was actually
more than James a "shaper" of American fiction.

1769   _____.   A Simplified Approach to James.   Great Neck,
New York: Barron, 1964.

1769.1 Abel, Robert H.   "Gide and Henry James: Suffering, Death,
and Responsibility," MwQ, 9 (1968), 403-416.
Contrasts Gide's view of suffering with that of James.

1770   Abrahams, William.   "In the Henry James Country," [poem],
in Vice Versa (1942).

1771   Adachi, Yasushi.   "Subjective Approach in Criticism,"
HiyRon, 14 (1963), 53-65.
On Henry James's moral sense.

1772   Adams, Henry.   Letters of Henry Adams, 1858-1891.   Worth-
ington Chauncey Ford, ed.   Boston and New York: Houghton
Mifflin, 1930, passim; London: Constable, 1930, passim.
Reminiscences.

1773   Adams, John R.   "Henry James: Citizen of Two Countries,"
TLS (London), (April 17, 1943), 188, 190.
Stresses James's Anglo-American vision.

1774   Adams, Percy G.   "Young Henry James and the Lesson of
His Master Balzac," RLC, 35 (July-September, 1961), 458-
467.
The influence of Balzac on James.

1775   Aiken, Conrad.   "James, Henry," A Reviewer's ABC:

<u>Collected Criticism of Conrad Aiken from 1916 to the Pres-</u>
<u>ent.</u> New York: Meridian Books, 1958, pp. 230-238.

1776   Albérès, R. M. "Aux sources du 'nouveau roman': L'im-
pressionnisme anglais," RdP, 69 (May, 1962), 74-86.
On the twentieth century English novel with comment on
James.

1777   Albright, Daniel. <u>An Account of the Discussion of Narrative</u>
<u>Technique from Poe to James.</u> Diss. Chicago University:
1957.

1777.1 Allen, Walter. <u>The English Novel: A Short Critical His-</u>
<u>tory.</u> New York: E. P. Dutton, 1955, pp. 311-313, passim.

1777.2 _____. <u>George Eliot.</u> London: Weidenfeld and Nicol-
son, 1965, passim.
The influence of George Eliot on Henry James.

1778   _____. <u>The Modern Novel: In Britain and the United</u>
<u>States.</u> New York: E. P. Dutton, 1964, passim.

1779   _____. "New Wine That Tastes Like Old," NYTBR (December 25, 1960), 1, 13.
Essay-review, <u>Parodies.</u> Dwight Macdonald, ed. 1960.

1780   _____. <u>Tradition and Dream: The English and American</u>
<u>Novel from the Twenties to Our Time.</u> London: Phoenix
House, 1964, passim.
Contains comparisons of later writers with James.

1781   _____. <u>The Urgent West: The American Dream and Mod-</u>
<u>ern Man.</u> New York: E. P. Dutton, 1969, passim.
Complexity of the American relationship with Europe, "the
main subject" of Henry James's fiction.

1782   Allingham, William. <u>William Allingham's Diary.</u> Fontwell,
Sussex: Centaur Press, Ltd. , 1967, p. 378.
Reiminiscence which reveals James as an "unmitigated
Cockney."

1783   Allott, Miriam. "Form versus Substance in Henry James,"
REL, 3 (January, 1962), 53-66.
A desire for "singleness of vision" in James's work is
"frustrated" by James's "presentation of the difficulty and
anomaly surrounding most attempts at efficient moral action."

1784   _____. "James Russel Lowell: A Link Between Tennyson and Henry James," RES, n. s., 6 (October, 1955), 399-
401.
Both James and Tennyson made use of a legend told them
by Lowell.

1785   _____. Novelists on the Novel. London: Routledge &
Kegan Paul, 1959; New York: Columbia U. P., 1962, passim.

1786   _____. "Symbol and Image in the Later Work of Henry
James," EIC, 3 (July, 1953), 321-336.
          Says James's symbols are "almost always connected with
his theme of appearance and reality."

1787   Altick, Richard D. "Henry James, Paris Correspondent,"
SatR, 41 (January 18, 1958), 18ff.

1788   _____. "The Spirit of Scholarship," in The Art of Literary Research. New York: W. W. Norton, 1963, p. 15.

1789   Alvarez, A. "Intelligence on Tour," KR, 21 (Winter, 1959),
23-33.
          Suggests that the travel sketches complement the novels.

1790   Anderson, Charles R. "Henry James's Fable of Carolina,"
SAQ, 54 (April, 1955), 249-257.

1791   _____. "James's Portrait of the Southerner," AL, 27
(November, 1955), 309-331.

1792   Andersen, Kenneth. "Mark Twain, W. D. Howells, and Henry James: Three Agnostics in Search of Salvation," MTJ,
15, i (Winter, 1970), 13-16.

1793   Anderson, Quentin. "The American Henry James: A Study
of the Novelist as a Moralist," DA, 14 (Columbia: 1954),
115-116.

1794   _____. The American Henry James. New Brunswick,
New Jersey: Rutgers University Press, 1957.
          A most useful study.

1795   _____. "The Coming Out of Culture," The Imperial Self:
An Essay in American Literary and Cultural History. New
York: Alfred A. Knopf, Inc., 1971, pp. 201-244.

1796   _____. "The Critic and Imperial Consciousness," New
Rep, 152 (April 17, 1965), 15-17.
          A comparison of Van Wyck Brooks and Henry James.

1797   _____. "Henry James, His Symbolism and His Critics,"
Scrutiny, 15 (December, 1947), 12-19.
          Cf., Quentin Anderson. "The Two Henry Jameses,"
Scrutiny, 14 (September, 1947), 242-251.

1798   _____. "Henry James and the New Jerusalem," KR, 8
(Autumn, 1946), 515-566.
          James as a moralist.

1799 _____. Introduction. <u>Henry James: Selected Short Stories.</u> New York: Rinehart, 1950; revised, 1957.

1800 _____. "Leon Edel's <u>Henry James</u>," VQR, 48 (Autumn, 1972), 621-630.

1801 _____. "The Two Henry Jameses," Scrutiny, 14 (September, 1947), 242-251.
Introductory article to Quentin Anderson, "Henry James, His Symbolism and His Critics," Scrutiny, 15 (1947), 12-19.

1802 _____. "Willa Cather: Her Masquerade," NewRep, 153 (November 27, 1965), 28-31.
The influence of Henry James on Willa Cather.

1803 Anderson, Sherwood. Letter to Van Wyck Brooks, <u>Letters of Sherwood Anderson.</u> Howard Mumford Jones and Walter B. Rideout, eds. Boston: Little, Brown & Co., 1953, pp. 102-103.
Derogatory criticism.

1804 Andreas, Osborn. <u>Henry James and the Expanding Horizon: A Study of the Meaning and Basic Themes of James's Fiction.</u> Seattle: University of Washington Press, 1948.
This work should certainly be consulted in any study of James's themes.

1805 Andrews, W. "Henry James, Edith Wharton, and the Age of Leisure," Harper, 230 (May, 1965), 137-140.

1806 Anon. "The Accents of the Master," TLS, 3138 (April 20, 1962), 264.
On editing James.

1807 Anon. "L'Atene dei James," FLe, 51 (December 18, 1955), 7.

1808 Anon. "Cher Maître and Mon Bon," TLS (September 25, 1948), 540.

1809 Anon. "The Death of Henry James," TLS (April 17, 1943), 187.
A memorial.

1810 Anon. "Gloom and Some Friendships," TLS, 1245-46 (October, 1969).

1811 Anon. "Gulf of Henry James," Nation, 111 (October 20, 1920), 441.

1812 Anon. "Henry James: A Last Glimpse," LivA, 301 (May 31, 1919), 541-543.
Reminiscences.

1813   Anon. "A Henry James Centenary Exhibition," CLQ, 1 (June, 1943), 33-44.

1814   Anon. "Henry James and the English Association," Scrutiny, 14 (December, 1946), 131-133.

1815   Anon. "Henry James Number," LittleR, 5 (August, 1918).

1816   Anon. "Henry James Reprints," TLS (February 5, 1949), 96.

1817   Anon. "The Matter of the Master," TLS, 3677 (September 15, 1972), 1060.

1818   Anon. "Mr. James' Variant," Atl, 94 (Summer, 1904), 426-427.

1819   Anon. "Notes," Nation, 86 (January 2, March 5, 1908), 11, 215.

1820   Anon. "Novels of Henry James," LivA, 310 (July 30, 1921), 267-271.

1821   Anon. "A Reviewer's Notebook," Freeman, 3 (August 24, 1921), 574-575; 4 (February 8, 1922), 526-527.

1822   Anon. "The World of Henry James," LivA, 289 (April 22, 1916), 229-232.

1823   Antush, John V. "Money in the Novels of James, Wharton, and Dreiser," DA, 29 (Stanford: 1968), 558A.

1824   _____. "Money as Myth and Reality in the World of Henry James," ArQ, 25 (Summer, 1969), 125-133.
        Indicates some of the ways James uses money "to move his plots, to motivate and expose his characters ... [and] to create a human condition in which his characters ... [are free to] find an Eden-like freedom to explore the potentials of human growth."

1825   Aoki, Tsuguo. "James ni okeru Hoshuha no Kankaku," EigoS, 118 (1972), 494-495.
        The conservative sense in James.

1826   Appignanesi, Lisa. Femininity and the Creative Imagination: A Study of Henry James, Robert Musil and Marcel Proust. New York: Harper & Row, 1973.
        An examination of the "myth of femininity" as revealed by a comparative study of James, Musil and Proust.

1826.1 "Appreciation," Spec, 116 (March 4, 1916), 312-313.

1827   Arader, Harry F. "American Novelists in Italy: Nathaniel

Hawthorne, Howells, James, and F. Marion Crawford," DA, 13 (Pennsylvania: 1953), 791.

1828   Arlos, Alma R.   "Our Doubt Is Our Passion": <u>Ambiguity in</u> <u>Three of the Later Novels of Henry James.</u>   Diss.   Radcliffe: 1962.

1829   Arnavon, C.   <u>Les Lettres Americaines Devant La Critique</u> <u>Française (1887-1917).</u>   Paris: 1952.

1829.1 Arsenescu, Adina.   "Henry James," Orizont, 12 (December, 1969), 55-59.

1830   Arvin, Newton.   "Henry James and the Almighty Dollar," H&H, 7 (April-May, 1934), 434-443.
        Maintains that James was not unaware of the social consequences of great wealth.

1831   _____.   <u>Herman Melville.</u>   The American Men of Letters Series.   William Sloane Associates, 1950, 21, 103, 202, passim.
        Comparisons.

1832   _____.   "Looking Backward with Henry James," NYTBR, (April, 1956), 1.
        Reminiscences.

1833   _____.   "The World of Henry James," Nation, 195 (November 10, 1962), 310-311.
        Essay-review, Leon Edel.   <u>The Conquest of London,</u> and <u>The Middle Years.</u>

1833.1 Aspiz, Harold.   <u>Mark Twain's Reading: A Critical Study.</u> Diss.   Los Angeles: University of California: 1949, pp. 203ff.
        Clemens' dislike of James.

1834   Asselineau, Roger.   "The French Stream in American Literature," YCGL, 17 (1968), 29-39.
        Says that James, as well as other American writers, borrowed techniques from French artists.

1835   Aswell, Edward Duncan.   "The Art of Aggression: The Short Fiction of Henry James, 1888-1898," DA, 25 (Berkeley, California: 1965), 4141.

1836   _____.   "James's Treatment of Artistic Collaboration," Criticism, 8 (Spring, 1966), 180-195.
        "... The most compelling conclusion ... is that James could never have viewed collaboration as a feasible or healthy artistic possibility."

1837   Atherton, Gertrude.   <u>Adventures of a Novelist.</u>   New York:

Liveright, Inc., 1932, pp. 107, 116.
Reminiscences and criticism.

1838 _____. The Bell in the Fog and Other Stories. New
York: Garrett Press, 1968, pp. 4-6.
A fictional tribute in the opening sketch of the Jamesian
hero.

1839 Aubry, G. Jean. Joseph Conrad, Life and Letters. Garden
City, New York: Doubleday, 1927, I, 270-271.
Conrad's criticism of James's work.

1840 Auchincloss, Louis. "James and Bourget: The Artist and
the Crank," in his Reflections of a Jacobite. Boston:
Houghton Mifflin Co., 1961, pp. 127-137.

1840.1 _____. "James and the Russian Novelists," in Reflections of a Jacobite. Boston: Houghton Mifflin Co., 1961,
pp. 157-171.

1841 _____. "A Reader's Guide to the Fiction of Henry James,"
Reflections of a Jacobite. Boston: Houghton Mifflin, 1961,
pp. 209-220.

1842 _____. "A Strategy for James Readers," Nation, 190
(April 23, 1960), 364-367.
Suggests the order in which James's works should be read.

1843 _____. "The World of Henry James," Show, 4 (July-
August, 1964), 49-55.
Assembles a few attractive and rare photographs.

1844 Auden, W. H. "At the Grave of Henry James," [poem], PR,
8 (July-August, 1941), 266-270.

1844.1 _____. "At the Grave of Henry James," in The Question
of Henry James. F. W. Dupee, ed. New York: Henry Holt,
1945, pp. 246-250.

1845 _____. "Henry James and the Artist in America," HarperM, 197 (July, 1948), 36-40.
Stresses James's integrity as an artist.

1846 Ayscough, John. "Of Some Americans," CathW, 116 (October, 1922), 41-55.

1846.1 Aziz, Maqbool, ed. Introduction. The Tales of Henry
James (1864-1869). Oxford: Clarendon Press, 1973, I,
xvii-1.

1846.2 B., H. S. "Henry James: American Criticism," N&Q, 176
(January 7, 1939), 8.

1847   "The Baffling Henry James," LitD, 52 (March 18, 1916), 714-715.

1847.1 Baker, Ernest A. The History of the English Novel: The Day Before Yesterday. London: Witherby, 1938, IX, 254-255.

1848   Baldwin, James. "As Much of the Truth as One Can Bear," Opinions and Perspectives. Francis Brown, ed. Boston: Houghton Mifflin, 1964, pp. 210-211, 214.

1849   Baldwin, Richard Eugene. "The Influence of Emerson on the Fiction of Henry James," DA, 28 (Berkeley, Calif.: 1967), 4162A.

1850   Ballou, Ellen B. "Scudder's Atlantic," HLB, 16 (October, 1968), 326-353.

1851   Banta, Martha. Henry James and the Occult: The Great Extension. Bloomington: Indiana University Press, 1972.

1852   _____. "The House of Seven Ushers and How They Grew: A Look at Jamesian Gothicism," YR, 57 (October, 1967), 56-65.
        Sees James as a practitioner of the New Gothicism which was tied "to psychological developments of the period."

1853   _____. "The Two Worlds of Henry James: A Study in the Fiction of the Supernatural," DA, 26 (Indiana: 1965), 1035-1936.

1854   Bantock, G. H. "Morals and Civilization in Henry James," CamJ, 7 (December, 1953), 159-181.
        The essential James is to be found "in those representatives of refined moral consciousness which accept their difference from the rest of society unsupported by a sense of affinity to anything except their own finer selves and the obligations which these impose."

1855   Barnet, Sylvan, Morton Berman, and William Burto, eds. "The Art of Fiction," The Study of Literature. Boston: Little, Brown & Co., 1960, pp. 93-116.

1855.1 Barnhart, Clarence L., with Assistance of William D. Halsey. "Henry James," The New Century Handbook of English Literature. Rev. ed., New York: Appleton-Century-Crofts, 1967, pp. 620-621.

1855.2 Barrell, Charles Wisner. "Genesis of a Henry James Story," SFQ, 6 (1945), 63-4.

1856   Barrett, Clifton Waller. "Some Bibliographical Adventures in Americana," BSAP, 44 (1st Qt., 1950), 21, 24.

"An exhaustive gathering of the first editions, English and
American, of the old master Henry James, is apt to ex-
haust the collector...."

1857   Barrett, Laurence. "Young Henry James, Critic," AL, 20
(January, 1949), 385-400.
Believes that aspects of James's later thinking are re-
vealed in his criticism.

1858   Barrie, J. M. ["Henry James"] The Greenwood Hat: Being a Memoir of James Anon [1885-1887]. Privately printed,
1930; New York: Scribner's, 1938, pp. 240ff.
Reminiscence of a meeting with James.

1859   Bashore, James Robert, Jr. "The Villains in the Major
Works of Nathaniel Hawthorne and Henry James," DA, 19
(Wisconsin: 1959), 2939.

1860   Bass, Eben Edward. "Ethical Form in the Fiction of Henry
James," DA, 23 (Pittsburgh: 1962), 1015.

1861   _____. "Henry James and the English Country House,"
MarkR, 2 (February, 1970), 4-10.
Considers the symbolism of names of various country
houses in James's fiction.

1862   _____. "Lemon-Colored Volumes and Henry James,"
SSF, 1 (Winter, 1964), 113-122.
On the stories James first published in The Yellow Book.

1863   Battersby, H. F. P. "Novels of Mr. Henry James," EdinbR,
197 (January, 1903), 59-85.

1863.1 Battilana, Marilla. Venezia Sfondo e Simbolo Nella Narrativa di Henry James. Milan: Laboratorio delle arti, 1971,
pp. 251f.

1864   Baugh, Albert C., ed. "The Modern Novel" [Henry James],
A Literary History of England. New York: Appleton-Century-Crofts, Inc., 1948, pp. 1547-1551.

1865   Baumgaertel, Gerhard. "The Reception of Henry James in
Germany," Sym, 13 (Spring, 1959), 19-31.

1866   Baumgartel, Werner. Henry James im Spiegel Moderner
Englischer Literaturkritik. Diss. Tübingen, 1954.

1867   Baxter, Annette K. "Independence vs. Isolation: Hawthorne
and James on the Problem of the Artist," NCF, 10 (December, 1955), 225-231.
"If James asked his artist to be but partially a man, and
Hawthorne that he be more than a man, each was apparently unwilling to grant the accessibility of other alterna-
tives...."

1868   Bay, André. "Une morale rayonnante," NL, 44 (juillet 21, 1966), 8.

1869   Bayley, John. The Characters of Love: A Study in the Literature of Personality. New York: Basic Books, 1961.

1870   Beach, Joseph Warren. The Method of Henry James. New Haven: Yale U. P., 1918; revised ed., Philadelphia: Albert Saifer, 1954; repr., 1964.
       An invaluable study of technique.

1871   _____. "Henry James," Cambridge History of American Literature. New York: Putnam's, 1921, p. 104; Macmillan, 1936, pp. 96-108.

1872   _____. "The Novel from James to Joyce," Nation, 232 (June 10, 1931), 634-636.

1873   _____. "The Sacred and Solitary Refuge," Furioso, 3 (1948), 23-27.
       Stresses theory.

1874   _____. "Subjective Drama: James," "Point of View: James," "Point of View: James and Others," "Point of View: James, Stendhal," in The Twentieth Century Novel. New York: Century Co., 1932; Appleton-Century, 1942, pp. 177-92, 193-203, 204-217, 218-228.

1875   Beachcroft, T. O. "James, Conrad, and the Place of the Narrator," The English Short Story (II). London: Published for the British Council and the National Book League by Longmans, Green & Co., 1964, pp. 14-18.

1876   _____. The Modest Art: A Survey of the Short Story in English. London: Oxford University Press, 1968.

1877   Beattie, Munro. "Henry James, Novelist," DR, 39 (Winter, 1960), 455-463.
       James's field said to be not myth or epic, but life.

1878   _____. "The Many Marriages of Henry James," Patterns of Commitment in American Literature. Marston LaFrance, ed. Toronto: Toronto U. P., 1967, pp. 93-112.
       "Marriage longed for or schemed for, marriage postponed, marriage thwarted, marriage triumphant," Beattie says, "defines and directs the action...."

1879   Beaver, Harold. "A Figure in the Carpet: Irony and the American Novel," Essays and Studies. London: John Murray, 1962, pp. 101-114.

1880   Bedford, Sybille. "Fantasy without Whimsy," SatR, 43 (November 19, 1960), 28-29.

Comparison of Muriel Spark and James.

1881 Beebe, Maurice L. The Alienation of the Artist: A Study
of Portraits of the Artist By Henry James, Marcel Proust,
and James Joyce. Diss. Cornell, 1953.

1882 _____, and William T. Stafford. "Criticism of Henry
James," MFS, 3 (Spring, 1957), 73-96.

1883 _____. "Henry James: The Ideal of Detachment," Ivory
Towers and Sacred Founts: The Artist as Hero in Fiction
from Goethe to Joyce. New York: New York U. P., 1964,
pp. 197-231, passim.
      Develops the thesis that "the artist is detached from one
      kind of life only that he may accept more fully and par-
      ticipate more completely in a different kind of life."

1884 _____. "Henry James and the Sophomore," CE, 14
(1952), 20-22.
      Cf., Fred B. Millett. "Henry James and the Undergradu-
      ate," CE, 14 (1952), 167-168; Arthur L. Scott. "A Pro-
      test against the James Vogue," CE, 13 (1952), 194-201.

1885 _____. "The Turned Back of Henry James," SAQ, 53
(October, 1954), 521-539.
      Bases an interpretation of James's alienation on the idea
      that every great artist as an artist is detached from so-
      ciety.

1886 Beer, Thomas. "Henry James and Stephen Crane," The
Question of Henry James. F. W. Dupee, ed. New York:
Henry Holt, 1945, pp. 105-107.

1887 _____. "Princess Far Away," SatRL, 1 (April 25,
1925), 701-702.
      Essay-review, Van Wyck Brooks. The Pilgrimage of
      Henry James. New York: 1925.

1888 Beerbohm, Max. "The Guerdon," Parodies: An Anthology
from Chaucer to Beerbohm--and After. Compiled with Introduction and Notes by Dwight Macdonald. New York: The
Modern Library, 1960, pp. 147-149.

1889 _____. "An Incident," Mainly on the Air. New York:
Alfred A. Knopf, 1958, pp. 131-133.
      A reminiscence.

1890 _____. "Jacobean and Shavian," Around Theatres. New
York: Knopf, 1930, pp. 260-265, 323-326. Repr., Henry
James: A Collection of Critical Essays. Leon Edel, ed.
Englewood Cliffs, New Jersey: Prentice-Hall, 1963, pp. 18-
26.

1890.1 _____. "The Mote in the Middle Distance," Christmas
       Garland. New York: Oxford U. P., 1936, pp. 3-10; repr.,
       in Question of Henry James. F. W. Dupee, ed. New York:
       Henry Holt, 1945, pp. 40-43.

1891   Beers, Henry A. Initial Studies in American Letters. New
       York: The Chautauqua Press, 1899, pp. 213ff.

1891.1 _____. An Outline Sketch of American Literature. New
       York: Chautauqua Press, 1887, pp. 271-274.
           James, having become "half-denationalized," had gained a
           curious "doubleness" in his point of view which enabled
           him to look at "America with the eyes of a foreigner and
           at Europe with the eyes of an American."

1892   Beker, Miroslav. "T. S. Eliot's Theory of Impersonality
       and Henry James: A Note," SRAZ, 27-28 (1969), 163-167.
           Points out that James's thoughts [in the Prefaces] on "the
           depersonalization of the artist" parallel those of the poet.

1893   Bell, Millicent. "Dream of Being Possessed and Possess-
       ing," MassR, 10 (Winter, 1969), 97-114.

1894   _____. "The Eagle and the Worm," LonM, 6 (July, 1966),
       5-46.
           James's appreciation of Edith Wharton.

1895   _____. "Edith Wharton and Henry James: The Literary
       Relation," PMLA, 74 (December, 1959), 619-637.
           Influence of James, and comparisons of techniques of the
           two writers.

1896   _____. Edith Wharton and Henry James: The Story of
       Friendship. London: Peter Owen, Ltd., 1966; New York:
       George Braziller, 1965.
           Though James was deeply sympathetic, the author finds no
           suggestion of a love affair between him and Mrs. Wharton.

1896.1 _____. "Henry James: The Man Who Lived," MassR, 14
       (Spring, 1973), 391-414.

1897   _____. "A James 'Gift' to Edith Wharton," MLN, 72
       (March, 1957), 182-185.

1898   Bell, Vereen M. "Character and Point of View in Represent-
       ative Victorian Novels," DA, 20 (Duke: 1960), 3741-42.
           Treats the subjective analysis of characters in the novels
           of James and others.

1899   Bennett, Arnold. "Henry James," in Books and Persons:
       Being Comments on a Past Epoch, 1908-1911. New York:
       Doran & Co., 1917, pp. 263-266.

1900   _____. "Henry James," in Things That Have Interested
        Me. First Series. New York: Doran, 1921, pp. 323-332.

1901   _____. The Journal of Arnold Bennett. [1896-1928]
        New York: Literary Guild, 1933, passim.

1902   _____. "Two Reputations," in Savour of Life: Essays in
        Gusto. New York: Doubleday, 1928, pp. 117-121.
            Reiminiscences.

1903   Bennett, Barbara L. The Ethics of Henry James's Novels.
        Diss. North Carolina: 1954.

1903.1 Bennett, Joan. George Eliot: Her Mind and Her Art.
        Cambridge: At the University Press, 1954, pp. 128-130.
        The influence of Eliot on James.

1904   Benson, Arthur Christopher. The Diary of Arthur Christo-
        pher Benson. Percy Lubbock, ed. New York: Longmans,
        1926.
            Reminiscence.

1905   _____. "Henry James," Cornhill, 40 (November, 1916),
        511-519.
            Authoritative remarks by a friend of many years.

1906   _____. "Lamb House, Rye," in Rambles and Reflections.
        London: 1926; New York: Putnam, 1926, pp. 29-37.

1907   _____. "Henry James," Memories and Friends. New
        York: Putnam, 1924, pp. 214-228.

1908   Benson, E. F. As We Were: A Victorian Peep Show. Lon-
        don, New York: Longmans, Green & Co., 1943, pp. 277-
        281, 283-284, passim.

1909   _____. Final Edition. London, New York: Appleton-
        Century, 1940, pp. 6-13, passim.
            Reminiscences.

1910   Bentzon, T. "Les Nouveaux Romanciers Américains: Henry
        James," RDM (May 1, 1883).
            An early interpretation from a French point of view.

1911   Bergonzi, Bernard. "An Early Wells Review of Henry
        James," TLS (April 18, 1958), 216.
            Reproduction and discussion of H. G. Wells' review in
            SatR, June 1, 1895.

1911.1   _____. "The Novelist and His Subject-matter," Listener,
        60 (September 18, 1958), 426-427.

1912   _____. The Situation of the Novel. Pittsburgh University

Press, 1970; London: Macmillan, 1970, passim.

1913 Berland, Alwyn. "Henry James," UKCR, 18 (Winter, 1950),
94-108.
   James's stories are largely "of victory of intelligence
   over circumstances...."

1914 _____. "Henry James and the Aesthetic Tradition," JHI,
23 (July-September, 1962), 407-419.
   Notes that James, Ruskin, and Arnold held similar attitudes toward art.

1915 _____. "Henry James and the Grand Renunciation." KM
4 (1958), 82-90.
   Treats the theme of renunciation in James.

1916 _____. Henry James and the Nature of Civilization.
Diss. Cambridge: 1953-54.

1917 _____. "James and Forster: The Morality of Class,"
CamJ, 6 (February, 1953), 259-280.

1918 Berry, Thomas Elliott. The Newspaper and the American
Novel, 1900-1969. Metuchen, New Jersey: Scarecrow Press,
1970, passim.

1919 Berryman, John. Stephen Crane. William Sloane Associates. The American Men of Letters Series, 2nd pr., 1950,
passim.

1920 Bersani, Leo. "The Jamesian Lie," PR, 36 (Winter, 1969),
53-79.
   The author of the article is concerned with the self-suf-
   ficiency of James's formal unities. James's "deceptively
   banal position that only execution matters means most pro-
   foundly that verisimilitude ... is the grace and the truth
   of a formal unity."

1921 _____. Point of View in Fiction: Studies of Narrative
Techniques. Diss. Harvard: 1957.

1922 _____. "Variations on a Paradigm," NYTBR (June 11,
1967), 6, 45.

1923 Berthoff, Warner. The Example of Melville. Princeton:
Princeton University Press, 1962, passim.
   Compares James and Melville.

1924 _____. The Ferment of Realism: American Literature,
1884-1919. New York: The Free Press, 1965, passim.

1925 _____. Fictions and Events: Essays in Criticism and
Literary History. New York: E. P. Dutton & Co., 1971,

pp. 157-160, 283-285.

1926   Berti, Luigo. "Saggio su Henry James," Inventario, 1
        (Autumn-Winter, 1946-1947), 77-88.

1927   Bertocci, Angelo. "The Labyrinthine Spirit: Henry James,"
        in Charles Du Bos and English Literature. New York:
        King's Crown Press, 1949, pp. 196-205.

1928   Bethurum, Dorothy. "Morality and Henry James," SR, 31
        (July-September, 1923), 324-330.

1929   Bewley, Marius. "Appearance and Reality in Henry James,"
        Scrutiny, 17 (Summer, 1950), 90-114.

1930   _____. The Complex Fate: Hawthorne, Henry James,
        and Some Other American Writers. London: Chatto and
        Windus, 1968, passim.

1931   _____. The Eccentric Design: Form in the Classic
        American Novel. New York: Columbia University Press,
        1959, pp. 220-258.

1932   _____. "Henry James and 'Life,'" HudR, 11 (Summer,
        1958), 167-185.
        Europe acts as a catalyst upon Americans in James's
        work, so that they may discover the "personal fulfillment
        which is life."

1933   _____. "James's Debt to Hawthorne, (I): The Blithedale
        Romance and The Bostonians," Scrutiny, 16 (Winter, 1949;
        Spring, 1950), 178-195.

1934   _____. "James's Debt to Hawthorne, (II): The Marble
        Faun and The Wings of the Dove," Scrutiny, 16 (1949), 301-
        317.

1935   _____. "James's Debt to Hawthorne (III): The American
        Problem," Scrutiny, 17 (Spring, 1950), 14-31.

1936   _____. Masks and Mirrors: Essays in Criticism. New
        York: Atheneum Publishers, c1949, 1970, passim.

1937   _____. "The Verb to Contribute," Spec, 6839 (July 24,
        1959), 114-115.
        Says that James stressed moral seriousness of art in
        early reviews.

1937.1 Bianchini, Angela. "Henry James e la Remington," NA,
        511, #2042 (February, 1971), 259-263.
        In 1897 writer's cramp caused James to acquire a type-
        writer and a typist.

1938   Biddle, Arthur William. "The Emerging Consciousness: A
        Study of the Development of the Centre of Consciousness in
        the Early Novels of Henry James," DAI, 31 (Michigan State:
        1970), 6046A.
            James sought a means of "dramatizing consciousness...."

1938.1 Biddle, Francis. "The Eagle and the Worm," SR, 75 (Sum-
        mer, 1967), 533-539.
            Essay-review, Millicent Bell. Edith Wharton and Henry
        James. New York: 1965.

1938.2 Bielenstein, Gabrielle Maupin. "Affinities for Henry James,"
        Meanjin, 16 (Winter, 1957), 196-199.

1939   Bier, Jesse. The Rise and Fall of American Humor. New
        York: Holt, Rinehart & Winston, 1968, pp. 390-393, pas-
        sim.

1939.1 Bierce, Ambrose. Wasp, 10 (February 17, 1883), 5.
            An attack on James and Howells.

1940   Birch, Brian. "Henry James: Some Bibliographical and Tex-
        tual Matters," Library, 20 (1965), 108-123.
            Cf. S. P. Rosenbaum, Library 21 (1966), 248-250; and
        Brian Birch, Library, 21 (1966), 250-252.

1940.1 Bishop, Ferman. "Henry James Criticizes 'The Tory Lov-
        er,'" AL, 27 (May, 1955), 262-264.

1941   Blackall, Jean F. Recurrent Symbolic Elements in the Nov-
        els of Henry James (1896-1901). Diss. Radcliffe: 1961.

1942   Blackmur, Richard P. "American Literary Expatriate,"
        The Lion and the Honeycomb: Essays in Solicitude and Crit-
        ique. New York: Harcourt, Brace, 1955, pp. 61-78.

1942.1 _____. "A Critic's Job of Work," The Double Agent:
        Essays in Craft and Elucidation. New York: Arrow Eds.,
        1935.

1943   _____. "In the Country of the Blue," KR, 5 (Autumn,
        1943), 595-617. Repr., The Question of Henry James. F.
        W. Dupee, ed. New York: 1945, pp. 191-211; Critiques
        and Essays on Modern Fiction. Ronald Press, 1952, pp.
        303-318.

1944   _____. "The Loose and Baggy Monsters of Henry James:
        Notes on the Underlying Classic Form in the Novel," Accent,
        11 (Spring, 1951), 129-146. Repr., in The Lion and the
        Honeycomb, pp. 268-288.

1945   _____. "Henry James," in The Literary History of the
        United States. Robert E. Spiller, et al, eds. New York:

Macmillan, 1948, pp. 1039-1064.

1946   Blanche, Jaques-Émile. "Henry James," La Revue Euro-
péenne, (August-September, 1923).

1947   Blanke, Gustav H. "Aristokratie und Gentleman in Englisch-
en und Amerikanischen Roman des 19. und 20. Jahrhunderts,"
G-RM, n. s., 13, #3 (July, 1963), 281-306.

1948   _____. "Henry James als Schriftsteller zwischen Amer-
ika und Europa," NS, 2 (1956), 59-71.

1949   Bleich, David. "Utopia: The Psychology of a Cultural Fantasy," DAI, 30 (New York University: 1970), 4935A-36A.

1950   Bliven, Naomi. "Books: Home, James," NY, 48 (April 29,
1972), 137f.

1951   _____. "Lessons in the Master," NY, 39 (September 7,
1963), 151-157.

1952   Blöcker, Günter. "Henry James," Merkur, 11 (August,
1957), 730-743.

1952.1 Blount, Joseph Donald. "Marcel Proust and Henry James in
the Tradition of Lyric Description," DA, 34 (South Carolina:
1973), 5956A-5957A.

1953   Bluen, Herbert. "The Poetry of Edgar Allan Poe," AryanP,
35 #7 (July, 1964), 316-319.
James found Poe's work worthless.

1954   Boas, Ralph Philip. The Study and Appreciation of Literature. New York: Harcourt, 1931, passim.

1954.1 Bocaz, Sergio Hernan. "La novelística de José Donoso y su
cosmogonia estética a través de los influencias principales:
Marcel Proust y Henry James," DAI, 33 (Colorado: 1972),
1714A.

1955   Bockes, Douglas Theodore. "The Late Method of Henry
James," DA, 14 (Syracuse: 1954), 2062.

1956   _____. The Late Method of Henry James. Ann Arbor:
No. 10,064, University Microfilms, 1954.

1957   Bogan, Louise. "Henry James on a Revolutionary Theme,"
Nation, 146 (April 23, 1938), 471-474. Repr., in Literary
Opinion in America. M. D. Zabel, ed. New York: 1951,
pp. 351-356.

1958   _____. "The Portrait of New England," Nation, 161 (December 1, 1948), 582-583.

1959   _____. Selected Criticism: Prose, Poetry. New York:
Noonday Press, 1955, pp. 112-121, 267-268, 295-301.

1960   _____. "The Silver Clue," Nation, 159 (December 23,
1944), 775-776.

1961   Bogosian, Ezekiel. The Perfect Gentleman: A Study of an
Esthetic Type in the Novels of Richardson, Jane Austen,
Trollope, and Henry James. Diss. University of California:
1937.

1962   Boit, Louise. "Henry James as Landlord," Atl, 178 (August,
1946), 118-121.
Reminiscences.

1963   Bompard, Paola. "Henry James e il problema del male,"
FLe, 11 (March 16, 1952), 4.

1964   Bontley, Thomas John. "The Aesthetics of Discretion: Sexuality in the Fiction of Henry James," DA, 27 (Stanford:
1966), 3446A-47A.

1965   Booth, Bradford A. "Henry James and the Economic Motif,"
NCF, 8 (September, 1953), 141-150.
"The heart of virtually every James novel and of many
short stories is a struggle for money or a squabble over
money."

1966   _____. "Form and Technique in the Novel," in The Reinterpretation of Victorian Literature. Joseph E. Baker, ed.
Princeton, New Jersey: Princeton U. P., 1950, pp. 94-95.
James saw the novel "not [as] a narrative but a represen-
tational work serving the same ends as the other arts.
It must have form, structure, style. But it did not
achieve these qualities without the sacrifice of others...."

1967   Booth, Wayne. "Henry James and the Unreliable Narrator,"
The Rhetoric of Fiction. Chicago: Chicago U. P., 1961, pp.
339-374.

1968   Borchers, Lotte. Frauengestalten und Frauenprobleme Bei
Henry James. (Ein Beitrag zur amerikanischen Literaturge-
schichte). Diss. Greifswald, 1929. (Published: Berlin,
1929).

1968.1 Borden, Diane M. Threads for the Labyrinth: Style and
Symbol in Henry James. Diss. Santa Cruz, Calif.: 1972.

1969   Borklund, Elmer. "Howard Sturgis, Henry James, and Bel-
chamber," MP, 58 (May, 1961), 255-269.

1970   _____. "Recent Approaches to Henry James," JGE, 16
(1965), 327-340.

Essay-review of recent books on James.

1970.1 Bosanquet, Theodora. "As I Remember Henry James,"
T&T, 35 (July 3, 1954), 875-876; 35 (July 10, 1954), 913-
914.
Reminiscences.

1971 _____. "Henry James," FnR, 101 (June, 1917), 995-
1009; LivA, 294 (August 11, 1917), 346-347.

1972 _____. "Henry James as a Literary Artist," Bookman,
45 (August, 1917), 571-581.

1973 _____. Henry James at Work. London: The Hogarth
Press, 1924; Garden City, New York: Doubleday, 1928, pp.
243-276.

1974 _____. "The Record of Henry James," YR, 10 (October,
1920), 143-156.

1974.1 [Bosanquet, Theodora.] "The Secret of Henry James's Style
as Revealed by His Typist," CurOp, 63 (August, 1917), 118.

1975 Boughton, Alice. "A Note by His Photographer," H&H, 7
(April-May, 1934), 478-49.
Reminiscences.

1976 Bowden, Edwin T. "In Defense of a Henry James Collection," LCUT, 6 (Winter, 1960), 7-12.

1977 _____. "Henry James and International Copyright Again,"
AL, 25 (January, 1954), 499-500.
Cf., Edna Kenton, H&H, 7 (1934), 537.

1978 _____. "Henry James and the Struggle for International
Copyright: An Unnoticed Item in the James Bibliography,"
AL, 24 (January, 1953), 537-539.
The item is a letter printed in the Critic, December 10,
1887.

1979 _____. The Novels of Henry James: An Approach Through
the Visual Arts. Diss. Yale: 1952.

1980 _____. The Themes of Henry James: A System of Ob-
servation Through the Visual Arts. (Yale Studies in English,
Vol. 132) New Haven: Yale U. P., 1956; 2nd pr., 1960.
A most important work which focuses on the arts in James.

1981 Bowen, Edwin W. "Henry James, the Realist: An Appreciation," MethR, 101 (May, 1918), 410-419.

1982 Boyd, E. A. "Henry James Self-Revealed," Freeman, 1
(August 25, 1920), 563-564.

1983 _____. "Henry James," Literary Blasphemies. New York: and London: Harper, 1927, pp. 213-226.

1984 Boynton, Percy H. A History of American Literature. Boston: New York: Ginn & Co., 1919, pp. 422ff, passim.

1984.1 Brack, O. M., Jr. "Mark Twain in Knee Pants: The Expurgation of Tom Sawyer Abroad," Proof, 2 (1972), 145-151.

1985 Bradford, Gamaliel. "Henry James," American Portraits: 1875-1900. Boston and New York: Houghton Mifflin Co., 1922, pp. 171-196.

1986 _____. "Portrait of Henry James," NAR, 213 (February, 1921), 211-224.

1987 Bradley, A. G. "Henry James as I Knew Him," JO'LW (December 18, 1936).

1987.1 Bragdon, Claude. "The Figure in Mr. James's Carpet," Critic, 44 (February, 1904), 146-150.

1988 _____. "A Master of Shades," Critic, 46 (January, 1905), 20-22.

. 1989 Brasch, James Daniel. "The Relation of Theme and Setting in the Major Novels of Henry James," DA, 20 (Wisconsin: 1959), 1011.

1990 Bree, Germaine. "Distrusting the Gaul," Nation, 198 (April 13, 1964), 377-379.

1991 Brewster, Henry. "Henry James and the Gallo-American," BottOs, 19 (Spring, 1957), 179-181.
An account of the friendship between James and Henry B. Brewster.

1992 Bridgman, Richard. "Henry James and Mark Twain," in The Colloquial Style in America. New York: Oxford U. P., 1966, pp. 78-130, passim.
Shows that James and Twain "corroborated and re-enforced one another's efforts" in using colloquial language to literary effect.

1993 Briggs, Anthony D. "Alexander Pushkin: A Possible Influence on Henry James," FMLS, 8 (January, 1972), 52-60.

1994 "British Tributes to Henry James," LitD, 52 (April 8, 1916), 970.

1994.1 Brkić, Svetozar. Tema 'medjunarodne situacije' i sukoba u delima Henri Džemza i Iva Andrića. Ivo Andrić, Institut za teoriju književnosti i umetnosti, Beograd, I, 1962, pp. 317-329.

1994.2 Broderick, John C. "Henry James and Gestation: A Reply,"
       CE, 21 (1960), 497-499.

1994.3 Brogan, D. W. "No Innocents Abroad," HarperB (July,
       1958), 86-87, 98.
           American travellers abroad, including James.

1994.4 Brogan, Denis. "The Last of Bloomsbury," Spec, 223
       (1969), 236.

1994.5 Brome, Vincent. Six Studies in Quarrelling. London:
       Cresset Press, 1958, p. 198.

1995   Bronson, Walter C. "Henry James, Jr.," A Short History
       of American Literature. Boston and New York: D. C.
       Heath & Co., Rev., and enlarged, 1900, 1919.

1995.1 [Brooke, Stopford.] Life and Letters of Stopford Brooke.
       L. P. Jacks, ed. New York: Scribner's, 1917, pp. 528-
       529.

1996   Brooks, Cleanth. "The American 'Innocence': In James,
       Fitzgerald, and Faulkner," Shenandoah, 16 (Autumn, 1964),
       21-37.
           Compares characters in the novels of the three writers.

1997   Brooks, Peter. "Melodramatic Imagination," PR, 39, #2
       (1972), 195-212.
           James's views of Balzac.

1997.1 Brooks, Van Wyck. An Autobiography. New York: E. P.
       Dutton & Co., Inc., 1965, pp. 428-429, passim.

1998   _____. The Confident Years: 1885-1915. London: J.
       M. Dent, 1955, passim; New York: E. P. Dutton, 1952,
       passim.

1999   _____. The Dream of Arcadia: American Writers and
       Artists in Italy. New York: E. P. Dutton, 1958, pp. 155-
       175.

2000   _____. The Flowering of New England, 1815-1865. New
       York: Modern Library, 1936, passim.

2001   _____. "Henry James: The American Scene," Dial, 75
       (July, 1923), 29-42.

2002   _____. "Henry James, the First Phase," Dial, 74 (May,
       1923), 433-450.

2003   _____. "Henry James of Boston," SatRL, 22 (July 13,
       1940), 3-4, 16-17.

2004 _____. New England: Indian Summer, 1865-1915. New
York: E. P. Dutton, 1940, pp. 224-249, 276-295, 395-408.

2005 _____. "Our Illustrious Expatriate," Freeman, 1 (April
28, 1920), 164-165.

2006 _____. The Pilgrimage of Henry James. New York: E.
P. Dutton, 1925; repr., New York: Octagon Books, 1972.
A study of James as an "expatriate novelist."

2007 _____. "The Pilgrimage," Days of the Phoenix. New
York: E. P. Dutton, 1957, pp. 175-182.

2007.1 _____. The Times of Melville and Whitman. London:
J. M. Dent; New York: E. P. Dutton, 1953, pp. 319-321.
Comparisons of themes in American writers, including
James.

2008 _____. "Two Phases of Henry James," The Question of
Henry James. F. W. Dupee, ed. New York: Henry Holt,
1945, pp. 120-127.

2009 Brophy, Brigid. "Henry James," in Don't Never Forget:
Collected Views and Re-Reviewers. New York: Henry Holt,
1967, pp. 203-208.
A reply to Maxwell Geismar, Henry James and His Cult.
1964.

2009.1 Brower, Reuben. The Fields of Light: An Experiment in
Critical Reading. New York: 1951, Oxford University
Press, passim.

2010 Brown, Ashley. "Landscape into Art: Henry James and
John Crowe Ransom," SR, 79 (April-June, 1971), 206-213.
Suggests a source of Ransom's Old Mansion in James.

2011 Brown, Clarence Arthur, comp. ["Henry James] "Realism
and Aestheticism: Introduction," Achievement of American
Criticism. New York: Ronald, 1954, pp. 386-390.

2012 Brown, Daniel R. "The Cosmopolitan Novel: James and
Lewis," SinLNL, 1, i (1969), 6-9.

2013 Brown, E. K. "The Fiction of Henry James," YR, n. s.,
34 (Spring, 1945), 536-539.

2014 _____. "James and Conrad," YR, 35 (Winter, 1946),
265-285.

2015 _____. "Two Formulas for Fiction: Henry James and
H. G. Wells," CE, 8 (October, 1946), 7-17.
Says that when H. G. Wells attacks James's novels as
over-unified, he is presenting a counterattack on behalf

of his own conception of the novel as a "ragbag" for presentation of the author's experiences and ideas.

2016   Brown, Francis, ed. <u>Opinions and Perspectives from the</u>
       <u>New York Times Book Review.</u> Boston: Houghton Mifflin,
       1964, passim.

2017   Brownell, William C. "Henry James," <u>American Prose Mas-</u>
       <u>ters.</u> New York: Scribner's, 1909; repr. , Cambridge,
       Mass. : Harvard U. P. , 1963, 339-398, passim.

2018   _____. "Henry James," Atl, 95 (April, 1905), 496-519.

2019   Bruccoli, Matthew J. "Fitzgerald, Brooks, Hemingway, and
       James," FitzN, 29 (Spring, 1965), 1-3.

2019.1 Brumm, Ursula. "Symbolism and the Novel," PR, 25
       (1958), 329-342. Repr. , in <u>The Theory of the Novel.</u> Philip
       Stevick, ed. pp. 354-368.

2019.2 Bruneau, Jean. "Une Lettre Inédité de Henry James à Gus-
       tave Flaubert Autour de Mockton Milnes, Lord Houghton,"
       RLC, 41 (October-December, 1968), 520-533.

2020   Brussel, I. R. <u>Anglo-American First Editions, Part II.</u>
       <u>West to East.</u> London and New York: 1936.
          Provides information as to first editions printed in Eng-
       land.

2021   Bryden, Ronald. "The Wounds of Judgment," Spec, 7037
       (May 10, 1963), 605.

2022   Brylowski, Anna Salne. "The House of Irony: A Study of
       Irony in Henry James," DA, 28 (Michigan State: 1967),
       5044A-45A.

2022.1 Buchan, Alexander M. "Edith Wharton and 'The Elusive
       Bright-Winged Thing,' " NEQ, 37 (September, 1964), 343-362.
          Comparison of the two authors as to technique.

2023   Buchanan, Robert. "The Modern Young Man as Critic,"
       URev, 3 (March, 1889), 355-359.

2024   Bufkin, E. C. "A Pattern of Parallel and Double: The Func-
       tion of Myrtle in <u>The Great Gatsby,</u>" MFS, 15, #4 (1969-
       1970), 517-524.
          The effects of Fitzgerald's technique are derived from Hen-
       ry James.

2025   Buitenhuis, Peter. "Aesthetics of the Skyscraper: The
       Views of Sullivan, James, and Wright," AQ, 9 (Fall, 1957),
       316-324.

2026 _____. The American Henry James. Diss. Yale: 1955.

2027 _____. "From Daisy Miller to Julia Bride: A Whole Passage of Intellectual History," AQ, 11 (Summer, 1959), 136-146.

2028 _____. The Grasping Imagination: The American Writings of Henry James. Toronto: Toronto University Press, 1970.

2028.1 _____, ed. Henry James: French Writers and American Women: Essays. Branford, Conn.: Compass Pub. Co., 1960.

2028.2 _____. "Henry James and American Culture," in Challenges in American Culture. Ray B. Brown, Larry N. Landrum, and William K. Bottorff, eds. Bowling Green, Ohio: Bowling Green Univ. Popular Press, 1970, pp. 199-208.

2028.3 _____. "Henry James on Hawthorne," NEQ, 32 (June, 1959), 207-225.

2029 Burde, Edgar J. "The Double Vision of Henry James: An Essay on the Three Late Novels," DAI, 31 (Claremont: 1970), 1753A.

2030 Burgess, Anthony. "Treasures and Fetters," Spec, 7078 (February 21, 1964), 254.
A comparison of James and Elizabeth Bowen.

2031 Burgess, C. F. "The Seeds of Art: Henry James's Donnée," L&P, 13 (Summer, 1963), 67-73.
Studies the recurrent pattern in James of a conscious external donnée.

2032 Burgess, Charles E. "Henry James's 'Big' Impression: St. Louis, 1905," MHSB, 27 (1970), 30-63.
Presents information about James and St. Louis.

2033 _____. "The Master and the Mirror," PLL, 7 (Fall, 1971), 382-405.
William Marion Reedy's Mirror emphasized James's style but labeled him an expatriate.

2034 Burke, Kenneth. The Philosophy of Literary Form: Studies in Symbolic Action. Louisiana State University Press, 1941, p. 264, passim.

2035 _____. A Rhetoric of Motives. New York: Prentice-Hall, 1950, pp. 116-117, 294-298.

2036 Burrell, John Angus. "Henry James: A Rhapsody of Youth," Dial, 63 (September 27, 1917), 260-262.

2037   Burstein, Frances Brownell. "The Picture of New England
        Puritanism Presented in the Fiction of Henry James," DA,
        25 (Boston Univ.: 1964), 2977-78.
            Finds that James's fictional treatment of Puritanism is
            "historically accurate and perceptive."

2038   Burt, Nathaniel. "Struthers Burt '04: The Literary Career
        of a Princetonian," PULC, 19 (Spring-Summer, 1958), 109-
        122.
            The influence of James.

2039   Burton, Richard. "Björnson, Daudet, James: A Study in
        the Literary Time-Spirit," in Literary Likings. Boston:
        Copeland & Day, 1898, pp. 107-109, 122-128.

2040   Buschges, Gisela. Die Kultureinwirkung Europas Auf Den
        Amerikaner Bei Henry James. Diss. Freiburg, 1952.

2041   Byatt, A. S. "Prophet and Boulder," NSt (January 2, 1970),
        16.
            Compares James and Browning.

2042   Bynner, Witter. "On Henry James' Centennial: Lasting Im-
        pressions of a Great Writer," SatRL, 26 (May 22, 1943), 23-
        28.

2043   _____. "A Word or Two with Henry James," Critic, 46
        (February, 1905), 146-148.

2044   Byrd, J. Scott. Writers and Artists in the Non-Fiction of
        Henry James. Diss. North Carolina: n. d.

2044.1 C., R. W. "James and Kipling," N&Q, 196 (June 9, 1951),
        260.

2045   Cady, Edwin H. The Light of Common Day: Realism in
        American Fiction. Bloomington: Indiana U. P., 1971, pas-
        sim.
            Through analyses of James and others, the author presents
            a more precise definition of realism.

2046   _____. The Realist at War: The Mature Years, 1885-
        1920, of William Dean Howells. Syracuse: Syracuse U. P.,
        1958, passim.

2047   _____. The Road to Realism: The Early Years, 1837-
        1885, of William Dean Howells. Syracuse U. P., 1956, pp.
        146-147, 152-154, passim.

2047.1 Cairns, Huntington, Allen Tate, and Mark Van Doren. Invi-
        tation to Learning. New York: Random House, 1941, pp.
        142-143, 178-180.

2048   Cairns, William B. "Character-Portrayal in the Work of
        Henry James," WSLL, 2 (Summer, 1918), 314-322.

2049   _____. "Meditations of a Jacobite," Dial, 60 (March 30,
        1916), 313-316.

2050   Calisher, Hortense. "A Short Note on a Long Subject: Hen-
        ry James," TQ, 10 (Summer, 1967), 57-59.
            James "never for one moment under-estimated the intelli-
            gence of his readers. There are some who will never
            forgive him for it."

2051   Cambon, Glauco. "The Negative Gesture in Henry James,"
        NCF, 15 (March, 1961), 335-343.
            James has his characters choose the "pure" in the form of
            a negation.

2052   _____. "L'ombra di Henry James," FLe, 15 (May 15,
        1960), 5.

2052.1 Campos, Christophe. The View of France from Arnold to
        Bloomsbury. London and New York: Oxford U. P., 1965.
            The relationship of writers, including James, to French
            literature.

2053   Canby, Henry Seidel. "He Knew His Women," SatRL, 34
        (November 10, 1951), 9-10, 34-36.
            James's characterization of women.

2054   _____. "Henry James," HarperW, 62 (March 25, 1916),
        291.

2055   _____. "Henry James," Definitions, First Series: Essays
        in Contemporary Criticism. New York: Harcourt, 1922;
        Port Washington, New York: Kennikat Press, Inc., 1967,
        pp. 278-281.
            "... The flat truth is that Henry James was not a novelist
            at all,... He was primarily a critic, the greatest Ameri-
            can critic since Poe...."

2056   _____. "Henry James and the Observant Profession,"
        SatRL, 33 (December 2, 1950), 11-12, 70-71.

2056.1 _____. "Henry James as a Critic," HarperW, 62 (March
        25, 1916), 291.

2057   _____. "Hero of the Great Know-How," The Saturday Re-
        view Gallery. New York: Simon and Schuster, 1959, p. 98.
            "... The reader feels sympathy with Henry James and his
            passion for the 'refinement' of culture ... when Mark
            [Twain] hangs signboards of consumers' goods on the towers
            of Camelot and the spires of the cathedrals."

2058 _____. "The Return of Henry James," SatRL, 31 (January 24, 1948), 9-10, 34-35.
A discussion of the renewed interest in Henry James based on recent volumes written or edited by F. O. Matthiessen.

2059 _____. "The Return of Henry James," SatRL, 31 (February 7, 1948), 27.
Error of SatRL, 31 (January 24, 1948), corrected.

2060 _____. The Short Story in English. New York: 1909, pp. 307-314.

2061 _____. "The Timelessness of Henry James," SatRL, 28 (October 20, 1945), 9-10.
Essay-review of The Short Stories of Henry James. Clifton Fadiman, ed. New York: 1945.

2062 _____. Turn West, Turn East: Mark Twain and Henry James. Boston: Houghton Mifflin, 1951.
The title indicates point of view.

2063 _____. Walt Whitman, an American: A Study in Biography. New York: Literary Classics, Inc., distributed by Houghton Mifflin, Boston: 1943, p. 281.
Discusses Henry James's review of Whitman's "Drum-Taps." "... It is a searching, caustic, somewhat condescending review...."

2064 Cantwell, Robert. "A Little Reality," H&H, 7 (April-June, 1934), 494-505.
Says that early in his career James wanted to be a realist and that he never altogether lost contact with the source of reality--the lower classes.

2064.1 _____. "No Landmarks," Sym, 4 (1933), 70-84. Also in Literary Opinion in America. Morton D. Zabel, ed. New York: 1937, pp. 530-541.

2065 _____. "The Return of Henry James," NewRep, 81 (December 12, 1934), 119-121.

2066 _____. "A Warning to Pre-War Novelists," NewRep, 91 (June 23, 1937), 177-180.
James and the war.

2066.1 Capellan, Angel. "Estudio estructural de las obras tempranas de Henry James," Atlántida, 53 (1971), 586-603.

2066.2 Cargas, Harry J. "Seeing, But Not Living: Two Characters from James and Wharton," NLauR, 1, ii (1972), 5-7.

2067 Cargill, Oscar. "Henry James and the Political Vocation," WestR, 18 (Spring, 1954), 199-208.

2068 _____. "Henry James as Freudian Pioneer," ChiR, 10 (Summer, 1956), 13-29.

2069 _____. "Henry James's 'Moral Policeman': William Dean Howells," AL, 29 (January, 1958), 371-398.
On the literary relationship of the two authors.

2070 _____. Introduction. The Novels of Henry James. New York: Macmillan, 1961.

2070.1 _____. "Occlusion and Refraction in Jamesian Criticism," NCF, 19 (December, 1964), 302-304.
Essay-review of Laurence Holland's The Expense of Vision, 1964, and Robert L. Gale's The Caught Image, 1964.

2071 _____. "William Dean Howells as Henry James's 'Moral Policeman,' " Toward a Pluralistic Criticism. Carbondale and Edwardsville: Southern Illinois U. P., 1965, pp. 69-94.

2072 Carter, E. S. "The Palpitating Divan," EJ, 39 (May, 1950), 237-242.

2073 Carter, Everett. "Henry James," Howells and the Age of Realism. Philadelphia and New York: Lippincott, 1954, pp. 249-263, passim.

2074 Cartinau, Virginia. "Aspecte ale romanului modern si con-temporan englez," ViR, 22, ix (1969), 93-103.
On James and others.

2075 Cary, Elizabeth Luther. "Henry James," Scribner's, 36 (Oc-tober, 1904), 394-400.

2076 _____. The Novels of Henry James: A Study. London and New York: Putnam's, 1905; New York: Haskell House, 1964.
Said by Zabel in The Portable Henry James to be the earliest book on James.

2076.1 Cary, Richard. "Henry James Juvenilia: A Poem and a Letter," CLQ, 9 (1970), 58-63.

2076.2 _____. "Vernon Lee's Vignettes of Literary Acquaint-ances," CLQ, 9 (September, 1970), 179-199.
Reproduces some of Vernon Lee's comments on Henry James.

2077 "The Case of Mr. James," Outlook, 111 (September 22, 1915), 175.
"... While we regret that Mr. James is no longer an American citizen, we see no reason for criticising in him what we commend in a foreigner."

2078   Castiglione, Luigi. "Profilo di James," FLe, 17 (September 23, 1962), 5.

2079   Catalani, G. "Henry James and American Criticism," N&Q, 176 (March 18, 1939), 194-195.

2079.1 [Cather, Willa] The World and the Parish: Willa Cather's Articles and Reviews, 1893-1902. William D. Curtin, ed. Lincoln: Nebraska U. P. , 1970, passim.
        James's influence on Cather.

2080   Cawelti, John G. "Form as Cultural Criticism in the Work of Henry James," Literature and Society. Bernice Slote, ed. Lincoln: Nebraska U. P. , 1964, pp. 202-212.

2081   Cestre, Charles. "La France dans l'oeuvre de Henry James," RAA, 10 (October, 1932), 1-13, 112-122.

2082   Chadderdon, Arnold H. "Comic Method in Henry James's Fiction," DA, 26 (Yale: 1965), 2205.
        A study of James's skill in assimilating alien elements and creating a free play of mind.

2082.1 Chan, Lois Mai. "Figures in the Carpet: A Study of Leading Metaphors in Six Realistic Novels," DA, 31 (Kentucky: 1970), 5354A.

2082.2 Chapman, R. W. "False Scent," TLS (October 19, 1940), 531.
        Cf. , G. M. Young and G. S. Ritchie, TLS (October 6, 1940), 543.

2082.3 Chapman, Sara Simmons. "Henry James' Developing Perspective of America: An Examination of the Tales," DAI, 31 (Ohio Univ.: 1970), 2908A.

2083   Chase, Richard. The Democratic Vista: A Dialogue on Life and Letters in Contemporary America. Garden City, New York: Doubleday & Co. , 1958, p. 65ff.

2084   _____. "James on the Novel vs. the Romance," The American Novel and Its Tradition. Garden City, New York: Doubleday Anchor Books, 1957, pp. 117-137.

2084.1 Chatman, Seymour. "Henry James et le style de l'intangibilité," Poetique, 6 (1971), 155-172.
        Excerpts from Chatman's longer study, tr. , Henry Quéré.

2085   _____. The Later Style of Henry James. Oxford: Basil Blackwell, 1972.

2086   Cherniak, Judith. "Henry James as Moralist: The Case of the Late Novels," CentR, 16 (Spring, 1972), 105-121.

2087   Cheshire, David, and Malcolm Bradbury. "American Real-
        ism and the Romance of Europe: Fuller, Frederic, Garland,"
        PAH, 4 (1970), 285-310.
            Incidental references to James, but also notation of simi-
            larities between Frederic and James.

2088   Chesterton, Gilbert Keith. Autobiography. New York:
        Sheed & Ward, 1936, pp. 222ff.

2089   _____. "Henry James," Common Man. London and New
        York: Sheed & Ward, 1950, pp. 144-148.
            Appreciative criticism.

2090   Chevallez, Abel. Le Roman Anglais de Notre Temps. Lon-
        don: 1921; English translation, New York: 1925.

2090.1 Chew, Samuel C. "The Modern Novel," [Henry James], A
        Literary History of England. Albert C. Baugh, ed. New
        York: Appleton-Century-Crofts, Inc., 1948, pp. 1547-1551.

2091   Chislett, William, Jr. "Henry James: His Range and Ac-
        complishment," Moderns and Near-Moderns. New York:
        Grafton Press, 1928, pp. 11-66.

2092   Chubb, Percival. "Mark Twain at Sundown: Side-Lights
        from Hardy, Meredith, and Henry James," MTQ, 5 (Spring,
        1943), 15-16, 18.

2092.1 Cieker, Rosemarie. Europa-America en Cuatro Novelas de
        Henry James. Diss. Univ. of Madrid: 1969.

2093   Cimatti, Pietro. "Romanzieri Americani," FLe, 15 (May 15,
        1960), 5.
            Discussion of James and others.

2094   Cixous, Hélène. "L'écriture comme placement: Henry
        James," Poétique, 1, i (1970), 51-63.

2095   Clair, John A. The Ironic Dimension in the Fiction of Hen-
        ry James. Diss. Western Reserve: 1964.

2096   _____. The Ironic Dimension in the Fiction of Henry
        James. Pittsburgh: Duquesne U. P., 1965.

2097   Clark, A. F. Bruce. "Henry James," UnivR, 18 (February,
        1919), 45-68.

2098   Clark, Edwin. "Henry James and the Actress," PacS, 3
        (Winter, 1949), 84-99.
            Provides a survey of James's adventures in drama.

2099   Clark, Harry Hayden, ed. Transitions in American Literary
        Criticism. Durham, North Carolina: Duke U. P., 1953, pas-
        sim.

2100   Clemens, Cyril. "Bret Harte and Henry James as Seen by
        Marie Belloc Lowndes," MTQ, 2 (Fall, 1937), 21-23.

2100.1 _____. "A Chat with William Lyon Phelps," MTQ, 6,
        #4 (1945), 5-7.
        Relates Phelps' conversations with James in regard to his
        dictation to a "dry-as-dust Scotsman" who showed no emo-
        tion.

2101   _____. "Henry James, 1843-1916," MTQ, 5 (Spring,
        1943), 1.

2102   _____. "A Visit to Henry James' Old Home," MTQ, 5
        (Spring, 1943), 9.
        Reminiscences which indicate James's personality.

2103   [Clemens, Samuel L.] Smith, Henry Nash, and William M.
        Gibson, eds., with assistance of Frederick Anderson. Mark
        Twain-Howells Letters. Cambridge, Mass.: Belknap Press
        of Harvard U. P., 1960, passim.

2104   Cohen, B. Bernard. "Henry James and the Hawthorne Cen-
        tennial," EIHC, 92 (July, 1956), 279-283.

2105   Colby, Frank Moore. "In Darkest James," Bookman, 16
        (November, 1902), 259-260.
        Also in Essays of the Past and Present, comp. by War-
        ner Taylor, New York: 1927, pp. 405-412; Robert P.
        Falk, American Literature in Parody. New York: 1955,
        pp. 129-132; Imaginary Obligations. New York: 1904,
        pp. 321-335; The Question of Henry James. F. W. Dupee,
        ed. New York: 1945, pp. 20-27.

2106   _____. "The Queerness of Henry James," Bookman, 15
        (June, 1902), 396-397.

2107   Coleman, Elizabeth. "Henry James's Criticism: A Re-eval-
        uation," DA, 28 (Columbia: 1965), 1428A-29A

2108   Collins, Norman. "Henry James," in The Facts of Fiction.
        London: 1932, pp. 228-236; New York: Dutton, 1933.

2109   Colum, Mary Gunning (Maguire). "The Outside Literatures
        in English: The Irish and the American," From These
        Roots: The Ideas That Have Made Modern Literature. New
        York: Scribner's, 1937, pp. 260-311.

2110   Colvert, James B. "Views of Southern Character in Some
        Northern Novels," MissQ, 18 (Spring, 1965), 59-68.
        Compares James's treatment of Southern character with
        that of other writers.

2111   Colvin, Sidney, ed. "Robert Louis Stevenson and Henry

James with Some Letters of Mrs. R. L. Stevenson," Scribner's, 75 (March, 1924), 315-326.

2112   Comer, C. A. P. "Evolution of Henry James," Critic, 34 (April, 1899), 338-342.

2113   Commager, Henry Steele. The American Mind: An Interpretation of American Thought and Character Since the 1880's. New Haven: Yale U. P., 1950, pp. 258-260, passim.
        Treats James as a novelist and as an expatriate.

2114   Conn, Peter James. "The Tyranny of the Eye: The Observer as Aggressor in Henry James's Fiction," DAI, 30 (Yale: 1969), 1556A.

2115   Connolly, Cyril. "Henry James," Previous Convictions: Selected Writings of a Decade. New York: Harper, 1963, pp. 218-220

2116   Conrad, Jessie. Joseph Conrad As I Knew Him. Freeport, New York: Books for Libraries Press, c1925, repr., 1970, passim.

2117   Conrad, Joseph. "Henry James: An Appreciation," NAR, 180 (January, 1905), 102-108; repr., 203 (April, 1916), 585-591.
        Repr., Notes on Life and Letters. New York: J. M. Dent, 1921, pp. 11-19; Question of Henry James. Dupee, ed., pp. 44-46; Henry James: A Collection of Critical Essays. Edel, ed., pp. 11-17.

2118   _____. "The Historian of Fine Consciences," in The Question of Henry James. F. W. Dupee, ed. New York: 1945, pp. 44-46.

2119   [Conrad, Joseph]. Life and Letters by G. Jean Aubry. Garden City, New York: Doubleday, 1927, I, 270-271.
        Conrad's letter to John Galsworthy in defense of James.

2120   Cook, Albert. "The Portentous Intelligent Stillness: James," The Meaning of Fiction. Detroit: Wayne State U. P., 1960, pp. 134-166.

2120.1 Cook, David A. "James and Flaubert: The Evolution of Perception," CL, 25 (Fall, 1973), 289-307.

2121   Cooper, Harold. "Trollope and Henry James," MLN, 58 (November, 1943), 558.

2122   Cooper, Suzana Regoleth. "Art as Deception: A Study of Some Fictional Characters of Thomas Mann and Henry James," DAI, 30 (Illinois: 1969), 3002A.

2123   Core, George Eric. "Everything the Shade of the Real: The
        Fiction of Henry James, 1902-1914," DAI, 32 (North Caro-
        lina University at Chapel Hill: 1971), 5223A.
            Concerns chiefly the great fiction of the late third period,
            1902-1904, and the novels and stories which followed in
            the last period, 1905-1914.

2124   Cornelius, Roberta D. "The Clearness of Henry James,"
        SR, 27 (January, 1919), 1-8.

2125   Cornwell, Ethel F. "The Jamesian Moment of Experience,"
        in The "Still Point": Theme and Variation in the Writings of
        T. S. Eliot, Coleridge, Henry James, Virginia Woolf, and
        D. H. Lawrence. New Brunswick, New Jersey: Rutgers U.
        P., 1962, pp. 126-158.

2126   Cowie, Alexander. "Henry James," The Rise of the Ameri-
        can Novel. New York: 1948, pp. 702-742.

2127   Cowley, Malcolm. "The Return of Henry James," NewRep,
        92 (January 22, 1945), 121-122.

2128   _____. "The Two Henry Jameses," NewRep, 112 (Febru-
        ary 5, 1945), 177-180.
            "The Return of Henry James," and "The Two Henry
            Jameses" both repr., in A Many-Windowed House. Car-
            bondale: Southern Illinois U. P., 1970.

2129   Cox, C. B. "Henry James and the Art of Personal Relation-
        ships," The Free Spirit: A Study of Liberal Humanism in
        the Novels of ... Henry James.... New York: Oxford U.
        P., 1963, pp. 38-73.
            The central theme is the failure of "liberalism" to deal
            with essential ethical problems.

2130   _____. "Henry James and Stoicism," Essays and Studies.
        (English Association), 8 (1955), 76-88.

2130.1 _____. "Henry James's Unravished Brides," Spec,
        (March 17, 1967), 29-30.

2130.2 Cox, James M. "Henry James: The Politics of Internation-
        alism," SoR, 8 (1972), 493-506.

2130.3 Coy Ferrer, Juan J. La Novelística de Henry James.
        Iniciación y Primera Madurez, 1864-1881. Diss. Univ. of
        Madrid: 1969.

2131   Coy, Javier. "Henry James en la crítica de los últimos
        treinta años," FMod, 6 (1966), 75-90.

2132   Crankshaw, Edward. "James the Obscured," NatlR, 229
        (July, 1947), 73-77.

2133   Crews, Frederick C. "Society and the Hero," in The Trage-
        dy of Manners, Moral Drama in the Later Novels of Henry
        James. New Haven: Yale U. P. , 1957, pp. 13-29.
        An important study of James's later period.

2134   Croly, Herbert. "Henry James and His Countrymen," Lamp,
        28 (February, 1904), 47-53, repr. , in The Question of Henry
        James. F. W. Dupee, ed. New York: 1945, pp. 28-40.
        James came to see that "he must deal with the vision and
        values of life as they appeared to him; and according to
        his moral outlook European life was life itself raised to a
        higher power, because more richly charged, more signifi-
        cantly composed and more completely informed."

2135   Cromer, Viris. "James and Ibsen," CL, 25 (Spring, 1973),
        114-127.
        James's views on Ibsen illustrate his "ideas on the theater
        at a moment when he was extremely conscious of it."

2136   Cromphout, G. Van. "Artist and Society in Henry James,"
        ES, 49 (April, 1968), 132-140.
        Sees James's stories of writers and artists as reflecting
        James's own dilemma which was also the dilemma of the
        age.

2137   Cross, Wilbur L. "Henry James and Impressionism," in
        The Development of the English Novel. New York: Macmil-
        lan, 1899, pp. 263-268.

2138   Crothers, S. M. "Henry James," Later Years of the Satur-
        day Club, 1870-1920. Mark Antony De Wolfe Howe, ed. New
        York: Houghton Mifflin, 1927, pp. 385-390.

2139   Crotty, Sister M. Madeleine. "The Mother in the Fiction of
        Henry James," DA, 23 (Fordham: 1962), 1698-99.

2140   Cummins, Elizabeth Keyser. "Henry James: Irony and the
        Limited Observer," DA, 29 (Claremont: 1968), 2670A.

2140.1 Cunliffe, J. W. English Literature in the Twentieth Century.
        New York: Macmillan, 1933; Freeport, New York: Books
        for Libraries Press, Essay Index Reprint Series, 1967, pp.
        204-207, 306-307, passim.
        James's views on the "new Georgian novelists" and, as
        well, his reaction to Rupert Brooke on English poets.

2141   Cunliffe, Marcus. The Literature of the United States. A
        Pelican Book. Middlesex: Penguin Books, 1954.
        Cunliffe's favorites appear to be James and Mark Twain.

2142   Cuny, Claude M. "Retour à Henry James," LetFran, 1275
        (March 19, 1969), 11-12.

2142.1 "Current Criticism of Henry James," Bookman, 26 (December, 1907), 357.

2143   Curti, Merle. The Growth of American Thought. 3rd ed.
        New York, Evanston, London: Harper & Row, 1964, pp.
        392, 509.

2144   Dahlberg, Edward, and Herbert Read. Truth Is More Sacred:
        A Critical Exchange on Modern Literature. New York:
        Horizon Press, 1961, pp. 121-148.

2145   Daiches, David. "Sensibility and Technique," KR, 5 (Autumn,
        1943), 569-579.
            States that James's moral sense is "dependent on his sense
            of aesthetic significance," and his technical skill enables
            him to make convincing a personal moral interpretation of
            human behavior.

2145.1   _____. Sensibilidad y Técnica. (Prefacio a una crítica
        de Henry James (Sensibility and Technique). Traducción de
        Soledad Salinas, Asomante, Vol. II, No. 3, 1946. El origi-
        nal se publicó en el número Homenaje a Henry James, de la
        Kenyon Review.

2146   D'Andrea, Antonio. "Il pragmatismo del James e le origini
        della filosofia contemporanea in America," Belfagor (Flor-
        ence), 3 (September, 1948), 525-540.

2146.1 Daniels, Earl. "James Editions," SRL, 10 (September 23,
        1933), 128.

2147   Dargan, E. Preston. "Henry James the Builder," NewRep,
        7 (June 17, 1916), 171-174.

2147.1 D'Arzo, Silvio. "Henry James (Di società, di uomini e
        fantasmi). Paragone, 1 (December, 1950), 13-21.

2147.2 Daugherty, Sarah Bowyer. "The Literary Criticism of Henry
        James, 1864-1884," DA, 34 (Pennsylvania: 1973), 5096A-97A.

2147.3 Daumier, Honoré. "Picture and Text," The Nature of Art.
        John Gassner and Sidney Thomas, eds. New York: Crown,
        1964, pp. 467-479.

2148   Dauner, Louise. "Henry James and the Garden of Death,"
        UKCR, 19 (Winter, 1952), 137-143.

2149   Davis, Robert Gorham. Instructor's Manual for Ten Modern
        Masters. New York: Harcourt, 1953, 2nd ed., 1959.

2150   Davray, Henry D. "Un déraciné Anglo-Américain: Henry
        James, d'après sa correspondance," MdF, 146 (February 15,
        1921), 68-84.

James's attitude toward French naturalism.

2151 Deakin, Motley F. The Picturesque in the Life and Work of Henry James. Diss. Univ. of California, Berkeley: 1961.

2152 _____. "The Real and Fictive Quest of Henry James," BuR, 14 (May, 1966), 82-97.
Shows that the quest motif in James's non-fiction sketches was utilized in much of his early fiction.

2152.1 Dean, Sharon Welch. "Lost Ladies: The Isolated Heroine in the Fiction of Hawthorne, James, Fitzgerald, Hemingway, and Faulkner," DAI, 34 (New Hampshire: 1973), 2616A.

2153 de Araujo, Victor. "The Short Story of Fantasy: Henry James, H. G. Wells, and E. M. Forster," DA, 27 (Washington: 1965), 200A.
In Chapter Two, the author considers seven of James's stories which treat the problem of evil, although "The Turn of the Screw" is not included.

2154 Debo, Elizabeth Lea. "The Narrator in Henry James, Joseph Conrad, and Ford Madox Ford," DAI, 32 (Nebraska: 1972), 3946A.

2155 Decker, Clarence R. The Victorian Conscience. New York: Twayne Publishers, 1952, passim.

2156 de la Mare, Walter. "Henry James," LivA, 289 (April 8, 1916), 122-125.

2157 _____. "Henry James," TLS, 951 (April, 1920), 217-218.

2158 Deland, Margaret. MTQ, Henry James Number, 5 (Spring, 1943), 2.
"... I objected to ... his occasional cataract of words-- words--words."

2159 de la Roche, Mazo. "Reading James Aloud," MTQ, 5 (Spring, 1943), 8.

2160 Delbaere-Garant, Jeanne. Henry James: The Vision of France. Paris: Société d'Editions (Les Belles Lettres), 1970, pp. 1-441.
A very significant work.

2161 Delétang-Tardif, Yanette. "Henry James," VAC, 14 (1950), 50-51.

2162 Demel, Erika von Elswehr. Die Wertwelt Von Henry James. Diss. Vienna: 1944.

2163 De Mille, George E. "Henry James," Literary Criticism in

America: A Preliminary Survey. New York: 1931, pp.
158-181.

2163.1 Denney, Reuel. "The Discovery of the Popular Culture,"
American Perspectives: The National Self-Image in the
Twentieth Century. Edited for the American Studies Assn.
by Robert E. Spiller and Eric Larrabee. Cambridge: Harvard U. P., 1961, 156-157.
James established a claim on the theme of "the poverty of
wishes" of the American people--the "poverty of aspira-
tions."

2164   De Santis, Alex. The English Fables of Henry James:
1895-1900. Diss. Princeton: n. d.

2165   Deurbergue, Jean. "Un romancier en porte-à-faux: Henry
James," Critique (Paris), 14 (June, 1956), 501-511.

2166   Dietrichson, Jan W. "Henry James and Emile Zola," in
Americana-Norvegica. Norwegian Contributions to American
Studies. Vol. II, Sigmund Skard, ed. Philadelphia: Penn-
sylvania U. P., 1968, II, 118-134.
Shows that Zola's influence on James "was not very im-
portant."

2167   _____. "The Image of Money in the Works of Henry
James," The Image of Money in the American Novel of the
Gilded Age. Oslo, Universitetsforlaget; New York: Humani-
ties Press, 1969, pp. 24-164.
A very comprehensive coverage of the financial aspects of
James's work.

2168   Diffené, Patricia. Henry James: Versuch Einer Würdigung
Seiner Eigenart. Diss. Marburg: 1939.

2169   _____. James: Versuch Einer Würdigung Seiner Eigenart.
Bochum, 1939. (Privately printed.)

2170   Ditsky, John. "The Watch and Chain of Henry James," UWR,
6 (Fall, 1970), 91-101.

2171   Dommergues, Pierre. "L'art romanesque de Henry James,"
Le Monde, 27 (March 7, 1970), iv.

2172   Donnelly, J. B. "Cultural Consolations During the Great
War," Topic, 12 (Spring, 1972), 22-34.
James and others felt that the post-war period would find
society surviving better than before 1914.

2173   Donovan, Alan B. The Sense of Beauty in the Novels of
Henry James. Diss. Yale: 1964.

2174   Dove, John Roland. "The Tragic Sense in Henry James,"

TSLL, 2 (Autumn, 1960), 303-314.
States that James was actually a tragedian who depicts
man as "the victim of his own ingenious trust in his fel-
low man," betrayed by the person to whom he is most
committed.

2175   Downing, F. "The Art of Fiction," Cw, 55 (December 28,
       1951), 297-299.

2176   Draper, Muriel. "I Meet Henry James," HarperM, 156
       (March, 1928), 416-421; also in Music at Midnight. New
       York and London: Harper, 1929, pp. 87-96.

2177   Draper, Ruth. The Art of Ruth Draper: Her Dramas and
       Characters. With Memoir by Morton Dauwen Zabel. Garden
       City, New York: Doubleday, 1960; London: Oxford U. P.,
       1960.
       A poem by Ruth Draper in honor of Henry James in Za-
       bel's Memoir.

2178   Drew, Elizabeth. The Novel: A Modern Guide to Fifteen
       English Masterpieces. New York: Dell Books, 1963, pp.
       224-244.

2179   Dryden, Edgar A. Melville's Thematics of Form: The
       Great Art of Telling the Truth. Baltimore: Johns Hopkins,
       U. P., 1968, pp. 12-18, passim.

2180   Dub, Friederike. Die Romantechnik Bei Henry James.
       Diss. Vienna: 1933.

2181   Duberman, Martin. James Russell Lowell. Boston: Hough-
       ton Mifflin, The Riverside Press, 1966, pp. 261-262, 335-
       336, passim.
       Lowell's friendship with James.

2181.1 Duffy, John J. "Ernest Dowson and the Failure of Deca-
       dence," URKC, 34 (October, 1967), 45-49.

2182   Dumitriu, Georgeta. "Aspecte ale metodei narative in ro-
       manul lui Henry James," RITL, 18 (1969), 235-247.

2182.1 _____. "Henry James teoretician al romanului. (Henry
       James the theorist of the novel.) In Studii de Literatură
       Universală Si Comparata. (Studies on World and Compara-
       tive Literature.) Bucharest: Editura Academiei Republicii
       Socialiste România: 1970.

2183   Dunbar, Viola Ruth. Studies in Satire and Irony in the
       Works of Henry James. Diss. Northwestern: 1942.

2184   Duncan, Hugh Dalziel. Language and Literature in Society:
       A Sociological Essay on Theory and Method in the Interpre-

tation of Linguistic Symbols. New York: Bedminster Press,
1961, p. 134, passim.
"... Henry James 'attaches' specific images to characters
whose social and moral status he defines clearly in the
course of the story."

2185   Duncan, Kirby Luther. "The Structure of the Novels of Henry James," DA, 28 (South Carolina: 1967), 2242A-43A.
Finds that thirteen of James's novels show a single "structure," i.e., "one or more central characters, and the two
opposing poles which he or they must choose between, attempt to synthesize, or reject."

2186   Dupee, Frederick W. "Approaches to Henry James," Literature in America. New York: Meridian Press, 1957, pp.
242-246.

2187   _____. Henry James: His Life and Writings. New York:
William Sloane Associates, c1951; revised for Anchor Books,
1956.
Contains critical material, as well as biographical.

2188   _____. "Henry James in the Great Grey Babylon," PR,
18 (March-April, 1951), 183-190.

2189   _____. "James for Americans," LonSpec, 6447 (January
18, 1952), 84.

2190   _____, ed. Introduction. The Question of Henry James.
New York: Henry Holt, 1945.
A significant work containing many important items.

2191   Dwight, H. G. "Henry James--'in His Own Country,'"
PutM, 2 (May, 1907), 164-170; (July, 1907), 433-442.
A helpful survey of critical opinions of the early twentieth
century.

2191.1 Dwyer, John Francis. "A Medium for Sexual Encounter:
Henry James's Return to the International Theme, 1899-1904,"
DAI, 33 (New York State Univ., Buffalo: 1972), 4408A-09A.

2191.2 Dyson, John Peter. "The Soft Breath of Consciousness: A
Critical Analysis of Some of the Later Tales of Henry
James," DAI, 32 (Princeton: 1972), 4608A.

2191.3 Eagleton, Terry. Exiles and Emigrés: Studies in Modern
Literature. New York: Schocken Books, 1970, passim.

2192   Eakin, Paul J. Henry James and the New England Consciousness. Diss. Harvard: 1966.

2192.1 Earnest, Ernest. "The American Ariel," SAQ, 65 (Spring,
1966), 192-200.

2193   Eastman, Richard M. A Guide to the Novel. San Francis-
       co: Chandler Pub. Co. , 1965, pp. 126-128, passim.

2194   Edel, Leon. "The Choice So Freely Made, " NewRep, 133
       (September 26, 1955), 26-28.
           "Life [for James] was good and it was evil; people were
       innocent, ... or, ... predatory and destructive. "

2195   _____. "The Enduring Fame of Henry James, " Opinions
       and Perspectives. Francis Brown, ed. Boston: Houghton
       Mifflin, 1964, pp. 102-109.
           "The Henry James 'revival' ... has been under way for
       the past two decades.

2196   _____. "The Exile of Henry James, " UTQ, 2 (July, 1933),
       520-532.

2197   _____, ed. General Introduction. The Complete Tales of
       Henry James. New York: J. B. Lippincott, 1962.

2198   _____. Henry James. (UMPAW, No. 4). Minneapolis:
       Minnesota U. P. , 1960.
           "... He [James] alone created the cosmopolitan novel in
       English...."

2199   _____, et al, eds. "Henry James, " Masters of American
       Literature. Shorter Edition, Boston: Houghton Mifflin, The
       Riverside Press, 1959, pp. 972-978.

2200   _____. "Henry James: The Americano-European Legend, "
       UTQ, 36 (July, 1967), 321-334.

2201   _____, ed. Henry James: The Future of the Novel.
       New York: Vintage Books, 1956.

2202   _____. "Henry James and Sir Sidney Waterlow: The Un-
       published Diary of a British Diplomat, " TLS (August 8, 1968),
       844-845.

2203   _____, ed. Introduction [to each volume]. The Bodley
       Head Henry James. London: Bodley Head, 1967-1972.

2204   _____, ed. Introduction. Henry James: A Collection of
       Critical Essays. Englewood Cliffs, New Jersey: Prentice,
       1963.
           Reprints seventeen essays on James without duplicating
       those in The Question of Henry James. F. W. Dupee,
       ed. 1945.

2205   _____, ed. Introduction and Notes. The Ghostly Tales of
       Henry James. New Brunswick, New Jersey: Rutgers U. P. ,
       1948.

2206   _____. Introduction. <u>Henry James: Selected Fiction.</u>
New York: Everyman's Library, 1953.

2207   _____. "Henry James," <u>Six American Novelists of the
Nineteenth Century.</u> Richard Foster, ed. (Repr., UMPAW).
Minneapolis: Minnesota U. P., 1968, pp. 191-225.

2208   _____, ed. New Introduction and Headnotes. <u>Henry
James: Stories of the Supernatural.</u> New York: Taplinger,
1970.
            Originally published as <u>The Ghostly Tales of Henry James.</u>
            1948.

2209   _____. "Henry James: The War Chapter, 1914-1916,"
UTQ, 10 (January, 1941), 125-138.
            Recounts James's anxiety as to the war and the resulting
            social awareness which came to him.

2210   _____, et al. "Henry James Number," MFS, 12 (Spring,
1966), 3-177.

2211   _____, and Gordon N. Ray, eds. <u>Henry James and H. G.
Wells: A Record of Their Friendship, Their Debate on the
Art of Fiction, and Their Quarrel.</u> Urbana: Illinois U. P.,
1958.

2212   _____. "Henry James and <u>The Nation,</u>" Nation, 201 (September 20, 1965), 237-240.
            From the first issue of the journal until 1880, Henry
            James contributed more than two hundred writings.

2213   _____. "Henry James and the Poets," Poetry, 62 (September, 1943), 328-334.
            A discussion of recent poems on Henry James.

2214   _____. "Henry James and Vernon Lee," PMLA, 69 (June,
1954), 677-678.

2214.1   _____. "Henry James Discoveries," TLS (July 29, 1939),
460.

2214.2   _____. "A Henry James Essay," TLS (May 24, 1941),
251, 253.

2215   _____. <u>The Henry James Reader.</u> New York: Scribner's, 1965.

2216   _____. "Hugh Walpole and Henry James: The Fantasy of
the 'Killer and the Slain,' " AI, 8 (December, 1951), 351-
369.

2217   _____. "The James Revival," Atl, 182 (September, 1948),
96-98.

2217.1 _____. "Jonathan Sturges," PULC, 15 (Autumn, 1953), 1-9.

2218 _____. "The Literary Convictions of Henry James," MFS, 3 (Spring, 1957), 3-10.
James was both a critic and a creator; as a critic he was concerned with the "consciousness of the artist."

2219 _____. "A Note on the Translation of Henry James in France," RAA, 7 (August, 1930), 539-540.

2220 _____. The Psychological Novel, 1900-1950. Philadelphia: Lippincott, 1955; New York: Grosset & Dunlap, 1964, passim.

2221 _____. "Speaking of Books: Henry James Looked Ahead," NYTBR (November 12, 1967), 2, 70-72.

2222 _____. "To the Poet of Prose," Book Week (February 27, 1966); repr., in MFS, 12, #1 (Spring, 1966), 3-6.
"James was the complete artist...."

2223 _____. "The Versatile James," Nation, 173 (November 10, 1951), 406-408.
Essay-review of The Portable Henry James. Morton Zabel, ed. 1951.

2224 Edelstein, Arnold Stanley. "The Triumph of Fantasy: Ambiguity and Ambivalence in the Fiction of Henry James," DAI, 33 (Berkeley: 1971), 271A-72A.

2225 Edelstein, Tilden G. Strange Enthusiasm: A Life of Thomas Wentworth Higginson. New Haven and London: Yale U. P., 1968, pp. 361-362, passim.
Reviews Higginson's criticism of James's work.

2226 Edgar, Pelham. "The Art of Henry James," NatlR, 83 (July, 1924), 730-739.

2227 _____. "Henry James, the Essential Novelist," QQ, 39 (May, 1932), 181-192.
Also: "The Essential Novelist? Henry James," in The Art of the Novel: From 1700 to the Present Time. New York: Russell & Russell, 1965, pp. 172-183.

2228 _____. "Henry James and His Method," PRSC, 12, Ser, 3 (1919), 225-240.

2229 _____. Henry James, Man and Author. London; Boston and New York: Russell & Russell, 1927, 1964.
Restates biographical material, but also provides a general summary of plots and themes.

2230   _____. "Three Novels of Henry James," DR, 4 (January, 1925), 467-475.

2231   Edmondson, Elsie. The Writer as Hero in Important American Fiction Since Howells (Howells, James, Norris, London, Farrell, Cabell). Diss. Michigan: 1954.

2232   Edwards, Herbert. "Henry James and Ibsen," AL, 24 (May, 1952), 208-223.
          Ibsen's influence on James.

2232.1   Edwards, Oliver. "Truthful James," The Times, (November 1, 1956), 13.

2233   Egan, Maurice Francis. "The Revelation of an Artist in Literature," CathW, 111 (June, 1920), 289-300.

2234   Egan, Michael. Henry James: The Ibsen Years. London: Vision, 1972; New York: Barnes & Noble, 1972.

2235   Elderdice, Robert A. Henry James's Revisions of His Early Short Stories and Short Novels. Diss. Maryland: 1952.

2236   Eliot, T. S. "Henry James," LittleR, 5 (August, 1918), 44-53.
          Repr., The Idea of the American Novel. Rubin and Moore, eds. New York: 1961, pp. 245-247; The Question of Henry James. Dupee, ed., pp. 108-119; Literature in America. Philip Rahv, comp. New York: 1967, pp. 221-230.

2237   _____. "Henry James," in The Shock of Recognition: The Development of Literature in the United States. Edmund Wilson, ed. New York: Doubleday, 1943; Farrar, Strauss and Cudahy, 1955, pp. 854-865.

2238   _____. "A Prediction in Regard to Three English Authors: Henry James, J. G. Frazer, F. H. Bradley," Vanity Fair (February, 1924).
          Excerpt repr., in Henry James: A Collection of Critical Essays. Leon Edel, ed. Englewood Cliffs, N.J.: 1963, pp. 55-56.

2239   Ellis, Stewart Marsh. "February Reverie: Henry James-- Thomas Moore," Mainly Victorian. New York: Hutchinson, 1925, pp. 205-208.

2240   Ellison, Ralph. "Society, Morality and the Novel," The Living Novel: A Symposium. Granville Hicks, ed. New York: Macmillan, 1957, pp. 58-91.

2241   Ellmann, Richard, and Charles Feidelson, Jr., eds. The Modern Tradition: Backgrounds of Modern Literature. New York: Oxford U. P., 1965.

2242   Elton, Oliver. "The Novels of Mr. Henry James," QR, 198
        (October, 1903), 358-379.
            Repr., in Modern Studies. London, New York: Arnold
            & Co., 1907; Freeport, New York: 1967, pp. 245-284.

2243   Emerson, Donald. "Henry James," Arts/Soc, 2 (n. d., ca.
        1963), 126-132.

2244   _____. "Henry James: A Sentimental Tourist and Rest-
        less Analyst," TWA, 52 (1963), 17-25.
            Illustrates how James's observation was supplemented by
            imagination.

2245   _____. "Henry James and the American Language," TWA,
        49 (December, 1960), 237-247.
            Emerson argues that James was really not unsympathetic
            toward American speech patterns.

2246   _____. Henry James and the Life of the Imagination.
        Diss. Wisconsin: 1950.

2247   _____. "Henry James and the Limitations of Realism,"
        CE, 22 (December, 1960), 161-166.

2248   _____. "Henry James on the Role of Imagination in Criti-
        cism," TWA, 51 (1962), 287-294.
            Show that from 1864 James's criticism became less dog-
            matic and more emphatic on the role of imagination.

2249   _____. "The Relation of Henry James's Art Criticism to
        His Literary Standards," TWA, 57 (1969), 9-19.
            A comprehensive survey of the limitations of James's art
            criticism in relation to his literary criticism.

2250   Emerson, Edward Waldo. "Henry James," in Early Years
        of the Saturday Club, 1855-1870. New York: Houghton, 1918,
        pp. 322-333.

2251   Engelberg, Edward. "James and Arnold: Conscience and
        Consciousness in a Victorian 'Künstlerroman,'" Criticism,
        10 (Spring, 1968), 93-114.
            Repr., in Henry James's Major Novels. Lyall Powers,
            ed. Michigan St. U. P., 1973, pp. 3-27. Demonstrates
            how James made use of Arnold's "distinctions between
            Hebraism and Hellenism ... the perfect dialectic for de-
            scribing his hero's conflict."

2251.1 _____. The Unknown Distance: From Consciousness to
        Conscience. Goethe to Camus. Cambridge: Harvard U. P.,
        1972, pp. 154-172, passim.

2252   Enkvist, Nils Erik. "Henry James and Julio Reuter: Two
        Notes," NM, 57 (December, 1956), 318-324.

2253   Erhart, Virginia. "Los fantasmas de Henry James ante la
       critica," in Asociacion Argentina de Estudios Americanos.
       Sextas Jornadas de Historia y Literatura Norteamericana y
       Rioplatense. 2 Vols. Buenos Aires: 1971, [not paged].

2252   Espey, John J. "The Major James," Ezra Pound's Mauber-
       ley. Berkeley, California: 1955, pp. 49-61.

2255   Fabris, Alberta. "La Francia di Henry James," SA, 9
       (1963), 173-226.
           The French influence on James's critical views.

2256   . Henry James e la Francia. (Biblioteca di Studi
       Americani, No. 18). Rome: Edizioni di Storia e Lettera-
       tura, 1969.
           After a biographical chapter, the author discusses James's
       early and mature criticism.

2257   Fadiman, Clifton, ed. Introduction. The Short Stories of
       Henry James. New York: Random House, Inc., 1945.

2258   . "En Kommentar till 'Europa,' " BLM, 17 (1948),
       99-100.

2259   . "The Revival of Interest in Henry James,"
       NYHTB, 21 (January 14, 1945), 1-2.
           "James ... is a modern writer, to be ranked with Joyce,
       Proust, Mann...."

2260   . "Three Notes on Henry James," in Party of One.
       Cleveland: World Publishing Co., 1955, pp. 154-175.

2261   Faison, E. Lane, Jr. "The Novelist as Art Critic," SatR,
       40 (June 1, 1957), 28.

2262   Falk, Robert P. "Henry James and the 'Age of Innocence,' "
       NCF, 7 (December, 1952), 171-188.
           On the American-European background of James's thought.

2263   . "Henry James's Romantic 'Vision of the Real,' "
       Essays Critical and Historical Dedicated to Lily B. Camp-
       bell. Berkeley and Los Angeles: 1950, pp. 137-152.
           James's early "realism" was a conscious effort to work
       out a synthesis in critical and artistic terms of the intel-
       lectual currents of the 1870's.

2264   , ed. Introduction. American Literature in Parody:
       A Collection of Parody, Satire and Literary Burlesque of
       American Writers Past and Present. New York: Twayne
       Publishers, 1955.

2265   . "Jacobites and Anti-Jacobites: Three Recent
       Studies of Henry James," NCF, 27 (September, 1972), 224-
       229.

Observes that the "spring issue (1934) of <u>Hound and Horn</u> marked the beginning of the Henry James 'revival.' "

2266 _____. "The Literary Criticism of the Genteel Decades, 1870-1900," <u>The Development of American Literary Criticism.</u> Floyd Stovall, ed. Chapel Hill: North Carolina U. P., 1955, pp. 113-157, passim.

2267 _____. "The Rise of Realism, 1871-1891," <u>Transitions in American Literary History.</u> Durham, North Carolina: Duke U. P., 1953, pp. 381-442.

2268 _____. "Henry James: Aesthetic Theories and Critical Methods," "James's Studio Stories: The Disinherited of Art," "James as Passionate Pilgrim and Disappointed Observer," "Social Adjustment and Literary Fulfillment: James, the Middle Years," in <u>The Victorian Mode in American Fiction, 1865-1885.</u> East Lansing: Michigan State U. P., 1965, pp. 54-66, 67-78, 79-91, 138-156.

2269 _____. "The Writers' Search for Reality," <u>The Gilded Age.</u> H. Wayne Morgan, ed. Rev. and enlarged ed., Syracuse U. P., 1970, pp. 223-237.

2270 Farnham, Mary Davis. "Henry James on Three Victorian Novelists: Concepts of the Novel," DAI, 31 (North Carolina, Chapel Hill: 1970), 6054A.

2271 _____. "Henry James on Three Victorian Novelists: Concepts of the Novel," <u>Proper Stations: Class in Victorian Fiction.</u> London: Faber, 1971.

2272 Farrell, James T. <u>Literature and Morality.</u> New York: Vanguard Press, [World Publishing Co.], 1946, passim.
"... the moral tone of sections of the upper classes in his [James's] own time" are reflected in James's work, but he was not a moralist "in any sense of the word."

2273 Farrer, Alison. "Watch, Ward, the Jamesian Themes," <u>Balcony,</u> 1 (1965), 23-27.

2274 "Father of Super-Realism," CurOp, 54 (June, 1913), 489-490.

2275 Fawcett, Edgar. "Henry James's Novels," PrincetonR, n. s., 14 (July, 1884), 68-86.
A very good summary of James's work to 1881.

2275.1 _____. "Henry James's Novels," PrincetonR, 14 (April, 1886), 59-68.

2276 Fay, Eliot G. "Balzac and Henry James," FR, 24 (February, 1951), 325-330.

A summary of James's public acknowledgments of Balzac's importance.

2277   _____. "Henry James as a Critic of French Literature," FAR, 2 (September, 1949), 184-193.

2278   Featherstone, Joseph L. "Mrs. Wharton and Mr. James," NewRep, 152 (May 29, 1965), 21-24.
James's influence on Mrs. Wharton.

2279   Feidelson, Charles, Jr., and Paul Brodtkorb, Jr., eds. Interpretations of American Literature. New York: Oxford U. P., 1959, passim.

2280   Feidelson, Charles, Jr. "James and the 'Man of Imagination' in Literary Theory and Structure: Essays in Honor of William K. Wimsatt. Frank Brady, John Palmer and Martin Price, eds. New Haven, Conn.: Yale U. P., 1973.

2281   _____. Symbolism and American Literature. Chicago: Chicago U. P., 1953, pp. 47-49, passim.
"The Jamesian technique is discovery as well as construction;... In his prefaces and notebooks James clearly assumed that his work lay in a realm of meaning equally distinct from his own ego and from the world of objective experience...."

2282   Feinstein, Herbert. "Two Pair of Gloves: Mark Twain and Henry James," AI, 17 (Winter, 1960), 349-387.
The symbolic use of gloves in the works of both writers.

2283   Feldman, Stephen Michael. "The Dynamics of Innocence in Henry James: A Guide to the Jamesian Vision," DA, 28 (Yale: 1967), 4626A-27A.

2284   Felstiner, John. "Max Beerbohm and the Wings of Henry James," KR, 29 (September, 1967), 449-471.
Felstiner notes that "Beerbohm's maturist values start in the comic dispute made up by his caricatures and parodies of Henry James." There were 15 caricatures and several parodies, and James seems to have been delighted with many of them.

2285   Fenollosa, Ernest. "Henry James," Instigations of Ezra Pound. Freeport, New York: Books for Libraries Press, 1920, repr., 1967, pp. 106-167.

2286   Ferguson, Alfred R. "The Triple Quest of Henry James: Fame, Art, and Fortune," AL, 27 (January, 1956), 475-498.
Although art is often said to be James's sole preoccupation, throughout his career James was apparently interested also in fame and fortune.

2287   Ferguson, Louis A.   "Henry James and Honoré de Balzac:
       A Comparative Study in Literary Techniques," DA, 29 (Ford-
       ham: 1967), 1537A.

2288   Fergusson, Francis.   "James's Idea of Dramatic Form,"
       KR, 5 (Autumn, 1943), 495-507.

2288.1 Fernandez, Diane. "Henry James et la symetrie," LN (June-
       July, 1969), 77-90.

2289   _____.   "Henry James, ou la richesse des possibles,"
       QuinLit, (February 16, 1970), 8-10.

2290   _____.   "Henry James Revisited," QuinLit, 68 (March,
       1969), 4-5.

2291   Fernando, Lloyd.   "The Radical Ideology of the 'New Wom-
       an,' " SoR, 2, #3 (1967), 206-222.
          Notes that "bad marriages" were the subject of novels by
          James and others.

2292   Fick, Otto W.   The Clue and the Labyrinth: The Mind and
       Temperament of Henry James. Diss. Chicago: 1954.

2293   Fiedler, Leslie A.   An End to Innocence: Essays on Culture
       and Politics. Boston: Beacon Press, 1948, 1955, pp. 196-
       197, 199-200, passim.
          James as a vital influence in modern literature.

2294   _____.   "The Revenge on Woman: from Lucy to Lolita,"
       Love and Death in the American Novel. Rev. ed.   New
       York: Stein & Day, 1966, pp. 288-295.
          "... it is not until Henry James that the Dark Lady-Fair
          girl archetype and the myth of the American in Europe are
          fused into a rich and unified subject...."

2294.1 Field, Mary Lee. "Henry James's Criticism of French Lit-
       erature," DAI, 33 (Wayne State Univ.: 1972), 2370A.

2295   Fielding, H. M.   "Henry James, the Lion," Reader, 5 (Feb-
       ruary, 1905), 364-367.

2296   Figuera, Angela.   Tres Escritores Norteamericanos: Mark
       Twain, Henry James, Thomas Wolfe. Madrid: Gredos,
       1961.

2297   Finch, George A.   The Development of the Fiction of Henry
       James from 1879 to 1886. Diss. New York University:
       1947.
          An abridgment of the dissertation published by New York
          U. P., 1949.

2298   _____, ed.   "James as a Traveler," Portraits of Places:

By Henry James. New York: Lear, Publishers, 1948, pp.
15-31.

2299   Finch, I. W. A Study of the Relationship Between Hawthorne
and James. Diss. Harvard: 1939.

2299.1 Fink, Guido. "I bambini terribili di Henry James," Para-
gone, #236 (1969), 4-28.

2300   Finkelstein, Sidney. "Six Ways of Looking at Reality,"
Mainstream, 13 (December, 1960), 31-42.
Contrasts descriptive passages from James with other
writers.

2301   Finney, Martha Collins. "The Mingled Vision: Point of
View in the Novels of Henry James, 1871-1890," DAI, 32
(Iowa: 1971), 1468A.

2302   Fiocco, A. "Un romanzo di James sul palcoscenio," FLe,
38 (September 24, 1950), 8.

2303   Firebaugh, Joseph J. "Coburn: Henry James's Photographer," AQ, 7 (Fall, 1955), 215-233.
James's collaboration with Alvin Langdon Coburn.

2304   _____. Henry James and the Law of Freedom. Diss.
Washington: 1952.

2305   _____. "The Pragmatism of Henry James," VQR, 27
(Summer, 1951), 419-435.
Interpretation of James as a pragmatist.

2306   _____. "The Relativism of Henry James," JAAC, 12
(December, 1953), 237-242.
James favored a relativistic rather than an absolute aes-
thetic according to Firebaugh.

2307   Fischer, William Coverly, Jr. "The Representation of Men-
tal Processes in the Early Fiction of William Dean Howells
and Henry James," DA, 28 (Berkeley, Calif.: 1967),
4597A-98A.

2307.1 _____. "William Dean Howells: Reverie and the Nonsym-
bolic Aesthetic," NCF, 25 (1970), 1-30.
A brief but noteworthy comparison of Howells' "graphic"
style and James's "symbolic uses of language that reach
behind appearance to metaphorical meanings."

2308   Fish, Charles Kelleway, Jr. "Henry James and the Craft of
Fiction: The Years of Exploration, 1864-1871," DA, 25
(Princeton: 1964), 3568.
An analysis of sixteen early stories and one novel showing
James's early experimentation with point of view and with

the contrasting materials of American and European life.

2309   Fitzpatrick, Kathleen. Henry James and the Influence of
        Italy. Sydney: Sydney University Press, 1968.

2310   FitzRoy, Almeric. Memoirs of Sir Almeric FitzRoy. Lon-
        don: Hutchinson & Co. , 1925, p. 278.

2311   Fleet, Simon. "The Nice American Gentleman," Vogue, 136
        (October 19, 1949), 183-185, 187.
                James is remembered in Sussex, not as a distinguished
                American author, but as the "very nice American gentle-
                man."

2312   _____. "In Search of Henry James at Rye," ModA, 9
        (Winter, 1964-1965), 69-76.

2313   Flestiner, John. "Max Beerbohm and the Wings of Henry
        James," KR, 29 (September, 1967), 450-471.
                Notes that Beerbohm's most outstanding parodies of James
                appear in "The Guerdon," A Peep Into the Past," and
                "The Mote in the Middle Distance."

2314   Flory, Sister Ancilla. "Rhythmic Configuration in the Late
        Style of Henry James," DA, 27 (Catholic University: 1966),
        3044A.
                Contains an analysis of deviations from rhythmic norms.

2315   Flower, Dean Scott. "The Art of the Nouvelle: Henry
        James," DA, 27 (Stanford: 1966), 179A.
                Traces James's indebtedness to masters of short fiction,
                and notes that James's nouvelles gave him flexibility with
                a narrow subject, the individual isolated from society.

2316   _____. Introduction. Great Short Works. New York:
        Harper & Row, 1966.

2317   _____. Henry James in Northampton: Visions and Re-
        visions. Northampton, Mass.: Friends of the Smith College
        Library, 1971.

2318   Flynn, T. E. "Henry James's Journey from the Interior,"
        DR, 51 (Spring, 1971), 96-104.
                Essay-review of Peter Buitenhuis, The Grasping Imagina-
                tion. Toronto: 1970.

2319   Fogle, Richard H. "Organic Form in American Criticism,
        1840-1870," in The Development of American Literary Criti-
        cism. Floyd Stovall, ed. Chapel Hill: North Carolina U.
        P. , 1955, pp. 82, 86.

2320   Foley, Richard N. The Critical Reputation of Henry James
        in American Magazines from 1866 to 1916. Diss. Catholic

University: 1943.
A most useful work for the study of James's reputation in
the nineteenth century and early twentieth.

2321 _____. Criticism in American Periodicals of the Works
of Henry James from 1866 to 1916. Washington, D.C.:
Catholic U. P., 1944. Repr., Folcroft, Pa.: Folcroft
Press, 1970.

2322 Follett, Helen Thomas, and Wilson Follett. "Henry James,"
Atl, 117 (June, 1916), 801-811.

2322.1 _____. "Henry James," Some Modern Novelists: Appreci-
ations and Estimates. Freeport, New York: Books for Libraries Press, 1967, pp. 75-98, passim. [First pub.,
1918.]

2323 Follett, Wilson. The Modern Novel. New York: Alfred A.
Knopf, 1918, 1923.

2324 _____. "The Simplicity of Henry James," AmR, 1 (May-
June, 1923), 315-325.

2325 Forbes, Elizabeth. "Dramatic Lustrum: A Study of the Ef-
fect of Henry James's Theatrical Experience on His Later
Novels," NEQ, 11 (1938), 108-120.
James's greater use of dramatic method after 1889-1896.

Ford, Madox Ford. See Hueffer, Ford Madox.
Hueffer was known as "Hueffer" until 1919, and thereafter
as "Ford."

2326 Forrester, Andrew D. Henry James et la France. Diss.
Lyon: 1949.

2327 Forster, E. M. Aspects of the Novel. New York: Harcourt,
Brace & World, 1927, repr., 1956, pp. 30-31; Essays in
Modern Literary Criticism. Ray B. West, ed. New York:
Rinehart, 1952, pp. 433-438.

2328 _____. "Henry James in the Galleries," NewRep, 135
(December 5, 1956), 24-25.

2328.1 _____. ["Henry James'] Listener, 62 (July 16, 1959),
103.

2328.2 Foster, Richard, ed. Six American Novelists of the Nineteenth Century. Minneapolis: University of Minnesota Press,
1968.

2329 Fox, Hugh. Henry James: A Critical Introduction. Cones-
ville, Iowa: 1968.
A useful work for the student.

2330 _____. "Henry James and the Antinomian James House-
hold: A Study of Selfhood and Selflessness," ArQ, 15
(Spring, 1959), 49-55.
Finds that although James was a moralist in the New England mystical tradition, he was "influenced by a much
more personal family tradition that agreed with the transcendentalists that selfhood was man's aim ... but modified
this selfhood to ultimately end in selfishness."

2331 Frailberg, Louis. Psychoanalysis: American Literary Criticism. Detroit: Wayne State U. P., 1960, p. 172, 192.

2332 Francis, Sister Mary. "Henry James' Theory of Literary Invention," Greyfriar Lectures. Second Series, 1959, pp. 3-
19.

2333 Frank, Charles P. Edmund Wilson. New York: Twayne
Publishers, 1970.
Expresses harsh criticism of Wilson's "The Ambiguity of
Henry James," Triple Thinkers. New York: 1948.

2333.1 Frank, Frederick S. "The Two Taines of Henry James,"
RLC, 45 (1971), 350-365.
Analyzes James's views of Taine and concludes that for
James Taine was always "a great hero-villain of letters, an
enviable intellect who was everything which the fine artist
ought to be and everything as well which the responsible
critic ought not to be."

2333.2 Frank, Joseph. "Henry James: The Real Thing," SR, 63
(Winter, 1955), 168-174.

2334 _____. The Widening Gyre: Crisis and Mastery in Modern Literature. New Brunswick, N.J.: Rutgers U. P.,
1963, p. 157.

2334.1 Frantz, Jean H. "Henry James and Saintine," N&Q, 7, n.s.
(1960), 266-268.

2334.2 Fraser, G. S. "The English Novel," The Twentieth-Century
Mind: History, Ideas, and Literature in Britain. C. B. Cox,
and Anthony Edward Dyson, eds. Oxford: Oxford U. P.,
1972, II [1918-1945], 374, 386-387.

2335 Fraser, John. "Leavis and Winters: A Question of Reputation," WHR, 26 (Winter, 1972), 1-16.
Notes that Leavis's professional reputation is still not se-
cure partly because of his critical opinions about James
and others.

2336 Frederick, John T. The Darkened Sky: Nineteenth-Century
American Novelists and Religion. Notre Dame, Indiana:
Notre Dame U. P., 1969, pp. 229-253.

In a chapter on James, Frederick concludes that James is "the most religious" of the six nineteenth-century American novelists he studies, if "we make our definition of religion broad enough."

2337   Freeman, Arthur. "Henry James and Dickens," TLS, 3,602 (March 12, 1971), 296.

2338   Freeman, John. "Henry James," The Moderns: Essays in Literary Criticism. New York: Crowell, 1917, pp. 219-241.

2339   Fricker, Robert. Der Moderne Englische Roman. Göttingen: Vandenhoeck and Ruprecht, 1958.

2340   Friedl, Herwig. Die Funktion der Bildlichkeit in den Kritischen und Theoretischen Schriften Von Henry James: Ein Entwurf Seiner Literaturtheorie. (BzJA.) Heidelberg: Winter, 1972.

2340.1 Friedling, Sheila. "Problems of Perception in the Modern Novel: The Representation of Consciousness in Works of Henry James, Gertrude Stein, and William James," DAI, 34 (Wisconsin: 1973), 3391A.

2341   Friedman, Alan. The Turn of the Novel. New York: Oxford U. P., 1966, pp. 176-177, passim.

2341.1 Friedman, Norman. "Forms of the Plot," JGE, 8 (1953), 241-253. Repr., Theory of the Novel. Philip Stevick, ed. New York: 1967, pp. 145-166.

2342   _____. "Point of View in Fiction: The Development of a Critical Concept. PMLA, 70 (1955), 1160-1184. Repr., The Theory of the Novel. Philip Stevick, ed. New York: 1967, pp. 108-137.

2343   Frierson, William C. "Henry James's Version of the Experimental Novel," The English Novel in Transition, 1885-1940. Norman, Oklahoma: Oklahoma U. P., 1942, pp. 107-115. Discussion of James's experimental method.

2344   _____. L'Influence du Naturalisme Français Sur Les Romanciers Anglais de 1885 à 1900. Paris: 1925. Discussion of the French influences upon James.

2344.1 "From the James Family Libraries," Bancroftiana (Berkeley, California), 52 (1972), 1-2. Additions to holdings, Bancroft Library, University of California, Berkeley.

2345   Fryckstedt, Olov W. In Quest of America: A Study of Howells' Early Development as a Novelist. Cambridge, Mass.: Harvard U. P., 1958, passim.

One aspect discussed in the above book is the influence of
James on Howells.

2346   Frye, Northrop. Anatomy of Criticism: Four Essays.
        Princeton, New Jersey: Princeton U. P., 1957, passim.

2347   Fuller, Henry Blake. "Howells or James?" Darrel Abel,
        ed. MFS, 3 (Summer, 1957), 159-164.

2347.1 _____. "Howells or James?" Howells: A Century of
        Criticism. Kenneth Eugene Eble, ed. Dallas: Southern
        Methodist U. P., 1962, pp. 34-40.

2348   Fullerton, Morton. "The Art of Henry James," QR, 212
        (April, 1910), 393-408; LivA, 265 (June 11, 1910), 643-652.
        Compares James and Balzac.

2349   Fussell, Edwin. "Hawthorne, James and 'The Common
        Doom,'" AQ, 10 (Winter, 1958), 438-453.
        Discussion of the feeling of isolation common to both
        writers.

2349.1 G., E. "Henry James on George Eliot," N&Q, 185 (July 31,
        1943), 76.

2349.2 Gabrielsen, Thor. "Henry James' gjenkomst," Edda, 53
        (1953), 131-144.

2350   Gale, Robert L. "Art Imagery in Henry James's Fiction,"
        AL, 29 (March, 1957), 47-63.
        "If one wishes to add the anonymous story 'A Tragedy of
        Error,' ... to the James canon ... the total [of images]
        is raised by 28 to 16,901 images in 135 works...."

2351   _____. The Caught Image: A Study of Figurative Lan-
        guage in the Fiction of Henry James. Diss. Columbia:
        1952.

2352   _____. The Caught Image: Figurative Language in the
        Fiction of Henry James. Chapel Hill: University of North
        Carolina Press, 1964.

2353   _____. "Evil and the American Short Story," AION-SG,
        1 (1958), 183-202.

2354   _____. "Freudian Imagery in James's Fiction," AI, 11
        (Summer, 1954), 181-190.

2355   _____. "Henry James," Eight American Authors: A Re-
        view of Research and Criticism. James Woodress, ed. Rev.
        ed. New York: Norton, 1971, pp. 321-375.

2356   _____. "Henry James and Chess," ChessL, 14 (December

5, 1959), 12.

2357 _____. "Henry James and Italy," SA, 3 (1957), 189-203.
Italy provided many scenes and images for James's fiction,
according to the author.

2358 _____. "Henry James and Italy," NCF, 14 (September,
1959), 157-170.
The contributions of Italy to James's fiction.

2359 _____. "Henry James's Dream Children," ArQ, 15
(Spring, 1959), 56-63.
Shows that James used his own childhood experiences and
memories to delineate certain degrees of awareness.

2360 _____. "Henry James's Imagistic Portrait of Henry
James," ForumH, 3 (Summer, 1961), 31-34.
Suggests that the art imagery in James's work indicates
that he saw himself most often as like a painter or dramatist.

2361 _____. "Names in James," Names, 14 (1966), 83-108.
Comments on James very early awareness that fictional
names may be potent aids to characterization.

2362 _____. "A Note on Henry James's First Short Story,"
MLN, 72 (1957), 103-107.
Believes that James's use of imagery in his first story indicates the consistency of his use of imagery throughout
his career.

2363 _____. Plots and Characters in the Fiction of Henry
James. Hamden, Conn.: Archon Books, 1965.
A valuable aid to students of James.

2364 _____. "Religious Imagery in Henry James's Fiction,"
MFS, 3 (Spring, 1957), 64-72.

2365 Gard, Roger, ed. Introduction, Headnotes, and Appendix.
Henry James: The Critical Heritage. London: Routledge &
K. Paul; New York: 1968.
An impressive collection of reviews, memoirs, and re-
marks in diaries and notebooks apropos Henry James.

2366 Gardner, Burdett. "An Apology for Henry James's 'Tiger-
Cat,'" PMLA, 68 (September, 1953), 688-695.
Henry James and Vernon Lee [Violet Paget].

2367 Gardner, Joseph H. "Dickens in America: Mark Twain,
Howells, James, and Norris," DAI, 30 (Berkeley, Calif.:
1970), 4409A-10A.

2368 Gargano, James W. "Henry James on Baudelaire," MLN,

75 (November, 1960), 559-561.
    Says that James upholds the need for morality in litera-
    ture when he characterizes some poems of Baudelaire's
    as "evil-smelling weeds."

2369   Garland, Hamlin. Hamlin Garland's Diaries. Donald Pizer,
       ed. San Marino, California: Huntington Library, 1968,
       passim.

2370   _____. "Henry James at Rye," Roadside Meetings. New
       York: Macmillan Company, 1930, pp. 454-465.
       An account of Garland's visit at Rye.

2370.1 _____. "Roadside Meetings of a Literary Nomad: Henry
       James, Lover of America," Bookman, 71 (July, 1930), 427-
       434.

2371   Garn, Dennis Stewart. "Experience Disengaged: Henry
       James's Use of the Romance," DAI, 32 (Michigan State Uni-
       versity: 1970), 429A.

2372   Garnier, Marie Reine. Henry James et la France. Diss.
       Strasbourg: 1927.

2372.1 _____. Henry James et la France. Paris: Honoré
       Champion, 1927.

2373   Garrett, Peter K. "The Creations of Consciousness," Scene
       and Symbol from George Eliot to James Joyce: Studies in
       Changing Fictional Mode. New Haven: Yale U. P., 1969,
       pp. 76-159.
       James's work is seen as occupying "a central position in
       the transition from traditional to modern fictional modes."

2374   _____. "Scene and Symbol: Changing Mode in the English
       Novel from George Eliot to Joyce," DA, 27 (Yale: 1967),
       4251A.

2375   Garst, Tom. "Beyond Realism: Short Fiction of Kipling,
       Conrad, and James in the 1890's," DAI, 30 (Washington Univ.:
       1969), 1167A.

2376   Gass, William H. "The High Brutality of Good Intentions,"
       Accent, 18 (Winter, 1958), 62-71.
       Repr., in Discussions of Henry James. Naomi Lebowitz,
       ed. Boston: 1962, pp. 89-95; Fiction and the Figures of
       Life. New York: 1970, pp. 177-190.

2377   _____. "A Spirit in Search of Itself," Fiction and the Fig-
       ures of Life. New York: Alfred A. Knopf, 1970, pp. 157-
       163.
       Compares Henry and William James.

2378   Gastón, Nilita Vientós. Introducción a Henry James. Puer-
        to Rico: Ediciones de la Torre, University of Puerto Rico,
        1956.

2379   Geary, Edward Acord. "A Study of the Androgynous Figure
        in the Fiction of Henry James," DAI, 32 (Stanford: 1971),
        1509A.

2379.1 Geismar, Maxwell. "Evading Art and Society," ChiR, 24
        (Spring, 1973), 85-92.

2380   _____. "Henry James and His Cult," LonM (April, 1964).
        Cf., Brigid Brophy. "Henry James," Don't Never Forget.
        New York: Holt, 1967, pp. 203-208.

2380.1 _____. Henry James and His Cult. London: Chatto &
        Windus, 1964.

2381   _____. "Henry James and the Jacobites," AmSch, 31
        (Summer, 1962), 373-381; 31 (1962), 656ff; 32 (Autumn,
        1962-Spring, 1963), 335.

2382   _____. Henry James and the Jacobites. Boston: Hough-
        ton Mifflin, 1963.

2383   _____. The Last of the Provincials: The American Novel,
        1915-1925. London: Secker & Warburg, 1947, passim.

2384   Géracht, Maurice Aron. "Windows on the House of Fiction:
        James's Perspectives on Some French and English Figures,"
        DAI, 31 (Wisconsin: 1970), 5401A.

2384.1 Gerard, Albert. "Introduction à Henry James," RN (June,
        1953), 651-657.

2385   Gerber, Richard. "Henry James," NeueR, 78, #2 (1967),
        307-317.
        James and the development of the novel.

2386   _____. "Die Magie der Namen bei Henry James," Anglia,
        81 (1963), 175-197.
        James's use of names.

2387   Gerould, Gordon Hall. "Explorers of the Inner Life," Pat-
        terns of English and American Fiction. Boston: 1942, pp.
        438-461; Reissued, New York: Russell & Russell, 1966.

2388   Gettmann, Royal A. "Landscape in the Novel," PrS, 45
        (Fall, 1971), 239-244.
        Notes that James advocated "close texture" in the novel,
        an element which can be achieved only if the landscape
        blends with the work.

2389   Ghiselin, Brewster. "Automatism, Intention, and Autonomy
        in the Novelist's Production," Daedalus, 92 (Spring, 1963),
        297-311.
            Comment on James and Lytle included.

2390   Gibson, Priscilla. "The Uses of James's Imagery: Drama
        Through Metaphor," PMLA, 69 (December, 1954), 1076-1084.

2391   Gide, André. "Henry James," YR, n. s., 19 (March, 1930),
        641-643.
            An unsent letter to Charles DuBos criticizing James.

2392   _____. "Henry James," in The Question of Henry James.
        F. W. Dupee, ed. New York: Holt, 1945, pp. 251-253.

2393   _____. The Journals of André Gide, 1889-1949, I: 1889-
        1924, II: 1924-1949. Justin O'Brien, trans. New York:
        Vintage Books, Inc., 1956, passim.

2394   Gilbert, E. L. "Kipling and James: A Note on Travel,"
        KilpingJ, 31 (1964), 7-9.

2395   Gill, Richard. "Tradition and an Individual Talent: The Lit-
        erary Background of the Country House in James's Fiction,"
        Happy Rural Seat: The English Country House and the Lit-
        erary Imagination. London and New Haven: Yale U. P.,
        1972, pp. 253-259.

2396   Gill, W. A. "Henry James and His Double," Atl, 100 (1907),
        458-466; FnR, 92 (October 1, 1909), 689-700.
            Pierre Carlet de Chamblain de Marivaux is the double.

2397   Gillen, Francis Xavier. "The Relationship of Rhetorical Con-
        trol to Meaning in the Novels of Henry James, Virginia
        Woolf, and E. M. Forster," DAI, 30 (Fordham: 1969),
        1525A.

2398   Gillespie, Gerald. "Novella, Nouvella, Novella, Short Novel?
        --A Review of Terms," Neophil, 51, #2 (April, 1967), 117-
        127; cont. to Neophil, 51, #3 (July, 1967), 225-229.
            An analysis of terms with reference to James and others.

2399   Gilman, Lawrence. "The Book of the Month," NAR, 201
        (May, 1915), 757-760.

2400   Gilman, Richard. "Americans Abroad," AH, 12 (October,
        1961), 9-27, 89-93.

2401   Gindin, J. J. "Howells and James," in Harvest of a Quiet
        Eye: The Novel of Compassion. Bloomington, Ind.: Indi-
        ana U. P., 1971, pp. 102-128.
            James's "increasing complexity and ... vast widening of
        the humanity involved in this definition of morality" the

author sees as a movement toward "compassion" in American fiction not to be equalled by examples of later
writers.

2402   Ginger, Ray. An Age of Excess: The United States from
1877 to 1914. New York: Macmillan, 1965.
Useful background for the interpretation of James's work.

2403   Giorcelli, Cristina. Henry James e L'Italia. Rome: Edizioni di Storia e Letteratura, 1969.

2404   Girling, H. K. "The Strange Case of Dr. James and Mr.
Stevenson," WascanaR, 3 (1968), 65-76.

2405   Gliddon, Gerald M. "James Incomplete," TLS (February 24,
1966), 148.
Cf., Hart-Davis, Rupert. "James Incomplete," TLS
(March 3, 1966), 167. Relative to editions.

2405.1   "Gloom and Some Friendships," TLS, 68 (October 30, 1969),
1245-1246.

2406   "Glorified Snobbishness of James," CurL, 43 (November,
1907), 526.

2407   Goetsch, Paul. Die Romankonzeption in England, 1880-1910.
(AF 94.) Heidelberg: Winter, 1967.

2408   Gohdes, Clarence. American Literature in Nineteenth-Century England. New York: Columbia U. P., 1944, passim.

2409   _____. "Henry James," The Literature of the American
People: An Historical and Critical Survey. A. H. Quinn,
ed. New York: Appleton-Century-Crofts, 1951, pp. 688-
700.

2410   Goldberg, M. A. " 'Things' and Values in Henry James's
Universe," WHR, 11 (Autumn, 1957), 377-385.
James presents details "indirectly, by suggestion, not by
description." He deals with the reality of consciousness
that views things and places with feelings.

2411   Goldsmith, Arnold L. Determinism, Free Will and Responsibility in the Works of Oliver Wendell Holmes, Henry James,
and Frank Norris. Diss. Wisconsin: 1953.

2412   _____. "Free Will, Determinism, and Social Responsibility in the Writings of Oliver Wendell Holmes, Sr., Frank
Norris, and Henry James," SDD-UW, 15 (1955), 610-612.

2413   _____. "Henry James's Reconciliation of Free Will and
Fatalism," NCF, 13 (September, 1958), 109-126.
James's relationship to nineteenth-century views.

2413.1 Gonzalez Pantin, Hilda Ana. La Función del Tiempo en la
Novelística de Henry James. Diss. Madrid: 1969.

2414   Goode, John, ed. Introduction. The Air of Reality: New
Essays on Henry James. New York: Methuen & Co., 1973.
A very pertinent survey of Jamesian criticism.

2415   _____. "The Art of Fiction: Walter Besant and Henry
James," Tradition and Tolerance in Nineteenth-Century Fiction: Critical Essays on Some English and American Novels.
David Howard, et al, eds. London: Routledge and K. Paul,
1966; New York: Barnes and Noble, 1967, pp. 243-281.

2416   _____. "Character and Henry James," NewRL, 40 (No-
vember-December, 1966), 55-75.

2417   Goodman, Charlotte Margolis. "Views of the Artist and His
Art in the Writing of Henry James," DAI, 32 (Brandeis:
1971), 2686A.

2418   Gordan, John D. "The Ghost at Brede Place," BNYPL, 56
(December, 1952), 591-596.

2419   Gordon, Caroline. "Henry James and His Critics," How to
Read a Novel. New York: Viking Press, 1957, pp. 111-
119, passim.

2420   Gosse, Edmund. "Henry James," Scribner's, 67 (April,
1920), 422-430, 548-557.

2421   _____. "Henry James," LonMerc, 1 (April, 1920), 673-
684; 2 (May, 1920), 29-41.

2422   _____. "Henry James," Aspects and Impressions. London: Cassell & Co., 1922; New York: Scribner's, 1922,
pp. 17-53.

2423   _____. The Life and Letters of Sir Edmund Gosse. Evan
Charteris, ed. London: William Heinemann, 1931, passim.
Letters of Sir Edmund Gosse to Henry James.

2423.1 Grabo, Carl H. The Technique of the Novel. New York:
Scribner's, 1928; Gordian Press, 1964, passim.

2424   Gragg, Perry Earl. "The Revelation of Consciousness: The
Psychology of William James and Five Novels of Henry
James," DA, 21 (Texas: 1961), 3097-98.

2425   Graham, Kenneth. English Criticism of the Novel: 1865-
1900. Oxford: At the Clarendon Press, 1965, pp. 108-113,
passim.

2426   Graham, R. B. Cunningham. "The Short Story," SatR, 108

(November 27, 1909), 662.
Remarks that Henry James and others are devoting them-
selves more and more to short pieces "and in them are
doing some of their finest work."

2427   Grana, Gianni.   "Henry James e la grande arte narrativa,"
FLe, 5 (March 4, 1956), 4-6.

2428   Grattan, Clinton Hartley.   "The Calm within the Cyclone,"
Nation, 134 (February 17, 1932), 201-203.
A brief estimate of James.

2429   Gray, James.   "Interpreting Genius," SatRL, 34 (December
1, 1951), 27.

2430   Green, Martin.   "Henry James and the Great Tradition,"
LonM, 2, n. s. (January, 1963), 32-45.

2430.1   _____.   "Henry James and the Great Tradition," in Re-
Appraisals: Some Commonsense Readings in American Literature.   New York: W. W. Norton, 1965, pp. 145-166.

2431   _____.   "Style in American Literature," CamR, 89,
#2151 (June 3, 1967), 385-387.
Essay-review of Richard Poirier's A World Elsewhere
New York: 1966, with application to James.

2432   Greene, George.   "Elizabeth Bowen: Imagination as Ther-
apy," Perspective, 14 (Spring, 1965), 42-52.
Henry James as "mentor" for Elizabeth Bowen.

2433   Greene, Graham.   "L'aspect religieux de Henry James,"
DieuV, 20 (1951), 105-114.

2434   _____.   Cinco Ensayos en La Niñez Perdida.   Ediciones
Criterio, Emecé, Buenos Aires, 1954.

2435   _____.   "Graham Greene on Henry James," Novelists on
Novelists.   Louis Kronenberger, ed.   New York: Doubleday,
1962, pp. 330-342.

2436   _____.   "Henry James," TR, (Paris), 29 (May, 1950),
9-22.

2437   _____.   "Henry James: The Religious Aspect," "The
Private Universe," Collected Essays.   London: Sydney;
New York: Viking, 1969, pp. 23-40; 41-53.

2438   _____.   "Henry James--An Aspect," Contemporary Essays.
Sylva Norman, ed.   London: Elkin Mathews and Marrot,
1933, pp. 65-75.

2439   _____.   "Henry James," The Lost Childhood and Other

Essays. London: Heinemann, 1951, pp. 21-30, 31-39, 49-50.

2440 _____. "The Private Universe," [originally entitled "Henry James: The Private Universe"], The English Novelists. Derek Verschoyle, ed. London: Chatto & Windus, 1936, pp. 215-228. Repr., Henry James: A Collection of Critical Essays. Leon Edel, ed., pp. 111-122.

2441 Greene, Philip Leon. "Henry James and George Eliot," DA, 24 (New York University: 1964), 4188-89.

2442 Gregory, Alyse. "A Superb Brief," American Criticism. William A. Drake, ed. New York: Harcourt, 1926, pp. 95-100.

2443 Grewall, Om Prakash. "Henry James and the Ideology of Culture: A Critical Study of The Bostonians, The Princess Casamassima and The Tragic Muse," DAI, 30 (Rochester: 1969), 5444A.

2444 Griffith, Albert J. Peter Taylor. (Twayne United States Authors Series, 168). New York: Twayne, 1970.
    The influence of James on Taylor, especially in matters of technique.

2445 Grigg, Womble Quay. "The Molds of Form: Comedy and Conscience in the Novels of Henry James," DA, 22 (Penn.: 1961), 1156-57.

2446 Gross, Theodore L. "Henry James: The Illusion of Freedom," The Heroic Ideal in American Literature. New York: Free Press, 1971, pp. 68-84.

2447 Grosskurth, Phyllis. "The World of Muriel Spark: Spirits of Spooks?" TamR, 39 (Spring, 1966), 62-67.
    Similarities in Spark and James.

2447.1 Grossman, Edward. "Henry James and the Sexual-Military Complex," Comm, 53, iv (1972), 37-50.

2448 Grossman, James. "The Face in the Mountain," Nation, 161 (September 8, 1945), 230-232.
    Parallels in the works of James found in the plays of George S. Kaufman.

2449 Grover, P. R. "Mérimée's Influence on Henry James," MLR, 63 (1968), 810-817.
    James gained from the French novelist "the construction of a well-conducted action, the conveying of emotion through significant detail, [and] the presence of strong passions."

2450   Grover, Philip. "Henry James and Several French Critics: Sources and Comparisons," PP, 11, #1 (1968), 45-52.

2451   Grumman, Joan Mary. "Henry James's Great 'Bad' Heroines," DAI, 33 (Purdue: 1972), 5177A.

2452   Guedalla, Philip. "The Crowner's Quest," NSt, 12 (February 15, 1919), 421-422.

2453   _____. Supers and Supermen: Studies in Politics, History and Letters. New York: Garden City Pub. Co., 1924, passim.

2454   "Gulf of Henry James," Nation, 111 (October 20, 1920), 441. "Across a vast gulf those who like Henry James view with contempt those who do not, and in return those who do not like him view with incredulity those who do. Neither his alleged obscurity nor his avowed cosmopolitanism explains this gulf...."

2455   Gullason, T. A. "The Jamesian Motif in Stephen Crane's Last Novels," Person, 42 (Winter, 1961), 77-84.

2456   Gullón, Richardo. "Imágenes del Otro, Homenaje a Angel del Rio. RHM, 31 (1965), 210-221.

2457   Gunn, Giles B. "Criticism as Repossession and Responsibility: F. O. Matthiessen and the Ideal Critic," AQ, 22 (1970), 629-648. Praises Matthiessen's pioneering work on James.

2458   Gunn, Peter. Vernon Lee: Violet Paget, 1856-1939. New York: Oxford U. P., 1964. James's relationship with the minor novelist-critic.

2459   Gunthner, Frantz. "Henry James--Le romancier comme critique," Le Monde, 27 (March 7, 1970), v.

2460   Gurko, Leo. The Angry Decade. New York: Dodd, Mead & Co., 1947, pp. 129-132.

2461   Gutscher, Marianne. Henry James und Walter Pater. Diss. Vienna, 1940.

2461.1 Gutwinski, Waldemar Franciszek. "Cohesion in Literary Texts: A Study of Some Grammatical and Lexical Features of English Discourse," DA, 30 (Conn.: 1970), 2990A.

2461.2 Gwiazda, Ronald E. The Spiral Staircase and the Blank Wall: Fantasy and Anxiety in Three Early Novels By Henry James. Diss. Columbia: 1972.

2461.3 H., J. "Henry James and Dumas Fils," N&Q, 185 (August

28, 1943), 132-133.

2462   Habegger, Alfred C. "Secrecy in the Fiction of Henry
        James," DA, 28 (Stanford: 1967), 1077A-1078A.

2462.1 Habicht, Louise Ann. Henry James and Joseph Conrad: A
        Study in Relationship. Diss. Brown U. : 1971.

2463   Hackett, Francis. "Henry James," Horizons: A Book of
        Criticism. New York: B. W. Huebsch, 1918, pp. 74-82.

2464   _____. "Henry James Revisited," On Judging Books: In
        General and in Particular. New York: John Day, 1947, pp.
        247-249.

2465   _____. "A Stylist on Tour," NewRep, 2 (May 1, 1915),
        320-321; repr., in Horizons: A Book of Criticism. New
        York: 1918, pp. 268-273.

2466   Hafley, James. "Malice in Wonderland," ArQ, 15 (Spring,
        1959), 5-12.
            Compares James and Poe.

2467   Hagemann, E. R. "Life Buffets (and Comforts) Henry James,
        1883-1916: An Introduction and an Annotated Checklist,"
        PBSA, 62 (2nd Qt. , 1968), 207-225.
            Provides a vast area of information as to James's reputa-
        tion in the time period specified.

2468   _____. " 'Unexpected Light in Shade Places': Henry
        James and Life, 1883-1916," WHR, 24 (Summer, 1970), 241-
        250.
            Much additional information as to James's reputation.

2469   Haight, Gordon S., ed. A Century of George Eliot Criticism.
        Boston: Houghton Mifflin Co. , 1965, passim.
            Shows James's estimate of George Eliot.

2470   Hale, Edward Everett. "Henry James," Dial, 60 (March 16,
        1916), 259-262.

2471   _____. "The Impressionism of Henry James," UCFP, 2
        (January, 1931), 3-17.

2472   _____. James Russell Lowell and His Friends. Boston:
        New York: Houghton Mifflin, 1898, 1901, p. 202.
            James listed as a member of the Saturday Club.

2473   _____. "The Rejuvenation of Henry James," Dial, 44
        (March 16, 1908), 174-176.

2474   Halifax, Viscount. "The British Ambassador Pays Tribute,"
        MTQ, 5, Henry James Number (Spring, 1943), [Title page].

Tribute to Henry James.

2475   Hall, Robert A., Jr. "Some Recent Books on Henry James,"
       AION-SG, 9 (1966), 49-64. [Sezione germanica]
       A survey of criticism on James during the 1960's.

2475.1 Hall, Sallie Jean. "The Integrated Self: A Reading of the
       Novels of Henry James," DAI, 32 (Florida: 1972), 5738A.

2476   Hall, William F. "Caricature in Dickens and James," UTQ,
       39 (1970), 242-257.
       Discussion of simple caricatures of likenesses and more
       subtle and complex caricatures of equivalence in James
       and Dickens.

2477   _____. Society and the Individual in the English Fictions
       of Henry James, 1885-1901. Diss. Johns Hopkins: 1954.

2477.1 Hallab, Mary Clark Yost. "Psychoanalytic Criticism of the
       Life and Works of Henry James," DAI, 32 (La. State:
       1971), 966A.

2478   Halleck, Reuben Post. "Henry James," History of American
       Literature. New York: American Book Co., 1911, pp. 376-
       378, passim.
       Calls James a leader in realistic fiction, his work the
       "quintessence of realism."

2479   Halverson, John. "Late Manner, Major Phase," SR, 79
       (Spring, 1971), 214-231.
       "The price James paid for his psychological and moral
       penetration [in later novels] was a retraite du mot. He
       loses sight altogether of the verbal splendors of his earli-
       er style."

2480   Hamblen, Abigail Ann. "Henry James and the Freedom
       Fighters of the Seventies," GaR, 20 (Spring, 1966), 35-44.

2481   _____. "Henry James and the Press: A Study of Pro-
       test," WHR, 11 (Spring, 1957), 169-75.
       James's dislike of the popular press.

2482   _____. "The Inheritance of the Meek: Two Novels by
       Agatha Christie and Henry James," Discourse, 12 (Summer,
       1969), 409-413.
       A comparison.

2483   _____. "The Jamesian Note in Edith Wharton's The Chil-
       dren," UKCR, 31 (1965), 209-211.
       Further consideration of James's relation to Edith Whar-
       ton.

2484   Hamilton, Clayton. "Disengaged," Forum, 41 (April, 1909),
       342-343.

2485   Hamilton Eunice C. "Biographical and Critical Studies of
        Henry James, 1941-1948," AL, 20 (January, 1949), 424-
        435.

2486   Hampshire, Stuart. "Henry James," Modern Writers, and
        Other Essays. London: Chatto & Windus; New York:
        Knopf, 1970, pp. 96-101.

2487   Hapgood, Norman. "Henry James," Literary Statesmen and
        Others: Essays on Men Seen from a Distance. London:
        Duckworth & Co., Chicago: H. S. Stone & Co., 1898, pp.
        193-208.

2488   _____. "Henry James," BachA, 3 (October, 1896), 477-
        488.

2489   Hardy, Barbara. "Total Relevance: Henry James," "The
        Matter of Treatment: Henry James," The Appropriate Form:
        An Essay on the Novel. London: University of London (Ath-
        lone Press), 1964, pp. 11-29, 30-50.
            A very pertinent analysis of James's techniques.

2490   _____. "The Change of Heart in Dickens' Novels," VS,
        5 (September, 1961), 49-67.
            Comparison of moral conversion in Dickens with that in
        James.

2491   _____, ed. Critical Essays on George Eliot. New York:
        Barnes & Noble, 1970, passim.
            Contains passages indicating points of contrast between
        Eliot and James.

2492   Hardy, Florence Emily. The Early Life of Thomas Hardy,
        1840-1891. New York: Macmillan Co., 1928, passim.
            Contains comments of Hardy as to James's work.

2493   _____. The Later Years of Thomas Hardy, 1892-1928.
        London: Macmillan; New York: Macmillan, 1930, St. Mar-
        tin's Press, 1962, pp. 167-168, passim.

2494   Harkins, E. F. "Henry James," Famous Authors. Boston:
        L. C. Page, 1901, pp. 91-105.

2495   _____. "Literary Career of Henry James," Little Pil-
        grimages Among Men Who Have Written Famous Books. Bos-
        ton: L. C. Page, 1902.

2496   Harkness, Bruce. "The Lucky Crowd--Contemporary British
        Fiction," EJ, 47 (October, 1958), 387-397.
            An interesting but incidental reference. Sees the fiction
        of the late 50's as a reaction to the work of such writers
        as James.

2497   Harland, Henry. "Mr. Henry James," Academy, 55 (No-
       vember 26, 1898), 339-340.
           The article shows appreciative Jamesian criticism by Mr.
           Harland, an expatriate American writer and editor of the
           Yellow Book.

2498   Harlow, Virginia. Thomas Sergeant Perry: A Biography
       and Letters to Perry from William, Henry, and Garth Wil-
       kinson James. Durham, North Carolina: Duke U. P., 1950,
       passim.

2499   _____. "Thomas Sergeant Perry and Henry James,"
       BPLQ, 1 (July, 1949), 43-60.
           Similarities in the attitudes of Thomas Sergeant Perry and
           Henry James, and their aspiration to "take refuge in the
           life of intelligence," combined to make their friendship
           "one of the fine examples of friendship between literary
           men."

2500   Harnack, Curtis. "Week of the Angry Artist...," Nation,
       204 (February 20, 1967), 245-248.
           Reports that the major objects of the participants' hostility
           were Henry James, the New Criticism, and the Old Left.

2501   Harrier, R. C. " 'Very Modern Rome'--An Unpublished Es-
       say of Henry James," HLB, 8 (1954), 125-140.
           Printed for the first time from holograph MS at Harvard.
           Shows James's love of Italy.

2502   Harris, Frank. My Life and Loves. Introduction by John
       F. Gallagher, ed. London: W. H. Allen, 1964, pp. 636-
       638.
           An account of a meeting with James.

2503   Harris, Joel Chandler. "Provinciality in Literature--A De-
       fense of Boston," in Joel Chandler Harris: Editor and Es-
       sayist: Miscellaneous Literary, Political and Social Writings.
       Julia Collier Harris, ed. Chapel Hill, North Carolina:
       North Carolina U. P., 1931, pp. 186-191.

2504   Harris, Wendell V. "English Short Fiction in the Nineteenth
       Century," SSF, 6 (Fall, 1968), 1-93.
           The work of James helped to bring the short story to ma-
           turity and popular recognition in England.

2505   Harrison, Henry Sydnor. "Henry James: 'Notes on Novel-
       ists, with Some Other Notes,' " YR, n. s., 4 (April, 1915),
       608-611.

2506   Harrison, Stanley R. "Through a Nineteenth-Century Look-
       ing Glass: The Letters of Edgar Fawcett," TSE, 15 (1967),
       107-157.
           Fawcett's letters indicate his literary judgments of James.

2507   Hart, James S. "Henry James's Later Novels: The Objecti-
       fying of Moral Life," DA, 14 (Stanford: 1954), 2346.

2508   Hart-Davis, Rupert. "James Incomplete," TLS (March 3,
       1966), 167.
          Has reference to the re-publication of James's work. Cf.,
          G. M. Gliddon, TLS (February 24, 1966), 148.

2509   Hartley, L. P. "Henry James," Sixteen Portraits of People
       Whose Houses Have Been Preserved by the National Trust.
       L. A. G. Strong, ed. London: Naldrett Press, 1951, pp.
       80-92.
          Lamb House in Rye.

2510   _____. "The Novelist's Responsibility," E&S, 15 (1962),
       88-100.
          Henry James given as an example of an author who ac-
          cepted a novelist's responsibility, which is the "acceptance
          of ethical standards."

2511   _____. "Henry James," The Novelist's Responsibility.
       London: Hamish Hamilton, 1967, pp. 177-183.
          "He [Henry James] accepted conventions, and conventional
          opinion, as an index and criterion of morality...."

2512   Hartman, Geoffrey H. "The Heroics of Realism," YR, 53
       (October, 1963), 26-35.
          Incidental remarks but pertinent: "... James obstacles
          himself; he refuses simply 'to know.' "

2513   Hartsock, Mildred E. "Henry James and the Cities of the
       Plain," MLQ, 29 (Summer, 1968), 297-311.

2514   Hartwick, Harry. "Caviar to the General," Foreground of
       American Fiction. New York: American Book Co., 1934,
       pp. 341-368.
          Discussion of a number of James's works.

2515   _____. "Henry James," A History of American Letters
       by Walter Fuller Taylor. New York: American Book Co.,
       1936, pp. 556-559.

2516   Harvey, J. R. Victorian Novelists and Their Illustrators.
       New York: University of New York Press, 1971, pp. 166-
       167, 176.
          Shows the inter-relationship between the novel and the il-
          lustrator.

2517   Harvey, Paul, comp., and ed. "Henry James," The Oxford
       Companion to English Literature. 4th ed. rev. Oxford:
       Clarendon Press, 1967, 424-425.

2518   Harvey, W. J. The Art of George Eliot. New York:

Oxford U. P., 1961, pp. 13-32, passim.

2519 _____. "The Human Context," Character and the Novel.
Ithaca, New York: Cornell U. P., 1965; repr. in Theory of
the Novel. Philip Stevick, ed. New York: 1967, pp. 231-
251.

2519.1 Hasler, Jörg. Switzerland in the Life and Work of Henry
James. The Cooper Monographs on English and American
Language and Literature, No. 10. Bern, Switzerland: A.
Franke, 1966.

2520 Hatcher, Harlan Henthorne. "America Catches Step," Cre-
ating the American Novel. New York: Farrar, 1935, pp.
12-20.

2520.1 Hawthorne, Julian, et al, eds. "Henry James," The Literature of All Nations and All Ages. Chicago and Philadelphia:
E. R. DuMont, 1898, Later published as The Masterpieces
and the History of Literature, Volume X, New York: Art Library Pub. Co., 1898. pp. 351-352.
    "He [Henry James] has been described by a critic as look-
    ing at America with the eyes of a foreigner, and at Europe
    with the eyes of an American.... The educated American
    seems to be rare in Mr. James's collection of charac-
    ters...."

2521 Hay, John. The Life and Letters of John Hay by William
Roscoe Thayer. Boston and New York: Houghton Mifflin,
c1908, 1916, I, 411, 416f.
    John Hay's letters to Howells about Henry James.

2521.1 Hayashi, Tetsumaro. "Henry James: A Semantic View of
His Short Stories," The Indian P.E.N., 33 (1967), 35-38.

2522 Hayne, Barrie S. The Divided Self: The Alter Ego as
Theme and Device in Brockden Brown, Hawthorne, and
James. Diss. Harvard: 1964.

2523 Hays, H. R. "Henry James, the Satirist," H&H, 7 (April-
June, 1934), 514-522.

2524 Haywood, J. C. How They Strike Me, These Authors. Philadelphia: 1877.
    Discussion of James's early development.

2525 Head, Ruth, ed. Pictures and Other Passages from Henry
James. New York: Stokes, 1917.
    "... not one of my contemporaries shares my enthusiasm
    [for James]."

2526 Heimer, Jackson W. The Lesson of New England: Henry
James and His Native Region. (Ball State Monograph 9,

Pubs. in Eng. 5). Muncie, Indiana: Ball State U. P. , 1967.
Shows James's attitude toward New England.

2527   Hellman, Geoffrey. "Profiles," NY, 47 (March 13, 1971),
        43-6.
        A good survey of Leon Edel's writing about Henry James.

2528   Hellman, George S. "Stevenson and Henry James, The Rare
        Friendship Between Two Famous Stylists," Century, n. s.
        89 (January, 1926), 336-345.

2529   Hemphill, George. "Hemingway and James," KR, 11 (Winter,
        1949), 50-60; Repr., Ernest Hemingway: Man and Hero, pp.
        329-339.
        Points of similarity in the two writers.

2530   Hendrick, Leo T. Henry James: The Late and Early Styles.
        Diss. Michigan, 1953.

2531   "Henry James," Outlook, 79 (April, 1905), 838-839; Reader,
        6 (August, 1905), 334-335.

2531.1 "Henry James: Citizen of Two Countries. An Anglo-Amer-
        ican Vision," TLS (April 17, 1943), 188, 190.

2531.2 "Henry James, Self-Revealed, LitD, 66 (July 10, 1920), 89-
        94.

2532   "Henry James Reprints," TLS (February 5, 1949), 96; John
        Lehmann and F. R. Leavis, TLS (February 12, 1949), 105;
        J. C. Maxwell, TLS (February 19, 1949), 121; A. J. Hoppé,
        TLS (February 26, 1949), 137; Leon Edel, TLS (March 12,
        1949), 169; David Garnett, TLS (March 19, 1949), 185.

2532.1 "Henry James and His Unfinished Work," Dial, 60 (March
        30, 1916), 316-317.

2532.2 "Henry James's Workshop," NewRep, 13 (December 1, 1917),
        119-121.

2533   Henry, John. "Henry James on George Eliot," N&Q, 185
        (October 9, 1943), 235-236.

2533.1 Heppenstall, Rayner. The Fourfold Tradition: Notes on the
        French and English Literatures with Some Ethnological and
        Historical Asides. New York: New Directions, 1961, Part
        II, 1900-1950, includes James, passim.

2534   Herrick, Robert. "Henry James," American Writers on
        American Fiction. John C. Macy, ed. New York: Horace
        Liveright, 1931, pp. 298-316.

2535   _____ . "Tolstoi and Henry James," YR, n. s. , 12

(October, 1922), 181-186.

2536 _____. "A Visit to Henry James," The Manly Anniversary Studies in Language and Literature. Chicago: 1923,
pp. 229-242.
    References to changes in James's style when he began
    dictation.

2537 Heston, Lilla A. "A Study of the Point of View in Three
Novels by Henry James: The Spoils of Poynton, The Wings
of the Dove, and The Golden Bowl," DA, 26 (Northwestern:
1965), 3533.

2538 Hicks, Granville. "Fugitives," The Great Tradition: An Interpretation of American Literature Since the Civil War.
New York: 1933, pp. 100, 105-124.

2539 _____. "The Shape of a Career," SatR, 41 (December
13, 1958), 38.
    Contrasts the productivity of James and Howells with that
    of Hemingway and Faulkner.

2540 _____. "The Novels of Henry James," SatR, 44 (August
5, 1961), 10.

2541 _____. "Vision Behind the Vision," SatR, 45 (November
3, 1962), 23.

2542 Higginson, Thomas Wentworth. "Henry James, Jr.," LitW,
10 (November 22, 1879), 383-384.
    Interesting as an early evaluation of James.

2543 _____. "Henry James, Jr., " Short Studies of American
Authors. Boston and New York: 1880, pp. 51-60.
    Appreciative interpretation of early work.

2544 _____. "Henry James, Jr.," The Question of Henry
James. F. W. Dupee, ed. New York: Henry Holt, 1945,
pp. 1-5.

2545 Higuchi, Hideo. "Henry James's Criticism of Fiction,"
Shur, 24 (1962), 24-38.
    James's views of imagination and form.

2545.1 Hill, John Edward. "Dialectical Aestheticism: Essays on
the Criticism of Swinburne, Pater, Wilde, James, Shaw, and
Yeats," DAI, 34 (Virginia: 1972), 3648A-49A

2545.2 Hill, John S. "Henry James: Fitzgerald's Literary Ances-
tor," FitzN, 40 (Winter, 1968), 6-10.

2546 Hinchliffe, Arnold P. "The Good American," TCL, 168
(December, 1960), 529-539.

2547   _____. Symbolism in the American Novel, 1850-1950:
An Examination of the Findings of Recent Literary Critics in
Respect of the Novels of Hawthorne, Melville, James, Hem-
ingway, and Faulkner. Diss. Manchester: 1962-1963.

2548   Hind, Charles Lewis. "Henry James," Authors and I. New
York: 1921, pp. 161-165.

2549   Hinz, Evelyn J. "Henry James's Names: Tradition, Theory,
and Method," CLQ, 9 (1972), 557-578.
In the significance James gives to names, the author says
he follows the tradition of the novelists of manners.

2550   _____. "The Imagistic Evolution of James's Businessmen," CRAS, 3 (Fall, 1972), 81-95.
Says James' portraits of the capitalist are usually associ-
ated with "appetite," but his changes of attitude toward
the type are evident in alterations of specific images.

2551   Hoag, Gerald Bryan. "Henry James and Formalist Criticism
of the Novel in English in the Twentieth Century," DA, 26
(Tulane: 1965), 2753.
Thinks James's concept of organic form is derived from
Coleridge.

2551.1 _____. Henry James and the Criticism of Virginia Woolf.
Wichita State University Bulletin No. 92. Wichita, Kansas,
1972.

2552   Hoare, Dorothy M. "Henry James," Some Studies in the
Modern Novel. London: Chatto and Windus, 1940, pp. 3-35.

2553   _____. "A Note on Henry James," NewAdel, 2 (March-
May, 1929), 247-248.

2554   Hocks, Richard Allen. "Henry James and Pragmatic Thought,"
DA, 28 (North Carolina: 1967), 3639A-40A.

2555   Hodgdon, David Crockett. "Henry James: The Texture of
Language in the Later Novels, 1897-1901," DAI, 32 (New
York State University at Binghamton: 1971), 434A.

2555.1 Hodge, Judith Bush. "The Essential Constant: A Focusing
Device in Selected Novels by Henry James," DAI, 33 (Pennsylvania: 1972), 1727A.

2556   Hofer, Ernest Harrison. "The Realization of Conscience in
the Later Henry James," DA, 21 (Cornell: 1960), 197.

2556.1 Hoffman, Frederick J. "The Expense and Power of Greatness: An Essay on Leon Edel's James," VQR, 39 (Summer,
1963), 518-528.

2557   _____. "Freedom and Conscious Form: Henry James
and the American Self," VQR, 37 (Spring, 1961), 269-285.

2558   _____. "Henry James, W. D. Howells, and the Art of
Fiction," The Modern Novel in America. Chicago: Henry
Regnery Co., 1951, pp. 1-30.

2559   Hoffmann, Charles George. "The Development toward the
Short Novel Form in American Literature, with Special Reference to Hawthorne, Melville and James," DA, 13 (Wisconsin: 1953), 380-381.

2560   _____. The Short Novels of Henry James. New York:
Bookman Associates, 1957.
          A good survey of criticism covering many of James's
          works.

2561   Holder, Alan. "The Lesson of the Master: Ezra Pound and
Henry James," AL, 35 (March, 1963), 71-79.
          Shows that Pound was an early appreciative critic of
          James.

2562   _____. "T. S. Eliot on Henry James," PMLA, 79 (September, 1964), 490-497.
          Notes that although Eliot often underestimated James's
          critical views, he valued James's fiction.

2563   _____. "Three Voyagers in Search of Europe: A Study
of Henry James, Ezra Pound, and T. S. Eliot," DA, 26
(Columbia: 1965), 1646-47.

2564   _____. Three Voyagers in Search of Europe: A Study of
Henry James, Ezra Pound, and T. S. Eliot. Philadelphia:
University of Pennsylvania Press, 1966.

2565   Holder, Alex. "On the Structure of Henry James's Metaphors," ES, 41 (October, 1960), 289-297.
          Divides James's images into three major categories:
          those of one metaphorical element, those of two, those of
          more than two.

2566   Holder-Barell, Alexander. The Development of Imagery and
Its Functional Significance in Henry James's Novels. Cooper
Monographs, No. 3, Bern, Francke Verlag, 1959.

2567   Holland, Laurence B. The Expense of Vision: Essays on
the Craft of Henry James. Diss. Harvard: 1965.

2568   _____. The Expense of Vision: Essays on the Craft of
Henry James. Princeton, New Jersey: Princeton U. P.,
1964.
          A valuable study of several novels.

2569   Holliday, Robert Cortes. "Henry James, Himself," Walking-
       Stick Papers. New York: George H. Doran Co., 1918, pp.
       121-129.
            An account of a casual meeting with James.

2570   Holman, C. Hugh. "Of Everything the Unexplained and Irre-
       sponsible Specimen: Notes on How to Read American Real-
       ism," GaR, 18 (Fall, 1964), 316-324.
            Both James and Howells, looking to Turgenev as literary
       master, "embraced a mimetic theory of art, in which the
       fidelity of the art object to its subject is its highest cri-
       terion."

2571   Hølmebakk, Gordon. "Romanen som redskap eller erkjen-
       nelse. Noen notater om forholdet mellom Henry James og
       H. G. Wells," Vinduet, 12, #1 (1958), 170-178.
            Discusses the conflicting views of James and Howells as
       to the art of the novel.

2572   Holroyd, Stuart. "Henry James," JO'LW, 5 (August 10,
       1961), 171-173.
            Notes that James's last novels foreshadowed the moral col-
       lapse of society which was partly responsible for the war.

2573   "Homage to Henry James," H&H, 7, #3 (April-June, 1934).

2574   Honig, Edwin. Dark Conceit: The Making of Allegory.
       Evanston, Illinois: Northwestern U. P., 1959, passim.
            The use of allegory by Romantic and modern writers, es-
       pecially James.

2575   _____. "In Defense of Allegory," KR, 20 (Winter, 1958).

2576   _____. "The Merciful Fraud in Three Stories of Henry
       James," TigE, 9 (October, 1949), 83-96.

2577   Hopkins, Gerard. Introduction. Selected Stories. London:
       Oxford University Press, 1957.

       Hopkins, Viola. See Winner, Viola Hopkins.

2578   Hönnighausen, Lothar. "The Velvet Glove-zur Erzähltechnik
       in Henry James' Spätwerk," GRM, 48 (1967), 307-22.

2579   Horne, Charles F. The Techniques of the Novel: The Ele-
       ments of the Art, Their Evolution and Present Use. New
       York and London: Harper & Row, 1908, passim.

2580   Horne, Helen. Basic Ideals of Henry James's Aesthetics as
       Expressed in the Short Stories Concerning Artists and Writers.
       Diss. Marburg: 1960.

2581   _____. Basic Ideals of James's Aesthetics as Expressed in the Short Stories Concerning Artists and Writers.   Marburg: Erich Mauersberger, 1960.

2582   Horrell, Joyce Tayloe. "A Shade of a Special Sense: Henry James and the Art of Naming," AL, 42 (May, 1970), 203-220.
Says that James's fictional use of names "can be convincingly discussed only in terms of their use in a particular story."

2583   Hoskins, Katherine. "Henry James and the Future of the Novel," SR, 54 (January-March, 1946), 87-101.

2584   Hough, Graham. "Books in General," NS&N, 37 (April 16, 1949), 382.

2585   _____. "Henry James," List, 73 (March 25, 1965), 447-449.
James's development as a novelist.

2586   _____. "Rejoinder," NS&N, 37 (May 14, 1949), 503.
Cf., F. R. Leavis, "Reply," NS&N, 37 (April 23, 1949), 406.

2586.1 Hovanec, Evelyn Ann. "Henry James and Germany," DAI, 34 (Pittsburgh: 1973), 2628A-29A.

2587   Hovey, Richard B. John Jay Chapman: An American Mind.
New York: Columbia U. P., 1959, pp. 118-119, 152-153, passim.
Comparisons of Chapman and James.

2588   Howard, David, John Lucas and John Goode, eds. "The Art of Fiction: Walter Besant and Henry James," Tradition and Tolerance in Nineteenth-Century Fiction: Critical Essays on Some English and American Novels. New York: Barnes & Noble, 1967, pp. 243-281.

2588.1 Howe, Helen. The Gentle Americans, 1864-1960: Biography of a Breed. New York: Harper & Row, 1965, pp. 91-92, passim.

2589   Howe, Irving. "Henry James's Return to America," New Rep, 157 (September 30, 1967), 23-26.
The changes James found when he returned to America in 1904.

2589.1 _____. "Henry James and the Political Vocation," WR, 18 (Spring, 1954), 199-208.

2590   _____. "The Political Vocation," Politics and the Novel.
New York: Horizon Press, 1957, pp. 139-156; World Pub. Co., Meridian Books, 1964, pp. 139-156.
"Henry James is a novelist of temptations ... but the

temptation of politics, which has haunted so many modern
writers, seems never to have troubled him at all...."

2591   Howe, M. A. DeWolfe. Memories of a Hostess: A Chronicle
        of Eminent Friendships Drawn Chiefly from the Diaries of
        Mrs. James T. Fields. Boston: Atlantic Monthly Press,
        1922, pp. 297-301, passim.
            Of special interest is the discussion of James's esteem
        for the work of Sarah Orne Jewett.

2592   Howells, William Dean. "Editor's Easy Chair," Harper's,
        102 (January, 1900), 318-320.

2593   _____. "Editor's Study," HarperNMM, 77 (October,
        1888), 799-800.
            Howells' early estimate of James.

2594   _____. "Henry James," Criticism and Fiction, and Other
        Essays. Clara Marburg Kirk and Rudolf Kirk, eds. New
        York: University Press, 1939, pp. 229-236.

2595   _____. "Mr. Henry James, Jr.," Century, n. s., 3 (No-
        vember, 1882), 25-29.
            The essay is relative to James's early development.

2596   _____. "Mr. Henry James's Later Work," NAR, 176
        (January, 1903), 125-137.
            According to Howells, James has "imagined few heroines
        acceptable to women...."

2597   _____. "Mr. Henry James's Later Work," NAR, 203
        (April, 1916), 572-584.

2598   _____. "Mr. Henry James's Later Work," [1903], in
        The Question of Henry James: A Collection of Critical Es-
        says. F. W. Dupee, ed. New York: 1945, pp. 6-19.

2599   _____. Life in Letters of William Dean Howells. Mil-
        dred Howells, ed. New York: Doubleday, 1928, passim.

2600   _____. "Literary Recollections," NAR, 195 (April, 1912),
        558-562.

2601   Hueffer, Ford Madox [Ford]. "Henry James," Mightier Than
        the Sword. London: George Allen and Unwin, 1938, pp. 13-
        37. Appeared in the United States under the title Portraits
        from Life. Boston: Houghton Mifflin, 1937.

2602   _____. "The Master," AmMerc, 36 (November, 1935),
        315-327.
            Appreciative criticism of James.

2603   _____. Henry James: A Critical Study. London: Mar-

tin Secker, 1913; New York: Dodd, Mead, 1916; repr.,
1964; New York: Octagon Books, 1972.

2604   _____. "Henry James: Novelists and Novels," Critical
Writings of Ford Madox Ford. Frank MacShane, ed. Lincoln: Nebraska U. P., 1964, pp. 107-126.

2605   _____. "Memories and Criticisms," Ancient Lights and
Certain New Reflections. London: Chapman & Hall, 1911.
Provides an early estimate of James.

2606   _____. "The Old Man," [1932] in The Question of Henry
James. F. W. Dupee, ed. New York: 1945, pp. 47-53.

2607   _____. "Techniques," SoR, 1 (1935-36), 20-35.

2608   _____. "Three Americans and a Pole," Scribner's, 90
(October 1931), 379-386.
As a personal friend of James, Ford's comments are note-
worthy.

2609   _____. "Thus to Revisit...," Dial, 69 (July, August,
September, 1920), 52-60, 132, 141, 239-246; 70 (January,
1921), 14-23.

2610   _____. "Two Americans--Henry James and Stephen Crane,"
LitR, 1 (March 19, 1921), 1-2; (March 26, 1921), 1-2.

2611   Huffman, James Richard. "The Sense of the Past in Henry
James," DAI, 32 (Michigan State: 1970), 434A.

2612   Hughes, Herbert L. Theory and Practice in Henry James.
Diss. Virginia: 1923.

2613   _____. Theory and Practice in Henry James. Ann Arbor:
Edwards Brothers, 1926.
James's early development.

2614   Humphrey, Robert. Stream of Consciousness in the Modern
Novel. Berkeley and Los Angeles: California U. P., 1954.
"The salient thing that differentiates him [James] from the
stream-of-consciousness writers is the fact that he describes the rational weighing of intelligence.... It lacks
the free-flowing, elliptic, and symbolic quality of true
stream of consciousness."

2615   Huneker, James Gibbons. "The Lesson of the Master,"
Bookman, 51 (May, 1920), 364-368.
Article indicates James's early development.

2616   _____. "A Note on Henry James," in Unicorns. New
York: Scribner's, 1917, pp. 53-66; also in Modern English

Essays. Ernest Rhys, ed. New York, 1922, V, 64-76.

2616.1 _____. Steeplejack. 2 vols. New York: Scribner's, 1922, passim.

2616.2 _____. Letters of James Gibbons Huneker. Josephine Huneker, ed. New York: Scribner's, 1922, passim.

2617 Hutchens, John K. "One Very Dark Night in the Life of Mr. Henry James," NYHTB (December 11, 1960), 32.

2618 Hutton, Virgil. "James Joyce's The Dead," E-WR, 2 (Winter, 1965-1966), 124-139.
      Compares James Joyce and Henry James.

2619 Hyde, H. Montgomery. "An Afternoon with Max," LS, 6693, pp. 445-447.
      A talk with Max Beerbohm about Henry James.

2620 _____. "Henry James and Theodora Bosanquet," Encounter, 39 (October, 1972), 6-12.

2621 Hyman, Stanley Edgar. The Armed Vision: A Study in the Methods of Modern Literary Criticism. Rev. ed. New York: Vintage Books, 1955, passim.

2622 Hynes, Samuel. "A Small Literary Monument," Cw, 77 (November 9, 1962), 172-174.
      James contribution to American literature.

2623 I., B. de C. "Henry James at Work," ManGW, 59 (September 23, 1948), 12.

2624 "If Henry James Had Written 'The Ring and the Book,' " LitD, 45 (September 21, 1912), 467-468.
      Discussion of James's views of this work.

2625 Iglesias, J. The Novelistic Art of Henry James. Diss. Univ. of Valladolid: 1971.

2626 "Ineradicable American in the Genius of the Most Misunderstood of Modern Novelists," CurOp, 60 (April, 1916), 280-281.
      The influence of Europe on James.

2627 Irwin, W. "After Reading a Chapter by Henry James," [poem], Critic, 46 (March, 1905), 220.

2628 Ishizaki, Ayako Tomii. The Psychological Novels of Henry James and Matsume Soseki. Diss. Pennsylvania: n. d.

2629 Isle, Walter Whitfield. "Experiments in the Novel: Henry James's Fiction, 1896-1901," DA, 22 (Stanford: 1962), 3645-46.

2630 _____. Experiments in Form: Henry James's Novels:
      1896-1901. Cambridge, Mass.: Harvard U. P., 1968.
           An intensive and useful study of the novels of the period
           designated.

2631 Izzo, Carlo. "Henry James Scrittore Sintattico," SA, 2 (1956),
      127-142.

2632 Jacobson, Dan. "Liberalism and Literature," NSt (March 1,
      1963), 312-314.
           James's view of life.

2633 James, Alice. Alice James, Her Brothers, Her Journal.
      Anna Robeson Burr, ed. New York: Dodd, Mead & Co.,
      1934, passim. Repr., Milford House, 1972.
           Contains much interesting material not merely biographical.

2634 _____. The Diary of Alice James. Leon Edel, ed. New
      York: Dodd, Mead & Co., 1964, passim.
           Contains much critical discussion of various works of Hen-
           ry James.

2635 "James, Henry, 1843-1916," [Editorial], MTQ, 5, (Spring,
      1943), 1.

2636 James, Henry. "George Eliot's Middlemarch," NCF, 8 (De-
      cember, 1953), 161-170.
           James's review of Middlemarch is reprinted for the first
           time since its appearnce anonymously in Galaxy, 15 (March,
           1873), 424-428.

2637 "James, Henry," Outlook, 112 (March 8, 1916), 541-542.

2638 "James and English Speech," Outlook, 83 (May 5, 1906),
      16-17.

2639 "James and Others on Browning," LitD, 44 (June 1, 1912),
      1159-1160.

2640 "James as a Literary Sphinx," CurL, 42 (June, 1907), 634-
      636.

2641 "James the Obscure," Newsweek, 47 (May 7, 1956), 110.

2642 "James Viewed by the Portrait Painter," LitD, 79 (Decem-
      ber 8, 1923), 29.
           A verbal portrait by Jacques Blanche, the French portrait
           painter, who painted a portrait of James.

2643 [James's Achievement], EdinR, 197 (January, 1903), 59-85.
           A sympathetic treatment of various works.

2644 "James's Impressions of New England," CurL, 39 (July, 1905,
      97-99.

2645   "Mr. James's Order of Merit," LitD, 52 (February 12,
        1916), 377.

2646   James, William. The Letters of William James. Henry
        James, II, ed. Boston: Atlantic Monthly Press, 1920, 2
        vols., passim.
        Much material other than biographical.

2647   _____. Introduction. The Literary Remains of Henry
        James, Upper Saddle River, New Jersey: Literature House,
        1970.

2648   _____. "The Third Manner," in American Literature in
        Parody: A Collection of Parody, Satire, and Literary Burl-
        esque of American Writers Past and Present. Robert P.
        Falk, ed. New York: Twayne Pubs., 1955, p. 134.
        William James's letter to Henry James relative to Henry's
        "third manner" of literary style.

2649   _____. ["The Third Manner"] The Selected Letters of
        William James. Elizabeth Hardwick, ed. New York: Far-
        rar, Straus and Cudahy, 1961, passim.

2649.1 Jarrett-Kerr, Martin. Studies in Literature and Belief.
        London: Garden City Press, n. d., p. 15.
        A brief but concise analysis of James's work "within the
        total Western outlook, an outlook largely shaped by Chris-
        tian theology."

2650   Jefferson, D. W. Henry James. New York: Barnes &
        Noble, 1961, 1965; Edinburgh and London: Oliver and Boyd,
        1960.
        A very helpful work.

2651   _____. Henry James and the Modern Reader. Edinburgh:
        Oliver and Boyd, 1964; New York: St. Martin's Press, 1964.

2652   Jellema, R. H. Victorian Critics and the Orientation of
        American Literature, with Special Reference to the Reception
        of Walt Whitman and Henry James. Diss. Edinburgh:
        1962-1963.

2653   Jenkins, Iredell. "The Aesthetic Object," RevMeta, 11, #1
        (September, 1957), 3-11.
        Has reference to James's women characters.

2654   Jennings, R. "Fair Comment," NC, 133 (May, 1943), 230.

2655   Johnson, Alice Evangeline. "A Critical Analysis of the Dis-
        located Character as Developed in the Novels of Henry
        James," DA, 17 (Wisconsin: 1957), 1763-64.

2656   _____. A Critical Analysis of the Dislocated Character

As Developed in the Major Novels of Henry James. Ann
Arbor: University Microfilms, Publication No. 21,854;
Microfilm, AC-1, 1957.

2657   Johnson, Arthur. "A Comparison of Manners," NewRep, 20
(August 27, 1919), 113-115.
Compares Henry James and Herman Melville.

2658   Johnson, Courtney, Jr. "The Problems of Sex in the Writings of Henry James," DA, 28 (Michigan: 1966), 679A-680A.
Sees in James "the solution to a character's sexual problems" as "inseparable from the solution to his moral, aesthetic, and spiritual" problems.

2659   Johnson, Lee Ann. "The Art of Characterization: James's
Depiction of the 'Protector' Figure," DAI, 33 (U.C.L.A.:
1972), 1685A.

2660   Johnson, Robert G. "A Study of the Style of Henry James's
Late Novels," DAI, 32 (Bowling Green State Univ.: 1971),
2092A.

2661   Jones, Dora M. "Henry James," LonQR, 126 (July, 1916),
117-120.

2662   Jones, Edith R. "Stephen Crane at Brede," Atl, 194, #1
(July, 1954), 57-61.
An account of James's visit at the Crane's and "how" the
play, "The Ghost at Brede," was "born."

2663   Jones, Granville Hicks. "The Jamesian Psychology of Experience, Innocence, Responsibility, and Renunciation in the Fiction of Henry James," DAI, 30 (Pittsburgh: 1969), 5447A.

2664   Jones, Howard Mumford. "An Altar of the Living," NewRep,
147 (November 17, 1962), 30ff.

2665   _____. The Theory of American Literature. Ithaca, New
York: Cornell, 1948; reissued with new concluding chapter
and revised bibliography, Ithaca, New York: Cornell U. P.,
1965, passim.

2666   Jones, Llewellyn. "Henry James and Spiritual Democracy,"
Humanist, 19, #3 (June, 1959), 156-164.
Sees James as a "spiritual democrat," unenvious of the
aristocrats he portrayed.

2666.1 Jones, M. "Balzac aux Etats-Unis," RLittComp, 24 (April,
1950), 228-230.

2667   Jones, Oliver P. "Fables of the Imagination: First-Person
Narrative in Henry James," DAI, 33 (S.U.N.Y., Buffalo:
1972), 1729A.

2668   Jones, T. H. "The Essential Vulgarity of Henry James,"
        AULLA Proceedings (August 19-26, 1964), 49-50.

2669   Jones, Walter Paul. An Examination of Henry James's The-
        ory and Practice of Fiction. Diss. Cornell: 1925.

2670   Jones-Evans, Mervyn. "Henry James's Year in France,"
        Horizon, 14 (July, 1946), 52-60. Also in Golden Horizon.
        Cyril Connolly, ed. British Book Centre, 1953, pp. 571-
        579.

2671   Jordan, Elizabeth. "Henry James at Dinner," MTQ, 5
        (Spring, 1943), 7.
            A meeting with James.

2672   _____. Three Rousing Cheers. New York and London:
        Appleton-Century, 1938, passim.

2673   Josephson, Matthew. "The Education of Henry James," "A
        'Passionate Pilgrim,' " "The Return of Henry James," Por-
        trait of the Artist as American. New York: Harcourt,
        1930; repr., Octagon Books, 1964, pp. 70-79, 98-138, 265-
        288.

2674   Jost, Edward F. "Love and Two Kinds of Existentialism,"
        EngRec, 16 (February, 1966), 14-18.

2675   K., Q. "Henry James's Workshop," NewRep, 13 (December
        1, 1917), 119-121.

2676   Kaman, John Michael. "The Lonely Hero in Hawthorne,
        Melville, Twain, and James," DA, 34 (Stanford: 1973),
        5974A-5975A.

2677   Kane, Patricia. "Mutual Perspective: James and Howells as
        Critics of Each Other's Fiction," MinnR, 7, #3 (1967), 331-
        341.
            Provides a survey of public and private critiques which
        James and Howells made of each other's works.

2678   Kariel, Henry S. "Notes: Rebellion and Compulsion: The
        Dramatic Pattern of American Thought," AQ, 14 (Winter,
        1962), 608-611.
            Calls for new studies of American thought which would re-
        examine Henry James and others.

2679   Karita, Motoshi. "Shosetsu to Denki no Shudai-sentaku to
        Imi," SophiaT, 17 (1968), 29-45.
            Matter and meaning in the fiction of James and Hawthorne.

2680   Karl, Frederick R. An Age of Fiction: The Nineteenth Cen-
        tury British Novel. New York: Farrar, 1964, passim.

2681   Kaufman, Marjorie R. "Henry James's Comic Discipline:
        The Use of the Comic in the Structure of His Early Fiction,"
        DA, 15 (Minnesota: 1955), 2534.

2682   _____. Henry James's Comic Discipline: The Use of the
        Comic in the Structure of His Early Fiction. Ann Arbor:
        University Microfilms, 1955, Publication No. 14,556.

2683   Kaul, A. N. The Action of English Comedy: Studies in the
        Encounter of Abstraction and Experience from Shakespeare
        to Shaw. New Haven and London: Yale U. P., 1970, passim.

2684   Kaul, R. K. "Henry James on the Creative Process,"
        RUSEng, 6 (1972), 33-44.

2685   Kay, Wallace G. "The Observer and the Voyeur: Theories
        of Fiction in James and Robbe-Grillet," SoQ, 9 (October,
        1970), 87-91.
            Comparisons and contrasts in the two writers.

2686   Kayser, von Rudolf. "Henry James: Ein europäischer
        Amerikaner," NSR, 18 (December, 1950), 480-484.
            Considers James's creative power as always European.

2687   Kazin, Alfred. Contemporaries. Boston and Toronto: Lit-
        tle, Brown & Co., Atlantic Monthly Press Book, 1924, 1962,
        p. 63.

2688   _____. On Native Grounds: An Interpretation of Modern
        American Prose Literature. New York: Reynal & Hitch-
        cock, 1942, pp. 10-11, 46-50, 438-439, passim.

2689   _____. " 'Our Passion Is Our Task,' " NewRep, 108
        (February 15, 1943), 215-218.
            Analysis of the affirmations of William and Henry James.

2690   _____. "A Procession of Children," AmSch, 33 (Spring,
        1964), 171-173, 176-178.
            "Henry James turns children into prodigies. They know
            too much for their age.... Only the solitariness of
            James's child characters makes them 'American.' "

2690.1 _____. "The Republic of the Spirit," Reporter, 33 (Aug-
        ust 12, 1965), 44, 47.
            Essay-review, Millicent Bell's Edith Wharton and Henry
            James. New York: 1965.

2691   _____. "William and Henry James: 'Our Passion Is Our
        Task' " The Inmost Leaf. New York: Harcourt, Brace,
        c1941, 1955, pp. 9-20.

2692   Kees, Weldon. "Henry James at Newport," [poem], Poetry,
        59 (October, 1941), 16-17.

2693   Kelley, Cornelia Pulsifer. The Early Development of Henry
       James. Diss. Illinois: 1930.

2694   _____. "The Early Development of Henry James," UISL-
       &L, 15 (1930), Nos. 1 and 2.

2695   _____. The Early Development of Henry James. Intro-
       duction by Lyon N. Richardson. Urbana: Illinois U. P.,
       1965.
       A most helpful study as to James's early work.

2696   _____. "Henry James on Zola," CLQ, 1 (1943), 44-51.

2697   Kellner, L. Geschichte der Nordamerikanischen Literatur.
       Berlin: 1913; English translation, New York: 1915.

2698   Kellogg, Gene. The Vital Tradition: The Catholic Novel in
       a Period of Convergence. Chicago: Loyola U. P., 1970, pp.
       111, 114, 115.
       James's influence on Graham Greene.

2699   Kenner, Hugh. "Critic of the Month: III--Ghosts and Bene-
       dictions," Poetry, 113 (November, 1968), 109-125.
       James's influence on Ezra Pound.

2700   Kenney, Blair G. "Henry James's Businessmen," CLQ, 9,
       #1 (March, 1970), 48-58.
       "It is surprising that only the most aesthetic, ... Henry
       James, is able to see beyond the stereotype, and to por-
       tray for us that virile figure in all his variety, in nobility
       as well as squalor...."

2701   Kenton, Edna. "Henry James and Mr. Van Wyck Brooks,"
       Bookman, (New York), 62 (October, 1925), 153-157.

2702   _____. "Henry James in the World," H&H, 7 (April-
       June, 1934), 506-513. Repr., The Question of Henry James.
       F. W. Dupee, ed. New York: 1945, pp. 131-137.
       Insists that James was international, at heart the citizen
       of no country.

2703   _____. Introduction. Eight Uncollected Tales of Henry
       James. New Brunswick, New Jersey: Rutgers U. P., 1950;
       Freeport, New York: Books for Libraries Press, 1971.

2704   Kettle, Arnold. An Introduction to the English Novel. Lon-
       don: Hutchinson, 1953, 2 vols. Rev. ed., 1967; New York:
       Harper & Row, 1968, passim.

2705   Keynes, Geoffrey. "Henry James in Cambridge," LonM, 6
       (March, 1959), 50-61.

2705.1 _____. Henry James in Cambridge. Cambridge:
       Heffer, 1967.

2706   King, Sister M. Judine. "An Explication of 'At the Grave of
        Henry James,' by W. H. Auden," Horizontes, 25 (1971), 61-
        65.

2707   Kinnaird, John. "The Paradox of an American 'Identity,' "
        PR, 25 (1958), 380-405.

2707.1 Kirby, David Kirk. "Some Implications of the Technique of
        Foreshortening in the Writings of Henry James," DAI, 32
        (Johns Hopkins: 1972), 6982A.

2707.2 _____. "Two Modern Versions of the Quest," SoHR, 5
        (1971), 387-395.

2708   Kirk, Clara M. " 'The Brighter Side' of Fiction--According
        to Howells and James," CE, 24 (March, 1963), 463-464.
        "Both Howells and James felt that gloom in fiction was not
        in itself a literary virtue."

2708.1 _____. W. D. Howells and Art in His Time. New Bruns-
        wick, New Jersey: Rutgers U. P., 1965, passim.

2708.2 Kleinbard, Elaine Zablotny. "Citadels of Withdrawal: Psy-
        chological Themes in the Tales of Henry James," DAI, 33
        (Yale: 1972), 2381A.

2709   Knight, Grant C. "Henry James and the Direct Impression,"
        The Strenuous Age in American Literature. Chapel Hill:
        North Carolina U. P., 1954, pp. 101-122.

2710   _____. "The Triumph of Realism: Henry James," The
        Novel in English: 1931, N. Y.: R. R. Smith, 1931, pp. 276-287.

2711   Knights, L. C. "Henry James and the Trapped Spectator,"
        SoR, 4 (January, 1939), 600-15. Repr. in Explorations: Es-
        says in Criticism. London: Chatto & Windus, 1947; New
        York: Stewart, 1947, pp. 174-189.

2712   Knox, George. "James's Rhetoric of 'Quotes,' " CE, 17
        (February, 1956), 293-297.
        James's use of quotation marks for certain words and
        phrases is not an expression of purism, according to
        Knox, but a device by which he achieves various rhetori-
        cal effects.

2713   Koch, Dorothy A. Morality in the Criticism of Henry James.
        Diss. Pittsburgh: 1933.

2714   Kocmanova, Jessie. "The Revolt of the Workers in the Nov-
        els of Gissing, James, and Conrad," BrSE, 1 (1959), 119-
        139.
        Says these novelists show awareness of the "working-class
        revolt," but that they fail to provide realistic portrayals

of this revolt because of their isolation.

2715   Kolb, Harold H., Jr. "The Illusion of Life: American Realism as a Literary Form in the Writings of Mark Twain, Henry James, and W. D. Howells in the Mid-1880's," DA, 29 (Indiana: 1968), 3102A.

2716   _____. The Illusion of Life: American Realism as a Literary Form. Charlottesville: Virginia U. P., 1969, passim.
Emphasis is placed on Henry James.

2716.1 Koljević, Svetozar. "Pustolovina svesti u romanu Henrija Džejmza." Putevi, Banja Kuka, No. 2, 3 (1961), 174-188, 258-286.

2717   Komota, Junzo. "Henry James--On His Early Works," EDK, 7 (January, 1962), 203-217. (In Japanese)
James's experience of life seen merely as impression or imagination.

2718   Kono, Yotaro. "The Victorian Realists in the United States: Henry James and William Dean Howells," Maekawa Shunichi Kyōju Kanreki Kinen-Ronbunshū. [Essays and Studies in Commemoration of Professor Shunichi Maekawa's Sixty-First Birthday.] Tokyo: Eihosha, 1968, pp. 177-190.

2719   Kornfeld, Milton Herbert. "A Darker Freedom: The Villain in the Novels of Hawthorne, James, and Faulkner," DA, 31 (Brandeis: 1970), 2883A.

2720   Koskimies, Rafael. "Novelists' Thoughts about Their Art," NM, 57 (1956), 148-159.
Discusses James among others.

2721   Kossman, Rudolph R. Henry James: Dramatist. Diss. University of Leiden: 1969.

2722   Kraft, James Louis. "The Early Tales of Henry James: 1864-1880," DA, 28 (Fordham: 1967), 4179A-80A.

2723   _____. The Early Tales of Henry James. Carbondale: Southern Illinois U. P., 1969.

2724   Kraft, Quentin G. "The Central Problem of James's Fictional Thought: From The Scarlet Letter to Roderock Hudson," ELH, 36 (June, 1969), 416-439.
"... we may conclude ... that ... James, like Hawthorne ... could not be satisfied with the simple choice of either freedom or morality; he seems to have sensed that life achieves its full human potential only in a synthesis combining ... both the one and the other...."

2725 _____. "Life Against Death in Venice," Criticism, 7
(Summer, 1965), 217-223.

2726 _____. "The Question of Freedom in James's Fiction,"
CE, 26 (February, 1965), 372-381.
Concludes that freedom in James often seems passive and
is usually limited, but is, nevertheless, real.

2727 _____. "A Study of Point of View in Selected Short Stories of Henry James," DA, 24 (Duke: 1963), 2-36.

2728 Kramer, Hilton. "Henry James in the Nineties," NewL, 52
(May 26, 1969), 14-16.

2729 Krehayn, Joachim. Henry James und Seine Stellung Zu England Oder der Bürger Auf der Suche Nach der Bürgerlichkeit.
Diss. Berlin (H): 1951.

2730 Kretsch, Robert W. "Political Passion in Balzac and Henry
James," NCF, 14 (December, 1959), 265-270.
Comparison of James and Balzac.

2731 Kretzschmar, Helmut. Der Begriff des "Consciousness" Bei
Henry James. Diss. Hamburg: n. d.

2732 Krickel, Edward Francis, Jr. "Henry James and America,"
DA, 16 (Vanderbilt: 1956), 538.

2733 _____. Henry James and America. Ann Arbor: University of Michigan Microfilms, 1956, Pub. No. 15797.

2733.1 Krishan, Bal. "Henry James and the Nature of the Nouvelle," DAI, 33 (Utah: 1972), 1688A.

2734 Kriticheskie etiudy (Gauel's i Dzhems) [Critical Studies of
Howells and James]. Kolos'ia, 1890, No. 4, pp. 267-273.

2735 Krook, Dorothea. Elements of Tragedy. New Haven and
London: Yale U. P., 1969, passim.

2735.1 _____. "The Madness of Art: Further Reflections on
the Ambiguity of Henry James," HUSL, 1 (Spring, 1973),
25-38.

2736 _____. "The Method of the Later Works of Henry James,"
LonM, 1 (July, 1954), 52-70.

2737 _____. The Ordeal of Consciousness in Henry James.
New York: Cambridge U. P., 1962; Reissued, 1967.
An excellent study.

2737.1 _____. "Principles and Method in the Later Work of
Henry James," Interpretations of American Literature.

Charles Feidelson, Jr., and Paul Brodtkarb, Jr., eds. New York: Oxford U. P., 1959, pp. 262-279.

2738   Kubal, David L. "Henry James and the Supreme Value," ArQ, 22 (Summer, 1966), 101-114.
The supreme value in James's work, says the author, is the practical intellect, which understands the limits of human endeavor but can still function.

2739   Küsgen, Reinhardt. Die Kurzgeschichten Henry James. Diss. Erlangen: n. d.

2740   Labrie, Ernest R. "Henry James's Idea of Consciousness," AL, 39 (January, 1968), 517-529.
A very helpful analysis of "consciousness" in the aesthetic and moral concepts of James.

2741   _____. "The Morality of Consciousness in Henry James," CLQ, 9 (1971), 409-424.

2742   _____. "The Power of Consciousness in Henry James," ArQ, 29 (Summer, 1973), 101-114.
"In the conflicts portrayed by Henry James, it is usually superior consciousness which provides the edge...."

2743   _____. "The Role of Consciousness in the Fiction of Henry James, 1881-1899," DA, 28 (Toronto: 1966), 1438A.

2744   _____. "Sirens of Life and Art in Henry James," LakeUR, 2 (1969), 150-169.
"For the artist in James's world, there would seem to be the necessity to be attracted to the siren of life...."

2744.1 LaFrance, Marston, ed. Patterns of Commitment in American Literature. Published in association with Carleton University of Toronto U. P., 1967.

2745   Landry, Lowell. "Genres of Short Fiction in the Works of Henry James," DAI, 31 (Tulane: 1970), 4776A.

2746   Lang, Andrew. Old Friends, Essays in Epistolary Parody. London and New York: Longmans, Green & Co., 1893, pp. 25-29.
Lang's parodistic allusion to Daisy Miller.

2747   Lang, Hans-Joachim. "Henry James, 1955-1958: Ein Literaturbericht," JA, 4 (1959), 191-219.

2748   La Roche, Mazo de. "Reading Henry James Aloud," MTQ, 5 (Spring, 1943), 8.
An appreciative note.

2749   Lauber, John. "The Contrast: A Study in the Concept of

Innocence," ELN, 1 (September, 1963), 33-37.
Tyler in his comedy anticipates Henry James.

2750   Lauer, Kristin. "Backdoor to James: The Nature of Plot-
ting," MichA, 3 (Spring, 1971), 107-111.
The romantic and tragic plots work together as well as in
opposition in James's novels.

2751   Laurence, Dan H. "A Bibliographical Novitiate: In Search
of Henry James," PBSA, 52 (1958), 23-33.
Describes his experiences in the compilation of the Edel
and Laurence Bibliography.

2752   _____. "Henry James and Stevenson Discuss 'Vile' Tess,"
CLQ, 3 (May, 1953), 164-168.
The first printing of the full text of the disapproving remarks of James and Stevenson on Tess of the D'Uber-
villes.

2753   Lavender, Kenneth Ernest. "Henry James: From Drama to
Metaphor: 1896-1904," DAI, 33 (Santa Barbara, Calif.:
1972), 1733A.

2754   Leach, Anna. "Henry James: An Appreciation," Forum
(May, 1916), 551-564.

2755   Leary, Lewis Gaston, ed. "Absent Things in American Life,"
American Literary Essays. New York: Crowell, 1960, pp.
37-38.

2756   Leary, Lewis. "Henry James," Criticism: Some Major
American Writers. New York: Holt, Rinehart & Winston,
1971, pp. 165-166.

2757   Leavis, F. R. "The Appreciation of Henry James," Scrutiny,
14 (Spring, 1947), 229-237.

2758   _____. "Comment," in The Complex Fate by Marius Bewley. New York: Gordian Press, 1967, p. 144.

2759   _____. "Henry James," The Great Tradition. London:
1948, pp. 126-172; Garden City, New York: Doubleday, 1954;
London: Penguin Books, 1962, pp. 141-191, 275-295.

2760   _____. "Henry James Reprints," TLS (February 5, 1949),
96.

2761   _____. "Henry James and the Function of Criticism,"
Scrutiny, 15 (Spring, 1948), 98-104. Repr., in The Common
Pursuit. London: Chatto & Windus, 1952, 1962; Penguin,
1963, pp. 223-232.
Cf., Quentin Anderson. "Henry James and the New Jerusa-
lem," KR, 8 (1946), 515-566.

2762   . "A Note on 'James as Critic,' " in <u>Henry James:</u> <u>Selected Literary Criticism.</u> Morris Shapira, ed. New York: Horizon Press, 1964, pp. xiii-xxiii.

2763   . Introduction. <u>The Complex Fate</u> by Marius Bewley. New York: Gordian Press, 1967, vii-xv.

2764   . "Reply," NS&N, 37 (April 23, 1949), 406.
Cf., G. Hough. "Work of Henry James," NS&N, 37 (April 16, 1949), 382; "Rejoinder," NS&N, 37 (May 14, 1949), 503.

2765 Leavis, Q. D. "Henry James: The Stories," Scrutiny, 14 (Spring, 1947), 223-229.

2765.1   . "Henry James's Heiress: The Importance of Edith Wharton," Scrutiny, 7 (December, 1938), 261-276.

2766   . "The Institution of Henry James," Scrutiny, 15 (December, 1947), 68-74.

2767   . "Note on Literary Indebtedness: Dickens, George Eliot, Henry James," HudR, 8 (Fall, 1955), 423-428.
Three uses of the "Roman scene" in fiction to illustrate two types of indebtedness.

2767.1 Lebowitz, Naomi. "The Counterfeiters and the Epic Pretence," UTQ, 33 (1964), 291-310.

2768   . <u>Discussions of Henry James.</u> Boston: Heath, 1962.

2769   . "Henry James and the Moral Imperative of Relationship," DA, 24 (Washington University (St. Louis): 1963), 300.

2770   . <u>The Imagination of Loving: Henry James's Legacy to the Novel.</u> Detroit: Wayne State University, 1965.
An important study.

2771 LeClair, Robert C. <u>Three American Travelers in England: James Russell Lowell, Henry James, and Henry Adams.</u> Diss. Pennsylvania: 1944.

2772   . <u>Three American Travelers in England: James Russell Lowell, Henry James, and Henry Adams.</u> Philadelphia: Privately printed, 1945.

2773   . <u>Young Henry James, 1843-1870.</u> New York: Bookman Associates, 1955.

2774 Lee, B. C. "A Felicity Forever Gone: Henry James's Last Visit to America," BAASB, 5 (December, 1963), 31-42.

Lee, Vernon - See Paget, Violet.

2775   Leeming, David Adams. "Henry James and the French Nov-
        elists," DAI, 32 (New York University: 1970), 5234A.

2776   _____. "Henry James and George Sand," RLC, 43 (Janu-
        ary-March, 1969), 47-55.
             Concludes "that James used Sand ... as a means of clari-
             fying his own aesthetic and as a means of demonstrating
             that morality in art must be derived from within the world
             of art...."

2777   Leighton, Lawrence. "Armor Against Time," H&H, 7 (Ap-
        ril-May, 1934), 373-384.
             Asserts that James lived in Europe, not because he hated
             America, but because he was out of sympathy with his
             age.

2778   Leisy, Ernest. "Der Erzählstandpunkt in der neueren eng-
        lischen Prosa," GRM, 6 (1956), 40-51.

2779   Leisy, Ernest Erwin. American Literature: An Interpreta-
        tive Survey. New York: Thomas Y. Crowell, 1929, pp.
        193-200, passim.

2780   Leonard, Vivien R. "An Introductory Study of Imagery in
        the Prefaces to the New York Edition of the Novels and Tales
        of Henry James," DA, 27 (Columbia: 1966), 1826A-27A.

2781   Lerner, Daniel, and Oscar Cargill. "Henry James at the
        Grecian Urn," PMLA, 66 (June, 1951), 316-331.
             Says that the myth of the cultural "limitations" of James
             was created by Ford Madox Hueffer and Rebecca West
             (1913-1916) who were not sufficiently read in either James
             or the classics to generalize on James's "deficiencies."

2782   Lerner, Daniel. "The Influence of Turgenev on Henry
        James," SlavR, 20 (American Series I) (December, 1941),
        28-54.
             Provides extensive evidence of the influence.

2783   Leslie, Shane. "A Note on Henry James," Horizon (June,
        1943), 405-413.

2784   Levin, Harry. Refractions: Essays in Comparative Litera-
        ture. New York: Oxford U. P., 1966, pp. 153-155, 194-
        196, 210-211, 216-218, passim.

2785   _____. Symbolism and Fiction. Charlottesville: Vir-
        ginia University Press, 1956, pp. 12-13.

2786   Levine, George. "Madame Bovary and the Disappearing Au-
        thor," MFS, 9 (Summer, 1963), 103-119.

Shows the influence of Flaubert.

2787   Le Vot, André. "Henry James--Le critique comme romancier," Le Monde, 27 (March 7, 1970), iv.

2788   Levy, Edward Richard. "Henry James and the Pragmatic
Assumption: The Conditions of Perception," DA, 25 (Illinois: 1964), 1212.

2789   Levy, Leo B. "Criticism Chronicle: Hawthorne, Melville,
and James," SoR, n. s., 2 (Spring, 1966), 427-463.

2790   _____. "Henry James and the Jews," Commentary, 26
(September, 1958), 243-249.

2791   _____. Versions of Melodrama in the Novels, Tales, and
Plays of Henry James: 1865-1897. Diss. (Berkeley, Calif.:
1954).

2792   _____. Versions of Melodrama. Berkeley, California:
University of California Press, 1957.

2793   Lewis, J. H. "The Difficulties of Henry James," Poet Lore,
39 (Spring, 1928), 117-119.

2794   Lewis, Naomi. "In Spite of Lit," TC, 978 (August, 1958),
114-125.

2795   Lewis, R. W. B. The American Adam. Chicago: University of Chicago Press, 1955.

2796   _____. "Hawthorne and James: The Matter of the
Heart," Trials of the Word: Essays in American Literature
and Humanistic Tradition. New Haven, Conn.: Yale U. P.,
1965, pp. 77-96.

2797   _____. "Henry James: The Theater of Consciousness,"
Trials of the Word. New Haven, Conn.: Yale U. P., 1965,
pp. 112-128.

2798   _____. "The Histrionic Vision of Henry James," JA, 4
1959), 39-51.

2799   _____. "The Tactics of Sanctity: Hawthorne and James,"
Hawthorne Centenary Essays. Roy Harvey Peace, ed. Columbus: Ohio State U. P., 1964, pp. 271-295.

2800   Lewis, Wyndham. "Henry James: The Arch-Enemy of 'Low
Company,' " Men without Art. London: 1934, pp. 138-157;
New York: Russell & Russell, 1964.

2801   Lewisohn, Ludwig. "The Rise of the Novel," Expression in
America. London and New York: Harper & Bros., 1932,
pp. 233-272.

2802   Leyburn, Ellen Douglass. <u>Strange Alloy: The Relation of</u>
        <u>Comedy to Tragedy in the Fiction of Henry James</u>. Chapel
        Hill: North Carolina University Press, 1968.
            Contains wide coverage of James's work.

2803   _____. "Virginia Woolf's Judgment of Henry James,"
        MFS, 5 (Summer, 1959), 166-169.

2803.1 Libby, Marion Jean Vlastos. "Self-Affirmation: The Chal-
        lenge to Self-Sacrifice in the Fiction of Henry James," DAI,
        32 (Stanford: 1971), 1478A.

2804   Lid, R. W. "Ford Madox Ford and His Community of Let-
        ters," PrS, 35 (Summer, 1961), 132-136.
            The influence of James on Ford Madox Ford.

2805   _____. "Tietjens in Disguise," KR, 22 (Spring, 1960),
        265-276.
            The influence of James on Ford Madox Ford.

2806   Liddell, Robert. "Percy Lubbock," KR, 29 (September,
        1967), 493-511.
            Discusses Lubbock's work on James.

2807   _____. "The Novelist as Mystic: 'The Song of Henry
        James,' " <u>A Treatise on the Novel</u>. London: Jonathan Cape,
        1947, repr., 1963, pp. 87-89. Also in <u>Robert Liddell on</u>
        <u>the Novel</u>. Chicago: Chicago U. P., 1947, 1953, pp. 77-79.

2807.1 _____. "The Spoken Word Transcended: Jane Austen and
        Henry James," <u>Some Principles of Fiction</u>. London: Jona-
        than Cape, 1953, repr., 1961, pp. 81-85.

2807.2 _____. "Verbal Flux: Henry James and Bradshaw,"
        <u>Some Principles of Fiction</u>. London: Jonathan Cape, 1953,
        repr., 1961, pp. 85-86.

2808   "Light on Darkest James," Nation, 85 (October 17, 1907),
        343-344.
            Found James's works difficult to read, but felt they were
            for those readers willing to "follow faintly marked paths
            of thought."

2809   Liljegren, Sten Bodvar. <u>American and European in the Works</u>
        <u>of Henry James</u>. Lund: Lund Universities Arsskrift, 1920,
        pp. 17-35.

2810   Lincecum, J. B. "A Victorian Precursor of the Stream-of-
        Consciousness Novels: George Meredith," SCB, 31 (Winter,
        1971), 197-200.
            The influence of Meredith's "stream-of-consciousness"
            technique on James and others.

2811   Lind, Ilse Dusoir. "Inadequate Vulgarity of Henry James,"
        PMLA, 66 (December, 1951), 886-910.

2812   Lind, Sidney E. "Henry James," TLS (November 27, 1948),
        667.

2813   _____. "Some Comments on B. R. McElderry's 'The
        Uncollected Stories of Henry James,' " AL, 23 (March, 1951),
        130-131.
            Cf., B. R. McElderry, AL, 21 (November, 1949), 279-
            291.

2814   _____. The Supernatural Tales of Henry James: Con-
        flict and Fantasy. Diss. NYU: 1948.

2815   Linn, James Weber, and Houghton Wells Taylor. A Fore-
        word to Fiction. New York and London: Appleton-Century,
        1935, pp. 39-43, 113-115, passim.

2816   Linneman, William R. "Satires of American Realism, 1800-
        1900," AL, 34 (March, 1962), 80-93.
            The professional humorists criticized the realists, espe-
            cially Henry James and William Dean Howells.

2817   Littell, Philip. "Books and Things," NewRep, 3 (July 3,
        1915), 234.

2818   _____. "Books and Things," ["Landscape in Henry
        James,"] NewRep, 6 (March 18, 1916), 191.

2819   _____. "Henry James as Critic," NewRep, 1 (November
        21, 1914), 26-28.

2820   _____. "Henry James's Quality," NewRep, 6 (March 11,
        1916), 152-154. Also in Books and Things. New York:
        Harcourt, Brace & Howe, 1919, pp. 215-223.

2821   _____. "Henry James's Way of Writing English," New-
        Rep, 13 (December 29, 1917), 254.

2822   Livesay, J. F. B. "Henry James and His Critics," DR, 7
        (April, 1927), 80-88.

2823   Lochhead, Marion. "Stars and Striplings: American Youth
        in the Nineteenth Century," QR, 297 (April, 1959), 180-188.
            Discussion of James and others.

2824   Lodge, David. "Strether by the River," Language of Fic-
        tion: Essays in Criticism and Verbal Analysis of the Eng-
        lish Novel. London: Routledge & Kegan Paul; New York:
        Columbia U. P., 1966, pp. 189-213.
            James's use of language.

2825   _____. The Novelist at the Crossroads and Other Essays
on Fiction and Criticism. Ithaca, New York: Cornell U. P.,
1971, passim.

2826   Logan, M. "Henry James," Nation, 57 (November 30, 1893),
416-417.

2827   Lombardi, Olga. "Il Mito Dell'America," NA, 508, #2030
(February, 1970), 274-280.

2828   Lombardo, Agostino, ed. L'Arte del Romanzo. Milano:
C. M. Lerici editore, 1959.

2829   _____. "La critica letteraria di Henry James," Belfagor,
14 (January 31, 1959), 23-38.

2830   _____. "Henry James, The American e il mito di Otello,"
Friendship's Garland: Essays Presented to Mario Praz on
His Seventieth Birthday. Roma: Edizioni di Storia e Lettera-
tura, 1966, II, 107-142.

2831   _____. La Ricerca del Vero: Saggi Sulla Tradizione Letteraria Americana. Roma: Ed. di storia e letteratura, 1961.

2832   Long, E. Hudson. Introduction. Henry James: Short Novels.
New York: Dodd, Mead, 1961.

2833   Loomis, Charles Battell. "An Attempt to Translate Henry
James," Bookman (New York), 21 (July, 1905), 464-466.

2834   _____. "Books and Authors," Sun (New York), (May 17,
1905).

2835   Loomis, Edward W. "Three Notes on Plot," Spectrum, 4,
#2 (Spring-Summer, 1960), 94-99.
        Comment on James and others.

2836   Lord, Catherine. "Aesthetic Unity," JP, 58 (1961), 321-327.

2837   Loreis, Hector-Jan. "De Wortels van de Nieuwe Roman,"
["The Roots of the New Novel"], NVT, 19 (April, 1966), 379-
408.
        Sees the "new novel" as growing out of the impressionism
        latent in the works of James and Conrad.

2838   Lowe, Alma L. The Travel Writing of Henry James. Diss.
Rice, 1955.

2839   Lowell, James Russell. "Henry James: James's Tales and
Sketches," The Function of the Poet, and Other Essays. Al-
bert Mordell, ed. Port Washington, New York: Kennikat
Press, 1967, pp. 105-114.

2839.1 _____. New Letters of James Russell Lowell. M. A.
DeWolfe, ed. New York: Harper's, 1932, p. 242.
Lowell's letter to Henry James.

2840 Lowery, Bruce. "Henry James et Marcel Proust," RdP, 71
(April, 1964), 74-82.
Parallels in technique and style between the two writers.

2841 _____. "Marcel Proust et Henry James," IeD, 216 (May
15, 1965), 20-23.

2842 _____. Marcel Proust et Henry James: Une Confrontation. Paris: Plon, 1964.

2843 Lowndes, Marie Belloc. "Henry James in War Time,"
MTQ, 5 (Spring, 1943), 8.
"... the outburst of the World War made him [James]
feel so passionately pro-Ally in sympathy that he felt the
only thing he could do was to adopt British citizenship...."

2844 Lubbock, Percy. The Craft of Fiction. London: Jonathan
Cape, 1921; New York: Viking, 1921, passim.

2845 _____. "Henry James," QR, 226 (July, 1916), 60-74;
LivA, 290 (September 16, 1916), 733-741.
The later novels of James mostly.

2846 _____. "The Mind of an Artist," in The Question of Hen-
ry James. F. W. Dupee, ed. New York: Henry Holt &
Co., 1945, pp. 54-69.
Originally the Introduction to The Letters of Henry James.
Percy Lubbock, ed. New York: 1921, 1970.

2847 _____. Portrait of Edith Wharton. New York: Appleton-
Century, 1947; repr., Kraus, 1969, passim.
A last "picture" of James and his friend.

2848 Lucas, E. V. Reading, Writing and Remembering: A Literary Record. New York: Harper & Bros., 1932, pp. 183-
185, passim.

2848.1 Lucas, John, ed. Introduction. Literature and Politics in
the Nineteenth Century. London: Methuen, 1971, passim.

2849 _____. "Manliest of Cities: The Image of Rome in Henry James," SA, 11 (1965), 117-136.

2850 _____. Henry James's Revisions of His Short Stories.
Diss. Chicago: 1949.

2851 Lüdeke, Henry. "Henry James," NSR, 1 (May, 1952), 34-
42.
Originally a chapter from the author's Geschichte der

Amerikanischen Literature.

2852   Lutwack, Leonard. "Mixed and Uniform Prose Styles in the
        Novel," JAAC, 18 (March, 1960), 350-357; repr., in The
        Theory of the Novel. Philip Stevick, ed. New York: 1967,
        pp. 208-219.

2852.1 Luxford, Ansel Frank, Jr. "Henry James's Forgotten
        Phase: A Critical Analysis of the Late Fiction," DAI, 32
        (Virginia: 1971), 4618A.

2853   Lyde, Marilyn Jones. Edith Wharton: Convention and Mor-
        ality in the Work of a Novelist. Norman, Oklahoma: Okla-
        homa U. P., 1959, pp. 118-119, 164-165, passim.

2854   Lydenberg, John. "American Novelists in Search of a Lost
        World," RLV, 27, #4 (1961), 306-321.
                Loss, betrayal, vain searching constitute the chief themes
                in the novels of James and others.

2855   _____. "Comment on Mr. Spilka's Paper," L&P, 14,
        (1964). Cf., Mark Spilka. L&P, 13 (1963), 105-111.

2856   Lynd, Robert. "Henry James," Old and New Masters. New
        York: Scribner's, 1919, pp. 70-85.

2857   _____. "The Literary Life," and "The Return of Henry
        James," in Books and Writers. New York: Macmillan,
        1952, pp. 8-12, 113-117.

2858   Lynen, John F. The Design of the Present: Essays on Time
        and Form in American Literature. New Haven and London:
        Yale U. P., 1969, passim.
                Incidental but perceptive remarks about James.

2859   Lynn, Kenneth S. "Attack on an Idol," Reporter, 29 (No-
        vember 7, 1963), 52, 54.
                Essay-review of Maxwell Geismar's Henry James and the
                Jacobites. Boston: 1962.

2859.1 _____, ed. The Comic Tradition in America. New
        York: Doubleday, 1958, pp. 351-352.

2860   Lyra, Franciszek, ed. "Correspondence of Helena Modrze-
        jewska (Modjeska) to Henry James," KN, 19 (1972), 89-96.

2861   Lytle, Andrew. "Impressionism, the Ego, and the First
        Person," Daedalus, 92 (Spring, 1963), 281-296.
                Comments on James and others.

2862   M. L. R. "Mr. Henry James, Jr., and His Critics,"
        LitW, 13 (January 14, 1882), 10-11.

2863   _____. "Tales of Three Cities," LitW, 15 (September, 1884), 308-309.

2864   Macaulay, Robie. " 'Let Me Tell You About the Rich...,' " KR, 27 (Autumn, 1965), 645-671.

2865   MacCarthy, Desmond. Experience. Freeport, New York: Books for Libraries Press (first pub., 1935), repr., 1968.

2866   _____. "Henry James," Portraits. New York: Oxford U. P., 1955, pp. 149-169.
Henry James as a "conscious artist."

2867   _____. "Henry James," NSt, 15 (May, 1920), 162-164.

2868   _____. "Money, Birth and Henry James," NSt, 9 (July 21, 1917), 375-376.

2869   _____. "Mr. Henry James and His Public," Independent (London) 6 (May, 1905), 105-110.

2869.1   _____. "Otherness," Sun Times, (February 27, 1949), 3.

2870   _____. "The World of Henry James," LivA, 339 (January, 1931), 491-498; SatRL, 8 (1931), 81-83.

2871   _____. "Two Short Reminiscences: Henry James and Rupert Brooke," Memories: Forewords By Raymond Mortimer and Cyril Connolly. New York: Oxford U. P., 1953, pp. 202-204.

2872   Macdonald, Dwight, comp. Parodies: An Anthology from Chaucer to Beerbohm--and After. New York: Modern Library, 1960, pp. 149-150.
Comments on the apt parody of James by Max Beerbohm, "The Guerdon."

2873   Macdonell, Annie. "Henry James as Critic," Bookman (New York), 4 (September, 1896), 20-22; repr., 43 (April, 1916), 219-222.

2874   _____. "Living Critics: Henry James," Bookman (London), 10 (June, 1896), 76-77.

2875   [Machen, Arthur]. "Arthur Machen Pays Tribute," MTQ, 5, #4 (Spring, 1943), 8.

2876   MacKenzie, Compton. "Henry James," L&L, 39 (December, 1943), 147-155.

2877   _____. Literature in My Time. London: Rich & Cowan, 1933, pp. 35-38, passim.

2878 _____. "Memories of Henry James," Cw, 51 (January 13, 1950), 394-397.

2879 _____. "My Meetings with Henry James," MTQ, 6, #1-5 (Summer-Fall, 1944), 6-7.

2880 Mackenzie, Manfred. "Communities of Knowledge: Secret Society in Henry James," ELH, 39 (March, 1972), 147-168.

2881 _____. "Henry James: Serialist Early and Late," PQ, 41 (April, 1962), 492-499.

2882 _____. "Obscure Hurt in Henry James," SoR, 3 (1968), 107-131.
"... the central psychological experience delineated [in James] is shame...."

2883 MacNaughton, William R. "The First-Person Fiction of Henry James," DAI, 31 (Wisconsin: 1970), 1805A-06A.

2884 Macy, John. "Henry James," The Spirit of American Literature. New York: Doubleday, 1913, pp. 324-339.

2885 Maguire, C. E. "James and Dumas, fils," MD, 10 (May, 1967), 34-42.

2886 Maini, Darshan Singh. "The Style of Henry James," IJES, 9 (1968), 18-29.

2887 Maixner, Paul. "Henry James and the Question of Formal Unity," DA, 27 (Columbia: 1966), 1828A.

2888 _____. "James on D'Annunzio--A High Example of Exclusive Estheticism," Criticism, 13 (Summer, 1971), 291-311.
Says that James attention to D'Annunzio indicates "an important advance in his critical thought...."

2889 Major, John C. "Henry James, Daudet, and Oxford," N&Q, 13 (February, 1966), 69-70.

2889.1 Malin, Irving. "The Authoritarian Family in American Fiction," Mosaic, 4, iii (1971), 153-173.
Presents James's concepts of family in a context of Hawthorne and others, but finds the father-son relationship "less important [in James] than the portrayal of powerful or powerless women...."

2890 _____. New American Gothic. Carbondale: Southern Illinois U. P., 1962, pp. 8-9, 79.
"... Hawthorne and James ... view the castle as the outpost of authoritarianism; the voyage as the flight from such authoritarianism into new directions of strength and love...."

2891   Mallet, Charles. Anthony Hope and His Books. London:
        Hutchinson & Co., 1935, p. 230.
        The subtlety of James in thought and language.

2892   Manley, John Matthews, and Edith Rickert. "The Old Mas-
        ters: Howells and James." Contemporary American Litera-
        ture: Bibliographies and Study Outlines. New York: Har-
        court, Brace & Co., 1922, 1929, pp. 3-8.

2893   Mariani, Umberto. "L'esperienza italiana di Henry James,"
        SA, 6 (1960), 221-253.

2894   _____. "The Italian Experience of Henry James," NCF,
        19 (December, 1964), 237-254.
        Contrasts James's early romanticism about Italy and his
        later use of symbolic impressions to express the quest for
        beauty and life.

2894.1 Marković, Vida. Conflict and Controversy Between Henry
        James and H. G. Wells. Zbornik radova, Beograd, 1969,
        pp. 197-216.

2894.2 _____. "Henry Džems," Savremenik (December, 1960),
        528-541.

2895   Markow, Georges. "Charles Du Bos et Henry James," RLC,
        25 (October-December, 1951), 436-448.

2896   _____. Henry James et la France (1843-1876). Diss.
        Paris: 1952.

2897   _____. Henry James. John Cumming, trans. Preface by
        André Maurois. New York: Minerva Press, 1969; Paris:
        Editions Universitaires, 1958.

2898   Marks, Robert. James's Later Novels: An Interpretation.
        New York: William-Frederick Press, 1960.

2899   Marsden, Malcolm M. "Discriminating Sympathy: Charles
        Eliot Norton's Unique Gift," NEQ, 31 (December, 1958), 463-
        483.

2900   Marsh, Edward Clark. "James: Auto-Critic," Bookman (New
        York), 30 (October, 1909), 138-143.

2901   _____. "Number of People--Henry James," Harper, 178
        (May, 1939), 575-576.

2901.1 Marshall, James Morse. "Patterns of Freedom in Henry
        James's Later Novels," DA, 23 (Syracuse: 1962), 634.

2902   Marshall, Margaret. "Notes by the Way," Nation, 156 (Ap-
        ril 24, 1943), 599ff.

2902.1 Martin, Harold C., ed.   Foreword.   Style in Prose Fiction.
       (English Institute Essays) New York: Columbia U. P.
       1959, passim.

2903   Martin, Jay.   "Henry James: The Wings of the Artist,"
       Harvests of Change: American Literature, 1865-1914,"
       Englewood Cliffs, New Jersey: Prentice-Hall, 1967, pp.
       310-364, passim.

2904   Martin, Robert K.   "Henry James and the Harvard College
       Library," AL, 41 (March, 1969), 95-103.
              James's borrowing from the Harvard College Library
       shows his interest not only in fiction, drama, and poetry,
       but also in history and biography.

2905   _____.   "Henry James and Rodolphe Töpffer: A Note,"
       RomN, 10, #2 (Spring, 1969), 245-246.
              James's acquaintance with Rodolphe Töpffer.

2906   Martin, Terence.   "Adam Blair and Arthur Dimmesdale: A
       Lesson from the Master," AL, 34 (May, 1962), 274-279.
              James's comparison of The Scarlet Letter with John Lock-
       hart's Adam Blair.

2906.1 Martineau, Barbara.   "Portraits Are Murdered in the Short
       Fiction of Henry James," JNT, 2 (1972), 16-25.
              James's use of the portrait which is destroyed.

2907   Martineau, Stephen Francis.   "Opposition and Balance: A
       Characteristic of Structure in Hawthorne, Melville, and
       James," DA, 28 (Columbia: 1967), 1441A.

2908   Marx, Leo.   The Machine in the Garden: Technology and
       the Pastoral Ideal in America.   New York: Oxford U. P.,
       1964, pp. 239-240, 350-353, passim.

2909   Mary Francis, Sister.   "Henry James's Theory of Literary
       Invention," Greyfriar Lectures.   Second Series, 1959, p. 3-
       19.

2910   Masback, Frederic Joseph.   "The Child Character in Haw-
       thorne and James," DA, 21 (Syracuse: 1960), 338.
              James and Hawthorne both saw the child as "an innocent
       exposed to an evil world."

2911   Matheson, Owen.   "Portraits of the Artist and the Lady in
       the Shorter Fiction of Henry James," DR, 48 (Summer,
       1968), 222-230.

2912   Matthews, Brander.   "Henry James, Book Reviewer,"
       NYTBR, (June 12, 1921).

2913   Matthiessen, Francis Otto.   The Achievement of T. S. Eliot:

An Essay on the Nature of Poetry. 3rd ed. London and
New York: Oxford U. P., 1958, passim.
James's influence on T. S. Eliot.

2914 _____. American Renaissance: Art and Expression in the
Age of Emerson and Whitman. New York: Oxford U. P.,
1941, pp. 292-305, 351-368.

2915 _____. "Henry James," in Responsibilities of the Critic:
Essays and Reviews. New York: Oxford U. P., 1952, pp.
230-233.

2915.1 _____. Henry James the Major Phase. New York: Oxford U. P., 1944.
An important study covering James's later works.

2916 _____. "Henry James's Portrait of the Artist," PR, 11
(Winter, 1944), 71-87.
James's portraits of the writer in various short stories
"dramatize the issue which is still our issue, the relation
of the artist to society."

2917 _____. Introduction. American Novels and Stories.
New York: Oxford U. P., 1945; A. A. Knopf, 1956.

2918 _____, ed. Introduction. Henry James: Stories of
Writers and Artists. Norfolk, Connecticut: New Directions,
1944.

2919 _____. "James and the Plastic Arts," KR, 5, #4 (1943),
533-550.
The influence of painting and the visual arts on James.

2920 _____. "Not Quite the Real Thing," NewRep, 113 (December 3, 1945), 766-768.
Essay-review of The Short Stories of Henry James. Sel.
and ed., by Clifton Fadiman. New York: 1945.

2920 Maugham, W. Somerset. "The Art of Fiction," The Art of
Fiction: An Introduction to Ten Novels and Their Authors.
Garden City, New York: Doubleday & Co., 1955, pp. 13-31,
passim.

2921 _____. ["Henry James"] Introduction. Tellers of Tales.
New York: Doubleday, 1939.

2922 _____. "Maugham on Henry James," SatR, 37 (December
4, 1954), 18.

2923 _____. "Some Novelists I Have Known," The Vagrant
Mood. London: Heinemann, 1952, pp. 197-209.

2924 Maurois, André. "Ecrivains américains," RdP, 54 (April,

1947), 9-24.
  Says that James will outlive many other writers of his
  day.

2925 _____. The Miracle of America. Trans. Denver and
  Jane Lindley. London and New York: Harper & Row, 1944,
  p. 346.
    Believes that James remained more American than he him-
    self suspected.

2926 _____. "Un puritain hérésiarque, Henry James," NL,
  1703 (April 21, 1960), 1, 4.

2927 Maves, Carl Edwin. "Sensuous Pessimism: Italy in the
  Work of Henry James," DAI, 30 (Stanford: 1969), 5450A-
  51A.

2928 _____. Sensuous Pessimism: Italy in the Work of Henry
  James. Bloomington: Indiana U. P. , 1973.

2929 Maxse, Mary. "Henry James: A Master of His Art,"
  NatlR (London), 113 (December, 1939), 773-778.

2929.1 Maxwell, J. C. "Henry James's 'Poor Wantons': An Unnoticed Version," NCF, 19 (December, 1964), 301-302.

2930 Mayer, Charles W. "Percy Lubbock: Disciple of Henry
  James," DA 29 (Michigan: 1968), 904A.

2930.1 Mayne, Ethel Coburn, LittleR, 5 (August, 1918), 2; repr.,
  The Little Review Anthology. New York: 1933, pp. 222-
  225.

2931 Mayoux, Jean-Jacques. "L'homme sans présent," LetN, 2
  (October, 1954), 547-558.
    On James's personality and art.

2931.1 Mays, Milton A. "Down-Town with Henry James," TSLL,
  14 (Spring, 1972), 107-122.

2932 _____. "Henry James, or, The Beast in the Palace of
  Art," AL, 39 (January, 1968), 467-487.
    Asserts that the "central theme of James's fiction is a
    failure to have 'lived'...."

2932.1 _____. "Henry James in Seattle," PacnNQ, 59 (October,
  1968), 186-189.

2933 _____. "Uptown and Downtown in Henry James's America: Sexuality and the Business-Society," DA, 26 (Minnesota: 1965), 6046.
    Emphasizes the social criticism in certain of James's
    novels in which James shows the difference between male

and female culture with the consequent blurring of woman's role.

2934   McCarthy, Harold T. _The Aesthetic of Henry James_. Diss. Harvard: 1950.

2935   _____. _Henry James: The Creative Process_. London: W. H. Allen, 1959; New York: Yoseloff, 1958.
An excellent study of James's methods and theories as indicated in many of his works.

2936   _____. "Henry James and the American Aristocracy," ALR, 4 (Winter, 1971), 61-71.
In some of James's characters finds similar characteristics--"highly puritan standards, a dread of sex, a distrust of foreigners ... and an assumed title to superiority and leadership."

2937   _____. "Henry James and 'The Personal Equation,' " CE, 17 (February, 1956), 272-278.
James believed that the true artist in prose applied "the personal equation" to his writing; therefore, every novelist of integrity would develop "a highly personal style."

2938   McCormick, John O. "The Rough and Lurid Vision: Henry James, Graham Greene and the International Theme," JA, 2 (1957), 158-167.

2939   McCullough, Bruce Welker. "The Novelist in Search of Perfection: Henry James," _Representative English Novelists: Defoe to Conrad_. New York and London: Harper & Bros., 1946, pp. 274-302.

2940   McDonald, James. "The Novels of John Knowles," ArQ, 23 (Winter, 1967), 335-342.
Comparison of Knowles' _Morning in Antibes_ with James's work in the confrontation of the innocent American with the complex and corrupt European culture.

2941   McDonald, Walter. "The Inconsistencies in Henry James's Aesthetics," TSLL, 10 (Winter, 1969), 585-597.

2942   McDougal, Edward D. "Henry James," TLS, (November 13, 1969), 1313.

2943   McDowell, Margaret B. "Edith Wharton's Ghost Stories," Criticism, 12 (Spring, 1970), 133-152.
States that Mrs. Wharton believed that "the effects which the writer should strive for in the supernatural tale resemble those of James...."

2944   McElderry, Bruce R., Jr. "Gertrude Atherton and Henry James," CLQ, 3 (November, 1954), 269-272.

2945   _____. "Hamlin Garland and Henry James," AL, 23 (January, 1952), 433-446.

2946   _____. Henry James. New York: Twayne's United States Authors Series, No. 79. New York: 1965.
A very helpful study.

2947   _____. "Henry James and the Whole Family," [Twelve popular writers collaborating on a serial for Harper's Bazaar], PacS, 4, #3 (Summer, 1950), 352-360.

2947.1   _____. "James' 'Woman of Genius,'" TLS (July 22, 1955), 413.
Requests the aid of readers in identifying the allusion. Cf., F. W. Bradbrook and Malcolm Elwin, ib., (July 29, 1955), 429; Hester Thackeray Fuller, ib., (August 5, 1955), 445; Percy Lubbock and Frank W. Bradbrook, ib., (August 12, 1955), 461; Susanne H. Nobbe, ib., (August 26, 1955), 493.

2948   _____. "The Uncollected Stories of Henry James," AL, 21 (November, 1949), 279-291.
An attempt to provide a concise statement of the whole of James's shorter fiction and to give brief evaluations of those stories excluded from the chief collected editions. Cf., Sidney E. Lind, AL, 23 (1951), 130-131.

2948.1 McElrath, J. R. "Thoreau and James: Coincidence in Angles of Vision?" ATQ, 11 (1971), 14-15.

2948.2 McFarlane, I. D. "A Literary Friendship: Henry James and Paul Bourget," CamJ, 4 (December, 1950), 144-161.

2949   McGill, Anna Blanche. "Henry James, Artist," Poet Lore, 16 (Winter, 1905), 90-96.

2950   McGill, V. J. "Henry James: Master Detective," Bookman (New York), 72 (November, 1930), 251-256.

2951   McGinty, Sister Mary C. "The Jamesian Parenthesis: Elements of Suspension in the Narrative Sentences of Henry James's Late Style," DA, 24 (Catholic U.: 1964), 4193.
States that James's sentences show every grade of variation.

2952   McIntyre, Clara F. "The Later Manner of Henry James," PMLA 27, n. s., 20 (1912), 354-371.
Surveys the early objections to the later style.

2953   McKenzie, Terence J. An Analysis of Henry James's Interpretation and Treatment of English Character, Culture, and Morals. Diss. Virginia: n. d.

2954   McLuhan, H. M.   "The Southern Quality," Southern Vanguard.
        Allen Tate, ed.   New York: Prentice-Hall, 1947, pp. 100-
        121.

2954.1 McMahon, Helen.   Criticism of Fiction: A Study of Trends
        in the Atlantic Monthly, 1857-1898.   New York: Bookman
        Associates, 1952, pp. 34-35, 100-101, passim.
        Provides an excellent survey of critical opinions concern-
        ing James's work from the then prominent critics.

2955   McManis, Jo Agnew.   "Edith Wharton's Hymns to Respect-
        ability," SoR, 7 (Fall, 1971), 986-993.
        Wharton's indebtedness to James.

2956   McNeir, Waldo, and Leo B. Levy, eds.   Studies in Ameri-
        can Literature.   Baton Rouge: Louisiana State U., 1960,
        passim.
        Contains essays on James and others.

2956.1 Melchiori, Barbara.   "Feelings about Aspects: Henry James
        on Pierre Loti," SA, 15 (1969), 169-199.

2957   _____.   "The Taste of Henry James," SA, 3 (1957), 171-
        187.

2958   Melchiori, Giorgio.   "Aspetti del simbolismo di Henry
        James," IlSim, 59 (1966), 169-190.

2959   _____.   "Aspetti del Simbolismo di Henry James," in
        Il Simbolismo nella Letteratura Nord-Americana: Atti del
        Symposium Tenuto a Firenze 27-29 Novembre, 1964.   Fi-
        renze: La Nuova Italia, 1965, pp. 169-190.

2960   _____.   "Browning e Henry James," in Friendship's Gar-
        land.   Roma: Edizioni di Storia e Letteratura, 1966, II,
        143-180.

2961   _____.   "Il dejeuner sur l'herbe di Henry James," SA,
        10 (1964), 201-228.
        James and the fine arts.

2961.1 _____.   "Due Manieristi: Henry James e G. M. Hopkins,"
        Lo Spettatore Italiano, 6 (January, 1953), 20-27.

2962   _____.   "The English Novelist and the American Tradi-
        tion (1955)," B. M. Arnett, tr.   SR, 68 (July, 1960), 502-
        515.
        The influence of James on L. P. Hartley's view of sin.

2963   _____.   "Henry James e Tennyson," Arte e Storia: Studi
        in Onore di Leonello Vincenti.   Torino: Giappichelli, 1965,
        pp. 339-360.

2964   _____. "Locksley Hall Revisited: Tennyson and Henry James," REL, 6 (October, 1965), 9-25.

2965   _____. "Two Mannerists: James and Hopkins," The Tightrope Walkers: Studies of Mannerism in Modern English Literature. London: Routledge & Kegan Paul, 1956, pp. 13-33, passim.

2966   _____. "Un Personaggio Di Henry James," SA, 2 (1956), 179-194.

2967   _____. "Shakespeare and Henry James," ShN, 17 (1967), 56.

2968   Mellow, James R. "James as Journalistic Critic," Cw, 65 (February 1, 1957), 469-470.

2968.1   _____. "Edith Wharton and Henry James," Cw, 82 (June 18, 1965), 417-418.
            Their friendship.

2969   Mellquist, Jerome. "From Henry James to Paul Rosenfeld," SR, 54 (October, 1946), 691-698.

2970   Meltzer, Sharon Bittenson. "The Fiction of Henry James, 1895-1901," DAI, 32 (Yale: 1970), 445A.

2971   Mencken, Henry Louis. The American Language: An Inquiry into the Development of English in the United States. 4th ed. New York: Alfred A. Knopf, 1963, passim.

2972   _____. A Book of Prefaces. New York: Alfred A. Knopf, 1917, 1922, passim.
            Incidental but very pertinent remarks as to James.

2973   _____. "Henry James," Mencken Chrestomathy. New York: Knopf, 1949, pp. 500-501.

2974   Mendilow, A. A. "The Position of the Present in Fiction: The Time Locus of the Reader," Time and the Novel. London: Peter Nevill, Ltd., 1952, passim.

2974.1 Menikoff, Barry. "Punctuation and Point of View in the Late Style of Henry James," Style, 4 (Winter, 1970), 29-47.
            Demonstrates that after 1900 James's punctuation "facilitate[s] his method of interior narration," with dashes and colons "functioning as loose ligatures that connect disaparate statements."

2975   _____. "Style and Point of View in the Tales of Henry James," DA, 28 (Wisconsin: 1966), 686A-87A.

2976   _____. "The Subjective Pronoun in the Late Style of

Henry James," ES, 52 (October, 1971), 436-441.

2977   Mews, Siegfried. "German Reception of American Writers
       in the Late Nineteenth Century," SAB, 34 (March, 1969),
       7-9.
           James was among the American writers who enjoyed great
       popularity in Germany in the last half of the 19th century.

2978   Michaud, Régis. "Henry James...," The American Novel
       Today: A Social and Psychological Study.   Boston: Little
       Brown & Co., 1928, pp. 47-54.
           Gives the man-without-a-country psychological interpreta-
       tion of James's work.

2979   _____. Mystiques et Réalistes Anglo-Saxon d'Emerson à
       Bernard Shaw.   Paris: 1918.

2979.1 _____. Le Roman Américain d'aujourd'hui.   Paris:
       1926.

2980   _____. "Un Splendide Exile: Henry James," Panorama
       de la Littérature Américaine Contemporaine.   Paris: Kra,
       1928, pp. 115-120.

2980.1 _____. "William et Henry James," RdF, (September,
       1922), 141-159.

2981   Miller, J. Hillis. "Some Implications of Form in Victorian
       Fiction," CLS, 3, #2 (1966), 109-118.

2982   Miller, James Edwin, ed. "The Art of Fiction," Myth and
       Method.   Lincoln: Nebraska U. P., 1960, pp. 3-27.

2983   _____. "Henry James: A Theory of Fiction," PrS, 45
       (1971), 330-356.

2984   _____, ed. Introduction. Theory of Fiction: Henry
       James.   Lincoln, Nebraska: Nebraska U. P., 1972.

2985   _____. Quests Surd and Absurd: Essays in American
       Literature.   Chicago and London: Chicago U. P., 1967, pp.
       55-56.
           "James sent his Americans across the sea to Europe where,
       in the shadows of the past, they took on moral configura-
       tions that appeared distinguishable and distinctive...."

2986   Miller, Perry. Nature's Nation.   Cambridge, Mass.: The
       Belknap Press of Harvard U. P., 1967, pp. 262-264, 274-
       275, passim.

2987   Miller, Raymond A., Jr.   Representative Tragic Heroines in
       the Work of Brown, Hawthorne, Howells, James, and Dreiser.
       Diss. Wisconsin: 1957. DA, 17 (Wisconsin: 1957), 2612-13.

2988   Miller, Warren. "Henry James in Hollywood," M&M, 2 (December, 1949), 81-83.

2989   Millett, Fred B. "Henry James and the Undergraduate," CE, 14 (1952), 167-168.
         Cf., Maurice Beebe, "Henry James and the Sophomore," CE, 14 (1952), 20-22.

2990   Millgate, Michael. American Social Fiction: James to Cozzens. Edinburgh: Oliver and Boyd; New York: Barnes & Noble, 1965, passim.
         Thinks that James never "solved the contradiction between his need to write about the business man and his inability to do so."

2991   _____. "Henry James and the Business Hero," American Social Fiction. Edinburgh: Oliver and Boyd, 1964, pp. 1-17.

2992   _____. "The Novelist and the Businessman: Henry James, Edith Wharton, Frank Norris," SA, 5 (1959), 161-189.

2993   Milman, Lena. "A Few Notes upon Mr. James," YB, 7 (October, 1895), 71-83.
         Appreciative criticism.

2993.1 Milton, Dorothy. The Unquiet Hearthside: A Study of the Parent-Child Relationship in the Fiction of Henry James. Diss. Chicago: 1968.

2994   Miner, Earl R. "Henry James's Metaphysical Romances," NCF, 9 (June, 1954), 1-21.
         James's stories with "marked qualities of moral intensity and psychological insight in the context of supernaturalism" can best be characterized as "metaphysical."

2995   Minter, Elsie Gray. "The Image in the Mirror: Henry James and the French Realists," DA, 24 (North Carolina: 1964), 3340-41.
         Treats knowledge of material, selection, and point of view.

2996   Mintzlaff, Dorothy. The Theme of the Unlived Life in the Fiction of Henry James. Diss. Michigan: n. d.

2996.1 Miroiu, Mihai. "The Makers of the Stream of Consciousness Novel," AnUBLG, 19 (1970), 137-149.

2997   Mix, Katherine Lyon. A Study in Yellow: The Yellow Book and Its Contributors. Lawrence: Kansas U. P., 1960, passim.

2998   Mizener, Arthur. The Sense of Life in the Modern Novel. Boston: Houghton Mifflin. The Riverside Press, Cambridge: 1964, passim.

2999   Mlikotin, Anthony Matthew. "The International Theme in the
        Novels of Turgenev and Henry James," DA, 22 (Indiana:
        1961), 873-874.

3000   _____. Genre of the "International Novel" in the Works of
        Turgenev and Henry James: A Critical Study. Los Angeles:
        University of Southern California Press, 1971.

3001   "The Modern Henry James," Newsweek, 26 (October 22, 1945),
        106-110.
            Discusses the James revival.

3001.1 Moeller, Charles. "Henry James et l'athéisme mondain,"
        RGB, (April, 1953), 907-923.

3002   Monroe, E. N. "Other Books," America, 95 (May 19, 1956),
        207.

3003   Monroe, N. Elizabeth. The Novel and Society: A Critical
        Study of the Modern Novel. Chapel Hill: North Carolina U.
        P., 1941, passim.

3004   Monteiro, George. "Addendum to Edel and Laurence: Henry
        James in Portuguese," PBSA, 65 (3rd Qt., 1971), 302-304.
            A list of James's works published in Portuguese will pro-
            vide a rudimentary basis for the study of James in a for-
            eign language.

3005   _____. "A Contemporary View of Henry James and Oscar
        Wilde, 1882," AL, 35 (January, 1964), 528-530.
            Harriet Loring, a socially prominent lady of Washington,
            described James and Wilde when they visited that city in
            1882.

3005.1 _____. "Hawthorne, James, and the Destructive Self,"
        TSLL, 4 (1962), 58-71.

3006   _____. "Henry James and the American Academy of Arts
        and Letters," NEQ, 36 (March, 1963), 82-84.
            Henry James was among those elected to the American
            Academy in January, 1905.

3007   _____. "Henry James and His Reviewers: Some Identifi-
        cations," PBSA, 63 (October, 1969), 300-304.

3008   _____. "Henry James and John Hay," BBr, 19 (1963),
        69-88.
            A literary and social relationship.

3009   _____. "Henry James and John Hay: A Literary and So-
        cial Relationship," DA, 28 (Brown: 1964), 1824A.

3010   _____. Henry James and John Hay: The Record of a

Friendship. Providence, Rhode Island: Brown University
Press, 1965.
   Brings together and supplements material published in a
   series of short articles.

3011   _____. "The New York Tribune on Henry James, 1881-
         1882," BNYPL, 67 (February, 1963), 71-81.

3012   Mooney, Stephen L. "James, Keats, and the Religion of
         Consciousness," MLQ, 22 (December, 1961), 399-401.

3012.1 Moore, George. Confessions of a Young Man. London:
         W. Heinemann, 1928.
            George Moore's estimate of Henry James.

3013   Moore, Marianne. "Henry James as a Characteristic Amer-
         ican," H&H, 7 (April-May, 1934), 363-372. Also in her
         Predilections. New York: Viking Press, 1955, pp. 21-31;
         Literary Opinion in America. Morton D. Zabel, ed. New
         York: 1937, pp. 225-233.

3014   Moore, Rayburn S. "The Full Light of Higher Criticism:
         Edel's Biography and Other Recent Studies of Henry James,"
         SAQ, 63 (Winter, 1964), 104-114.
            Shows the revival of interest in James.

3015   Mordell, Albert, ed. Discovery of Genius: William Dean
         Howells and Henry James. New York: Twayne, 1961.

3016   Morgan, Alice. "Henry James: Money and Morality," TSLL,
         12 (1970), 75-92.
            Shows the "apparently necessary connection between renunci-
            ation of love, passion, or marriage, and certain financial
            attitudes."

3017   Morgan, Louise. "The Weakness of Henry James," Outlook
         (London), 57 (February 6, 1926), 89.

3018   Morley, Robert. "Meetings with Some Men of Letters," QQ,
         39 (February, 1932), 67-71.

3019   Morris, Lloyd. "Melancholy of the Masters," Postscript to
         Yesterday. New York: 1947, 89-106.

3020   Morris, Wright. "Use of the Past: Henry James," The Ter-
         ritory Ahead. New York: Harcourt, Brace & Co., 1957,
         pp. 93-112, 187-214.

3021   Morrison, Peggy Ann R. "The Connoisseur in the Novels of
         Henry James," DAI, 34 (Brandeis: 1972), 3660A.

3021.1 Morrison, Sister Kristin. "James's and Lubbock's Differing
         Points of View," NCF, 16 (December, 1961), 245-255.

3021.2 Morse, John T., Jr. <u>Life and Letters of Oliver Wendell</u>
<u>Holmes.</u> Boston and New York: Houghton Mifflin, 1896,
I, 243.
Holmes listed Henry James as a member of the Saturday
Club.

3022   Morse, Samuel French. <u>Wallace Stevens</u>. New York: Pe-
gasus, 1970.
Shows that Stevens closely resembled James in approach-
ing life as a means to art.

3023   Mortimer, Raymond. "Henry James," Horizon, 7 (May,
1943), 314-329.

3024   Moss, Leonard Jerome. "Transitional Devices in Henry
James," CEA, 22 (February, 1960), 1, 6, 12.

3025   Mossman, Robert Edward. "An Analytical Index of the Literary and Art Criticism by Henry James," DA, 27 (Pittsburgh: 1966), 1790A.
Provides a most useful Index to James's prose: reviews,
critical essays, prefaces, lectures, notebooks, and letters.

3026   "The Most Brilliant Light Yet Thrown on the Great Henry
James Question," CurOp, 63 (December, 1917), 407-408.
James's style.

3027   Moult, Thomas. "Dedicated to Art," EngR, 31 (August,
1920), 183-186.

3028   Mowat, Robert Balmain. "On Both Sides of the Atlantic,"
<u>Americans in England</u>. New York: Houghton Mifflin, 1935,
pp. 202-226.

3029   Mowbray, J. P. "The Apotheosis of Henry James," Critic,
41 (November, 1902), 409-414.

3030   Mull, Donald Locke. "Sublime Economy: Money as a Symbolic Center in Henry James," DA, 27 (Yale: 1966), 2537A.
States that James used money to symbolize the power and
commercial limits put upon the imagination.

3030.1 _____ . <u>Henry James's "Sublime Economy": Money as</u>
<u>Symbolic Center in the Fiction.</u> Middletown, Conn.: Wesley-
an U. P., 1973.

3031   Munford, Howard M. "Der geteilte Strom: Zur Kunstauf-
fassung von Henry James," TuK, 15 (1967), 12-21.

3032   Munzar, Jiri. "Graham Greene, Essayist," PP, 14, #1
(1971), 30-38.
Comparison with James's view of good and evil.

3033   Murakami, Fujio. "The Question of the Aesthete in Henry
        James," JimK, 11 (1960), 104-114.

3034   Murphy, Edward F. Henry James and Katherine Anne Porter:
        Endless Relations. Diss. Ottawa: 1959.

3035   Murray, Donald M. "The Balcony, the Pond, and the Lit-
        erary Traveler," AntiochR, 25 (Summer, 1965), 333-336.
            "In the James novel, places are ... firmly fixed as sym-
        bols in the substance of action and theme."

3036   _____. The Critical Reception of Henry James in English
        Periodicals, 1875-1916. Diss. New York University: 1951.

3037   _____. "Henry James and the English Reviewers, 1882-
        1890," AL, 24 (March, 1952), 1-20.
            Shows that the reviewers steadily cooled toward James be-
        cause of a preference for romance rather than realism,
        and a "surprisingly consistent objection to James's works on
        moral grounds," as well as the "strictly national preju-
        dice against the upstart American."

3038   _____. "Henry James in the Advanced Composition
        Course," CE, 25 (October, 1963), 26-30.
            Describes his successful use of "The Art of Fiction," and
        other James criticism as guides for students writing fic-
        tion."

3039   _____. "James and Whistler at the Grosvenor Gallery,"
        AQ, 4 (Spring, 1952), 49-65.
            Although James and Whistler "both took new and similar
        directions in the eighties, there was no meeting of minds
        between them. James the critic was too conservative on
        the subject of painting to make this possible."

3040   Mustanoja, Tauno F. "W. Somerset Maugham Portrays Hen-
        ry James," NM, 52 (April, 1951), 99-103.

3041   Nadal, Ehrman Syme. "Personal Recollections of Henry
        James," Scribner's 68 (July, 1920), 89-97.

3042   Nagel, Paul C. This Sacred Trust: American Nationality,
        1798-1898. New York: Oxford U. P., 1971, pp. 214-215,
        passim.
            Traces James's attitude and feelings about America.

3043   Narkevich, A. Iu. Genri Dzhems (25 let so dnia smerti).
        (Bibliograficheskaia spravka) [Henry James (25th anniver-
        sary of his death). (Bibliographic note)]. Literaturnoe
        obozrenie, 1941, No. 4, p. 79.

3044   Nassauer, Gertrud. Die Frauengestalten Bei Henry James
        Als Spiegel Seiner Weltanschauung. Diss. Munich: ca. 1933.

3045   Neff, John C. "Henry James the Reporter," NMQ, 8 (February, 1938), 9-14.
        A discussion of the relation of James's style to modern reporting.

3046   Neider, Charles. Introduction. Short Novels of the Masters. New York: Rinehart, 1948, pp. 11-17.

3047   Neifer, Leo J. "Durrell's Method and Purpose of Art," WisSL, 3 (1966), 99-103.
        Compares Lawrence Durrell and Henry James.

3048   Nettels, Elsa. "The Drama of Consciousness: The Role of the Central Intelligence in Selected Novels of Henry James," DA, 21 (Wisconsin: 1960), 615-616.

3048.1   _____. "James and Conrad on the Art of Fiction," TSLL, 14 (Fall, 1972), 529-543.
        A study of the letters and essays of the two writers indicates their agreement on essential points.

3049   Nevius, Blake. Edith Wharton: A Study of Her Fiction. Berkeley and Los Angeles: California U. P., 1953, pp. 27-28, 30-36, 54-55. passim.

3050   Newbolt, Henry. The Later Life and Letters of Sir Henry Newbolt. Margaret Newbolt, ed. London: Faber & Faber, 1942, p. 270.
        Derogatory criticism.

3051   Newburgh, M. L. H. "Mr. Henry James, Jr., and His Critics," LitW, 13 (January 14, 1882), 10-11.

3051.1 Newcomer, Alphonso Gerald. "Henry James," American Literature. Chicago: Scott, Foresman, 1901, 1908, pp. 298-299.
        "... Americans ... have often resented his [James's] portrayals as inaccurate or at least as unfair to the truest types of American manhood and womanhood...."

3052   Newlin, Paul A. "The Uncanny in the Supernatural Short Fiction of Poe, Hawthorne, and James," DA, 28 (U.C.L.A.: 1967), 5064A-65A.

3053   Newman, Charles. "The Lesson of the Master: Henry James and James Baldwin," YR, 56 (1967), 45-59.

3054   Niall, Brenda. "Prufrock in Brownstone: Edith Wharton's The Age of Innocence," SoRA, 4, #3 (1971), 203-214.

3055   Nicholas, Charles Andrew. "Henry James's Personal Theory of Art," DAI, 32 (Michigan: 1971), 1522A.

3056   Niemi, Pearl C. "The Art of Crime and Punishment," MFS,
        9 (Winter, 1963-1964), 291-313.
            Parallels to be found in James.

3057   Niess, Robert J. "Henry James and Emil Zola: A Parallel,"
        RLC, 30 (January-March, 1956), 93-98.

3058   Noble, David W. "The Realists: Mark Twain, William Dean
        Howells, Henry James," The Eternal Adam and the New
        World Garden: The Central Myth in the American Novel
        Since 1830. New York: George Braziller, 1968, pp. 49-98.

3059   Noel, France. Henry James, Peintre de la Femme. Diss.
        Paris: 1942.

3059.1 _____. Henry James, Peintre de la Femme. Alençon:
        Poulet-Malassis, 1942.

3060   Nonaka, Ryō. "On Consciousness in Henry James's Work,"
        EngL (Waseda), 20 (January, 1962), 5-19.
            Discusses narrative point of view.

3061   Norman, Sylva (Mrs. Edmund C. Blunden). "Before the Dis-
        solution," FnR, n. s., 161 (May, 1947), 380-382.

3062   _____, ed. Introduction. Contemporary Essays. Lon-
        don: Elkin Mathews & Marrot, 1933.

3063   Norton, Charles Eliot. Letters of Charles Eliot Norton.
        Boston and New York: Houghton Mifflin, 1913, passim.

3064   "The Novels of Henry James," LivA, 262 (September 11,
        1909), 691-696; LivA, 310 (July 30, 1921), 267-271.

3065   Nowell-Smith, Simon. "First Editions, English and Ameri-
        can," Library, 20 (March, 1966), 68.
            Examples of the publication of James's works indicate that
            there is often no clear-cut priority between English and
            American editions.

3066   _____, ed. "The Legend," The Legend of the Master:
        Henry James. London: Constable; New York: Scribner's,
        1948, pp. xxi-xlvi.

3067   _____. "Mr. H--," TLS (December 28, 1946), 643.
            Illustrates the improbability of identification of "L'Ameri-
            cain H--" in Flaubert's letter of July 3, 1874, with Henry
            James.

3068   _____. "Without Benefit of Bibliography: Some Notes on
        Henry James," BC, 7 (Spring, 1958), 64-67.

3069   Nuhn, Ferner. "The Enchanted Kingdom of Henry James,"

The Wind Blew from the East: A Study in the Orientation of American Culture. New York: Harper, 1942, pp. 87-163.

3070 _____. "Henry Adams and the Hand of the Fathers," Literature in America. Philip Rahv, ed. Cleveland and New York: World Pub. Co. , 1967, pp. 247-250.
Compares Henry James and Henry Adams.

3071 Nyren, Dorothy, ed. "Henry James," A Library of Literary Criticism: Modern American Literature. New York: Ungar, 1960, pp. 248-254.

3072 O'Brien, E. J. The Advance of the American Short Story. New York: 1923.
Influences upon James.

3072.1 O'Brien, Ellen Tremper. Henry James and Aestheticism. Diss. Harvard: 1969.

3073 O'Connor, Frank. [Pseud. , for Michael O'Donovan] "Transition: Henry James," The Mirror in the Roadway: A Study of the Modern Novel. New York: Knopf, 1956, repr. , 1964, pp. 223-235, passim.

3074 O'Connor, William Van. An Age of Criticism, 1900-1950. Chicago: Regnery, 1952, pp. 58-63, passim.

3075 _____. "The Novel of Experience," and "The Narrator as Distorting Mirror," The Grotesque: An American Genre, and Other Essays. Carbondale: So. Illinois U. P. , 1916, 1962, pp. 37-46, 78-91, passim.

3076 O'Faolain, Sean. The Short Story. London: 1924, p. 102; New York: Devin-Adair, 1951, passim.
Sees Henry James as the last great teller of stories.

3077 _____. "O'Faolain on James," Storytellers and Their Art. New York: Doubleday (Anchor Book), 1963, pp. 343-352.

3078 O'Grady, Walter. "On Plot in Modern Fiction: Hardy, James, and Conrad," MFS, 11 (Summer, 1965), 107-115.
Finds James's fiction well balanced, the flow of his fiction constantly "inward. "

3079 Okita, Hagime. "From Henry James to Willa Cather," Albion, 8 (November, 1961), 132-145.
The influence of James on Cather's work, especially the technique.

3080 Oliver, Clinton. "Henry James as a Social Critic," AR, 7 (Summer, 1947), 243-258.

3081   O'Neill, John Patrick. "The Story in It: The Design of Ac-
        tion and Situation in Henry James's Fiction," DAI, 32 (Stan-
        ford: 1971), 927A.

3081.1 _____. Workable Design: Action and Situation in the
        Fiction of Henry James. Port Washington, New York: Ken-
        nikat Press, 1973.

3082   Onishi, Akio. "An Approach to Henry James: Through an
        'International' Trilogy," BungR, 12 (January, 1963), 1-45.

3083   Orage, Alfred Richard. "Henry James," Readers and
        Writers, 1917-1921. New York: Knopf, 1922, pp. 9-13.
        Henry James, a "mentalized phenomena."

3084   _____. "Henry James and the Ghostly," Little Review
        Anthology. Margaret Anderson, ed. New York: Hermitage,
        1953, pp. 230-232.

3085   _____. "James' Play of Minds," Selected Essays and
        Critical Writings. H. Read and D. Saurat, eds. New York:
        1935, pp. 85-88.

3086   Orcutt, William Dana. "Celebrities off Parade: Henry
        James," CSMM, 26 (August 24, 1934), 12.

3087   _____. "Friends Through Type," In Quest of the Perfect
        Book: Reminiscences and Reflections of a Bookman. Bos-
        ton: Little, 1926, pp. 73-107.

3088   _____. "From My Library Walls," CSMM, 35 (August 17,
        1943), 7.

3089   _____. "From a Publisher's Easy Chair," Celebrities Off
        Parade. Willett, 1935, pp. 192-233.

3090   _____. "Redundancy of Henry James," From My Library
        Walls: A Kaleidoscope of Memories. New York: Longmans,
        1945, pp. 134-138.

3091   Ortmann, Amei. "Henry James: Ein Leben für die Litera-
        tur," TuK, 15/16 (1967), 1-11.

3092   Otake, Masaru. "On Henry James," Jin-ShR, 2 (Winter,
        1962), 17-69.

3093   Otsu, Eiichiro. "Ghost Novels of Henry James," Critica, 5
        (March, 1962), 34-52.

3094   "Our Great Renunciator," LitD, 51 (August 28, 1915), 405-
        406.
            Quotations are given from various papers indicating the
            public reaction to James's renunciation of his American
            citizenship.

3094.1 Oxford and Asquith, Earl of. "Anglo-American Relations before the War: Henry James," Memories and Reflections,
1852-1927. Boston: Little, Brown & Co., 1928, pp. 331-
337.

3095   Pacey, W. C. D. "Henry James and His French Contemporaries," AL, 13 (November, 1941), 240-256.
On the French influences.

3096   Paget, Violet [Pseud., Vernon Lee]. "Lady Tal," Vanitas:
Polite Stories. New York: Lovell, Coryell & Co., 1892.
An Ambiguous portrait of James in the story.

3097   Palache, John G. "The Critical Faculty of Henry James,"
UCC, 26 (October, 1924), 399-410.

3098   Parkes, Henry Banford. The American Experience: An Interpretation of the History and Civilization of the American
People. 2nd ed. rev. New York: Knopf, 1955, pp. 261-
265, passim.

3099   _____. "The James Brothers," SR, 56 (1948), 323-328.
A good survey of the contribution of both.

3100   Parquet, Mary Ellen. "Henry James: The Bliss and the
Bale," DA, 20 (Nebraska: 1959), 303-304.

3101   Parrington, Vernon Louis. "Henry James and the Nostalgia
of Culture," Main Currents in American Thought. New York:
1930, III, 239-241; also in The Question of Henry James.
F. W. Dupee, ed. New York: 1945, pp. 128-130.

3102   Pastalosky, Rosa. "Nathaniel Hawthorne: Entre Henry James
y el psicoanálisis," in Asociación Argentina de Estudios
Americanos. Sextas Jornadas de Historia y Literatura Norteamericana y Rioplatense. 2 Vols. Buenos Aires.

3103   Paterson, John. "The Language of 'Adventure' in Henry
James," AL, 32 (November, 1960), 291-301.

3104   Patrick, Michael D. "Henry James's Literary Criticism,"
IllQ, 35 (December, 1972), 20-33.

3105   Pattee, Fred Lewis. The Development of the American Short
Story: An Historical Survey. New York and London: Harper
& Bros., 1923, pp. 194-208, passim.

3106   _____. "Henry James," A History of American Literature
with a View to the Fundamental Principles Underlying Its Development. New York and Boston: Silver, Burdett & Co.,
1896, pp. 429-432.

3107   _____. History of American Literature Since 1870. New

York: Century Co., 1915, pp. 186-197, passim.

3108 _____. The New American Literature, 1890-1930. New
York: Cooper Square Pubs., 1968, passim.

3108.1 Paul, Sherman. Edmund Wilson: A Study of Literary Vocation in Our Time. Urbana: Illinois U. P., 1965, pp. 17-
18, 36-38, 216-217, passim.

3109 Pauly, Thomas Harry. " 'The Travel Sketch-Book and the
American Author': A Study of the European Travelogues of
Irving, Longfellow, Hawthorne, Howells, and James," DAI,
32 (Berkeley, Calif.: 1971), 928A.

3110 Payne, William Morton. "Henry James," Dial, 5 (December, 1884), 206-207; Dial, 27 (July, 1899), 21.

3111 Pecnik, B. "Henry James," Republika, 8 (May, 1952), 329-
330.

3112 Penfield, Lida S. Henry James and the Art of the Critic.
Diss. Boston: 1938.

3113 Pennell, Joseph. The Adventures of an Illustrator. Boston:
Little, Brown & Co., 1925; London: Fisher Unwin, 1925,
passim.

3114 _____. "In London with Henry James," Century, 103
(February, 1922), 543-548.

3115 Perrin, Noel. "The Henry James Papers," NY, 36 (November 12, 1960), 191-198.

3116 Perry, Bliss. And Gladly Teach. Boston and New York:
Houghton Mifflin, 1935, passim.
Remarks that he did not much like the much-discussed
"third manner" of Henry James.

3117 _____. "The American Mind," The American Mind and
American Idealism. Boston and New York: Houghton Mifflin, 1912, passim.
Asserts that Henry James portrayed with "unrivalled psychological insight the Europeanized American of the eigh-
teen-seventies and eighties."

3118 _____. "Commemorative Tribute to Henry James,"
Academy Notes and Monographs. New York: 1922. (Prepared for the American Academy of Arts and Letters.)

3119 _____. A Study of Prose Fiction. Boston and New York:
Houghton Mifflin, 1902, passim.

3120 Perry, F. M. "Henry James: Master of Indirection," in

Story-Writing: Lessons from the Masters. New York: Holt, 1926, pp. 140-179.

3121   Perry, Ralph Barton. "Henry James in Italy," HGM, 41 (June, 1933), 189-200.

3122   _____. "The James Collection," HUL, 4 (March, 1942), 74-79.

3123   _____. The Thought and Character of William James. Boston and Toronto: Little, Brown & Co., 1935, passim. Includes comment by William as to the work of Henry James.

3124   Peterich, Werner. Henry James und Das Literarische Experiment. Diss. Munich: n. d.

3125   Peterson, Dale Earl. "One Much-Embracing Echo: Henry James' Response to Ivan Turgenev," DAI, 31 (Yale: 1971), 1524A.

3126   Peterson, William S. "Henry James on Jane Eyre," TLS, No. 3,622 (July 30, 1971), 919-920.

3127   Petesch, Natalie M. "The Ceremony of Innocence: A Study of Narrative Techniques in Henry James," DA, 23 (Texas: 1962), 1687-88.

3128   Phelps, Gilbert. The Russian Novel in English Fiction. London: Hutchinson, 1956, pp. 61-87.

3129   Phelps, William Lyon. "Henry James," YR, 5 (July, 1916), 783-797.

3130   _____. "Henry James," The Advance of the English Novel. New York: Dodd, Mead & Co., 1922, pp. 302-330, passim.

3131   _____. "Henry James: America's Analytical Novelist," LaHJ, 40 (November, 1923), 174-175.

3132   _____. "Henry James," Autobiography with Letters. London and New York: Oxford U. P., 1939, pp. 550-564, passim.

3133   _____. "James," in Howells, James, Bryant, and Other Essays. New York: Macmillan, 1924, pp. 123-155.

3134   Phillips, John Nova. "A Twaddle of Graciousness," BottOs, 19 (Spring, 1957), 195-202.

3135   Pier, F. "Pale Adventurers," HarperW, 54 (December 10, 1910), 35.

3136   Pierhal, Armand. "Henry James, le Civilisé," HeM, 6
        (March, 1951), 413-420.

3137   Pilkington, John, Jr. Henry Blake Fuller. Twayne United
        States Authors Series, 175. New York: Twayne, 1970,
        passim.
            Discusses Fuller's admiration for James.

3138   Pisapia, Biancamaria. "George Eliot e Henry James," SA,
        13 (1967), 235-280.

3139   Pitkin, Walter B. The Art and the Business of Story Writ-
        ing. New York: Macmillan, 1912, p. 38.

3140   Pizer, Donald. "A Primer of Fictional Aesthetics," CE, 30
        (April, 1969), 572-580.

3141   _____. Realism and Naturalism in Nineteenth-Century
        American Literature. Carbondale and Edwardsville: South-
        ern Illinois U. P., 1966, pp. 3-10, passim.
            Discusses the realism in James.

3142   Plante, Patricia R. "Edith Wharton: A Prophet Without Due
        Honor," MWQ (1962), 16-22.
            Edith Wharton's debt to Henry James.

3143   Pochmann, Henry A. "Henry James," German Culture in
        America: Philosophical and Literary Influences, 1600-1900.
        Madison: Wisconsin U. P., 1957, pp. 442-477.

3144   _____, and Gay Wilson Allen, eds. Masters of American
        Literature. New York: Macmillan, 1949, I, 541-547.

3145   Podhoretz, Norman. "Edmund Wilson, the Last Patrician--
        I," Reporter, 19 (December 25, 1958), 25-28.
            Says that Edmund Wilson devoted his writing career to the
        support of values of such men as Henry James.

3146   _____. "Edmund Wilson, The Last Patrician--II," Re-
        porter, 20, #1 (January 8, 1959), 32-35.

3147   Poirier, Richard. The Comic Sense of Henry James: A
        Study of the Early Novels. New York: Oxford U. P., 1960.
            An excellent study of novels before 1881.

3148   _____. Fiction of Comedy and the Early Henry James.
        Diss. Harvard: 1959.

3149   _____. "The Performing Self," in The Performing Self:
        Compositions and Decompositions in the Languages of Con-
        temporary Life. New York: Oxford U. P., 1971, pp. 86-
        111.

3150 _____. "Visionary to Voyeur: Hawthorne and James,"
A World Elsewhere: The Place of Style in American Literature. New York: Oxford U. P., 1966, pp. 93-143, passim.

3151 _____. "What Is English Studies, and If You Know What
That Is, What Is English Literature?" PR, 37 (1970), 37-
41.
Compares Herbert Marcuse and James for having similar
"relevance."

3152 Porte, Joel. "James," The Romance in America: Studies
in Cooper, Poe, Hawthorne, Melville, and James. Middle-
town, Conn.: Wesleyan U. P., 1969, pp. 193-226.
Discusses early, middle and late examples of James's
"most characteristic" contributions to the form.

3153 Porter, Katherine Anne. "The Days Before," in The Days
Before. New York: Harcourt, Brace, 1952, pp. 3-22.
Discusses James's "force of persuasion expressed in the
individual vivid images of the past wherever encountered
...."

3154 _____. "The Days Before," KR, 5 (Autumn, 1943), 481-
494.

3155 Porter, Kathleen Zamloch. "The Epistemological Novels of
Joseph Conrad and Henry James," DA, 34 (Syracuse: 1973),
6654A-55A.

3156 Pouillon, Jean. "Henry James," TM, 118 (October, 1955),
549-560.

3157 Poulet, Georges. "Henry James," The Metamorphoses of the
Circle. Tr., Carley Dawson and Elliott Coleman. Baltimore, Maryland: Johns Hopkins Press, 1966, 307-320.

3158 _____. Studies in Human Time. Tr., Elliott Coleman.
Baltimore: Johns Hopkins Press, 1956, pp. 350-354.

3159 Pound, Ezra. ABC of Reading. Norfolk, Conn.: 1934, p.
90; New York: J. Laughlin, 1960.

3160 _____. "In Explanation," "Brief Note," and "The Middle
Years," LittleR, 5 (August, 1918), 5-41.

3161 _____. "Henry James," The Literary Essays of Ezra
Pound. T. S. Eliot, ed. London and New York: New Directions, 1954, pp. 295-338, passim.

3162 _____. "Henry James," Make It New. New Haven, Conn.:
Yale U. P., 1935, pp. 251-307.

3163 _____. "Henry James," Instigations. New York: Books

for Libraries Press, 1920, pp. 106-167. Repr., Chicago:
Regnery, 1960; New York: Books for Libraries, 1967.

3164 _____. The Letters of Ezra Pound. D. D. Paige, ed.
New York: Harcourt, Brace, 1950, p. 125.

3165 _____. "The Middle Years," LittleR, 5 (August, 1918),
5-41.

3166 _____. "Moeurs Contemporaines, VII" Personae. New
York: 1950, p. 181.

3167 _____. The Pisan Cantos in The Cantos of Ezra Pound.
New York: New Directions, 1948, 1970.
          Cantos LXXIV and LXXIX, p. 11 and p. 66, respectively,
          have allusions to Henry James.

3168 Powers, Lyall H. Guide to Henry James. Columbus, Ohio:
Charles E. Merrill (Merrill Guides.), 1969.

3169 _____, ed. Introduction. Henry James's Major Novels:
Essays in Criticism. East Lansing: Michigan State U. P.,
1973.
          An excellent collection of essays.

3170 _____. Henry James: An Introduction and Interpretation.
New York: Holt, Rinehart and Winston, 1970.

3171 _____. "Henry James and the Ethics of the Artist,"
TSLL, 3 (August, 1961), 360-368.

3172 _____. "Henry James and French Naturalism," DA, 16
(Indiana: 1955), 341.

3172.1 _____. Henry James and French Naturalism. Ann Arbor:
University Microfilms, 1956, No. 14,664.

3173 _____. Henry James and the Naturalist Movement. Michigan: Michigan State U. P., 1972.

3174 _____. "Henry James and Zola's Roman Experimental,"
UTQ, 30 (October, 1960), 16-30.

3175 _____. "Henry James's Antinomies," UTQ, 31 (January,
1962), 125-135.
          The fundamental antimony is related to the familiar ten-
          sion in James's work between America and Europe.

3176 _____. "James's Debt to Alphonse Daudet," CL, 24
(Spring, 1972), 150-162.

3177 _____. "Preoccupations of Henry James," Nation, 184
(June 29, 1957), 571-572.

3178   Powys, John Cowper. "Henry James," Suspended Judg-
        ments: Essays on Books and Sensations. New York: 1916,
        pp. 367-398.
            "People do not and perhaps never will ... converse with
            one another quite so goldenly...."

3179   _____. "John Cowper Powys on Henry James," Little
        Review Anthology. Margaret Anderson, ed. New York:
        Hermitage House, 1953, pp. 28-30.

3180   Pratt, Cornelia Atwood. "Evolution of Henry James," Critic,
        n. s., 31 (April, 1899), 338-342.

3181   Pratt, William C., Jr. "Revolution without Betrayal: Hen-
        ry James, Pound, Eliot, and the European Tradition," DA,
        17 (Vanderbilt: 1957), 2600.

3181.1 _____. Revolution without Betrayal. Nashville, Tenn.:
        Vanderbilt U. P., 1957.

3181.2 Prausnitz, Walther G. The Craftsmanship of Henry James:
        A Study of the Critical Reviews 1864-1884. Diss. Chicago:
        1957.

3182   Preston, Harriet Waters. "The Latest Novels of Howells
        and James," Atl, 91 (January, 1903), 77-82.

3183   Price, Lawrence Marsden. The Reception of United States
        Literature in Germany. Chapel Hill: North Carolina U. P.,
        1966, pp. 157-158, passim.

3184   Priestley, J. B. Literature and Western Man. New York:
        Harper & Bros., 1960, pp. 357-362, passim.

3185   Pritchard, John Paul. "The Realists: Henry James," Criti-
        cism in America: An Account of the Development of Critical
        Techniques from the Early Period of the Republic to the Mid-
        dle Years of the Twentieth Century. Norman, Oklahoma:
        Oklahoma U. P., 1956, pp. 175-184.
            "James saw indecency in literature as a danger to literary
            art no less than to public morals...."

3186   Pritchett, V. S. "Babcockism," NSt, 59 (June 11, 1960),
        863-864.

3187   _____. "Birth of a Hermaphrodite," NSt (November 30,
        1962), 779-780.

3187.1 _____. Books in General. New York: Harcourt, 1952,
        pp. 43-49.

3188   _____. "Great Horse-faced Bluestocking," TriQ, 11 (Oc-
        tober 11, 1968), 463-464.

Notes that James referred to George Eliot as a "great
horse-faced blue-stocking."

3188.1 _____. "The Writer as Traveller," NS&N, 51 (June 16,
1956), 693-694.

3189   Purdy, Strother B. "Henry James's Abysses: A Semantic
Note," ES, 51 (October, 1970), 424-433.
An attempt "to plot the occurrence" of the word abyss,
and "to characterize it semantically throughout James's
work."

3190   _____. "Henry James and the Mot Juste," WisSL, 6
(1969), 118-125.
James as "a marked linguistic innovator."

3191   _____. "Henry James and the Sacred Thrill," PQ, 48
(1969), 247-260.
Examines the variety of James's use of the word sacred
in his later works.

3191.1 _____. "Henry James, Gustave Flaubert, and the Ideal
Style," Lang&S, 3 (1970), 163-184.

3192   _____. "Henry James's Use of Vulgar," AS, 42 (February, 1967), 45-50.
Demonstrates James's variety of use of the word vulgar,
proving "the far greater range that the word had for him
than it has for us."

3193   _____. "The Language of Henry James with Emphasis on
His Diction and Vocabulary," DA, 21 (Wisconsin: 1960), 626.

3194   Putt, S. Gorley. "Henry James and Dickens," TLS, 3599
(February 19, 1971), 213; No. 3602 (March 12, 1971), 296;
3604 (March 26, 1971), 352.

3195   _____. "James the First," Eng, 14, #81 (Autumn, 1962),
93-96.
The early stories indicate later economy of phrase, contrasting and comic use of deliberate verbosity, and greater
sophistication of language.

3196   _____. "A Henry James Jubilee, II," CM, 162 (1947),
284-297.

3197   _____. Henry James: A Reader's Guide. London:
Thames & Hudson; Ithaca, New York: Cornell U. P., 1966;
new edition, Harmondsworth, Penguin (Peregrine Books),
1968.

3198   _____. " 'Cher Maitre' and 'Mon Bon': Henry James,
Man and Legend," Scholars of the Heart: Essays in

Criticism. London: Faber and Faber, 1962, pp. 141-235.

3199   Quinn, Arthur Hobson. "Henry James and the Fiction of International Relations," American Fiction: An Historical and Critical Survey. New York and London: 1936, pp. 279-304.

3200   _____, ed. The Literature of the American People: An Historical and Critical Survey. New York: Appleton-Century-Crofts, 1951, passim.

3201   _____. The Soul of America: Yesterday and Today. Pennsylvania U. P., 1932, passim.

3202   Quvamme Børre. "Henry James," Edda (Oslo), 44 (January-June, 1944), 73-85.

3203   Rahv, Philip. "Attitudes toward Henry James," NewRep, 108 (February 15, 1943), 220-224; in American Literary Essays. New York: 1960, pp. 153-158; Image and Idea. Norfolk, Conn.: 1959, pp. 63-70; Literature and the Sixth Sense. Boston: 1969, pp. 95-103; The Question of Henry James. F. W. Dupee, ed. New York: 1945, pp. 273-280.

3204   _____. "The Cult of Experience in American Writings," PR, 7 (1940), 412-424. Also in Image and Idea. Norfolk: New Directions, 1949, pp. 42-70; Literary Opinion in America. Morton D. Zabel, ed. New York: 1951, pp. 550-560.

3205   _____. "The Heiress of All the Ages," PR, 10 (May-June, 1943), 227-247. Also in Image and Idea. Rev. ed. New York: New Directions, 1957, pp. 51-76; Literature and the Sixth Sense. Boston: 1969, pp. 104-125.

3206   _____. "Henry James: The Banquet of Initiation," Discovery of Europe: The Story of American Experience in the Old World. Boston: Houghton Mifflin Co., Riverside Press, 1947, pp. 269-271.

3207   _____, ed. Introduction. Eight Great American Short Novels. New York: Berkley Publishing Co., 1963, p. 11.

3208   _____, ed. Introduction and Headnotes. The Great Short Novels of Henry James. New York: Dial Press, 1944; Toronto: Longmans.

3209   _____. Introduction. Literature in America. New York: World Publishing Co., 1962, passim.

3210   _____. "Pulling Down the Shrine," The Myth and the Powerhouse. New York: Farrar, Straus and Giroux, c1949, 1965, pp. 202-208, passim.

3211   Raleigh, John Henry. "The English Novel and the Three

Kinds of Time," <u>Perspectives in Contemporary Criticism.</u>
New York: Harper & Row, 1968, pp. 42-49, passim.

3212   _____. "Henry James," <u>Matthew Arnold and American</u>
<u>Culture.</u> Berkeley, Calif.: California U. P., (University
of California English Studies, No. 17), 1957, pp. 17-46.

3213   _____. "Henry James: The Poetics of Empiricism,"
PMLA, 66 (March, 1951), 107-123.
       Interprets James in reference to Locke.

3213.1 _____. "Henry James: The Poetics of Empiricism,"
<u>Time, Place, and Idea: Essays in the Novel.</u> Carbondale:
Southern Illinois U. P., 1968, pp. 3-24.

3214   _____. "The Novel and the City: England and America
in the Nineteenth Century," VS, 11 (March, 1968), 291-328.
       The different views of the city in England and America
       provided by James and other writers.

3215   Ramadan, A. M. <u>The Reception of Henry James's Fiction in</u>
<u>the English Periodical Between 1875 and 1890.</u> Diss. Lon-
don: 1959-1960.

3216   Ramsey, Roger. "The Available and the Unavailable 'I':
Conrad and James," ELT, 14 (1971), 137-145.

3217   Ranald, Ralph Arthur. "Henry James and the Social Question: 'Freedom' and 'Life' in the Social Novels of the 1880's,"
DA, 23 (Princeton: 1963), 2531-32.

3218   Randell, Wilfred L. "The Art of Mr. Henry James," FnR,
99 (April, 1916); also in LivA (July, 1916), 281-299.

3219   _____. "Henry James as Humanist," FnR, n. s., 110
(Spring, 1921), 459-469.

3220   Raskin, Jonah. "Henry James and the French Revolution,"
AQ, 17 (Winter, 1965), 724-733.
       Shows that James was more concerned with social prob-
       lems than is usually thought.

3221   Raunheim, John Peter. "A Study of the Revisions of the
Tales of Henry James Included in the New York Edition,"
DAI, 33 (N.Y.U.: 1972), 733A.

3222   Ray, Gordon N. "The Importance of Original Editions,"
<u>Nineteenth-Century English Books: Some Problems in Bibli-</u>
<u>ography.</u> Urbana, Ill.: Illinois U. P., 1942, passim.

3223   Read, Herbert. "Henry James," <u>Collected Essays in Lit-</u>
<u>erary Criticism.</u> London: Faber and Faber, 1938, pp.
361-362. New York: Horizon Press, 1956.

Discusses James's treatment of Puritanism.

3224 _____. "Henry James," The Nature of Literature. New
York: Horizon Press, 1956, pp. 354-368. [Published in
England as Collected Essays.

3225 _____. "Henry James," The Sense of Glory: Essays in
Criticism. New York: Harcourt, 1930, pp. 206-208; Cambridge, England: 1929.

3226 _____. "Two Notes on a Trilogy," Tenth Muse: Essays
in Criticism. Freeport, New York: Books for Libraries
Press, 1969, pp. 189-197.

3227 Reardon, John. "Hemingway's Esthetic and Ethical Sports-
men," UR, 34 (October, 1967), 13-23.
Jamesian parallels in Hemingway.

3228 Recchia, Edward J. "Form and the Creative Process: Lesson and Example in Eleven of Henry James's Artist Tales,"
DAI, 30 (Ohio State: 1969), 2495A-96A.

3229 "Recent Acquisitions--Manuscripts," PULC, 30, #1 (Autumn,
1968), 55-63.
Manuscripts acquired by Princeton Library from July 1,
1967, to June 30, 1968, include materials relating to
James.

3230 Reck, Andrew J. Introduction to William James: An Essay
and Selected Texts. Bloomington and London: Indiana U. P.,
1967, pp. 11-12, passim.

3231 Redman, Ben Ray. "New Editions," SatR, 34 (September 29,
1951), 15.
Essay-review of Morton Zabel's The Portable Henry
James. New York: 1951.

3232 Reedy, William Marion. "Henry James," Mirror, 25 (March
3, 1916), 1.

3233 _____. "Henry James at His Worst," Mirror, 11 (March
7, 1901), 3.

3234 _____. "A New Year's Sermon," Mirror, 7 (December
30, 1897), 2.
The influence of James, a "foreigner."

3234.1 Rees, Richard. For Love or Money: Studies in Personality and Essence. London: Secker and Warburg, 1960, passim.

3235 Reid, Stephen A. The Role of Technique in Henry James's
Later Novels. Diss. Berkeley, California: 1961.

3236   Reilly, Robert J.   "Henry James and the Morality of Fic-
        tion," AL, 39 (March, 1967), 1-30.
        A good study which won the Norman Foerster Prize for
        the best article published in AL during 1967.

3237   _____. "Henry James and the Morality of Fiction,"
        Criticism: Some Major American Writers. Sel. by Lewis
        Leary. New York: Holt, Rinehart and Winston, 1971, pp.
        167-192.

3237   Reinhart, Charles S.   "Henry James," HarperW, 34 (June,
        14, 1890), 471-472.

3239   "Religion and Henry James," N&Q, 184 (May 8, 1943), 271-
        272.

3240   Rest, Jaime.   "Henry James y el arte de la novela," Aso-
        ciación Argentina de Estudios Americanos. Sextas Jornadas
        de Historia y Literatura Norteamericana y Rioplatense.   2
        Vols. Buenos Aires, 1971.

3241   Revol, E. L.   Reseña de "The Question of Henry James,"
        Sur, 1946, 142.

3242   Rexroth, Kenneth.   "Henry James and H. G. Wells," Assays.
        Norfolk, Conn.: New Directions, 1961, pp. 114-117.

3243   Rice, Loree McConnell.   "Henry James's Theory of the Nov-
        el," DAI, 31 (Oklahoma State: 1970), 6022A.

3244   Richardson, Lyon N., ed.   Henry James: Representative Se-
        lections, with Introduction, Bibliography, and Notes.   New
        York: American Writer Series, 1941; Urbana: Illinois U. P.,
        1966.
        The introductory critical essay presents "a careful account
        of the developments of the mind of Henry James, with es-
        pecial references to events influencing his literary work...."

3245   Richardson, S. D.   "Henry James as a Novelist," Harvard
        M, 2 (April, 1886), 59.
        An early estimate.

3246   Riddel, Joseph N.   "F. Scott Fitzgerald, the Jamesian In-
        heritance, and the Morality of Fiction," MFS, 11 (Winter,
        1966), 331-350.
        James's influence on Fitzgerald.

3247   Roberts, James Deotis.   Faith and Reason: A Comparative
        Study of Pascal, Bergson, and James.   Boston: Christopher
        Publishing House, 1962, passim.

3248   Roberts, James L.   "An Approach to Evil in Henry James,"
        ArQ, 17 (Spring, 1961), 5-16.

3249   Roberts, Louise A.   Henry James's Criticism of Nineteenth-
       Century America. Diss. Chicago: 1946.

3250   Roberts, Morley.   "Meetings with Some Men of Letters,"
       QQ, 39 (February, 1932), 65-70.

3251   Roberts, Morris.   "Henry James and the Art of Foreshorten-
       ing," RES, 22 (July, 1946), 207-214.
           Discussion of the narrative function of the dramatic meth-
       od.

3252   _____.   Henry James's Criticism. Cambridge, Mass.:
       Harvard U. P., 1929; New York: Haskell House, 1965.
       An indispensable study.

3253   _____.   "Henry James's Final Period," YR, 37 Septem-
       ber, 1947), 60-67.
       The aspects of maturity in James's late fiction.

3254   _____.   Henry James's Literary Criticism. Diss. Har-
       vard: 1928.

3255   Robinson, Jean Joseph.   "Henry James and Schulberg's The
       Disenchanted," MLN, 67 (November, 1952), 472-473.

3256   Roditi, Edouard.   "Fiction as Allegory," Oscar Wilde.   Nor-
       folk, Conn.:   New Directions, 1947, pp. 99-124.

3257   _____.   "Oscar Wilde and Henry James," UKCR, 15
       (Autumn, 1948), 52-56.

3258   Rogers, Robert.   "The Beast in Henry James," AI, 13
       (Winter, 1956), 427-454.
       Sees the "beast" as representing guilt.

3259   _____.   A Psychoanalytic Study of the Double in Litera-
       ture.   Detroit: Wayne State U. P., 1970, pp. 70-72, 99-
       108, 113-114, passim.

3260   Roscoe, E. S.   "Henry James at the Reform Club," Book-
       man (New York), 60 (January, 1925), 584-585.

3261   Rose, Alan M.   "Conrad and the Sirens of the Decadence,"
       TSLL, 11 (Spring, 1969), 795-810.
       Attitude of James and Conrad toward the Decadence.

3262   Roselli, Daniel N.   "Max Beerbohm's Unpublished Parody of
       Henry James," RES, 22 (February, 1971), 61-63.
           Discusses Beerbohm's parody of James "pencilled" at an
       unknown date in his copy of James's Terminations.

3263   Rosenbaum, S. P.   "Henry James and Creativity: 'The Log-
       ic of the Particular Case,' " Criticism, 8 (1966), 44-52.

3264   Rosenfeld, Paul. "The Henry James Revival," Cw, 43 (Jan-
        uary 11, 1946), 329-332.
                Discusses the causes of the revival of interest in Henry
        James.

3265   Rosenzweig, Saul. "The Ghost of Henry James: A Study in
        Thematic Apperception," C&P, 12 (December, 1943), 79-100.
        Repr., in PR, 11 (Fall, 1944), 435-455; Art and Psychoanaly-
        sis. William Phillips, ed. New York: Cirterion Books,
        1957, pp. 89-111.

3266   Ross, Maude Cardwell. "Moral Values of the American
        Woman as Presented in Three Major American Authors,"
        DA, 25 (Texas: 1965), 5262-63.
                Three authors are James, Hawthorne, and Faulkner.

3267   Rothenstein, William. Men and Memories. New York:
        Coward-McCann, 1932, p. 173.

3268   Rourke, Constance. "The American," American Humor: A
        Study of the National Character. New York: Harcourt, 1931,
        pp. 235-265; repr., The Question of Henry James. F. W.
        Dupee, ed. New York: 1945, pp. 138-159.
                The American character abroad.

3269   Rouse, H. Blair. "Charles Dickens and Henry James: Two
        Approaches to the Art of Fiction," NCF, 5 (September, 1950),
        151-157.

3270   Routh, Harold Victor. "George Romanes," Towards the
        Twentieth Century: Essays in the Spiritual History of the
        Nineteenth. New York: Macmillan, 1937, pp. 335-336,
        339.

3271   Rovit, Earl. "James and Emerson: The Lesson of the Mas-
        ter," AmSch, 33 (Summer, 1964), 434-440.

3272   Rowe, John C. "Restless Analysts: Henry Adams and Henry
        James: A Study in the Function of Modern Symbolism,"
        DAI, 33 (N.Y. State U., Buffalo: 1972), 1739A-40A.

3273   Roy, Claude. "Anton Tchekhov et Henry James," NRF, 20
        (November, 1962), 876-887.

3274   Rubin, Louis D., Jr., and John Rees Moore, eds. Intro-
        duction. The Idea of an American Novel. New York:
        Thomas Y. Crowell, 1961, pp. 243-257.

3275   Ruhm, Herbert. "The Complete Tales of Henry James,"
        SR, 71 (1963), 675-680.

3276   Ruland, Richard. The Rediscovery of American Literature:
        Premises of Critical Taste, 1900-1940. Cambridge, Mass.:

Harvard U. P. , 1967, pp. 78-81, 255-265, passim.

3277   Rupp, Richard H. <u>Celebration in Postwar American Fiction,</u>
        <u>1945-1967.</u> Coral Gables, Fla.: Miami U. P. , 1970, pas-
        sim.
        James not an influence after World War II.

3278   Russell, John. "Books in General," NS&N, 29 (May 26,
        1945), 339.

3279   _____. "Henry James and His Architect," ArchR (March,
        1943).

3280   _____. "Henry James and the Leaning Tower," NS&N,
        25 (April 17, 1943), 254-255.

3281   Ryan, Marjorie. "Forster, James, and Flaubert: A Paral-
        lel," N&Q, 8 (March, 1961), 102-103.

3282   Rypins, Harold L. "Henry James in Harley Street," AL,
        24 (January, 1953), 481-492.
        An attempt to identify Sir Luke Strett.

3283   Saalbach, R. P. "Literature and Morality," PMLA, 86 (Oc-
        tober, 1971), 1031.

3284   Sabiston, Elizabeth J. "The Provincial Heroine in Prose
        Fiction: A Study in Isolation and Creativity," DAI, 30
        (Cornell: 1969), 1150A.

3285   Sachs, Viola. "Uwagi o Amerykanskim 'Romansie,' " PrH,
        10, #2 (1966), 87-93.
        Henry James was the first great American writer who re-
        verted to the "classical tradition" of the novel.

3286   Sackville-West, Edward. "James: An American in Europe,"
        SatRL, 34 (January 20, 1951), 24-25.

3287   _____. "The Personality of Henry James," <u>Inclinations.</u>
        London: Secker & Warburg, 1949, pp. 42-71; New York:
        Kennikat Press, 1945, 1967, pp. 42-71.

3288   Salisbury, Howard E. "Wish-Fulfillment as Moral Crisis in
        the Fiction of Henry James," DA, 24 (Washington: 1963),
        304.
        Shows the disparity between wish and reality by compari-
        son of leading characters who are "outsiders."

3289   Salomon, Roger B. "Realism as Disinheritance: Twain,
        Howells, and James," AQ, 16 (Winter, 1964), 531-544.
        Shows that, unlike Twain and Howells, James refused to
        separate objectivity from a sense of the past. An apt
        discussion of the fusion of present and past.

3290   . "Time and the Realists," Intellectual History in America. Cushing Strout, ed. New York: Harper, 1969, pp. 47-59.

3291 Samokhvalov, N. I. Genri Dzheims [Henry James]. Uchenye zapiski Krasnodarskogo pedagogicheskogo instituta, 1956. vyp. 18. Filologiia, pp. 106-129.

3292 Sampson, George. "Letters in Criticism," Bookman (London), 58 (May, 1920), 76-77.

3293 Samuel, Irene. "Henry James on Imagination and the Will to Power," BNYPL, 69 (February, 1965), 117-130.
The unimaginative, wilful characters often appear to succeed, but "their obtuseness is their triumph and their doom."

3294 Samuels, Charles Thomas. The Ambiguity of Henry James. London, Chicago, Urbana, Ill.: Illinois U. P., 1971.
The central problem, the author states, is "how to assert the essential difference between good and evil without oversimplifying their opposition, how to establish the validity of moral judgments without ignoring personal bias."

3295 Sandeen, Ernest. "The Wings of the Dove and The Portrait of a Lady: A Study of Henry James's Later Phase," PMLA, 69 (December, 1954), 1060-1075.
Discusses James's increasing ability to handle "moral ambiguities."

3296 Sanders, Thomas E. The Discovery of Fiction. Glenview, Illinois: Scott, Foresman & Co., 1967, pp. 299-302, 331-361, passim.

3297 Sanford, Charles L. "Henry James and the American Rush of Experience," The Quest for Paradise: Europe and the American Moral Imagination. Urbana: Illinois U. P., 1961, pp. 203-227.
Discusses the myth of Eden in American Literature, with special emphasis on Henry James.

3298 Sanna, Vittoria. "I primi racconti di Henry James: 1864-1872," AION-SG, 5 (1962), 213-248.

3299   . "I romanze di Edith Wharton e la narrativa Jamesian," SA, 10 (1964), 229-291.
Considers Wharton's work an extension of James.

3300 Sasaki, Miyoko. "Henry James ni mirareru Aku e no Ichi Kosatsu," Oberon, 34 (1971), 72-80.
James's study of evil.

3300.1 Sassoon, Siegfried. Meredith. New York: Viking Press, 1948, passim.

3301   Sauer, Edwin H. Henry James: The Symbols of Morality
        in the Novels of the Middle Period, 1881-1900. Diss. Cin-
        cinnati: 1951.

3302   Saul, Frank Joseph. "Autobiographical Surrogates in Henry
        James: The Aesthetics of Detachment," DAI, 30 (Johns Hop-
        kins: 1969), 2549A.

3302.1 Savelli, Giovanni. "Posizione di Henry James," Humanitas,
        4 (March, 1949), 322-325.

3303   Saveson, Marilyn B. The Influence of Emile Zola upon the
        Theory and Practice of Some English Novelists of His Time.
        [Henry James and others]. Diss. Cambridge: 1956.

3304   Sayre, Robert F. The Examined Self: Henry Adams and
        Henry James and American Autobiography. Diss. Yale:
        1962.

3305   _____. The Examined Self: Benjamin Franklin, Henry
        James, Henry Adams. Princeton, New Jersey: Princeton
        U. P. , 1964.
            Discusses the friendship between James and Adams and its
        influence on certain of James's stories.

3306   Scanlon, Lawrence E. "Henry James's 'Compositional Re-
        source and Value Intrinsic,' " ForumH, 4, #1 (1963), 13-19.
            Asserts that James's aesthetic includes a theory devel-
        oped by Horatio Greenough as early as 1843.

3307   Schelling, Felix Emmanuel. "Some Forgotten Tales of Henry
        James," Appraisements and Asperities as to Some Contempo-
        rary Writers. New York: Lippincott, 1922, pp. 169-174.

3308   Scheyer, Ernst. The Circle of Henry Adams. Detroit:
        Wayne State U. P. , 1970, pp. 25-26, 134-137, passim.
            Henry Adams and Henry James.

3309   Schlesinger, Arthur M. , Jr. , and Morton White, eds.
        Paths of American Thought. London: Chatto & Windus, 1964,
        pp. 59-60, 247-249, passim.

3310   Schneider, Isidor. "The Rediscovery of Henry James," New
        Masses, 55 (May 28, 1945), 23-24.

3311   Scholes, James Bert. "American and British Criticism of
        Henry James: 1916-1953," DA, 22 (North Carolina: 1962),
        2798-99.
            "The rise of James's literary reputation is closely related
        to the prominence of analytical criticism, which since the
        1930's has been an increasingly important mode of criti-
        cism...."

3312   Schuhmann, Kuno. "Ethik und Ästhetik im Spätwerk von
        Henry James," JA, 15 (1970), 77-87.

3313   Schulte, Rainer Ortwin. "Henry James and Marcel Proust:
        A Study in Sensibility," DA, 26 (Michigan: 1965), 3352.

3314   Schultz, Elizabeth Avery. "Henry James and the Impossible
        and Irresistible Romance," DA, 28 (Michigan: 1967),
        5069A-70A.

3315   Schuyler, Montgomery. "Henry James," NYTBR, 13 (Janu-
        ary 11, 18, 1908), 5, 30.

3316   _____. "Henry James's Short Stories," Lamp, 26 (Ap-
        ril, 1903), 231-235.

3317   Schwertman, Mary Pogue. "Henry James's Portraits of
        Ladies," DA, 29 (North Carolina, Chapel Hill: 1969),
        2282A.

3318   Scott, Arthur L. "A Protest against the James Vogue,"
        CE, 13 (January, 1952), 194-201.
            States that James is devoid of "those prerequisites of a
            great writer: passion, energy, gusto, love of life."
            Cf., Maurice Beebe, CE, 13 (1952), 455-457; Fred B.
            Millett, CE, 14 (1952-53), 167-168.

3319   Scott, Dixon. "Henry James," Bookman (London), 43 (March,
        1913), 299-306.

3320   _____. "In Defence of Henry James," Bookman (London),
        45 (March, 1914), 302-307.

3321   _____. "Henry James," Men of Letters. London: 1916;
        New York: Hodder & Stoughton, 1923, pp. 78-110.

3322   Scott-James, Rolfe Arnold. "Above the Battle," Fifty Years
        of English Literature, 1900-1950, with a Postscript, 1951 to
        1955. New York: Longmans, 1956, pp. 54-74.

3323   Scudder, Horace E. "A Few Story-Tellers, Old and New,"
        Atl, 72 (November, 1893), 693-699.

3324   _____. "James, Crawford, and Howells," Atl, 57 (June,
        1886), 850-857.

3324.1 Sears, Donald A., and Margaret Bourland. "Journalism
        Makes the Style," JQ, 47 (1970), 504-509.

3325   Sears, Sallie. The Negative Imagination: Form and Per-
        spective in the Novels of Henry James. Ithaca, New York:
        Cornell U. P., 1968.
            A significant study.

3326   Segal, Ora. The Lucid Reflector: The Observer in Henry
       James's Fiction. New Haven: Yale U. P., 1970.
       Comprehensive coverage of James's works.

3327   Seldes, G. V. "Henry James: An Appreciation," HarvardM,
       53 (December, 1911), 92-100.

3327.1 Senanu, K. E. "Anton Chekov and Henry James," IbandanSE,
       2, #1 (1970), 182-197.

3328   Shahane, V. A. "Formative Influences on E. M. Forster,
       Henry James--A Study in Ambivalence," OJES, 1, #1 (1961),
       39-53.

3329   Shapira, Morris. "The Artist and the Artistic," CamR, 78
       (June 15, 1957), 711-712.

3330   _____, ed. Henry James: Selected Literary Criticism.
       London: Heinemann, 1963; New York: Horizon Press, 1964.

3331   Sharma, O. P. "The Albany Cousin and Two Heroines of
       Henry James," Indian Essays in American Literature: Pa-
       pers in Honour of Robert E. Spiller. Sujit Mukherjee, and
       D. V. K. Raghavacharyulu, eds. Bombay: Popular Praka-
       shan, 1969, pp. 149-165.

3332   Sharp, Sister M. Corona. The Confidante in Henry James:
       Evolution and Moral Value of a Fictive Character. Notre
       Dame, Indiana: Notre Dame U. P., 1963.

3333   _____. "Fatherhood in Henry James," UTQ, 35 (April,
       1966), 279-292.
       Finds the fathers in James's works usually the tyrants,
       adventurers, and vanquished.

3334   _____. "The Role of the Confidante in Henry James,"
       DA, 23 (Notre Dame: 1962), 2139-40.

3335   Sherman, Stuart Pratt. "Aesthetic Idealism of Henry James,"
       Nation, 104 (April 5, 1917), 393-399.

3336   _____. "The Aesthetic Idealism of Henry James," On
       Contemporary Literature. New York: Holt & Co., 1917,
       pp. 226-255. Also in The Question of Henry James. New
       York: 1917, pp. 70-91.

3337   _____. "Henry James," The Columbia University Course
       in Literature. New York: Columbia U. P., 1929, XVIII,
       218-233.

3338   _____. "The Special Case of Henry James," WeeklyR,
       (July 7, 1920); repr., in The Emotional Discovery of Amer-
       ica. New York: Farrar, c1932; Freeport, New York:

Books for Libraries Press, 1970, pp. 35-47.

3339   Shine, Muriel Gruber.   "Children, Childhood, and Adoles-
       cence in the Novels and Tales of Henry James," DA, 29
       (N. Y. U.:   1967), 273A-4A.

3340   _____.   The Fictional Children of Henry James.   Chapel
       Hill: North Carolina U. P. , 1969.
       Although James's earlier children are analyzed, central
       attention is given to the Jamesian children of the 1890's.
       A most useful study.

3341   Shitsu, Iwase.   "The American Scene and James's Creative
       Method," SELit (Japan), 46 (March, 1970), 141-152.

3342   Short, Raymond W.   "Henry James World of Images,"
       PMLA, 68 (September, 1953), 943-960.
       A study of "the areas of existence of experience most
       used by James as sources for his imagery...."

3343   _____.   "The Sentence Structure of Henry James," AL,
       18 (May, 1946), 71-88.
       The suitability of sentence structure to James's purpose.

3344   _____.   "Some Critical Terms of Henry James," PMLA,
       65 (September, 1950), 667-680.

3345   Shroeder, John W.   "The Mothers of Henry James," AL,
       22 (January, 1951), 424-431.
       Finds the "archetypal mother-quest as integrative symbol-
       ic element" in certain stories.

3346   Shulenberger, Arvid.   "Henry James as a Minor Novelist,"
       NatlR, 14 (February 26, 1963), 166-167.
       Essay-review, The Conquest of London and The Middle
       Years.   Leon Edel, ed.   Derogatory criticism: James
       both as a novelist and as critic considered a "minor fig-
       ure."

3347   Shulman, Robert.   "Henry James and the Modern Comedy of
       Knowledge," Criticism, 10 (Winter, 1968), 41-53.

3348   Silverstein, Henry.   "Utopia of Henry James," NEQ, 35 (De-
       cember, 1962), 458-468.

3349   Simms, L. Moody, Jr.   "Henry James and the Negro Ques-
       tion," AN&Q, 10, #8 (April, 1972), 127-128.

3350   Simon, Irene.   "Jane Austen and The Art of the Novel," ES,
       43 (June, 1962), 225-239.
       Compares Austen and Henry James.

3351   Simon, Jean.   "Les Exiles"--[Henry James], Le Roman

Américain Aux XXe Siecle.   Paris: Boivin, 1950, pp. 45-
51.

3352   Simon, John Kenneth. "A Study of Classical Gesture: Henry James and Madame de Lafayette," CLS, 3 (1966), 273-
283.

3353   Singh, Brijarj. "A Study of the Concepts of Art, Life and
Morality in the Criticism of Five Writers from Pater to
Yeats," DAI, 32 (Yale: 1971), 3331A-32A.
Henry James, one of the writers studied.

3354   Sklepowich, Edward A. "The Play of Tone: Henry James
and the Concept of Social Artifice," DAI, 32 (Virginia:
1971), 4633A-34A.

3355   Slabey, Robert M. "Henry James and 'The Most Impressive
Convention in All History,' " AL, 30 (March, 1958), 89-102.
James and Catholicism.

3356   Smalley, Evelyn Garnaut. The Henry James Yearbook.
Boston: R. G. Badger, 1911; London: J. J. Dent & Co.,
Ltd., 1912.

3357   Smith, Bernard. "The Quest of Beauty," Forces in American Criticism: A Study of the History of American Thought.
New York: Harcourt, Brace, 1939, pp. 185-228.

3358   Smith, Henry Nash. "The Morals of Power: Business Enterprise as a Theme in Mid-Nineteenth Century American
Fiction," Essays on American Literature in Honor of Jay B.
Hubbell.   Clarence Gohdes, ed.   Durham, N.C.: Duke U. P.,
1967, pp. 90-91.

3359   Smith, Herbert F.   Richard Watson Gilder.   Twayne United
States Authors Series, #166.   New York, Twayne Pubs.,
1970.
Contains a discussion of the professional relationship of
James and Gilder, editor of Scribner's Monthly Magazine,
and then editor of its successor, the Century Monthly
Magazine.

3360   Smith, J. Oates. "Henry James and Virginia Woolf: The
Art of Relationships," TCL, 10 (October, 1964), 119-129.
In James, knowledge is gained through "relentless witness-
ing"; in Woolf, through "the desperate effort to transcend
time."

3361   Smith, James Harry, and Edd Winfield Parks, eds. "Henry
James," Great Critics. 3rd ed., rev. and enl. New York:
Norton, 1951, pp. 648-651.

3362   Smith, Janet Adam. "Henry James and R. L. Stevenson,"

LonMerc, 34 (September, 1936), 412-420.
An account of the relationship between the "two most conscious novelists of their time."

3363   _____, ed. Introduction. <u>Henry James and Robert Louis</u>
<u>Stevenson: A Record of Friendship and Criticism</u>. London:
Rupert Hart-Davis, 1948; New York: Macmillan, 1949.

3364   _____. "That One Talent," NS&N, 52 (October 13, 1956),
455-456.
Essay-review of John L. Sweeney's <u>Henry James: The</u>
<u>Painter's Eye, 1956.</u>

3365   Smith, Logan Pearsal. "The Expatriates," <u>Unforgotten</u>
<u>Years</u>. Boston: Little, Brown & Co., 1939, pp. 263-296.

3366   _____. "Notes on Henry James," Atl, 172 (August, 1943),
75-77.

3367   _____. "Slices of Cake," NS&N, 25 (June 15, 1943), 367-
368.

3367.1 Smith, Martha Stribling. "A Study of the Realistic Treatment of Psychic Phenomena in Selected Fiction of William
Dean Howells, Hamlin Garland, Henry James, Frank Norris,
and Theodore Dreiser," DAI, 33 (North Carolina, Chapel
Hill: 1972), 1743A-44A.

3368   Smith, S. Stephenson. "The Psychological Novel," in <u>The</u>
<u>Craft of the Critic</u>. New York: Thomas Y. Crowell, 1931,
pp. 185-190.

3369   Smith, William Francis, Jr. "Sentence Structure in Three
Representative Tales of Henry James," DAI, 31 (Michigan
State: 1970), 3520A.

3370   Smyth, Albert Henry. "Henry James on American Speech,"
BookN, 23 (July, 1905), 856.

3371   Snell, Edwin Marion. <u>The Modern Fables of Henry James</u>.
Cambridge, Mass.: Harvard U. P., 1935.

3372   Snell, George. "Henry James: Life Refracted by Temperament," <u>The Shapers of American Fiction, 1798-1947</u>. New
York: Cooper Square Publishers, 1961, pp. 129-140.

3373   Snow, Lotus. "The Pattern of Innocence through Experience
in the Characters of Henry James," UTQ, 22 (April, 1953),
230-236.

3374   _____. "Some Stray Fragrance of an Ideal: Henry
James's Imagery for Youth's Discovery of Evil," HLB, 14
(Winter, 1960), 107-125.

3375 Sobiston, Elizabeth J. "The Provincial Heroine in Prose Fiction: A Study in Isolation and Creativity," DA, 30 (Cornell: 1969), 1150A.

3376 Solomon, Eric. "Joseph Conrad, William Faulkner, and the Nobel Prize Speech," N&Q, 14 (July, 1967), 247-248.
Says that Faulkner in the 1950 Nobel Prize Speech drew heavily upon Conrad's appreciation of Henry James.

3377 _____. Stephen Crane in England: A Portrait of the Artist. Columbus: Ohio State U. P., 1964, pp. 67-89.

3378 Solomon, Jan Kadetsky. "The Puritan, the Gentleman, and the Artist: A Study of the Conflict Between Ethics and Aesthetics in the Novels of Henry James," DA, 25 (Michigan: 1964), 7278-79.

3379 Sölter, Ursula. Die Romanauffassung Bei Henry James und in der Englischen Literaturkritik der 1920er Jahre. Diss. Mainz, 1956.

3380 Spackman, William M. On the Decay of Humanism. New Brunswick, New Jersey: Rutgers U. P., 1967, pp. 33-81.
Essays on James and others.

3381 Spanos, B. The Essential Henry James: The American Years, 1843-1870. Diss. London: 1954-1955.

3382 Sparshott, F. E. "An Aspect of Literary Portraiture," EIC, 15 (July, 1965), 359-360.

3383 Specker, Heidi. "The Change of Emphasis in the Criticism of Henry James," ES, 29 (April, 1948), 33-47.

3384 Spencer, Benjamin T. "The Jamesian Resolution," The Quest for Nationality: An American Literary Campaign. Syracuse U. P., 1957, pp. 308-312, passim.

3385 _____. "Pound: The American Strain," PMLA, 81, #7 (December, 1966), 457-466.

3386 Spender, Stephen. "Henry James," and "Henry James and the Contemporary Subject," The Destructive Element: A Study of Modern Writers and Beliefs. London: Jonathan Cape, 1935, pp. 11-110, 189-200.

3387 _____. "A Modern Writer in Search of a Moral Subject," LonMerc, 31 (December, 1934), 128-133.

3388 _____. "The School of Experience in the Early Novels," H&H, 7 (April-May, 1934), 417-433; revised and repr., The Destructive Element.

3389 _____. "The Unconscious," The Destructive Element. London: 1935, pp. 67-98.

3390 _____. "A World Where the Victor Belonged to the Spoils," NYTBR (March 12, 1944), 3.

3391 Spiller, Robert E. "Art and the Inner Life: Dickinson, James," Cycle of American Literature: An Essay in Historical Criticism. New York: Macmillan, 1955, pp. 163-183.

3392 _____. "Artist of Fiction," SatR, 39 (June 9, 1956), 19-20.

3393 _____. "Henry James," in Eight American Authors: A Review of Research and Criticism. Floyd Stovall, ed. New York: Norton, 1963, pp. 364-418. [See also revised edition, 1971, "Henry James," by Robert L. Gale.]

3394 _____, et al, eds. "Henry James," Literary History of the United States. Rev. ed. in one volume. New York: Macmillan, 1960, pp. 1039-1064.

3395 _____. "Seer of the Gem-like Flame," SatR, 36 (May 9, 1953), 13-14.

3396 _____. The Third Dimension: Studies in Literary History. New York: Macmillan Co.; London: Collier-Macmillan, 1965, pp. 86, 114-115.
     Comparison of Henry James and Stephen Crane.

3397 Squire, J. C. "Henry James and His Unfinished Work," Dial, 60 (March 30, 1916), 316-318.

3398 Squire, John Collings. "Henry James's Obscurity," Books in General. London: Heinemann, 1919, pp. 179-184.

3399 Stader, Karl-Heinz. Die Bewusstseinskunst Von Henry James. Diss. Bonn: 1953.

3400 Stafford, William T. "The American Critics of Henry James: 1864-1943," DA, 21 (Kentucky: 1961), 2722.

3400.1 _____. "The Americanism' of Henry James: Quentin Anderson and Van Wyck Brooks," WR, 22 (Winter, 1958), 155-160.

3401 _____. "Emerson and the James Family," AL, 24 (January, 1953), 433-461.
     The significance of Emerson to various members of the family.

3401.1 _____. "Henry James," American Literary Scholarship: An Annual: 1969. J. Albert Robbins, ed. Durham, N.C.:

Duke U. P. , 1971, pp. 89-107.

3401.2 _____. "Henry James," American Literary Scholarship:
An Annual: 1968. J. Albert Robbins, ed. Durham, N.C. :
Duke U. P. , 1970, pp. 84-99.

3402 _____. "Henry James the American: Some Views of His
Contemporaries," TCL, 1 (July, 1955), 69-76.
An excellent survey of contemporary criticism.

3403 _____. "James Examines Shakespeare: Notes on the Nature of Genius," PMLA, 73 (March, 1958), 123-128.

3404 _____. "Lowell 'Edits' James: Some Revisions in
French Poets and Novelists," NEQ, 32 (March, 1959), 92-
98.
In the second edition of this book James heeded some
criticisms Lowell made about the first edition.

3405 _____. "The Two Henry Jameses and Howells: A Bib-
liographical Mix-up," BB, 21 (January-April, 1955), 135.
Cf. , Austin Warren. "James and His Secret," SatRL, 8
(May 28, 1932), 759.

3406 _____. "William James as a Critic of His Brother Henry," Person, 40 (Autumn, 1959), 341-353.
William disliked Henry's choice of subject matter and
style.

3406.1 Stallman, R. W. , and Lillian Gilkes, eds. Stephen Crane:
Letters. New York: New York U. P. , 1960, pp. 243-244,
passim.
Provides an account of the play, "The Ghost at Brede
Place," in which James is said to have collaborated.

3407 Stanford, Derek. "A Larger Latitude: Three Themes in the
'Nineties Short Story," ConR, 210 (February, 1968), 96-104.

3408 Staub, A. W. "The Well-Made Failures of Henry James,"
SoSpJ, 37 (Winter, 1961), 91-101.

3409 Steegmuller, Francis. "Flaubert's Sundays: Maupassant and
Henry James," Cornhill, 163 (Spring, 1948), 124-130.

3410 Steen, James T. "The Vision of Henry James," CSE, 7
(1963), 55-65; repr. , in Lectures on Modern Novelists.
Arthur T. Broes, et al, eds. Pittsburgh, Pa.: 1963, pp.
55-65.

3411 Stegner, Wallace, ed. The American Novel from James
Fenimore Cooper to William Faulkner. New York: Basic
Books, 1965, passim.

3412   Stein, Gertrude. "Henry James," Four in America. New
        Haven, Connecticut: Yale U. P., 1947, pp. 119-159; repr.,
        Freeport, New York: Books for Libraries Press, 1969.

3413   Stein, Roger B. John Ruskin and Aesthetic Thought in Amer-
        ica, 1840-1900. Cambridge: Harvard U. P., 1967, pp.
        210-217.

3414   Steinkamp, Egon. Das Fremdheitserlebnis bei Henry James.
        Die Mächte Europa und Amerika im Leben und Werk des
        Schriftstellers. Diss. Münster: 1956.

3415   Stephens, Robert O., and James Ellis. "Hemingway, Fitz-
        gerald, and the Riddle of 'Henry's Bicycle,' " ELN, 5 (Sep-
        tember, 1967), 46-49.

3415.1 Stern, J. P. On Realism. London and Boston: Routledge
        & Kegan Paul, 1973, pp. 116f, 163f, passim.
           James's realism derives not from "some esoteric hang-
        up," but from the "relation of the total to life."

3416   Stevens, George. "The Return of Henry James: Exploring
        the Relationship Between James and His Audience," SatRL,
        28 (March 3, 1945), 7-8, 30, 32-33.

3416.1 Stevens, Harriet S. "Lo que James sabía," Torre, 13, 49
        (1965), 171-193.

3417   Stevenson, Elizabeth. The Crooked Corridor: A Study of
        Henry James. New York: Macmillan Co., 1949; London:
        1950.
           A very complete coverage of James's works.

3417.1 Stevenson, Lionel. The English Novel: A Panorama. Bos-
        ton: Houghton Mifflin, Riverside Press, Cambridge: 1960,
        pp. 394-396, 417-418, 511-512, passim.

3418   _____. The History of the English Novel. New York:
        Barnes & Noble, 1967, passim.

3419   _____. The Ordeal of George Meredith: A Biography.
        New York: Scribner's, 1953, pp. 268-269, 317-318, passim.

3420   Stevenson, Robert Louis. "Humble Remonstrance," from
        "Memories and Portraits," in Essays: A Selection. New
        York: Coward-McCann, 1950, pp. 365-375.

3421   Stevick, Philip. "The Theory of Fictional Chapters," WHR,
        20 (1966), 231-241; repr., in The Theory of the Novel. New
        York: 1967, pp. 171-184.

3422   Stewart, John Innes Mackintosh. "Henry James," Eight Mod-
        ern Writers. Oxford History of English Literature. New

York: Oxford U. P. , 1963, XII, 71-121.

3423   Stewart, Randall. American Literature and Christian Doc-
        trine. Baton Rouge, La. : Louisiana State U. P. , 1958,
        pp. 15-19, 102-106, passim.

3424   _____. "The Moral Aspects of Henry James's 'Interna-
        tional Situation,' " UnivR, 9 (Winter, 1943), 109-113; repr. ,
        in Regionalism and Beyond. George Core, ed. Nashville:
        Vanderbilt U. P. , 1968, pp. 178-184.

3425   Stokes, D. "Honors for Henry James," CSMM (June 17,
        1950), 14.

3426   Stone, Donald David. The English Novel in the 1880's:
        George Meredith, Henry James, and the Development of
        Modern Fiction. Diss. Harvard: 1968.

3426. 1 _____. "Henry James and the Americanization of English
        Fiction," and "Conclusion: Two Novelists," Novelists in a
        Changing World. Cambridge: Harvard U. P. , 1972, pp.
        173-331, 332-337.

3427   Stone, Edward. The Battle and the Books: Some Aspects of
        Henry James. Athens, Ohio: Ohio U. P. , 1964.

3427. 1 _____. "From Henry James to John Balderston: Rela-
        tivity and the '20's," MFS, 1 (May, 1955), 2-11.

3428   _____. "Henry James," A Certain Morbidness: A View
        of American Literature. London: Feffer & Simons; Carbon-
        dale and Edwardsville: Southern Illinois U. P. , 1969, 2nd
        pr. , 1970, pp. 43-52, passim.

3429   _____, ed. Henry James: Seven Stories and Studies.
        New York: Appleton-Century-Crofts, 1961.

3430   _____. Henry James and His Sense of the Past. Diss.
        Duke: 1950.

3431   _____. "Henry James and Rome," BPLQ, 3 (April, 1951),
        143-145.

3432   _____. "Poe In and Out of His Time," ESQ, 31 (2nd Qt. ,
        1963), 14-17.

3433   _____. "James's 'Jungle': The Seasons," UKCR, 21
        (Winter, 1954), 142-144.
        Considers the imagery of the months and seasons implicit
        in names of the characters.

3434   _____. Voices of Despair: Four Motifs in American Lit-
        erature. Athens: Ohio U. P. , 1966, pp. 106-107, passim.

3435   Stovall, Floyd. <u>American Idealism.</u> Norman, Oklahoma:
        Oklahoma U. P., 1943, pp. 121-123, passim.

3436   _____. "The Decline of Romantic Idealism, 1855-1871,"
        <u>Transitions in American Literary History.</u> Harry Hayden
        Clark, ed. Durham, North Carolina: Duke U. P., 1953,
        pp. 352-353, passim.

3437   _____, ed. Introduction. <u>The Development of American
        Literary Criticism.</u> Chapel Hill: North Carolina U. P.,
        1955, passim.

3438   _____, ed. <u>Eight American Authors: A Review of Re-
        search and Criticism.</u> New York: W. W. Norton, 1963; re-
        vised ed., 1971, James Woodress, ed.

3439   Strong, Leonard Alfred George. "James and Joyce," <u>Per-
        sonal Remarks.</u> London: Nevill, 1953; New York: Live-
        right, 1953, pp. 184-189.

3440   Strout, Cushing. "Henry James and the International Theme
        Today," SA, 13 (1967), 281-297.

3441   Struble, George G. "Henry James and the Rise of the Cos-
        mopolitan Spirit in American Literature," <u>Proceedings of the
        IVth Congress of the International Comparative Literature As-
        sociation.</u> François Jost, ed. Fribourg, 1964. 2 Vols.
        The Hague: Mouton, 1966, pp. 80-85.

3442   "Style of Henry James," Nation, 102 (March 2, 1916), 244-
        255.

3443   "Suffragette Ignorance of Henry James," LitD, 48 (June 27,
        1914), 1545.

3444   Summerhayes, Donald C. <u>The Relation of Illusion and Real-
        ity to Formal Structure in Selected Works of Fiction By Na-
        thaniel Hawthorne, Melville, and James.</u> Diss. Yale: n.d.

3445   Sumner, Nan and Nathan. "A Dickinson-James Parallel,"
        RS, 39 (1971), 144-147.

3446   Sutton, Walter. <u>Modern American Criticism.</u> Englewood
        Cliffs, New Jersey: Prentice-Hall, Inc., 1963, passim.

3447   Swan, Michael. "Boasting of Henry James," and "Henry
        James and H. G. Wells: A Study of Their Friendship Based
        on Their Unpublished Correspondence," <u>A Small Part of
        Time: Essays on Literature, Art, and Travel.</u> Chester
        Springs, Pa.: Dufour, 1961, pp. 139-145, 41-57.

3448   _____. <u>Henry James.</u> (British Council Pamphlet) Lon-
        don: Longmans, Green, 1950; Arthur Barker, 1952; Revised,
        1957.

3449   . "Henry James and the Heroic Young Master," LonM, 2 (May, 1955), 78-86; HarperB, 89 (September, 1955), 226-227, 270, 272.

3450   , ed. Introduction. Selected Short Stories. Baltimore: Penguin Books, 1963.

3451   . Introduction. Ten Short Stories. London: J. Lehmann, 1948; Chester Springs, Pa.: Dufour Editions, 1948.

3452   . A Small Part of Time. London: Jonathan Cape, 1957, pp. 43-57, 139-145, 173-204.

3453 Swartz, David L., Jr. "Bernard Shaw and Henry James," ShawR, 10 (May, 1967), 50-59.

3454 Sweeney, John L. "The Demuth Pictures," KR, 5 (Autumn, 1943), 522-532.
Suggests that Demuth's pictures throw light on James's literary method.

3455   , ed. Introduction. The Painter's Eye: Notes and Essays on the Pictorial Arts By Henry James. Cambridge, Mass.: Harvard U. P., 1956.
A very helpful study.

3455.1 Sweetapple, R. "Accepting the Unacceptable," Australasian Universities Language and Literature Association: Proceedings and Papers of the Twelfth Congress Held at the University of Western Australia, February 5-11, 1969. A. P. Treweek, ed. [Sydney]: AULLA, 1970.
A study of the double in James's short stories.

3455.2 Swinden, Patrick. "Registration," [Henry James], Unofficial Selves: Character in the Novel from Dickens to the Present Day. New York: Barnes & Noble, 1973, pp. 100-119, passim.
Discusses the criticism of John Bayley.

3456 Swinnerton, Frank. "Artful Virtuosity: Henry James," The Georgian Scene: A Literary Panorama. New York: Farrar, 1934, pp. 19-39.

3457   . Authors I Never Met. London: Allen and Unwin, 1956, pp. 17-24.

3458   . Figures in the Foreground: Literary Reminiscences, 1917-1940. Garden City, New York: Doubleday & Co., 1964, p. 25, passim.

3459   . "From Henry James to Gissing," Background with Chorus: A Footnote to Changes in English Literary

Fashion Between 1901 and 1917. New York: Farrar, Straus and Cudahy, 1956, pp. 118-136.

3460   _____. "Henry James," Spectator, 170 (April 9, 1943), 336.

3461   _____. "Henry James' Superb Performance," MTQ, 5 (Spring, 1943), 2.

3462   Switzer, John W. Henry James's Debt to Hawthorne. Diss. Missouri: n. d.

3463   "Symposium in Honor of William and Henry James," New Rep, 108 (February 15, 1943), 215-230.

3463.1   Takahashi, Masao, ed. A Study of Henry James's Novels. Tokyo: Hokuseido, 1966.

3464   Takano, Fumi. "The Women in the Novels of Henry James," TsudaR, 3 (November, 1958), 3-13.

3465   Takuwa, Shinji. "Hawthorn, James, and Soseki: The Sense of Sin," SELL, 12 (January, 1962), 13-28.

3466   Tallman, Warren E. "Dramas of a High Civilization. Pre-liminary Studies in Henry James's Fiction," DA, 19 (Washington: 1958), 799.

3466.1   Taniguchi, Rikuo, ed. Henry James. Tokyo: Kenkyusha, 1967.

3467   Tanner, Tony. City of Words: American Fiction, 1950-1970. New York: Harper & Row, 1971, pp. 416-418, pas-sim.

3468   _____. "Distorting James," Encounter, 19 (November, 1962), 84-86.
         Essay-review of Dorothea Krook's The Ordeal of Conscious-ness in Henry James. New York: 1962.

3469   _____, ed. Henry James: Modern Judgments. London: Macmillan, 1968; Nashville: Aurora Pubs. , 1970.

3470   _____. "Henry James and Henry Adams," TriQ, 11 (1968), 91-108.
         An important comparison of the two writers. States that it was Adams's intention "to unravel the secrets of nature," James's "to explore the mystery of his own consciousness."

3470.1   _____. "James in the Terrible Tank," Spectator, 222 (1969), 240-241.

3471   _____. "James's Little Tarts," Spectator, #7019

(January 4, 1963), 19.
Essay-review, Leon Edel, ed. The Complete Tales of
Henry James. Vols. 3 and 4. New York: 1962.

3471.1 _____. "Henry James's Subjective Adventurer," Essays
and Studies of English Association. London: New Series, 16,
1963.

3472 _____. "The Literary Children of James and Clemens,"
NCF, 16 (December, 1961), 205-218.

3473 _____. "Henry James," The Reign of Wonder: Naivety
and Reality in American Literature. Cambridge: Cambridge
U. P., 1965, pp. 259-335.
An excellent study of James.

3473.1 Tate, Allen. "Three Commentaries: Poe, James, Joyce,"
SR, 58 (Winter, 1950), 1-15.

3474 Taylor, Christy M. "The Pictorial Element in the Theory
and Practice of Henry James," DA, 15 (Stanford: 1955),
1860-61.

3475 Taylor, Gordon O. "The Friction of Existence: Henry
James," The Passages of Thought: Psychological Representation in the American Novel, 1870-1900. New York: Oxford U. P., 1970, pp. 42-84.

3476 Taylor, Walter Fuller. "Fiction as Fine Art: Henry James
(1843-1916)," A History of American Letters. New York:
American Book Co., 1936, pp. 289-294; Chicago: Regnery,
1956, pp. 261-268.

3476.1 Tedford, Barbara Wilkie. "Henry James's Admiration of
Ivan Turgenev, an Early Influence 'Ineradicably Established,' "
DAI, 31 (Pittsburgh: 1970), 2404A.

3477 Teichgraeber, Stephen E. "The Treatment of Marriage in
the Early Novels of Henry James," DA, 28 (Rice: 1967),
1830A.
Finds that James's characters "can be definitely placed ...
regarding their relative merits and degrees of awareness
and sensitivity through a study of their ideas about the
manner in which they attempt marriage."

3478 Terras, Victor. "Turgenev's Aesthetic and Western Realism," CL, 22 (1970), 19-35.

3479 Terrie, Henry L., Jr. "Henry James and the 'Explosive
Principle,' " NCF, 15 (March, 1961), 283-299.
James's method and structure in presenting action.

3480 _____. "Pictorial Method in the Novels of Henry James,"

DA, 16 (Princeton: 1955), 343-344.

3481 Thayer, William Roscoe. The Life and Letters of John Hay. Boston and New York: Houghton Mifflin, 1916, pp. 411f, 416f.

3482 "Thersites"--"Talk on Parnassus," NYTBR (May 24, 1949), 7, 27.
Henry James, Herman Melville, and Franz Kafka in an imaginary conversation.

3483 Thomas, Amory A. "Henry James à Paris," IeD, 161 (May 15, 1962), 25-29.

3484 Thomas, Jean Landers. "The Technical Synthesis of Henry James: A Study of the Method of 'The Major Phase,'" DAI, 32 (New York: 1971), 4027A.

3485 Thomas, William A. Henry James: A Study in Realism from the Beginnings in the First Quarter of the Nineteenth Century to 1870. Diss. Pennsylvania: 1934.

3486 Thomas, William B. "The Novelist's Point of View: A Study of the Technique of Henry James," DA, 29 (Bowling Green: 1968), 1236A.

3487 Thompson, Edward Raymond [pseud.]. "Henry James and Max Beerbohm," Portraits of the New Century (The First in Ten Years). London: E. Benn, Ltd., 1928; Garden City, New York: Doubleday, Doran, 1928, pp. 282-299.

3488 Thompson, Francis. Literary Criticism. T. L. Connolly, ed. New York: Dutton, 1948, pp. 298-306.

3489 Thorberg, Raymond. "Henry James and 'The New England Conscience,'" N&Q, 16 (June, 1969), 222-223.
Notes that James first used the phrase in 1879.

3490 _____. "Terror Made Relevant: James's Ghost Stories," DR, 47 (Summer, 1967), 185-191.
The terror in James's ghost stories the author finds in the "consciousness which may be called the soul."

3491 Thorp, Willard. Foreword. The Madonna of the Future, and Other Early Stories. New York: New American Library, 1962.

3492 Thurber, James. "Onward and Upward with the Arts: On the Wings of Henry James," NY, 35 (November 7, 1959), 184-197.

3493 _____. "The Wings of Henry James," Lanterns and Lances. London: Hamish Hamilton, 1961, pp. 88-105.

3494   Ticknor, Caroline. Glimpses of Authors. Boston: Houghton Mifflin, 1922, passim.

3495   Tilford, John E., Jr. "James the Old Intruder," MFS, 4
(Summer, 1958), 157-164.

3495.1 Tilley, Arthur. "The New School of Fiction," NatlR, 1 (April, 1883), 257-268.
A response to William Dean Howells. Cf., William Dean
Howells. "Henry James, Jr.," Century, 3 (November,
1882), 25-29; and QR, 45 (January, 1883), 212-217.

3496   Tillotson, Geoffrey. "Henry James and His Limitations,"
Criticism and the Nineteenth Century. New York: Barnes
& Noble, 1952, pp. 244-269.

3497   _____, and Kathleen Tillotson. Mid-Victorian Studies.
London: Athlone Press, 1965, passim.

3497.1 _____, and Miriam Allott. "Symbol and Image in the
Later Work of Henry James," EIC, 3 (October, 1953), 476.

3497.2 Tillotson, Kathleen. The Tale and the Teller. London:
Rupert Hart-Davis, 1959, passim.

3498   Tillyard, E. M. W. "Interlude: Henry James," The Epic
Strain in the English Novel. Fair Lawn, New Jersey: Essential Books, 1958, pp. 121-125.

3498.1 Tilton, Eleanor. Foreword. Henry James: The Marriages
and Other Stories. New York: American Library, 1961.

3499   Tindall, William York. The Literary Symbol. Bloomington:
Indiana U. P., 1955, 2nd printing, 1960, passim.

3500   _____. "Stream of Consciousness," Forces in Modern
British Literature, 1885-1946. New York: Knopf, 1947, pp.
283-317.

3501   Tintner, Adeline R. "The Museum World," [originally, "The
Spoils of Henry James,"] Henry James: A Collection of
Critical Essays. Englewood Cliffs, New Jersey: Prentice-
Hall, 1963, pp. 139-155.

3502   _____. "The Spoils of Henry James," PMLA, 61 (March,
1946), 239-251.
On James's interest in art.

3503   Tochihara, Tomoo. "The Question of Henry James's International Theme: A Study of James's Novels between 1871
and 1881," Ronko, 8 (1961), 128-138.

3504   Todasco, Ruth Taylor. "The Humanism of Henry James: A

Study of the Relation between Theme and Imagery in the
Later Novels," DA, 25 (Texas Tech.: 1964), 3559.

3505   Tompkins, Jane, ed. Introduction. Twentieth-Century Interpretations. Englewood Cliffs, New Jersey: Prentice-
Hall, 1970, passim.

3506   Tooker, L. Frank. "As I Saw It from an Editor's Desk:
The Fiction of the Magazine," Century, 108 (June, 1924),
260-271.

3506.1 Toser, Basil. "Meeting Henry James," MTQ, 6 (Summer-
Fall, 1943), 16.

3507   Townsend, Frank H. "Mark Twain and Henry James: Im-
plications for School Programs," The Teacher and American
Literature: Papers Presented at the 1964 Convention of the
National Council of Teachers of English. Lewis Leary, ed.
Champaign, Ill.: National Council of Teachers of English,
1965, pp. 144-148.
Response of twelfth grade students to certain works of the
two authors.

3508   Tracy, Bruce Philip. "Henry James's Representation of Inner Consciousness in Meditation Scenes from the Late Novels," DAI, 32 (Michigan State: 1971), 1533A.

3509   Traill, H. D. "The Papers of Basil Fillimer," YellowB, 5
(April, 1895), 19-32.
Cf., Wendell V. Harris. "English Short Fiction in the
Nineteenth Century," NCF 6 (1968), 1-93. Harris called
the above "one of the best parodies of James."

3510   Traschen, Isadore. "An American in Paris," AL, 26
(March, 1954), 67-77.

3511   _____. "Henry James and the Art of Revision," PQ, 35
(January, 1956), 39-47.

3512   Trent, William Peterfield, et al, eds. "Henry James,"
The Cambridge History of American Literature. New York:
Macmillan, 1936; Cambridge, England: At the University
Press, 1921, pp. 96-108, passim.

3513   Trilling, Lionel. "An American View of Two Literatures,"
Books, 263 (August, 1951), 178-181.

3514   _____. "Dreiser and the Liberal Mind," Nation, 162
(April 20, 1946), 466ff.

3515   _____, ed. Introduction. Literary Criticism: An Introductory Reader. New York: Holt, Rinehart and Winston,
1970, passim.

3516 _____. "The Jameses," TLS, 3685 (October 20, 1972), 1257.
Asserts that Edel has misinterpreted William James's letter refusing election to the American Academy of Arts and Letters, and that Edel consequently has misinterpreted William's feeling for his brother Henry.

3517 _____. The Liberal Imagination: Essays on Literature and Society. London: 1951; New York: Viking Press, 1951, Doubleday, 1957.

3518 _____. "Manners, Morals, and the Novel," Approaches to the Novel: Materials for a Poetics. Robert Scholes, ed. San Francisco: Chandler Publishing Co., rev. ed., 1961, pp. 121-136.

3518.1 _____. "A Note on Art and Neurosis," PR, 12 (Winter, 1945), 41-48.

3519 _____. The Opposing Self: Nine Essays in Criticism. New York: Viking Press, 1955, passim.

3520 _____. "Our Hawthorne," PR, 31 (Summer, 1964), 329-351.
A revised version of the Afterword in Hawthorne Centenary Essays. Roy Harvey Pearce, ed. 1964. Discusses James's criticism of Hawthorne.

3521 Troy, William. "The Altar of Henry James," NewRep, 108 (February 15, 1943), 228-230. Repr., in The Question of Henry James. F. W. Dupee, ed. New York: 1945, pp. 267-272; in William Troy: Selected Essays. Stanley E. Hyman, ed. Rutgers U. P., 1967, pp. 58-64.

3522 _____. "Henry James and Young Writers," Bookman (New York), 73 (June, 1931), 351-358.
Young writers can learn more from Henry James than from other writers; particularly, they will learn "the deepest meaning of the phrase 'the integrity of the artist.'"

3523 _____. "The Lesson of the Master," and "The New Generation," in William Troy: Selected Essays. Stanley Hyman, ed. New Brunswick, N.J.: 1967, pp. 45-57, 79-91.

3524 Tuttleton, James W. "Edith Wharton: Form and the Epistemology of Artistic Creation," Criticism, 10 (1968), 334-351.

3525 _____. "Henry James and Edith Wharton: Fiction as the House of Fame," MASJ, 7 (Spring, 1966), 25-36.

3526 Tweedy, Katherine. "Jane Austen's Novel and the Novel of Henry James," VJUS, 11 (1938), 74-82.

3527   "Two Frontiersmen," Nation, 90 (April, 1928), 422-423.

3528   Tyler, Parker. Every Artist His Own Scandal: A Study of
        Real and Fictive Heroes. New York: Horizon Press, 1964,
        pp. 209-255.

3529   _____. "Texts Out of Context," ChiR, 12 (Spring, 1958),
        67-73.
        States that James's letters to the New York Tribune re-
        veal his relation to the American reader.

3530   Tytell, John. "Henry James: From Omniscience to Inner
        Reality. The Experimental Novels, 1895-1901," DAI, 30
        (New York University: 1968), 343A.

3530.1 _____. "Henry James and the Romance," MarkR, 5
        (May, 1969), 1-2.

3530.2 _____. "The Jamesian Legacy in The Good Soldier,"
        SNNTS, 3 (Winter, 1971), 365-373.
        The influence of James on Ford Madox Ford's story.

3531   Uhlig, Helmut. "Henry James Deutsch," T&Z, 2 (Spring,
        1955), 262-266.
        Henry James in Germany.

3532   Ulanov, Barry. "The Novel," in The Two Worlds of Amer-
        ican Art: The Private and the Popular. New York: Mac-
        millan, 1965, pp. 209-283, passim.

3533   Underwood, John Curtis. "Henry James: Expatriate," Lit-
        erature and Insurgency: Ten Studies in Racial Evolution.
        New York: M. Kennerley, 1914, pp. 41-86.

3534   Unrue, Darlene Harbour. "Henry James and Gothic Romance,"
        DAI, 32 (Ohio State: 1971), 4028A.

3534.1 Urnov, M. "Uells protiv Dzheimsa. 'Spor o romane i pis-
        atel'skom masterstve. [Wells versus James. The Quarrel
        about the novel and the writer's talent.] VL, 7 (1966), 92-
        112.

3535   Vaid, Krishna B. The Tales of Henry James: A Critical
        Study. Diss. Harvard: 1961.

3536   _____. Technique in the Tales of Henry James. Cam-
        bridge, Mass.: Harvard U. P., 1964.
        A most helpful study covering many of James's works.

3537   Vallette, Jacques. "Une amitié littéraire et sa fin," MdF,
        1140 (August, 1958), 706-708.
        On Henry James and H. G. Wells.

3538 _____. "Croissance de Henry James," MdF, 1124 (April, 1957), 706-709.

3539 _____. "Du nouveau sur Henry James," MdF, No. 1082 (October, 1953), 333-334.

3540 VanDerBeets, Richard. "A Note on Henry James's 'Western Barbarian,' " WHR, 17 (Spring, 1963), 175-178.

3541 Vanderbilt, Kermit. The Achievement of William Dean Howells: A Reinterpretation. Princeton, New Jersey: Princeton U. P., 1968, passim.

3542 _____. Charles Eliot Norton: Apostle of Culture in a Democracy. Cambridge, Mass.: Belknap Press of Harvard U. P., 1959, pp. 225-226, passim.

3543 _____. "James, Fitzgerald, and the American Self Image," MassR, 6 (Winter, 1965), 289-304.

3544 Van Doren, Carl. "Henry James," The American Novel, 1789-1939. New York: 1921; rev., and enlarged, New York: Macmillan, 1940, pp. 188-220.

3545 Van Ghent, Dorothy. The English Novel: Form and Content. New York: Rinehart, 1953, pp. 211-228, 428-439; Harper Torchbooks, 1961, pp. 211-228.

3546 Van Nostrand, Albert D. "The Dense Totality of Henry James," Everyman His Own Poet: Romantic Gospels in American Literature. New York: McGraw, 1968, pp. 149-174.

3547 Vann, J. Don, ed. Critics of Henry James. (Readings in Literary Criticism, No. 18). Coral Gables, Florida: Miami U. P., 1972.

3548 Vedder, Henry Clay. "Henry James," American Writers of Today. Boston and New York: Silver, Burdett & Co., 1894, 1910, pp. 69-86, passim.

3549 Vientós Gastón, Nilita. Introducción a Henry James. Ediciones de la Torre. Universidad de Puerto Rico, 1956.

3550 "Visit to America," Reader, 5 (February, 1905), 360.

3551 Vitelli, James R. Van Wyck Brooks. New York: Twayne, 1969.
        Discussion of Brooks' The Pilgrimage of Henry James. 1925.

3552 Vivas, Eliseo. "Henry and William James: Two Notes," KR, 5 (Autumn, 1943), 580-594.

Says the novelist illustrates his brother's doctrine of the stream of consciousness and "pure experience."

3553 _____. "Henry and William," Creation and Discovery: Essays in Criticism and Aesthetics. New York: Noonday Press, 1955, pp. 15-28.

3554 _____. Henry y William James, Asomante. Vol. II, No. 3, 1946. Traducción de Nilita Vientós Gastón. El original aparece en el nímero-Homenaje de la Kenyon Review.

3555 Volpe, Edmond L. "The Childhood of James's American Innocents," MLN, 71 (May, 1956), 345-347.
Suggests that the childhood of James's cousins was the source of the American Innocents, the protagonists in James's novels.

3556 _____. "Henry James and the Conduct of Life: A Study of the Novelist's Moral Values," DA, 14 (Columbia: 1954), 1735.

3557 _____. Henry James and the Conduct of Life: A Study of the Novelist's Moral Values. Ann Arbor: University Mictofilms, 1954, AC-1, #8848.

3558 _____. "James's Theory of Sex in Fiction," NCF, 13 (Spring, 1958), 36-47.
James's treatment of sex was delicate, subtle, the author says, in keeping with James's "artistic aim": "to portray man's inner world as skillfully and artistically as the French writers had depicted man's sensual and physical existence."

3559 Von Klemperer, Elizabeth G. The Fiction of Henry James and Joseph Conrad in France: A Study in Penetration and Reception. Diss. Radcliffe: 1958.

3560 Vorpahl, Ben M. "Henry James and Owen Wister," PMHB, 95 (1971), 291-338.

3560.1 Wadden, Anthony T. "The Novel as Psychic Drama: Studies of Scott, Dickens, Eliot, and James," DAI, 31 (Iowa: 1970), 4737A.

3561 Wade, Allan, ed. Introduction. The Scenic Art. New Brunswick, New Jersey: Rutgers U. P., 1948.

3562 Wagenknecht, Edward. Cavalcade of the American Novel: from the Birth of the Nation to the Middle of the Twentieth Century. New York: Henry Holt & Co., 1952, pp. 173-174, 265-266, 333-334, passim.

3563 _____. "Of Henry James and Howells, 1925," VQR, 1

(October, 1925), 453-460.

3564 _____. "The Mark Twain Papers and Henry James: The Treacherous Years," SNNTS, 2 (Spring, 1970), 88-98.
Essay-review of The Mark Twain Papers and Edel's The Treacherous Years, 1895-1901.

3565 _____. "Our Contemporary Henry James," CE, 10 (December, 1948), 123-132.
An excellent survey of James's ideas.

3566 Wager, Willis. American Literature: A World View. New York: New York U. P., 1968, pp. 145-156.

3567 Wagner, Linda Welshimer. "The Dominance of Heredity in the Characterizations of Henry James," SDR, 2 (Spring, 1965), 69-77.
An analysis of some of James's main characters.

3568 "Waiting for a Critic," SatRL, 10 (April 14, 1934), 628.

3569 Walbridge, Earle. Index and Key to Literary Characters Drawn from Life. New York: H. W. Wilson Co., p. 15.

3570 Walbrook, H. M. "The Novels of Henry James," FnR, n. s., 127 (May, 1930), 680-691.

3571 Walcutt, Charles Child. "The Illusion of Action in Henry James," Man's Changing Mask. Modes and Methods of Characterization in Fiction. Minneapolis: Minnesota U. P., 1966, pp. 175-211.
According to Walcutt, James initiated the "aesthetic notion of objectivity," that is, the practice of allowing "scene and dialogue" to "speak for themselves, without auctorial commentary or explanation."

3572 Waldock, A. J. A. "Henry James," James, Joyce, and Others. Williams & Norgate, Ltd., 1937; repr., Freeport, New York: Books for Libraries, 1967, pp. 1-29.

3573 Walker, Don D. "The Gun and Lasso of Henry James," WHR, 17 (Spring, 1963), 178-180.
The Western detail and imagery James gained from reading Owen Wister and Bret Harte.

3574 _____. "Wister, Roosevelt and James: A Note on the Western," AQ, 12 (Fall, 1960), 358-366.

3575 Walker, William E., and Robert L. Welker, eds. Reality and Myth: Essays in American Literature in Memory of Richmond Croom Beatty. Nashville: Vanderbilt U. P., 1964, pp. 190-191, passim.
A comparison of James and Evelyn Scott.

3576   Wallace, Irving. Fabulous Originals. New York: Knopf,
        1956, pp. 46-80.

3577   Wallace, Ronald William. "Henry James and the Comic
        Form: A Study of the Major Novels," DAI, 32 (Michigan:
        1971), 4029A.

3578   Walpole, Hugh. "Henry James, A Reminiscence," Horizon,
        1 (February, 1940), 74-80.

3579   _____. "Mr. Oddy," All Souls' Night: A Book of Stories.
        New York: Doubleday, Doran & Co. , 1933, pp. 129-152.
        A fictional reminiscence of the later James.

3580   Walsh, William. "Henry James and a Sense of Identity,"
        Listener, 62 (August 6, 1959), 205-206.

3581   _____. "A Sense of Identity in a World of Circumstances:
        The Autobiography of Henry James," A Human Idiom: Litera-
        ture and Humanity. New York: Barnes & Noble, 1964, pp.
        52-73.

3582   _____. The Use of Imagination: Educational Thought and
        the Literary Mind. London: Chatto & Windus, 1959; New
        York: Barnes & Noble, 1960, passim.

3583   Walter, Eugene. "A Rainy Afternoon with Truman Capote,"
        IntroB, 2 (December, 1957), 1-2.
        Capote comments on literary figures who influenced him,
        one of whom was James.

3584   Walters, Dorothy Jeanne. "The Theme of Destructive Inno-
        cence in the Modern Novel: Greene, James, Cary, Porter,"
        DA, 21 (Oklahoma: 1961), 2300-01.

3585   "The War and the Literary Style of Henry James," LitD, 50
        (April 3, 1915), 752-753.
        Quotations from various newspapers to show the relation-
        ship between the war and James's literary style.

3586   Ward, Joseph A. "Evil in the Fiction of Henry James," DA,
        18 (Tulane: 1958), 2151-52.

3587   _____. "Henry James and the Nature of Evil," TCL, 6
        (July, 1960), 65-69.

3588   _____. "Henry James and the Nature of Evil," Critical
        Approaches to American Literature. Ray B. Browne and
        Martin Light, eds. New York: Thomas Y. Crowell, 1965,
        II, 119-125.

3589   _____. "Henry James's America: Versions of Oppres-
        sion," MissQ, 12 (Winter, 1959-1960), 30-44.

Notes that in much of James's work America is a land of
innocence, but "there is also the America of oppression
in James's work."

3590 _____. The Imagination of Disaster: Evil in the Fiction
of Henry James. Lincoln: Nebraska U. P., 1961.

3591 _____. "The Ineffectual Heroes of James's Middle Period," TSLL, 2 (Autumn, 1960), 315-327.

3592 _____. "James's Idea of Structure," PMLA, 80 (September, 1965), 419-426.
Finds James developing from a Neo-classical appreciation
of form to an organicist view wherein opposites may be
reconciled.

3593 _____. "Picture and Action: The Problem of Narration
in James's Fiction," RUS, 51 (Winter, 1965), 109-123.
Defines James's problem as the subordination of action to
picture.

3594 _____. The Search for Form: Studies in the Structure of
James's Fiction. Chapel Hill: North Carolina Press, 1967.
To some extent this volume may be considered a companion study to the author's Imagination of Disaster, for, in
both books, the conclusion is that James's ultimate position about morality and technique is a pragmatic one.
Both books are excellent and comprehensive studies.

3595 _____. "Social Criticism in James's London Fiction,"
ArQ, 15 (Spring, 1959), 36-48.
Asserts that in James's London fiction between 1897 and
1901, society rather than the individual is the villain.

3596 Ward, Mary Augusta [Mrs. Humphrey Ward]. "The Villa
Barberini: Henry James," A Writer's Recollections. London and New York: Harper Bros., 1918, pp. 201-210.

3597 Warren, Austin. "Henry James," The New England Conscience. Ann Arbor: Michigan U. P., 1966, pp. 143-156.

3598 _____. "Henry James: Symbolic Imagery in the Later
Novels," Rage for Order: Essays in Criticism. Chicago:
Chicago U. P., 1948, pp. 142-161. Repr., in A Collection
of Critical Essays. Leon Edel, ed., pp. 123-138, and Discussions of Henry James. Naomi Lebowitz, ed., pp. 96-
105.

3599 _____. "James and His Secret," SatRL, 8 (May 28,
1932), 759.
Cf., William T. Stafford. "The Two Henry Jameses and
Howells: A Bibliographical Mix-up," BB, 21 (1955),
135.

3600   _____. "Myth and Dialectic in the Later Novels," KR,
5 (Autumn, 1943), 551-568.

3601   _____. "Myth and Dialectic in the Later Novels of Henry
James," Kenyon Critics: Studies in Modern Literature.
John Crowe Ransom, ed. Cleveland: World Pub. Co.,
1951, pp. 42-57.

3602   _____. "The Nature and Modes of Narrative Fiction,"
Approaches to the Novel: Materials for a Poetics. Robert
Scholes, ed. San Francisco: Chandler Pub. Co., 1961, pp.
5-21, passim.

3603   Warren, R. P., ed. "The Henry James Number," KR, 5
(Autumn, 1943), 481-617.

3604   Wasiolek, Edward. "Tolstoy's The Death of Ivan Illyich and
Jamesian Fictional Imperatives," MFS, 6 (Winter, 1960-
1961), 314-324.

3605   Wasserstrom, William. Heiress of All the Ages: Sex and
Sentiment in the Genteel Tradition. Minneapolis: Minnesota
U. P., 1959, pp. 56-67, 87-98, passim.

3606   Watanabe, Hisayoshi. "Past Perfect Retrospection in the
Style of Henry James," AL, 34 (May, 1962), 165-181.
As the past perfect tense replaces the narrative past
tense in James's later novels, "physical action is progres-
sively replaced by thought, the event by retrospective consciousness of it."

3607   Waterlow, S. P. "Memories of Henry James," NSt, 26
(February 6, 1932), 514-515.

3608   _____. "The Work of Henry James," IndendentRev, 4
(November, 1904), 236-243; (January, 1905).

3609   Watson, George. "Henry James," The Literary Critics: A
Study of English Descriptive Criticism. New York: Barnes
& Noble, 1964, pp. 148-160.

3610   Watt, Ian. The British Novel: Scott Through Hardy. New
York: Appleton-Century-Crofts, 1970, passim.

3611   _____. "Conrad, James and Chance," Imagined Worlds:
Essays on Some English Novels and Novelists in Honour of
John Butt. Maynard Mack and Ian Gregor, eds. London:
Methuen & Co., 1968, pp. 301-322.

3612   _____. "The Leavises on Dickens," Listener, 85 (March
11, 1971), 298-301.
Dickens compared with other writers including James.

3613 _____. The Rise of the Novel. Berkeley and Los Angeles: California U. P. , 1959, passim.

3614 _____. The Victorian Novel: Modern Essays in Criticism. New York: Oxford U. P. , 1971, pp. 324-336.

3615 Waugh, Arthur. "The Art of Henry James," Tradition and
Change: Studies in Contemporary Literature. New York:
Dutton, 1919, pp. 246-252. Also, London: 1919.

3616 Webb, Howard W. , Jr. "Recent Scholarship on Mark Twain and
Henry James," The Teacher and American Literature: Papers
Presented at the 1964 Convention of the National Council of
Teachers of English, Lewis Leary, ed. Champaign, Ill. : Nat.
Council of Teachers of English, 1965, pp. 134-143.

3617 Weber, Carl J. "Hardy and James," HLB, 16 (January,
1968), 18-25.
        The relationship between the two writers. Also, letters
        from Hardy, one to James, two about James.

3618 Weber, Carl J. "Henry James and His Tiger-Cat," PMLA,
68 (September, 1953), 672-687.
        James's reaction to the hostile portrait of himself in Vio-
        let Paget's "Lady Tal." Cf. , Leon Edel, PMLA, 69
        (1954), 677-678; Burdett Gardner, PMLA, 68 (1953), 688-695.

3619 _____. "Henry James and Thomas Hardy," MTQ, 5
(Spring, 1943), 3-4.

3620 _____. "A Unique Henry James Item," CLQ, 2 (April,
1948), 123.

3621 Webster, Norman W. "Mrs. Humphry Ward: A Retrospect,"
Cornhill, 1059 (Spring, 1969), 223-233.

3622 Wegelin, Christof. "Edith Wharton and the Twilight of the
International Novel," SoR, 5 (1969), 398-418.

3623 _____. "Hemingway and the Decline of International Fiction," SR, 73 (Winter, 1965), 284-298.
        Hemingway in contrast to James.

3624 _____. "Henry James: The Expatriate as American,"
Sym, 9 (Spring, 1955), 46-55.
        James's expatriate attitudes were rooted firmly in Amer-
        ican ideas and in his "American consciousness."

3625 _____. "Henry James and the Aristocracy," NwR, 1
(Spring, 1958), 5-14.
        James distinguished between European "culture" and Amer-
        ican "character."

3626   _____. The Image of Europe in Henry James. Dallas,
             Texas: Southern Methodist U. P. , 1958.
                     A thorough study stressing the relation of "the fine con-
                     sciousness and the fine conscience. "

3627   _____. "The Rise of the International Novel," PMLA, 77
             (June, 1962), 305-510.
                     Insists that James was anticipated in this genre by other
                     novelists. Cf. , Oscar Cargill, PMLA, 73 (1958), 418-
                     425.

3628   Weimann, Robert. "Erzählerstandpunkt und point of view.
             Zu Geschichte und Aesthetik der Perspektive in englischen
             Roman," ZAA, 10, #4 (1962), 369-416.
                     Comments on James in the light of these terms.

3629   Weimer, David R. The City as Metaphor. New York:
             Random House, 1966, pp. 34-51.

3630   Weinstein, Philip M. Henry James and the Requirements of
             the Imagination. Harvard U. P. , 1971; London: Oxford U.
             P. , 1971.
                     The central thesis is James's continuous concern with con-
                     flict between imagination and experience.

3631   _____. Open Windows and Closed Doors: Imagination and
             Experience in the Fiction of Henry James. Diss. Harvard:
             1968.

3632   Weismann, Leopoldine. Edith Whartons Romankunst und ihre
             Beeinflussung durch Henry James. Diss. Vienna: 1947.

3633   Weithaus, Sister Barbara M. , O.S. F. "Represented Dis-
             course in Selected Novels of Henry James," DAI, 31 (Catho-
             lic U. : 1970), 407A-08A.

3634   Wellek, René. "Henry James," A History of Modern Criti-
             cism, 1750-1950. New Haven: Yale U. P. , 1965, IV, 213-
             237.

3635   _____. "Henry James's Literary Theory and Criticism, "
             AL, 30 (November, 1958), 293-321.
                     James's critical theory allowed him "to characterize sensi-
                     tively and evaluate persuasively a wide range of writers. "

3635. 1   _____, and Austin Warren. Theory of Literature. New
             York: Harcourt, Brace & World (A Harvest Book), 3rd ed.
             1956, passim.

3636   Wells, Anna Mary. Dear Preceptor: The Life and Times of
             Thomas Wentworth Higginson. Boston: Houghton Mifflin, The
             Riverside Press, Cambridge: 1963, pp. 259-260, passim.
                     Has reference to Higginson's essay on Henry James.

3637   Wells, Carolyn. "A Limerick by Henry James," American
        Literature in Parody. Robert P. Falk, ed. New York:
        Twayne Publishers, 1955, p. 135.

3638   Wells, H. G. "Of Art, of Literature, of Mr. Henry James,"
        Boon, the Mind of the Race, The Wild Asses of the Devil,
        and The Last Trump: Being a First Selection from the Lit-
        erary Remains of George Boon, Appropriate to the Times.
        Prepared for Publication by Reginald Bliss, with an Ambigu-
        ous Introduction by H. G. Wells. New York: George H.
        Doran Co., 1915, pp. 86-130.
            Repr., in Henry James and H. G. Wells. Leon Edel and
            Gordon Ray, eds. 1958, pp. 244-247. And in The Idea
            of the American Novel. Louis Rubin and John Moore,
            eds. 1961, pp. 248-250.

3639   _____. Experiment in Autobiography: Discoveries and
        Conclusions of a Very Ordinary Brain (Since 1866). New
        York: Macmillan, 1934, passim.

3640   _____. " 'A Magnificent but Painful Hippopotamus,' "
        American Literature in Parody. Robert P. Falk, ed. New
        York: Twayne Publishers, 1955, p. 133.

3641   _____. "Wells and Henry James," NS&N, 25 (June 12,
        1943), 385.
            A brief letter in which Wells insists that his pen portrait
            of James was "good-tempered guying."

3642   "Wells vs. James," Newsweek, 51 (April 28, 1958), 99.
        Essay-review of Leon Edel and Gordon Ray's Henry
        James and H. G. Wells. Urbana, Ill.: 1958.

3643   Welsh, Alexander. "The Allegory of Truth in English Fic-
        tion," VS, 9 (September, 1965), 7-28.

3644   West, Ray B., Jr., and Robert Wooster Stallman. The Art
        of Modern Fiction. New York: Rinehart, 1949, pp. 583-
        593.

3644.1 West, Ray B., Jr., ed. Essays in Modern Literary Criti-
        cism. New York: Rinehart, 1952, passim.

3645   _____. The Short Story in America, 1900-1950. Chi-
        cago: Regnery, 1952, pp. 1-27.

3646   West, Rebecca [pseud.]. "Nonconformist Assenters and In-
        dependent Introverts," The Court and the Castle: Some
        Treatment of a Recurrent Theme. New Haven: Yale U. P.,
        1957, pp. 203-207.

3647   _____. "Early Impressions [of Henry James]," Modern
        Writers at Work. Josephine Ketcham Piercy, ed. New

York: Macmillan, 1930, pp. 184-188.

3648   . Henry James. London: Nisbet, 1916; New York:
Henry Holt & Co., 1916; reissued by Kennikat Press, 1968.
A survey of James's life and works.

3649   . "Reading Henry James in War Time," NewRep,
2 (February 27, 1915), 98-100.

3650   [West, Rebecca.] "Rebecca West Dethrones Some of Our
Literary Idols," CurOp, 61 (November 4, 1916), 343-344.

3651   Westcott, Glenway. "A Sentimental Contribution," H&H, 7
(April-May, 1934), 523-534.
Comment on Henry James and his influence.

3652   Whalley, George. Poetic Process. London: Routledge &
Kegan Paul, 1953, passim.

3653   Wharton, Edith. "A Backward Glance," LaHJ, 51 (October,
1933), 19, 73, 78, 80; also in A Backward Glance. London
and New York: Appleton-Century, 1934, pp. 305-311, passim.
Comments by a novelist who knew James well.

3653.1   . "Henry James in His Letters," QR, 234 (July-
October, 1920), 188-202.

3654   . The Writing of Fiction. New York: Scribner's
1925, passim.

3655   "What James Went Through," Time, 51 (May 3, 1948), 100,
102, 103.
Essay-review of Simon Nowell-Smith's Henry James: The
Legend of the Master. New York: 1948.

3656   Wheelwright, John. "Henry James and Stanford White,"
H&H, 7 (April-May, 1934), 480-493.

3656.1 White, J. William. "Professor White's Interpretation of
Henry James's Action," Spectator, 115 (August 14, 1915),
204-205.

3657   White, Morton Gabriel, and Lucia White. "The Visiting
Mind: Henry James," The Intellectual Versus the City:
From Thomas Jefferson to Frank Lloyd Wright. Cambridge,
Mass.: Harvard U. P., 1962, pp. 75-94.

3658   White, Richard Grant. "Recent Fiction," NAR, 128 (January, 1879), 101-106.

3659   White, William. "Unpublished Henry James on Whitman,"
RES, n.s., 20 (August, 1969), 321-322.

A letter from James, November 9, 1898, to Dr. John
Johnston acknowledging receipt of Johnston's Diary Notes
of a Visit to Walt Whitman and Some of His Friends.
Manchester, 1898.

3660   Whitmore, Paul E.   "The Image of the City in the Art of
Henry James," DA, 30 (Fordham: 1969), 1579A.

3661   "Who Owns Henry James," Time, 80 (November 30, 1962),
98.
Essay-review, Leon Edel's The Conquest of London and
The Middle Years. 1962.

3662   Wiesenfarth, Brother Joseph, F.S.C. "Henry James and the
Dramatic Analogy: A Study of the Major Novels of the Middle Period," DA, 23 (Catholic Univ. of America: 1962), 241.

3663   _____. Henry James and the Dramatic Analogy: A Study
of the Major Novels of the Middle Period. New York: Fordham U. P., 1963.

3663.1 _____. "Henry James: Action and the Art of Life,"
FourQ, 15 (January, 1966), 18-26.

3664   _____. "Illusion and Allusion: Reflections in 'The Cracked
Looking-Glass,' " FourQ, 12 (November, 1962), 30-37.
Comparison of Katherine Anne Porter and Henry James.

3665   Willett, Maurita. "Henry James's Indebtedness to Balzac,"
RLC, 41 (April-June, 1967), 204-227.

3666   Willey, Frederick. "The Free Spirit and the Clever Agent in
Henry James," SoR, 2 (Spring, 1966), 315-328.

3667   Williams, Blanche Colton. "The Depth of Henry James,"
MTQ, 5 (Spring, 1943), 5-6.
Calls James "the first great technician in fiction."

3667.1 Williams, Harold Herbert. Modern English Writers: Being
a Study of Imaginative Literature, 1890-1914. London:
Sidgwick & Jackson, 1918, 1925; New York: Knopf, 1919.

3667.2 Williams, Owen P. D. "The Three 'R's,' " TLS (February
5, 1949), 89.

3668   Williams, Raymond. "The Parting of the Ways," The English Novel from Dickens to Lawrence. New York: Oxford
U. P., 1970, pp. 119-139.
Describes James's works as moral presentations of human
problems in which "human speech ... has never been better rendered."

3669   Williams, Stanley Thomas. "Cosmopolitanism in American

Literature before 1880," The American Writer and the European Tradition. Margaret Denny and William H. Gilman, eds. Minneapolis: Minnesota U. P., 1950, pp. 45-62.

3670   _____. "Henry James," The Pageant of America: The American Spirit in Letters. London: Oxford U. P.; New Haven: Yale U. P., 1926, pp. 261-264.

3671   Wilson, Angus. "Evil in the English Novel," KR, 29 (March, 1967), 167-194.

3672   Wilson, Edmund. "The Ambiguity of Henry James," H&H, 7 (April-June, 1934), 385-406. Repr., The Question of Henry James. F. W. Dupee, ed. New York: 1945, pp. 160-190; Psychoanalysis and American Fiction. Irving Malin, ed. New York: 1965, pp. 143-186; elaborated in The Triple Thinkers. New York: Oxford U. P., 1948, pp. 48-132.

3673   _____. "The Exploration of James," NewRep, 50 (March 16, 1927), 112-113.
            Essay-review of Pelham Edgar's Henry James: Man and Author. London: 1927.

3674   _____. "Henry James and Auden in America," NY, 22 (September 28, 1946), 85-87.

3675   _____. "The Last Phase of Henry James," PR, 4 (February, 1938), 3-8.

3676   _____. "Meeting with Max Beerbohm," Encounter, 21 (December, 1963), 16-22.
            Notes that Beerbohm loved Henry James despite his caricatures of James.

3677   _____. "New Documents on the Jameses," NY, 23 (December 13, 1947), 133-137.
            Essay-review of The Notebooks of Henry James. F. O. Matthiessen and Kenneth Murdock, 1955; and F. O. Matthiessen's The James Family. 1961.

3678   _____. "The Novels of Henry James," NewRep, 44 (October 14, 1925), 203.

3679   _____. Patriotic Gore: Studies in the Literature of the American Civil War. New York: Oxford U. P., 1962, pp. 585-587, 661-665, 667-670, 699-700, passim.

3680   _____. "The Pilgrimage of Henry James," NewRep, 42 (May 6, 1925), 283-286.
            Essay-review, Van Wyck Brooks' The Pilgrimage of Henry James. New York: 1925.

3681   _____. "The Pilgrimage," The Shores of Light. New

York: Farrar, Straus & Young, 1952, pp. 217-228.

3682 _____. "The Vogue of Henry James," NY, 20 (November 25, 1944), 84-89.

3683 Wilson, Harris, ed. Introduction. Arnold Bennet and H. G. Wells: A Record of a Personal and Literary Friendship. Urbana, Ill.: Illinois U. P., 1960, passim.

3684 Wilson, Jack Hamilton. "George Eliot in America, Her Vogue and Influence, 1858-1900," DA, 27 (North Carolina: 1966), 190A.

3685 Wilson, James Southall. "Henry James and Herman Melville," VQR, 21 (Spring, 1945), 281-286.

3686 Wilson, Richard. "Henry James and 'The Note Absolute,'" EBST, 4 #4 (Session 1958-59 [1966]), 31-35.
    Asserts that James was unmoved by criticism, convinced that he had struck "the note absolute,"--a phrase James used in The Ambassadors.

3687 Wilson, Woodrow. "Henry James on 'Newspaper English,'" CurL, 39 (August, 1905), 155.

3688 Wilt, Napier, and John Lucas, eds. Americans and Europe: Selected Tales of Henry James. Boston: Houghton Mifflin, 1965.

3689 Winner, Viola Hopkins. "The Art of Seeing: Art Themes and Techniques in the Work of Henry James," DA, 21 (New York: 1961), 2275-6.

3689.1 _____. Henry James and the Visual Arts. Charlottesville, Va.: Virginia U. P., 1970.

3690 _____. "Pictorialism in Henry James's Theory of the Novel," Criticism, 9 (Winter, 1967), 1-21.
    Explains how James's knowledge of art affected his conception of fiction in theory and practice, and also provides a "Glossary of Art Metaphors."

3691 _____. "Visual Art Devices and Parallels in the Fiction of Henry James," PMLA, 76 (December, 1961), 561-574.
    Influence of the fine arts in James's fiction.

3692 Winslow, Cedric. Henry James and the Dilemma of the American Tradition. Diss. NYU: n. d.

3693 Winters, Yvor. "Henry James and the Relation of Morals to Manners," AmR, 9 (October, 1937), 482-503, repr., Maule's Curse: Seven Studies in the History of American Obscurantism. Norfolk, Conn.: Swallow Press, 1938, 1947, pp. 169-216.

James is "much more than a mere portrayer of the American abroad; his work partakes in a considerable measure of the allegorical character of Hawthorne."

3694 _____. "Maule's Well or Henry James and the Relation of Morals to Manners," In Defense of Reason. New York: Swallow Press, 1947, pp. 300-343.

3695 Wirsing, Sibylle. "Ein Souverain des Melodrams. Henry James in seinen Romanen und Notizbüchern," Der Monat, 18, Heft 218 (1966), 58-72.

3695.1 Wister, Fanny Kemble. "Caroline Lewis and Henry James," PMHB, 95 (1971), 330-350.

3696 "With Two Countries," Time, 44 (December 4, 1944), 100-104.
Review-article, The Great Short Novels of Henry James. Philip Rahv, ed. New York: 1944.

3697 Wolf, Howard Robert. "Forms of Abandonment in Henry James," DA, 28 (Michigan: 1967), 5031A-32A.

3698 Wolfe, Don M. The Image of Man in America. 2nd ed. New York: Thomas Y. Crowell, 1970, passim.

3699 Woodard, James E., Jr. "Pragmatism and Pragmaticism in James and Howells," DAI, 31 (New Mexico: 1970), 408A.

3699.1 Woodcock, George. "Henry James and the Conspirators," SR, 60 (Spring, 1952), 219-229.

3700 Woodress, James L., Jr. Howells and Italy. Durham, North Carolina: Duke U. P., 1952, passim.

3701 Woodward, Robert H. "Punch on Howells and James," ALR, 3 (1970), 76-77.

3701.1 Woolf, Leonard. "Henry James and the Young Men," Listener, 62 (July, 1959), 53-54; E. M. Forster, ib., 62 (July 16, 1959), 103.

3702 Woolf, Virginia. "Henry James," Death of the Moth, and Other Essays. London: Hogarth Press, 1942, pp. 83-100; New York: Harcourt, 1942, pp. 129-155.

3702.1 _____. "Henry James," Collected Essays. New York: Harcourt, Brace & World, 1967; London: Hogarth, 1966, pp. 267-292, passim.

3703 _____. "Henry James's Ghost Stories," Granite and Rainbow. New York: Harcourt, 1958, pp. 65-72.

3704   _____. A Writer's Diary: Being Extracts from the Di-
            ary of Virginia Woolf. Leonard Woolf, ed. New York:
            Harcourt, Brace & Co., 1953, passim.

3705   "The World of Henry James," LivA, 289 (April 22, 1916),
            229-233.

3706   Wright, Austin McGiffert. The American Short Story in the
            Twenties. Chicago: Chicago U. P., 1961, passim.

3707   Wright, Edgar. Mrs. Gaskell: The Basis for Reassessment.
            London and New York: Oxford U. P., 1965, pp. 173-175,
            263-264, passim.

3708   Wright, Nathalia. "Henry James and the Greenough Data,"
            AQ, 10 (Fall, 1958), 338-343.
                 Notes that James's association with the Geenough family
            in Europe was "responsible for the development of some
            of his most distinctive characterizations and the creation
            of some of his greatest scenic effects."

3709   _____. "The Moral Field: James," American Novelists
            in Italy: The Discoverers--Allston to James.   Philadelphia:
            Pennsylvania U. P., 1965, pp. 198-248.
                 Traces James's long and deep interest in Italy.

3710   Wright, Walter F. The Madness of Art: A Study of Henry
            James. Lincoln: Nebraska U. P., 1962.
                 A very extensive study.

3711   Wyatt, Bryant N. "Naturalism as Expedience in the Novels
            of Frank Norris," MarkR, 2 (February, 1971), 83-87.
                 Comparison of James and Norris.

3712   Wyatt, Edith. "Henry James: An Impression," NAR, 203
            (April, 1916), 592-599; repr., in Great Companions. New
            York: Appleton-Century, 1917, pp. 83-99.

3713   Yeazell, Ruth Bernard. "The Late Style of Henry James:
            A Study of Style in the Novel," DAI, 32 (Yale: 1971),
            7016A.

3714   Young, Filson. "A Bunch of Violets," EngR, 22 (April,
            1916), 317-320; LivA, 289 (May 27, 1916), 568-569.

3715   Young, Frederic Harold. The Philosophy of Henry James,
            Sr. New York: Bookman Associates, 1951, p. 215, passim.
                 Calls attention to the influence of Henry James, Sr., on
            Henry James, Jr.

3715.1   Young, G. M., and G. S. Ritchie. ["False Scent,"], TLS
            (October 9, 1940), 543.
                 Cf., R. W. Chapman, "False Scent," TLS (October 19, 1940),
            531.

3715.2 Young, Mahonri Sharp. "Duveneck and Henry James: A
Study in Contrasts," Apollo, 112 (1970), 210-217.

3715.3 Young, Thomas Daniel, and Ronald Edward Fine. "Henry
James," American Literature: A Critical Survey. New
York: American Book Co., 1968, II, 198-212, 275-300.

3716   Young, Vernon. "The Question of James," ArQ, 1 (Winter,
1945), 57-62.

3717   Zabel, Morton Dauwen. "The Act of Life," NewRep, 134
(April 30, 1956), 25-26.
        Essay-review, The Selected Letters of Henry James.
        Leon Edel, ed. New York: 1955.

3718   _____. "Henry James: The Act of Life," Craft and Character in Modern Fiction. New York: Viking, 1957, pp.
114-143.

3719   _____, ed. Introduction. The Art of Travel: Scenes and
Journeys in America, England, France and Italy from the
Travel Writings of Henry James. Garden City, New York:
Doubleday Anchor, 1958, pp. 1-48.

3720   _____, ed. Introduction. Fifteen Short Stories. New
York: Bantam Books, 1961.

3720.1 _____. Introduction. Henry James: In the Cage and
Other Tales. Garden City, New York: Doubleday, 1958.

3721   _____. " 'Henry James' Place,' " Nation, 156 (April 24,
1943), 597-599.
        Suggests that Washington Place, New York City, be re-
        named "Henry James' Place."

3722   _____. Historia de la Literatura Norteamericana. Capí-
tulo XI, Losada, Buenos Aires: 1950.

3723   _____, ed. Literary Opinion in America: Essays Illus-
trating the Status, Methods, and Problems of Criticism in
the United States in the Twentieth Century. 3rd ed., rev.,
New York: Harper (Harper Torchbooks), 1962, 2 vols., pp.
47-50. (1st ed., 1937).

3723.1 _____. "Memoir," The Art of Ruth Draper: Her Dramas and Characters. Garden City, New York: Doubleday
& Co., 1960, pp. 1-114.

3724   _____. "Poetics of Henry James," Poetry, 45 (February,
1935), 270-276.

3725   _____. "The Poetics of Henry James," The Question of
Henry James. F. W. Dupee, ed. New York: 1945, pp.
212-217.

3726 _____, ed. Introduction. <u>The Portable Henry James</u>.
New York: Viking Press, 1956.

3727 Zauli-Naldi, Camilla. "James e Trollope," SA, 3 (1957),
205-219.

3728 Ziff, Larzer. "Literary Absenteeism: Henry James and
Mark Twain," <u>The American 1890's: Life and Times of a
Lost Generation.</u> New York: Viking Press, 1966, pp. 50-
72, passim.

3729 _____. "The Literary Consequences of Puritanism,"
ELH, 30 (1963), 293-305.

3730 Zolla, Elemire. "Henry James e i morti," Elsinore, 3
(1966), 49-71.

IV. BIBLIOGRAPHY

3731   Anon. "The Soho Bibliography of Henry James," CLQ, Ser. IV (1958), 277-279.

3732   Auchincloss, Louis. "Bibliography," Reflections of a Jacobite. Boston: Houghton Mifflin, 1961, pp. 209-220.

3732.1   Baker, Ernest A., and James Packman. "Henry James," A Guide to the Best Fiction. New York: Macmillan, 1932, pp. 263-266.

3733   Battersby, H. F. P. "Novels of Mr. Henry James," EdinbR, 197 (January, 1903), 59-85.

3734   Beach, Joseph Warren. "Bibliographical Note," and "Supplement to Bibliographical Note," The Method of Henry James. Philadelphia: Albert Saifer, 1954, pp. 272-276, 281-283.

3735   _____. "Henry James," in Cambridge History of American Literature. New York: c.1921, 1947, III, 98-108, IV, 671-675.

3736   Beebe, Maurice, and W. T. Stafford. "Criticism of Henry James: A Selected Check List with an Index to Studies of Separate Works," MFS, 3 (Spring, 1957), 73-96.

3737   _____. "Criticism of Henry James: A Selected Checklist," MFS, 12 (Spring, 1966), 117-177.

3738   Bell, Inglis F., and Jennifer Gallup. A Reference Guide to English, American and Canadian Literature. Vancouver: University of British Columbia Press, 1971.

3739   Birch, Brian. "Henry James: Some Bibliographical and Textual Matters," Library, 20 (June, 1965), 108-123.

3740   Blanck, Jacob. "Henry James," Bibliography of American Literature. 5 Vols. New Haven: Yale U. P., 1955-1969, V, 117-181.

3741   _____, ed. Merle Johnson's American First Editions. 4th ed., revised and enlarged. Waltham, Mass.: Mark Press, 1965, pp. 282-286.

3742   Bowden, Edwin T. "In Defense of a Henry James Collec-
        tion," LCUT, 6 (Winter, 1960), 7-12.

3743   _____ . "Henry James and the Struggle for International
        Copyright: An Unnoticed Item in the James Bibliography,"
        AL, 24 (January, 1953), 537-539.

3744   Brenni, Vito J. , comp. "Henry James," American English:
        A Bibliography. Philadelphia: Pennsylvania U. P. , 1964,
        pp. 22-23.

3745   Brooks, Van Wyck. [Bibliographical Footnotes]. The Dream
        of Arcadia: American Writers and Artists in Italy, 1760-
        1915. New York: Dutton, 1958.

3745.1 Cary, Elizabeth Luther see King, Frederick A.

3745.2 [Catalogue of Exhibition 24, October 8-December, 1946],
        Gazette of Grolier Club 2, 1947.

3746   Clair, John A. "A Selected Bibliography," The Ironic Di-
        mension in the Fiction of Henry James. Pittsburgh: Du-
        quesne U. P. , 1965, pp. 129-140.

3747   Coleman, Arthur, and Gary R. Tyler, comps. "Bibliogra-
        phy," Drama Criticism: A Checklist of Interpretation Since
        1940 of English and American Plays. 2 Vols. Denver:
        Alan Swallow, 1966, I, 98, 401, 420.

3747.1 Cook, Dorothy, and Isabel S. Monro, comps. "Henry
        James," Short Story Index: An Index to 60,000 Stories in
        4,320 Collections. New York: H. W. Wilson Co. , 1953,
        pp. 693-695.

3747.2 Cotton, Gerald B. and Hilda Mary McGill. "Henry James,"
        in Fiction Guide: British and American. Archon Books and
        Clive Bingley, 1967, p. 15.

3748   Cranfill, Thomas Mabry, and Robert Lanier Clark, Jr. An
        Anatomy of "The Turn of the Screw." Austin, Texas: Tex-
        as U. P. , 1965.

3749   Daniels, Earl. "Bibliography of Henry James," TLS (April
        20, 1933), 276.

3750   Dunbar, Viola R. "Addenda to 'Biographical and Critical
        Studies of Henry James, 1941-1948,'" AL, 20 (January, 1949),
        424-435," AL, 22 (March, 1950), 56-61.

3751   Edel, Leon, and Dan H. Laurence, eds. A Bibliography of
        Henry James. London: Rupert Hart-Davis, 1957; 2nd ed. ,
        revised. Soho Bibliographies. London: Rupert Hart-Davis,
        1961.

3752   Edel, Leon. <u>Henry James</u>. Philadelphia: Lippincott, 1953,
        pp. 337-344; London: Hart-Davis, pp. 345-351.

3753   _____. <u>Henry James: A Collection of Critical Essays</u>.
        Englewood Cliffs, New Jersey: Prentice Hall, 1965, pp.
        184-186.

3754   _____. <u>Henry James: Les Années Dramatiques</u>.   Paris:
        Jouve & Co., 1931, pp. 245-252.

3755   _____, ed.   Introduction and Notes.   <u>Henry James: Se-
        lected Fiction</u>.   New York: Dutton, 1953, xxi-xxiv.

3756   _____, and Lyall H. Powers.   "Henry James and the <u>Ba-
        zar</u> Letters," BNYPL, 62 (February, 1958), 75-103.

3757   _____.   "A Note on Translations of Henry James in
        France," RAA, 7 (1930), 539-540.

3758   Eichelberger, Clayton L., comp., assisted by Karen L.
        Bickley, et al.   <u>A Guide to Critical Reviews of United States
        Fiction, 1870-1910</u>.   Metuchen, New Jersey: Scarecrow
        Press, 1971, pp. 177-182.

3759   Ferguson, Alfred R.   "Some Bibliographical Notes on the
        Short Stories of Henry James," AL, 21 (November, 1949),
        292-297.

3760   Foley, P. K.   "James, Henry," <u>American Authors, 1795-
        1895: A Bibliography of First and Notable Editions Chrono-
        logically Arranged with Notes</u>.   New York: Milford House,
        Inc., 1969, pp. 155-157.

3761   Foley, Richard Nicholas.   <u>Criticism in American Periodicals
        of the Works of Henry James from 1866 to 1916</u>.   Washing-
        ton: Catholic University of America Press, 1944; repr.,
        Folcroft, Pa.: Folcroft Press, 1970.

3762   Fullerton, Bradford M.   <u>Selective Bibliography of American
        Literature, 1775-1900: A Brief Estimate of the More Impor-
        tant American Authors</u>.   New York: W. F. Payson, 1932,
        pp. 159-161.

3763   Gale, Robert L.   "Henry James," <u>American Literary Scholar-
        ship: An Annual, 1970</u>.   J. Albert Robbins, ed.   Durham,
        North Carolina: Duke U. P., 1972, pp. 90-115.

3764   _____.   "Henry James," <u>Eight American Authors</u>.   James
        Woodress, et al, eds.   New York: Revised ed., Norton,
        1972, pp. 321-375.

3765   Gerstenberger, Donna, and George Hendrick.   <u>The American
        Novel, 1789-1959: A Checklist of Twentieth Century</u>

Criticism. Denver: Allan Swallow, 1961, pp. 141-164.

3765.1 _____. The American Novel: 1789-1959: A Checklist of Twentieth Century Criticism on Novels Written Since 1789. Vol. II. Criticism Written 1960-1968. Denver: Allan Swallow, 1970, pp. 189-218.

3766   Gold Star List of American Fiction; Fiftieth Anniversary Edition, 1966. Syracuse, New York: Syracuse Public Library, 1966, p. 21.

3767   Gomme, Laurence. "American First Editions: Henry James, 1843-1916," PubW, 104 (August 11, 1923), 498-499.

3768   Grattan, C. Hartley. The Three Jameses: A Family of Minds. New York: Longmans, Green & Co., 1932, pp. 369-373.

3769   The Grolier Club. One Hundred Influential American Books Printed Before 1900: Exhibition at the Grolier Club, April 18-June 16, 1947, pp. 10, 115-116. [Repr., with permission of original publisher, Kraus Reprint Corporation. New York: 1967.]

3770   Hagemann, E. R. "Life Buffets (and Comforts) Henry James, 1883-1916: An Introduction and Annotated Checklist," PBSA, 62 (April-June, 1968), 207-225.

3771   Hall, Susan Corwin, Comp. Hawthorne to Hemingway: An Annotated Bibliography of Books from 1945 to 1963 about Nine American Authors. Robert H. Woodward, ed. New York: Garrett Pub. Co., 1965, pp. 36-44, passim.

3772   Hamilton, Eunice C. "Bibliographical and Critical Studies of Henry James, 1941-1948," AL, 20 (January, 1949), 424-435.

3773   Harkness, Bruce. "Bibliography and the Novelistic Fallacy," SB, 12 (1959), 59ff.

3774   Havlice, Patricia P. "Henry James," Index to American Author Bibliographies. Metuchen, New Jersey: Scarecrow Press, 1971, pp. 90-91.

3775   Hoffman, Charles G. "Bibliography," The Short Novels of Henry James. New York: Bookman Associates, 1957, pp. 133-139.

3776   Holman, Clarence Hugh, comp. "Henry James," The American Novel Through Henry James. New York: Appleton-Century-Crofts, 1966, pp. 44-53, passim.

3776.1 Houghton, Walter E., ed. "Henry James," The Wellesley Index to Victorian Periodicals, 1824-1900. London: Routledge,

1966; Toronto U. P. , 1966, p. 953, passim.

3777   Howard-Hill, T. H. Bibliography of British Literary Bibli-
        ographies. Oxford: At the Clarendon Press, 1969, pp.
        371-372.

3778   Jefferson, D. W. "Bibliography," Henry James. New York:
        Barnes & Noble, c1960, 1965, pp. 114-120.

3779   Johnson, Merle. American First Editions: Bibliographic
        Checklists of the Works of 146 American Authors. Rev. ,
        and enlarged. New York: R. R. Bowker Co. , 1932, pp.
        197-201.

3780   _____. "Henry James," Merle Johnson's American First
        Editions. Bibliographic Checklists of the Works of 199 Amer-
        ican Authors. 3rd ed. , revised by Jacob Blanck. New
        York: R. R. Bowker Co. , 1936, pp. 260-264.

3781   Johnson, Richard Colles, and G. Thomas Tanselle. "Ad-
        denda to Bibliographies of James [and others]: Haldeman-
        Julius 'Little Blue Books' as a Bibliographical Problem,"
        PBSA, 66 (1st Qt. , 1972), 66.

3781.1 _____. " 'James,' The Haldeman-Julius 'Little Blue
        Books,' as a Bibliographical Problem," PBSA, 64 (1st Qt. ,
        1970), 29-78.

3782   Johnson, Thomas H. "Henry James" [Bibliograph], Literary
        History of the United States. Robert Spiller, ed. New York:
        1948, III, 584-590.

3783   Kaplan, Louis, comp. , in association with James Tyler
        Cook, Clinton E. Colby, Jr. , and Daniel C. Haskell. A
        Bibliography of American Autobiographies. Madison: Wis-
        consin U. P. , 1961, p. 152.

3784   Kelley, Cornelia Pulsifer. "Bibliography of the Early Devel-
        opment of Henry James," and "A Supplemental Bibliography,"
        The Early Development of Henry James. Urbana: Illinois
        U. P. , 1965, pp. 301-304, 305-314.

3785   Kenton, Edna. "Some Bibliographical Notes on Henry James,"
        H&H, 7 (April-June, 1934), 535-540.
            Cf. , Edwin T. Bowden. "Henry James and International
        Copyright Again," AL, 25 (1954), 499-500.

3786   King, Frederick A. "Bibliography," The Novels of Henry
        James: A Study by Elizabeth Cary. New York: Haskell
        House, 1964, pp. 189-215.

3787   Kraft, James. "An Unpublished Review by Henry James,"
        SB, 20 (1967), 267-273.

Text of the review, with notes of James's revisions.

3788   Laurence, Dan H.   "A Bibliographical Novitiate: In Search
        of Henry James," PBSA, 52 (1st Qt. , 1958), 23-33.

3788.1 Leary, Lewis. Articles on American Literature, 1900-1950.
        Durham: Duke U. P. , 1954, pp. 155-163.

3789   _____. Articles on American Literature, 1950-1967.
        Carolyn Bartholet and Catherine Roth, assistants. Durham,
        North Carolina: Duke U. P. , 1970, pp. 296-324.

3790   LeClair, Robert Charles. Three American Travellers in
        England: James Russell Lowell, Henry Adams, Henry James.
        Philadelphia: Pennsylvania U. P. , 1945, pp. 216-219.

3791   _____. Young Henry James, 1843-1870. New York:
        Bookman Associates, 1955, pp. 455-462.

3792   Libman, Valentina A. Russian Studies of American Litera-
        ture: A Bibliography. Robert V. Allen, trans. Clarence
        Gohdes, ed. Chapel Hill, North Carolina: North Carolina
        U. P. , 1969, pp. 106, 110.

3793   Manley, John Matthews, and Edith Rickert. "The Old Mas-
        ters: Howells and James," Contemporary American Litera-
        ture: Bibliographies and Study Outlines. New York: Har-
        court, Brace & Co. , 1922, 1929.

3794   Mathews, J. Chesley. "Bibliographical Supplement," Eight
        American Authors: A Review of Research and Criticism by
        Jay B. Hubbel and Others. New York: W. W. Norton, 1963.

3795   Matthiessen, Francis Otto, and Kenneth Ballard Murdock,
        eds. The Notebooks of Henry James. New York: Oxford
        U. P. , 1947.

3796   McElderry, Bruce R. "Henry James," American Literary
        Scholarship: An Annual, 1963. James Woodress, ed. Dur-
        ham, North Carolina: Duke U. P. , 1965, pp. 64-71.

3797   _____. "Henry James," American Literary Scholarship:
        An Annual, 1964. James Woodress, ed. Durham, North
        Carolina: Duke U. P. , 1966, pp. 62-72.

3798   _____. "Henry James," American Literary Scholarship:
        An Annual, 1965. James Woodress, ed. Durham: Duke
        U. P. , 1967, pp. 69-81.

3799   _____. "Henry James," American Literary Scholarship:
        An Annual, 1966. Durham: Duke U. P. , 1968, pp. 65-78.

3800   _____. "The Published Letters of Henry James: A

Survey," BB, 20 (January-April, 1952), 165-171; (May-August, 1952), 187.

3801 _____. "The Uncollected Stories of Henry James," AL, 21 (November, 1949), 279-291.
   Cf., S. E. Lind. "Reply," AL, 23 (March, 1951), 130-131.

3802 McMahon, Helen. Criticism of Fiction: A Study of Trends in "The Atlantic Monthly," 1857-1898. New York: Bookman Associates, 1952.
   Contains list of reviews of James's novels in Atlantic Monthly in the period designated.

3803 Monteiro, George. "Addendum to Edel and Laurence: Henry James's 'Future of the Novel,' " PBSA, 63 (April, 1969), 130.
   Notes that James's essay was first published in the Saturday Review of Books and Arts, a weekly supplement to the New York Times, August 11, 1900, p. 541.

3804 _____. "Henry James and His Reviewers: Some Identifications," PBSA, 63 (1969), 300-304.

3805 _____. "William Dean Howells: Two Mistaken Attributions," PBSA, 56 (1962), 254-257.

3805.1 Moore, Rayburn S. "The Full Light of Higher Criticism: Edel's Biography and Other Recent Studies of Henry James," SAQ, 63 (Winter, 1964), 104-114.

3806 Mossman, Robert E. "An Analytical Index of the Literary and Art Criticism of Henry James," DA, 27 (Pittsburgh: 1966), 1790A.

3807 Narkevich, A. Iu. "Genri Dzhems (25 let so dnia smerti). (Bibliograficheskaia spravka)." [Henry James (25th anniversary of his death). (Bibliographic note)]. Literaturnoe obozrenie, 1941, no. 4, p. 79. (Signed: A. N.) Russian studies.

3808 Nilon, Charles H. "Henry James," Bibliography of Bibliographies in American Literature. New York and London: R. R. Bowker & Co., 1970, pp. 105-108.

3809 Northup, Clark Sutherland. "Henry James," A Register of Bibliographies of the English Language and Literature. New York: Hafner Publishing Co., 1962, p. 214.

3810 Nowell-Smith, Simon. "Bibliography," The Legend of the Master. New York: Scribner's, 1947, pp. 172-176.

3811 _____. "Without Benefit of Bibliography," BC, 7 (Spring, 1958), 64-67.

3812   Okita, Hajime. Henry James Bibliography in Japan.   Kyoto:
        Showado, Apollon-sha, 1958.

3813   Phillips, LeRoy. A Bibliography of the Writings of Henry
        James. Boston: Houghton Mifflin, 1906; New York: Coward
        McCann, 1930; Burt Franklin, 1968.

3814   Powers, Lyall H. Selected Bibliography. Henry James: An
        Introduction and Interpretation. New York: Barnes & Noble,
        1970, pp. 150-160.

3815   _____. Selected Bibliography. Henry James's Major Nov-
        els: Essays in Criticism. East Lansing, Michigan: Michi-
        gan State U. P. , 1973, pp. 459-461.

3816   Richardson, Lyon N. , ed. Bibliography and Notes. Henry
        James: Representative Selections. London: 1947, pp. 288-
        303; New York: American Book Co. , 1941, xci-cxi.

3817   _____. Bibliography. The Question of Henry James.   F.
        W. Dupee, ed. New York: 1945, pp. 281-297.

3818   Robbins, J. Albert, ed. American Literary Scholarship: An
        Annual, 1968. Durham, North Carolina: Duke U. P. , 1970.

3819   _____, ed. American Literary Scholarship: An Annual,
        1969. Durham, North Carolina: Duke U. P. , 1971.

3820   _____, ed. American Literary Scholarship: An Annual
        1970. Durham, North Carolina: Duke U. P. , 1972.

3821   Roberts, Morris. Bibliography. Henry James Criticism.
        Cambridge: Harvard U. P. , 1929, pp. 121-125; New York:
        Haskell House, 1965.

3821.1 _____. "Henry James," SR, 57 (July, 1949), 521-525.

3822   Russell, John R. "The Henry James Collection," URLB, 11
        (Spring, 1956), 50-52.

3823   Sears, Sallie. Bibliography. The Negative Imagination.
        Ithaca, New York: Cornell U. P. , 1968, pp. 223-227.

3824   Segal, Ora. Selected Bibliography. The Lucid Reflector:
        The Observer in Henry James's Fiction. New Haven: Yale
        U. P. , 1970, pp. 241-257.

3825   Short Story Index. Firkins, Ina Ten Eyck, comp. , 1923-
        1936; Fidell, Estelle A. , comp. , 1956-1969. New York: H.
        W. Wilson Co. , 1923-1969.

3826   [Shorter, Clement, ed.] "Bibliography of Henry James," in
        "Letters to an Editor," by Henry James. [London: 1916],
        pp. 13-16.

3827   Slack, Robert C. , ed. "Henry James," Bibliographies of
        Studies in Victorian Literature. Urbana: University of Illi-
        nois Press, 1967.

3828   "Some Bibliographical Notes of Henry James," H&H, 7
        (1934), 535-540.

3829   Spiller, Robert E. , et al. Literary History of the United
        States. 2 vols. New York: Macmillan, 1962, pp. 584-590;
        Supplement, pp. 144-148.

3830   Stafford, William T. "Henry James," American Literary
        Scholarship: An Annual, 1967. James Woodress, ed. Dur-
        ham, North Carolina: Duke U. P. , 1969, pp. 73-85.

3831   _____. "Henry James," American Literary Scholarship:
        An Annual, 1968. J. Albert Robbins, ed. Durham, North
        Carolina: Duke U. P. , 1970, pp. 84-99.

3832   _____. "Henry James," American Literary Scholarship:
        An Annual, 1969. J. Albert Robbins, ed. Durham, North
        Carolina: Duke U. P. , 1971, pp. 89-107.

3833   _____. "Henry James," American Literary Scholarship:
        An Annual, 1971. J. Albert Robbins, ed. Durham, North
        Carolina: Duke U. P. , 1972, pp. 86-103.

3834   _____, ed. Perspectives on James's "Portrait of a Lady":
        A Collection of Critical Essays. New York: New York U.
        P. , 1967, pp. 297-303.

3835   _____. "The Two Henry Jameses and Howells: A Biblio-
        graphical Mix-up," BB, 21 (January-April, 1955), 135.
        Correction of error in standard bibliographies which list
        Austin Warren's article, "James and His Secret," SRL,
        8 (May 28, 1932), 959, as dealing with Henry James, Jr.

3836   Stallman, Robert Wooster. Bibliographical Note. The Houses
        That James Built and Other Literary Studies. East Lansing:
        Michigan State U. P. , 1961, pp. 252-254.

3837   Stevenson, Elizabeth. The Crooked Corridor. New York:
        Macmillan, 1949, pp. 164-166.

3837.1 Stewart, John I. M. Eight Modern Writers. Vol. XII of
        The Oxford History of English Literature. Oxford: Claren-
        don Press, 1963.

3838   Stone, Herbert Stuart, comp. First Editions of American
        Authors: A Manual for Book Lovers. Kennebunkport, Maine:
        Milford House, 1970, pp. 114-116.

3838.1 Stott, R. Toole. "Letter to the Editor," [Re: Dan H.

Laurence's A Bibliographical Novitiate,"] PBSA, 52 (1958), 329-330.

3839   Stovall, Floyd, et al. "Selected Bibliographies: Henry James," Eight American Writers. New York: W. W. Norton, 1963, pp. 1602-1605.

3840   Stratman, Carl J., comp. Bibliography of the American Theatre, Excluding New York City. Loyola U. P., 1965, p. 137.

3841   Swan, Michael. Henry James. Bibliographical Series of Supplements to British Book News on Writers and Their Work. No. 5. London: Longmans, Green, 1950; revised 1957; repr., 1964.

3842   Tanselle, G. Thomas. "The Descriptive Bibliography of American Authors," SB, 21 (1968), 1-24.

3843   Taylor, Walter Fuller. A History of American Letters. Boston: American Book Co., 1936, pp. 556-559. [Subsequent editions entitled: The Story of American Letters]

3844   Temple, Ruth Z., comp., and ed. "Henry James," Twentieth Century British Literature: A Reference Guide and Bibliography. New York: Frederick Ungar Pub. Co., 1968.

3845   Thurston, Jarvis, and O. B. Emerson, et al. Short Fiction Criticism: A Checklist of Interpretation Since 1925 of Stories and Novelettes (American, British, Continental), 1800-1958. Denver: Alan Swallow, 1960, pp. 94-115.

3846   Tompkins, Jane, ed. Selected Bibliography. Twentieth Century Interpretations of "The Turn of the Screw" and Other Tales: A Collection of Critical Essays. Englewood Cliffs, New Jersey: Prentice-Hall, 1970.

3847   Trent, William Peterfield, et al. Cambridge History of American Literature. New York: G. P. Putnam's Sons, 1917-1921, IV, 671-675.

3848   Vallette, Jacques. "Petite Bibliographie de Henry James depuis la Guerre," MdF, No. 1067 (July, 1952), 528-531.

3849   Van Patten, Nathan. "Henry James," An Index to Bibliographies and Bibliographical Contributions Relating to the Work of American and British Authors, 1923-1932. Stanford U. P.; London: Humphrey Milford, 1934, p. 133.

3850   Walker, Warren S., comp. Twentieth Century Short Story Explication: Interpretations, 1900-1960, Inclusive, of Short Fiction Since 1800. Hamden, Conn.: The Shoe String Press, 1961, pp. 166-204.

3850.1 _____. Twentieth-Century Short Story Explication: Supplement I. Interpretations Since 1960 of Short Fiction Since
1800. Hamden, Conn.: Shoe String Press, 1963, pp. 52-65.

3850.2 _____. Twentieth-Century Short Story Explication: Supplement II. Interpretations, April 1, 1963-December 31,
1964. Hamden, Conn.: Shoe String Press, 1965, pp. 72-
86.

3851   Watson, George, ed. "Henry James," The New Cambridge
Bibliography of English Literature, 1800-1900. Cambridge:
Cambridge U. P., 1969, III, 992-1000.

3852   West, Rebecca. Henry James. New York: Henry Holt,
1916, pp. 119-126.

3853   Wiesenfarth, Joseph. Henry James and the Dramatic Analogy. New York: Fordham U. P., 1963, pp. 135-139.

3854   Willen, Gerald, ed. A Casebook on "The Turn of the
Screw." New York: Thomas Y. Crowell, 1960; 2nd ed.,
1969.

3855   _____, ed. Bibliography. Henry James: "The American." New York: Thomas Y. Crowell Co., 1972.

3856   Woodress, James. "Henry James," American Bibliography,
PMLA, 70 (1955), 170-17; 71 (April, 1956), 174-175; 72
(April, 1957), 254-255; 73 (1958), 204; 74 (May, 1959), 172;
75 (1960), 253; 76 (1961), 207-209.

3857   _____. Dissertations in American Literature, 1891-1966.
Revised and enlarged with the assistance of Marian Koritz.
Durham, North Carolina: Duke U. P., 1968.

3858   _____, et al. American Literary Scholarship: An Annual, 1963. Durham: Duke U. P., 1965, pp. 64-71.

3859   _____, et al. American Literary Scholarship: An Annual, 1964. Durham: Duke U. P., 1966, pp. 62-72.

3860   _____, et al. American Literary Scholarship: An Annual, 1965. Durham: Duke U. P., 1967, pp. 69-81.

3861   _____, et al. American Literary Scholarship: An Annual, 1966. Durham: Duke U. P., 1968, pp. 65-78.

3862   _____, et al. American Literary Scholarship: An Annual, 1967. Durham: Duke U. P., 1969, pp. 73-85.

3863   Wright, Austin, ed. "Henry James," Bibliographies of Studies in Victorian Literature for the Ten Years, 1945-1954.
Urbana, Illinois: Illinois U. P., 1956.

3864   Wright, Lyle H. "Henry James," American Fiction: 1876-
1900. A Contribution Toward a Bibliography. San Marino,
California: Huntington Library Press, 1966, pp. 292-294.

3865   Wright, Walter F. Selected Bibliography. The Madness of
Art: A Study of Henry James. Lincoln: Nebraska U. P.,
1962, pp. 255-266.

Abandonment: 180, 3697
About, Edmond: 1574, 1742
Achievement: 1577
Action: 872, 999, 1102, 3081,
   3571, 3593
Adam and Eve: 203, 790
Adams Henry: 8, 9, 10, 11, 12,
   23, 38, 1653, 1712, 1740,
   1772, 1794, 1795, 1998, 2028,
   2187, 2352, 2630, 2634, 2737,
   2802, 3010, 3070, 3304, 3305,
   3308, 3417, 3470, 3630
Adams, John: 38, 3626
Adventure: 1074, 1115, 3103
Aeschylus: 2352, 2568
The Aesthete (See also: Decadence): 194, 295, 1072, 1158,
   1877, 1914, 3033, 3689
Aesthetics and Aesthetic Values:
   127, 151, 180, 305.2, 750,
   952, 1071, 1072, 1142.1, 1158,
   1229, 1914, 1964, 2025, 2306,
   2307.1, 2380.1, 2382, 2545.1,
   2580, 2581, 2737, 2836, 2887,
   2934, 2935, 2941, 3033, 3140,
   3072.1, 3170, 3283, 3302,
   3306, 3312, 3335, 3336, 3378,
   3413, 3689
The "Affective Fallacy": 934.3,
   941, 942
Agassiz, Louis: 23, 38, 1998,
   2187
Age: 1493
Agnosticism: 787.1, 1792
Alcott, A. Bronson: 8, 9, 23,
   38, 1795, 1998, 2187, 2695,
   2773
Alcott, Louisa May: 8, 9, 23,
   1756, 1998, 2634, 2695, 2773
Alienation: 1881, 1885, 2380,
   2380.1, 2382
Allegory: 108, 236.1, 358, 384,

550, 586, 1229, 1877, 2560,
   2568, 2574, 2575, 3255, 3643
Allusion, Literary: 615, 682,
   1753, 3664
Ambiguity: 285, 413, 795, 886,
   1197, 1298, 1412, 1425, 1828,
   2094, 2224, 2262, 2333, 2380,
   2735.1, 2737, 2802, 3069,
   3294, 3326, 3630, 3672
Ambivalence: 630, 795, 2224,
   3328
America and American Life: 186,
   186.1, 783, 2134, 2191, 2192.1,
   2908, 2936, 3249, 3341
America and Europe: 229, 250,
   418, 1773, 1980, 2006, 2007,
   2075, 2076, 2200, 2242, 2293,
   2400, 2538, 2686, 2769, 2809,
   2998, 3028, 3069, 3117, 3286,
   3385, 3402, 3414, 3417, 3510,
   3667, 3669, 3688
America and Henry James:
   2083.3, 2732, 2733, 2925,
   3042, 3382, 3402, 3417
   3382, 3402, 3417
The American Business Man:
   210, 565, 1823, 2007.1, 2990
American Character: 2075, 3201
American Culture: 492, 2028.2,
   2568
The American Dream: 262 ·
The American Experience: 3098
American Gentility: 465
The American Girl: 34, 421,
   449.1, 450, 457, 460, 461.1,
   2650, 3417, 3626
American Gothic: 2890
American Identity: 991, 2707
American Innocence: 189, 189.1,
   418, 439, 440, 454, 1996,
   2749, 2795, 2940, 3207, 3286,
   3473, 3555, 3589

American Romanticism: 3351
American Self-Image: 235, 3543
American Thought: 2678, 3309
American Tradition: 3692
The American Type: 235, 255,
    871, 1823, 2007.1, 3268
The American Woman: 1635,
    2028.1, 3266, 3571
The American Writer: 1925
Analogy, dramatic: 3662, 3663
Analysis, psychological: 3130,
    3326, 3417
Ancestry, James's: 5.4
Andersen, Hendrik Christian
    (Sculptor): 1665, 1728
Anglo-American: 1663, 1670,
    2150, 3094.1, 3145
Antimonism: 93, 3175
Anti-Semitism: 2380, 2380.1
Anxiety: 2461.2
Appearance(s): 537, 1191, 1486,
    1929, 1930, 3630
Architecture: 2568, 3689
Aristocracy, American: 2936,
    3625, 3626
Aristocracy, European: 3625
Aristotle: 38
Arnold, Matthew: 8, 9, 10, 11,
    12, 38, 301, 980, 2198, 2251,
    2352, 2634, 2695, 2737, 2773,
    3326, 3689
Art: 43, 210, 243, 497, 500,
    575, 631, 676, 783, 950, 1092,
    1118, 1156, 1160.1, 1269, 1862,
    1887, 1904, 1914, 1937, 1980,
    1985, 1986, 2010, 2031, 2050,
    2122, 2171, 2226, 2243, 2249,
    2261, 2286, 2348, 2350, 2352,
    2376, 2376.1, 2379.1, 2380,
    2380.1, 2382, 2417, 2568,
    2673, 2720, 2744, 2784, 2887,
    2892, 2929, 2931, 2932, 2961,
    2965, 3025, 3027, 3047, 3055,
    3056, 3129, 3353, 3391, 3417,
    3476, 3501, 3502, 3518.1,
    3532, 3548, 3615, 3630, 3638,
    3670, 3689, 3710
Art of Fiction, James's Art:
    1640.1, 2049, 2051, 2099,
    2175, 2179, 2558, 3048.1,
    3218, 3269, 3417, 3660
The Artist: 8, 298, 512, 606,
    621, 650, 949, 959, 977, 1007,

1072, 1076, 1162, 1248, 1502.1,
    1840, 1857, 1862, 1867, 1881,
    1883, 1885, 1892, 1943, 2028,
    2044, 2136, 2222, 2233, 2380,
    2382, 2417, 2802, 2846, 2866,
    2870, 2903, 2911, 2916, 2937,
    2949, 3170, 3171, 3175, 3197,
    3228, 3329, 3378, 3392, 3394,
    3417, 3501, 3630, 3638, 3689
The Artist in America: 709,
    1845, 2345, 2673, 2918
Artist, James as Literary Artist:
    1972, 2222, 2226, 2249, 3615
Arts, Visual and Pictorial: 414,
    1979, 3455
Atherton, Gertrude: 2944
Auden, William H.: 2352, 2380.1,
    2706, 3674
Augier, Emile: 1082.1
Austen, Jane: 8, 9, 38, 872,
    1795, 2028, 2187, 2229, 2352,
    2560, 2634, 2650, 2737, 2770,
    3325, 3350, 3526
Author Intrusion: 169
Authority: 3630
Athenaeum Club: 9, 10

Babcockism: 3186
Balance: 847, 2907
Balderston, John: 1080, 3427.1
Baldwin, James, Influence of
    Henry James: 3053
Balzac, Honore de: 8, 9, 10,
    11, 12, 23, 38, 96, 170,
    170.1, 237.1, 301, 528, 591.1,
    813, 904, 922, 929, 1133,
    1740, 1774, 1785, 1794, 1795,
    1997, 2028, 2155, 2187, 2229,
    2276, 2287, 2348, 2352,
    2380.1, 2382, 2568, 2630,
    2666.1, 2695, 2730, 2737,
    2770, 2773, 2802, 2995, 3252,
    3326, 3336, 3536, 3548, 3665,
    3689.1
Baudelaire, Charles: 38, 2368,
    2695, 2770, 2792, 3325, 3536,
    3689.1, 3710
Beardsley, Aubrey: 10, 1740,
    2187
Beauty: 315, 2173, 3417, 3357
Beerbohm, Max: 11, 12, 1139.4,
    1187, 1406, 2187, 2284,

Beerbohm, Max (cont.): 2313,
2352, 2619, 3262, 3487, 3676
Beholder: 1532
Benedict, Clare--Collection of
Letters: 1683
Bennett, Arnold: 57, 1899, 1900,
1901, 1902
Benson, Arthur Christopher:
1904, 1905, 1906, 1907
Bergson, Henry: 23, 38, 3247
Berry, Walter: 1690
Besant, Walter: 2415, 2588
The Bible: 2568
Biblical: 1164
Bierce, Ambrose: 23
Birth (Station in Life): 37.2,
2868
Blake, William: 1794, 1795,
2773, 3325, 3630
Blanche, Jacques (Portrait
Painter): 2642
Blindness: 333
Bodley Head Edition: 2203
Boott, Elizabeth: 8, 9, 10, 11,
12, 301
Boott, Francis: 8, 9, 10, 11, 12,
301, 2634
Bosanquet, Theodora: 1740, 1971,
1972, 1973, 1974, 1974.1,
2187, 2229, 2620, 2792
Boston: 2003, 2028, 2382
Bouget, Paul: 10, 11, 12, 38,
614, 1740, 1840, 2187, 2198,
2229, 2560, 2634, 2712, 2737,
2773, 2948.1
Bouget, Mme. Paul (Minnie): 11,
12, 1740
Bowen, Elizabeth: 2030, 2432
Brewster, Henry B.: 785, 1664,
1991
Britten, Benjamin: 625, 1371
The Brontes: 11, 12, 301, 1167,
2028, 2229, 2352, 3126, 3325,
3536
Brooke, Stopford: 1727
Brooks, Van Wyck: 1796, 2019,
2701
Brownson, Orestes Augustus:
301, 1795
Browning, Elizabeth Barrett: 9.
10, 11, 12, 38, 301, 1740,
2634, 2773
Browning, Robert: 8, 10, 11, 12,

38, 301, 682, 933, 1740,
2041, 2187, 2198, 2229, 2352,
2568, 2624, 2634, 2639, 2681,
2695, 2773, 2960, 3417,
2689.1
Bulwer-Lytton, Edward: 301,
2792
Bunyan, Paul: 1795, 2568
Burne-Jones, Sir Edward: 2028,
2634, 3689
Burns, Robert: 2352
Business Man: 565, 2550, 2700,
2933, 2991, 2992 (See also:
The American Business Man)
Business Enterprise as Theme:
3358
Byron, George Gordon: 9, 10,
12, 38, 301, 2568

Calvinism: 8
Cambridge: 1695, 2705, 2705.1
Camus, Albert: 2770, 3325
Cannibalism, emotional: 1804,
2380.1, 2382
Capitalism: 2568
Capote, Truman: 3583
Caricature: 2476, 2568
Carlyle, Thomas: 8, 10, 12, 23,
38, 1794, 1795, 2028, 2187,
2695, 2773
Castration (See "Obscure Hurt")
Cather,Willa: 1802, 2079.1,
2352, 2380, 2383, 3003, 3079,
3562
Catholicism: 2352, 2438, 3355,
3417
Centennial, James's: 1654, 1773,
1813, 2042, 3603
Cervantes, Don Quixote: 2352,
2695, 3326
Cervantes Saavedra, Miguel: 9,
38, 2229
Chance: 1243, 3611
Change of Heart: 2695
Channing, William Ellery: 38,
1795
Chapman, John Jay: 1795, 2587
Characters and Characterization:
102, 183.2, 350, 363, 372,
401.1, 535, 655, 729, 807,
867, 894, 1011.1, 1135, 1271,
1557.1, 1869, 1898, 2017,

Characters and Characterization
(cont): 2048, 2049, 2051,
2053, 2082, 2099, 2110, 2122,
2363, 2380, 2382, 2416, 2519,
2560, 2655, 2656, 2659, 2870,
2911, 2953, 3200, 3201, 3286,
3317, 3332, 3334, 3345, 3373,
3417, 3442, 3523, 3567, 3569,
3571, 3591, 3705, 3708
Characterization and Southern
Characters: 405, 1790, 1791,
2110, 2954
Characterization, Women: 2027,
2028.1, 2130.1, 2152.1, 2267,
2291, 2294, 3317, 3464
Chekhov, Anton: 2630, 3252,
3273, 3327.1
Cherbuliez, Victor: 428, 470,
862, 2695, 3689
Chess and James: 2355
The Child, Childhood and Adolescence: 359, 513, 1260, 1286,
1307, 1389, 1390.1, 1417,
1495, 1502, 2352, 2359, 2380,
2382, 2690, 2910, 3339, 3340,
3472, 3555
Child, Francis James: 301
Choric (commentator, observer,
or prophet): 3326
Christ: 3326
Christie, Agatha: 1543, 2482
Church: 3417 (See also: Catholicism)
The City: 176.2, 261, 371, 911,
915, 2025, 2032, 2849, 3214,
3629, 3657, 3660
The Civil War and James: 8,
1925, 2028, 2187, 2380.1,
2382, 3417, 3648
Civilization: 375, 1854, 1916,
2089, 3417, 3466, 3501 (See also: Morals and Morality)
Clarity in James: 2124
Class: 879, 1917
Clemens (See Twain, Mark)
Coburn, Alvin Langdon (James's
photographer): 2303
Coleridge, Samuel Taylor: 1388,
1740, 1795, 2028, 2352, 2737,
3417
Colette, Sidonie Gabrielle Claud-
ine: 135
Collaboration: 1836, 2352

Collections of Books, Letters,
Manuscripts: 1704, 1660,
1683, 1684, 1696, 1697, 1976,
3122, 3229
Collections of Stories: The Better Sort, 12; Embarrassments,
11, 12, 38; The Finer Grain,
12; The Soft Side, 11, 12;
Terminations, 11, 12, 1740,
2006, 2380.1, 3015; The Two
Magics, 11, 1740, 2229, 2380.1,
2630
Collins, Wilkie: 301, 2792
Comedy and the Comic: 171.2,
216.1, 219, 290, 409.1, 465,
487, 490.1, 465, 487, 490.1,
496, 572.2, 692, 1000.1,
1107, 1479, 2082, 2242, 2445,
2568, 2681, 2682, 2683, 2802,
2859.1, 3147, 3148, 3186,
3326, 3347, 3577
Commitment: 734, 2744
Confidante: 846, 2560, 3326,
3332, 3334 (See also Observer)
Confidence: 1464, 2352, 2695
Conflict: 2814
Conrad, Joseph: 23, 38, 542,
929, 1085, 1525, 1667.1,
1694, 1794, 1839, 2014, 2038,
2116, 2117, 2118, 2119, 2187,
2198, 2227, 2229, 2462.1,
2560, 2630, 2770, 3261, 3325,
3376, 3559, 3590, 3611
Conscience: 174, 980, 980.1,
1096, 2118, 2155, 2251, 2251.1,
2445, 2556, 3523 (See also
Consciousness and the Unconscious)
Conscience, the New England Conscience: 174, 174.1, 412,
3489, 3597
Consciousness (See also Conscience): 38, 163, 316, 318, 566,
633, 636, 758, 768, 811, 907,
1050.1, 1059, 1078, 1096,
1795, 1796, 1860, 1938, 2191.2,
2192, 2220, 2251, 2251.1,
2340.2, 2342, 2380, 2382,
2410, 2424, 2614, 2731, 2737,
2740, 2741, 2742, 2743, 2770,
2796, 2797, 2802, 2810, 2866,
2970, 2974, 2984, 2996.1,
3012, 3048, 3060, 3213.1,

Consciousness (cont.): 3326, 3417, 3468, 3470, 3500, 3508, 3532, 3552, 3553

Conversation as a Device: 3417 (See also Dialogue and Language)

Conversion Experience: 172

Cooper, James Fenimore: 23, 38, 301, 1795, 2187, 2028, 2352, 2568, 2773, 3626

Copyright - International: 1977, 1978

Cosmopolitanism: 2012, 2032, 2198, 2625, 3129, 3441, 3624, 3626, 3669

The Craft of James: 262, 2308, 3181.2, 3456, 3461, 3476, 3542, 3615

Crane, Stephen: 23, 731, 1184, 1886, 2028, 2352, 2455, 2560, 2610, 2662, 3377, 3396, 3406.1

Crawford, Francis Marion: 9, 301, 690, 1678, 1679, 3324

Crawford, Thomas (American Sculptor): 981

Creative Process and Creativity: 252.1, 2684, 3228, 3263, 3284, 3341, 3375, 3417

The Critic: 359, 2054, 2055, 2056.1, 3113

Criticism (of James's Criticism): 527.1, 603.2, 706, 1857, 2107, 2147.2, 2218, 2294.1, 2380.1, 2382, 2761, 2762, 2819, 2822, 2873, 2900, 2968, 3025, 3051, 3252, 3254, 3311, 3383, 3400, 3536

Cruikshank, George: 301

Culture, European: 3417

Culture, General: 374, 532.1, 822.1, 888, 1152, 1795, 1949, 2017, 2040, 2057, 2172, 2293, 2443, 2784, 3101, 3213.1, 3417, 3529

Cult, Jamesian (See Revival of Interest in Henry James)

Curtis, George: 8, 301

Dante, Alighieri: 8, 9, 10, 11, 12, 38, 301, 1794, 1795, 2352, 2568

Dark Ladies: 391, 1343, 1560

Darkness in Henry James: 1529, 2105, 2808, 3710

Darwin, Charles: 9, 10, 12, 23, 38, 301, 1528, 2380.1, 2382

Daudet, Alphonse: 8, 9, 10, 11, 12, 38, 301, 394, 1703, 1740, 2028, 2187, 2198, 2229, 2380.1, 2382, 2568, 2695, 2770, 2773, 2889, 2995, 3010, 3176, 3689.1

Daumier, Honore: 38, 301, 2568

Davenport, Marcia: 2052

Da Vinci, Leonardo: 38, 301

de Lafayette, Madame: 3352

Death: 427, 895, 916, 988, 1494.1, 1550, 1769.1, 2148

Decadence: 194, 2181.1, 2242, 3261 (See also Aesthetes)

Decorum (See Freedom)

Defoe, Daniel: 8, 9, 2568

de Goncourt Brothers: 3252, 3326

Democracy: 384, 547, 2568, 2666

Demonic: 1292 (See also Gothic and Supernatural)

Demuth, Charles: 1234, 3454

Design: 1010 (See also Form and Structure)

Despair: 3434 (See also Determinism)

Detachment: 621, 1883, 1885, 2560, 3302

Determinism: 812, 2411, 2412, 2413

Development of Henry James: Early Development: 8, 9, 37, 410, 464, 707, 1781, 1794, 1857, 1870, 1910, 1938, 2002, 2006, 2007, 2008, 2017, 2023, 2039, 2049, 2062, 2090, 2091, 2099, 2127, 2128, 2134, 2147, 2147.2, 2150, 2187, 2221, 2229, 2235, 2242, 2275, 2307, 2308, 2325, 2338, 2344, 2348, 2372, 2372.1, 2380, 2417, 2422, 2461.2, 2470, 2473, 2487, 2495, 2524, 2530, 2542, 2530, 2542, 2543, 2560, 2613, 2615, 2650, 2681, 2682, 2693, 2694, 2695, 2717, 2722, 2723, 2727, 2754, 2773, 2809, 2817, 2818, 2884, 2912, 2979.1,

Development of Henry James
(cont.) 3030.1, 3041, 3072,
3097, 3107, 3133, 3148, 3180,
3195, 3200, 3218, 3245, 3252,
3307, 3336, 3388, 3394, 3477,
3512, 3544, 3548, 3615, 3648,
3667.1
Middle Period: 10, 11, 1870,
3073, 3160, 3165, 3301, 3394,
3512, 3591, 3662, 3663, 3681
Later Phase: 12, 34, 131,
257.1, 352, 707, 1066.2, 1571,
1763, 1786, 1795, 1828, 1837,
1870, 1955, 1956, 1998, 2008,
2029, 2085, 2086, 2113, 2123,
2127, 2128, 2133, 2187, 2191.2,
2242, 2254, 2297, 2314, 2325,
2470, 2479, 2507, 2530, 2555,
2556, 2560, 2572, 2596, 2597,
2598, 2650, 2736, 2737, 2737.1,
2759, 2845, 2852.1, 2866,
2898, 2901.1, 2903, 2915.1,
2951, 2952, 2974.1, 2976,
3015, 3182, 3200, 3251, 3253,
3295, 3394, 3476, 3484, 3497,
3504, 3508, 3512, 3598, 3600,
3601, 3675, 3681, 3686, 3713
Dialectic: 3600, 3601
Dialogue: 1016, 1870, 1992,
2229, 2560, 3120, 3633
Dickens, Charles: 8, 9, 10, 11,
12, 23, 38, 301, 805, 904.2,
913.1, 913.2, 913.3, 1033,
1740, 1794, 1795, 2028, 2187,
2229, 2337, 2352, 2367,
2380.1, 2382, 2476, 2490,
2568, 2630, 2695, 2737, 2767,
2773, 2792, 2935, 3194, 3252,
3269, 3326, 3417, 3612, 3325,
3689.1
Dickinson, Emily: 23, 38, 3445
Diction: 3190, 3191, 3192, 3193
(See also Language)
Diplomacy: 152.1
Disaster: 3590
Discourse: 688, 3633 (See also
Dialogue and Language)
Discretion: 1964
Disease and James, 827, 933.2,
1542
Disinheritance, Theme of: 2380.1
Disraeli, Benjamin (Earl of Bea-
consfield): 9, 10, 2792

Dissertations, Dissertation Ab-
stracts and Dissertation Ab-
stracts International: 52, 61,
101, 108, 119.1, 127, 131,
146, 171.1, 188, 231, 245,
263, 299, 304, 305.2 306, 307,
307.3, 400, 504, 545, 547.1,
555, 558.1, 562.2, 564.1,
572.1, 634.1, 666, 678.1, 698,
798, 840, 842.1, 865, 910,
920, 987, 1048, 1055, 1097,
1108, 1125, 1126, 1138, 1152,
1217.1, 1286, 1296, 1394,
1473, 1483, 1495, 1527, 1532,
1537, 1539, 1544, 1557.1,
1582, 1625, 1683, 1736.2,
1737, 1737.1, 1737.2, 1748,
1752, 1762.1, 1765.1, 1777,
1793, 1823, 1827, 1828, 1833.1,
1835, 1849, 1853, 1859, 1860,
1866, 1881, 1898, 1903, 1916,
1921, 1938, 1941, 1949, 1952.1,
1955, 1961, 1964, 1968, 1968.1,
1979, 1989, 2022, 2026, 2029,
2037, 2040, 2044, 2082, 2082.1,
2082.3, 2095, 2107, 2114,
2122, 2123, 2139, 2140, 2151,
2152.1, 2153, 2154, 2162,
2164, 2168, 2173, 2180, 2183,
2185, 2191.1, 2191.2, 2192,
2224, 2231, 2235, 2246, 2270,
2283, 2287, 2292, 2294.1,
2297, 2299, 2301, 2304, 2307,
2308, 2314, 2315, 2320, 2326,
2340.2, 2351, 2367, 2371,
2374, 2375, 2379, 2384, 2397,
2411, 2417, 2424, 2441, 2443,
2445, 2451, 2461, 2461.1,
2461.2, 2462, 2462.1, 2475.1,
2477, 2477.1, 2507, 2522,
2530, 2547, 2551, 2554, 2555,
2555.1, 2556, 2559, 2563,
2567, 2580, 2586.1, 2611,
2612, 2628, 2629, 2652, 2655,
2658, 2659, 2660, 2663, 2667,
2669, 2676, 2681, 2693, 2707.1,
2708.2, 2715, 2719, 2722, 2727,
2729, 2731, 2732, 2733.1, 2739,
2743, 2745, 2753, 2769, 2771,
2775, 2780, 2788, 2791, 2803.1,
2814, 2838, 2850, 2852.1, 2883,
2887, 2896, 2901.1, 2907, 2910,
2927, 2930, 2933, 2934, 2951,

2953, 2970, 2975, 2987,
2993.1, 2995, 2996, 2999,
3009, 3021, 3025, 3030, 3034,
3036, 3044, 3048, 3052, 3055,
3059, 3072.1, 3081, 3100,
3109, 3113, 3124, 3125, 3127,
3148, 3172, 3181, 3181.2,
3193, 3215, 3217, 3221, 3228,
3235, 3243, 3249, 3254, 3272,
3284, 3288, 3301, 3302, 3303,
3304, 3311, 3313, 3314, 3317,
3334, 3339, 3353, 3354,
3367.1, 3369, 3375, 3378,
3379, 3381, 3399, 3400, 3414,
3426, 3430, 3444, 3462, 3466,
3474, 3476.1, 3477, 3480,
3484, 3485, 3486, 3504, 3508,
3530, 3534, 3535, 3556, 3559,
3560.1, 3577, 3584, 3586,
3631, 3632, 3633, 3660, 3662,
3684, 3689, 3692, 3697, 3699,
3713
Disunity: 376
Divorce: 1502.2
Donnee, James's: 2013, 2031,
2935
Dostoevsky, Fyodor: 23, 38,
928, 1785, 1795, 2187, 2229,
2380.1, 2382, 2935, 3056
The Double in Literature: 633,
2024, 3259
Dowson, Ernest: 194, 2181.1
Drama and the Dramatic Effect:
10, 314, 549, 572.1, 1339,
1418, 1607, 1611, 1621, 1622,
1626, 1633, 1870, 1871, 2098,
2133, 2288, 2325, 2390, 2568,
2721, 2753, 3417, 3560.1,
3662
Dramatic Method: 2380.1, 2382,
2560, 2802, 3251
Dramatization: 430, 437, 1146,
1170, 1171, 1204, 1244, 1256,
1277, 1309, 1310, 1314, 1335,
1348, 1354, 1356, 1418, 1428,
1573, 1575, 1597, 1602, 1603,
1604, 1611.1, 1625, 2133
Dream, Use of: 1521, 2380.1,
3417
Dreiser, Theodore: 23, 38, 2028,
2380.1, 2382, 3514, 3325
Dreyfus, Alfred: 38
DuBos, Charles du: 1927, 2391,

2392, 2895
Dumas, Alexandre (fils): 8, 9,
10, 11, 38, 209, 301, 890,
984.1, 976, 1082.1, 1740,
1758.1, 2028, 2380.1, 2382,
2461.3, 2630, 2695, 2792,
2885, 2935, 3325
Dumas, Alexandre (pere): 10,
38
Du Maurier, George: 9, 10, 11,
12, 301, 1740, 2028, 2198,
2695, 2773, 2935, 3689.1
Durrell, Lawrence: 3047
Durrenmatt, Friedrich: 1292
Duty: 781, 1539

Early Years of Henry James: 3,
8, 28, 34, 37, 43, 44, 3069,
3155, 3670 (See also Development: Early Years)
The Economic Age: 1931, 2382
Economic Motif: 1965, 2380.1,
2802 (See also Money)
Economy of Style, James's: 3479
Eden: 1261 (See also Adam and
Eve)
Edgeworth, Maria: 2695
Editing: 1806
Editions: 53, 60, 86, 87, 110,
129, 144, 145, 146, 969,
1003, 1006, 1124, 1125, 1714,
1788, 1816, 1856, 1976, 1990,
2020, 2146.1, 2204, 2405,
2508, 2560, 2780, 3065, 3222,
3229; New York Edition: Items
listed under section thus entitled, but see also: 10, 11,
12, 110, 230, 969, 1788,
2303, 2630
Edwards, Jonathan: 38, 301,
1794, 1795
Effect: 314, 548
Egotism and the Ego: 764,
1015.1, 2380, 2382, 2522,
2861, 3417
Eliot, George: 8, 9, 10, 11, 12,
23, 38, 78.1, 301, 398, 508,
532, 534, 759.1, 802, 804,
805, 806, 813, 1033, 1167,
1740, 1777.2, 1794, 1795,
1903.1, 2028, 2187, 2270,
2349.1, 2352, 2380, 2382,

Eliot, George (cont.): 2441, 2469, 2491, 2518, 2533, 2568, 2630, 2634, 2636, 2695, 2737, 2767, 2770, 2773, 2935, 3138, 3188, 3252, 3326, 3417, 3684, 3689

Eliot, T. S.: 78.1, 119, 278, 497, 1795, 2028, 2187, 2352, 2380.1, 2382, 2562, 2563, 2564, 2568, 2737, 2770, 2913, 3325, 3590, 3626

Embrace, Meaning of in James's Fiction: 3630

Emerson, Ralph Waldo: 8, 9, 10, 11, 12, 23, 38, 301, 646, 1794, 1795, 1849, 2028, 2187, 2198, 2380.1, 2382, 2568, 2770, 2773, 2935, 3252, 3271, 3401, 3417, 3590, 3626, 3630, 3689

Epictetus: 2935, 3252

Empiricism: 3213 (See also Experience)

Ending, Inconclusive: 3326

England: 2382, 2771, 2772, 3417, 3626

Epic: 1441, 3498, 2767.1

Epistemology: 88.1, 152, 468, 3155, 3326

Ethics: 151, 650, 1860, 1870, 1903, 2380.1, 2510, 2511, 3171, 3312, 3378 (See also Morality)

Europe (See America and Europe)

Europe and Europeans (European Tradition): 38, 43, 229, 483, 871, 1919, 1980, 2092.1, 2143, 2242, 2258, 2293, 2345, 2380, 2510, 2511, 2514, 2563, 2564, 2611, 2784, 2802, 2903, 2985, 3069, 3101, 3181, 3195, 3206, 3384, 3417, 3428, 3626

Evil: 173, 582, 583, 776, 783, 1198, 1232, 1250, 1250.1, 1290, 1294, 1338, 1345, 2353, 2802, 3214, 3248, 3374, 3410, 3586, 3587, 3588, 3590, 3671, 3710

Existence: 3475 (See also Life)

Existentialism: 338, 1019, 2674

Expatriate, James as: 1942, 2005, 2006, 2007, 2033, 2062, 2075, 2112, 2191.3, 2196,

2980, 3098, 3233, 3365, 3523, 3533, 3624

Experience: 1094, 1306, 1485, 1507.1, 2125, 2380.1, 2382, 2663, 2683, 3075, 3204, 3213, 3297, 3373, 3388, 3630

Exploitation: 3630

Expressionism: 2380.1, 2382, 2568, 3639

Fable: 205, 1804, 2667, 3371

The Fair Lady: 391 (See also the Dark Lady)

Fairy Tale Aspect: 386, 831, 3417, 3630

The Fall (See Unfortunate Fall)

Fame: 2286

Family Pattern and Relationships: 2380.1, 2889.1

Fantasy: 1183, 1880, 1949, 2147.1, 2153, 2224, 2253, 2461.2, 2814

Fastidiousness: 3630

Fatalism: 1494.1, 2413 (See also Determinism)

Fatherhood in James: 574, 2413, 333

Faulkner, William: 1795, 2352, 2380.1, 2382, 2539, 2568, 2630, 2770, 2985, 3325, 3376, 3590, 3626, 3630

Fawcett, Edgar: 2506

Femininity and Feminism: 1826, 3571

The Feminist Movement: 369, 372, 377, 385.1, 398, 404.1, 2380.1, 2382 (See also Women Suffrage)

Fielding, Henry: 8, 38, 1740, 1785, 2695

Fields, Mr., and Mrs. James T.: 8, 301, 2187, 2591, 2773

Figures of Speech: 3417 (See also Imagery and Symbolism)

Films: 1618 (See also Specific Works)

First Person, Use of: 276, 2861, 2883, 2976

Fitzgerald, F. Scott: 5, 105, 198, 235, 423, 2019, 2024, 2187, 2545.2, 2568, 3246, 3415, 3543

Flaubert, Gustave: 8, 9, 10, 11, 12, 23, 38, 147, 301, 527.3, 813, 889, 1635, 1666, 1794, 2019.2, 2120.1, 2187, 2420, 2422, 2568, 2695, 2770, 2773, 2786, 2995, 3067, 3191.1, 3252, 3281, 3326, 3409, 3415, 3689

The Fool as Character: 3417

Fordham Castle: 2352

Foreshadowing: 196

Foreshortening, Art of: 573, 2707.1

Form: 321.1, 329, 519, 539, 545, 574, 627, 993, 1110, 1150, 1476, 1498.1, 1517, 1783, 1860, 1944, 1966, 2034, 2080, 2288, 2319, 2545, 2557, 2568, 3081, 3228, 3306, 3325, 3394, 3577, 3594, 3630

Forster, E. M.: 147, 1917, 2153, 3281, 3328, 3689

Fortune: (See Money)

The Fourth Manner of James: 560

France, Influence of: 527, 1834, 2081, 2160, 2219, 2255, 2256, 2277, 2294.1, 2326, 2372, 2372.1, 2382, 2449, 2450, 2533.1, 2667.1, 2670, 2775, 2896, 2995, 3417, 3523, 3559, (See also French Influence on Literature)

France, Anatole: 1740, 2229, 3417

Franklin, Benjamin: 8, 9, 38

Frederic, Harold: 2087

Freedom and Free Will: 118, 734, 812, 824, 875, 993, 1055, 1137, 1161.1, 2021, 2304, 2411, 2412, 2413, 2446, 2557, 2726, 2901.1, 3217, 3630, 3666

French Influence: 660, 1834, 1991, 2028.1, 2081, 2150, 2155, 2255, 2256, 2277, 2344, 2384, 2770, 2775, 2995, 3015, 3095, 3523

French Naturalism: 2344, 2345, 3172, 3172.1, 3326

French Revolution, James's Attitude toward: 3220

French Translations of James: 2219

Freud, Sigmund: 9, 11, 1168, 1209, 1246, 1247, 1279, 1291, 1377, 1384, 1394, 1414, 1794, 1964, 2028, 2068, 2352, 2354, 2380.1, 2560, 3325

Freudian Imagery: 2354

Fry, Roger: 3689.1

Fuller, Henry Blake: 1768, 3137

Fuller, Margaret: 8, 23, 301, 1795, 2773, 3626

Gainsborough, Thomas: 2352

Gallo-American: 1663, 1991.1

Galsworthy, John: 2229

The Garden: 1286

Garland, Hamlin: 2945, 3626

Gaskell, Mrs. Elizabeth Cleghorne: 1167, 1756, 2695, 2935

Gautier, Theophile: 8, 9, 11, 23, 38, 301, 1740, 2695, 2770, 3252, 3689.1

Genius, Nature of: 362, 408

Genteel Tradition: 124, 473, 2266, 3605

Gentleman Type: 1961, 3378

German Culture and James: 3143

Germany, James's Reception in: 11, 1865, 2586.1, 2977, 3183, 3531, 3626

Gestation: 740, 770, 793, 1994.2

Gesture: 672, 1446

Ghost Stories: 1208, 1319, 1430, 2205, 2208, 2943, 3093, 3490, (See also Gothic and Supernatural)

Ghost(s): 634, 1301 (See also Supernatural)

Ghost Story Element: 2380.1, 2382, 2935, 3084, 3417

"The Ghost" at Breda: 2418, 2662, 3406.1, 3689

Gide, André: 8, 11, 38, 1769.1, 1785, 1795, 2380.1, 3325

The Gilded Age: 405

Girl (See The American Girl)

Gissing, George: 903, 2229, 2630

Gladstone, William Ewart: 11, 1740, 2634

Glasgow, Ellen: 3003

Goethe, Wolfgang von: 8, 9, 11,
38, 301, 1258, 1794, 1795,
2028, 2352, 2695, 3252, 3626
Goncourt, Edmond de: 2935,
2995
Good and Evil: 1290, 1411,
2447, 3032, 3417
Good Intentions: 776
Goodness: 3417
Gosse, Sir Edmund: 8, 9, 10,
11, 12, 23, 38, 1682, 1723,
1740, 2028, 2187, 2198, 2229,
2380.1, 2382, 2420, 2421,
2422, 2423, 2695, 3010, 3325,
3417, 3689.1
Gothic and Gothicism: 1195,
1337, 1851, 1852, 1853, 2028,
2568, 2890, 3285, 3534 (See
also Ghost Stories and Supernatural)
Grace: 1557
Grammar (See Language): 973,
1379
Greeley, Horace: 8, 38, 301,
3626
Greene, Graham: 667, 2028,
2630, 2698, 2938, 3032, 3062,
3590
The Greenoughs: 877, 3708
Griffiths, T.: 1283
Griswold, Rufus: 8
Guilt: 297, 346, 3258
Guthrie, Thomas Anstey: 690

Hallucination: 1392, 1395
Hamlet: 1740, 1794, 2380.1,
3252
Hardy, Thomas: 9, 10, 11, 12,
321, 968, 1699, 1794, 2028,
2187, 2229, 2352, 2492, 2493,
2630, 2695, 2752, 2770, 3252,
3417, 3617, 3619
Harte, Bret: 2028, 2100, 3573,
3626
Hartley, L. P. 2962
Hawthorne, Nathaniel: 8, 9, 10,
11, 12, 23, 38, 301, 336,
342, 344, 365, 384, 534,
637.1, 649, 651, 659, 661,
735, 994, 1044, 1138, 1186,
1369, 1459.1, 1523, 1523.1,
1740, 1794, 1795, 1933, 1934,

1935, 2028.1, 2104, 2126,
2187, 2229, 2299, 2349, 2352,
2380.1, 2382, 2560, 2568,
2630, 2679, 2695, 2773, 2796,
2799, 2906, 2910, 3102, 3150,
3276, 3325, 3326, 3423, 3462,
3465, 3520, 3536, 3590, 3626
Hay, John: 10, 11, 818, 1708.1,
1709, 1710, 1712, 2028, 2521,
3008, 3009, 3010, 3481
Hemingway, Ernest: 1795, 2019,
2352, 2380.1, 2382, 2529,
2539, 3227, 3325, 3415, 3623
Heredity in Characterization:
867, 1011.1, 3567
The Hero: 344, 347, 401, 425,
427, 556, 621, 788, 882,
1509, 1838, 1883, 2133, 2231,
2676, 2880, 2990, 2991, 2992,
3417, 3591
Heroics: 1287
The Heroine: 426, 441, 446,
739, 784, 840, 864, 870,
2152.1, 2380.1, 2382, 2451,
2987, 3205, 3284, 3331, 3375
Higginson, Thomas Wentworth:
38, 2028, 2225, 2352, 3636
History: 93.1, 183, 2382
History, Intellectual: 638
Hogarth, William: 9, 11, 301
Holmes, Justice Oliver Wendell:
9, 10, 11, 12, 38, 1685,
1740, 2773
Holmes, Oliver Wendell (Jr.):
8, 9, 10, 11, 12, 38, 301,
1740, 2028, 2187, 2382, 2773,
3021.2, 3626
Hopkins, Gerard Manley: 2961.1,
2965
Horror: 1427 (See also Supernatural)
Howe, Julia Ward: 11, 12, 301,
1740, 2187, 2352, 2773
Howells, William Dean: 8, 9,
10, 11, 12, 23, 38, 301, 444,
845, 1686, 1689, 1740, 1768,
1792, 2004, 2028, 2047, 2069,
2071, 2073, 2103, 2187.1,
2229, 2269, 2307.1, 2345,
2347, 2347.1, 2352, 2380,
2382, 2558, 2560, 2568, 2592,
2593, 2594, 2595, 2596, 2597,
2598, 2599, 2600, 2630, 2677,

Howells, William Dean (cont.):
2688, 2695, 2708, 2718, 2734,
2737, 2770, 2773, 2802, 3010,
3015, 3182, 3252, 3324, 3325,
3326, 3405, 3417, 3541, 3563,
3599, 3626, 3701, 3728
Hugo, Victor: 8, 9, 11, 38, 301,
2568, 2695, 2773, 3252
Humanism: 3219, 3380, 3504,
3521
Humor: 221, 1794, 1939, 2651,
2802, 3268, 3417
Huneker, James Gibbons: 2615,
2616, 2616.1, 2616.2
Hunt, Leigh: 9
Hunt, William Morris: 8, 301,
2187, 2773
Huxley, Thomas Henry: 9, 11, 23

Ibsen, Henrik: 10, 11, 12, 1717,
1740, 2062, 2135, 2187, 2229,
2232, 2234, 2352, 2568, 2630,
2737, 3252, 3325
Idealism: 811, 821, 1535, 2446,
2678, 2802, 3335, 3336, 3374,
3435, 3436, 3630
Identity, American: 991, 2707
Identity Crisis: 858
Identity, Sense of: 90.1, 226,
916, 3580, 3581
Illusion: 397, 615, 2380.1, 2382,
3444, 3664
Imagery: 71, 89, 111, 150, 166,
350, 358, 373, 558, 581, 637,
771, 839, 1007, 1129, 1162,
1269, 1270, 1376, 1548, 1572,
1749, 1752, 1786, 2167, 2184,
2350, 2351, 2352, 2354, 2360,
2362, 2364, 2390, 2560, 2565,
2566, 2737, 2780, 2995, 3258,
3326, 3342, 3374, 3417, 3433,
3497, 3504, 3573, 3598, 3630
(See also Symbolism)
Imagination, Use of: 55, 151.1,
336.1, 574.1, 585.1, 895, 925,
988, 1077, 1092, 1506, 1826,
1835, 1997, 2028, 2031, 2246,
2248, 2280, 2318, 2432, 2545,
2667, 2717, 2770, 2802, 2984,
3293, 3325, 3410, 3417, 3517,
3582, 3590, 3630, 3631, 3710
Immortality: 38, 3417

Impressionism: 1776, 2028,
2471, 2861, 2961, 2984, 3521
Incest: 2380.1 (See also Darkness in James)
Independence: 1867, 3630 (See
also Freedom)
Indirection: 1139
The Individual: 737, 2477
Initiation: 1492
Innocence: 109, 198, 419, 433,
439, 440, 458, 483, 578, 760,
1255, 1294, 1487, 1488, 1493,
2262, 2283, 2293, 2560, 2663,
2802, 3127, 3206, 3286, 3373,
3417, 3584, 3630
Integration: 844
Intention: 1577
The International Novel: 190,
1580, 3627 (See also Internationalism)
Internationalism and International
Theme: 176.1, 190, 370, 407,
585, 660, 664, 667, 719, 720,
880.1, 992, 1580, 1581, 1804,
1891, 1932, 2028, 2191.1,
2345, 2560, 2611, 2625, 2702,
2802, 2809, 2903, 2938, 2999,
3000, 3069, 3082, 3110, 3170,
3199, 3200, 3326, 3394, 3417,
3424, 3440, 3503, 3548, 3622,
3623, 3670, 3688
Invention, Literary: 2909
Irony: 130, 150, 281, 315, 503,
673, 810, 831, 868, 961,
1127, 1139, 1879, 2022, 2095,
2096, 2140, 2183, 2560, 2568,
2737, 2802, 2970, 3326
Irving, Washington: 8, 9, 23,
38, 301, 2028, 2062, 2695,
2773, 3626
Isolation: 1867, 3284, 3375,
3630
Italy, Influence of: 8, 1827,
2309, 2357, 2358, 2380, 2382,
2403, 2501, 2893, 2894, 2927,
2928, 3121, 3417, 3431, 3626,
3709

Jacobean and Shavian: 1874, 1890
Jacobites: 629, 1841, 1874, 2028,
2049, 2265, 2381, 2382
The James Family: 2, 2.1, 14,

The James Family (cont.): 20, 23, 25.1, 26.1, 33.1, 35.1, 38, 46.1, 48.3, 301, 241, 1936, 2187, 2634, 3401, 3516, 3677
James, Alexander Robertson (Nephew): 10, 12, 2634
James, Alice (sister): 5.1, 5.2, 8, 7.2, 9, 10, 11, 12, 38, 301, 1740, 1936, 2035.1, 2062, 2187, 2380.1, 2366, 2634, 2773, 3417
James, Augustus (uncle): 8, 301, 2773
James, Catherine Barber (grandmother): 8, 301, 2187, 2773
James, Catherine (cousin): 301
James, Catherine Margaret (aunt): 8, 301, 2187
James, Edward (uncle): 301
James, Ellen King (aunt): 301
James, Garth Wilkinson (brother): 8, 9, 10, 11, 12, 38, 301, 1740, 2187, 2380.1, 2634, 2773
James, Gertrude (cousin) (Mrs. James H. Pendleton): 301
James, Henry (father): 8, 9, 10, 11, 12, 23, 38, 47, 301, 1740, 2187, 2380.1, 3715
James, Henry ("Harry," nephew): 8, 10, 11, 12, 38, 1740, 2187, 2380.1
James, Howard (uncle): 8, 301
James, Jeannette ("Janet," aunt) (Mrs. William H. Barker): 301
James, John Barber (uncle): 8, 301
James, John Vanderburgh (cousin): 301
James, Lydia Lush (cousin, Mrs. Henry Mason): 301
James, Marie Bay (cousin, Mrs. Charles Robert): 301
James, Mary Helen (cousin, Mrs. Alfred Grymes): 301
James, Mary Margaret ("Peggy," niece): 10, 12, 38
James, Mary Robertson (Mrs. Vaux, niece): 12, 38
James, Mary R. Walsh (mother): 8, 9, 10, 11, 38, 301, 1740

James, Robert (uncle): 301
James, Robert W. (cousin): 301
James, Robertson (brother): 8, 9, 11, 12, 38, 301, 2187, 2773
James, William (brother): 1.1, 2, 8, 9, 10, 11, 12, 14, 23, 38, 43, 47, 52, 301, 1192, 1740, 2187, 2352, 2630, 2634, 2646, 2647, 2648, 2649, 2689, 2691, 2695, 2773, 3123, 3406, 3516, 3552, 3554
James, William, Jr. (nephew): 8, 10, 12, 38, 1740
James, (Mrs. William -Alice Howe Gibbens): 9, 10, 11, 12, 38, 2187
James, William (grandfather): 8, 10, 11, 301, 2187, 2773
Jewett, Sarah Orne: 11, 12, 1658, 2591
Jews: 11, 417, 2380.1, 2382, 2790
Johnson, Dr. Samuel: 12, 38
Journalism, James's Attitude toward Journalism and Reporting: 1787, 1918, 2320, 2321, 2380.1, 2382, 2881, 2968, 3045, 3215, 3728
Journals: Atlantic Monthly: 8, 9, 10, 11, 12, 1758.2, 1850, 2028, 2187, 2380.1, 2382, 2695, 2773, 2954.1, 3010, 3417; Century Magazine: 9, 10, 11, 12, 2028, 2187, 3359; Cornhill: 8, 9, 10, 12, 301, 420, 2187, 2695, 2773, 3010; Cosmopolitan: 10, 11; English Illustrated: 9, 10, 11; Fortnightly Review: 10, 3010; The Galaxy: 8, 9, 2028, 2695, 2773; Harper's Baza[a]r: 1674; Harper's Monthly: 1, 2187, 2380.1, 2382; Harper's Weekly: 10, 11, 2187; Life: 1767, 2467, 2468; Lippincott's Magazine: 9, 12, 2695; Little Review: 2930.1, 3084; Macmillan's: 9, 10, 2187, 2380.1, 2382, 2695; The Mirror: 2033; The Nation: 8, 9, 10, 301, 2028, 2212, 2695, 2773, 3010, 3417; North American Review:

Journals: North American Review
(cont): 8, 9, 11, 12, 301,
2028, 2187, 2380.1, 2382,
2695, 2773, 3417; Once-a-Week:
8, 301, 2773; Pall Mall Ga-
zette: 9, 11, 12; Punch: 9,
10, 11, 301, 2028, 2773, 3701;
Revue des Deux Mondes: 8, 9,
10, 11, 12, 301, 2695, 2773,
3417; Scribner's Magazine: 9,
10, 11, 12, 2028, 2187, 2695,
3359; New York Tribune: 9,
10, 11, 1673, 3010, 3011,
3529; The World (New York):
10, 11, 12; The Yellow Book:
10, 11, 12, 56, 1862, 1908,
2187, 2453, 2630, 2993, 2997,
3010, 3689.1
Joyce, James: 11, 38, 110.1,
345, 873, 1795, 2187, 2380.1,
2382, 2618, 3325, 3439
Judgment: 824
Juvenilia: 1667, 2076.1

Kafka, Franz: 11, 1795, 2770,
3482, 3590
Kant, Immanuel: 38, 1794, 1795
Kaufman, George S. 2448
Keats, John: 9, 10, 12, 566,
923, 1795, 2352, 2770, 3012,
3325, 3417, 3590, 3630
Kemble, Frances Anne: 8, 9, 10,
11, 12, 38, 301, 1740, 2028,
2187, 2380.1, 2382, 2634,
3010
Kierkegaard, Soren: 1795, 3417
Kingsley, Charles: 1756, 2352,
2695
Kipling, Rudyard: 10, 11, 12,
23, 38, 2044.1, 2187, 2198,
2394, 2935, 3252, 3417
The Kiss: 844
Knowledge: 535, 692, 1261, 3347
Knowles, John: 2940

LaFarge, John: 23, 1698, 2187,
2198
Lamb, Charles: 8, 12
Lamb House: 11, 31, 32, 1906,
1908, 2229, 2311, 2352, 2509,
3417

Landscape, James's Use of:
243, 640, 2010, 2388, 2818
Language, Linguistics, and Word
Play: 122, 131, 133, 141,
141.1, 152, 171, 213, 315,
415, 475.1, 523, 548, 554,
557, 607, 634.1, 678.1, 784.1,
822, 919, 951, 973, 1016,
1379, 1558, 1634, 1651, 1834,
1967, 1992, 2014, 2085, 2245,
2307.1, 2351, 2352, 2555,
2568, 2651, 2668, 2712, 2778,
2802, 2807.1, 2807.2, 2821,
2824, 2825, 2872, 2891,
2931.1, 2951, 2971, 2972,
2976, 3103, 3149, 3156, 3189,
3190, 3191, 3192, 3193, 3343,
3344, 3369, 3370, 3385, 3581,
3687
Laughter: 2802 (also see Humor)
Lee, Vernon (See Paget)
Leisure, Age of: 1805
Lewis, Caroline: 3695.2
Lewis, Sinclair: 66, 2012, 2229
Liberalism: 2632
Life, James's Treatment of:
307.3, 322, 485, 507, 659,
727, 735, 768, 783, 838, 872,
971, 993, 1100, 1550, 1931,
2051, 2194, 2560, 2715, 2716,
2744, 2802, 2998, 3217, 3353,
3372, 3391, 3417, 3475, 3556,
3557, 3569, 3630, 3663.1,
3717, 3718
Light: 1066
A Limerick (by Henry James):
3637
Limitations of Henry James:
3496, 3630
Lincoln, Abraham: 8, 9, 12, 38,
301, 2028
Linguistics (See Language)
Lockhart, John G.: 2906
Longfellow, Henry Wadsworth:
8, 9, 10, 11, 12, 23, 38, 301,
2028, 2187, 3325, 3417, 3626
Louvre (Palais du): 8, 12, 301,
2187, 2380.1, 2382, 3417
Love: 338, 432, 535, 781, 916,
1539, 1559.1, 1804, 1869,
2380.1, 2382, 2674, 2770,
3234.1
Lowell, James Russell: 8, 9,

Lowell, James Russell (cont.):
10, 11, 12, 23, 38, 301,
527.2, 1014, 1518, 1740, 1784,
1794, 1795, 2181, 2229, 2472,
2695, 2839, 2839.1, 3010,
3404

Macaulay, Thomas Bagington: 38
Madness: 1131, 2735.1, 3710
Magazines: 3506 (See Journals)
Magic and Miracles: 563, 3630
Malamud, Bernard: 674
Malice: 783
The Maltese Cross: 1104
Mann, Thomas: 2122
Manners, Tragedy of: 74.1,
2133, 2382, 2568, 2657, 3518,
3693, 3694
Marivaux, Pierre Carlet de
Chamblain: 2396
The Market Place: 1540
Marriages, Treatment of in
James: 701.1, 1063, 1118.1,
1878, 2291, 3477, 3511, 3630
Materialism: 889 (See Money)
Matter and Meaning: 35
Maugham, W. Somerset: 12,
3040, 3536
Maupassant, Guy de: 9, 10, 11,
12, 38, 718, 1740, 2187, 2229,
2352, 2420, 2560, 2568, 2695,
2770, 2773, 2935, 2995, 3252,
3326, 3409, 3536, 3630
McKinley, William: 38
Meaning: 545, 682, 2679 (See
also Matter and Meaning)
Meaning, Metaphorical: 545, 1121
Melancholy: 3019
Melodrama: 225, 810, 1180,
1590, 1617, 2791, 2792, 2802,
3417
Melville, Herman: 8, 12, 23, 38,
401, 587, 1794, 1831, 1923,
2028, 2179, 2187, 2352, 2380.1,
2382, 2560, 2568, 2657, 2935,
3325, 3482, 3590, 3685
Memorials and Memorial Tributes
to James: 33, 1809, 1844,
1847, 1994, 2177, 2236, 2470,
2622, 2902, 3118, 3196, 3232,
3425, 3463, 3568, 3721,
3723.1, 3724, 3725

Memory, Use of: 3417
Meredith, George: 8, 9, 10, 11,
12, 38, 804, 1163, 1740,
2187, 2227, 2229, 2352, 2630,
2695, 2770, 2810, 3252, 3442
Mérimée, Prosper: 8, 9, 23,
38, 301, 2028, 2187, 2449,
2450, 2568, 2695, 3252
Metamorphosis: 563
Metaphor: 100, 106, 176.2, 217,
330, 369, 559, 568.2, 1134,
2085, 2390, 2565, 2753, 3326,
3417 (See also Imagery and
Symbolism)
Metaphysical Aspect: 1121, 2994,
3600, 3601
Methods: 143, 252.1, 348, 1870,
1024, 1131, 1955, 1956, 2082,
2228, 2343, 2380.1, 2603,
2621, 2736, 2737.1, 3341,
3484, 3571 (See also Technique)
Michelangelo, Buonarroti: 8, 38,
2352, 2568, 2695
Mill, John Stuart: 38, 1794
Millais, John Everett: 301
Miller, Henry: 1795, 2380.1
Millionaires: 201, 228.2, 2007.1
(See Money)
Molière, Jean Baptiste Poquelin:
38, 2082, 2352
Money: 37.2, 201, 228.2, 489,
1173, 1460, 1823, 1824, 1830,
1965, 2167, 2286, 2352, 2380.1,
2868, 3016, 3030, 3030.1,
3179, 3234.1, 3417, 3630
Monologue, Interior: 562.2,
2047.1
Monomyth: 590
Montégut, Emile: 8, 9, 2695
Moore, George: 8, 3012.1
Morality and Moral Sense: (See
also Religion and Religious Aspect): 63, 70, 88.1, 93.1,
104, 127, 150, 151, 281, 316,
360, 361, 418, 575, 751.1,
837, 842.1, 879, 952, 974, 993,
1109, 1119, 1120, 1121, 1126,
1129, 1468, 1494, 1771, 1789,
1793, 1794, 1798, 1854, 1857,
1868, 1870, 1890, 1903, 1917,
1928, 1937, 1980, 2014, 2049,
2069, 2071, 2086, 2105, 2133,

2155, 2240, 2262, 2272,
2330, 2376, 2376.1, 2425,
2507, 2560, 2572, 2713,
2741, 2769, 2887, 2962,
2994, 3016, 3214, 3236,
3237, 3246, 3266, 3283,
3288, 3301, 3332, 3334,
3353, 3358, 3374, 3387,
3424, 3518, 3556, 3557,
3558, 3668, 3693, 3694,
3695, 3709, 3728
Morbidity: 3428
Morris, William: 8, 9, 2198,
2695, 2935, 3417
Mothers and Mother-quest: 2139,
3345
Motifs: 389, 3434
Motives: 1119, 2035
Movies: 1182, 1306, 2988 (See
also Films and Specific
Works)
Musset, Alfred de: 1740, 2187,
2352, 2695, 2773
Mystery: 834, 1036
Mystic, Novelist as: 2807,
2807.1
Myth: 484, 1824, 3600, 3601

Naivety: 3473
Names, James's Use of: 192,
350, 372, 406, 951, 1105,
1861, 2361, 2386, 2549,
2582, 3433
Napoleon, Louis Bonaparte: 8,
9, 11, 12, 38, 3417
Narration: 76, 1077, 2182,
1538.1, 2427, 2568, 2667,
3326, 3593, 3602, 3604 (Also see Technique)
Narrator: 276, 280, 296, 376,
501, 524, 944, 1062, 1069,
1522, 1875, 2017, 2154,
2342, 2560, 2737, 2802,
3075, 3326, 3630 (See also
Confidante and Observer)
Nationalism: 2130.2, 2163.1,
2200, 3384, 3417
Nationalism: 331, 2028, 2155,
2344, 2380.1, 2382, 2770,
2935, 3141, 3172, 3173,
3521 (See also French Naturalism)

Nature: 1092, 3417
Negative Gesture: 332
Negative Imagination: 574.1
Negroes: 2380.1, 2382, 3349
Neuroses: 354
New England and Henry James:
368, 368.1, 1958, 2192, 2526,
2644, 3417, 3489
The "New School" of Fiction:
3495.1
The New York Edition: (See under section entitled "New York
Edition")
Newman, John Henry: 38
Norris, Frank: 3711
Norton, Charles Eliot: 8, 9, 10,
11, 12, 23, 38, 301, 1740,
2028, 2187, 2198, 2229, 2695,
2773, 2899, 2935, 3252, 3417,
3542, 3689.1
Norton, Grace: 8, 9, 10, 11, 12,
38, 301, 1740, 2028, 2187,
2229, 2802, 3417
The Nouvelle, Development of:
2380, 2382, 2398, 2559, 2733.1,
3326
The Novel, Development of: 488,
529, 530, 1776, 1778, 1847.1,
1864, 1872, 1877, 1912, 2012,
2084, 2090.1, 2126, 2137,
2193, 2201, 2207, 2220, 2227,
2230, 2240, 2271, 2323, 2328.2,
2341, 2342, 2380, 2382, 2385,
2425, 2489, 2496, 2551, 2552,
2559, 2568, 2583, 2585, 2604,
2770, 2792, 2801, 2807, 2837,
2939, 2982, 3128, 3130, 3131,
3243, 3285, 3303, 3350, 3411,
3417, 3417.1, 3418, 3419,
3426, 3497, 3498, 3499,
3518, 3544, 3545, 3562, 3602,
3610, 3613, 3614, 3668
The Novel, Experimental Form:
2629, 2630, 3530
The Novel, International: 3622,
3623, 3627 (See also Internationalism)

Objective Center: 1143
The "Obscure Hurt" to Henry
James: 5, 2380.1, 2882,
3415

The Observer: 163, 547.1, 669, 972, 1027, 1045, 1532, 2062, 2114, 2140, 2685, 3326, 3417, 3630 (See also Confidante, Narrator, and Spectator)

The Occult: 1851, 1852, 1853 (See also Ghosts, Gothic, and Supernatural)

Omniscience: 3530

Omniscient Author: 3326

Opera: 1364, 1371, 1372, 1561, 1618

The Order of Merit: 2645

Osgood, James R.: 1682, 1719

Paget, Violet (pseud., Vernon Lee): 10, 12, 978, 982, 1680, 1733, 2076.2, 2214, 2366, 2458, 3096, 3618

Painting and Painters, Influence on James: 193, 2568, 3689.1 (See also Visual and Pictorial Arts)

Palmer, George Herbert: 23

Parable: 502, 1058, 1060, 3326

Parallel: 1164, 2024

Paris: 65, 230, 1787, 2352, 3417, 3483, 3510 (See France and French Influence)

Parodies: 1070, 1139.4, 1164, 1178, 1185, 1254, 1779, 1888, 1890.1, 2264, 2568, 2649, 2746, 2872, 3262, 3509, 3637, 3638, 3640

Pascal, Blaise: 531, 3247

Passion: 837, 1120, 3630

Past, Sense of and Use of: 138, 255.1, 712.1, 1078.1, 1804, 2560, 2611, 3020, 3417, 3430

Pastoral and Pastoralism: 389, 487, 822.1, 1286

Pater, Walter: 9, 11, 12, 2199, 2380, 2382, 2461, 2568, 2935, 3252, 3417, 3689.1

Pathos: 2802, 3417

Pattern: 136 (See Form and Structure)

Peirce, Charles Saunders: 9, 23, 38, 2935

The Pell-Clarkes: 9, 301, 1718

Perception: 1635, 2340.2

Perfectibility in Man: 3417

Perry, Lilla Cabot (Mrs. Thomas Sergeant Perry): 1706

Perry, Thomas Sergeant: 8, 9, 10, 12, 23, 38, 301, 1794, 2028, 2187, 2229, 2380, 2382, 2498, 2499, 2773, 2792, 3689.1

Perspective: 3325

Pessimism: 809, 2927, 2928

Philosophy and Philosophical Values: 3417, 3715

Pictorial, Picturesque, and Visual Arts: 250, 1641, 2151, 2770, 3410, 3474, 3480, 3593, 3689, 3690

Place: 536, 725, 823.1, 2706, 3213.1, 3721 (See also Setting)

Plato: 38, 1795, 2737

The Play within the Play: 922

Playwright, James as: 1586, 1587, 1588, 1596, 1600, 1601, 1604, 1605, 1606, 1609, 1610, 1610.1, 1610.2, 1614, 1615, 1616, 1617, 1621, 1622, 1627, 1628, 1629, 1630

Plot: 100, 121, 140, 757, 1087, 1271, 2341.1, 2363, 2462, 2568, 2750, 2835, 3078, 3156 (See also Form and Structure)

Poe, Edgar Allan: 8, 9, 12, 23, 38, 301, 347, 1794, 1795, 1953, 2028, 2187, 2352, 2466, 2568, 2695, 2773, 3325, 3326, 3432, 3536, 3630, 3689.1

Poems about Henry James: 1.7, 1770, 1844, 1844.1, 2177, 2213, 2627, 2692

Poetry in James: 15.2, 848, 1293, 3417, 3724

Point of View: 59.1, 125, 167, 176.1, 199, 325, 407, 558.1, 808, 999, 1010, 1106, 1108, 1207.1, 1303, 1544, 1870, 1874, 1898, 1921, 1967, 2017, 2028, 2301, 2308, 2342, 2352, 2560, 2727, 2769, 2815, 2859.1, 2913, 2974.1, 2975, 3021.1, 3060, 3417, 3486, 3571, 3628

Political Themes and Politics: 38, 370, 392, 880.1, 893, 897, 898, 903, 904, 2067, 2130.2, 2589.1, 2590, 2632, 2666, 2848.1, 3417

Pope, Alexander: 2028
Porter, Katherine Anne: 354.1,
  3034, 3664
Portraits: 1516, 2360, 2906.1,
  2911.2, 2916
Portraiture, Literary: 798, 849,
  3382
Pound Ezra: 12, 38, 256, 311,
  2028, 2187, 2254, 2380.1,
  2382, 2453, 2561, 2563, 2564,
  2568, 2699, 2770, 3159, 3160,
  3161, 3162, 3163, 3164, 3165,
  3166, 3167, 3385
Poverty: 2382, 3417
Power: 27, 2556.1, 3293, 3358,
  3417
Praed, Rosa: 732
Pragmaticism: 3699
Pragmatism: 312, 390, 2305,
  2554, 2788, 2935
Pre-Raphaelites: 10, 2935,
  3689.1 (See also Dante Gabriel Rossetti)
The Press, and James: 420,
  2320, 2321, 2481, 3036, 3037,
  3506, 3529, 3687
Pride: 357, 766
Proust, Marcel: 8, 10, 11, 12,
  38, 1952.1, 1954.1, 2187,
  2840, 2841, 2842, 3313, 3326,
  3523, 3630, 3689.1
Provincialism: 379, 2606, 2802,
  3284
Psyche and Psychical: 589, 1367
Psychology and the Psychological:
  180, 334, 630.1, 795, 860,
  1011, 1043, 1168, 1242, 1307,
  1367, 1389, 1400, 1414, 1453,
  1482.1, 1877, 1949, 2099,
  2220, 2387, 2477.1, 2628,
  2663, 2708.2, 2882, 2978,
  3259, 3352, 3368, 3475,
  3560.1
Puritanism: 65, 878, 2028, 2037,
  2051, 2926, 3223, 3326, 3378,
  3417, 3423, 3729
Pushkin, Alexander Sergeevich:
  1993
Pynchon, Thomas: 1312

Queerness in James: 2105, 2106,
  2802 (See also Darkness in

James)
The Quest Motif: 347, 433,
  1312, 1432, 2152, 2286,
  2707.2

Raconteur: 3326 (See also Narrator)
Radicalism: 879.2
Raisonneur: 3326
Ransom, John Crowe: 2010
Reade, Charles: 8, 1740, 2695
Reading Aids: 236.1, 356,
  1139.3, 1769, 1842, 2009.1,
  2159, 2215, 2363, 2419, 2651,
  2748, 2865, 3159, 3168, 3197,
  3710, 3726
Realism and Reality: 309, 331,
  390.1, 390, 441.1, 537, 811,
  889, 919, 950, 1049, 1118,
  1191, 1287, 1432, 1486, 1824,
  1877, 1924, 1929, 1930, 1981,
  1984, 1998, 2017, 2045, 2046,
  2047, 2064, 2073, 2082.1,
  2087, 2099, 2123, 2155, 2247,
  2263, 2266, 2267, 2269, 2274,
  2300, 2345, 2375, 2380, 2382,
  2410, 2414, 2425, 2478, 2512,
  2568, 2570, 2666, 2678, 2710,
  2715, 2716, 2718, 2770, 2802,
  2816, 2892, 2995, 3058, 3141,
  3185, 3289, 3290, 3306, 3326,
  3415.1, 3417, 3444, 3473,
  3485, 3530, 3575, 3613, 3728,
Rebellion: 2678
Rebirth: 184
Reciprocity: 1496, 1540
Redemption: 1492, 2568
Redundancy: 3090
Reedy, William Marion: 2033
Refinement: 323, 327
Reflection: 1047
Reform Club: 12
Relativism: 1080, 2306
Religion and Religious Aspects:
  358, 2336, 2364, 2433, 2439,
  3239, 3417
Reminiscences: 14, 19, 42, 683,
  1772, 1782, 1812, 1832, 1843,
  1844.1, 1858, 1889, 1899,
  1900, 1901, 1904, 1905, 1906,
  1907, 1908, 1909, 1919, 1962,
  1970.1, 1973, 1975, 1987,

Reminiscences (cont.): 2042,
    2088, 2092, 2102, 2116,
    2138, 2158, 2176, 2177,
    2250, 2310, 2311, 2312,
    2365, 2369, 2370, 2370.1,
    2420, 2453, 2492, 2502,
    2525, 2548, 2569, 2588.1,
    2591, 2602, 2608, 2609,
    2619, 2662, 2671, 2672,
    2687, 2699, 2705.1, 2871,
    2876, 2878, 2879, 2930.1,
    2945, 3006, 3018, 3041,
    3086, 3087, 3088, 3089,
    3114, 3115, 3132, 3134,
    3167, 3187, 3250, 3260,
    3267, 3282, 3300.1, 3366,
    3367, 3415, 3419, 3420,
    3457, 3494, 3506.1, 3578,
    3579, 3596, 3607, 3647,
    3652, 3653, 3667, 3683,
    3712, 3713
Renaissance: 3689.1
Renunciation: 1126.1, 1570.1,
    2663, 3571
Repetition: 1992
Reprints: 2532, 2760
Reputation, James's: 15.2, 34,
    1902, 2033, 2061, 2195, 2320,
    2321, 2335, 2365, 2454, 2467,
    2468, 2525, 2869, 2924, 3008,
    3014, 3029, 3036, 3037, 3050,
    3183, 3196, 3203, 3383, 3400,
    3402, 3469, 3579, 3682
Responsibility: 1102, 1769.1,
    1549.1, 2411, 2412, 2457,
    2510, 2511, 2663, 3417
Retrospection 1012, 3606
Reuter, Julio: 2252
Revelation: 1870
Revenge: 184, 660.1
Reverie: 2307.1
Reviewers of Henry James: 1759,
    2320, 2321, 3036, 3037 (See
    also Reputation)
Revisions: 17.1, 110, 144, 187.2,
    197, 223, 231, 232, 233, 399,
    429, 527.2, 703, 707, 798,
    800, 995, 1124, 1476, 1480,
    2235, 2850, 3326, 3404, 3511
    (See also Style)
Revival of Interest in Henry James:
    1252, 1736.2, 1877, 2058, 2059
    2065, 2127, 2142, 2195, 2198,

    2217, 2259, 2265, 2290,
    2380.1, 2382, 2857, 3001,
    3014, 3264, 3286, 3310, 3318,
    3416, 3492, 3493, 3682
Revolt and Revolution: 903, 906,
    1145, 1957, 1959, 2568, 2714,
    3181, 3181.1, 3417 (See also
    Rebellion)
Reynolds, Sir Joshua: 38, 2352,
    3326, 3689
Rhythm: 3499 (See also Style)
Ribot, Theodule A.: 1659
Riviere, Henri: 861
Robbe-Grillet, Alain: 2685
Robbins, Elizabeth: 10, 11, 12,
    1608
Romance: 205, 476, 1870, 2084,
    2371, 2770, 3314, 3417, 3530.1
Romanticism: 331, 1049, 2770,
    3326, 3417, 3630
Rome: 1638, 2352, 2849, 3417,
    3431 (See also Italy)
Roosevelt, Theodore: 38, 3574,
    3575.1
Rossetti, Dante Gabriel: 8, 10,
    12, 38, 301, 1004, 2935,
    3689 (See also Pre-Raphael-
    ites)
Rousseau, Jean Jacques: 9, 38,
    2380.1
Ruskin, John: 8, 9, 12, 38,
    301, 1519, 1794, 2028, 2198,
    2568, 2695, 2773, 2935, 3252,
    3413, 3417, 3689
Russian Novelists and James:
    1840.1, 2734, 3272
Russian Studies of James: 41,
    595, 2734, 3043, 3291
Rye: 14, 37.1, 2028, 2312,
    2370, 2370.1, 3417 (See also
    Lamb House)

Sacrifice: 2568
Saint-Beuve, Charles Augustin:
    8, 9, 38, 111, 2187, 2248,
    2450, 2568, 2695, 2770, 2935,
    3252, 3689
Salvation: 313, 1792
Sand, George: 8, 9, 11, 12, 23,
    38, 1740, 1754, 2017, 2028,
    2187, 2229, 2352, 2568, 2695,
    2770, 2773, 2776, 2935, 3252

Sandberg, Carl: 2229
Santayana, George: 23, 38, 1795, 2568, 2770
Sargent, John Singer (Portrait painter): 9, 10, 12, 38, 1740, 2198, 2229, 2352, 2568, 2935, 3010
"Sarto, Andrea del": 2352, 2695
Sartre, Jean-Paul: 3325
Satire: 687, 688, 2183, 2382, 2523, 2560, 2802, 2816, 3354, (See also Irony)
The Saturday Club: 3021.2
Scene and Scenic Presentation: 2373, 2374, 2560, 3417, 3561
Schopenhauer, Arthur: 38, 885
Science: 1528, 3417
Scott, Sir Walter: 8, 10, 11, 38, 1756, 1785, 2352, 2568, 2695
Sculpture and Sculptors: 3689.1
Secrecy: 2462
Seeing: 333 (See Vision)
Self-destructive: 344, 3005.1
Self-development, self-fulfillment, and self-realization: 3630
Selflessness: 2330
Self-release: 3630
Self-restraint: 3630
Self-sacrifice: 2803.1, 3630
Sensibility: 160, 331, 755, 974, 1230.1, 1582, 2145, 2145.1, 2382, 2770, 3313, 3417
Sensuousness: 3417
Serialization: 126, 208, 2881 (See also Journals)
Setting: 911, 1989, 2560, 3213.1
Sex and Sexuality: 795, 866, 1964, 2034, 2105, 2191.1, 2380.1, 2382, 2513, 2658, 2933, 3417, 3558, 3630 (See also Morality)
Shakespeare, William: 8, 9, 10, 11, 12, 38, 116, 301, 362, 1794, 2352, 2447.1, 2560, 2568, 2695, 2737, 2773, 2792, 2967, 3325, 3326, 3403, 3417, 3536, 3590
Shaw, George Bernard: 8, 9, 10, 11, 12, 38, 594, 1795, 2568, 2630, 3326, 3453
Shelley, Percy Bysshe: 9, 10, 12, 38, 2229, 2352, 2568, 3590, 3630
Shock, Value of: 3417
The Short Story, Development of: 1876, 1995, 2060, 2153, 2235, 2353, 2426, 2504, 2560, 2745, 2765, 3072, 3105, 3120, 3316, 3407, 3645, 3706
Short Stories, Collections of: 636.1, 656, 665, 1799, 2235, 2257, 2577, 2703, 3195, 3275, 3429, 3450, 3451, 3720, 3720.1
Silence: 1558
Simplicity: 2324
Sin: 3465 (See also Evil and Morality)
Situations, Use of as Figures of Speech: 3081, 3417
Slang: 554 (See Language)
Smollett, Tobias: 8, 38, 2028, 2352, 2560, 2695, 3326
Society, American: 263, 2001, 2991
Society and Social Criticism: 38, 245, 317, 326, 378, 384, 393, 400, 418, 441, 701.1, 783, 891, 912, 952, 1063, 1118.1, 1400, 1582, 1789, 1885, 1947, 2133, 2136, 2147.1, 2184, 2240, 2262, 2266, 2291, 2294, 2330, 2379.1, 2380.1, 2382, 2412, 2477, 2538, 2714, 2790, 2864, 2880, 2933, 2954, 2978, 2990, 2991, 3003, 3080, 3175, 3217, 3220, 3309, 3354, 3358, 3394, 3417, 3443, 3517, 3595
Society, Southern: 405, 2954
Sources: 295.1, 320, 342, 406.1, 682, 773 (See also Specific Works)
The Southerner (Type): 363
Spanish-American War: 11
Spark, Muriel: 1880, 2447
Spectator: 613, 2711, 3630 (See Confidante, Narrator and Observer)
Speech: 2931.1 (See also Dialogue and Language)
Spencer, Herbert: 23, 38
Staël, Madame de: 8, 9
Stendhal, Henri-Marie Beyle: 12, 38, 2187, 2352, 2695, 3689.1

Sterne, Laurence: 12, 2695,
3326
Stevens, Wallace: 3022
Stevenson, Robert Louis: 8, 9,
10, 11, 12, 23, 38, 45.1, 301,
353, 1278, 1699, 1724, 1785,
2028, 2111, 2187, 2198, 2229,
2270, 2352, 2380, 2382, 2404,
2528, 2568, 2630, 2752, 2770,
3362, 3363, 3417, 3536,
3689.1
Stevenson, Mrs. Robert Louis:
12, 905, 2111
Stoicism: 2130
Story, William Wetmore (person):
9, 11, 12, 38, 1515.1, 1740,
1794, 2187, 2380, 2380.1,
2784, 3063, 3308, 3608, 3626,
3689.1, 3710
Stowe, Harriet Beecher: 8, 11,
12, 2028, 2773
Stream of Consciousness: 2154,
2342, 2810, 2996.1 (See also
Technique)
Structure: 308, 386, 471, 496,
496.1, 567, 680, 847, 1009,
1010, 1222, 1484, 1563, 2185,
2280, 2397, 2560, 2681, 2682,
2907, 3213.1, 3417, 3444,
3592, 3594 (See also Form)
Study Aids: 95, 228, 329, 521,
677, 717, 754, 756, 1093,
1139.3, 1311, 1424, 1472,
1842, 1855.1, 1855, 2178,
2363, 2570, 2748 (See also
Reading Aids)
Style: 131, 249, 249.1, 250,
305.1, 352, 441.1, 547.1,
584, 664, 707, 800, 965, 973,
992, 1012, 1229.1, 1480, 1531,
1532, 1538, 1763, 1984, 1992,
1995.1, 2018, 2033, 2084.1,
2085, 2314, 2324, 2380, 2382,
2431, 2463, 2470, 2479, 2528,
2530, 2536, 2560, 2568, 2815,
2852, 2875, 2886, 2902.1,
2951, 2952, 2975, 2976, 2993,
3026, 3045, 3120, 3150, 3161,
3181.2, 3190, 3189, 3195,
3191.1, 3195, 3200, 3213.1,
3233, 3324.1, 3326, 3380,
3417, 3442, 3479, 3548, 3585,
3606, 3608, 3670, 3713, 3724

Subjects: 2603 (See Themes)
Substance: 1783
Suffering: 1769.1, 2802
The Suffragette Movement: 3443
Supernatural: 697, 698, 1355,
1361, 2205, 2208, 2438, 2737,
2814, 2921, 2943, 3052, 3084,
3093, 3265, 3417, 3490, 3703
(See also Ghosts, Gothic, and
Occult)
Suspense, Use of: 1870, 3417
Swedenborg, Emanuel: 8, 9, 10,
12, 23, 38, 301, 1794, 1795,
2187
Swinburne, Algernon Charles:
8, 9, 12, 301, 1756, 1795,
2380, 2382, 2695, 2935, 3252,
3417
Switzerland: 2519.1, 3417
Symbolism and Symbols: 150,
200, 281, 543, 576, 1056,
1134, 1257, 1290, 1389, 1541,
1569, 1786, 1797, 1941, 2019.1,
2148, 2184, 2281, 2282, 2307.1,
2314, 2373, 2374, 2547, 2560,
2568, 2666, 2780, 2785, 2958,
2959, 3301, 3326, 3417, 3497,
3499, 3521, 3598, 3600 (See
also Imagery)

Taine, Hippolyte: 8, 9, 11, 12,
38, 2028, 2248, 2333.1, 2568,
2695, 3689.1
Taste: 989, 1440, 1455, 2560,
2957
Tate, Allen: 1385
Taylor, Peter: 2444
Tchekhov, Anton: 3272
Teaching Aids: 292.1, 480,
480.1, 521, 525.2, 714, 940,
1424, 1472, 1884, 2149, 2989,
3038, 3151, 3318, 3337, 3507,
3616
Techniques: 34, 68, 76, 245,
304, 352, 376, 573, 755, 822,
974, 1230.1, 1280, 1297, 1407,
1777, 1870, 1874, 1921, 1966,
2082, 2145, 2145.1, 2228,
2281, 2287, 2425, 2579, 2607,
2612, 2613, 2769, 2786, 2791,
2792, 2844, 3024, 3078, 3127,
3170, 3235, 3251, 3486, 3535,

Techniques (cont.): 3536, 3630,
    3667, 3689.1
Television: 1404 (See also Dra-
    matization and Theatre)
Temperament: 2292, 2603
Temple, Mary (Minny): 8, 9, 10,
    11, 12, 36, 38, 301, 848,
    1572, 1740, 2028, 2187, 2229,
    2380.1, 2382, 2630, 2737,
    2773, 3417, 3590, 3626, 3630
Temptation(s): 3630 (See also
    Self-Restraint)
Tennyson, Alfred, Lord: 8, 9,
    10, 11, 12, 38, 301, 640,
    710, 1014, 1518, 1784, 2028,
    2187, 2198, 2352, 2380.1,
    2382, 2681, 2695, 2963, 2964,
    3010, 3326, 3417
Terror: 3490 (See also Ghosts
    and Supernatural)
Textual: 53, 59.2, 87, 129, 175,
    176, 181, 182, 187.2, 188,
    189.2, 214, 319, 412, 526,
    537.1, 718.1, 828, 1462,
    1816, 1940, 2508 (See also
    Editions)
Thackeray, William Makepeace:
    8, 9, 10, 11, 12, 23, 38,
    301, 813, 1740, 2028, 2187,
    2352, 2382, 2568, 2695, 2737,
    2770, 2773, 3326, 3626
Theatre: 1393, 1402, 1594,
    1596, 1598, 1599, 1605,
    1608, 1613, 1619, 1620,
    1623, 1624, 1629, 1630,
    1632, 1633, 1634, 1717,
    2135, 2187, 2325, 2328,
    3689.1, (See also Dramatiza-
    tion and Television
Themes: 34, 156, 156.1, 157,
    158, 245, 304, 313, 329,
    330, 367, 581, 655, 660,
    694, 776, 879.3, 1145, 1475,
    1804, 1862, 1915, 1957, 1959,
    1980, 1989, 2021, 2125, 2129,
    2242, 2273, 2380.1, 2382,
    2522, 2560, 2603, 2650, 2653,
    2708.2, 2854, 2938, 2999,
    3000, 3265, 3286, 3358, 3394,
    3407, 3417, 3440, 3471, 3503,
    3504, 3523, 3584, 3646, 3689,
    3705, 3710, 3705
Themes, American: 34, 2650

Themes, English: 34, 2650
Theology: 2649.1
Theory and Theories of Henry
    James: 314, 1873, 2182.1,
    2280, 2332, 2612, 2613, 2669,
    2909, 2983, 3243, 3306, 3474,
    3635, 3635.1, 3690
The Third Person: 2352 (See
    also Style)
Thoreau, Henry David: 8, 9,
    23, 38, 1794, 1795, 2028,
    2187, 2380.1, 2382, 2773,
    2948.1, 3590, 3626
Time, Use of: 80, 88, 156,
    156.1, 157, 158, 200, 336.1,
    693, 782, 2974, 3158, 3211,
    3213.1, 3290 (See also Tech-
    nique)
Time-Spirit: 2039
Timing, Gift of: 3417
Titian, (Vecellio Tiziano): 1794,
    2352, 2695
Tocqueville, Alexis de: 1795,
    2028, 2187, 2380.1, 2382,
    2568
Tolstoy, Leo: 23, 38, 869,
    1785, 2380.1, 2382, 2535,
    3325, 3326
Tone: 1870 (See also Style)
Töpffer, Rodolphe: 2905
Towers, Roberts: 674
Tradition: 426, 1914, 1925,
    2241, 2430, 2430.1, 2538,
    2568
Tradition, American: 3692
Tradition, Literary: 1433
Tragedy and the Tragic Sense:
    392.1, 2174, 2568, 2802,
    2735, 3417, 3630
Tragedy of Manners: 2133
Transcendentalism and Trans-
    cendalists: 378, 2187, 2382
Transitional Devices: 822,
    3024 (See also Style)
Translations of Henry James's
    Works into Other Languages:
    183, 198.1, 228.1, 2219,
    2833, 3004
Travel, Influence of: 1789,
    2244, 2298, 2394, 2771, 2772,
    2838, 3035, 3109, 3188.1,
    3719
Trollope, Anthony: 8, 9, 10,

Trollope, Anthony (cont.): 11, 12, 23, 38, 301, 791, 1466, 1740, 1756, 1785, 1795, 2028, 2121, 2270, 2352, 2380.1, 2382, 2695, 2770, 3252, 3326, 3626, 3727

Truth: 1127, 3417, 3643

Turgenieff, Ivan: 8, 9, 10, 11, 12, 23, 38, 813, 881, 885.1, 892, 928, 1721, 1740, 1785, 2028, 2155, 2187, 2198, 2229, 2345, 2352, 2380, 2382, 2420, 2560, 2568, 2630, 2695, 2782, 2792, 3010, 3125, 3326, 3476.1, 3478, 3590

Twain, Mark: 8, 10, 11, 12, 23, 38, 184, 234, 796, 797, 1257, 1490, 1792, 1833.1, 1984.1, 1992, 2062, 2092, 2103, 2187, 2282, 2352, 2380.1, 2568, 2630, 2634, 3010, 3472, 3564, 3626

Tweedy, Edmund and Mary: 8, 9

The Two Henry Jameses: 1801, 2128, 3405, 3599

The Unconscious: 633, 2154, 3389 (See also Consciousness)

The "Unfortunate Fall": 337

Unity: 127, 481, 666, 2836, 2887, 3082 (See also Form, Structure, and Style)

Universality: 628

Universities: Cambridge, 11, 301, 1695, 2705, 2705.1; Harvard, 11, 301, 2028; Notre Dame, 12; Oxford, 11, 12, 2889; Yale, 11, 301

Utopia: 591, 1949, 3348

Vampires and Vampirism: 1062, 3326 (See also Ghosts and Supernatural)

Van Dyke, Sir Anthony: 2352

Victorian Mode: 2028, 2268 (see also Style)

Villains: 1530, 1859 (See also Characterization)

Villainy: 1549.1

Visual and Visual Arts: 414, 1979, 1980, 2056, 2919, 3689, 3689.1, 3690, 3691 (See also Pictorial)

Vinci, Leonardo da: 2695

Vision(s): 17.1, 262, 333, 441.1, 667, 668, 1556, 1557, 2029, 2263, 2283, 2301, 2317, 2531.1, 2541, 2567, 2568, 2798, 2938, 2948.1, 3410

Vocabulary: 3189, 3190, 3192, 3193 (See also Language)

The Voyeur: 2685

Vulgarity: 691, 2811, 2668, 3192, 3595

Walpole, Sir Hugh: 11, 12, 2216, 2229, 2737, 3417

War, World War I: 11, 2066, 2172, 2209, 2352, 2843, 3417, 3585, 3649

Ward, Mrs. Humphrey: 10, 11, 12, 2187, 2198, 2229, 2380.1, 2382, 3417, 3621

Waterlow, Sir Sydney: 13

Weakness of Henry James: 3017

Wealth: 2382 (See also Money)

Wells, Herbert George: 11, 12, 23, 38, 1729, 1911, 2015, 2211, 2229, 2380.1, 2382, 2568, 2571, 2737, 2825, 2894.1, 3242, 3325, 3417, 3447, 3534.1, 3537, 3626, 3638, 3639, 3640, 3641, 3642, 3689.1

West, Rebecca: 38, 2352, 2792, 3590

"Western Barbarian": 234, 3540

Western Imagery: 3573, 3574 (See Imagery)

Wharton, Edith: 8, 11, 12, 38, 1694, 1734, 1735, 1740, 1805, 1894, 1895, 1896, 1897, 1938.1, 1998, 2022.1, 2028, 2066.2, 2187, 2198, 2227, 2229, 2278, 2483, 2560, 2630, 2737, 2765.1, 2773, 2802, 2847, 2853, 2943, 2955, 2968.1, 3003, 3049, 3054, 3142, 3299, 3325, 3326, 3417, 3524, 3525, 3562, 3590, 3622, 3626, 3632, 3652, 3653, 3653.1, 3654

Whistler, James McNeill: 10, 12,

Whistler, James McNeill (cont.):
38, 3039
White, Stanford: 3656, 3656.1
Whitman, Walt: 8, 10, 12, 23,
38, 1794, 1795, 2028, 2063,
2187, 2380.1, 2382, 2568,
2695, 2773, 3252, 3417, 3590,
3626, 3659
Wilde, Oscar: 9, 10, 11, 12,
38, 2028, 2187.1, 2380, 2382,
2737, 3005, 3257, 3536, 3590
Willis, Nathaniel Parker: 983
Wish-Fulfillment: 1126, 1468,
3288
Wister, Owen: 1661, 2028, 3560,
3573, 3574
Wonder: 315
Woman, Womanhood, and Women
Characters: 788, 839.1, 855,
871, 2027, 2028.1, 2053,
2139, 2267, 2294, 2331, 2382,
2653, 2911, 3059, 3059.1,
3317, 3345, 3464, 3728
Woman, The American Woman:
3266, 3571
Woolf, Virginia: 9, 10, 11, 12,
38, 2551.1, 2568, 2630, 2770,
2803, 3003, 3325, 3360, 3702,
3702.1, 3703, 3704
Wordsworth, William: 8, 11, 12,
38, 1795, 2028, 2352, 2737,
3326, 3590, 3630
Wren, Sir Christopher: 1740
Writer as Hero: 2231

Yearbook, Henry James: 3356
Yeats, William Butler: 2028,
3417, 3590
Young Writers and James: 1778,
3522
Youth: 422, 744, 2036, 3374,
3417, 3630

Zola, Emile: 8, 9, 10, 11, 12,
23, 38, 301, 678, 1740, 2028,
2160, 2166, 2187, 2198, 2382,
2422, 2560, 2568, 2630, 2695,
2696, 2770, 2773, 2995, 3010,
3057, 3174, 3303, 3326, 3590,
3689.1, 3710, 3730

INDEX OF CRITICS

Aagemann, E. R. , 1767
Abel, Darrell, 721, 1767.1,
 1768, 1769
Abel, Robert H. , 1769.1
Abrahams, William, 1770
Adachi, Yasushi, 1771
Adams, Henry, 1653, 1772
Adams, John R. , 294, 1773
Adams, Percy G. , 1774
Adams, Robert M. , 328
Ahnebrink, Lars, 264
Aiken, Conrad, 1775
Alberes, R. M. , 1776
Albright, Daniel, 1777
Aldrich, C. Knight, 1166
Aldridge, John W. , 1
Alexander, Charlotte Anne,
 52
Alexander, Elizabeth, 1586
Alexandrescu, Sorin, 415.1
Allen, Gay Wilson, 1.1
Allen, Walter, 722, 723, 1777.1,
 1777.2, 1778, 1779, 1780,
 1781
Allingham, William, 1782
Allott, Miriam, 532, 640, 1014,
 1017, 1167, 1516, 1517,
 1518, 1519, 1783, 1784,
 1785, 1786
Altick, Richard D. , 53, 969,
 1787, 1788
Alvarez, A. , 1789
Amacher, Richard E. , 1434
Andersen, Kenneth, 54, 1792
Anderson, Charles R. , 363, 724,
 725, 964, 1790, 1791
Anderson, Quentin, 1.2, 1.3,
 532.1, 533, 599, 726, 727,
 944, 1018, 1168, 1793, 1794,
 1795, 1796, 1797, 1798, 1799,
 1800, 1801, 1802
Anderson, Sherwood, 1803

Andreach, Robert J. , 531, 1019
Andreas, Osborn, 1020, 1169,
 1804
Antush, John V. , 183, 1823,
 1824
Anzilotti, Rolando, 416
Aoki, Tsugio, 55, 1519.1, 1825
Aplash, Madhu, 729
Appignanesi, Lisa, 1826
Arader, Harry F. , 1827
Archibald, William, 1170, 1171
Arlos, Alma R. , 1828
Arms, George, 358, 417
Arnavon, Cyrille, 1172, 1829
Arsenescu, Adina, 1829.1
Arvin, Newton, 364, 1173, 1830,
 1831, 1832, 1833
Ashmore, Basil, 1084
Ashton, Jean Willoughby, 299
Aspiz, Harold, 1833.1
Asselineau, Roger, 1834
Aswell, Edward Duncan, 606,
 1174, 1835, 1836
Atherton, Gertrude, 1520, 1837,
 1838
Atkinson, Brooks, 1175
Aubry, G. Jean, 1085, 1839
Auchincloss, Louis S. , 55.1,
 1086, 1442, 1840, 1840.1,
 1841, 1842, 1843, 3732
Auden, W. H. , 1.7, 239, 240,
 1844, 1844.1, 1845
Austin, Deborah, 483
Ayscough, John, 1846
Aziz, Maqbool, 520, 718.1,
 1846.1

B. , H. S. , 1846.2
Backus, Joseph M. , 183.1
Bailey, John, 1656
Baker, Ernest A. , 1176, 1847.1,
 3732.1

Baker, Robert S., 1142.1
Baldwin, James, 1848
Baldwin, Richard Eugene, 1849
Ballorain, Rolande, 1177
Ballou, Ellen B., 1850
Bangs, John Kendrick, 1178
Banta, Martha, 184, 697, 698, 1485, 1851, 1852, 1853
Bantock, G. H., 1854
Bareiss, Dieter, 534
Barnes, Howard, 1179, 1589
Barnet, Sylvan, 1855
Barnhart, Clarence L., 1855.1
Barrell, Charles Wisner, 1855.2
Barrett, Clifton Waller, 1856
Barrett, Laurence, 1857
Barrie, J. M., 1858
Barzun, Jacques, 2, 300, 1180, 1590
Bashore, James Robert, Jr., 1859
Baskett, Sam S., 273
Bass, Eben, 56, 308, 484, 1860, 1861, 1862
Battersby, H. F. P., 1863, 3733
Battilana, Marilla, 1863.1
Baugh, Albert C., 1864
Baumgaertel, Gerhard, 497, 1865
Baumgärtel, Werner, 1866
Baxter, Annette K., 418, 1867
Bay, André, 1868
Bayley, John, 535, 1869
Baym, Nina, 1087
Bazzanella, Dominic J., 730
Beach, Joseph Warren, 185, 497.1, 1021, 1022, 1181, 1737.4, 1738, 1870, 1871, 1872, 1873, 1874, 3734, 3735
Beachcroft, T. O., 1875, 1876
Beams, David W., 1078
Beardsley, Monroe, 329
Beattie, Munro, 1877, 1878
Beaver, Harold, 1879
Bebeau, Donald, 536
Beck, Ronald, 330
Beckley, Paul V., 1182
Bedford, Sybille, 1183, 1880
Beebe, Maurice L., 621, 1023, 1881, 1882, 1883, 1884, 1885, 3736, 3737
Beer, Thomas, 731, 1184, 1886, 1887
Beerbohm, Max, 604.2, 1185,

1591, 1888, 1889, 1890, 1890.1
Beers, Henry A., 1186, 1891, 1891.1
Behrman, S. N., 1187
Beker, Mirosley, 1892
Bell, Inglis F., 3738
Bell, Millicent, 1521, 1893, 1894, 1895, 1896, 1896.1, 1897
Bell, Vereen, 1898
Bellman, Samuel Irving, 674, 1164
Bellringer, Alan W., 1024, 1088, 1089, 1090, 1143
Bement, Douglas, 518, 1435
Bennett, Arnold, 57, 515, 516, 1899, 1900, 1901, 1902
Bennett, Barbara L., 1903
Bennett, Joan, 58, 1903.1
Benson, Arthur Christopher, 1904, 1905, 1906, 1907
Benson, E. F., 1188, 1657, 1908, 1909
Bentzon, T., 1910
Bercovitch, Sacvan, 970
Bergonzi, Bernard, 1911, 1911.1, 1912
Berkelman, Robert, 945
Berkley, James, 1443
Berland, Alwyn, 59, 59.1, 879, 1189, 1913, 1914, 1915, 1916, 1917
Bernard, F. V., 186
Bernard, Kenneth, 688, 946
Berner, Robert L., 1190
Berry, Thomas Elliott, 1918
Berryman, John, 1919
Bersani, Leo, 1522, 1920, 1921, 1922
Berthoff, Warner, 1025, 1923, 1924, 1925
Berti, Luigo, 1926
Bertocci, Angelo, 1927
Bertolotti, David Santo, 1736.2
Bethurum, Dorothy, 1928
Bewley, Marius, 2.1, 241, 365, 419, 485, 537, 599.1, 659, 971, 1191, 1192, 1193, 1194, 1486, 1487, 1488, 1523, 1634, 1763, 1929, 1930, 1931, 1932, 1933, 1934, 1935, 1936, 1937
Beyer, William, 1592

Bhatnagar, O. P. , 186.1
Bianchini, Angela, 1937.1
Bicanic, Sonia, 420, 1444
Bickley, Karen L. , 3758
Bicknell, Percy, 3
Biddle, Arthur William, 1938
Biddle, Francis, 1938.1
Bielenstein, Gabrielle Maupin,
    732, 1938.1
Bier, Jesse, 1939
Bierce, Ambrose, 1939.1
Birch, Brian, 59.2, 60, 537.1,
    1940, 1523.1, 3739
Birkhead, Edith, 1195
Bishop, Ferman, 1658, 1940.1
Bixler, J. Seelye, 1659, 1660
Black, James O. , 61
Blackall, Jean Frantz, 607, 1026,
    1027, 1941
Blackmur, Richard P. , 62, 62.1,
    187, 270, 274, 538, 626, 733,
    932, 1028, 1029, 1091, 1144,
    1196, 1197, 1445, 1524, 1744,
    1745, 1746, 1747, 1942,
    1942.1, 1943, 1944, 1945
Blanche, Jacques-Emile, 1946
Blanck, Jacob, 3740, 3741
Bland, D. S. , 366
Blanke, Gustan H. , 1947, 1948
Blasing, Mutlu, 187.1
Blehl, Vincent F. , 734
Bleich, David, 539, 1949
Bliven, Naomi, 3.1, 1950, 1951
Blöcker, Gunter, 1952
Blotner, Joseph L. , 879.1
Blount, Joseph Donald, 1952.1
Bluefarb, Sam, 879.2
Bluen, Herbert, 1953
Boas, Ralph Philip, 1954
Bocaz, Sergio Hernan, 1954.1
Bochner, Jay, 735
Bockes, Douglas Theodore, 1955,
    1956
Bode, Carl, 1661
Bogan, Louise, 367, 368, 368.1,
    879.3, 1145, 1957, 1958, 1959,
    1960
Bogosian, Ezekiel, 1961
Boit, Louise, 1962
Bompard, Paola, 540, 1963
Bonincontro, Marilia, 736
Bontly, Thomas John, 63, 1198,
    1964

Booth, Bradford A. , 1965, 1966
Booth, Wayne C. , 1200, 1967
Borchers, Lotte, 1968
Borden, Diane M. , 1968.1
Borklund, Elmer, 1969, 1970
Bosanquet, Theodora, 187.2,
    520.1, 1201, 1970.1, 1971,
    1972, 1973, 1974, 1974.1
Bosch, Louis Alan, 188
Bottkol, Joseph M. , 275, 486
Boughton, Alice, 1975
Bouraoui, H. A. , 660
Bourland, Margaret, 3324.1
Bowden, Edwin T. , 694, 737,
    738, 1976, 1977, 1978, 1979,
    1980, 3742, 3743
Bowen, Edwin W. , 1981
Bowen, Elizabeth, 1202
Bowman, Sylvia E. , 739
Boyd, E. A. , 1982, 1983
Boynton, Percy H. , 1984
Brack, O. M. , Jr. , 1984.1
Bradbury, Malcolm, 2087
Bradford, Gamaliel, 1985, 1986
Bradley, A. G. , 1987
Bragdon, Claude, 498, 541, 1662,
    1987.1, 1988
Brasch, James Daniel, 1989
Brebner, Adele, 1489
Bredvold, Louis I. , 692.1
Bree, Germaine, 1990
Breit, Harvey, 1738.1
Brennan, Joseph G. , 64
Brenni, Vito J. , 3744
Brewster, Dorothy, 65, 1203
Brewster, Henry, 1663, 1664,
    1991
Bridgman, Richard, 1992
Briggs, A. D. , 1993
Britten, Benjamin, 1204
Brkić, Svetozar, 1994.1
Broderick, John C. , 740, 1092,
    1994.2
Brogan, D. W. 1994.2
Brogan, Denis, 1994.4
Brome, Vincent, 1665, 1994.5
Bronson, Walter C. , 1205, 1995
Brooke, Stopford, 1995.1
Brooks, Cleanth, 189, 189.1,
    1996
Brooks, Peter, 1997
Brooks, Sydney, 4
Brooks, Van Wyck, 242, 617,

1030, 1082, 1082.1, 1511.1,
1755, 1997.1, 1998, 1999,
2000, 2001, 2002, 2003,
2004, 2005, 2006, 2007,
2007.1, 2008, 3745
Brophy, Brigid, 2009
Broun, Heywood, 641, 1206
Brower, Reuben, 2009.1
Brown, Ashley, 243, 2010
Brown, Clarence Arthur, 2011
Brown, Daniel Russell, 66, 2012
Brown, E. K., 67, 542, 741,
1525, 2013, 2014, 2015
Brown, Francis, 2016
Brown, Ivor, 1146
Brown, John Mason, 1207
Brown, R. Christiani, 1526
Brownell, William Cary, 742,
2017, 2018
Bruccoli, Matthew J., 5, 216,
2019
Brumm, Ursula, 543, 2019.1
Bruneau, Jean, 1666, 2019.2
Brussel, I. R., 2020
Bryd, Scott, 619.1
Bryden, Ronald, 2021
Brylowski, Anna S[alne], 276,
2022
Bryson, Lyman, 168
Buchan, Alexander M., 2022.1
Buchanan, Robert, 2023
Buckler, William, 675
Bufkin, E. C., 2024
Buitenhuis, Peter, 244, 421, 487,
600, 622, 638, 743, 1635,
2025, 2026, 2027, 2028, 2028.1,
2028.2, 2028.3
Burde, Edgar J., 2029
Burgess, Anthony, 2030
Burgess, C. F., 2031
Burgess, Charles E., 2032, 2033
Burke, Kenneth, 2034, 2035
Burlingame, Roger, 1031
Burnham, P., 244.1
Burns, Landon C., Jr., 1032
Burr, Anna Robeson, 5.1
Burrell, Angus, 65, 1991
Burrell, John A., 422, 744, 2036
Burstein, Frances Brownell,
2037
Burt, Nathaniel, 2038
Burtner, William Thomas, Jr.,
245

Burton, Richard, 2039
Busch, Frieder, 68
Buschges, Gisela, 2040
Butler, John F., 1093
Butterfield, R. W., 189.2
Byatt, A. S., 2041
Byers, John R., Jr., 1207.1
Bynner, Witter, 2042, 2043
Byrd, J. Scott, 543.1, 544,
1437, 1438, 2044

C., R. W., 2044.1
Cady, Edwin Harrison, 331, 2045,
2046, 2047
Cairns, Huntington, 2047.1
Cairns, William B., 2048, 2049
Calisher, Hortense, 2050
Cambon, Glauco, 332, 1446,
1490, 2051, 2052
Cameron, Kate, 1208
Cameron, Kenneth Walter, 600.1
Campos, Christophe, 2052.1
Canady, Nicholas, Jr., 423
Canavaggia, Marie, 499
Canavan, Thomas L., 933.2
Canby, Henry Seidel, 2053, 2054,
2055, 2056, 2056.1, 2057,
2058, 2059, 2060, 2061, 2062,
2063
Cantwell, Robert, 654, 2064,
2064.1, 2065, 2066
Capellan, Angel, 2066.1
Cargas, Harry J., 2066.2
Cargill, Oscar, 69, 69.1, 190,
424, 745, 746, 747, 880,
1033, 1147, 1148, 1209, 1210,
1447, 2067, 2068, 2069, 2070,
2070.1, 2071, 2781
Carnell, Corbin S., 1210.1
Carter, E. S., 2072
Carter, Everett, 2073
Cartinau, Virginia, 2074
Cary, Elizabeth Luther, 640.2,
1211, 2075, 2076
Cary, Joyce, 1094
Cary, Richard, 1667, 2076.1,
2076.2
Castellanos, Rosario, 1212
Castiglione, Luigi, 2078
Catalani, G., 2079
Cather, Willa, 2079.1
Cawelti, John G., 2080

Cazan, Ileana, 748
Cecil, L. Moffitt, 70
Cervo, Nathan A., 660.1
Cestre, Charles, 2081
Chadderdon, Arnold H., 2082
Chaignon la Rose, Pierre de, 1756
Chan, Lois M., 749, 2082.1
Chanda, A. K., 750
Chapman, John, 1213
Chapman, R. W., 2082.2
Chapman, Sara Simmons, 1015.1, 2082.3
Chartier, Richard, 71
Chase, Richard, 72, 751, 1214, 2083, 2084
Chatman, Seymour, 2084.1, 2085
Chauhan, P. S., 751.1
Chen, Lucy M., 1527
Cherniak, Judith, 2086
Cheshire, David, 2087
Chesterton, Gilbert Keith, 1215, 2088, 2089
Chevallez, Abel, 2090
Chew, Samuel C., 2090.1
Chislett, William, 601, 1216, 2091
Chubb, Percival, 2092
Cieker, Rosemarie, 2092.1
Cimatti, Pietro, 2093
Cixous, Hélène, 2094
Clair, John A., 191, 2095, 2096, 3746
Clark, A. F. Bruce, 752, 2097
Clark, Donald L., 525.1
Clark, E., 1593
Clark, Edwin, 2098
Clark, Harry Hayden, 1528, 2099
Clark, Robert, Jr., 1224, 1225, 1226, 1227
Clark, Robert Lanier, Jr., 3748
Clemens, Cyril, 2100, 2100.1, 2101, 2102
Clemens, Katherine, 5.2
Clemons, Samuel Langhorn (See Mark Twain), 369.1, 2103
Clemons, Walter, 5.3
Clurman, Harold, 1217
Coffin, Tristram P., 425
Cohen, B. Bernard, 2104
Colby, Frank Moore, 1083, 1529, 2105, 2106
Cole, Robert C., 1217.1

Coleman, Arthur, 3747
Coleman, Elizabeth, 2107
Coleman, J., 1218
Coleman, Robert, 1219
Coles, Merivan R., 545
Collins, Carvel, 1220
Collins, Norman, 2108
Colognesi, Silvana, 309
Colum, Mary Gunning (Maguire), 2109
Colvert, James B., 2110
Colvin, Sidney, 2111
Commager, Henry Steele, 2113
Comer, C. A. P., 2112
Conger, Sydney M., 1530
Conn, Peter James, 333, 972, 2114
Connolly, Cyril, 2115
Connolly, Francis X., 1096
Conrad, Joseph, 1667.1, 2116, 2117, 2118, 2119
Cook, Albert, 2120
Cook, Alton, 1221
Cook, David A., 1635.1, 2120.1
Cook, Dorothy, 3747.1
Cook, George A., 192
Coon, Peter J., 972
Cooney, Seamus, 310, 973
Cooper, Frederick Taber, 73, 246
Cooper, Harold, 2121
Cooper, Suzana Regoleth, 2122
Core, George Eric, 2123
Cornelius, Roberta D., 2124
Cornillon, Susan K., 385.1
Cornwell, Ethel F., 2125
Costello, Donald P., 1220
Cotton, Gerald B., 3747.2
Coursen, Herbert R., Jr., 74
Coward, T. R., 1668
Cowie, Alexander, 2126
Cowley, Malcolm, 1223, 2127, 2128
Cowser, John, 5.4
Cox, C. B., 546, 571.2, 753, 2129, 2130, 2130.1
Cox, James M., 370, 880.1, 2130.2
Coy Ferrer, Juan J., 1448, 2130.3
Coy, Javier, 2131
Craig, G. Armour, 754
Cranfill, Thomas Mabry, 1224,

1225, 1226, 1227, 3748
Crankshaw, Edward, 2132
Crawford, William, 547
Creeth, Edmund, 193
Crews, Frederick C., 74.1, 2133
Croly, Herbert, 2134
Cromer, Viris, 2135
Cromphout, G. Van, 2136
Cromwell, Agnes Whitney, 75
Cross, Wilbur L., 2137
Crothers, S. M., 2138
Crotty, Sister M. Madeleine,
    2139
Crow, Charles R., 1531
Crowl, Susan, 547.1, 1229,
    1229.1, 1532
Crowther, Bosley, 1230
Cummins, Elizabeth Keyser, 934,
    2140
Cunliffe, J. W., 2140.1
Cunliffe, Marcus, 2141
Cuny, Claude M., 2142
Curti, Merle, 2143

D'Agostino, Nemi, 1594
Dahlberg, Edward, 1669, 2144
Daiches, David, 755, 974, 1230.1,
    2145, 2145.1
Daly, Joseph Francis, 1595
D'Andrea, Antonio, 2146
Daniel, Robert, 329
Daniels, Earl, 2146.1, 3749
Daniels, Howell, 618
Dankleff, Richard, 1097
Dargan, E. Preston, 2147
D'Arzo, Silvio, 2147.1
Daugherty, Sarah Bowyer, 2147.2
Daumier, Honoré, 2147.3
Dauner, Louise, 2148
D'Avanzo, Mario L., 682
Davis, Douglas M., 1231
Davis, J., 76
Davis, O., 425.1
Davis, Robert Gorham, 714, 2149
Davray, Henry D., 1670, 2150
Deakin, Motley F., 426, 2151,
    2152
Dean, Sharon Welch, 2152.1
Deans, Thomas R., 77
de Araujo, Victor, 2153
De Bellis, Jack, 1232
De Blois, Frank, 1233

Debo, Elizabeth Lea, 2154
Decker, Clarence R., 2155
DeFalco, Joseph M., 589
De la Mare, Walter, 2156, 2157
Deland, Margaret, 2158
de la Roche, Mazo, 2159
Delbaere-Garant, Jeanne, 627,
    881, 2160
Delétang-Tardif, Yanette, 2161
Demel, Erika von Elswehr, 2162
DeMille, George E., 2163
Demuth, Charles, 1234
Denney, Reuel, 2163.1
Dent, A., 1235
Derleth, August, 1236
DeSantis, Alex, 2164
Deurbergue, Jean, 2165
DeVoto, Bernard, 1237
Dickins, Bruce, 1449
Dickinson, Thomas H., 1238
Dietrichson, Jan W., 2166,
    2166.1
Diffené, Patricia, 2168, 2169
Ditsky, John, 2170
Dixson, Robert J., 756
Dobree, Valentine, 1450
Dolmatch, Theodore B., 1239
Domaniecki, Hildegard, 1240,
    1241
Dommergues, Pierre, 2171
Donnelly, J. B., 2172
Donoghue, Dennis, 311, 757
Donovan, Alan B., 1671, 2173
Dooley, D. J., 78
Dorris, George E., 78.1
Dort, B., 79
Dove, George N., 1242
Dove, John Roland, 758, 882,
    2174
Dow, Eddy, 406
Downing, F., 2175
Draper, Muriel, 2176
Draper, Ruth P., 427, 2177
Drew, Elizabeth, 759, 2178
Drucker, Leon, 1098
Dryden, Edgar A., 2179
Dub, Friederike, 2180
Duberman, Martin, 2181
Dubler, Walter, 883
Duffy, John J., 194, 2181.1
Dumitriu, Gheorgeta, 759.1,
    2182, 2182.1
Dunbar, Olivia Howard, 640.3,
    1649

Dunbar, Viola Ruth, 6, 428, 429,
    975, 976, 2183, 3750
Duncan, Hugh Dalziel, 2184
Duncan, Kirby Luther, 2185
Duncan-Jones, E. E., 1243
Dunlap, George A., 371
Dunn, Albert O., 80
Dupee, Frederick W., 7, 80.1,
    301, 429.1, 760, 1533, 1596,
    2186, 2187, 2188, 2189, 2190
Duras, Marguerite, 341
Durham, F. H., 1597
Durham, Frank M., 430
Durkin, Sister Mary Brian, 965
Durr, Robert A., 81
Dwight, H. G., 2191
Dwyer, John Francis, 2191.1
Dyne, Michael, 1244
Dyson, A. E., 1490.1
Dyson, John Peter, 2191.2

Eagleton, Terry, 2191.3
Eakin, Paul J., 2192
Earnest, Ernest, 977, 2192.1
Eastman, Richard M., 2193
Edel, Leon, 7.1, 7.2, 7.3, 8, 9,
    10, 11, 12, 13, 14, 15, 15.1,
    15.2, 82, 83, 84, 85, 85.1,
    86, 87, 88, 195, 247, 247.1,
    265, 265.1, 271, 277, 311.1,
    431, 487.1, 527, 528, 547.2,
    593, 695, 699, 704, 761, 762,
    763, 764, 765, 883.1, 978,
    979, 1034, 1035, 1078.1,
    1083.1, 1099, 1099.1, 1140,
    1141, 1149, 1245, 1246, 1451,
    1474, 1474.1, 1490.2, 1533.1,
    1598, 1599, 1600, 1601, 1636,
    1637, 1642, 1643, 1644, 1645,
    1671.1, 1672, 1673, 1674,
    1675, 1676, 1736.3, 1736.4,
    1748, 1748.1, 1757, 1764,
    2194, 2195, 2196, 2197, 2198,
    2199, 2200, 2201, 2202, 2203,
    2204, 2205, 2206, 2207, 2208,
    2209, 2210, 2211, 2212, 2213,
    2214, 2214.1, 2214.2, 2215,
    2216, 2217, 2217.1, 2218,
    2219, 2220, 2221, 2222, 2223,
    2532, 3751, 3752, 3753, 3754,
    3755, 3756, 3757
Edelstein, Arnold Stanley, 1100,

    2224
Edelstein, Tilden G., 2225
Edgar, Pelham, 16, 272, 766,
    1677, 2226, 2227, 2228, 2229,
    2230
Edmondson, Elsie, 2231
Edwards, Herbert, 2232
Edwards, Oliver, 883.2, 2232.1
Efrom, Arthur, 1247
Egan, Maurice Francis, 1248,
    2233
Egan, Michael, 2234
Eichelberger, Clayton L., 3758
Elderdice, Robert A., 2235
Eliot, Thomas Stearns, 602,
    2236, 2237, 2238
Elliott, G. P., 884
Ellis, David, 17
Ellis, James, 3415
Ellis, Stewart Marsh, 2239
Ellison, Ralph, 2240
Ellman, Richard, 2241
Elton, Oliver, 1249, 1534, 2242
Emerson, Donald, 1764.1, 2243,
    2244, 2245, 2246, 2247, 2248,
    2249
Emerson, Edward Waldo, 2250
Emerson, O. B., 3845
Enck, John J., 548
Engelberg, Edward, 980, 980.1,
    2251
Engstrom, Susanne, 88.1
Enkvist, Nils Erik, 2252
Erhart, Virginia, 2252.1
Espey, John J., 278, 2253
Evans, Oliver, 1250
Evans, Patricia, 89

Fabris, Alberta, 248, 2255, 2256
Fadiman, Clifton, 334, 656, 689,
    934.1, 947, 1251, 1252, 1452,
    2257, 2258, 2259, 2260
Fagin, Nathan B., 1253
Fahey, Paul, 1491
Faison, E. Lane, Jr., 2261
Falk, Robert P., 767, 1150, 1254,
    1255, 2262, 2263, 2264, 2265,
    2266, 2267, 2268, 2269
Farnham, Mary Davis, 2270, 2271
Farrell, James T., 2272
Farrer, Alison, 1475, 2273
Fawcett, Edgar, 2275, 2275.1

Fay, Eliot G., 2276, 2277
Fay, Gerard, 1256
Featherstone, Joseph L., 2278
Feidelson, Charles, Jr., , 500, 676,
    768, 2241, 2279, 2280, 2281
Feinstein, Herbert, 1257, 2282
Feldman, Stephen Michael, 2283
Felheim, Marvin, 521
Felstiner, John, 2284
Fenollosa, Ernest, 2285
Fenton, Edna, 1602
Ferguson, Alfred R., 2286, 3759
Ferguson, Louis A., 2287
Fergusson, Francis, 549, 550,
    1603, 1604, 2288
Fernandez, Diane, 2288.1, 2289,
    2290
Fernando, Lloyd, 2291
Feuerlicht, Ignace, 1258
Fick, Otto W., 2292
Fiderer, Gerald, 90, 1101
Fiedler, Leslie A., 432, 1259,
    1260, 1492, 2293, 2294
Field, Mary Lee, 2294.1
Fielding, H. M., 2295
Figuera, Angela, 2296
Finch, George A., 501, 878.1,
    2297, 2298
Finch, I. W., 2299
Fine, Ronald Edward, 3715.3
Fink, Guido, 2299.1
Finkelstein, Sidney, 1036, 2300
Finn, C. M., 90.1
Finney, Martha Collins, 2301
Fiocco, A., 2302
Firebaugh, Joseph J., 312, 551,
    885, 1261, 1535, 2303, 2304,
    2305, 2306
Fischer, William C., Jr., 2307,
    2307.1
Fish, Charles Kelleway, Jr., 655,
    1139, 1476, 2308
Fisher, Neil H., 91, 769
Fitzpatrick, Kathleen Elizabeth,
    1261.1, 2309
FitzRoy, Almeric, 2310
Fleet, Simon, 2311, 2312
Flestiner, John, 2313
Flinn, H. G., 770
Flory, Sister Ancilla, 2314
Flower, Dean Scott, 17.1, 2315,
    2316, 2317
Flynn, T. E., 2318

Foff, Arthur, 948
Fogle, Richard H., 2319
Foley, P. K., 3760
Foley, Richard Nicholas, 770.1,
    1037, 2320, 2321, 3761
Follett, Helen Thomas, 2322,
    2322.1
Follett, Wilson, 1038, 1039,
    1262, 1263, 2322, 2323, 2324
Folsom, James K., 1040
Forbes, Elizabeth L., 1605, 2325
Ford, Ford Madox (See Hueffer,
    Ford Madox)
Forde, Sister Victoria, 279
Forrester, Andrew D., 2326
Forster, E. M., 93, 2327, 2328,
    2328.1
Foster, Richard, 2328.2
Fox, Hugh, Jr., 93, 2329, 2330
Fraiberg, Louis, 2331
France, Wilmer Cave, 1649.1
Francis, Sister Mary, 2332
Frank, Charles P., 2333
Frank, Frederick S., 2333.1
Frank, Joseph, 17.2, 1151,
    2333.2, 2334
Franklin, Rosemary F., 272.1
Frantz, Jean H., 406.1, 608,
    609, 2334.1
Fraser, G. S., 2334.2
Fraser, John, 1266, 2335
Frederick, John T., 771, 2336
Frederiksen, Bodil F., 93.1
Freedman, William A., 628
Freeman, Arthur, 885.1, 2337
Freeman, John, 1267, 2338
Fricker, Robert, 2339
Friedl, Herwig, 2340
Friedman, Alan, 2341
Friedman, Norman, 2341.1, 2342
Friend, Albert C., 610
Friend, Joseph H., 772
Frierson, William C., 2343, 2344
Friese, Fränze, 94
Fryckstedt, Olov W., 2345
Frye, Northrop, 2346
Füger, Wilhelm, 611
Fukuma, Kin-ichi, 886
Fuller, Henry Blake, 2347,
    2347.1
Fullerton, Bradford M., 3762
Fullerton, Morton, 2348
Furbank, P. N., 1606

Fussell, Edwin, 2349

G., E., 2349.1
Gabriel, Gilbert W., 1268
Gabrielsen, Thor, 2349.2
Gale, Robert L., 49, 95, 552,
  686, 690, 702, 773, 949, 981,
  1041, 1142, 1269, 1270, 1271,
  1678, 1679, 1749, 2350, 2351,
  2352, 2353, 2354, 2355, 2356,
  2357, 2358, 2359, 2360, 2361,
  2362, 2363, 2364, 3763, 3764
Galloway, David, 774
Gallup, Jennifer, 3738
Gard, A. R., 553
Gard, Roger, 1042, 2365
Gardner, Burdett, 982, 1680,
  2366
Gardner, Joseph H., 2367
Garg, Neera, 775
Gargano, James W., 96, 196,
  313, 433, 1102, 1272, 1493,
  1494, 2368
Garis, Robert, 18, 97
Garland, Hamlin, 1650, 2369,
  2370, 2370.1
Garland, Robert, 1273
Garn, Dennis Stewart, 2371
Garnett, David, 19, 477, 2532
Garnier, Marie Reine, 2372,
  2372.1
Garrett, Peter K., 2373, 2374
Garst, Tom, 2375
Gass, William H., 20, 612, 776,
  2376, 2377
Gastón, Nilita Vientós, 2378
Geary, Edward Acord, 2379
Gegenheimer, Albert Frank, 707
Geismar, Maxwell, 20.1, 98,
  335, 629, 777, 1043, 1044,
  1274, 1536, 2379.1, 2380,
  2380.1, 2381, 2382, 2383
Geist, Stanley, 434
Genda, Shuighi, 1274.1
Géracht, Maurice Aron, 2384
Gerard, Albert, 2384.1
Gerber, John C., 99
Gerber, Richard, 2385, 2386
Gerould, Gordon Hall, 1275,
  2387
Gerstenberger, Donna, 3765,
  3765.1

Gettmann, Royal A., 197, 480,
  2388
Ghiselin, Brewster, 1103, 1750,
  2389
Gibbs, Wolcott, 1276
Gibson, Priscilla, 2390
Gibson, William M., 100, 417,
  435
Gide, André, 502, 2391, 2392,
  2393
Gifford, Henry, 1607
Gilbert, E. L., 2395
Gilbert, Justin, 1277
Gilkes, Lillian, 3406.1
Gill, Richard, 2395
Gill, W. A., 2396
Gillen, Francis Xavier, 314,
  2397
Gillespie, Gerald, 2398
Gilman, Lawrence, 683, 1681,
  2399
Gilman, Richard, 2400
Gindin, J. J., 2401
Ginger, Ray, 2402
Gioli, Giovanna M., 435.1
Giorcelli, Cristina, 2403
Girgus, Sam B., 1494.1
Girling, H. K., 315, 554, 1278,
  2404
Gleckner, Robert T., 661
Gliddon, Gerald M., 2405
Goddard, Harold C., 1279
Goetsch, Paul, 2407
Gohdes, Clarence, 2408, 2409
Goldberg, M. A., 2410
Goldfarb, Clare R., 372
Goldfarb, Russell M., 1476.1
Goldsmith, Arnold L., 1104,
  1105, 2411, 2412, 2413
Goldstein, Sallie Sears, 101, 555,
  1537
Gomme, Laurence, 3767
Gonzalez Pantin, Hilda Ana,
  2413.1
Goode, John, 102, 1538, 2414,
  2415, 2416, 2588
Goodman, Charlotte Margolis,
  983, 2417
Goodspeed, Edgar J., 436
Gordan, John D., 2418
Gordon, Caroline, 103, 556,
  2419
Gordon, David J., 1151.1, 1453

Gosse, Edmund, 21, 1280, 2420,
    2421, 2422, 2423
Gossman, Ann, 503
Gottschalk, Jane, 336
Gould, Cecil, 22
Gow, Ronald, 1477
Grabo, Carl H. , 103.1, 1281,
    1538.1, 2423.1
Gragg, Perry Earl, 2424
Graham, Kenneth, 2425
Graham, R. B. Cunningham, 2426
Grana, Gianni, 2427
Grattan, Clinton Hartley, 23,
    1608, 2428, 3768
Gray, James, 2429
Green, David B. , 373
Green, Martin, 2430, 2430.1,
    2431
Greene, Bertram, 437
Greene, George, 2432
Greene, Graham, 24, 778, 779,
    780, 1282, 1609, 1610, 2433,
    2434, 2435, 2436, 2437, 2438,
    2439, 2440
Greene, Mildred S. E. , 781, 1539
Greene, Philip Leon, 1106, 2441
Greenwood, di Clarissa, 1765
Greet, Thomas Y. , 1495
Gregor, Ian, 316
Gregory, Alyse, 2422
Grenander, M. E. , 782, 887, 984
Gretton, M. Sturge, 1751
Grewall, Om Prakash, 374, 888,
    1152, 2443
Griffin, Robert J. , 522
Griffith, Albert J. , 2444
Griffith, John, 934.2
Griffiths, T. , 1283
Grigg, Womble Quay, 2445
The Grolier Club, 3769
Gross, Barry, 198
Gross, Theodore L. , 2446
Grosskurth, Phyllis, 24, 2447
Grossman, Edward, 375, 2447.1
Grossman, James, 2448
Grosso, Luigi, 1478
Grover, P. R. , 603, 889, 2449
Grover, Philip, 2450
Grumman, Joan Mary, 2451
Guedalla, Philip, 2452, 2453
Gullason, T. A. , 2455
Gullón, Richardo, 2456
Gunn, Giles, 2457

Gunn, Peter, 2458
Gunthner, Frantz, 2459
Gurko, Leo, 523, 1454, 2460
Gutscher, Marianne, 2461
Gutwinski, Waldemar F. , 2461.1
Gwiazda, Ronald E. , 2461.2

H. , J. 890, 984.1, 2461.3
Haas, Herta, 198.1
Habegger, Alfred, 376, 1082.1,
    1496, 1540, 2462
Habicht, Louise Ann, 2462.1
Hackett, Francis, 249, 249.1,
    517, 2463, 2464, 2465
Hafley, James, 783, 2466
Hagan, John, 1541
Hagemann, E.R. , 2467, 2468,
    3770
Haggard, H. Rider, 784
Haggin, B. H. , 1284
Hagopian, John, 438, 934.3, 935
Haight, Gordon S. , 2469
Hale, Edward Everett, 1736.2,
    2470, 2471, 2472, 2473
Halifax, Viscount, 2474
Hall, James, 480.1, 525.2, 592
Hall, Robert A. , Jr. , 2475
Hall, Sallie Jean, 2475.1
Hall, Susan Corwin, 3771
Hall, William F. , 250, 317,
    1153, 2476, 2477
Hallab, Mary Clark Yost, 2477.1
Halleck, Reuben Post, 2478
Halliburton, D. G. , 891
Halperin, John W. , 557, 784.1
Halpern, Martin, 785
Halsey, William D. , 1855.1
Halverson, John, 2479
Hamblen, Abigail Ann, 377, 378,
    408, 439, 558, 1497, 1542,
    1543, 2480, 2481, 2482, 2483
Hamilton, Clayton, 1285, 2484
Hamilton, Eunice C. , 25, 892,
    2485, 3772
Hampshire, Stuart, 25.1, 2486
Han, Pierre, 481
Haney, Charles Williams, 1286
Hansot, Elizabeth, 336.1
Hapgood, Norman, 2487, 2488
Hardy, Barbara, 2489, 2490, 2491
Hardy, Florence E. , 2492, 2493
Harkins, E. F. , 2494, 2495
Harkness, Bruce, 2496, 3773

Harland, Henry, 2497
Harlow, Virginia, 2498, 2499
Harnack, Curtis, 2500
Harrier, Richard C. , 1638, 1682,
    2501
Harris, Frank, 2502
Harris, Joel Chandler, 379, 2503
Harris, Marie P. , 1651
Harris, Wendell V. , 2504
Harrison, Henry Sydnor, 692.1,
    2505
Harrison, Stanley R. , 2506
Hart, James D. , 1286.1
Hart, James S. , 2507
Hart-Davis, Rupert, 2508
Hartley, L. P. , 2509, 2510, 2511
Hartman, Geoffrey, 1287, 2512
Hartsock, Mildred, 26, 104, 280,
    318, 359, 380, 893, 1107, 2513
Hartwick, Harry, 2514, 2515
Harvey, J. R. , 2516
Harvey, Paul, 2517
Harvey, William J. , 786, 787,
    894, 2518, 2519
Harvitt, Hélène, 985
Haslam, Gerald, 381
Hasler, Jörg, 1683, 1684, 2519.1
Hassan, Ihab, 440
Hastings, Katherine, 26.1
Hatcher, Harlan Henthorne, 2520
Hatcher, Joe B. , 594
Havens, Raymond D. , 319, 605,
    700, 986, 1015
Havighurst, Walter, 677
Havlice, Patricia P. , 3774
Hawkins, William, 1288
Hawthorne, Julian, 787.1, 2520.1
Hay, John, 2521
Hayashi, Tetsumaro, 2521.1
Haycraft, Howard, 1289
Hayne, Barrie S. , 2522
Hays, H. R. , 2523
Haywood, J. C. , 2524
Head, Ruth, 2525
Healy, Kathleen, 352.1
Heilbrun, Carolyn, 788
Heilman, Robert B. , 1290, 1291,
    1292, 1293
Heimer, Jackson W. , 2526
Hellman, Geoffrey, 2527
Hellman, George S. , 2528
Hemphill, George, 2529
Hendrick, Leo T. , 2530
Henrick, George, 3765

Henry, John, 2533
Heppenstall, Rayner, 2533.1
Herrick, Robert, 1736.5, 2534,
    2535, 2536
Herx, Mary Ellen, 590
Heston, Lilla A. , 558.1, 1108,
    1544, 2537
Hetherington, Hugh W. , 475.2
Hicks, Granville, 26.2, 272.3,
    2538, 2539, 2540, 2541
Hicks, Priscilla Gibson, 1737
Higginson, Thomas Wentworth,
    2542, 2543, 2544
Highet, Gilbert, 715, 1739
Higuchi, Hideo, 2545
Hill, Hamlin, L. , Jr. , 320
Hill, John Edward, 2545.1
Hill, John S. , 105, 2545.2
Hinchliffe, Arnold, 1045, 2546-7
Hind, Charles Lewis, 2548
Hinz, Evelyn J. , 2549, 2550
Hirsch, David H. , 441
Hoag, Gerald Bryan, 2551, 2551.1
Hoare, Dorothy M. , 2552, 2553
Hocks, Richard Allen, 2554
Hodgdon, David Crockett, 2555
Hodge, Judith Bush, 2555.1
Hofer, Ernest Harrison, 2556
Hoff, Lloyd M. , 987
Hoffa, William, 303, 304
Hoffman, Frederick J. , 27, 895,
    988, 2556.1, 2557, 2558
Hoffman, Michael J. , 441.1
Hoffmann, Charles G. , 1046, 1047,
    1294, 1295, 2559, 2560, 3775
Hofmann, Gert, 504, 1048, 1296
Hoftund, Sigmund, 199
Hogarth, Basil, 1297
Hogsett, Elizabeth A. , 336.2
Holder, Alan, 106, 642, 2561,
    2562, 2563, 2564
Holder, Alex, 559, 2565
Holder-Barrell, Alexander, 2566
Holland, Laurence B. , 1545,
    1545.1, 2567, 2568
Holleran, James V. , 360
Holiday, Robert Cortes, 2569
Holloway, John, 321, 442
Holman, Clarence H. , 2570, 3776
Hølmebakk, Gordon, 2571
Holroyd, Stuart, 2572
Honig, Edwin, 2574, 2575, 2576
Hönnighausen, Lothar, 1439, 2578
Hopkins, Gerard, 2577

Hopkins, Viola - See Winner, Viola Hopkins
Hoppé, A. J., 2532
Horne, Charles F., 2579
Horne, Helen, 950, 2580, 2581
Horowitz, Floyd R., 108, 200
Horrell, Joyce Tayloe, 2582
Hoshioka, Motoko, 1298
Hoskins, Katherine, 529, 2583
Hough, Graham, 2584, 2585, 2586
Houghton, Donald E., 443
Houghton, Walter E., 1757.1, 3776.1
Houser, Zelma Large, 28
Hovanec, Evelyn Ann, 2586.1
Hovey, Richard B., 2587
Howard, David, 381.1, 2588
Howard-Hill, T. H., 3777
Howe, Helen, 2588.1
Howe, Irving, 201, 251, 252, 382, 896, 897, 898, 2589, 2589.1, 2590
Howe, M. A. DeWolfe, 1685, 2591
Howells, Mildred, 444, 1686, 2599
Howells, William Dean, 445, 445.1, 446, 447, 448, 449, 449.1, 603.1, 655.1, 708, 965.1, 1736.3, 2592, 2593, 2594, 2595, 2596, 2597, 2598, 2599, 2600
Hoxie, Elizabeth F., 450
Hudson, Gertrude R., 1515, 1687
Hudspeth, Robert N., 109
Hueffer, Ford Madox [Also known as Ford Madox Ford], 1264, 1265, 2601, 2602, 2603, 2604, 2605, 2606, 2607, 2608, 2609 2610
Huffman, James Richard, 2611
Hughes, Helen A., 1299
Hughes, Herbert L., 2612, 2613
Humma, John B., 450.1
Humphrey, Robert, 2614
Humphreys, S. M., 110
Huneker, James Gibbons, 642, 2615, 2616, 2616.1, 2616.2
Huneker, Josephine, 2616.2
Hunt, Thomas G., 1109
Hutchens, John K., 2617
Hutton, Virgil, 110.1, 2618
Hux, Samuel, 281
Hyde, H. Montgomery, 29, 30, 31, 32, 1646, 1647, 1648, 2619, 2620

Hyman, Stanley Edgar, 2621
Hynes, Joseph Anthony, Jr., 1498, 1515.1
Hynes, Samuel, 33, 2622

I., B. de C., 2623
Iglesias, J., 2625
Irle, Gerhard, 1300
Irwin, W., 2627
Ishizaki, Ayako Tomii, 2628
Isle, Walter Whitfield, 321.1, 695.1, 1048.1, 1049, 1110, 1498.1, 1611, 2629, 2630
Itagaki, Konomu, 1546
Ives, C. B., 1301
Iwase, Shitsuyu, 252.1, 524
Izak, Emily K., 1111
Izzo, Carlo, 2631

Jacobson, Dan, 2632
James, Alice, 2633, 2634
James, E. Anthony, 451
James, Henry, 202, 272.2, 281.1, 321.2, 452, 452.1, 453, 560, 560.1, 715.1, 789, 899, 935.1, 965.2, 990, 1112, 1154, 1499, 1547, 1611.1, 1612, 1689, 1690, 1691, 1692, 1751.1, 2635, 2636, 2645
James, William, 253, 560.1, 1693, 2646, 2647, 2648, 2649
Jarrett-Kerr, Martin, 2649.1
Jefferson, D. W., 34, 2650, 2651, 3778
Jefferson, Douglas, 1500
Jellema, R. H., 2652
Jenkins, Iredell, 2653
Jennings, R., 2654
Jennings, Richard, 1302
Johnson, Alice Evangeline, 2655, 2656
Johnson, Arthur, 2657
Johnson, Courtney, Jr., 203, 337, 630, 790, 2658
Johnson, Lee Ann, 1478.1, 2659
Johnson, Merle, 3779, 3780
Johnson, Richard Colles, 3781, 3781.1
Johnson, Robert G., 2660
Johnson, Thomas H., 3782
Jones, Alexander E., 1303
Jones, Dora M., 2661
Jones, Edith R., 262
Jones, Granville Hicks, 2663

Jones, Howard Mumford, 34.1,
    1304, 2664, 2665
Jones, Leonidas M., 525
Jones, Llewellyn, 2666
Jones, M., 2666.1
Jones, Oliver P., 2667
Jones, T. H., 2668
Jones, Walter P., 2669
Jones-Evans, Mervyn, 2670
Jordan, Elizabeth, 1512, 2671,
    2672
Josephson, Matthew, 709, 1305,
    2673
Jost, Edward F., 338, 2674
Juan, Epifanio San, Jr., 110.2

K., Q., 695.2, 1613, 2675
Kael, Pauline, 1306
Kaman, John Michael, 2676
Kamerbeck, J., Jr., 111
Kane, Patricia, 2677
Kane, Robert J., 649, 900
Kanzer, Mark, 505
Kaplan, Charles, 662
Kaplan, Louis, 3783
Kar, Annette, 454
Kariel, Henry S., 2678
Karita, Motoshi, 35, 2679
Karl, Frederick R., 1694, 2680
Katan, M., 1307
Kaufman, Marjorie R., 2681,
    2682
Kaul, A. N., 2683
Kaul, R. K., 2684
Kay, Wallace G., 2685
Kaye, Julian B., 112, 322, 506,
    1050
Kayser, von Rudolf, 2686
Kazlin, Alfred, 113, 2687, 2688,
    2689, 2690, 2690.1, 2691
Keating, P. J., 900.1
Kees, Weldon, 2692
Kehler, Harold, 951
Kelley, Cornelia Pulsifer, 2693,
    2694, 2695, 2696, 3784
Kellner, L., 2697
Kellogg, Gene, 2698
Kennedy, Ian, 455
Kenner, Hugh, 2699
Kenney, Blair Gates, 204, 791,
    2700
Kenney, William, 936, 1456

Kenton, Edna, 114, 1308, 1614,
    2701, 2702, 2703, 3785
Keown, Eric, 1309, 1310
Kerner, David, 339
Kettle, Arnold, 792, 2704
Key, Howard C., 770, 793
Keynes, Geoffrey, 1695, 2705,
    2705.1
Kimball, Jean, 561, 1548
Kimbrough, Robert, 1311
Kimmey, John L., 383, 901, 902,
    1155
King, Frederick A., 3786
King, Kimball, 1615
King, Sister M. Judine, 2706
Kinnaird, John, 991, 2707
Kinoian, Vartkis, 115, 794
Kirby, David Kirk, 696, 1312,
    2707.1, 2707.2
Kirk, Clara M., 2708, 2708.1
Kirk, Rudolf, 1696, 1697
Kirkham, E. Bruce, 663
Kleinbard, Elaine Zablotny,
    2708.2
Kleinberg, Seymour, 795
Knapp, Daniel, 948
Knieger, Bernard, 716
Knight, Arthur, 1313
Knight, Grant C., 1314, 1315,
    1316, 2709, 2710
Knights, L. C., 613, 2711
Knoepflmacher, U. C., 116
Knoll, Robert E., 481.1
Knox, George, 117, 205, 966,
    1317, 2712
Koch, Dorothy A., 2713
Koch, Stephen, 1549
Kocmanová, Jessie, 903, 2714
Kohli, Raj K., 796, 797
Kolb, Harold H., Jr., 2715,
    2716
Koljević, Svetozar, 2716.1
Komota, Junzo, 2717
Kono, Yotaro, 2718
Korg, Jacob, 282
Kornfeld, Milton Herbert, 1549.1,
    2719
Koskimies, Rafael, 2720
Kossick, Shirley, 487.2
Kossman, Rudolph R., 1616, 2721
Kozol, Clara Barbara, 1697.1
Kraft, James Louis, 254, 340,
    664, 992, 1758, 2722, 2723,
    3787

Kraft, Quentin G., 118, 993, 1550, 2724, 2725, 2726, 2727
Kramer, Cheris, 680
Kramer, Dale, 680
Kramer, Hilton, 2728
Krause, Sydney J., 798, 799, 800
Krehayn, Joachim, 2729
Kretsch, Robert W., 904, 2730
Kretzschmar, Helmut, 2731
Krickel, Edward F., Jr., 2732, 2733
Krishan, Bal, 2733.1
Krishna, Rao N., 323
Kronenberger, Louis, 1457, 1457.1
Krook, Dorothea, 266, 562, 562.1, 801, 1050.1, 1318, 1551, 1551.1, 2735, 2735.1, 2736, 2737, 2737.1
Krutch, Joseph Wood, 206
Kubal, David L., 2738
Kudo, Yoshimi, 119
Kuhn, Bertha M., 717
Küsgen, Reinhardt, 2739

L. R. F. O., 1051
Labor, Earle, 952
Labrie, Ernest Ross, 2740, 2741, 2742, 2743, 2744
LaFarge, John, 1698
LaFrance, Marston, 2744.1
Lainoff, Seymour, 507, 508, 937, 953
Lamb, Lynton, 1458
Landry, Lowell, 2745
Lane, Margaret, 1319
Lang, Andrew, 2746
Lang, Hans-Joachim, 1320, 2747
Lang, P. H., 1552
Langbaum, Robert, 904.1
Lanier, Henry Wysham, 1321
Lanier, Sidney, 456
La Roche, Mazode, 2748
Larrabee, Harold A., 35.1, 2749
Las Vergnas, Raymond, 1459, 1553
Lauber, John, 2749
Lauer, Kristin Olson, 119.1, 562.2, 2750
Laurence, Dan H., 1699, 2751, 2752, 3751, 3788
Lavender, Kenneth Ernest, 2753
Leach, Anna, 1322, 2754

Leary, Lewis Gaston, 1699.1, 2755, 2756, 3616, 3788.1, 3789
Leavis, Frank Raymond, 119.2, 488, 802, 803, 804, 904.2, 993.1, 1478.2, 1501, 1501.1, 1501.2, 1638.1, 2532, 2757, 2758, 2759, 2760, 2761, 2762, 2763, 2764
Leavis, Q. D., 478, 805, 1322.1, 2765, 2765.1, 2766, 2767
Lebowitz, Naomi, 563, 1052, 1554, 2767.1, 2768, 2769, 2770
LeClair, Robert Charles, 36, 37, 2771, 2772, 2773, 3790, 3791
Lee, B. C., 2774
Lee, Brian, 120, 564, 1555
Leeming, David Adams, 2775, 2776
Leggett, Glenn, 329
Lehmann, John, 283, 2532
Leighton, Lawrence, 2777
Leisy, Ernest, 2778, 2779
Leonard, Vivien Rose, 1737.1, 1752, 2780
Lerner, Daniel, 2781, 2782
Leslie, Shane, 2783
Levin, Gerald, 324
Levin, Harry, 1323, 2784, 2785
Levine, George, 2786
LeVot, André, 2787
Levy, Babette May, 604.3
Levy, Edward Richard, 2788
Levy, Leo B., 409, 509, 1053, 1324, 1325, 1479, 1617, 2789, 2790, 2791, 2792, 2956
Lewis, Eugene, 1326
Lewis, J. H., 2793
Lewis, Naomi, 2794
Lewis, R. W. B., 1556, 1557, 2795, 2796, 2797, 2798, 2799
Lewis, Wyndham, 2800
Lewisohn, Ludwig, 1327, 2801
Leyburn, Ellen Douglass, 2802, 2803
Leyris, Pierre, 937.1
Libby, Marion Jean Vlastos, 2803.1
Libman, Valentina A., 3792
Lid, R. W., 2804, 2805
Liddell, Robert, 121, 1328, 1329, 2806, 2807, 2807.1

Liebman, Sheldon W. , 807, 808
Lief, Leonard, 717.1
Liljegren, Sten Bodvar, 1330, 2809
Lincecum, J. B. , 2810
Lind, Ilse Dusoir, 691, 1673, 2811
Lind, Sidney E. , 933, 1331, 2812, 2813, 2814
Linn, James Weber, 1332, 2815
Linneman, William R. , 2816
Littell, Philip, 684, 684.1, 692.3, 1054, 1700, 2817, 2818, 2819, 2820, 2821
Livesay, J. F. B. , 2822
Lochhead, Marion, 2823
Lockridge, Ernest H. , 1156
Lodge, David, 122, 2824, 2825
Logan, Annie R. M. , 123
Logan, M. , 2826
Lombardi, Olga, 2827
Lombardo, Agostino, 2828, 2829, 2830, 2831
Long, E. Hudson, 2832
Long, Robert E. , 124, 384, 385, 1459.1, 1618
Loomis, Charles Battell, 2833, 2834
Loomis, Edward W. , 2835
Loomis, Roger S. , 525.1
Lord, Catherine, 2836
Lord, James, 341
Loreis, Hector-Jan, 2837
Love, Alma Louise, 479, 1765.1, 2838
Lowell, James Russell, 207, 2839, 2839.1
Lowery, Bruce, 2840, 2841, 2842
Lowndes, Marie Belloc, 2843
Lubbock, Percy, 125, 325, 1701, 1702, 2844, 2845, 2846, 2847
Lucas, E. V. , 905, 2848
Lucas, John, 1113, 1114, 1459.2, 2588, 2848.1, 2849, 2850, 3688
Lucas, William John, 906
Lucke, Jessie R. , 342
Ludeke, Henry, 2851
Ludwig, Richard, 665
Luecke, Sister Jane Marie, 907
Lutwack, Leonard, 2852
Luxford, Ansel Frank, Jr. , 2852.1
Lyde, Marilyn Jones, 2853
Lydenberg, John, 809, 1333, 1334, 2854, 2855
Lynd, Robert, 643, 2856, 2857
Lynen, John F. , 2858
Lynn, Kenneth S. , 2859, 2859.1
Lynskey, Winifred, 356
Lyra, Franciszek, 2860
Lytle, Andrew, 2861

M. L. H. , 638.1, 2862, 2863
Macauley, Robie, 489, 1460, 2864
MacCarthy, Desmond, 37.2, 701, 2865, 2866, 2867, 2868, 2869, 2869.1, 2870, 2871
Macdonald, Dwight, 1335, 2872
Macdonell, Annie, 2873, 2874
Machen, Arthur, 1336, 2875
MacKenzie, Compton, 2876, 2877, 2878, 2879
Mackenzie, Manfred, 126, 208, 630.1, 810, 1337, 2880, 2881, 2882
MacNaughton, William R. , 2883
Macy, John, 2884
Maddocks, Melvin, 37.3
Magalaner, Marvin, 481.2
Maglin, Nan B. , 385.1
Maguire, Charles E. , 209, 1758.1, 2885
Maini, Darshan Singh, 2886
Maixner, Paul Roger, 127, 666, 2887, 2888
Major, John C. , 1703, 2889
Male, Roy R. , Jr. , 1338
Malin, Irving, 2889.1, 2890, 3672
Mallet, Sir Charles, 2891
Manley, John Matthews, 2892, 3793
Mann, Jona J. , 457
Marcell, David W. , 811
Mariani, Umberto, 2893, 2894
Marković, Vida, 2894.1, 2894.2
Markow, Georges, 2895, 2896, 2897
Marks, Robert, 2898
Marks, Sita P. , 564.1, 1557.1, 1558
Marovitz, Sanford E. , 994

Marquardt, William F., 954
Marsden, Malcolm M., 2899
Marsh, Edward Clark, 1737,
  2900, 2901
Marshall, James Morse, 1055,
  2901.1
Marshall, Margaret, 1339, 2902
Martin, Harold C., 2902.1
Martin, Jay, 2903
Martin, Robert K., 2904, 2905
Martin, Terence, 938, 2906
Martin, W. R., 386
Martineau, Barbara, 1139.1,
  2906.1
Martineau, Stephen Francis,
  2907
Marx, Leo, 2908
Mary Francis, Sister, 2909
Masback, Frederic Joseph, 2910
Matheson, Gwen, 2911
Mathews, J. Chesley, 3794
Matsuhara, Iwao, 955
Matthews, Brander, 692.4, 1619,
  2912
Matthiessen, Francis Otto, 38,
  128, 812, 813, 814, 1740,
  2913, 2914, 2915, 2915.1,
  2916, 2917, 2918, 2919, 2920,
  3795
Maugham, W. Somerset, 2920,
  2921, 2922, 2923
Mauriac, François, 387, 388
Maurois, André, 2924, 2925,
  2926
Maves, Carl Edwin, 2927, 2928
Maxse, Mary, 2929
Maxwell, J. C., 129, 995, 2352,
  2929.1
Mayer, Charles W., 2930
Maynard, Reid, 130
Mayne, Ethel Coburn, 2930.1
Mayoux, Jean-Jacques, 2931
Mays, Milton A., 631, 943.5,
  2931.1, 2932, 2932.1, 2933
Mazzella, Anthony J., 814.1
McCarthy, Harold T., 1340,
  2934, 2935, 2936, 2937
McClary, Ben Harris, 1704
McCloskey, John C., 1502
McCormick, John O., 667, 2938
McCullough, Bruce Welker, 130.1,
  2939
McDonald, James, 2940

McDonald, Walter R., 2941
McDougal, Edward D., 1620,
  2942
McDowell, B. D., 1559
McDowell, Margaret B., 2943
McElderry, Bruce R., Jr., 267,
  458, 696.1, 939, 943.3, 1138,
  1139.2, 1480, 1513, 1705,
  2944, 2945, 2946, 2947,
  2947.1, 2948, 3796, 3797,
  3798, 3799, 3800, 3801
McElrath, J. R., 2948.1
McFarlane, I. D., 614, 2948.2
McGill, Anna Blanche, 2949
McGill, Hilda Mary, 3747.2
McGill, V. J., 2950
McGinty, Sister Mary Carolyn,
  131, 2951
McIntyre, Clara, 1737.1, 2952
McKenzie, Terence J., 2953
McLane, James, 1706
McLean, Robert C., 132, 284,
  389, 668, 669, 1115, 1559.1
McLuhan, H. M., 2954
McMahon, Helen, 955.1, 1758.2,
  2954.1, 3802
McManis, Jo Agnew, 2955
McMaster, Juliet, 815, 1341
McMurray, William, 390, 390.1
McNeir, Waldo, 2956
Megroz, R. L., 1342
Melchiori, Barbara, 2956.1, 2957
Melchiori, Giorgio, 640.1, 710,
  1056, 2958, 2959, 2960, 2961,
  2961.1, 2962, 2963, 2964,
  2965, 2966, 2967
Meldrum, Ronald M., 391, 1343,
  1560
Mellard, James M., 285
Mellow, James R., 2968, 2968.1
Mellquist, Jerome, 2969
Meltzer, Sharon Bittenson, 2970
Mencken, Henry Louis, 2971,
  2972, 2973
Mendelsohn, Michael, 459
Mendilow, A. A., 2974
Menikoff, Barry, 2974.1, 2975,
  2976
Mercer, Caroline G., 565
Mews, Siegfried, 2977
Michael, Mary Kyle, 133
Michaels, Herbert S., 594.1,
  1707

Michaud, Régis, 1708, 2978,
2979, 2979.1, 2980, 2980.1
Milano, Paolo, 1344
Miller, Betty, 184
Miller, J. Hillis, 2981
Miller, James E., Jr., 268,
2982, 2983, 2984, 2985
Miller, Perry, 2986
Miller, Raymond A., Jr. 2987
Miller, Theodore C., 392
Miller, Warren, 2988
Millett, Fred B., 816, 1139.6,
2989
Millgate, Michael, 209.1, 2990,
2991, 2992
Mills, A. R., 817
Milman, Lena, 2993
Milton, Dorothy, 2993.1
Miner, Earl R., 2994
Minter, Elsie Gray, 2995
Mintzlaff, Dorothy, 2996
Miroiu, Mihai, 2996.1
Mitchell, Juliet, 1502.1
Mitgang, Herbert, 620, 620.1
Mix, Katherine Lyon, 2997
Mizener, Arthur, 134, 2998
Mlikotin, Anthony Matthew, 2999,
3000
Moeller, Charles, 3001.1
Monro, Isabel S., 3747.1
Monroe, E. N., 3002
Monroe, N. Elizabeth, 3003
Monteiro, George, 50, 344, 460,
461, 530, 818, 819, 908, 909,
996, 997, 1157, 1708.1, 1709,
1710, 1711, 1712, 1759, 3004,
3005, 3005.1, 3006, 3007,
3008, 3009, 3010, 3011, 3803,
3804, 3805
Montgomery, Judith H., 819.1
Montgomery, Marion, 820
Moody, A. D., 821
Mooney, Stephen L., 566, 3012
Moore, D., 1561
Moore, George, 3012.1
Moore, John Rees, 3274
Moore, John Robert, 210
Moore, Marianne, 3013
Moore, Rayburn S., 39, 3014,
3805.1
Mordell, Albert, 1639, 1760,
3015
Morgan, Alice, 3016

Morgan, Louise, 3017
Morley, Robert, 3018
Morooka, Hirashi, 998
Morris, Lloyd, 3019
Morris, Wright, 255, 255.1,
3020
Morrison, Peggy Ann R., 3021
Morrison, Sister Kristin, 3021.1
Morse, John T., Jr., 3021.2
Morse, Samuel French, 3022
Mortimer, Raymond, 1057, 3023
Moses, Montrose, Jr., 1713
Moss, Leonard Jerome, 822,
3024
Mossman, Robert Edward, 3025,
3806
Motoda, Yuichi, 1344.1
Moult, Thomas, 3027
Mowat, Robert Balmain, 3028
Mowbray, J. P., 3029
Moynahan, Julian, 822.1
Mudrick, Marvin, 135
Muecke, D. C., 1562
Mueller, Lavonne, 956
Mukherji, Nirmal, 823, 823.1,
1345
Mull, Donald Locke, 824, 3030,
3030.1
Mulqueen, James E., 136, 567,
1563
Munford, Howard M., 3031
Munson, Gorham, 957
Munzar, Jiri, 3032
Murakami, Fugio, 295, 568, 1158,
3033
Murdock, Kenneth, 286, 1346,
1740, 3795
Murphy, Edward F., 3034
Murray, Donald M., 461.1, 825,
3035, 3036, 3037, 3038, 3039
Mustanoja, Tauno F., 3040
Mutarelli, Giorgio, 40
Myers, Robert Manson, 1116

Nadal, E. S., 3041
Nagel, Paul C., 3042
Naik, M. K., 586.1
Nakazato, Haruhiko, 711, 1461
Namekata, Akio, 826, 1117
Narkevich, A. Iu, 41, 3043,
3807
Nash, Deanna C., 568.2

Nassauer, Gertrud, 3044
Nathan, Monique, 137
Neff, John C., 3045
Neider, Charles, 286.1, 3046
Neifer, Leo J., 3047
Nelson, Carl, 326
Netherby, Wallace, 392.1
Nettels, Elsa, 138, 999, 3048, 3048.1
Nevius, Blake, 3049
Newbolt, Henry, 3050
Newburgh, M. L. H., 3051
Newcomer, Alphonso Gerald, 3051.1
Newlin, Paul A., 1000, 3052
Newman, Charles, 3053
Newman, Franklin, 521
Newton, J. M., 827
Niall, Brenda, 3054
Nicholas, Brian, 316
Nicholas, Charles Andrew, 475.3, 3055
Nicoloff, Philip L., 657
Niemi, Pearl C., 3056
Nies, Frederick J., 910
Niess, Robert J., 678, 3057
Nilon, Charles H., 3808
Noble, David W., 3058
Noble, James Ashcroft, 705
Noda, Hisashi, 211
Noel, France, 3059, 3059.1
Nonaka, Ryo, 3060
Norman, Sylva, 3061, 3062
Normand, Jean, 139, 212
Northrup, Clark Sutherland, 1350, 3809
Norton, Charles Eliot, 3063
Norton, Rictor Carl, 1350.1, 1350.2
Nowell-Smith, Simon, 42, 644, 828, 967, 1714, 3065, 3066, 3067, 3068, 3810, 3811
Nuhn, Ferner, 569, 1352, 3069, 3070
Nyren, Dorothy, 3071

O'Brien, E. J., 3072
O'Brien, Ellen Tremper, 3072.1
Ochshorn, M. G., 570
O'Connor, Frank, 3073
O'Connor, William Van, 3074, 3075

O'Faolain, Sean, 958, 3076, 3077
Offen, Susan, 829
O'Grady, Walter, 140, 3078
Ohmann, Carol, 463
Okita, Hagime, 3079, 3812
Okoshi, Tishiko, 1118
O'Leary, Sister Jeanine, 911
Oliver, Clinton F., 393, 912, 913, 3080
O'Neill, John P., 3081, 3081.1
Onishi, Akio, 407, 719, 720, 3082
Orage, Alfred Richard, 1353, 3083, 3084, 3085
Orcutt, William Dana, 3086, 3087, 3088, 3089, 3090
Ortmann, Amei, 3091
Otake, Masuru, 3092
Otsu, Eiichiro, 3093
Owen, Elizabeth, 327, 571
Oxford and Asquith, Earl of, 3094.1
Ozick, Cynthia, 1058

Pacey, W. C. D., 3095
Packman, James, 3732.1
Paget, Violet [pseud., Vernon Lee], 141, 141.1, 213, 3096
Paik, Nak-Chung, 1059
Palache, John G., 3096.1
Panter-Downes, Mollie, 287
Parker, Hershel, 214
Parkes, Henry Bamford, 3098, 3099
Parks, Edd Winfield, 3361
Parquet, Mary Ellen, 3100
Parrington, Vernon Louis, 3101
Pastalosky, Rosa, 3102
Paterson, John, 3103
Patrick, Michael D., 527.1, 603.2, 706, 1639.1, 3104
Pattee, Fred Lewis, 3105, 3106, 3107, 3108
Patterson, Rebecca, 670, 830
Paul, Sherman, 3108.1
Paulding, Gouverneur, 305
Pauly, Thomas Harry, 3109
Payne, James Robert, 305.1
Payne, William Norton, 3110
Peacock, Ronald, 1621
Pearce, Brian, 1462

Pearce, Roy Harvey, 215, 216
Pearson, Gabriel, 571.1
Pečnik, B., 3111
Pelswick, Rose, 1354
Pendo, Mina, 1463
Penfield, Lida S., 3112
Pennell, Joseph, 479.1, 3113,
   3114
Penzoldt, Peter, 1355
Perloff, Marjorie, 831
Perlongo, Robert A., 1060
Perosa, Sergio, 1079
Perrin, Edwin N., 571.1
Perrin, Noel, 1715, 3115
Perry, Bliss, 1061, 3116, 3117,
   3118, 3119
Perry, F. M., 3120
Perry, Ralph Barton, 43, 3121,
   3122, 3123
Peterich, Werner, 3124
Peterson, Dale Earl, 3125
Peterson, William S., 3126
Petesch, Natalie M., 3127
Petnovich, Michael, 399
Petty, G. R., 435
Phelan, Kappo, 1356
Phelps, Gilbert, 3128
Phelps, William Lyon, 464, 1357,
   1761, 3129, 3130, 3132, 3133
Phillips, John Nova, 1716, 3134
Phillips, LeRoy, 1762, 3813
Phillips, Norma, 1062
Phillips, Robert S., 288
Piccinato, Stefania, 1564
Pickering, Samuel F., 295.1
Picon, Gaëtan, 1652
Pier, F., 3135
Pierhal, Armand, 3136
Pilkington, John, Jr., 3137
Pisapia, Biancamaria, 3138
Pitkin, Walter B., 3139
Pizer, Donald, 3140, 3141
Plante, Patricia R., 3142
Pochmann, Henry A., 3143, 3144
Podhoretz, Norman, 3145, 3146
Poirier, Richard, 216.1, 409.1,
   490, 490.1, 832, 833,
   1000.1, 1464, 3147, 3148,
   3149, 3150, 3151
Popkin, Henry, 217, 1622, 1623
Porat, Tsfira, 1357.1
Porcher, Frances, 1502.1
Porte, Joel, 3152

Porter, Katherine Anne, 44,
   3153, 3154
Porter, Kathleen Zamloch, 3155
Pouillon, Jean, 3156
Poulet, Georges, 3157, 3158
Pound, Ezra, 256, 623, 623.1,
   3159, 3160, 3161, 3162, 3163,
   3164, 3165, 3166, 3167
Powers, Lyall H., 394, 510,
   650, 834, 835, 959, 1159,
   1160, 1674, 3168, 3169, 3170,
   3171, 3172, 3172.1, 3173,
   3174, 3175, 3176, 3177, 3814,
   3815
Powys, John Cooper, 1358, 3178,
   3179
Pratt, Cornelia Atwood, 3180
Pratt, William C., Jr., 3181,
   3181.1
Prausnitz, Walther G., 1762.1,
   1762.2, 3181.2
Preston, Harriet Waters, 218,
   491, 618.1, 3182
Price, Lawrence Marsden, 3183
Price, Reynolds, 1565
Priestley, J. B., 3184
Pritchard, John Paul, 1359, 3185
Pritchett, V. S., 219, 257, 410,
   492, 1741, 3186, 3187,
   3187.1, 3188, 3188.1
Purdy, Strother B., 415, 1016,
   3189, 3190, 3191, 3191.1,
   3192, 3193
Putt, S. Gorley, 395, 395.1,
   594.2, 624, 624.1, 701.1,
   712, 712.1, 913.1, 913.2,
   913.3, 914, 914.1, 914.2,
   933.1, 939.1, 1001, 1001.1,
   1063, 1079.1, 1079.2, 1118.2,
   1160.1, 1360, 1502.3, 1566,
   1567, 1567.1, 3194, 3195,
   3196, 3197, 3198

Quinn, Arthur Hobson, 1361,
   3199, 3200, 3201
Quinn, Patrick F., 1119
Quvamme, B., 3202

Raeth, Claire J., 960, 1064
Rahv, Philip, 396, 572, 1465,
   3203, 3204, 3205, 3206, 3207,

3208, 3209, 3210
Raleigh, John H., 915, 3211,
    3212, 3213, 3213.1, 3214
Ramadan, A. M., 3215
Rambeau, James J., 257.1
Ramsey, Roger, 3216
Ranald, Ralph Arthur, 1065,
    3217
Randall, D. A., 836
Randall, John H., III, 465
Randell, Wilfred L., 3218, 3219
Rao, Adapa R., 1361.1
Rao, Krishna N., (See also
    Krishna, Rao N.), 1002
Raskin, Jonah, 3220
Raunheim, John Peter, 1737.2,
    3221
Ray, Gordon N., 1003, 3222
Raymond, John, 1466
Read, Sir Herbert Edward, 142,
    1568, 1669, 3223, 3224, 3225,
    3226
Reaney, James, 1066
Reardon, John, 3227
Recchia, Edward J., 3228
Reck, Andrew J., 3230
Reddick, Bryan D., 572.1
Redgrave, Michael, 288.1
Redlich, Rosemarie, 258, 1469
Redman, Ben Ray, 3231
Reed, Glenn, 1362
Reed, John Q., 143
Reed, K. T., 289
Reedy, William Marion, 3232,
    3233, 3234
Rees, Richard, 1363, 3234.1
Reid, Charles, 1364
Reid, Forrest, 1365
Reid, Stephen A., 345, 837,
    1120, 3235
Reilly, Robert J., 3236, 3237
Reinhart, Charles S., 3237
Reinman, Donald H., 296
Rest, Jaime, 3240
Revol, E. L., 3241
Rexroth, Kenneth, 3242
Rice, Loree McConnell, 3243
Richards, Bernard, 143.1,
    1066.1
Richardson, Lyon N., 3244, 3816,
    3817
Richardson, S. D., 3245
Richmond, Lee J., 572.2

Rickert, Edith, 2892, 3793
Riddel, Joseph N., 3246
Ritchie, G. S., 3715.1
Robbins, J. Albert, 3818, 3819,
    3820
Roberts, James Deotis, 3247
Roberts, James L., 837.1, 3248
Roberts, Louise A., 3249
Roberts, Morley, 3250
Roberts, Morris, 269, 573,
    1066.2, 1366, 1640, 1640.1,
    3251, 3252, 3253, 3254, 3821,
    3821.1
Robins, Elizabeth, 1624, 1717
Robinson, Edwin Arlington, 645
Robinson, Jean Joseph, 686.1,
    3255
Robson, W. W., 1161
Rochner, J., 838
Roddman, Philip, 1467
Rodenbeck, John, 839
Roditi, Edouard, 511, 3256,
    3257
Roellinger, Francis X., 1367
Rogers, Robert, 346, 632, 3258,
    3259
Rollins, A. W., 466
Roper, Alan H., 1121
Roscoe, E. S., 3260
Rose, Alan M., 574, 3261
Roselli, Daniel N., 1139.4, 3262
Rosenbaum, Stanford Patrick,
    144, 145, 220, 1122, 1123,
    1124, 1125, 1481, 1718, 1719,
    3263
Rosenberry, Edward H., 651
Rosenfeld, Paul, 3264
Rosenfeld, Claire, 633
Rosenzweig, Saul, 3265
Ross, L., 289.1
Ross, Maude Cardwell, 3266
Ross, Morton L., 361
Rothenstein, William, 3267
Rountree, Benjamin C., 671
Rourke, Constance, 221, 3268
Rouse, H. Blair, 3269
Routh, Harold Victor, 3270
Rovit, Earl, 634, 646, 3271
Rowe, John Carlos, 1569, 3272
Roy, Claude, 3273
Rubin, Louis D., Jr., 1368,
    1368.1, 3274
Ruhm, Herbert, 411, 639, 3275

Ruland, Richard, 3276
Rupp, Henry R. , 146, 1436
Rupp, Richard H. , 3277
Russell, John R. , 1720, 3278,
    3279, 3280, 3822
Ryan, Marjorie, 147, 3281
Rypins, Harold L. , 1570, 3282

Saalbach, R. P. , 3283
Saalburg, Leslie, 147.1
Sabiston, Elizabeth J. , 839.1,
    840, 3284
Sachs, Viola, 3285
Sackville-West, Edward, 493, 841,
    842, 1067, 1067.1, 3286, 3287
Sale, William, 525.2
Salisbury, Howard E. , 842.1,
    1126, 1468, 3288
Salomon, Roger B. , 3289, 3290
Salzberg, Joel, 347, 916
Samokhvalov, N. I. , 3291
Sampson, George, 3292
Sampson, Martin W. , 99, 148,
    467, 619
Samuel, Irene, 3293
Samuels, Charles Thomas, 1068,
    1068.1, 1082.1, 1126.1, 1139.3,
    1369, 1369.1, 1468.1, 1502.4,
    1570.1, 3294
Sandeen, Ernest, 843, 1571, 3295
Sanders, Thomas E. , 3296
Sanford, Charles L. , 3297
San Juan, Epifanio, Jr. , 149
Sanna, Vittoria, 1370, 3298, 3299
Sasaki, Miyoko, 3300
Sassoon, Siegfried, 3300.1
Sauer, Edwin H. , 3301
Saul, Frank J. , 305.2, 3302
Savelli, Giovanni, 3302.1
Saveson, Marilyn B. , 3303
Sayre, Robert Freeman, 306,
    306.1, 3304, 3305
Scanlon, Lawrence E. , 3306
Schelling, Felix Emmanuel, 3307
Scherman, David E. , 258, 1469
Scherting, John, 1005
Scheyer, Ernst, 3308
Schieber, Alois J. , 307
Schlesinger, Arthur M. , Jr. , 3309
Schneider, Daniel J. , 150, 1127,
    1161.1
Schneider, Isidor, 3310

Schneider, Sister Lucy, 222, 844
Schneider, Marcel, 625, 1371
Scholes, James Bert, 3311
Scholes, Robert, 512
Schonberg, Harold C. , 1372
Schorer, Mark, 1373
Schrero, Elliot M. , 1069
Schuhmann, Kuno, 151, 3312
Schulte, Rainer Ortwin, 3313
Schultz, Elizabeth Avery, 397,
    3314
Schulz, Max F. , 223
Schuyler, Montgomery, 3315, 3316
Schwertman, Mary Pogue, 3317
Scoggins, James, 297
Scott, Arthur L. , 3318
Scott, Clement, 594.3
Scott, Dixon, 3319, 3320, 3321
Scott, R. H. F. , 45
Scott-James, Rolfe Arnold, 3322
Scudder, Horace E. , 397.1, 845,
    960.1, 3323, 3324
Seaman, Owen, 1070
Sears, Donald A. , 3324.1
Sears, Sallie, 151.1, 574.1,
    3325, 3823
Segal, Ora, 357, 652, 3326, 3824
Segnitz, T. M. , 718
Seiffert, Alice, 1374.1
Seldes, G. V. , 3327
Selig, Robert L. , 398
Senanu, K. E. , 3327.1
Sewell, Richard B. , 940
Seznac, Jean, 1721
Shahane, V. A. , 3328
Shapira, Morris, 3329, 3330
Sharma, O. P. , 3331
Sharp, Robert L. , 45.1
Sharp, Sister M. Corona, 574.2,
    846, 3332, 3333, 3334
Shaw, George Bernard, 596, 597
Sherman, Stuart Pratt, 1071,
    1722, 3335, 3336, 3337, 3338
Shine, Muriel G. , 3339, 3340
Shitsu, Iwase, 3341
Short, Raymond W. , 940, 3342,
    3343, 3344
Shorter, Clement, 3826
Shou (Shaw), B. , 595
Shriber, Michael, 152, 468
Shroeder, John W. , 3345
Shucard, Alan R. , 152.1
Shulenberger, Arvid, 3346

Shulman, Robert, 519, 692, 3347
Shuman, R. B., 1723
Shumsky, Allison, 224, 1006, 1737.3
Siegel, Eli, 1375
Siegel, Paul N., 1376
Sigaux, Gilbert, 153
Silver, John, 1377
Silverstein, Henry, 591, 3348
Simms, L. Moody, Jr., 3349
Simon, Irene, 3350
Simon, Jean, 3351
Simon, John Kenneth, 672, 3352
Singh, Brijraj, 3353
Sklepowich, Edward A., 3354
Slabey, Robert M., 1378, 1379, 3355
Slaughter, Martina, 1380
Smalley, Evelyn Garnaut, 3356
Smith, Bernard, 3357
Smith, Charles R., 647
Smith, Frances E., 348
Smith, Henry Nash, 3358
Smith, Herbert F., 399, 3359
Smith, J. Oates, 3360
Smith, James Harry, 3361
Smith, Janet Adam, 1724, 3362, 3363, 3364
Smith, Logan Pearsall, 1128, 3365, 3366, 3367
Smith, Martha Stribling, 3367.1
Smith, Roland M., 1381
Smith, S. Stephenson, 3368
Smith, Thomas F., 847
Smith, William Francis, Jr., 475.4, 634.1, 678.1, 3369
Smyth, Albert Henry, 3370
Snell, Edwin Marion, 3371
Snell, George, 1382, 3372
Snow, Lotus, 575, 848, 1007, 1129, 1162, 1572, 3373, 3374
Sobiston, Elizabeth J., 3375
Solomon, Eric, 1383, 3376, 3377
Solomon, Jan Kadetsky, 3378
Solotaroff, Theodore, 400
Sölter, Ursula, 3379
Spackman, William M., 3380
Spanos, Bebe, 917, 1008, 3381
Sparshott, F. E., 849, 3382
Speck, Paul, 1009
Specker, Heidi, 3383
Spencer, Benjamin T., 3384, 3385

Spencer, James L., 576
Spender, Stephen, 577, 1130, 3386, 3387, 3388, 3389, 3390
Spilka, Mark, 941, 942, 1384
Spiller, Robert E., 307.1, 1725, 3391, 3392, 3393, 3394, 3395, 3396, 3829
Squire, J. C., 1726, 3397, 3398
Squires, Radcliffe, 1385
Stader, Karl-Heinz, 3399
Stafford, William T., 225, 225.1, 362, 469, 527.2, 850, 1640.2, 1753, 3400, 3400.1, 3401, 3401.1, 3401.2, 3402, 3403, 3404, 3405, 3406, 3736, 3830, 3831, 3832, 3833, 3834, 3835
Stallman, Robert Wooster, 154, 155, 156, 156.1, 157, 158, 851, 852, 853, 854, 3406.1, 3644, 3836
Standley, F. L., 1727
Stanford, Derek, 3407
Stanford, Donald E., 1386
Stanzel, Franz K., 158.1, 159
Starkie, Enid, 527.2
Staub, A. W., 3408
Steegmuller, Francis, 3409
Steen, James T., 3410
Steer, Helen Vane, 1625
Steger, Wallace, 3411
Stein, Gertrude, 3412
Stein, Roger B., 3413
Stein, William Bysshe, 160, 290, 855, 943, 1072, 1073, 1131
Steinhoff, William, 521
Steinkamp, Egon, 3414
Steinmann, Martin, 525.2
Stephens, Robert O., 3415
Stern, J. P., 3415.1
Stevens, A. Wilber, 259
Stevens, George, 3416
Stevens, Harriet S., 1503, 3416.1
Stevenson, Elizabeth, 45.2, 3417, 3837
Stevenson, Lionel, 3417.1, 3418, 3419
Stevenson, Robert Louis, 3420
Stevick, Philip, 3421
Stewart, John Innes Mackintosh, 856, 1640.3, 3422, 3837.1
Stewart, Randall, 857, 3423, 3424
Stoehr, Taylor, 918, 919

Stokes, D. , 3425
Stokes, John, 1151. 1
Stoll, Elmer Edgar, 1388
Stone Albert E. , 161, 1389, 1390. 1
Stone, Donald David, 3426, 3426. 1
Stone, Edward, 349, 350, 470, 482, 635, 653, 680. 1, 943. 1, 960. 2, 1080, 1081, 1482, 3427, 3427. 1, 3428, 3429, 3430, 3431, 3432, 3433, 3434
Stone, Geoffrey, 401
Stone, Herbert Stuart, 3838
Stone, William B. , 614. 1
Stott, R. Toole, 3838. 1
Stovall, Floyd, 636, 636. 1, 3435, 3436, 3437, 3438, 3839
Strandberg, Victor H. , 226, 858
Stratman, Carl J. , 3840
Strong, Leonard Alfred George, 3439
Strout, Cushing, 3440
Struble, George G. , 3441
Summerhayes, Donald C. , 3444
Sumner, Nan, 3445
Sumner, Nathan, 3445
Sutton, Walter, 3446
Swan, Michael, 227, 291, 647. 1, 1391, 1504, 1728, 1729, 3447, 3448, 3449, 3450, 3451, 3452, 3841
Swartz, David L. , Jr. , 3453
Sweeney, John L. , 1641, 3454, 3455
Sweetapple, R. , 3455. 1
Swinden, Patrick, 3455. 2
Swinnerton, Frank, 162, 3456, 3457, 3458, 3459, 3460, 3461
Switzer, John W. , 3462
Szala, Alina, 228

Tadokoro, Nobushige, 471, 1392
Takahashi, Masao, 3463. 1
Takahashi, Michi, 1010
Takano, Fumi, 228. 1, 3464
Takuwa, Shinji, 3465
Tallman, Warren E. , 3466
Taniguchi, Rikuo, 3466. 1
Tanner, Tony, 46, 163, 494, 578, 604, 859, 1074, 3467,

3468, 3469, 3470, 3470. 1, 3471, 3472, 3473
Tanselle, G. Thomas, 3781, 3781. 1, 3842
Tartella, Vincent, 526
Tate, Allen, 51, 164, 351, 2047. 1, 3473. 1
Taylor, C. , 1573
Taylor, Christy M. , 3474
Taylor, Gordon O. , 165, 860, 1011, 1482. 1, 3475
Taylor, H. W. , 1332
Taylor, Marion A. , 228. 2
Taylor, Ross M. , 518, 1435
Taylor, Walter Fuller, 3476, 3843
Tedford, Barbara Wilkie, 3476. 1
Teichgraeber, Stephen E. , 3477
Temple, Ruth Z. , 3844
Terras, Victor, 3478
Terrie, Henry L. , 166, 3479, 3480
Tharp, Louise Hall, 1730
Thayer, William Roscoe, 3481
Theobald, John R. , 579
Thomas, Amory A. , 3483
Thomas, Glen R. , 1394
Thomas, Jean Landers, 3484
Thomas, William A. , 3485
Thomas, William B. , 167, 3486
Thompson, Edward Raymond, 3487
Thompson, Francis, 260, 580, 3488
Thomson, A. W. , 1395
Thomson, Fred C. , 637
Thorberg, Raymond, 355, 412, 861, 1139. 5, 1574, 1742, 3489, 3490
Thorp, Willard, 526. 1, 679, 1396, 3491
Thurber, James, 168, 1397, 1575, 3492, 3493
Thurston, Jarvis, 3845
Tick, Stanley, 229
Ticknor, Caroline, 402, 639. 1, 3494
Tilford, John E. , Jr. , 169, 3495
Tilley, Arthur, 3495. 1
Tilley, Wesley H. , 920, 920. 1
Tilley, Winthrop, 1132
Tillotson, Geoffrey, 3496, 3497, 3497. 1
Tillotson, Kathleen, 3497. 2

Tillyard, E. M. W., 921, 3498
Tilton, Eleanor, 681, 3498.1
Tindall, William York, 1398,
    3499, 3500
Tintner, Adeline R., 170, 170.1,
    170.2, 591.1, 921.1, 922,
    923, 1133, 1134, 1441, 3501,
    3502
Tochihara, Tomoo, 3503
Todasco, Ruth Taylor, 581, 3504
Tomlinson, M., 1626
Tompkins, Jane P., 352, 693,
    1399, 3505, 3846
Tooker, L. Frank, 3506
Toor, David, 961
Toser, Basil, 3506.1
Tournadre, C., 1400
Towsend, Frank H., 3507
Trachtenberg, Allan, 261, 262
Trachtenberg, Stanley, 1401
Tracy, Bruce Philip, 3508
Traill, H. D., 3509
Traschen, Isadore, 230, 231,
    232, 233, 3510, 3511
Travis, Mildred K., 637.1
Trent, William Peterfield, 3512,
    3847
Trewin, J. C., 1402
Tribble, Joseph L., 862
Trieschmann, Margaret, 582
Trilling, Lionel, 46.1, 403, 404,
    604.1, 604.2, 924, 925, 926,
    927, 943.2, 3513, 3514, 3515,
    3516, 3517, 3518, 3518.1,
    3519, 3520
Troy, William, 1403, 3521, 3522,
    3523
Truss, Tom J., Jr., 1165
Tuttleton, James W., 3524, 3525
Tuveson, Ernest, 1403.1
Tweedy, Katherine, 3526
Tyler, Gary R., 3747
Tyler, James, 3783
Tyler, Parker, 513, 513.1, 1075,
    1076, 1576, 3528, 3529
Tytell, John, 476, 1505, 3530,
    3530.1, 3350.2

Uhlig, Helmut, 3531
Ulanov, Barry, 3532
Underwood, John Curtis, 3533
Unrue, Darlene Harbour, 3534

Untermeyer, Louis, 46.2
Updike, John, 1406
Urnov, M., 3534.1
Uroff, M. D., 962
Uzzell, Thomas H., 1407

Vaid, Krishna B., 3535, 3536
Vallette, Jacques, 3537, 3538,
    3539, 3848
Van Aken, Paul, 1408
Van Cromphout, Gustaaf, 1577
Van Der Beets, Richard, 234,
    3540
Vanderbilt, Kermit, 235, 3541,
    3542, 3543
Vandermoere, H., 495
Vandersee, Charles, 703
Van Doren, Carl, 1409, 3544
Van Doren, Mark, 1410, 1470,
    2047.1
Van Ghent, Dorothy, 863, 863.1,
    3545
Van Kaam, Adrian, 352.1
Van Nostrand, Albert D., 3546
Vann, J. Don, 3547
Van Patten, Nathan, 3849
Vedder, Henry Clay, 471.1, 3548
Veeder, William R., 171, 1483
Verney, Lady F. P., 864
Vidan, Ivo, 928, 929
Vientós Gastón, Nilita, 3549
Vincec, Sister Stephanie, 1578
Vitelli, James R., 3551
Vivas, Eliseo, 3552, 3553, 3554
Voegelin, Eric, 1411, 1412, 1413
Volpe, Edmond Loris, 472, 481.2,
    865, 866, 1135, 1754, 3555,
    3556, 3557, 3558
Von Klemperer, Elizabeth G.,
    3559
Vorpahl, Ben M., 46.3, 3560

Wadden, Anthony T., 171.1,
    3560.1
Wade, Allan, 1627, 1628, 3561
Wade, David, 648
Wagenknecht, Edward, 3562,
    3563, 3564, 3565
Wager, Willis, 3566
Wagner, Linda Welshimer, 867,
    1011.1, 3567

Walbridge, Earle F., 1514, 1731, 3569

Walbrook, H. M., 1629, 1630, 1631, 3570

Walcutt, Charles Child, 404.1, 3571

Waldock, Arthur John Alfred, 1414, 3572

Walker, Don, 3573, 3574

Walker, Warren S., 3850, 3850.1, 3850.2

Walker, William E., 3575

Walkley, Arthur Bingham, 598, 1632, 1732

Wallace, Irving, 292, 3576

Wallace, Jack E., 868

Wallace, Ronald William, 171.2, 1163, 3577

Walpole, Hugh, 1415, 3578, 3579

Walsh, William, 307.2, 1506, 3580, 3581, 3582

Walt, James, 353

Walter, Eugene, 3583

Walters, Dorothy Jeanne, 3584

Walters, Margaret, 327.1

Ward, Alfred C., 598.1, 1416

Ward, Joseph A., 172, 173, 496, 496.1, 583, 673, 1484, 1579, 3586, 3587, 3588, 3589, 3590, 3591, 3592, 3593, 3594, 3595

Ward, Mary Augusta (Mrs. Humphrey Ward), 3596

Warren, Austin, 47, 174, 174.1, 3597, 3598, 3599, 3600, 3601, 3602, 3635.1

Warren, R. P., 3603

Wasiolek, Edward, 869, 1507, 3604

Wasserstrom, William, 473, 3605

Watanabe, Hisayoshi, 584, 1012, 3606

Watanabe, Toshiro, 870

Waterlow, S. P., 3607, 3608

Watkins, Floyd C., 236

Watson, George, 3609, 3851

Watt, Ian, 175, 176, 3610, 3611, 3612, 3613, 3614

Watts, Richard, Jr., 1417

Waugh, Arthur, 3615

Weales, Gerald, 1418, 1471

Webb, Howard W., 3616

Weber, Carl J., 968, 1733, 3617, 3618, 3619, 3620

Webster, Norman W., 3621

Wegelin, Christof, 48, 176.1, 585, 871, 1580, 1581, 1581.1, 3622, 3623, 3624, 3625, 3626, 3627

Weiman, Robert, 3628

Weimer, David R., 48.1, 176.2, 3629

Weinstein, Philip M., 585.1, 871.1, 1013, 1076.1, 1077, 1507.1, 3630, 3631

Weismann, Leopoldine, 3632

Weithaus, Sister Barbara, M., O.S.F., 3633

Welker, Robert L., 3575

Wellek, René, 3634, 3635, 3635.1

Wells, Anna Mary, 3636

Wells, Carolyn, 3637

Wells, H. G., 3638, 3639, 3640, 3641

Welsh, Alexander, 586, 3643

Wertham, Frederic, 354

Wescott, Glenway, 1419, 3651

West, Katharine, 1420

West, Muriel, 1421, 1422

West, Ray B., Jr., 236.1, 3644, 3644.1, 3645

West, Rebecca, 3646, 3647, 3648, 3649, 3650, 3852

Westbrook, James Seymour, Jr., 1582

Westbrook, Perry D., 514, 687

Wexford, Jane, 292.1

Whalley, George, 3652

Wharton, Edith, 1583, 1734, 1735, 3653, 3653.1, 3654

Wheelwright, John, 3656

White, J. William, 3656.1

White, Lucia, 3657

White, Morton Gabriel, 3657

White, Richard Grant, 474, 3658

White, Sidney Howard, 263

White, William, 3659

Whitford, Robert Calvin, 1736

Whitmore, Paul E., 3660

Wiesenfarth, Brother Joseph, 48.2, 354.1, 615, 872, 1077.1, 1136, 3662, 3663, 3663.1, 3664, 3853

Wilcox, Thomas W., 293

Wilde, Oscar, 1423

Wilding, Michael, 873, 874

Wilkins, M. S., 930

Willen, Gerald, 237, 1424, 1472, 3854, 3855
Willett, Maurita, 237.1, 3665
Willey, Frederick, 875, 1137, 3666
Williams, Blanche Colton, 3667
Williams, Harold Herbert, 3667.1
Williams, Orlo, 177
Williams, Owen P. D., 3667.2
Williams, Paul O., 876
Williams, Raymond, 3668
Williams, Stanley Thomas, 3669, 3670
Williamson, Marilyn L., 178
Wilson, Angus, 3671
Wilson, Edmund, 48.3, 413, 1425, 1426, 1427, 1742.1, 3672, 3673, 3674, 3675, 3676, 3677, 3678, 3679, 3680, 3681, 3682
Wilson, Harris W., 1508, 3683
Wilson, Jack Hamilton, 3684
Wilson, James Southall, 587, 3685
Wilson, R. B. J., 1584
Wilson, Richard, 3686
Wilson, Woodrow, 3687
Wilt, Napier, 3688
Winner, Viola Hopkins, 107, 298, 989, 1440, 1455, 3689, 3689.1, 3690, 3691
Winslow, Cedric, 3692
Winsten, Archer, 1428
Winters, Yvor, 3693, 3694
Wirsing, Sibylle, 3695
Wise, James N., 179
Wister, Fanny Kemble, 3695.1
Woelfel, Karl, 1473
Wolf, Howard Robert, 180, 1509, 3697
Wolfe, Don M., 3698
Wolff, Robert Lee, 1429
Wood, Ann, 475
Woodard, James E., Jr., 3699
Woodcock, George, 931, 3699.1
Woodress, James, 3700, 3856, 3857, 3858, 3859, 3860, 3861, 3862
Woodward, Comer Vann, 405
Woodward, Robert H., 3701
Woolf, Leonard, 3701.1
Woolf, Virginia, 414, 685, 1430, 1585, 1585.1, 1585.2, 1736.1, 3702, 3702.1, 3703, 3704

Woolson, Constance Fenimore, 475.1
Worden, Ward S., 1510, 1511, 1743
Worsley, T. C., 1431
Wright, Austin McGiffert, 687.1, 3706, 3863
Wright, Edgar, 3707
Wright, Lyle H., 3864
Wright, Nathalia, 877, 3708, 3709
Wright, Walter F., 588, 658, 713, 878, 963, 1432, 3710, 3865
Wyatt, Bryant N., 3711
Wyatt, Edith, 3712
Wyld, Lionel D., 1633

Yeazell, Ruth Bernard, 3713
Young, Filson, 3714
Young, Frederic Harold, 3715
Young, G. M., 3715.1
Young, Mahonri Sharp, 3715.2
Young, Robert E., 181, 182
Young, Thomas Daniel, 3715.3
Young, Vernon, 3716
Yu, Frederick Y., 1432.1

Zabel, Morton D., 272.4, 616, 1766, 3717, 3718, 3719, 3720, 3720.1, 3721, 3722, 3723, 3723.1, 3724, 3725, 3726
Zauli-Naldi, Camilla, 3727
Zietlow, Edward R., 238
Ziff, Larzer, 3728, 3729
Zimmerman, Everett, 1433
Zolla, Elemire, 3730